Warsaw. The Jewish Metropolis

IJS STUDIES IN JUDAICA

CONFERENCE PROCEEDINGS OF THE
INSTITUTE OF JEWISH STUDIES,
UNIVERSITY COLLEGE LONDON

Series Editors

Mark Geller
François Guesnet
Ada Rapoport-Albert

VOLUME 15

The titles published in this series are listed at *brill.com/ijs*

FRONTISPIECE Bernardo Belotto, known as Canaletto, *Bridgettine Church and the Arsenal*, 1775. *Detail presenting Jews standing in front of a small manor house on the corner of Długa and Bielańska streets, Royal Castle in Warsaw (fot. Andrzej Ring).*

Warsaw. The Jewish Metropolis

*Essays in Honor of the 75th Birthday
of Professor Antony Polonsky*

Edited by

Glenn Dynner and François Guesnet

BRILL

LEIDEN | BOSTON

This paperback was originally published in hardback as Volume 15 in the series IJS.

Warsaw. the Jewish metropolis : essays in honor of the 75th birthday of professor Antony Polonsky / edited by Glenn Dynner and François Guesnet.
    pages cm. — (IJS studies in Judaica ; volume 15)
    Includes bibliographical references and index.
    ISBN 978-90-04-29180-5 (hardback : alk. paper) — ISBN 978-90-04-29181-2 (e-book) 1. Jews—Poland—Warsaw—History. 2. Jews—Poland—Warsaw—Social conditions—History. 3. Jews—Poland—Warsaw—Economic conditions—History 4. Jews—Poland—Warsaw—Intellectual life. 5. Warsaw (Poland)—Ethnic relations. I. Dynner, Glenn, 1969- editor. II. Guesnet, François, editor. III. Polonsky, Antony, honoree. IV. Title: Jewish metropolis.

DS134.64.W36 2015
305.892'4043841—dc23

2015005127

Typeface for the Latin, Greek, and Cyrillic scripts: "Brill". See and download: brill.com/brill-typeface.

ISSN 1570-1581
ISBN 978-90-04-32842-6 (paperback, 2017)
ISBN 978-90-04-29180-5 (hardback, 2015)
ISBN 978-90-04-29181-2 (e-book, 2015)

Copyright 2015 by Koninklijke Brill NV, Leiden, The Netherlands.
Koninklijke Brill NV incorporates the imprints Brill, Brill Hes & De Graaf, Brill Nijhoff, Brill Rodopi and Hotei Publishing.
All rights reserved. No part of this publication may be reproduced, translated, stored in a retrieval system, or transmitted in any form or by any means, electronic, mechanical, photocopying, recording or otherwise, without prior written permission from the publisher.
Authorization to photocopy items for internal or personal use is granted by Koninklijke Brill NV provided that the appropriate fees are paid directly to The Copyright Clearance Center, 222 Rosewood Drive, Suite 910, Danvers, MA 01923, USA. Fees are subject to change.

This book is printed on acid-free paper.

Contents

Acknowledgements VIII
Notes on the Contributors IX
List of Illustrations and Maps XIV

Introduction   1

PART 1
The Rise of the Metropolis

1 Illegal Immigrants: The Jews of Warsaw, 1527–1792   19
   Hanna Węgrzynek

2 Merchants, Army Suppliers, Bankers: Transnational Connections and the Rise of Warsaw's Jewish Mercantile Elite (1770–1820)   42
   Cornelia Aust

3 In Warsaw and Beyond: The Contribution of Hayim Zelig Slonimski to Jewish Modernization   70
   Ela Bauer

4 The Garment of Torah: Clothing Decrees and the Warsaw Career of the First Gerer *Rebbe*   91
   Glenn Dynner

5 From Community to Metropolis: The Jews of Warsaw, 1850–1880   128
   François Guesnet

6 An Unhappy Community and an Even Unhappier Rabbi   154
   Shaul Stampfer

7 Distributing Knowledge: Warsaw as a Center of Jewish Publishing, 1850–1914   180
   Nathan Cohen

8   In Kotik's Corner: Urban Culture, Bourgeois Politics and the Struggle for Jewish Civility in Turn of the Century Eastern Europe   207
    Scott Ury

9   Hope and Fear: Y.L. Peretz and the Dialectics of Diaspora Nationalism, 1905–12   227
    Michael C. Steinlauf

10 "Di Haynt-mishpokhe": Study for a Group Picture   252
    Joanna Nalewajko-Kulikov

11 A Warsaw Story: Polish-Jewish Relations during the First World War   271
    Robert Blobaum

12 The Capital of "Yiddishland"?   298
    Kalman Weiser

13 The Kultur-Lige in Warsaw: A Stopover in the Yiddishists' Journey between Kiev and Paris   323
    Gennady Estraikh

14 Enduring Prestige, Eroded Authority: The Warsaw Rabbinate in the Interwar Period   347
    Gershon Bacon

15 From Galicia to Warsaw: Interwar Historians of Polish Jewry   370
    Natalia Aleksiun

16 Negotiating Jewish Nationalism in Interwar Warsaw   390
    Kenneth B. Moss

PART 2
Destruction of the Metropolis and Its Aftermath

17 The Polish Underground Press and the Jews: The Holocaust in the Pages of the Home Army's *Biuletyn Informacyjny*, 1940–1943   437
    Joshua D. Zimmerman

18 "The Work of My Hands is Drowning in the Sea, and You Would Offer Me Song?!": Orthodox Behaviour and Leadership in Warsaw during the Holocaust   467
Havi Dreifuss

19 The Warsaw Ghetto in the Writings of Rachel Auerbach   496
Samuel Kassow

20 Stories of Rescue Activities in the Letters of Jewish Survivors about Christian Polish Rescuers, 1944–1949   515
Joanna B. Michlic

21 The Politics of Retribution in Postwar Warsaw: In the Honor Court of the Central Committee of Polish Jews   539
Gabriel N. Finder

22 The End of a Jewish Metropolis? The Ambivalence of Reconstruction in the Aftermath of the Holocaust   562
David Engel

23 The Reconstruction of Jewish Life in Warsaw after the Holocaust: A Case Study of a Building and Its Residents   570
Karen Auerbach

24 In Search of Meaning after Marxism: The *Komandosi*, March 1968, and the Ideas that Followed   590
Marci Shore

25 "*Context is Everything*." Reflections on Studying with Antony Polonsky   613
Yohanan Petrovsky-Shtern

Name Index   617

Acknowledgements

The current volume is an outgrowth of a conference held at University College London on June 22–25, 2010, at the Institute of Jewish Studies at University College, London. We would like to thank the initial sponsors and supporters of that conference, including the Embassy of the Republic of Poland; Dr. Hanna Gronkiewicz-Waltz, President of the City of Warsaw; The American Association for Polish-Jewish Studies, Cambridge, MA; Fondation pour la Mémoire de la Shoah, Paris; The Adam Mickiewicz Institute, Warsaw; The Department of Culture, City of Warsaw; The Polish Cultural Institute, London; The Littauer Foundation, New York; The Littman Library of Jewish Civilization; The Institute for Polish Jewish Studies, Oxford; The Jewish Historical Institute, Warsaw; and The Polin Museum for the History of Polish Jews, Warsaw. The conference would scarcely have been possible without their support. We also would like to acknowledge the diligence of the staff at the UCL Institute of Jewish Studies, particularly Sara Ben-Isaac. We are grateful to all speakers, chairs and commentators at the conference, notably to Professor Norman Davies for his opening keynote, and to all contributors to the present volume. In addition, we thank Lindsey Taylor-Guthartz for her careful translation of Havi Dreifuss' article, Jim Dingley for his contribution to copy-editing this volume, and Anastasiya Novatorskaya who, with the support of the office of the Dean of Studies at Sarah Lawrence College, compiled the Name Index. We are grateful to the staff at Brill Academic Publishers for their exemplary support in putting together this large volume—Jennifer Pavelko assisted us at the beginning, with Katelyn Chin, Meghan Connolly and Paige Sammartino taking good care to complete the task. Finally, we would like to thank Professor Antony Polonsky, who has inspired this volume with his decades-long devotion to the field of Polish Jewish Studies. It is to him that we dedicate this volume.

Notes on the Contributors

Karen Auerbach
is Assistant Professor and Stuart E. Eizenstat Fellow at the University of North Carolina in Chapel Hill. She is author of *The House at Ujazdowskie 16: Jewish Families in Warsaw after the Holocaust* (Indiana University Press, 2013).

Natalia Aleksiun
is Associate Professor of Modern Jewish History, Touro College, Graduate School of Jewish Studies; and Assistant Professor, Institute of History, Polish Academy of Sciences. She is author of *Where to? The Zionist Movement in Poland, 1944–1950* (in Polish; Warsaw, 2002), and co-editor of *Polin* 20, devoted to the memory of the Holocaust.

Cornelia Aust
is Wissenschaftlicher Mitarbeiter at the Leibniz-Institute for European History in Mainz. She is author of "Between Amsterdam and Warsaw. Commercial Networks of the Ashkenazic Mercantile Elite in Central Europe," *Jewish History* 27.1 (2013): 41–71.

Gershon Bacon
is an associate professor in the Jewish History Department at Bar-Ilan University, where he holds the Marcell and Maria Roth Chair in the History and Culture of Polish Jewry. He is the author of, among other works, *The Politics of Tradition: Agudat Yisrael in Poland, 1916–1939* (Jerusalem, 1996; revised and expanded Hebrew version, 2005), and the forthcoming *The Jews of Modern Poland, 1772–2000*, to be published by the University of California Press.

Ela Bauer
teaches at Kibbutzim College in Tel Aviv. She is author of *Between Poles and Jews: The Development of Nahum Sokolow's Political Thought* (Jerusalem: Magnes Press, 2005); and "The Ideological Roots of the Polish Jewish Intelligentsia."

Robert Blobaum
is Eberly Family Distinguished Professor of History at West Virginia University. He is editor of *Antisemitism and its Opponents in Modern Poland* (Ithaca, NY: Cornell University Press, 2005), and author of *Rewolucja: Russian Poland, 1904–1907* (Ithaca, NY: Cornell University Press, 1995) and *Feliks Dzierżyński and the*

SDKPiL: A Study in the Origins of Polish Communism (Boulder and New York: East European Monographs and Columbia University Press, 1984).

Nathan Cohen
is Associate Professor of Literature of the Jewish People at Bar Ilan University. He is author of *Sefer, Sofer v'iton: merkaz ha-tarbut ha-yehudit b'varsha, 1918–1942* (Jerusalem Magnes Press, 2003).

Havi Dreifuss
is Senior Lecturer in the Department of Jewish History, Tel Aviv University, and director of the Center for the Research of the Holocaust in Poland at the Yad Vashem International Institute for Holocaust Research. She is author of *We Polish Jews? The Relations between Jews and Poles during the Holocaust—The Jewish Perspective* (in Hebrew; Yad Vashem, 2010); and *Changing Perspectives on Polish-Jewish Relations during the Holocaust* (Yad Vashem, 2012).

Glenn Dynner
is Professor of Religion and Chair of Humanities at Sarah Lawrence College. He is author of *Men of Silk: The Hasidic Conquest of Polish Jewish Society* (Oxford University Press, 2006); and *Yankel's Tavern: Jews, Liquor and Life in the Kingdom of Poland* (Oxford University Press, 2013). He is editor of *Holy Dissent: Jewish and Christian Mystics in Eastern Europe* (Wayne State University Press, 2011); and co-editor of *Polin* 27: "Jews in the Kingdom of Poland."

David Engel
is Greenberg Professor of Holocaust Studies, Professor and Chair of Hebrew and Judaic Studies, and Professor of History at New York University and a Senior Fellow of the Goldstein-Goren Diaspora Research Center at Tel Aviv University. His books include *In the Shadow of Auschwitz* (University of North Carolina Press, 1987), *Facing a Holocaust* (University of North Carolina Press, 1993), *Between Liberation and Flight* (in Hebrew; Tel Aviv, 1996), *Zionism: A Short History of a Big Idea* (Harlow, 2008), and *Historians of the Jews and the Holocaust* (Stanford, 2010). He has been an editor of the journal *Gal-Ed: On the History and Culture of Polish Jewry* since 1985.

Gennady Estraikh
is Associate Professor of Yiddish Studies at Skirball Department of Hebrew and Judaic Studies, New York University. His publications include *Soviet Yiddish: Language Planning and Linguistic Development* (Oxford University Press, 1996); *In Harness: Yiddish Writers' Romance with Communism*, (Syracuse University

Press, 2005); *Yiddish in the Cold War* (Legenda, 2008); and *Yiddish Literary Life in Moscow* (in Russian, forthcoming).

Gabriel N. Finder

is Associate Professor of Germanic Languages and Literatures and Director of the Jewish Studies Program at the University of Virginia. He is author of *Jewish Honor Courts: Revenge, Retribution, and Reconciliation in Europe and Israel after the Holocaust*, ed. Laura Jockusch and Gabriel N. Finder (Detroit: Wayne State University Press, forthcoming 2015).

François Guesnet

is Reader in Modern Jewish History at University College London. He is author of *Polnische Juden im 19. Jahrhundert: Lebensbedingungen, Rechtsnormen und Organisation im Wandel* (Cologne, Vienna: Böhlau Verlag, 1998) and edited *Der Fremde als Nachbar: Polnische Positionen zur jüdischen Präsenz. Texte seit 1800* (Frankfurt am Main: Suhrkamp Verlag, 2009) and, with Gwenyth Jones, *Antisemitism in an Era of Transition: Traditions and Impact in Post-Communist Poland and Hungary* (Frankfurt am Main: Peter Lang Verlag, 2014).

Samuel Kassow

is Northam Professor of History, Trinity College, Hartford CT. He is author of *Students, Professors and the State in Tsarist Russia 1884–1917* (University of California Press, 1989); and *Who will write our History: Emanuel Ringelblum and the Oyneg Shabes Archive* (Indiana University Press, 2007).

Joanna B. Michlic

is Lecturer in Contemporary History, Bristol University, and Director of the HBI (Hadassah-Brandeis Institute) Project on Families, Children, and the Holocaust at Brandeis University. She is author of *Poland's Threatening Other: The Image of the Jew from 1880 to the Present* (University of Nebraska, 2008). Together with John-Paul Himka she co-edited *Bringing the Dark to Light: The Memory of the Holocaust in Postcommunist Europe* (University of Nebraska, 2013), and edited the forthcoming *Jewish Families in Europe, 1939-Present: History, Representation, and Memory*.

Kenneth B. Moss

is Felix Posen Associate Professor of Jewish History and Director, Stulman Program in Jewish Studies at The Johns Hopkins University. He is author of *Jewish Renaissance in the Russian Revolution* (Harvard, 2009), currently being translated into Hebrew for publication by the Zalman Shazar Center.

Joanna Nalewajko-Kulikov
is Assistant Professor, Department for the History of Intelligentsia, Institute of History, Polish Academy of Sciences and author of *Strategies of Survival: Jews on the Aryan Side in Warsaw* (in Polish, Warsaw 2004); and *Citizen of Yiddishland: About Jewish Communists in Poland* (in Polish, Warsaw 2009). She recently co-edited *Lesestunde/Lekcja czytania* (in Polish and German, Warsaw, 2013); and is author of a forthcoming book on *Haynt* (1908–1939).

Yohanan Petrovsky-Shtern
is Crown Family Professor of Jewish Studies at Northwestern University. He is also a Fulbright Specialist on East Europe; a Fellow at the Harvard Ukrainian Research Institute; an Honorary Visiting Professor at the Free Ukrainian University in Munich; and an honorary doctor of the National University Kyiv Mohyla Academy in Kyiv. He has published over one hundred articles and six books, including *The Golden-Age Shtetl: a New History of Jewish Life in East Europe* (Princeton, 2014), nominated for Pulitzer Prize.

Marci Shore
is Associate Professor of history at Yale University. She is the translator of Michał Głowiński's *The Black Seasons* (Northwestern University Press, 2005), and the author of *Caviar and Ashes: A Warsaw Generation's Life and Death in Marxism, 1918–1968* (Yale University, 2006), and *The Taste of Ashes: The Afterlife of Totalitarianism in Eastern Europe* (Crown Publishers, 2013).

Shaul Stampfer
is the Rabbi Edward Sandrow Professor of Soviet and East European Jewish History at the Hebrew University. He is the author of *Families, Rabbis and Education: Traditional Jewish Society in Nineteenth-Century Eastern Europe* (2010) and of *Lithuanian Yeshivas of the Nineteenth Century* (2012)—both published by the Littman Library of Jewish Civilization.

Michael Steinlauf
is Professor of History and Director of the Holocaust and Genocide Studies Program at Gratz College in Philadelphia. He is the author of *Bondage to the Dead: Poland and the Memory of the Holocaust* (Syracuse University Press, 1997) and a contributing editor to the YIVO *Encyclopedia of Jews in Eastern Europe*.

Scott Ury
is Senior Lecturer in Tel Aviv University's Department of Jewish History, where he is also Director of the Roth Institute for the Study of Contemporary

Antisemitism and Racism. He is author of *Barricades and Banners: The Revolution of 1905 and the Transformation of Warsaw Jewry* (Stanford, 2012). He is also co-editor of volume 24 of the annual *Polin* on "Jews and Their Neighbors in Eastern Europe since 1750," as well as a volume published by Routledge entitled *Cosmopolitanism, Nationalism and the Jews of East Central Europe* (2014).

Hanna Węgrzynek
is Chief Specialist for Research and Historical Projects at the Museum of the History of Polish Jews in Warsaw. She is the author of books and articles devoted to the history of Jews in Poland including *The Jewish "Black Legend": Blood Libel Trials in Old Poland* (in Polish; Warsaw, 1995); *History and Culture of Polish Jews: A Reference Book* (in Polish; Warsaw, 2000—jointly with Alina Cała and Gabriela Zalewska); *Milles ans des Juifs en Pologne* (Warsaw, 2004).

Kalman Weiser
is the Silber Family Professor of Modern Jewish Studies at York University in Toronto. He is the author of *Jewish People, Yiddish Nation. Noah Prylucki and the Folkists in Poland* (University of Toronto Press, 2011), co-editor of *Czernowitz at 100. The First Yiddish Language Conference in Historical Perspective* (Lexington Books, 2010), and co-editor of a new, revised edition of Solomon Birnbaum's 1979 *Yiddish: a Survey and a Grammar* (University of Toronto Press, 2015).

Joshua D. Zimmerman
is Associate Professor of History and the Eli and Diana Zborowski Professorial Chair in Holocaust Studies at Yeshiva University in New York. He is the author of *The Polish Underground and the Jews, 1939–1945* (Cambridge University Press, 2015), *Poles, Jews and the Politics of Nationality: The Bund and the Polish Socialist Party in Late Tsarist Russia, 1892–1914* (University of Wisconsin Press, 2004), as well as the editor of two contributed volumes: *Contested Memories: Poles and Jews during the Holocaust and its Aftermath* (Rutgers University Press, 2003) and *Jews in Italy under Fascist and Nazi Rule, 1922–1945* (Cambridge University Press, 2005).

List of Illustrations and Maps

Frontispiece: Bernardo Belotto, known as Canaletto, *Bridgettine Church and the Arsenal*, 1775 (detail).

1   Aleksander Lesser, *The Funeral of the Five Fallen in 1861* (1861).   9
2   Rosh Hashanah greeting postcard.   12
3   Bernardo Belotto, known as Canaletto, *Krakowskie Przedmieście seen from the Column of King Sigismund III*, 1767–1768.   27
4   Map: Places of origin of Warsaw Jews according to 1778 Census, created by Hanna Węgrzynek and Robert Chmielewski (2011).   32
5   Map: Warsaw in 1778—Places of Residence of Jews, created by Hanna Węgrzynek and Robert Chmielewski (2011).   36
6   Leon Hollaenderski: A Warsaw Jew and his Wife (1846).   101
7   Examples of Russian Merchant Dress Presented to the Warsaw Police, 1847.   111
8   Maksymilian Fajans: Funeral procession of the archbishop of Warsaw, Antoni Melchior Fijałkowski (d. 5 October 1861).   147
9   Yehudah Pen: The Watchmaker (1914).   253
10 Map: The Polish Republic in the Interwar Period, ca. 1930s.   297
11 Cover illustration to *Erd-vey* (Earth-woe), by Israel Joshua Singer (1922).   337
12 Cartoon "A General Electoral Bloc" (*Der sheygets*, Warsaw 1930).   401
13 Tearoom of a Po'ale Tsiyon home for workers in the Praga suburb, Warsaw, ca. 1920s.   425
14 Tłomackie Street Synagogue (1875; Leandro Marconi), Warsaw.   436
15 Ruins of the Tłomackie Street Synagogue, Warsaw, 1940s.   503

Introduction

In 1989, Antony Polonsky devoted an edition of the journal *Polin: Studies in Polish Jewry*, then in its third year of publication, to the history of what was once the largest Jewish community in the world, Warsaw Jewry. The edition was soon expanded into a stand-alone book, co-edited with Wladyslaw Bartoszewski, entitled *The Jews in Warsaw: A History* (Oxford: Basil Blackwell, 1991).[1] Together, these collections of essays constituted the first major project on the history of Warsaw Jewry since the appearance of Jacob Shatzky's three-volume *Geshikhte fun yidn in varshe* (A History of Jews in Warsaw) four decades earlier.[2]

Shatzky's history of the Jews of Warsaw had been magisterial but flawed. It had covered multiple facets of Jewish life in the Polish capital in extremely rich detail, but was at times speculative and under-documented. Moreover, it ended with the year 1896, with a planned fourth volume remaining unwritten owing to the author's growing pessimism about contemporary interest in his subject. "For whom am I slaving?" Shatzky wrote a colleague, echoing the lament of the nineteenth-century maskil Judah Leib Gordon. "My people is dead, my theme is a dead one and I am dead-tired."[3] Polonsky and Bartoszewski's *Jews in Warsaw*, in contrast, was fired with optimism sparked in the immediate aftermath of the fall of Poland's Communist regime and the triumph of Solidarity. Optimism seems to have driven the contributors' selection of topics: foreseeing a new Polish-Jewish rapprochement, many highlighted the process of Jewish Polonization and integration throughout the city's history while struggling to understand why many Warsaw Jews had failed to become "Poles of the Mosaic persuasion."

---

1 Wladyslaw Bartoszewski and Antony Polonsky (eds.), *The Jews in Warsaw: A History* (Oxford: Basil Blackwell, 1991). According to Professor Polonsky, "Wladek Bartoszewski and I were struck that we had the material for a separate volume on Warsaw and Blackwells, who had done well out of the [Abraham] Lewin diary, were eager to go ahead." They also received generous support from Jack Fliderbaum, "who was very keen for a volume on Warsaw." Private correspondence by email, October 10, 2013. See also the major entry by Antony Polonsky: "Warsaw," in Gershon D. Hundert (ed.), *YIVO Encyclopedia on Jews in Eastern Europe* (2 vols.; New Haven, CN; London: Yale University Press, 2008), 2: 1993–2004. This encyclopedia will be referred to throughout this volume as *YIVO Encyclopedia on Jews in Eastern Europe*.
2 Jacob Shatzky, *Geshikhte fun yidn in varshe* (3 vols.; New York: YIVO, 1947–53). It should be noted that Hillel Zeidman wrote a history of Warsaw Jewry that remains unpublished.
3 For an account of Shatzky's saga of writing the three volumes and compiling sources for a fourth, which involved the author's "mental collapse," see Robert Moses Shapiro, "Jacob Shatzky, Historian of Warsaw Jewry," in Bartoszewski and Polonsky, *Jews in Warsaw*, 363–76.

The current volume, an outgrowth of a conference held at University College London in 2010, builds upon both of these major edifices. In addition to addressing the problem of the failure of large-scale Polonization in Warsaw treated so effectively in *Jews in Warsaw*, contributors to this volume pursue the axiomatic side of the question that seemed to preoccupy Shatzky: what other forms, if not Polonization, did Jewish expression assume in Warsaw? Our efforts reflect a special gratitude towards Professor Polonsky, who over the last thirty years almost single-handedly created a forum where scholars from Poland, Israel, North America, Britain, and elsewhere could investigate the rich, varied, often poignant history of Polish Jewry in an atmosphere free of acrimony and apologetics, in particular in the pages of the journal *Polin*. Hence our decision to dedicate a volume on Jewish history in Warsaw—the scene of major Jewish cultural developments and the very capital of Polish Jewish modernity—to its preeminent historian, Antony Polonsky.

A Jewish Metropolis

The history of the Jews of Warsaw is arguably the history of the first true metropolis in diasporic Jewish history. Such a designation is first of all about numbers: for many years during the course of the 19th century, the Polish capital was home to the largest Jewish settlement in the world, and remained among the largest two or three communities in the decades before the Holocaust. However, a metropolis is also about diversity, and Jewish Warsaw, though perhaps appearing to outsiders as an opaque mass of Eastern European Jews, was a highly differentiated community consisting of Jews who had arrived from the small and larger Polish towns; Jews who had come from German territories during the short-lived Prussian rule; and waves of Jews moving to the Polish capital from the Pale of Settlement and, eventually, from the Soviet Union. Warsaw was also the arena for the emergence of clearly identified religious and secular-oriented sub-communities which were rather about religious and cultural choices, e.g., whether to adhere to the ideals of a Europeanized appearance, the New Jewish Politics (Zionism, Jewish Socialism, Diaspora Nationalism), or the various Hasidic and non-Hasidic traditionalist enclaves. Consonant with contemporary post-secular theory, Jewish modernity in Warsaw coexisted, however uneasily, with potent manifestations of counter-modernity.[4]

---

4 On traditionalist-secularist coexistence in contemporary cities, see for example Saba Mahmood, *Politics of Piety: The Islamic Revival and the Feminist Subject* (Princeton, NJ: Princeton University Press, 2005). On traditionalism and public religion today, see José

Although the boundaries between these diverse Jewish identifications remained permeable, they also offered basic ways to define, reject, or confirm allegiances. These 'narcissisms of small differences' were on full display in a community which was so self-contained—not in the least from a point of view of location in Jewish enclaves in the north of the city—and which created limited but highly symbolic forms of interaction with the neighbouring non-Jewish communities. The Polish capital would function as a quintessential metropolis especially with regard to those cultural and religious identifications: on the one hand, consolidating sub-communities by allowing them to attain a critical mass, but on the other hand forcing them to confront cultural difference, Jewish and non-Jewish. Thus, Warsaw became a major Hasidic center while exposing members of Hasidic communties to alternative lifestyles, e.g., new forms of political mobilization through nationalism or social-democracy that were more potent than they were in the provinces. Warsaw would also become an arena for testing new roles for Jewish women, as rebellious students in institutions of secondary and higher education, as political organizers, and sometimes as primary breadwinners for their families within a more traditional milieu.

This striking heterogeneity was not least due to Warsaw's emergence as a major center of Jewish economic involvement, in both international trade and industry. For several decades, Warsaw would form a point of intersection between East and West, offering leading positions for foreign and native entrepreneurs and bankers. These diverse elites would be among the central players in the young Jewish metropolis, which already by the mid-19th century had ceased to conform to the traditional model of a centralized community with steep hierarchies. The Jewish metropolis was also a site of *bricolage*, of testing new forms of Jewish political, religious, and civil leadership, with only modest attempts to maintain an appearance of uniformity. Authoritarian Russian rule created challenging conditions for developing functional and efficient charitable, religious and educational institutions—even though it may be argued that from the demise of the January Uprising of 1863–64 until the end of the Russian occupation in World War One it was easier for the Jews of Warsaw to develop such institutions than for the Polish majority.

Lastly, it was the Warsaw metropolis that forced Jews to rise to considerable challenges like mass pauperization and deprivation during the Great War and the growing acrimony of Polish-Jewish confrontations after the re-emergence

---

Casanova, *Public Religions in the Modern World* (Chicago, IL: University of Chicago Press, 1994); and Dipesh Chakrabarty, *Habitations of Modernity: Essays in the Wake of Subaltern Theory* (Chicago, IL: University of Chicago Press, 2002).

of an independent Polish state. Although antisemitism undoubtedly embittered Jewish life in the Polish capital, the Jewish community itself offered refuge through its sheer numbers, its freedom of religious and political expression relative to Soviet cities, and, above all, its resources for defense and reassertion, at least until the German occupation during World War Two annihilated this unique community of opposites.

The Beginnings of Jewish Warsaw

The first phase of Jewish settlement in Warsaw ended almost as soon as it began. Not long after the first recorded Jewish presence in 1414, Warsaw's Christian residents attempted to fend off Jewish economic competition by instigating a series of expulsions (1455, 1483, and 1498). And in 1527, when the Mazovia (Mazowsze) province was incorporated into the Polish Crown, King Zygmunt granted Christian residents a *de non tolerandis Judaeis* privilege, thereby banning Jews from the city. Lest there be any misunderstanding, King Zygmunt August reiterated his ban in 1570. "No Jew, Jewess, Jewish child or servant (be the latter Jewish or Christian) shall dwell with property or wares within the limits of Old Warsaw or New Warsaw," began his series of decrees. To be on the safe side, he demarcated a two-mile buffer zone around the city that was to be free of Jewish residence and trade.[5]

But Warsaw, which became the capital of the Polish-Lithuanian Commonwealth in 1596, offered too many economic opportunities for a resourceful, landless Jewish population. In her chapter in the present volume, Hanna Węgrzynek finds evidence of an "enormous, unofficial Jewish community in Warsaw during the period when the *de non tolerandis Judaeis* law was in force." In addition to noble-owned jurisdictions (*jurydyki*) within Warsaw, where historians have already noted a Jewish presence, Węgrzynek uncovers a substantial illegal Jewish presence in several neighborhoods in Warsaw proper, including sacrosanct Old Warsaw. Notwithstanding their official absence, the Jews of Warsaw grew from an estimated 2,500 people in 1764 to 3,534 by 1778, and to 6,750 by 1792. This may mean that Warsaw, already at that moment in time, was home to the largest concentration of Jews in all of Poland-Lithuania and, together with Amsterdam and Prague, one of the largest in all of Europe.

Becoming a legal community was another matter. Debates over Jewish settlement in Warsaw raged throughout the Four Year Sejm (1788–92), a last-ditch attempt to reform the Polish-Lithuanian Commonwealth after its first partition

---

5 Bartoszewski and Polonsky, *Jews in Warsaw*, 3–4.

by Russia, Prussia, and Austria. These debates were accompanied by violent protests by Warsaw's Christian residents, which included a major riot on May 16, 1790,[6] as well as a major political effort by leading Polish-Lithuanian Jewish communities to secure a legal status.[7] The May 3rd Constitution nevertheless remained silent on the issue of Jewish settlement in Warsaw and, to make matters worse for Warsaw's Jews, abolished the noble jurisdictions that had served as their refuge. During Tadeusz Kościuszko's uprising against Poland's rapacious neighbours in 1794, in the wake of a second partition of Poland-Lithuania, Berek Joselewicz (1764–1809), a Jewish leaseholder of Lithuanian origin, formed a Jewish armed unit in order to contribute to the defence of the Polish capital. His efforts became a powerful *lieu de mémoire* of Polish-Jewish history.[8]

During the Era of the Partitions

Jewish status in Warsaw was only regulated after the third partition, when Poland-Lithuania had been effectively reduced to a Russian, Prussian, Austrian, and, briefly, French colony. On December 21, 1799, the Prussian regime that had ruled over Warsaw since 1796 established that Jews who had arrived in the city after 1796 were to pay an annual tribute (210,000 zlotys) while Jews arriving there after that date would be subject to a ticket charge of one zloty per day. In 1802, the Prussian regime extended formal rights to entire Jewish populations in all towns under its dominion, including Warsaw.[9] The official recognition of what was already possibly the largest concentration of Jews in Europe seems to have helped raise Warsaw's international profile. As Cornelia Aust shows in her chapter, a select group of Jewish merchants, army suppliers, and entrepreneurs were attracted there, helping to ensure the emergence of Warsaw as a

---

6 See Krystyna Zienkowska, " 'The Jews Have Killed a Tailor': The Socio-political Background of a Riot in Warsaw in 1790," in Bartoszewski and Polonsky, *Jews in Warsaw*, 127–50.
7 Artur Eisenbach (ed.), *Materiały do dziejów Sejmu Czteroletniego*, vol. 6 (Wrocław: Zakład narodowy im. Ossolińskich, 1968), passim; Jacob Goldberg, "Pierwszy ruch polityczny wśród Żydów polskich: plenipotenci żydowscy w dobie Sejmu Czteroletniego," in Jerzy Michalski (ed.), *Lud żydowski w narodzie polskim* (Warszawa: Instytut Historii PAN, 1994), 7–18.
8 A reflection on Joselewicz in the broader context of Jews and their relationship to military service see Derek Penslar, *Jews and the Military: a History* (Princeton, NJ: Princeton University Press, 2013), 56–57.
9 Artur Eisenbach, "Jews in Warsaw at the End of the 18th Century," in Bartoszewski and Polonsky, *Jews in Warsaw*, 106–7.

commercial and financial center in Eastern Europe with ties to western centers like Prussia and Amsterdam.

Warsaw reemerged in the early nineteenth century as the capital of an ambiguously reconstituted "Poland." Both the Duchy of Warsaw (1807–1814) and its successor state, the Kingdom of Poland (1815–1918), were technically autonomous and constitutional. But as neither Napoleon, as the ultimate ruler of the Duchy of Warsaw, nor the tsars, as the "kings" of the Kingdom of Poland, were willing to countenance a truly autonomous Polish state, the situation is probably better described as a kind of "soft" colonialism. This was particularly the case of the Kingdom of Poland, where the tsars routinely violated its constitutional guarantees, suppressed Polish nationalism, ignored Polish governmental representatives, and proceeded to all but remove Polish autonomy in the wake of two major Polish uprisings, 1830–1 and 1863–4. The hollowness of that autonomy was also reflected in Jewish policy which, despite numerous debates on the "Jewish question" by Polish publicists, was usually determined by tsarist decree.[10] Nevertheless, the Kingdom of Poland did retain a pronounced Polish character and, together with the Galician capitals of Kraków and Lwów, it was to form the main setting of the Polish national struggle, with Warsaw at its epicenter.

In this tumultuous atmosphere, Jewish aspirations continued to diverge internally. Western-oriented Jews like Isaac Flatau, who had arrived in Warsaw during the Prussian occupation, established a "modern," German-style synagogue in 1802 which, from 1859, offered sermons in Polish by Rabbi Marcus Jastrow. Jewish government clerks like Jacob Tugendhold and Antoni Eisenbaum, who championed outright Polonization, helped lay the groundwork for integration by establishing Jewish elementary and secondary schools and, in 1826, a modern Rabbinical School for training a modern, integrationist rabbinate.[11] However, the removal of Hebrew instruction from the elementary

---

10   Several Polish scholars have begun referring to the situation in the Kingdom of Poland and Galicia as one of colonization, though the situation was not comparable to colonial rule in, say, India or Latin America. For recent examples, see the essays in Krzysztof Stępnik and Dariusz Trześniowski, *Studia postkolonialne nad kulturą i cywilizacją Polską* (Lublin: Wydawnictwo Uniwersytetu Marii Curie-Skłodowskiej, 2010); and the special issue of *Historyka* 42 (2012), "Postcolonial Galicia: Prospects and Possibilities," available at http://historyka.edu.pl/en/article/art/historica-2012–29/ (consulted on 4/30/14). On the struggle between Polish publicists, conservative landowners, and the tsarist state over Jewish policy, see Glenn Dynner, *Yankel's Tavern: Jews, Liquor, and Life in the Kingdom of Poland* (New York: Oxford University Press, 2013).

11   See Antony Polonsky, *The Jews in Poland and Russia* (3 vols.; Oxford: Littman Library of Jewish Civilization, 2009–12), 1: 294–5; Zofia Borzymińska, *Szkolnictwo Żydowskie w*

school curricula and the exclusion of the study of the Talmud from the Rabbinical school curriculum alienated not only Warsaw's tradition-oriented majority but also maskilim—proponents of the transnational Hebraist movement known as Haskalah—who sought a more moderate synthesis between Jewish and European culture along rationalist lines.[12] Ela Bauer's chapter illuminates the Haskalah career of Hayyim Zelig Slonimski, charting his efforts to disseminate scientific knowledge in Hebrew to the East European Jewish masses. His stewardship of the Hebrew periodical *Ha-tzefirah* and a Jewish Public Library helped create a gateway to modernity for more traditional Polish Jews, though his eventual return to Russia may reflect the comparatively small scale of Haskalah in the kingdom. More successful were the kingdom's Jewish advocates of outright Polonization. While their Rabbinical School failed to produce rabbis who were acceptable to the Jewish masses, they did establish a Polish synagogue on Nalewki Street, a majestic "Great Synagogue" at Tłomackie Street, a Jewish Hospital and orphanage, and Polish Jewish periodicals like *Jutrzenka* (The Dawn, 1861–3) and *Izraelita* (Israelite, 1866–1913).[13]

Warsaw was also a major incubator of East European Jewry's quintessential movement of counter-modernity, Hasidism. While Hasidism's spectacular growth in a major urban center might seem counter-intuitive, Polish Hasidic leaders managed to attract some of Warsaw's most prominent Jewish mercantile and banking elites by granting them a sense of belonging and influence commensurate with their wealth.[14] In addition to developing a popular

---

Warszawie, 1831–1870 (Warszawa: ŻIH, 1994); and Michał Galas, *Rabbi Marcus Jastrow and his Vision for the Reform of Judaism* (trans. Anna Tilles; Boston, MA: Academic Studies Press, 2013), 25–46.

12   For a definition of Haskalah that reflects the scholarly consensus, see Shmuel Feiner, "Towards a Historical Definition of Haskalah," in Feiner and David Sorkin (eds.), *New Perspectives on the Haskalah* (London: Littman, 2001), esp. 185; and Michael Stanislawski, *For Whom Do I Toil? Judah Leib Gordon and the Crisis of Russian Jewry* (Oxford: Oxford University Press, 1988), 4.

13   See Martin Wodziński, *Hasidism and Haskalah in the Kingdom of Poland* (London: Littman Library of Jewish Civilization, 2005), 154–255; and Alexander Guterman, "The Congregation of the Great Synagogue in Warsaw: its Changing Social Composition and Ideological Affiliations," *Polin* 11 (1998): 112–26.

14   On the role of the Jewish mercantile elite in fomenting the spread of Hasidism into Warsaw and beyond, see Glenn Dynner, *Men of Silk: The Hasidic Conquest of Polish Jewish Society* (New York: Oxford University Press, 2006), esp. chapters 1 and 3; and François Guesnet, "Thinking Globally, Acting Locally: Joel Wegmeister and Modern Hasidic Politics in Warsaw," *Quest: Issues in Contemporary Jewish History. Journal of Fondazione CDEC* 2 (October 2011): www.quest-cdecjournal.it/focus.php?id=222.

earth-bound form of mysticism centered around charismatic *tzaddikim* (*rebbes* in Yiddish), Hasidim established prayer houses and yeshivas throughout the city, as well as courts within towns in close proximity to Warsaw.[15] As Glenn Dynner's chapter on the "clothing decrees" suggests, heavy-handed government attempts to reform the Jewish population by imposing modern modes of dress inadvertently strengthened the hand of Hasidic leaders like R. Isaac Meir Alter, the future Gerer *rebbe*.

The diversification of communal authority was one of several transformative processes that were gaining in momentum, as François Guesnet argues in his chapter on demographic growth, institutional development, and communal and political reconfigurations in the third quarter of the nineteenth century—a period which, the author suggests, witnessed the emergence of a multi-polar and multi-cultural Jewish metropolis. The growing heterogeneity also affected the city's religious leadership. Shaul Stampfer shows how tensions between Hasidim and Mitnaggdim undermined the tenure of Warsaw's chief rabbi, R. Jacob Gesundheit. An affluent non-Hasidic traditionalist who served as Warsaw's chief rabbi from 1870, Gesundheit was forcibly deposed in 1873 by a curious coalition of Ger Hasidim and Jewish integrationists, which marked the end of the Warsaw chief rabbinate itself.

Warsaw in this period gained renown as the focal point of Jewish mobilization for Polish patriotic causes, particularly before and during the 1863 Polish uprising against the tsar. Artists and writers have exalted this moment of Polish and Jewish fraternization—note, for example, the iconic Alexander Lesser painting of Warsaw's chief rabbi, R. Dov Ber Meisels, imagined accompanying the Archbishop of Warsaw at the funeral of the first victims of the demonstrations in 1861 that foregrounded the insurrection [see fig. 1]. Jewish historians, for their part, have avidly studied the estimated 2,000 Jews, mainly from Warsaw, who volunteered for Polish units. Such works celebrate Warsaw as a site of Polish-Jewish integration.[16]

---

15   Eleonora Bergman, *"Nie masz bóżniczy powszechnej:" Synagogi i Domy Modlitwy w Warszawie od końca XVIII do początku XXI wieku* (Warszawa: DiG, 2007), 136–57 and 91; Shaul Stampfer, "Hasidic Yeshivas in Interwar Poland," in idem, *Families, Rabbis, and Education: Traditional Jewish Society in Nineteenth-Century Eastern Europe* (Oxford and Portland, OR: Littman Library of Jewish Civilization, 2010), 252–74.

16   Artur Eisenbach, *The Emancipation of the Jews in Poland, 1780–1870* (Oxford: Blackwell, 1991), 433–39; Abraham Duker, "Jewish Participants in the Polish Insurrection of 1863," in George Alexander Kohut (ed.), *Studies and Essays in honor of Abraham A. Neuman* (Philadelphia, PA: E. J. Brill, 1962); N.M. Gelber, "Antayl fun yidn in oyfshtand fun 1863," *Lodzsher visnshaftlekhe shriftn* 1 (1938): 264–6. On the cultural reverberations of Jewish participation, see Magdalena Opalski and Israel Bartal, *Poles and Jews: A Failed*

FIGURE 1   *Aleksander Lesser*, The Funeral of the Five Fallen in 1861 *(1861)*.

Less commonly explored is Warsaw's transformation, from the perspective of Diaspora Jewry, into a pronounced Jewish metropolis with a varied publishing industry that churned out rich and diverse works in Hebrew, Yiddish, and to a lesser extent, Polish. As Nathan Cohen outlines in his chapter, the Warsaw Jewish printing enterprise included works on the sciences, medicine, lexicography, belle lettres, and *shund* literature. This intellectual variety, fueled by a major "Litvak" influx in the late-nineteenth century, helped transform Warsaw into an epicenter of Hebrew and Yiddish revival and a leading center of Jewish culture.

Notwithstanding Warsaw Jewry's increasing fragmentation, the community experienced a genuine cultural renaissance during the first half of the twentieth century. A major catalyst was the Russian Revolution of 1905, a transformative experience for civil society throughout the Russian Empire but resonating with particular force in the Kingdom of Poland, its capital, and its capital's

---

Brotherhood (Hanover, NH: Brandeis University Press, 1992), esp. 103; and Israel Bartal, *The Jews of Eastern Europe, 1772–1881* (Philadelphia, PA: University of Pennsylvania Press, 2002), 87. See also the documents in A. Eisenbach, D. Fajnhauz, and A. Wein (eds.), *Żydzi a powstanie styczniowe: materiały i dokumenty* (Warszawa: PWN, 1963); Zofia Borzymińska, *Dzieje żydów w Polsce: wybór tekstów źródłowych XIX wieku* (Warszawa: ŻIH, 1994), 113–24; and the appendix to Shatzky, *Geshikhte fun yidn in varshe*, II.

Jewish community.[17] The Jewish youth who streamed into the city influenced, and were themselves influenced by, the young metropolis. Scott Ury points to the hitherto neglected role of Warsaw's Jewish public sphere, nurtured by numerous coffee houses, many of which were open on the Sabbath. These coffee houses, Ury argues, served as commercial covers for vociferous political and social debates among the city's newly-arrived, unattached youth and, unlike the Hasidic *shtiblekh*, eluded religious authorities.

One of the most robust developments in Warsaw was the creation of secular Yiddish culture. A host of writers and cultural brokers, many of whom were "Litvaks," began to forge the vernacular language of Polish Jewry into an instrument of modernization, perhaps most importantly by means of the Yiddish press: no less than eleven Yiddish journals and newspapers had appeared by 1907.[18] Key to the flourishing of secular Yiddish Warsaw was the man who, according to Michael Steinlauf, stood at the "prophetic center of modern Yiddish culture," I.L. Perets. Through his publications in the periodical *Der Veg*, argues Steinlauf, Perets battled Polonizing Jews who, "with the quiet partnership of Ger and other Hasidic dynasties," he felt, were suppressing the national potential of Polish Jewry. Yet anchored as he was in his Diasporic Yiddish world, Perets remained skeptical of the utopian promises of Jewish Socialists, not to mention Zionists. Nevertheless, as Joanna Nalewajko-Kulikov argues, the Zionist Yiddish daily *Haynt* became absolutely integral to Warsaw Jewish life. Most *Haynt* contributors, she finds, were multi-lingual young men from a traditional milieu who had attained a university education, thus embodying a convergence of traditionalism and secularization that proved powerfully resonant.

In the Interwar Period

While Warsaw's Jewish population had risen impressively during the course of the nineteenth century (from 72,776 in 1864, to 210,526 in 1897), so had

---

17 Stefani Hoffman and Ezra Mendelsohn (eds.), *The Revolution of 1905 and Russia's Jews* (Philadelphia, PA: University of Pennsylvania Press, 2008); François Guesnet, "Revolutionary Hinterland: Transformations of Jewish Associational Life in the Kingdom of Poland, 1904–06," in Franziska Schedewie et al. (eds.), *The Russian Revolution of 1905 in Transcultural Perspective: Identities, Peripheries, and the Flow of Ideas* (Bloomington, IN: Slavica Publishers, 2013), 105–120.

18 For a conceptualization of literary production that takes into account an array of figures and institutions beyond writers themselves, see Pierre Bourdieu, *The Field of Cultural Production: Essays on Art and Literature* (ed. Randal Johnson; New York: Columbia University Press, 1993), 29–73.

Warsaw's Catholic population (from 131,808 in 1864, to 347,565 in 1897). Both Jews and Christians—including especially emancipated serfs—were drawn in by employment opportunities afforded by Warsaw's growing industrial arena, which consisted of metal-working, chemicals, textiles, foodstuffs, and clothing.[19] Proportionally, the Jewish population of Warsaw had remained stable at around 33 percent throughout the entire nineteenth century.[20] Jewish migration to the capital city was thus part of a more general urbanization trend, notwithstanding the alarm expressed in certain government circles.[21] The Jewish proportion did rise rather dramatically in Warsaw during the first decade of the twentieth century, peaking at 39.18 percent (306,061) by 1910. However, it declined by 3 percent per decade thereafter thanks to Jewish emigration, bottoming out at 29 percent (375,000) in 1939.[22] Claims that Warsaw was being "Judaized steadily and invaded by people unable to support themselves" are thus exaggerated.[23]

As the suppression of many forms of Jewish culture commenced in Soviet Russia during the interwar period, Warsaw's importance for the cultivation of Jewish artistic, intellectual, and religious life would only increase [see fig. 2]. This cultural effervescence occurred in the midst of a struggle over the very nature of the newly independent Polish state—was such a state to be Polish in an exclusive, ethnic national sense, or Polish in a way that made room for alternate expressions of ethnicity and religion? The relatively large-scale Jewish emigration from Poland throughout the early twentieth century reflected the temporary predominance of the former, xenophobic view and attendant interethnic tensions, which spawned economic boycotts and collective anti-Jewish violence. Robert Blobaum traces the "downhill slide in Polish-Jewish

---

19 See Bartoszewski and Polonsky, "Introduction," *Jews in Warsaw*, 19; see also Bina Garntsarska-Kedary, *Helkam shel ha-yehudim be'hitpathut ha-ta'asiyah shel varshe be'shanim 1816/20–1914* (Tel Aviv, 1985); Stanisław Koszutski, *Rozwój ekonomiczny Królestwa Polskiego w ostatnim trzydziestoleciu 1870–1900* (Warszawa: Nakład Księgarni Naukowej, 1905).

20 Stephen D. Corrsin, "Aspects of Population Change and of Acculturation in Jewish Warsaw at the End of the Nineteenth Century: The Censuses of 1882 and 1897," in Bartoszewski and Polonsky, *Jews in Warsaw*, 214. See also some fascinating data in Corrsin's monograph *Warsaw before the First World War* (New York: Columbia University Press, 1989), "Tables."

21 A report from 1845 used the allegedly disproportionate Jewish migration to justify the current residential restrictions in the city. See AGAD, KRSW 202, 168–170.

22 Piotr Wróbel, "Jewish Warsaw before the First World War," and Edward Winot Jr., "Jews in Inter-war Warsaw," in Bartoszewski and Polonsky, *Jews in Warsaw*, 255, Table 1, and 292, Table 1.

23 See Norman Davies, *God's Playground: A History of Poland* (2 vols.; New York: Oxford University Press, 2005), 2: 150.

FIGURE 2   *Rosh Hashanah greeting postcard. The postcard depicts a Reform and an Orthodox Jew shaking hands. The Yiddish verse reads: "'German' [Reform Jew] or Hasid, rich or poor, / Be brotherly and shake hands! / May you be inscribed for the new year—/ Whoever or whatever you are!" Published by Verlag Jehudia, Warsaw. From the Archives of the YIVO Institute for Jewish Research, New York. Courtesy of YIVO.*

relations in Warsaw" to the First World War, isolating food shortages and the stereotype of Jewish "food profiteers" as a major source of suspicions and recriminations. Nevertheless, Blobaum notes a striking absence of collective anti-Jewish violence in Warsaw during the Great War, in contrast to a city like Lwow, which he attributes to the smooth transitions of power occurring in Warsaw as it emerged as capital of a newly independent Poland in 1918.

In the wake of the First World War, Warsaw continued to develop as a site of Yiddish belles lettres, emerging as a center that arguably outpaced Vilna. This was to a great extent the result of the division of East European Jewry between the Soviet Union and Poland. Kalman Weiser, in his chapter, explains that the estrangement of Soviet from non-Soviet spheres in the 1920s necessitated a western capital of "Yiddishland." Despite the continued presence of Polonizing influences, Warsaw emerged as Vilna's main rival for Yiddish literary production thanks, in part, to a huge influx of Litvaks. Genady Estreikh illustrates a similar process with respect to Kiev, home to the Kultur-Lige, an organization created to nourish an autonomous or "nationalistic" Yiddish culture. Estreikh charts the transplant of the Kultur-Lige from Kiev to Warsaw in 1921 after its suppression by the new Soviet regime.

There were other reasons besides Yiddish publishing enterprises and the Litvak influx for the diversification of Warsaw's Jewish milieu. Gershon Bacon argues for the emergence of new forms of religious authority and of orthodox leadership, both formal and informal, within Warsaw. Natalia Aleksiun describes the influx from Galicia of a generation of Polish Jewish intellectuals who devoted themselves to the writing of Polish Jewish history in order to demonstrate Jewish belonging in an atmosphere of rising xenophobia and antisemitism. Then there was the New Jewish Politics, a subject treated throughout the pages of *Polin*, Professor Polonsky's seminal *Jews in Poland and Russia*, and other major monographs.[24] Kenneth Moss provides a distinctive addition to that literature by measuring the elusive size and influence of Jewish political movements. Emphasizing the fluidity of allegiances and attachments, Moss argues that Zionism nevertheless became a point of reference for a host of other kinds of nationalism thanks to the concrete presence of Zionist personalities, sports teams, conferences, and central branch offices in Warsaw. At the same time, he notices that Zionism's adversaries, including

---

24 Antony Polonsky, *The Jews in Poland and Russia*, vol. 3: *1914–2008* (London: Littman Library of Jewish Civilization, 2012). See also Ezra Mendelsohn, *Zionism in Poland: The Formative Years, 1915–1926* (New Haven, CT and London: Yale University Press, 1982); and idem, *The Jews of East-Central Europe between the World Wars* (Bloomington, IN: Indiana University Press, 1983), 11–84.

Bundists and Hasidim, sustained their own politically-charged subcultures by means of similarly visible and elastic institutions.

The Destruction of Warsaw Jewry and Its Aftermath

In August, 1939, a month before the German invasion of Poland that marked the beginning of World War II and the end of the heyday of Polish Jewry, 359,827 Jews resided in Warsaw. While they composed only 28.2 percent of Warsaw's population by now, they still constituted the second largest Jewish community in the world, after New York City, and the largest in Europe. Under German occupation, Warsaw Jewry's demographic status was at turns bloated by forcible influxes from surrounding towns and villages and emaciated through starvation, disease, and death. The new Governor of the District of Warsaw, Ludwig Fischer, completed the ghettoization of the Jews of Warsaw by November 15, 1940. By January of the next year, around 410,000 Jews were crammed into north-central Warsaw.[25]

The problem of overcrowding was ultimately resolved in the worst way imaginable. The mass deportation of 310,000 Warsaw Jewish men, women, and children to their deaths in Treblinka II in the summer and autumn of 1942, the heroic stand taken by many of the remaining 35,000 Jews in the Warsaw Ghetto, and the attempt to flee and hide by an almost equal number, have received excellent treatment by historians, including the late Yisrael Gutman.[26] The chapters here, however, expand historical investigation of the tragedy in important ways.

Joshua Zimmerman finds that the underground newspaper of the Polish Home Army, *Biuletyn Informacyjny*, consistently reported on Nazi atrocities

---

25 Bartoszewski, "The Martyrdom and Struggle of the Jews in Warsaw under German Occupation, 1939–43," in Bartoszewski and Polonsky, *Jews of Warsaw*, 312–48.

26 See Israel Gutman, *Resistance: The Warsaw Ghetto Uprising* (New York: Mariner Books, 1998); idem, *The Jews of Warsaw, 1939–1943: Ghetto, Underground, Revolt* (Bloomington, IN: Indiana University Press, 1982). More recently, see Samuel Kassow, *Who Will Write Our History? Emanuel Ringelblum, the Warsaw Ghetto, and the Oyneg Shabes Archive* (Bloomington, IN: Indiana University Press, 2007); and Gunnar Paulsson, *Secret City: The Hidden Jews of Warsaw, 1940–1945* (New Haven, CN: Yale University Press, 2003). Searing diary accounts include Emanuel Ringelblum, *Notes from the Warsaw Ghetto* (New York: Ibooks, 2006); Abraham Lewin, *A Cup of Tears: A Diary of the Warsaw Ghetto* (ed. Antony Polonsky; London: Fontana Press, 1990); and Chaim Kaplan, *Scroll of Agony: The Warsaw Diary of Chaim A. Kaplan* (Bloomington, IN: Indiana University Press, 1999).

against Jews with empathy and outrage, challenging our conception of Polish attitudes during the destruction of Warsaw Jewry. Havi Dreifus undertakes an examination of the neglected attitudes and behavior of religious leaders, including Hasidic *rebbes*, in the Warsaw Ghetto. Those leaders, rather than interpreting the decline of religious observance in the ghetto as deriving from the current tragedy, insisted instead that religious laxity was its very cause. Samuel Kassow examines the precious testimony of Rachel Auerbach, who reported on the horrific daily events like her more famous colleague Emmanuel Ringelblum but focused much more on the everyday Jews and individual artists and intellectuals who lent vibrancy to a dying Jewish Warsaw. He also illustrates Auerbach's unrelenting efforts to organize and regroup Jewish social self-help, most importantly in the '*Aleynhilf*' (Jewish Social Selfhelp), a network of Jewish charities attempting to maintain at least minimal communal structures in the ghetto. Joanna Michlic's chapter reinserts Polish Christians into the story of Warsaw Jewish survival by examining early postwar requests for compensation to the Central Committee of Polish Jews (CKŻP) written by Christian Polish rescuers and the Jews they had saved. Michlic argues that such letters often reveal humanitarian motivations and uncommon courage among Polish rescuers.

What emerged out of the rubble of Jewish Warsaw? The Jewish metropolis was no more—a mere 7,111 Jews were recorded residing in Warsaw by August of 1945. But Jewish life began to reconstitute itself there, however slowly. Gabriel Finder describes how the Central Committee of Polish Jews was instrumental in enabling Polish Jewry to try fellow Jews suspected of excessive collaboration with the Nazi regime by means of "honor courts." At the same time, David Engel finds that a natural reemergence of a Jewish community was stunted by policies of the new Polish government which, seeking legitimacy by presenting itself and its capital as being as "Polish" as possible, purposely diverted Jewish returnees and funds to other cities.

Nevertheless, in an echo of the pre-modern situation, an embryonic Jewish community stubbornly reestablished itself. Karen Auerbach points to a kind of residential identity among postwar Warsaw Jews, illustrated through a handful of Jewish families who worked for publishing houses of the communist government and chose to move into the same apartment building at 16 Ujazdowskie Avenue. However, if an ideological commitment to the communist regime initially bound such Warsaw Jewish families together, disappointment with the regime's repressiveness seems to have united their children's generation. Marci Shore describes how intellectuals like Adam Michnik, Jan Gross, and other intellectuals of mainly Jewish origin coalesced around the philosopher Leszek Kołakowski and, beginning in 1968, articulated a principled opposition to the regime. The latter, desperate for survival, drew attention to their Jewish roots and pressured many to leave, effectively purging Warsaw of Jews yet again.

The rise of the Solidarity movement and the fall of a divisive communist regime in 1989 represents a kind of new beginning, shadowed as it may be by the scale of past tragedy. A proud, visible Jewish life in Warsaw and throughout Poland seems in evidence now, and a Museum of the History of Polish Jews, with Professor Polonsky as its Chief Historian, has opened during the preparation of this volume. Students in Polish institutions of higher learning are eagerly studying the shared Polish-Jewish history, and their investigation of this shared past increasingly reflects an impressive linguistic range, including Hebrew and Yiddish. Finally, archives and holdings containing rich sources on Polish Jewish history have become newly accessible, making possible many of the essays in the current volume. The project of writing Polish Jewish history all over again, which Professor Polonsky has so energetically encouraged over the past decades, is now well underway.

Glenn Dynner and François Guesnet

PART 1

The Rise of the Metropolis

∴

CHAPTER 1

Illegal Immigrants: The Jews of Warsaw, 1527–1792

Hanna Węgrzynek

On April 18, 1788, Zelman Abramowicz of Biała, a 59-year-old Jewish resident in Warsaw accused of theft, supplied his interrogators with the following biographical information:

> From birth I lived with my parents until I was 15. When they died, I went to the town of Ema [probably Jena] to my faithless uncle Moszek and stayed with him for two years. From there I got to Berlin, where I stayed for four years teaching Jewish children. From Berlin I returned to the town of Mszczonów and taught children there for two years. After that I got married in Biała and became a merchant, and continued in that occupation for 30 years. Having failed in commerce, I went to Szmul [Zbytkower] in Praga as a slaughterhouse clerk and worked for him for a year. I came here to Warsaw four years ago.... I earn a living here from buying and selling secondhand goods.[1]

Next, Zelman's 23-year-old son, Majorek Zelmanowicz, was called on to tell his story:

> I have no craft skills. From birth I lived with my parents [in Biała] until the age of 11, when I went into service in the town of Węgrów with the Jewish merchant Leyzer and worked for him as an apprentice for seven years. After leaving him I went to Sochaczew and married the daughter of the faithless Josek Lewkowicz, and lived seven years with my parents-in-law in the village of Waliszew in the Gostynin area. From there I came with my wife to Warsaw to my brother Abramek, who is a translator at Warsaw Castle Royal Court. He had promised to find me a tavern I could manage on the outskirts of the city, but I have nothing so far, since Abramek has not yet been able to arrange anything, and I have been here in Warsaw for half a year.[2]

---

1 Archiwum Główne Akt Dawnych (Central Archives of Historical Records) [AGAD], Archiwum Królestwa Polskiego [AKP] 311.
2 AGAD, AKP 311.

These rich depositions provide rare perspectives on Jewish domestic and economic life in Warsaw during the eighteenth century. But their mere existence is intriguing, as well: in this period, as in previous centuries, Jewish residence in Warsaw was technically illegal.

Zelman and his son Majorek were not alone. They were part of an enormous, underground Jewish community in Warsaw during the period when the *de non tolerandis Judaeis* law was in force, i.e., the period when Jews were theoretically not allowed to live in Warsaw. The issue is not uncomplicated. This lengthy period of illegal residence was characterized by an ongoing rivalry between Warsaw Jews, who attempted to attain rights to legal residence, and Catholic townspeople, who spared no effort to prevent it. At the same time, new sources suggest that Jewish residence in Warsaw was in certain cases actually made possible by members of the latter group, in addition to members of the nobility and clergy. This chapter tells the story of how, with the complicity of Catholic nobles, merchants and clergy alike, Warsaw came to contain the largest concentration of Jews in the Polish-Lithuanian Commonwealth, and perhaps in all of Europe, long before Jewish residence there was even legal.

A History of the Settlement and Expulsion

The study of the early history of Warsaw Jewry remains in its infancy.[3] Jews had lived in Warsaw since at least the beginning of the fifteenth century, according

---

3 The history of Warsaw Jews in medieval and modern times was the subject of several studies by Emanuel Ringelblum, e.g. *Żydzi w Warszawie: Od czasów najdawniejszych do ostatniego wygnania w r. 1527* (Warszawa: Towarzystwo Miłośników Historii, 1932). While the overall importance of his published monograph on the topic has to be acknowledged, some of his findings are in need of verification and revision. See my articles "Żydzi w Warszawie przed XIX wiekiem," in *Żydzi Warszawy: Materiały konferencji w Żydowskim Instytucie Historycznym w 100 rocznicę urodzin Emanuela Ringelbluma* (Warszawa: Żydowski Instytut Historyczny, 2000), 27–41; and "Czy w 1483 r. książę mazowiecki Bolesław V wygnał Żydów z Warszawy? Możliwości interpretacji dokumentów miejskich," *Acta Universitatis Wratislaviensis, Historia* CLXXI (2005): 513–51. Less known is an additional study by Ringelblum on the history of Warsaw Jews, which covers the period from 1527 to the end of the eighteenth century. It was never completed and survives in manuscript form, in Yiddish, and is held in the collections of the Jewish Historical Institute in Warsaw. See Archiwum Żydowskiego Instytutu Historycznego w Warszawie (Archive of the Jewish Historical Institute in Warsaw), Archiwum Ringelbluma 401–404. See also Artur Eisenach, *Z dziejów ludności żydowskiej w Polsce w XVIII i XIX wieku* (Warszawa: Państwowy Instytut Wydawniczy, 1983); and Jacob Shatzky, *Geshikhte fun yidn in varshe*, vol. 1 (New York: YIVO, 1947), both of which have yet to

to the oldest surviving records, in both Old and New Warsaw.[4] At that point, the latter were effectively two separate towns, to judge by a census of Jews made in 1423[5] and extant bills of exchange, including those signed in Hebrew.[6] The turning point for Warsaw Jews came when the Mazovia (Mazowsze) province was incorporated into the Polish Crown from 1526 to 1529. As part of the incorporation act, King Sigismund I granted Warsaw's Christian residents the privilege of *de non tolerandis Iudaeis*, banning their Jewish competitors from the Old and New Towns as well as the suburbs.[7]

The king justified his decision by invoking vague "ancient customs" from the times of the Mazovian prince without stating the exact date or origins of those customs. This has given rise to much speculation about a supposed original document by Mazovian princes banning Jewish presence in Warsaw, as well as documents supposedly subsequently expelling Warsaw Jews during the fifteenth and early sixteenth centuries.[8] Yet we know of no such documents; nor are they quoted in Sigismund the First's charter according to accepted legal practice of the day.

The suspicious legal basis for the 1527 ban suggests that the motivation behind it was much more economic than constitutional. Internal conflicts had been intensifying in Warsaw since the end of the fifteenth century as patricians endeavored to strengthen their position at the expense of princely authority. Warsaw Jews were directly subordinate to the authority of the Mazovian princes and resided in those princes' domain, which was excluded from municipal jurisdiction. Consequently, Jews could engage in trade and crafts against the

---

be exhaustively analyzed. Note also my lecture, "The Jews in Warsaw under the Law of the *Non Tolerandis Judaeis* presented at the Thirteenth World Congress of Jewish Studies," the Hebrew University of Jerusalem, August 2001.

4 The oldest records are found in *Księga ziemi czerskiej—Liber Terrae Cernensis 1404–1425* (ed. Jan Tadeusz Lubomirski; Warszawa, 1879), 46; *Księga ławnicza miasta Nowej Warszawy*, vol. 1 (1416–1485) (ed. Adam Wolff; Wrocław: Zakład Narodowy im. Ossolińskich, 1960), passim; *Księga radziecka miasta Starej Warszawy*, vol. 1 (1447–1527) (ed. Adam Wolff; Wrocław: Zakład Narodowy im. Ossolińskich, 1963), passim.

5 AGAD, Księgi ziemskie i grodzkie warszawskie, 1; Hanna Zaremska, *Żydzi w średniowiecznej Polsce: Gmina krakowska* (Warszawa: Instytut Historii PAN, 2011), 255.

6 AGAD, Księgi ziemskie i grodzkie warszawskie, 2.

7 AGAD, Dokumenty pergaminowe 1557; Teodor Wierzbowski, *Przywileje królewskiego miasta stołecznego Starej Warszawy 1376–1772* (Warszawa: Towarzystwo Naukowe Warszawskie, 1913), 35; Ringelblum, *Żydzi w Warszawie*, 144.

8 Hilary Nussbaum, *Szkice historyczne z życia Żydów w Warszawie* (Warszawa, 1881; reprint Warszawa: Wydawnictwa Artystyczne i Filmowe, 1989), 4; Karol Mórawski, *Kartki z dziejów Żydów warszawskich* (Warszawa: Książka i Wiedza, 1993), 9; Ringelblum, *Żydzi w Warszawie*, 17.

wishes of municipal authorities.⁹ The town council strove, by means of guilds, to restrict the number of persons engaged in trade. The law of *de non tolerandis Judaeis* should therefore be seen as the culmination of a battle waged by traders and craftsmen to preserve the monopoly of the Christian guilds.

Zygmunt I's constitutional innovation was probably influenced by the growing religious conflict in the region, as well. In 1525, Prince Janusz of Mazovia issued a ban on Lutherans living and practicing their faith anywhere in the Mazovian Duchy under threat of death and confiscation of property.[10] A few months later, the prince prohibited residents of the Wizna land from maintaining contacts with the rebellious Prusy province.[11] His goal in both cases was to protect his estate from the Reformation, and his decrees had the desired effect: the influence of Protestantism in Mazovia was subsequently weakened. It seems that the fear of the Lutheran heresy affected policies towards Jews, since later bans on Protestants and Jews residing in Warsaw were formulated jointly within the same documents. Joint bans were adopted by the Warsaw land councils in 1679, 1682, and 1689[12] and by King Jan III Sobieski in 1678.[13]

The decision to introduce the *de non tolerandis Judaeis* law in Warsaw may have drawn upon the example of the Prussian towns. A ban on Jewish residence had been introduced in the Royal Prussia district upon its incorporation into the Polish crown in 1454. Prussian and Mazovian towns were very closely related in their economy and governance. For example, the Warsaw townspeople were interested in having their appellations from the judgments of the municipal court heard in Toruń (in Royal Prussia), not by the Prince of Mazovia. Like their Prussian counterparts, the Warsaw townspeople wanted to use their incorporation into the Polish Crown to strengthen their position, hence their efforts to remove those Jews who were not subject to the jurisdiction of the municipal authorities.

Warsaw's mayors and councils consistently guarded the city's privileges, persuading successive Polish kings to confirm the ban on Jewish residence. Zygmunt August did so in 1570; Stefan Batory in 1580; Zygmunt III in 1609; Władysław IV in 1636 and 1648; Jan Kazimierz in 1667; Jan Sobieski III in 1693;

---

9   Ringelblum, *Żydzi w Warszawie*, 39.
10 AGAD, Archiwum Zamoyskich [AZ] 3004.
11 Tomasz Strzembosz, *Tumult warszawski 1525 roku* (Warszawa: Państwowe Wydawnictwo Naukowe, 1959), 29.
12 AGAD, AZ 3004.
13 AGAD, Dokumenty papierowe 1092.

and August 11 in 1699.[14] The Warsaw Land Councils adopted similar resolutions in response to the townspeoples' demands on several occasions, including in 1613,[15] 1649, 1667, 1673, and 1692.[16]

Warsaw Jews, for their part, made consistent efforts to have the law lifted or to evade it one way or another ever since the granting of *de non tolerandis Judaeis* law in 1527. The first step was to obtain exemptions. Exception was made in the initial 1527 document for the royal customs officer and, importantly, the homeowner Moyse and his wife and children. It was noted, however, that no other Jews except for his closest family could live there. Another important breach came in 1570, when King Zygmunt August confirmed the *de non tolerandis Judaeis* law for Warsaw.[17] While Jews were banned from living in Old and New Warsaw and as far as 2 miles away from the river on both banks, they were now permitted to stay in the town and trade whenever the *Sejm* was in session. Yet another exception was made for Jewish army suppliers, while Jews serving the royal court in other capacities received special authorization to remain in Warsaw whenever the monarch was in residence. According to the spirit of a document drawn up by King Stefan Batory in 1580, Jews serving the Commonwealth had free access to the city. Undoubtedly to the chagrin of customs officers and tax collectors, many Jews, it seems, took advantage of the document's wording and posed as royal servants in order to come legally to Warsaw.[18]

From the middle of the sixteenth century, Warsaw began playing an increasingly vital role in the political and economic life of the country. The economic development of the city was enhanced by the presence of important political institutions and the city's location on the Vistula, one of the most important waterways used to ship goods to Gdańsk (Danzig). Between 1540 and 1589 thirteen out of thirty-eight *Sejm* sessions took place in Warsaw, more than anywhere else.[19] In keeping with the law of 1569, all the general assemblies of the Crown and Lithuania and, since 1573, free elections of the monarch, took place in Warsaw. The town's appeal grew yet more once it was designated as

---

14 AGAD, Dokumenty pergaminowe 1618, 1627, 1651, 2016; AGAD, Dokumenty Papierowe 1119; AGAD, AZ 3004.
15 AGAD, AZ 3004.
16 Adam Kaźmierczyk, *Sejmy i sejmiki szlacheckie wobec Żydów w drugiej połowie XVII wieku* (Warszawa: Wydawnictwo Sejmowe, 1994), 74.
17 AGAD, Dokumenty pergaminowe 1618; Wierzbowski, *Przywileje królewskiego miasta*, 86.
18 AGAD, Dokumenty pergaminowe 1627; Wierzbowski, *Przywileje królewskiego miasta*, 101.
19 *Historia sejmu polskiego*, vol. 1: *Do schyłku szlacheckiej Rzeczypospolitej* (ed. Jerzy Michalski; Warszawa: Państwowe Wydawnictwo Naukowe, 1984), 179.

the capital in 1596. It is hardly strange that Jews were keen to receive the right to legal residence in what was at once the country's new capital and a rapidly emerging trade center. Nor were their efforts always disappointed. The presence of the royal court and deputies accompanied by their retinues and the influx of politically active noblemen caused serious provisioning issues, which probably lay at the root of concessions made to individual Jews.

The Jewish influx into Warsaw was now considerable, to judge by complaints issued by municipal authorities and references by successive monarchs. Jews were put up as guests in the houses of merchants and members of other social groups, moving Zygmunt August (in 1570) and Stefan Batory (in 1580) to include a ban on renting rooms to Jews in houses owned by townspeople, clergy and noblemen, as well as rooms in districts that were royal property, backed by threats of punishment for non-compliance, in their decrees.[20] The new restrictions concerned not only Old and New Warsaw but also Blech, located on the left bank of the river, and the right-bank town of Praga where weavers were occupied with bleaching cloth.[21] They were apparently never enforced, however. The position of the nobility was simply too strong.

Already in the early seventeenth century, Jews were increasingly welcome guests on the estates of nobles and sometimes even clergy. In view of the growing political importance of Warsaw, many influential Polish and Lithuanian families purchased residences there. In 1559, the nobility was granted the right to acquire real-estate in cities, which led to the momentous establishment of independent noble estates (*jurydyki*) within urban centers that lay outside of municipal jurisdiction. Crucially, Jews could reside on these independent estates, thereby vitiating even the most impressive proscriptions on Jewish urban settlement. By 1640, for example, Jews resided in a house belonging to the Lithuanian Hetman (possibly Janusz Radziwiłł).[22] In the first half of the seventeenth century, Jews attempted to settle in the district of Praga, particularly in Skaryszew, which belonged to the Płock bishops and was granted *jurydyka* status in 1641. Whole communities of Jews would eventually spring up within those noble jurisdictions, which—as is well-known among Polish Jewish historians—functioned as Trojan horses for Jewish urban settlement.[23]

---

20 AGAD, Dokumenty pergaminowe 1618, 1627; Wierzbowski, *Przywileje królewskiego miasta*, 86, 101.

21 AGAD, Warszawa ekonomiczna [WE] 13; Aleksander Wejnert, *Starożytności Warszawy*, vol. 6 (Warszawa, 1858), 137, 144, 161; *Źródła do dziejów Warszawy: Rejestry podatkowe i taryfy nieruchomości 1510–1770*, vol. 1 (Warszawa, Państwowe Wydawnictwo Naukowe, 1963), 125.

22 AGAD, Dokumenty papierowe, 1642.

23 Adam Jarzemski [Jarzębski], *Gościniec abo krótkie opisanie Warszawy* (sine loco, 1643), 7.

Relatively few reports exist on the economic activities of Jews in Warsaw in the second half of the sixteenth and the entire seventeenth century. Sebastian Miczyński described Warsaw Jews as traders and moneylenders who offered their goods for sale in shops and taverns.[24] To judge by the acts issued in 1646 by Władysław IV and in 1650 by Jan Kazimierz, Jews were also producing and selling liquor.[25] They were, furthermore, accused of serving as "fences" for stolen goods and thereby contributing to the spread of theft.[26] A more charitable opinion was presented by Adam Jarzemski [Jarzębski], author of the first guidebook to Warsaw (published in 1643).[27] Jarzębski pointed out that one could buy a greater variety of goods from the Jews at very low prices and pawn items with them. He also admired their thrift and diligence. It may be assumed that most Jews seeking to work in Warsaw were people of little affluence and influence, but they seem to have been quite industrious. They presumably posed the biggest threat to Christian merchants, whom they repeatedly undersold.

As zealously as the townspeople tried to maintain laws against Jewish residence in Warsaw, Jews worked to get those laws lifted. They quoted general privileges, which assured them free residence and the freedom to conduct trade and crafts in the entire state. Their efforts were particularly energetic during the first half of the seventeenth century, when the controversy over their right to live and work in Warsaw was considered by the royal courts of Zygmunt III in 1628 and Władysław IV in 1646.[28] Acting on behalf of the Jews in the latter case was a delegation consisting of five persons originating from Lublin and Łuków, while Warsaw was represented by an influential citizen serving as the liquor tax collector. Both sides invoked their rights and privileges. Even the papal nuncio Mario Flonardi became involved, reporting to Rome that only thanks to his intervention did King Władysław refrain from lifting the *de non tolerandis Judaeis* law in Warsaw, and grumbling that the Jews had managed to gain the support of many dignitaries, including Catholics.[29] Ultimately, Władysław IV confirmed the law in Warsaw twice, in 1636 and 1648, banning Jews from living in the town and within a two-mile radius of its borders, including the districts

---

24 Sebastian Miczyński, *Zwierciadło Korony Polskiej* (Kraków, 1618), 35.
25 AGAD, WE 13; AGAD, AZ 3004.
26 AGAD, AZ 3004.
27 Jarzemski, 7.
28 AGAD, AZ 3004.
29 *Acta Nuntiaturae Polonae*. Tomus XXV. *Marius Filonardi (1635–1643)*, vol. 2 (*1 XI 1636–31 X 1637*), (ed. Theresia Chynczewska-Hennel; Cracoviae: Polska Akademia Umiejętności, 2006), no. 133.

of Praga and Skaryszew.[30] Violators could expect severe punishment, in the form of a fine of two thousand Hungarian zlotys.

But Władysław's acts, like those of his predecessors, still contained concessions. For example, he permitted the Jewish syndic Marc Nekel to reside in Warsaw together with his wife and children.[31] In all likelihood, all syndics, in order to both effectively represent the interests of the Jewish community before the king and his officials and efficiently convey royal decrees to Jews, must have had the right to reside in Warsaw. In 1669 Jencz Moszkowicz and Aron Oszyjowicz were granted this right,[32] as were Moysen and his half-brothers Elijah and Solomon in 1682.[33] Presumably they could even stay in the city when the royal court was not in residence.

In the second half of the seventeenth century, successive rulers confirmed the *de non tolerandis Judaeis* law. The Warsaw municipal authorities repeatedly reminded citizens of the ban on receiving Jews without informing the mayor, and reminded potential violators that they were subject to fines of up to one hundred zlotys.[34] Jews were threatened with the confiscation of their goods and even punishment by death.[35] Yet these decisions did little to deter the Jewish population thanks, among other things, to changes in the social structure of Warsaw. At the turn of the seventeenth century predominantly noble jurisdictions (*jurydyki*) were created, one after the other. The gentry, in search of new sources of profit, allowed Jews to settle in their jurisdictions. This symbiosis encouraged a rapid growth in Warsaw's Jewish population irrespective of explicit, continually reiterated royal decrees.[36]

In the second half of the eighteenth century Jews undertook fresh efforts to have their residence in Warsaw legalized. The political climate was more favorable owing to the 1764 electoral *Sejm* (parliament), which began addressing the issue of urban reform. At the same time, Warsaw was undergoing rapid development. Whereas in 1764 the city had barely 30,000 inhabitants, that number had risen to 115,000 by 1792 (although the official census only listed 81,000). Two years later, at the time of the Kościuszko Uprising (1794), it

---

30   AGAD, Dokumenty pergaminowe 1651.
31   AGAD, Dokumenty papierowe 990.
32   Janina Morgenstern, "Regesty z Metryki Koronnej i sigillat do historii Żydów w Polsce 1669–1696," *Biuletyn Żydowskiego Instytutu Historycznego* 60 (1969): 79.
33   AGAD, AZ 3004.
34   AGAD, WE 536; 537.
35   AGAD, AZ 3004.
36   A. Wejnert, *Starożytności Warszawy*, vol. 1 (Warszawa, 1848), 170, 241; *Encyklopedia Warszawy* (Warszawa: Państwowe Wydawnictwo Naukowe, 1994), 300.

FIGURE 1.3
Bernardo Belotto, known as Canaletto, *Krakowskie Przedmieście seen from the Column of King Sigismund III*, 1767–68. *Detail presenting Jewish merchants, Royal Castle in Warsaw (fot. Andrzej Ring).*

probably exceeded 150,000. Never again would the Warsaw population grow so rapidly.[37] The city limits had to be significantly extended. During an epidemic in 1770, the Lubomirski embankments (named after the Crown Marshall of the time) were built to strengthen sanitary controls. They enclosed suburban areas belonging to numerous *jurydyki* owned by nobility, clergy or the king, as well as fields and gardens. In connection with their construction, new streets and squares were laid out and extensive work was done on clearance, paving streets, and developing a sewage system. Warsaw was transformed from a medieval town to a modern metropolis whose administrative limits were marked by the Lubomirski embankments until the period of the First World War.

The development of Warsaw in the eighteenth century stimulated new architectural projects by the monarchs of the Saxonian Wettin dynasty, August II and III, as well as by the last king of Poland, Stanisław August Poniatowski. These monarchs also actively supported industrial development. During the reign of Stanisław August, there were around 300 factories in operation throughout the Polish-Lithuanian Commonwealth, about a quarter of which (70 to 80) were located in Warsaw. In 1784, the city contained 169 industrial

---

37 Marian Marek Drozdowski and Andrzej Zahorski, *Historia Warszawy*. Część 1: *do 1864* (Warszawa: Wydawnictwo Jeden Świat, 2004), 91; Andrzej Zahorski, *Warszawa w powstaniu kościuszkowskim* (2nd ed.; Warszawa: Wiedza Powszechna, 1985), 15; Barbara Grochulska, *Warszawa na mapie Polski stanisławowskiej: Podstawy gospodarcze rozwoju miasta* (Warszawa: Wydawnictwo Uniwersytetu Warszawskiego, 1980), 25.

buildings: 66 breweries, 27 mills, 31 brickworks, and 45 warehouses and stores.[38] Those may not be very impressive figures compared with contemporary London or Paris, but Warsaw could now rival such cities as Berlin (population 170,000) or the somewhat larger St. Petersburg (population 220,000). Warsaw also stood out among other Polish towns, most of which had no more than 1,000 to 2,000 inhabitants (Hubert Vautrin, who travelled in Poland in 1778, reported that "In truth, most of the settlements that are here called towns do not even deserve to be called townships: most of them are inhabited exclusively by Jews and serfs").[39]

The gradual development of Warsaw's industry drew new settlers, who in turn contributed to the construction boom and the growing demand for food and artisanal products. Economic development was abetted by Warsaw's position as a centre of political life, the place where the King resided and the *Sejm* met, as well as by its cultural activity, notably educational and literary. Little wonder that numerous foreigners settled there. During the reign of the Saxon monarchs, mainly Germans but also Frenchmen readily found employment as teachers. Above all, large numbers of Polish-Lithuanian nobles, burghers and peasants moved to Warsaw, as did Jews, who formed an increasingly numerous group within a rapidly growing population. Jewish predominance was supported in practice, if not in theory, by the Saxon monarchs, who avidly employed Jewish factors and craftsmen. Alongside these highly qualified specialists, less skilled Jews like Zelman and his son, cited in the introduction, began to stream into Warsaw in search any type of work.

According to the census of 1764, over 2500 Jews lived in Warsaw by this time, possessing an uncertain legal status.[40] On the basis of the Diet Constitution of 1775 Jews could settle on wastelands and assume the emphyteutic lease of royal, noble and clergy properties, both in Warsaw and throughout the Mazovian Voyewodship.[41] This decree could be interpreted in such a way that neutralized the *de non tolerandis Judaeis* law, thereby opening opportunities for Jewish settlement in hitherto forbidden areas. In response to the enormous

---

38 Drozdowski and Zahorski, *Historia Warszawy*, 91; Zahorski, *Warszawa w powstaniu kościuszkowskim*, 24.

39 Hubert Vautrin, "Obserwator w Polsce," in Wacław Zawadzki (ed.), *Polska stanisławowska w oczach cudzoziemców* (2 vols.; Warszawa: Państwowy Instytut Wydawniczy, 1963), 1:708.

40 R. [Raphael] Mahler, "Tsol un tseshpraytung fun di yidn in varshe," *Landkentnish: tsaytshrift far fragn fun Landkentnish un turistik, geshikhte fun yidishe yeshuvim, folklor un etnografie* 2 (Warsaw) 1934: 43.

41 *Volumina Legum*, vol. 8 (ed. Jozafata Ohryzko; St. Petersburg, 1860), 95; E. [Emanuel] Ringelblum, "A yidishe debate in poylishn seym yor 1775," *YIVO bleter. Hodesh: shrift fun yidishn visnshaftlekhn institut* 1 (1931): 426–31.

influx of Jews, a new *jurydyka* rather boldly named "New Jerusalem" was established outside the Lubomirski embankments in 1775.[42] Five years later, King Stanisław August Poniatowski settled Jews on his properties in Golędzinów on the right-bank of the Vistula river, next to Praga.[43]

Hiding in Plain Sight: The Warsaw Jewish Community in the Late 18th Century

Traveling in the Polish Lithuanian Commonwealth at the beginning of the 1790s, Fryderyk Schulz observed: "They have found a kind of second homeland in Poland, and there is a huge crowd of them in Warsaw."[44] A more critical traveler, Nathaniel William Wraxall, wrote in 1778:

> Warsaw is likewise crowded with Jews, who form a considerable portion of the inhabitants. They wear a distinguishing dress, and derive a very precarious subsistence from the arts of fraudulent commerce, most of them being extremely poor. From time to time they are plundered, exiled, imprisoned, and massacred: yet, under such accumulated vexations, they continually multiply, and are here found in far greater numbers than even at Amsterdam.[45]

One must constantly remind oneself that these reports referred to a largely underground, if substantial and highly developed, Jewish community in Warsaw. As mentioned earlier, Jews lived in numerous *jurydyki*. It is certain that they had their own official representatives, since the 'syndic' begins to appear in sources from 1759.[46] They probably also had fully functioning communal

---

42 Tymoteusz Lipiński, "Wiadomość o Nowej Jerozolimie," *Biblioteka Warszawska: pismo poświęcone naukom, sztukom i przemysłowi* 4 (1845): 403–407; Krystyna Zienkowska, "Spór o Nową Jerozolimę," *Kwartalnik Historyczny* 93.2 (1986): 351–76.

43 AGAD, Metryka Koronna, 296: 148v–150; AGAD, Archiwum Rodzinne Poniatowskich, 396; Maurycy Horn, *Regesty dokumentów i ekscerpty z Metryki Koronnej do historii Żydów w Polsce 1697–1795*, vol. 2: *Rządy Stanisława Augusta (1764–1795)*, part 2: *1780–1794* (Wrocław—Warszawa—Kraków—Gdańsk: Ossolineum, 1988), 22.

44 Fryderyk Schulz, *Podróże Inflantczyka z Rygi do Warszawy i po Polsce w latach 1791–1793* (ed. Wacław Zawadzki; Warszawa: Czytelnik, 1956), 78.

45 Nathaniel William Wraxall, "Wspomnienia z Polski," in Zawadzki (ed.), *Polska stanisławowska*, 1: 494 (see footnote 39).

46 E. Ringelblum, "Yidn in varshe in 18tn y"h, un zeyer rekhtlekh-gezelshaflekhe lage," *Historishe shriftn fun YIVO* 2 (1937).

and religious institutions. We know of the existence of prayer houses, at least at Pociejów (1790), as well as the presence of rabbis there as early as the 1770s.[47] However, the spectacular census of 1778, containing 50 pages of tables with names of Jews living in Warsaw, provides the most detailed picture of the Warsaw Jewish community before its formal readmission.[48]

It is not entirely clear what factors led directly to compilation of the 1778 census, which might help us better gauge the reliability of its data. As is well known, figures provided for taxation purposes are often lower than reality, while a very different picture emerges if the document was deployed in the struggle for legal residence in the city.[49] It seems that the census was compiled on the recommendation of the *Commissio Boni Ordinis* [Commission on Good Order], which, from its establishment in 1765, strove to unify the towns' legal status and to strengthen their position. The commission achieved some success through the agreement to unite New Warsaw with Old Warsaw, subject to certain conditions, namely the resolution of the problem of *jurydyki*. King Stanisław August Poniatowski issued a recommendation on both matters on 23 March, 1778.[50] The compilation of a list of Jews living in Warsaw was probably connected with these initiatives, for the king proposed that the rights of *jurydyki* owners should remain intact but that their residents should henceforth be subject to the jurisdiction of the municipal courts. This would, of course, have applied to their Jewish populations as well.

The 1778 census is not an unknown document, but historians have barely appreciated its comprehensiveness and exploited its rich data. Over 3,534 persons are mentioned by name—not only male heads of household but also their wives, children and servants. Information is supplied about places of origin and places of residence in Warsaw. Unfortunately, the census does not include data on age, occupation, or economic endeavor. Nevertheless, it not only constitutes a valuable statistical source but permits us to follow the migratory process, proving decisively that the majority of Jews in Warsaw had moved to the city in the recent past. This impression is confirmed in the court records of the Marshal's Jurisdiction for 1788, which demonstrate that the

---

47 *Materiały do dziejów Sejmu Czteroletniego*, vol. 1 (ed. Janusz Woliński, Jerzy Michalski, Emanuel Rostworowski; Wrocław: Zakład Narodowy Ossolińskich, 1955), 327.
48 AGAD, Archiwum Publiczne Potockich [APP], 93.
49 See Adam Teller, "Warunki życia i obyczajowość w żydowskiej dzielnicy Poznania w pierwszej połowie XVII wieku," in Jerzy Topolski and Krzysztof Modelski, eds., *Żydzi w Wielkopolsce na przestrzeni dziejów* (Poznań: Wydawnictwo Poznańskie, 1999), 60.
50 Władysław Smoleński, *Komisya Boni Ordinis Warszawska, 1765–1789* (Warszawa: Towarzystwo Miłośników Historii, 1913), 35.

majority of Jews had been present in the city for not more than 20 years, that is, from around 1768.[51] Significantly, these records contain information about Jews born in Warsaw, as well as Jewish marriages contracted there.[52]

According to the 1778 census, while new residents came from almost 190 different locales, most came from only a few localities, above all Lublin (over 15%) and Cracow (over 10%), two of the largest cities in the Polish-Lithuanian Commonwealth. Many also came from private, noble-owned towns like Pinczów (around 5%), Opatów (5%), Siemiatycze, Koniecpol, and Wodzisław. Many of these places lay relatively close to each other within the Świętokrzyskie region of northern Little Poland. The newcomers' economic conditions varied. The main reason for migration from these locales was probably overpopulation and the consequent need to look for new sources of income. Many such towns were located near rivers that served as main communication routes. A small subsection of Warsaw's Jewish immigrants came from abroad, including Amsterdam and Dresden. The majority lived in the most prestigious parts of the city, such as Krakowskie Przedmieście.

The 1778 census paints an unexpected picture of Jewish topography, for it only partially upholds the prevailing assumption that Jews settled in the noble-owned *jurydyki*. A significant portion of Jews actually lived on property belonging to their greatest rivals, Christian townspeople. Many of the latter were bakers, carpenters and merchants, although it is not always possible to determine their precise occupations and social origins. At first glance, the motivation of such Christian townspeople seems obvious enough. Jewish tenants brought in money, and probably significantly more than the market rate because of their illegal status. However, it would still seem counterproductive to help one's economic rivals in any way, no matter what the immediate financial gain. Their willingness to do so forces us to reconsider the diachronic nature of Jewish—Christian economic rivalry in the city. A large urban center like Warsaw offered opportunities for economic diversity and symbiosis that traversed ethnic boundaries. Not every Christian merchant and artisan, it turns out, was in direct competition with every Jew.

The 1778 census reveals relatively few large concentrations of Jews—the number of Jews exceeded 50 on only ten properties—residing in small houses in groups of a dozen or so. But some of the larger concentrations of Jews appeared where we might least expect them. Most surprisingly, Jews lived in the Old Town within the city walls, a blatant breach of the privilege *de non tolerandis Judaeis*. A total of 152 Jews lived in three properties on Jezuicka Street,

---

51 AGAD, AKP, 311.
52 AGAD, AKP 302, 311, 312.

MAP 1.1   *Places of origin of Warsaw Jews according to 1778 Census, created by Hanna Węgrzynek and Robert Chmielewski (2011).*

ILLEGAL IMMIGRANTS

and 138 Jews were living in the Jezierski annex alone. Jews lived in various parts of the city within the Lubomirski embankments, in both the most exposed places, such as Krakowskie Przedmieście (186 people), and in more peripheral locations like Czerniakowska Street and Krochmalna, Żelazna, Pawia and Kacza Streets, only recently laid out. Interestingly, these places usually coincide with the later centers of Jewish settlement and religious life as indicated on Eleonora Bergman's map of the sites of synagogues and prayer houses at the close of the 19th century.[53]

In 1778, Jews could be found in 143 buildings on 41 of Warsaw's 192 streets.[54] The greatest concentration and by now the very symbol of contemporary Jewish Warsaw was in the Pociejowski Palace on Senatorska Street, which, according to the 1778 census, housed 716 Jews. The cramped conditions defy imagination, especially as there was a bustling flea market in the courtyard. As court records show, the place did not enjoy the best reputation: the fact that many Jews traded in secondhand goods there provoked accusations that they were fencing stolen objects.

The Gołubskie estate at the junction of Senatorska and Bielańska Streets, a property belonging to the Golub *starosta* M. W. Grudzieński, was a more prestigious address. With at least 359 Jewish residents, it was the second largest concentration of Jews. Here, too, there were many shops. The character of the place was determined, however, by the social composition of the residents, a relatively large number of whom were widows. The syndic of the Warsaw Jews and his assistants lived there, as well, and their presence bestowed a sense of relative security. The next largest Jewish concentration was the Tłomackie mansion on Bielańska Street, where 207 Jews resided.

The center of Warsaw Jewish life was the area containing Senatorska and Bielańska Streets. A total of 1,597 Jews lived there, almost half of the city's 3,534 Jews. Fryderyk Schulz, mentioned earlier, described this enclave as follows:

> Beyond Tłumackie lies the Jewish quarter. Jews, as we know, deal in all kinds of second-hand articles, but here, during Sejm sessions, they are allowed to sell new goods in shops, and part of Senatorska Street has been settled by them. Here they deal especially in furs, canvas, cotton

---

53   Eleonora Bergman, *"Nie masz bóżnicy powszechnej": Synagogi i domy modlitwy w Warszawie od końca XVIII do początku XXI wieku* (Warszawa: Wydawnictwo DiG, 2007), inserted map VI: Synagogi/domy modlitwy [Synagogues and prayer houses] 1869.

54   *Taryfa Miasta Warszawy składki na koszary na rat sześć cztermiesięcznych w Roku 1784 ułożona percepty z kwitami zgodną okazuiąca* (sine loco et anno).

goods, silk, dresses, and the like. They sell them cheaply, and the shops are always full of customers.[55]

Surprisingly, Marywil, situated next to Pociejów at the junction of Senatorska Street and present-day Wierzbowa Street, is not mentioned in this context in the 1778 census. We know from travelers' accounts and other sources that many Jews settled in Marywil at the beginning of the 1790s and had shops there: "Hotels, restaurants, bookshops, artists of all kinds, craftsmen and Jews live together, even the masons have a meeting hall here," Schulz observed, "on the ground floor, shops are rented out, especially to Jews."[56] This observation suggests that the census data may well underestimate Warsaw's Jewish presence.

Another surprising discovery is that Jews were residing in *army barracks* in Warsaw, including barracks in Wielopole and on Krakowskie Przedmieście, with the number of Jews living in the latter reaching 128 by the time of the 1778 census. It is hard to say who authorized the residence of so large a number of undocumented and un-tolerated civilians in military buildings, but it is possible that their presence was only temporary in light of tax documents reflecting that other properties used as military quarters were rented out only while the troops were away.[57] Equally surprisingly, the census indicates that many Jews were residing on estates belonging to Catholic clergy. 165 Jews lived in a manor house (which had the appearance of any country manor) belonging to a priest named Janas in the jurisdictional enclave of Aleksandria. Another 23 Jews lived in a tenement building on Długa Street belonging to one of the abbots, and another 21 in a manor house on Żabia Street belonging to a priest named Jabłunowski.

Many Jews lived in the area by the Vistula River, predominately in two *jurydyki*. 209 Jews lived in Aleksandria, established by Aleksander Zasławski below Nowy Świat street during the 17th century. Significantly fewer—thirty Jews—resided on the site of the royal estate of Stanisławów at the base of the hill. Later sources suggest that this was a particularly important place for the economic activity of Warsaw Jews. Tariff records from 1784 indicate a Jewish warehouse by Leszyczynski Street, on the border between Stanisławów and Aleksandria on land belonging to the capital city of Warsaw. This was a warehouse for goods transported to the city via the Vistula. This duty was levied on

---

55   Schulz, *Podróże Inflantczyka*, 75.
56   Ibid., 91.
57   AGAD, AKP 307.

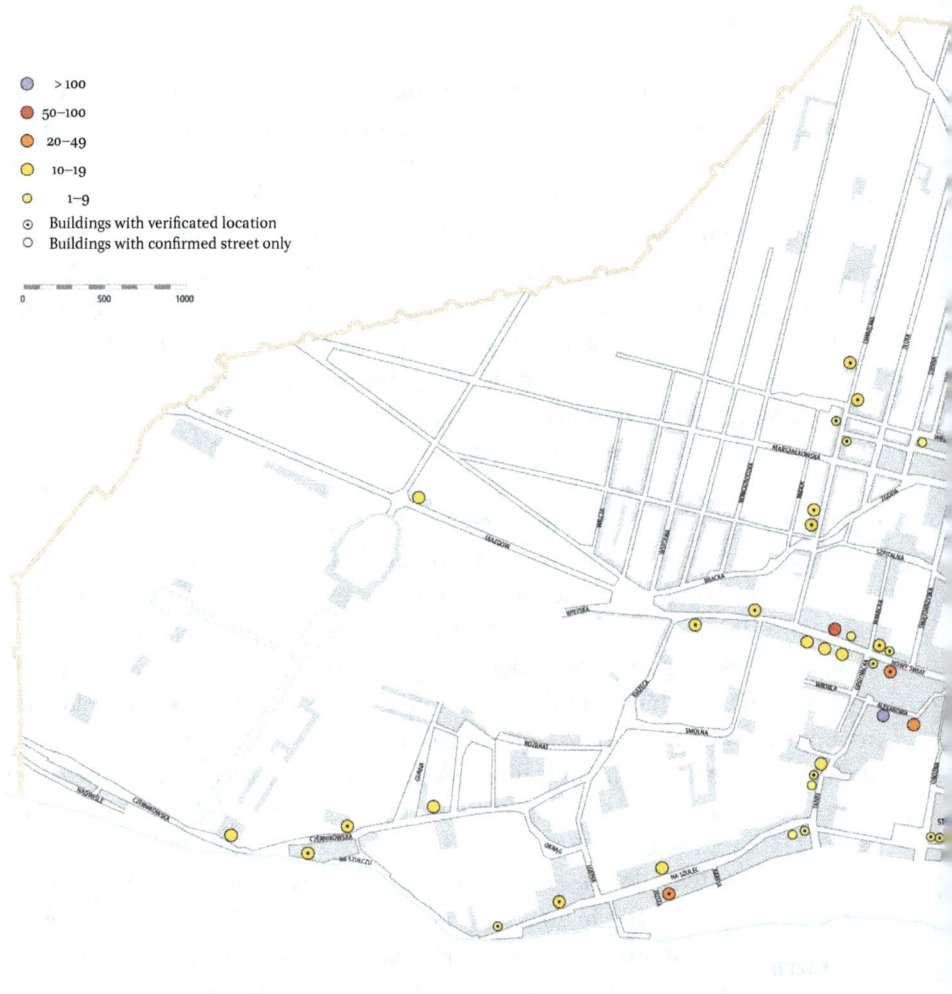

MAP 1.2   *Warsaw in 1778—Places of Residence of Jews, created by Hanna Węgrzynek and Robert Chmielewski (2011).*

Jews by the Great Marshal of the Crown [Marszałek Wielki Koronny] in 1775, and again in 1784.[58]

A tax quota three times larger reflects a second, undoubtedly much larger, Jewish warehouse located on Pokorna Street.[59] In a later period, this place would form an enduring part of the history of the Warsaw Jewish community. Easy access to mercantile ports was a probable reason for the settlement of significant groups of Jews not only in the Old City neighborhood by Bugaj street and Mariensztat, but also on the peripheral Solec and Czerniakowska streets. From 1784 tariff records it becomes clear that there were numerous magnate-owned stores, a number of which were probably used by Jewish merchants.

Who were the Jews of eighteenth-century Warsaw? Their typical family structure, according to the census, was unusual for Polish Jewry. Most were single individuals, sometimes accompanied by servants. They were probably business agents or merchants of various types who had not yet decided on a permanent change of residence. It was only after they had been in Warsaw for many years and consolidated their position in the city that they decided to bring their families to join them. This scenario is confirmed by other sources, particularly court records. Another large group of Warsaw Jews consisted of childless married couples. Although we lack information as to age, we may assume they were young people on the cusp of an independent existence, an assumption confirmed by the court records of the Marshal's Jurisdiction. Finally, there was a noticeably large number of single women. Most may be assumed to have been widows, since they lived in Warsaw with their children. But we occasionally find single women without children, accompanied by their servants, probably engaged in trade on their own behalf. The relatively large number of women suggests that Warsaw had become an important Jewish matchmaking center.

While the 1778 census does not give an unequivocal answer to the question of what brought Jews to Warsaw, it does suggest that economic prospects were a prime motive. More exhaustive information on the subject is found in the legal records of the Marshal's Jurisdiction. The documents that have survived—two of which are cited in the introduction to this chapter—may justly be termed the oldest biographies of Warsaw Jews. Their rare and colourful testimonies evince the difficult existence of Warsaw Jews, caused not only by their insecure legal status but also by the corruption and drunkenness of the syndics and their assistants (szkolniks/*shamashim*).[60] For example, Icek

---

58   AGAD, Metryka Litewska VII, 70; *Ordynacya dla miasta Warszawy względem Żydów* ([Warszawa], 1784), § 20.
59   *Taryfa Miasta Warszawy* (see footnote 54).
60   AGAD, AKP 314.

Mortkowicz, a carter from Zasław, reported that he was spending the night with many other Jews on Ogrodowa Street by Mosiek of Zychlin. This place was probably well known to the szkolniks as an illegal Jewish residence, for when they came that evening they forced every Jew present to give them half a zloty and, after collecting the money, sent someone to fetch vodka (*gorzałka*). Icek Mortkowicz complained that because he refused to give them money he was accused of stealing horses.[61]

We are struck, as well, by the great mobility of these Jews and their frequent changes of place of residence within the city. At the same time, the biographies deposed before the court by non-Jews—nobles, townspeople and peasants— reveal that this mobility was not unique to Jews. It is also worth noting that the punishments for crimes committed by Jews were similar or identical to those imposed on Christian townspeople. Only members of the nobility were treated more leniently. A first offence was punished by confinement for a few days or so in the Marshal's prison and a few dozen lashes. The next offence resulted in expulsion beyond the city embankments and a ban on returning to Warsaw. This provides further confirmation that the presence of Jews in the city, while not formally regulated, was tacitly endorsed.

Most Jews who came into conflict with the law were traders in second-hand goods which, as mentioned earlier, left them particularly vulnerable to accusations of selling stolen property. When Jews were caught in criminal acts, they often explained that they had been unable to engage in any craft and had been drawn into crime by poverty. Fawel Szłamowicz, an 18-year-old from Lublin accused of pickpocketing, testified: "I didn't have no money for bread and I was hungry."[62] This sentence, spoken in colloquial Polish and distinct from the notarial style of court documents, raises the question of the cultural character of Warsaw Jewry. Clearly, the Yiddish language was already dominant in the 1770s. This is evident from the form of the given names recorded in the 1778 census and from the Yiddish-sounding place names, such as Mezhyrich for Międzyrzec or Shedlich for Siedlce. Few Jews spoke Polish, a fact indicated by the employment of an interpreter in the Warsaw Castle judge court.[63] Thus, we can say with reasonable certitude that a center of Yiddish culture was beginning to take shape in Warsaw as early as the second half of the 18th century under the influence of its large linguistic community.

The residential situation in Warsaw was undoubtedly a factor leading to deliberations on the legal status of the Jewish population during the Four-Year

---

61 Ibid.
62 AGAD, AKP 311.
63 Ibid.

Sejm (1788–1792), the famous parliamentary session aimed at reforming the Polish-Lithuanian Commonwealth before its eventual dissolution. The Sejm's deliberations on Jewish residence did not produce radical reform, but this does not mean that no change occurred. The subsequent regulation of urban rights and the abolition of the jurisdictional enclaves proved momentous for them.[64] Visible proof of this is provided in the 1792 census of Warsaw, which classified the residents of each property under four headings: nobility, clergy, townspeople, and Jews (of whom there were now over 6,800!), a taxonomy that signifies an official acceptance of Warsaw's Jewish presence.[65] Nevertheless, most Warsaw Jews were still not entitled to acquire houses in contrast to the Praga suburb, where we find Szmul Zbytkower himself among the owners of houses on Targowa Street (his situation was rather exceptional).[66]

In 1792, the topography appears significantly altered from that of 1778. Jews were no longer living within the city walls, which seems to indicate that the law *de non tolerandis Judaeis* was being more strictly enforced. However, a relatively small group of Jews had now settled just outside the walls, on Bugaj and Brzozowa Streets. In 1792, significantly fewer Jews were present on Krakowskie Przedmieście, mainly in the Cadet Corps barracks. It is possible that this was the result of new regulations excluding Jews from specific streets, especially the most prestigious. The largest concentration of Jews was still to be found on Senatorska Street, where Jews lived in nearly every palace and house. Often they were the exclusive renters, i.e. in Jabłonowski palace the prince lived with his family and 23 Jewish tenants (probably in an adjacent house).

One more change that strikes the reader of the 1792 census is that places of origin of persons listed are now rarely indicated. This omission could mean that, in the fifteen years following 1778, Jews living in Warsaw had come to be regarded as locals rather than newcomers. The 1792 census also indicates that most Warsaw Jews were now artisans, although a significant group is shown as not possessing any means of steady sustenance.

Conclusion

From 1778 to 1792, illegal Jewish residence in Warsaw had come to be accepted as a fact of life. The legal situation of the city itself changed over the same

---

64 "Prawo o miastach z 18 kwietnia 1791 r.," in Jerzy Kowecki (ed.), *Konstytucja 3 Maja 1791* (Warszawa: Państwowe Wydawnictwo Naukowe, 1990), 131.
65 AGAD, WE 16, 17, 18.
66 AGAD, WE 745.

period, the decisive factors being the new Law on the Cities (Free Royal Cities act) and the resulting abolition of *jurydyki*,[67] which opened the way for a transfer of administrative responsibility and the pursuit of a more consistent policy for the whole urban area. The situation of the Jews, however, did not change nearly as much: they did not receive rights similar to those of the townspeople, while their illegal residence in the city was still tacitly accepted. Thus it was that, in the second half of the 18th century, Warsaw had become home to the largest concentration of Jews in the Polish-Lithuanian Commonwealth, and perhaps even in all of Europe, but remained an illegal—if tolerated—community. The actual Jewish presence in Warsaw provides a cautionary tale to scholars attempting to discern the real meaning and actual implementation of Jewish legislation in pre-partition Poland-Lithuania.

---

67 "Prawo o miastach," 131. See footnote 64.

CHAPTER 2

Merchants, Army Suppliers, Bankers: Transnational Connections and the Rise of Warsaw's Jewish Mercantile Elite (1770–1820)

Cornelia Aust

Introduction

In the summer of 1783, Jacob Prager, a Jewish wholesale merchant in Amsterdam, wrote to his brother Yehiel in London:

> Let God, be He Blessed, guard [us] from bad times. In one moment one may lose [all] that one has acquired in 50 years. This country has lost much of its commerce by this deplorable war and we fear that we shall not in our lifetime again do such flourishing business as in the past, because demand has virtually disappeared and all seafaring monarchies receive merchandise directly from East and West.[1]

As Gedalia Yogev has also shown for the case of the Prager family in Amsterdam and London, the decline of the Amsterdam staple-market hurt many Jewish merchants. At least for some time—during the second half of the eighteenth century—Amsterdam merchants were kept afloat by the business in bills of exchange. Nevertheless, by the end of the century, the city also lost its position as the preeminent financial market of Europe to London, which left a deep impact on Jewish and Protestant merchants and bankers alike.[2] These episodes form a key part of the relatively well-known story of the economic decline of Amsterdam, the parallel rise of London, and Jewish westward migration.

---

1 Quoted from Gedalia Yogev, *Diamonds and Coral: Anglo-Dutch Jews and Eighteenth-Century Trade* (Leicester: Leicester University Press, 1978), 246–47.
2 Marjolein 't Hart, Joost Jonker and Jan Luiten Van Zanden (eds.), *A Financial History of the Netherlands* (Cambridge: Cambridge University Press, 1997), 58–61; Youssef Cassis, *Capitals of Capital: A History of International Financial Centres, 1780–2005* (Cambridge: Cambridge University Press, 2006), 9–14; Jan De Vries and A.M. van der Woude, *The First Modern Economy: Success, Failure, and Perseverance of the Dutch Economy, 1500–1815* (Cambridge and New York: Cambridge University Press, 1997), 136.

However, the traditional scholarly conception of Jewish westward migration has somewhat obscured the close ties that remained between Amsterdam and Central and Eastern Europe for a time. In its role as financial capital and premier provider of credit, Amsterdam was crucial to the financial market in Central and, indirectly, Eastern Europe. Only toward the end of the eighteenth century did the decline of the Dutch economy and the political changes caused by the second and third partitions of Poland (in 1793 and 1795) weaken ties between Amsterdam and Central Europe and Poland. At the same time, one can detect the rise of a new Jewish mercantile and financial elite in Warsaw during this period.[3] A similar claim can be made for Berlin a bit earlier and for St. Petersburg somewhat later. Thus, the development that will be described here was not an isolated phenomenon, but part of a larger emergence of new financial centers in Central and Eastern Europe, accompanied by the rise of new Jewish mercantile and financial elites who did not, however, sever their connections to the West.

The rise of the new Jewish mercantile elite in Warsaw was somewhat parallel, though on a much smaller scale, to the rise of London's Jewish mercantile elite, both of which occurred at the expense of Amsterdam. Two phenomena were crucial to the rise of Warsaw's Jewish mercantile elite from the 1770s to the 1820s: migration and shifting occupational profiles. In contrast to the common westward depiction of Jewish migration, the temporary or constant migration of Jewish merchants, army suppliers, and bankers eastward, particularly to Warsaw, contributed significantly to the city's formation. At the same time, one can detect an occupational shift from commerce to army supplying and eventually to banking during this period. These migrations and occupational shifts had an important impact on commercial networks across Europe, and can only be understood within their wider European context.

Recognition of these changes necessitates a reframing of the rise of Warsaw as a Jewish metropolis and especially as a center of Jewish financing in nineteenth-century Eastern Europe. This reframing will have the added benefit of helping us overcome the traditional, exclusive focus on the relationship between Jewish communities and local non-Jewish authorities. Though important in the immediate context of mercantile activities, this focus has

---

3   For a more detailed analysis of these developments, see Cornelia Aust, "Commercial Cosmopolitans: Networks of Jewish Merchants between Warsaw and Amsterdam, 1750–1820" (Ph.D. thesis, University of Pennsylvania, 2010).

long clouded the importance of transnational connections across continental Europe for the ascendancy of a Jewish community like Warsaw.[4]

In the mid-eighteenth century, Warsaw would still not have seemed the most natural place for the rise of a new Jewish commercial elite in the space of a century. The Polish capital held a privilege *de non tolerandis Judaeis* since 1527 (see chapter 1 of this volume). Jews were only allowed to stay in Warsaw during the annual meetings of the Polish Sejm, usually six weeks per year in order to provide participating nobles with supplies and services. Banned from living in the city, some Jews settled on its outskirts on *jurydiki*, estates belonging to Polish magnates.[5] Warsaw itself, though the Polish capital, seat of the Polish king, and meeting place of the Sejm, was still a relatively peripheral place economically. Its merchants were mostly active in local trade in the first half of the eighteenth century and its location was too far from the larger European trade routes.[6] Only in the 1770s did international trade intensify, thanks to credit from Amsterdam.[7]

At the same time, Warsaw suddenly began to emerge as one of the larger European cities. Though it could not yet compete with a city like Amsterdam and its approximately 220,000 inhabitants by the end of the eighteenth century, the population of Warsaw more than quadrupled in less than half a century, from about 24,000 inhabitants in 1754 to about 110,000 in 1792. This was mainly a result of immigration to the capital from villages and small towns in the vicinity of Warsaw, and to a lesser degree from the rest of Poland and abroad during the last years of Stanisław August's reign.[8]

In terms of trade, the numbers of merchants from Warsaw visiting the fairs at Leipzig bespeak not only the growth of Leipzig as a center of commercial exchange but also the more active involvement of Warsaw merchants in transnational trade. In 1756, only eight Jewish and 20 non-Jewish merchants from the Polish capital visited the fair; ten years later there were already 182 Jewish and 60 non-Jewish merchants, while their numbers rose to 549 and

---

4 On the importance of a trans-national approach, see Moshe Rosman, "Jewish History across Borders," in *Rethinking European Jewish History* (ed. Jeremy Cohen and Moshe Rosman; Oxford and Portland, OR: The Littman Library of Jewish Civilization, 2009), 15–29.

5 Artur Eisenbach, "The Jewish Population in Warsaw at the Turn of the Eighteenth Century," *Polin* 3 (1988): 46–77. See also Hanna Węgrzynek's contribution to this volume.

6 Barbara Grochulska, *Warszawa na mapie Polski stanisławowskiej: Podstawy gospodarcze rozwoju miasta* (Warsaw: Wydawnictwo Uniwersytetu Warszawskiego, 1980), 18–20, 130–31.

7 Maria Bogucka et al., *Warszawa w latach 1526–1795* (Warsaw: Państwowe Wydawnictwo Naukowe, 1984), 332–33.

8 Grochulska, *Warszawa na mapie Polski stanisławowskiej*, 25–26. Bogucka et al., *Warszawa w latach 1526–1795*, 272–73.

98 respectively in 1789.[9] This shows not only a generally stronger presence of Warsaw merchants, but the growing importance of Warsaw Jewish merchants, though many were probably involved in retail trade rather than in whole sale commerce. Paradoxically, it was only around the Four Year Sejm and the 1794 Kościuszko uprising that Warsaw, despite the political disintegration of Poland, became a capital in every sense, politically, culturally, and no less economically.[10]

With the growth of the city, Warsaw attracted a growing number of Jews in the last third of the eighteenth century, a number of them equipped with the privilege of "supplier to the royal court" (*serwitorat*). Though they were not equal in stature to Central European Court Jews,[11] their closeness to the king and the economic opportunities that attended this position made the move to Warsaw—temporarily or permanently—quite attractive. In addition to the aforementioned noble estates (*jurydiki*) where Jews were allowed to settle, a growing number lived in Praga (not to be confused with the Czech city of Prague), a suburb of Warsaw where settlement restrictions were not strictly enforced and where seventy Jews were counted as permanent residents in 1765. Ten years later, when the restriction of settlement in Praga was officially abolished, the facts on the ground were legally ratified. In the following years, the number of Jews rose constantly despite the political upheavals of the last decades of the Polish-Lithuanian Commonwealth and the partitions of Poland. A census of Jews in Warsaw, or more precisely of the estates outside the city walls, came to over 3500 Jewish inhabitants in 1778, many living on central streets like Senatorska, Bielańska, Długa, Nalewki, Krakowskie Przedmieście, and Nowy Świat.[12] Similar to the general migration patterns to Warsaw, most were Jews from small towns in the vicinity of Warsaw and from Poland in general, but also from abroad. In the years to come, Jews used villages and small towns in the county of Warsaw, noble settlements (*jurydiki*) and Praga "as stepping stones for migration into Warsaw."[13]

---

9   Grochulska, *Warszawa na mapie Polski stanisławowskiej*, 85.
10 Bogucka et al., *Warszawa w latach 1527–1795*, 566–67.
11 On the question of court Jews in Eastern Europe see Gershon Hundert, "Was there an East European Analogue to Court Jews?" in *The Jews in Poland* (ed. Andrzej K. Paluch; Kraków: Jagiellonian University, 1992), 67–75.
12 "Konskrypcia Żydów dot. Żydów m. Warszawy, 1778," Archiwum Główne Akt Dawnych [AGAD], Archiwum Publiczne Potockich, syg. 93, mf. no. 17867. See also chapter 1 in this volume.
13 Artur Eisenbach, "The Jewish Population in Warsaw," 48. This was based on a new constitution for the Jews in Mazowia from 1775 that allowed them to settle on royal ground (emphyteutic ground), except for Warsaw itself. See also Artur Eisenbach, "Status prawny

Although wealthy merchants, army suppliers, and entrepreneurs constituted only a small minority among the Jews who settled in Warsaw at the turn of the nineteenth century, they were of crucial importance for the rise of Warsaw as a commercial and financial center in Eastern Europe in general and as a Jewish metropolis in particular. After briefly examining the case of the banker Simon Symons to illustrate transnational connections to Amsterdam and their decline, I will focus on three figures who exemplify the rise of the small Jewish mercantile elite in Warsaw: Itzig Jacob from Flatow (Złotów), Judyta Jakubowiczowa (Zbytkower), and Berek Szmul (Sonnenberger). Itzig Jacob from Flatow (Złotów) is better known as Izaak Flatau, the banker and founder of the Warsaw synagogue in Daniłowiczowska Street. His rise from a small sub-contractor to one of the most important army suppliers in the border region between Prussia and Poland and eventually one of the first Jewish bankers in Warsaw provides not only a glimpse into the economic rise and occupational shifts within the emerging Jewish elite of Warsaw but puts them into the context of legal limitations and changing borders between Prussia and the Polish-Lithuanian Commonwealth.

His mother-in-law Judyta Jakubowiczowa (Zbytkower) further exemplifies the transition from army supplying to banking and illustrates the nature and importance of transnational familial and commercial connections. Like her son-in-law, Judyta moved from Prussia to Warsaw, though earlier, in search of economic opportunities as well as a secure legal status. Judyta's stepson, Berek Szmul (Sonnenberger) exemplifies the move of Jewish entrepreneurs in Warsaw into another economic field—the leasing of state monopolies, as well as a shift of Jewish commercial networks eastward. Being religiously observant and a supporter of Hasidism, he also complicates the picture of a uniformly acculturated Jewish elite.

Trans-European Ties: From Amsterdam to Warsaw

Among the Jewish immigrants to Warsaw was a small group of already successful and affluent Jewish merchants and bankers who were drawn to Warsaw during the reign of Stanisław August Poniatowski. They came from

---

ludności żydowskiej w Warszawie w końcu XVIII i na początku XIX wieku," *BŻIH* 39 (1961): 3; idem, "Żydzi warszawscy i sprawa żydowska w XVIII w.," *Nadbitka* 3 (1975): 231–33. On numbers of Jews in the Polish-Lithuanian Commonwealth in general see Raphael Mahler, *Yidn in amolikn poyln in likht fun tsifern: di demografishe un sotsyal-ekonomishe struktur fun yidn in kroyn-poyln in akhtsentn yorhundert*, (2 vols. Varshe: Yidish bukh, 1958).

various Prussian towns, Hamburg and even Amsterdam to supply the court and individual nobles with luxury goods and credit. Among them were Wolfgang Heymann from Breslau (Wrocław) and the banker Simon Symons from Amsterdam, who exemplifies the ties between Ashkenazic merchants and bankers in Amsterdam and their coreligionists as well as non-Jewish merchants in Central and Eastern Europe.[14]

Although Ashkenazic merchants and bankers in Amsterdam focused on the opportunities that opened west of Amsterdam with the new markets and the rising financial center of London, many retained their business ties or built new ones in Central and (mostly indirectly) in Eastern Europe throughout the eighteenth century. After all, most Ashkenazic Jews in Amsterdam possessed roots in Central and Eastern Europe, whether their ancestors had lived in the Dutch capital for generations or had just arrived in the previous decades.[15] Coming from Amsterdam, Simon Symons first married into one of the most affluent Jewish families in Frankfurt/Oder before moving on to Warsaw. His family in Amsterdam and especially his uncles Benjamin and Samuel Symons sought to extend their business in two directions—to the east and the west. They mainly facilitated this goal through marriage strategies. Their ancestors had lived in Amsterdam since the early seventeenth century, and they were mostly involved in the trade in bills of exchange and diamonds as well as providing financial services.[16] They belonged to the small affluent elite of the Ashkenazi community in Amsterdam, though the volume of their business activities was not comparable to those of the most affluent

---

14 During the seventeenth century Amsterdam merchants had strong ties to Danzig (Gdańsk) in particular: Maria Bogucka, "Attempts to Break the Monopoly of Gdańsk in Polish Trade," *Studia Historiae Oeconomicae* 23 (1998): 117–19. See also Jonathan I. Israel, *European Jewry in the Age of Mercantilism, 1550–1750* (3rd ed.; Oxford and Portland, OR: The Littman Library of Jewish Civilization, 1998), 142–43 and 204–5. On the financial and commercial ties during the Seven Years War between Amsterdam and Central Europe, see Isabel Schnabel and Hyun Song Shin, "Liquidity and Contagion: The Crisis of 1763," *Journal of the European Economic Association* 2.6 (2004): 929–68, esp. 933–39.

15 Moses A. Shulvass, *From East to West: The Westward Migration of Jews from Eastern Europe during the Seventeenth and Eighteenth Centuries* (Detroit, MI: Wayne State University Press, 1971), 41–42, 44, 50. According to Shulvass, most Polish Jews who entered the strata of relatively wealthy Jewish merchants and bankers in Amsterdam had already arrived in the seventeenth century. On the immigration of Ashkenazi Jews to Amsterdam in the seventeenth century, see Yosef Kaplan, "Amsterdam and Ashkenazic Migration in the Seventeenth Century," *Studia Rosenthaliana* 23.2 (1989): 22–44.

16 Aust, "Commercial Cosmopolitans," 90–91, 96–101.

Sephardic merchants and bankers.[17] Their banking activities and trade in bills of exchange stretched from St. Petersburg and Riga in the East through all of Central Europe to London, Italy, France, the Ottoman Empire, and as far west as Suriname. To strengthen their connections to the west, they married into the Boas family in The Hague. To maintain their family business to the east, they used marriage strategies that closely mirrored the way they structured their business undertakings. Benjamin Symons' son Abraham became responsible for the family's business in Central and Eastern Europe. Moreover, Abraham Symons' uncle Berend Symons sent one of his two sons to Frankfurt/Oder, where he married Hendele, daughter of the affluent merchant Pincus Moses Schlesinger, in 1758.[18] This marriage tie was advantageous for both sides. Simon Symons began a shared business with his brother-in-law Levin Pincus Schlesinger, the Schlesingers received easier access to the credit market in Amsterdam, and the Symons family extended its ties to one of the most important Jewish families in the textile trade in Prussia. The benefits of the marriage arrangement were mutual. The financial capital and far reaching commercial connections of Levin Pincus Schlesinger's and Simon Symons' shared business allowed them to offer their services to the Polish king, who made them court suppliers in 1765.[19] When in Warsaw, Simon Symons provided credit to Polish nobles, supplied the king with diamonds, and held close business contact with his family in Amsterdam and Frankfurt/Oder as well as to cities like Danzig and Breslau.

With their businesses, the Schlesingers and other Jewish merchants in Frankfurt/Oder and elsewhere in Prussia as well as in Leipzig toward the end of the eighteenth century fulfilled a crucial function of transferring credit and

---

17   For the economic activities of Amsterdam Jewry in general, see Herbert Ivan Bloom, *The Economic Activities of the Jews in Amsterdam in the Seventeenth and Eighteenth Centuries* (Williamsport, PA: The Bayard Press, 1937). In 1743, at the age of 33, Benjamin Symons was listed among the ten wealthiest taxpayers in the Ashkenazi community, with an annual income of 2,500 guilders, partly accumulated through his trade in jewels and precious metals. Ibid., 177–178.

18   "Juden Acta betreffend die jährlich einzureichenden Juden Tabellen (1748–1759)," Stadtarchiv Frankfurt/Oder, Abteilung I, VII, 107, 325v–326. His marriage with Hendele is listed in "D.T.P. Ondertrouwen," Gemeentearchief Amsterdam [further: GAA], mf. 741, 420. Ignacy Schiper erroneously refers to Simon Symons as a brother of Benjamin and Samuel Symons. Schiper also mentions a fourth brother, Jacob Symons, who does not appear in any primary source: Ignacy Schiper, *Dzieje handlu żydowskiego na ziemiach polskich* (Warszawa: Nakładem Centrali Związku Kupców w Warszawie, 1937; repr., Kraków: Krajowa Agencja Wydawnicza, 1990), 302.

19   "Metryka Koronna, 1764–1780, KK 18 [mf. A-6083]," AGAD, Metryka Koronna, 171.

money across the continent. They acquired credit in Amsterdam via bills of exchange and transferred the credit to Jewish merchants from Eastern Europe, who usually paid in cash and could not rely directly on bills of exchange to Amsterdam, as most East European cities (with the exception of St. Petersburg) were not yet integrated legally into the European circulation of bills of exchange. The absence of regulations on the trade in bills of exchange as well as the mistrust of merchants in the Polish legal system enhanced the preference for cash payments from East European merchants at fairs like Leipzig and Frankfurt/Oder.[20]

Although both a bankruptcy wave of Christian banking houses in Warsaw in 1793 and the declining commercial role of Amsterdam were not directly linked, they occurred simultaneously and jointly contributed to the rise of a new and mostly Jewish banking elite in nineteenth-century Warsaw. In Amsterdam, the banking crises of 1763 and 1773 forced many bankers out of the trade in bills of exchange. It was often Jewish bankers who remained in the business until the last decade of the eighteenth century. Christian bankers, in contrast, increasingly provided government loans after the end of the Seven Years War in 1763, extending credit to German states, Sweden, Poland, and Russia, a trend that reaches back to the first half of the eighteenth century.[21] None of the Ashkenazic Jewish bankers was involved officially in the many large state loans issued to Poland between 1777 and 1792 by the large Christian banking houses in Amsterdam. The only Jewish bankers in the Netherlands involved in state loans in that period were Abraham and Simeon Boas from The Hague, who issued small loans to Austria, Denmark, Spain, Sweden, and Bohemia.[22] Most Jewish merchant-bankers, it seems, did not have the financial resources.

It appears that the 1763 crisis did not hit the Symons family substantially. When Benjamin Symons passed away that year, his sons Abraham and Emmanuel joined the firm and became partners of their uncle Samuel Symons in 1769. Abraham Symons regularly traveled to Warsaw and Danzig in the

---

20 Markus A. Denzel (ed.), *Geld- und Wechselkurse der deutschen Messeplätze Leipzig und Braunschweig (18. Jahrhundert bis 1823)* (vol. 10 of *Währungen der Welt*; eds. Jürgen Schneider et al.; Stuttgart: Franz Steiner, 1994), 5, 13–16; Markus A. Denzel, "Zahlungsverkehr auf den Leipziger Messen vom 17. bis zum 19. Jahrhundert," in *Leipzigs Messen 1497–1997: Gestaltwandel—Umbrüche—Neubeginn* (2 vols.; eds. Hartmut Zwahr, Thomas Topfstedt and Günter Bentele; Köln: Böhlau, 1999), 1:149–65.

21 De Vries and Van der Woude, *The First Modern Economy*, 142–43; 't Hart, Jonker and Van Zanden (eds.), *A Financial History of the Netherlands*, 59.

22 James C. Riley, *International Government Finance and the Amsterdam Capital Market, 1740–1815* (Cambridge and New York: Cambridge University Press, 1979), 139, 151, 165, 183, 248, 195.

following decade, while Emmanuel took care of the business with Western Europe, closely working with the Boas family of The Hague. After 1780 the track of Abraham Symons and the family's connection to Central and Eastern Europe gets lost. Simon Symons continued his business in Warsaw, where he went bankrupt and died in 1793.[23]

The year 1793 was a turning point in the history of banking in Warsaw. Though a general shift occurred throughout Europe that weakened the position of Protestant banking networks, it was spurred on by the bankruptcy of the major Christian, and mostly Protestant, banking houses in Warsaw that year. This disaster was brought on by the combination of a general downturn of the European economy, including the bankruptcy of a number of English and Dutch banks, and the escalating political turmoil in Poland. When rumors occurred in 1793 that the Tepper banking house was encountering difficulties due to defaults by the Polish government, creditors began attempting to withdraw their capital. The failure came as a shock and brought other Warsaw banks like Schultz and Cabrit down as well.[24] Eventually, all traditional Warsaw banking houses ceased to exist, leaving a considerable vacuum.

Thus, the first half of the 1790s saw the convergence of several momentous events: the steep decline of Amsterdam as a hub for commercial credit, the eruption of a major banking crisis in Warsaw, and the outbreak of political upheavals that would soon result in the dismemberment of Poland-Lithuania and its subjugation to the absolutist monarchs of Russia, Prussia, and Austria. These tectonic shifts ended the close, triangular commercial relationship between Amsterdam in the West, the Central European marketplaces (which functioned as brokers), and Warsaw in the East. The bankruptcy of Simon Symons was symptomatic of its breakdown.

The Rise of Army Suppliers in Warsaw

Though long-distance connections retained some importance after these events, the new Jewish commercial elite of the early nineteenth century in Warsaw emerged from a geographically closer circle. Jewish merchants and suppliers, who often initially traded in small quantities of goods, were able to exploit the opportunities that emerged out of the partitions of Poland, the regular movements of troops, and the need for army supplies that could not be

---

23   Aust, "Commercial Cosmopolitans," 220–21.
24   Barbara Grochulska, "Echos de la faillite des banques de Varsovie," *Annales Historiques de la Révolution Française* 53.4 (1981): 529–40.

provided locally. Here we find a third group of Jewish immigrants to Warsaw, in addition to those from Polish towns in its vicinity and those from larger Central European cities. These Jewish immigrants came to Warsaw from the formerly Polish territories that were now occupied by Prussia. Itzig Jacob (Izaak Flatau) belonged to this group of immigrants, a group driven not only by economic but by legal considerations. In his search for settlement rights and economic opportunities, Itzig Jacob followed the expanding Prussian state on what one might call an upward journey to the East.

Although historians have agreed in recent years that the synagogue Itzig Jacob opened in his (or more accurately, his wife's) house was not a "reformed" synagogue in accordance with any German model, his image as a wealthy Prussian banker who moved to Warsaw for business remains intact.[25] His story is, however, much more complex. He was born into a well-to-do merchant family in Flatow, probably before the first partition of Poland in 1772. In Prussian times, when Flatow was part of the so-called Netze district, his six brothers held privileges in Flatow and Gumbinnen (Gusev) as affluent merchants trading in velvet, silk and other textiles and visiting the fairs in Frankfurt/Oder. Itzig Jacob himself lacked a settlement privilege and tried to settle at various places in West- and later South Prussia while supplying the Prussian army with meat, grain, and feed.[26]

Itzig Jacob's first attempt to establish himself in Allenstein (Olsztyn) failed at the beginning of the 1780s, even though he offered to provide the local textile manufactory with material and purchase 4000 pieces of cloth from it annually. The wool manufacturers of Allenstein requested a concession for him, but the central government would not abandon its restrictive policy.[27] Eventually, it was Itzig Jacob's transnational connections that helped him overcome the legal obstacles inherent in Prussia's strict settlement regulations. Itzig Jacob maintained multiple ties to Poland, some probably established by his family before the first partition. He used his connections not only for the trade in wool and leather, but also for his increasingly predominant business—army

---

25 See Jürgen Hensel, "Wie 'deutsch' war die 'fortschrittliche' jüdische Bourgeoisie im Königreich Polen?" in *Symbiose und Traditionsbruch: deutsch-jüdische Wechselbeziehungen in Ostmittel- und Südosteuropa (19. und 20. Jahrhundert)* (eds. Hans Hecker and Walter Engel; Essen: Klartext Verlag, 2003), 135–72, here 142.

26 Aust, "Commercial Cosmopolitans," 54.

27 "Acta wegen des von dem Juden Isaac Jacob aus Flatow intendirten Etablissements in der Stadt Allenstein," Geheimes Preußisches Staatsarchiv Berlin [henceforth: GStA], II. HA, Abt. 7, Ostpreußen und Litauen, II Materien, no. 4709, 8–9, 17–22. His petition was finally rejected in 1782.

supplying. His contact with Szmul and Judyta Jakubowicz, the two wealthiest and most successful Jewish entrepreneurs in Warsaw, proved of crucial importance. When he tried to settle in Soldau (Działdowo), a Prussian town close to the Polish border, he informed the government

> that the wise Polish Court-Jew Schmul in Warsaw, who owns large noble estates in the vicinity of the capital, gave me the formal agreement to marry his oldest daughter though on the condition that I will settle as *Schutz-Jude* [protected privileged Jew]—if not in Warsaw—then at least in Soldau. I received this confirmation personally in Warsaw during my recent successful business trip involving Polish leather [...].[28]

Although Itzig Jacob never obtained the requested settlement privilege, he nevertheless did marry Szmul's daughter in 1796 and settle in Warsaw, which had just fallen under Prussian rule. This marriage was not only prestigious; it also solved his settlement issues when Szmul Jakubowicz and his wife Judyta obtained a general privilege for Prussia in 1798 that provided legal security to their daughters and sons-in-law.[29]

Itzig Jacob's supply patterns illustrate the importance of transnational connections for an army supplier. Immediately after the 1793 partition, Itzig Jacob had moved to Łowicz in newly occupied South Prussia, from where he supplied Prussian troops. During the Kościuszko uprising of 1794, he and his future father-in-law, Szmul Jakubowicz Zbytkower, who joined him in Łowicz, supplied the Russian army. After his intermezzo there, he moved to Posen in 1795 and successfully negotiated a large contract for supplying the Prussian army in South Prussia with oats, rye, flour, hay and straw. He shared the contract with Salomon Neumann, from his former domicile Łowicz, and with Michael Schweitzer and Itzig Kempner from Breslau in Silesia, since the scale of the business was too large to take on alone. The partners' geographic distribution helped them provide supplies from outside of South Prussia, in this case from Galicia, Silesia and the area of Sandomierz.[30]

---

28   "Acta betr. Das Gesuch des jüdischen Handlungs-Bedienten Itzig Jacob, um Bewilligung eines Schutz-Privilegii auf die Stadt Soldau," GStA, II. HA, Abt. 7, II Materien, no. 4717, 1v–2.

29   The general privilege of 1798 is pictured in Krzysztof Teodor Toeplitz, *Rodzina Toeplitzów: książka mojego ojca* (Warszawa: Wydawnictwo Iskry, 2004), 42.

30   "Die Angelegenheiten der Entrepreneurs, 1798–1803," AGAD, Generalne Dyrektorium. Departament Prus Południowych IX, no. 256.

Within a decade, Itzig Jacob had risen from a small local sub-contractor to a major supplier of multiple armies. He probably began by supplying meat, as he once mentions that he was a butcher, and then moved to grain, leather, and other goods imported from Poland.[31] Notwithstanding the restrictive policies of the Prussian government in the newly occupied territories,[32] Itzig Jacob quite literally capitalized on the expansionist nature of the Prussian state. Moreover, the case of Itzig Jacob underscores the importance of transnational familial networks not only for commercial reasons but also for overcoming legal obstacles. Thus, Itzig Jacob thrived under the specific conditions of the European borderlands, where transnational ties across rapidly shifting political borders were of crucial importance to providing supplies. Moreover, the changed political borders in the wake of the partitions of Poland brought large numbers of troops into the area, which required consistent and reliable supplies. Here (and similarly in the area of Alsace-Lorraine)[33] it was not so much far-flung transnational ties as the ability to work with other—primarily Jewish—merchants across changing political boundaries that allowed for commercial success.

After his move to Warsaw, Itzig Jacob was able to capitalize on the banking crisis of 1793 to make his own entry into banking. Like Jewish merchant-suppliers in Alsace-Lorraine, he and other Jewish entrepreneurs in Warsaw were helped by their preeminence in army supplying, which put them in an excellent position to exploit the bankruptcies of the Christian banking houses. The field was now almost entirely open to newcomers. The political unrest after 1793, the second and third partition of Poland, the Kościuszko uprising, and the city's capture by Prussia in 1796 may have created logistical and financial difficulties for Jewish entrepreneurs and diminished their assets, but these events also allowed them to enter banking, and they proved willing to assume the risks it entailed. The need for cash among Polish noble owners of extensive estates

---

31 "Acta wegen des von dem Juden Isaac Jacob aus Flatow intendirten Etablissements in der Stadt Allenstein," GStA, II. HA, Abt. 7, Ostpreußen und Litauen, 11 Materien, no. 4709, 1.

32 On the Prussian policies in the new territories, see Manfred Jehle, " 'Relocations' in South Prussia and New East Prussia: Prussia's Demographic Policy towards the Jews in Occupied Poland 1772–1806," *Leo Baeck Institute Year Book* 52 (2007): 23–47; Jürgen Heyde, "Zwischen Polen und Preußen: die jüdische Bevölkerung in der Zeit der Teilungen Polens," in *Fremde Herrscher—fremdes Volk: Inklusions- und Exklusionsfiguren bei Herrschaftswechseln in Europa* (eds. Helga Schnabel-Schüle and Andreas Gestrich; Frankfurt/Main: Peter Lang, 2006), 297–332.

33 On the rise of Jewish army suppliers in the Alsace-Lorraine region, see Michael Graetz, "Aliyato ve-shkiato shel sapak ha-tsava ha-yehudi: kalkalah yehudit be-etot milhamah," *Zion* 56 (1991): 255–73.

that could function as security provided a great deal of opportunity for aspiring bankers. The Prussian government had introduced in 1793 a mortgage system in its Polish territories, rendering this business more profitable. As nobles began entering their properties into mortgage books, the system allowed them to receive long-term loans and mortgage their estates systematically.[34]

Itzig Jacob was among the first to take advantage of these new opportunities. We do not know exactly when he entered the banking business after his move to Warsaw in 1796. However, contemporary and later sources generally refer to him as a wealthy "Prussian" banker, and archival records refer to banking activities from 1803.[35] In 1805, the estate owner Damasius of Krajewski, in need of cash to pay off his brother in the process of splitting their parents' estate, decided to "travel to Warsaw to [...] the well known merchant and banker [*Négotiant*] Itzig Jacob Flatau."[36] Thus, by the beginning of the nineteenth century Itzig Jacob had already achieved the reputation of an important Warsaw banker.

Though Itzig Jacob availed himself of the new opportunities in Warsaw at the turn of the nineteenth century, he continued to rely on other sources of income, as well. In addition to army supplying, he owned inns and was probably involved in the leasing of monopolistic rights to produce and sell alcohol (*propinacja*). Similarly, his ownership of a brickworks factory suggests attempted inroads into manufacturing.[37] By his death in 1806, his credit operations were significant, but did not yet constitute a full-fledged banking house. Similarly, other Jewish entrepreneurs who had moved to Warsaw by the late eighteenth century, such as his partner Moses Aron Fürstenberg and his wife's

---

34   Adelheid Simsch, *Die Wirtschaftspolitik des preussischen Staates in der Provinz Südpreussen 1793–1806/07* (Berlin: Duncker & Humblot, 1983), 208; Albert A. Bruer, *Geschichte der Juden in Preußen (1750–1820)* (Frankfurt/Main and New York: Campus, 1991), 161.

35   "Prozess des Starosten Joseph von Niemojewski gegen den Landesältesten Jacob Lewin in Marienwerder wegen der letzterem übertragenen drei Obligationen in Höhe von 62,000 Rtlr. des Bankiers Itzig Jacob Flatau," GStA, I. HA, Rep. 7C, no. 6N10, Fasz. 16.

36   "Beschwerde des Gutsbesitzers Damasius von Krajewski in seinem Prozess gegen den Juden Itzig Jacob Flatau wegen einer Obligation, 1805," GStA, I. HA, Rep. 7C, no. 34g, Fasz. 367. The term "Négotiant" was used for merchants trading in goods and money as well as for bankers. Johann Georg Krünitz, s.v. "Kaufmann," *Oekonomische Encyclopaedie oder Allgemeines System der Staats-, Stadt-, Haus- u. Landwirthschaft* (vol. 36; Berlin: Joachim Pauli, 1786), 496–97.

37   "Kancelaria Andrzeja Kalinowskiego," Archiwum Państwowe m.st. Warszawa [further: APW], syg. 23 [mf. S-980], 17, 23, 29, 41.

brother-in-law Leib Oesterreicher, traded in obligations and provided credit without moving into full-fledged banking.[38]

The Move into Banking

A shift from army supplying into full-fledged banking occurred after 1815, a process epitomized by Itzig Jacob's mother-in-law, Judyta Jakubowiczowa (Zbytkower). She was the daughter of Levin Buko in Frankfurt/Oder, born shortly after 1750 into one of the wealthiest and most influential merchant families in the city.[39] Probably owing to Prussian settlement restrictions, she moved to Warsaw in the late 1770s as a result of her marriage to the much older Szmul Jakubowicz (Zbytkower). Until his death in 1800,[40] Szmul Jakubowicz and his wife Judyta were closely involved in the trade and processing of agricultural products. When they acquired a large piece of royal land in Targówek, on the Praga side of the Vistula in 1780, they received full rights of usage, including an already existing windmill, the right to erect new buildings, and the right to produce and sell alcohol.[41] In addition, they established a tannery, a slaughterhouse and a textile manufactory on these grounds.[42] The motivation for

---

38 "Kancelaria Teodora Czempińskiego," APW, syg. 8, no. 874. "Kancelaria Przeździeckiego," APW, syg. 7, no. 19, 23, 26. "Kancelaria Aleksandra Engelke," APW, syg. 2, no. 165; syg. 10, no. 1362.

39 Aust, "Commercial Cosmopolitans," 93.

40 Usually 1801 is given as his year of death. Prussian records, however, prove that he had already passed away in the fall of 1800. "Die Gesuche verschiedener Juden um allgemeine Privilegien und Konzessionen auf Südpreußen," AGAD, Generalne Dyrektorium. Departament Prus Południowych I, no. 896, 133.

41 "Prawo Emphiteutyczne na Grunta w Dobrach Ziemskich Targowku," AGAD, Archiwum Królestwa Polskiego, syg. 357 [mf. 19541]. Legally, they acquired the land based on Emphyteutic law, which meant that the legal title to the land remained with the king but the right of usage was fully heritable and salable. Szmul, Judyta and their descendants received the land for 40 years in 1780, but obtained perpetual rights to the land in 1796. "Protokuł Przywilejów y Konsensów na Grunta Prawem Emphiteutycznym rozdane w Dobrach Targowska, Golendzinowa y Klucza Jabłońskiego," AGAD, Archiwum Potockich z Jabłonny, no. 47, 10.

42 Emanuel Ringelblum, "Shmuel Zbitkover," *Zion* 3, 3–4 (1938): 246–66, 337–55, here 340–41. One needs to rely on Ringelblum here, since most of the archival sources were destroyed during World War II. See also Anna Michałowska, "Szmul Jakubowicz Zbytkower," *BŻIH* 162–163 (1992): 79–90, esp. 84–85. According to Ringelblum, the slaughterhouse also processed pork. The tannery was established after Poland had banned the export of untanned hides in 1789 to stimulate manufacturing within the country. The slaughterhouse

establishing these businesses probably emerged from their commercial ventures and was closely tied to their interests as merchants and army suppliers.

Their business was not, however, limited to local operations. Judyta maintained close business connections with family members and fellow Jewish merchants from Frankfurt/Oder for decades; for example with her brother, Philip Levin Buko, who moved eastward as well to supply the Russian army while residing in Grodno. Eventually, her brother settled in the Prussian town of Memel (on the Baltic Coast, now Klaipėda) after settlement restrictions were lifted in 1812 with the partial emancipation of Prussian Jewry. Even more importantly, she maintained close business ties with the army supplier and banker Jacob Herz Beer in Berlin, son of Herz Beer, the wealthiest Jewish merchant and one of the communal leaders in Frankfurt/Oder.[43]

The Napoleonic Wars provided even more abundant opportunities for army suppliers like Judyta Jakubowiczowa, who not only supplied French and Polish troops in Warsaw, but Russian and Prussian troops as well. But only those willing and able to supply provisions reliably, to acquire them at least partly from outside the Duchy of Warsaw, and to extend credit and patiently await repayment, could survive in the business. Increasingly, it was Jewish suppliers who financed the armies by temporarily forgoing payments or by accepting state obligations. With the increasing payment in obligations, however, the supply of feed and food was not only a question of logistics anymore, but one of credit.

The importance of the role of credit in army supplying can be seen in the cases of both Judyta and her stepson Berek Szmul (Sonnenberg), two of the main suppliers to the Polish Army during the Napoleonic Wars. Lists of suppliers for all districts of the Duchy of Warsaw from December of 1810 and January of 1811, who received state obligations in March and April of 1811, confirm the important role of Jews among suppliers, who constituted a clear majority and worked on a much larger scale than Christian suppliers. Due to the financial difficulties of the Duchy of Warsaw, all supplies were paid in state obligations

---

was situated in close proximity to the large ox markets in Praga. In addition to trading in cattle, Szmul had offered to provide meat slightly below market prices on the condition that he receives a monopoly for supplying Warsaw with meat, a request he was granted in 1789. Emanuel Ringelblum, "Żydzi w świetle prasy warszawskiej wieku XVIII-go," *Miesięcznik Żydowski* 2, 6–12 (1932): 489–518, 42–85, 299–317, esp. 62–63.

43 Aust, "Commercial Cosmopolitans," 123–25. Jacob Herz Beer, a great grandson of the Court Jew Jost Liebmann, was involved in the supply of South-Prussian troops during the Polish insurrection of 1794. On Beer see Steven M. Lowenstein, *The Berlin Jewish Community: Enlightenment, Family, and Crisis, 1770–1830* (New York: Oxford University Press, 1994), 91, 107, 137.

at this point.⁴⁴ Already in November 1808, the state council of the Duchy of Warsaw noted severe problems with the supply of meat, other food, vodka, and wood to the army since many of the suppliers who remained unpaid refused to ship any further supplies. The council lamented the rising prices of supplies, but also pointed to a fundamental problem: the lack of cash led to diminished competition among suppliers and thus made the acquisition of goods on credit more expensive. Although there were attempts to get rid of Berek Szmul because of his allegedly overpriced supplies, the council concluded:

> In the end, it will be impossible to release this meat supplier [Berek Szmul] from his contract as demanded because it would be difficult to find another one who would be willing to take on these supplies due to irregular payments. One has to try by all means to satisfy him and other suppliers, because otherwise the provision of the repositories will collapse completely.⁴⁵

Berek Szmul and many other suppliers were still awaiting payment for their supplies years later; thus, army supplying meant providing long-term credit to the government.

After years of political unrest and changing rulers, the end of the Napoleonic Wars and the creation of the Kingdom of Poland in 1815 brought more stability. Although the Congress of Vienna postponed the dreams of a resurrection of an independent Polish state and essentially confirmed the partitions, the Kingdom of Poland enjoyed an increased political stability. This stability, which meant the relative absence of war for a few decades, diminished the profitability of army supplying and encouraged Jewish entrepreneurs to move into banking. The move was most pronounced in the case of Judyta Jakubowiczowa, who dropped out of army supplying after 1815 completely to concentrate her efforts in banking. The magnitude of her banking enterprise can be reconstructed relatively well from notarial records and the inventory of her assets that was drawn up after her death under the supervision of tax assessors. According to this inventory, her assets amounted to two and a half million Polish złotys plus

---

44 "Memoriał Ministra Woyny, 05. April 1811," AGAD, Rada Ministrów Księstwa Warszawskiego, serja 2-go, 115, 80–85.

45 Bronisław Pawłowski and Tadeusz Mencel (eds.), *Protokoły Rady Stanu Księstwa Warszawskiego*, t. 2, cz.1 (Toruń: Towarzystwo Naukowe w Toruniu, 1965), 208–9. See also Glenn Dynner, *Men of Silk: The Hasidic Conquest of Polish Jewish Society* (New York: Oxford University Press, 2006), 100.

an additional million in outstanding assets.[46] Similar to her son-in-law Samuel Antoni Frankel, who converted to Christianity with his family in 1806, she continued to cooperate closely with Prussian bankers, first and foremost with Herz Beer in Berlin. Nevertheless, political changes seem to have influenced the geographical orientation of her banking business or at least strengthened her business ties within the formerly Polish territories and to Russia, ties that she had maintained since the last quarter of the eighteenth century. In Warsaw, she had business ties with local Jewish and non-Jewish banking houses like those of Epstein & Levi and Piotr Steinkeller.[47] She held debt obligations from the government of the Kingdom of Poland as well as from a large merchant bank in St. Petersburg, but her international business was limited primarily to St. Petersburg and Berlin.[48] Though her career was originally built on her own mobility and transnational connections, primarily to Prussia and Russia, the rise of Warsaw as a financial center for the Kingdom of Poland may have limited the importance of those foreign connections.

Judyta Jakubowiczowa primarily served local clients, primarily Polish nobles, who were in constant need of credit. Examples of her regular clients were the widow Alexandra Lubomirski and the brothers Władysław and Tadeusz Ostrowski. Credit to local nobles was usually provided for two or three months or up to one year at five percent interest.[49] That most loans after 1822 were made in Russian rubles is noteworthy, as it may suggest that Judyta's business was becoming increasingly Russian-oriented. Her debtors may have increasingly adapted to the political circumstances, as well.[50] Moreover, the state remained an important client of these early Jewish banking houses, as seen in Samuel Antoni Fraenkel's loan of 150 million złotys to the Kingdom of Poland in 1833.[51]

Members of her close and large family, some of whom converted to Christianity, sustained the banking business and became part of the new

---

46   On the inventory of her house, firm, and assets, see Artur Eisenbach and Jan Kosim, "Akt masy spadkowej Judyty Jakubowiczowej," *BŻIH* 39 (1961): 88–143.

47   Ibid., 117–21.

48   The obligations are listed in the inventory of her assets. See Eisenbach and Kosim, "Akt masy spadkowej Judyty Jakubowiczowej," 121–37.

49   Aust, "Commercial Cosmopolitans," 240.

50   The ruble became the only valid currency in the Kingdom of Poland after 1850. After the 1831 uprising a form of hybrid coins was issued that carried dual values in kopeks and groszy. Paul D. Van Wie, *Image, History, and Politics: The Coinage of Modern Europe* (Lanham, MD: University Press of America, 1999), 96–97.

51   François Guesnet, "Banking," in *YIVO Encyclopedia of Jews in Eastern Europe* (2010), http://www.yivoencyclopedia.org/article.aspx/Banking (accessed January 19, 2012).

financial elite of Warsaw and the Kingdom of Poland as a whole throughout the nineteenth century. Her extended family included the Fraenkel, Toeplitz, and Bergson families. Other families in this circle, like the Kronenbergs and Epsteins, could look back on a similar story of immigration to Warsaw at the beginning of the nineteenth century.[52] After the brief lapse of multiple transnational connections of Jewish bankers in Warsaw, reflected in the case of Judyta Jakubowiczowa, these banking families rejoined transnational banking networks during the second half of the nineteenth century.

The Leasing of State Monopolies

The leasing of state monopolies as a field of entrepreneurial endeavor ties closely into two areas of economic activity undertaken by members of the mercantile elite in Warsaw and the Kingdom of Poland. First, leasing state monopolies was another arena of state service and was structurally comparable to army supplying. Second, moving into monopoly leases was not a radical occupational shift, as it was based on one of the major occupations of Jews in the Polish-Lithuanian Commonwealth, namely, the leasing of noble-owned enterprises (*arenda*). Jews leased noble estates or specific taxes, but in the eighteenth century they figured most prominently in leasing the right to produce and sell alcohol, a move into monopoly leasing from nobles though not yet from the state.[53] This form of leaseholding, marking the close integration of Jews into the feudal system of the Polish-Lithuanian Commonwealth, continued into the nineteenth century. The move into the lease of state monopolies

---

52   On these families, see for example Toeplitz, *Rodzina Toeplitzów* (see note 29); Szymon Askenazy (ed.), *Leopold Kronenberg: monografia zbiorowa* (Warsaw: Druk K. Kowalewskiego, 1922); Ryszard Kołodziejczyk, *Portret warszawskiego milionera* (Warsaw: Książka i Wiedza, 1968).

53   According to Gershon Hundert, over half of rural and a quarter of urban Jews earned their income primarily in this field by the 1760s. Jews dominated the production and sale of alcohol in villages and held leases on mills, breweries, distilleries, and taverns in towns. See his *Jews in Poland-Lithuania in the Eighteenth Century: A Genealogy of Modernity* (Berkeley: University of California Press, 2004), 32–33, 42–43; idem, *The Jews in a Polish Private Town: The Case of Opatów in the Eighteenth Century* (Baltimore, MD: Johns Hopkins University Press, 1992), 64–67. On the continuation of leaseholding in the nineteenth century see Judith Kalik, "Leaseholding," YIVO *Encyclopedia of Jews in Eastern Europe*, 1: 1003; Adam Teller, *Kesef, koah, ve-hashpa'ah: ha-yehudim ba-ahuzot bet radzivil be-lita ba-me'ah ha-18* (Jerusalem: Merkaz Zalman Shazar le-Toldot Yisrael, 2006), 128–29.

by mercantile elites suggests a partial shift away from the close Jewish connection to the nobility in favor of a closer connection to the state, although many members of the Jewish elite continued their dealings with nobles, especially in the field of money lending.

The transition of Berek Szmul, the aforementioned army supplier and son of Szmul Jakubowicz,[54] and his business partners into leasing the salt monopoly from the Duchy of Warsaw and then from the Kingdom of Poland is case in point. This move built on his prior economic activities. We have seen the active role Berek Szmul played in army supplying, especially in the supply of meat, often salted meat. He was also involved in the leasing of estates from Polish nobles in the Warsaw and Siedlce provinces of the Duchy of Warsaw.[55]

The inroads made by Polish Jewish entrepreneurs into the supply of salt were a product of the late eighteenth-century political shifts. The two main sources of salt—namely, the formerly Polish mines in Sambor and Wieliczka—became possessions of the Habsburg Empire after the first partition of Poland in 1772. In the Duchy of Warsaw and the Kingdom of Poland, the salt monopoly was leased privately. The fact that the major mines were situated outside the state may have contributed to Jewish prominence in the business, as Jewish entrepreneurs could use their transnational networks to import salt.

The contracts from notarial records show that salt supplying was a major business, one which the state was interested in leasing out completely so as to profit from high margins owing to its monopoly and high taxes. At the same time, salt supplying offered high-volume business opportunities for entrepreneurs in Warsaw and later in Cracow.[56] The volume of the salt trade was too immense to be fulfilled solely by any one individual merchant. Thus, in addition to contracts with the Polish state, we primarily find partnership agreements between various Jewish entrepreneurs who combined their efforts.

The salt supply from Galicia required relations with Jewish entrepreneurs on the other side of the border who were familiar with the administration and logistics of the salt business in the Habsburg Empire. In 1811, Berek Szmul signed a contract with Izaak Wolff Rapoport, a merchant from Lwów,

---

54 For the most details on Berek Szmul see Dynner, *Men of Silk*, 89–116, and Marcin Wodziński, "Legat Berka Sonnenberga czyli o zaskakującej karierze mimowolnego dobroczyńcy," *Studia Judaica* 7.1 (2004): 139–62.

55 "Kancelaria Walentego Skorochód-Majewskiego," APW, syg. 36 [mf. S-353], no. 2572/253, 151–160v.

56 Jan Kosim, *Losy pewnej fortuny: Z dziejów burżuazji warszawskiej w latach 1807–1830* (Wrocław: Zakład Narodowy imienia Ossolińskich, Wydawnictwo Polskiej Akademii Nauk, 1972), 213.

who held a contract with the Austrian government for an annual purchase of 100,000 barrels of salt from the mines in Galicia.[57] Berek Szmul agreed to purchase 50,000 barrels from Rapoport and to transport them to storage facilities throughout the Duchy of Warsaw. The contract, which was confirmed in June 1811 by Rapoport's agent Joseph Zwilling from Lwów, also stipulated that Berek Szmul was not allowed to purchase salt from any other source.[58]

It appears that the volume of the business soon exceeded Berek Szmul's financial (and likely organizational) capacities. In attempting to ground his business on more secure financial footing and increase the scale of his operation, he joined forces with Salomon Markus Posner, who would become his closest business associate. Moreover, he and Izaak Wolff Rapoport established the Southern Salt Trade Company in June 1811.[59] The long and detailed contract, in Polish and German, was signed in Warsaw by both entrepreneurs, who each held two sevenths of the company, and by Salomon Markus Posner, Josef Schwartzmann, and Lazer Zuker from Jaroslav in Galicia. Each of the latter held another seventh of the company, and their financial shares, losses, and benefits in the company were divided accordingly. The contract regulated the working of the company into the smallest detail and offers a glimpse into how this partnership was established.[60]

The contract also shows how these Jewish businessmen operated across political borders. The company was to buy and sell salt from the mine in Sambor in Galicia for the following eight years, and company associates were responsible for transporting the salt over land and water to the storages in the Duchy of Warsaw. We see here an ethnic network at work, functioning transnationally and transcending kinship ties. What mattered were acquaintance and prior shared business interests, useful ties to non-Jewish officials, geographic location, and experience in the salt trade. Presumably, being Jewish was expected but was not a precondition or qualification. All the company

---

57 "Kancelaria Jana Marczyńskiego," APW, syg. 14 [mf. S-119], no. 1785/76, 187–194. One barrel (beczek) equaled between 77 and 78 kg, thus the contract was about 7,700 tons of salt. The amount is somewhat inexact since the contract stipulated a barrel of either 140 Viennese pounds or 165 Berlin pounds; one Viennese pound was about 561 grams, a Berlin pound about 467 grams. See also Kosim, *Losy pewnej fortuny*, 214.
58 "Kancelaria Jana Marczyńskiego," APW, syg. 15 [mf. S-120], no. 274, 677–680.
59 Salomon Markus Posner lived in the same building as Berek Szmul on Królewska Street (land registry no. 1066) in Warsaw. In February 1811 Berek authorized Posner to pick up 20,000 barrels of salt from Galicia as part of his contract with Rapoport. "Kancelaria Jana Marczyńskiego," APW, syg. 14 [mf. S-119], no. 1813/104, 254–255.
60 Ibid., syg. 17 [mf. S-122], no. 2443/64, 130a–142v.

partners had been previously involved in the salt trade and most had done business with the Polish or Austrian governments.

The reasons for the company's termination in 1816 remain unclear, but may have been related to the political changes of 1815 and the formation of the Kingdom of Poland.[61] The end of the Napoleonic Wars changed not only the political landscape but also the conditions for Berek Szmul and his fellow entrepreneurs, who had supplied the Duchy of Warsaw with salt. Though it is impossible to fully reconstruct the ensuing developments, it seems that Berek Szmul and the banker Samuel Antoni Frankel had designs on a general salt monopoly for all of the Kingdom of Poland.[62] Earlier, in 1813, Berek Szmul and Frankel had cooperated in the purchase of salt from a Galician mine in Wieliczka, and in 1816 they joined forces to establish a salt monopoly in the Kingdom of Poland after the previous monopoly had been dismantled between 1813 and 1815.[63] It appears that Frankel used his connections to Prussia to add supplies of white salt from Prussia to the contract, thereby extending the geographic reach of the business.[64]

Although a few Christian entrepreneurs, like Piotr Steinkeller from Cracow, were involved in the salt monopoly,[65] the business was a typical example of a Jewish economic niche. The Jewish entrepreneurs' informal networks translated into formal contracts, without which businesses of this scale could not have operated, even within kin and ethnic networks. In contrast to the relatively weak economic position and local social cohesiveness of Christian Polish entrepreneurs, Jewish suppliers profited from their transnational connections to Jewish entrepreneurs in Galicia and Prussia and from their well-established ties to Polish officials, which they had forged as army suppliers. However, Berek

---

61   Ibid., syg. 31 [mf. S-137], no. 6102/517, 816–817; syg. 34 [mf. S-140], no. 6957/322, 809–810; no. 6958/ 323, 811–812; 6960/325, 815–816.

62   She and Frankel had converted to Catholicism in 1806. Frankel founded the banking house S.A. Frankel, which soon operated on a European scale. Kazimierz Reychman, *Szkice genealogiczne* (Warszawa: F. Hoesick, 1936; repr., Warszawa : Wydawnictwo Artystyczne i Filmowe, 1985), 18, 73.

63   "Kancelaria Walentego Skorochód-Majewskiego," APW, syg. 36 [mf. S-353], no. 2569/250, 137–139v; Ryszard Kołodziejczyk, *Piotr Steinkeller: kupiec i przemysłowiec 1799–1854* (Warszawa: Państwowe Wydawnictwo Naukowe, 1963), 37.

64   Aust, "Commercial Cosmopolitans," 250.

65   Piotr Steinkeller (the father) had tried to enter the salt business already during Napoleonic times, but only in 1825 did his son Piotr Steinkeller succeed in receiving a contract together with Konstantyn Wolicki. While Fraenkel and Posner were still involved in the salt business, more Christian entrepreneurs entered the business in the later 1820s. Kołodziejczyk, *Piotr Steinkeller*, 39.

Szmul's business, despite its success, was much less transnational than that of his father—it seems to have been limited mainly to his contacts in Galicia. When it did extend to Prussia, it was apparently through the agency of Samuel Antoni Frankel and not through the salt business.[66] This more regional focus did not, however, prevent Berek Szmul from becoming part of the new financial Jewish elite in Warsaw.

The New Mercantile Elite

This new mercantile and financial elite constituted a small minority of Warsaw Jewry, of course. The majority of Jewish immigrants to the city, most of them from the vicinity of Warsaw, remained poor or managed to accumulate only moderate wealth. Thus, one might wonder about the relationship between the small minority of wealthy merchants, army suppliers, and bankers and the majority of Jews in Warsaw at the late eighteenth and early nineteenth centuries. This question might be addressed on different levels: economically, socially, culturally, and legally.

Economically, their relationship is difficult to describe due to a lack of source material. It seems reasonable to assume that Jewish merchants and suppliers engaged less wealthy Jewish merchants as sub-suppliers and other Jews for many other tasks, such as transportation. Berek Szmul and his partners, for example, used Galician Jews to ship salt on rafts from Galicia into the Duchy of Warsaw. A contract with the government stipulated explicitly that it was the entrepreneurs' responsibility to ensure that such Jews would return to Galicia.[67]

The wealthy provided the poor with charity, as was common within Jewish communities. Both the last wills of Judyta Jakubowiczowa and of her stepson Berek Szmul provide ample evidence of their involvement in charity for both Jews and non-Jews, though presumably not entirely voluntarily in Berek Szmul's case.[68] In her will Judyta Jakubowiczowa bequeathed considerable

---

66 From the files of the Christian banking house Eichborn in Breslau to which Frankel had close ties, it appears that Berek Szmul was not in direct contact with Eichborn and that any financial transaction between Berek Szmul and Eichborn went through Samuel Antoni Frankel. See "Bankhaus Eichborn: Korrespondenz mit Samuel Antoni," Archiwum Państwowe we Wrocławiu, Oddział Kamieniec Ząbkowicki, Dom Bankowy Eichborn, no. 513, 96; no. 514, 13–13v; no. 516, 119; no. 516, 11–16, 27.
67 "Kancelaria Aleksandra Engelke," APW, syg. 1 [mf. S-523], no. 16, 58.
68 The first version of Judyta Jakubowiczowa's last will is dated February 27th; the second March 5th 1829. The differences between them are minimal. The copies used here were preserved in the notarial records "Kancelaria Kowalewskiego," APW, syg. 8, no. 675,

amounts to charity, divided between Jews and Christians, although the sum for Jewish institutions was about one third higher than that for non-Jewish institutions. She even stipulated that a gift of 5,000 gulden was to be distributed to the poor "without regard to religion" during her burial, which seems a rather unusual decision.[69] Moreover, as the case of Berek Szmul and others show, one cannot easily divide Warsaw Jewry into two groups—a more or less acculturated minority and a traditionalist majority. Following Glenn Dynner, one may suggest that immigrant entrepreneurs like Judyta Jakubowiczowa and Itzig Jacob tended to know European languages and orient themselves toward their non-Jewish cultural and social environment, while native-born entrepreneurs like Szmul Jakubowicz and his son Berek Szmul tended to remain more traditionalist and sometimes supported Hasidism.[70]

The example of Itzig Jacob and Moses Aron Fürstenberg shows that members of the elite were very well aware of the image the Polish administration had of the traditionalist Jewish majority. Moreover, it seems they at least partly accepted this image. During the Prussian era at the beginning of the nineteenth century, many wealthy Jewish merchants, bankers, and entrepreneurs took the opportunity to move further into the inner streets of the city. In 1801 Itzig Jacob together with Moses Aron Fürstenberg rented the Cracow Palace on Senatorska Street for ten years.[71] In 1806 the magistrate instructed the Jews of Warsaw to move from the city's inner streets to the outer ones within two years.[72] Itzig Jacob and Moses Aron Fürstenberg argued three points to secure

---

159–163v. Altogether, Berek Szmul's descendents gave 219,000 złotys to Jewish institutions, 20,000 złotys to Christian institutions in general, and 2,500 złotys to the Institute of the Deaf. Marcin Wodziński has shown that this was due to pressure imposed onto his family. See his "Legat Berka Sonnenberga," 139–62.

69 The Jewish hospital in Warsaw and the Jewish Society for Clothing the Poor received the total sum of 27,000 gulden, three Christian charitable organizations shared 19,000 gulden. Another fund of 2,500 gulden was set aside for the education of children "without regard to religion," but poor members of her family had to be given preference. "Kancelaria Kowalewskiego," APW, syg. 8, no. 675, 160v–161v.

70 Dynner, *Men of Silk*, 116. On the question of acculturation see also Agnieszka Jagodzińska, *Pomiędzy: akulturacja żydów Warszawy w drugiej połowie XIX wieku* (Wrocław: Wydawnictwo Uniwersytetu Wrocławskiego, 2008), 254–62.

71 On Fürstenberg see Schiper, *Dzieje handlu żydowskiego*, 369. Fürstenberg belonged to the traditional establishment of the Jewish community.

72 Stefan Kieniewicz, "The Jews of Warsaw, Polish Society, and the Partitioning Powers, 1795–1861," *Polin* 3 (1988): 102–21, esp. 106. See also Eleonora Bergman, *"Nie masz bóżnicy powszechnej:" Synagogi i domy modlitwy w Warsawie od końca XVIII do początku XXI wieku* (Warsaw: Wydawnictwo DiG, 2007), inserted map II.

their right to remain in the Cracow Palace, which was situated north of the centrally located Saxon Garden (Ogród Saski). First, they had invested a sizeable sum in repairs for the building. Second, they noted that according to the original contract Jews were not allowed to reside in the building, while they merely rented spaces for trade. Their third point was, however, most intriguing: they assumed that the measure was taken to expel poor Jews due to their "uncleanliness" (*Unreinlichkeit*), and proclaimed that this designation should certainly not apply to them.[73] This incident displays their sense of belonging to a (Jewish) elite.

Legal status, especially settlement privileges, became the most important distinction (alongside wealth) between the wealthy minority and the poorer majority of Warsaw Jewry. As Jews had been forbidden to settle in the city of Warsaw since 1527, increasing numbers of Jews of different socio-economic strata settled in growing numbers in Praga and on noble estates (*jurydiki*) throughout the second half of the eighteenth century. This migration did not remain uncontested. The most prominent example was the tearing down of "Nowa Jerozolimska" (New Jerusalem), where prince August Sułkowski had sought to establish a Jewish settlement and commercial center in 1774.[74] This was part of a larger conflict about the question of Jewish settlement in Warsaw between the burghers and nobles. Throughout the Four Years Sejm, Jewish settlement in Warsaw remained a matter of dispute. The burghers tried to prevent any softening of the privilege *de non tolerandis Judaeis*, while representatives of the Jews of the provinces and Warsaw sought to receive the right to settle 300 Jewish families within the boundaries of Warsaw and to allow them free trade in their petition (*Pokorna Prośba od Żydów Warszawskich*) in 1789. The petitioners, emphasizing their utility in national and international trade, offered a onetime payment of 180,000 złotys and annual payment of 3,000 thalers.[75] The petition thus employed an early modern mercantile argument predicated on economic utility and would have primarily applied to the wealthier strata of Warsaw Jewry. Similar to the proposition of 1789, delegations led by Simon Symons and David Königsberger offered the king 20,000 thalers (360,000 złotys)

---

73 "Die Umquartierung der Juden von den inneren in die äußeren Straßen Warschaus 1806," AGAD, Generalne Dyrektorium. Departament Prus Południowych VI, no. 3399.

74 Eisenbach, "The Jewish Population in Warsaw," 47; Kieniewicz, "The Jews of Warsaw," 104.

75 Artur Eisenbach, Jerzy Michalski, Emanuel Rostworowski and Janusz Woliński (eds.), *Materiały do dziejów sejmu czteroletniego* (vol. 6; Wrocław: Zakład Narodowy imienia Ossolińskich, 1969), 129–132. See also François Guesnet. "Politik der Vormoderne: 'Shtadlanuth' am Vorabend der polnischen Teilungen," *Jahrbuch des Simon-Dubnow-Instituts* 1 (2002): 235–55, esp. 251.

for the settlement of 130 families in Warsaw.[76] This offer suggests that Jewish mercantile elites followed traditional patterns of intervention: employing the argument of Jewish economic utility for themselves, and in this case not even demanding general settlement rights for Jews in Warsaw, let alone general emancipation.

Under Prussian rule, the situation did not change drastically. Although no expulsions were carried out in Warsaw itself, the legal department of the Prussian general governing body (*General-Direktorium*) confirmed that the *privilegium de non tolerandis Judaeis* had to be respected.[77] To exercise some form of control, Prussia introduced a system of so-called day-tickets (*Tageszettel*) in 1799.[78] Obviously, members of the wealthy Jewish mercantile elite had much greater means to evade restrictive legislation. Holding a Prussian general privilege (*Generalprivileg*), Judyta Jakubowiczowa and other well-to-do entrepreneurs were able to purchase property in Warsaw.

Economic power, however, had its limits. Despite Itzig Jacob's economic success, he remained dependent on his wife's general privilege, which she had received through her parents' Prussian general privilege (*Generalprivileg*) of 1798. Her death would have consigned Itzig Jacob to the lower category of a tolerated Jew. Although he invoked his strong economic position and his position as representative of the Jewish community in Warsaw, he did not receive a privilege of his own from the Prussian administration until at least 1804.[79] This also meant that the house on Daniłowiczowska Street, where Itzig Jacob opened his prayer house, legally belonged to his wife, who was allowed to purchase property based on the general privilege attained by her parents.

Despite the political transition from Prussian rule to the Napoleonic Duchy of Warsaw and eventually the tsarist Kingdom of Poland, each regime implemented a similar residential policy in Warsaw. They strove to keep Jews away from the central streets of the city as much as possible, as we have seen in the Prussian example above. The government of the Duchy of Warsaw thought to keep Jews outside the inner city by introducing, in 1809, the so-called *rewir*,

---

76 Eisenbach et al. (eds.), *Materiały do dziejów sejmu czteroletniego*, 340–42, 379, 382.
77 Jehle, "'Relocations'," 45.
78 This allowed for the permanent settlement of Jews who had entered Warsaw before 1796 while latecomers had to pay high taxes to receive the same right and whoever arrived after 1799 was obliged to pay a day-ticket charge to reside in the city temporarily. Eisenbach, "The Jewish Population in Warsaw," 58.
79 "Die Gesuche verschiedener Juden um allgemeine Privilegien und Konzessionen auf Südpreußen," AGAD, Generalne Dyrektorium. Departament Prus Południowych I, no. 896, 133–138, 147–152, 157–174, 192–197.

a zone of streets on which Jews were allowed to live. Only a small number of well-to-do merchants, bankers, and entrepreneurs, relative to the growing number of Jews in Warsaw, were allowed to live on streets outside the *rewir*.[80] In both the Duchy of Warsaw and the Kingdom of Poland, however, wealth, economic success, and proximity to non-Jewish authorities could not overcome all obstacles, especially when petitioners refused to adopt what was considered non-Jewish attire, among them Berek Szmul and his wife Temerel. Although Berek Szmul claimed in a petition from 1815 that he had received the right to settle anywhere in Warsaw from the Saxon king and Duke of Warsaw in 1810, notarial records suggest otherwise. Berek and Temerel probably moved from Praga to Warsaw in the first decade of the nineteenth century. According to notarial records, Berek Szmul officially lived in Zakroczymska Street (no. 1856) until 1810, one of the streets north of the old city that became off-limits to Jews in 1809.[81] The following year, Berek Szmul moved to the Bielinski Palace (no. 1066) in Królewska Street. The building belonged to the then-Minister of Justice Feliks Łubieński, who allowed a number of Jews to settle on his family's property in the outbuildings of the palace situated on the part of the street open to Jews.[82] In 1821, when more streets in Warsaw were declared off-limits, all of Królewska Street was included. Neither Berek Szmul nor his business partner Samuel Marcus Posner, who belonged to the conservative establish-

---

80 On the *rewir* see Adam Wein, "Żydzi poza rewirem żydowskim w Warszawie (1809–1862)," BŻIH 41 (1962): 45–70.

81 For the 1815 petition see "Akta Kommissyi Rządowey Spraw Wewnętrznych i Policyi," AGAD, Komisya Rządowa Spraw Wewnętrznych, no. 6628, 212. Addresses become easier to trace after 1808, when notarial offices opened. "Kancelaria Andrzeja Kalinowskiego," APW, syg. 1 [mf. S-957], no. 98, 265. "Kancelaria Jana Wincentego Bandtkie," APW, syg. 4a, no. 332, 135. "Kancelaria Jana Marczyńskiego," APW, syg. 11 [mf. S-116], no 1106/91, 224.

82 The palace was centrally located right at the southern edge of the Saxon Garden at the corner of Królewska and Marszałkowska Street. Jews had lived there back in the eighteenth century, as it was noble land and thus the settlement restrictions for the city of Warsaw did not apply. "Kancelaria Teodora Czempińskiego," APW, syg. 10, no 1253, 443; Jarosław Zieliński, *Atlas dawnej architektury ulic i placów Warszawy: Śródmieście historyczne*, vol. 8: *Pl. Krasińskich—Kwiatowa* (Warsaw: Towarzystwo Opieki nad Zabytkami, 2002), 74, 77. Królewska was off-limits only from Krakowskie Przedmieście to Mazowiecka Street: Jakób Kirszrot, *Prawa żydów w Królestwie Polskim: Zarys historyczny* (Warsaw: Nakład Zarządu Warszawskiej Gminy Starozakonnych, 1917), 99. See also Bergman, *"Nie masz bóżnicy powszechnej,"* 37, inserted map III. Sometimes the palace is also called Łubieński Palace. On the acquisition of houses and the right of settlement in certain parts of Warsaw, see also Dynner, *Men of Silk*, 103–104, 106. "Kancelaria Walentego Skorochód-Majewskiego," APW, syg. 3 [mf. S-320], no. 150, 110–110v. "Kancelaria Przeżdzieckiego," APW, syg. 7, no. 19, 27. "Kancelaria Jana Wincentego Bandtkie," APW, syg. 11b, no. 1046, 53; syg. 26b, no. 2536, 1.

ment of the community, appear to have received an exemption, as both moved away the same year.[83] Thus, they shared the fate of the majority of Warsaw Jewry, including acculturated poor Jews who were not granted the privilege to live outside the *rewir* because they did not meet the wealth requirements of the Kingdom of Poland.[84] Though wealth was significant in many cases, the situation of Berek Szmul and others indicates that wealth and close economic relations to government circles of the Duchy of Warsaw as well as the Kingdom were not necessarily decisive in gaining exemptions from government decrees.

Conclusion

To return to the laments of Jacob Prager in Amsterdam in the 1780s, the foregoing analysis has shown that the decline of Amsterdam's position as the major European center of commerce and financial services coincided with the rise of new commercial and financial centers. This was not only true for London, but on a smaller scale for Warsaw and other Central and later Eastern European cities. The decline of Amsterdam's role in trans-European commerce was not decisive for the rise of a new mercantile Jewish elite in Warsaw, but it helped wean Jewish merchants and bankers in Central and Eastern Europe off of western credit, at least temporarily. This may also explain the more transnational as opposed to trans-European connections of members of the new Jewish mercantile elite in the first decades of the nineteenth century, a development that was likely aggravated by political shifts and the increasing economic and political integration of the Kingdom of Poland into the Russian Empire.

These transnational connections and migrations to Warsaw enabled the rise of a new Jewish mercantile elite. In the former Polish territories that were occupied by Prussia following the partitions of Poland, particularly in Warsaw, the close involvement of Jewish merchants trading in raw materials and agricultural products prepared them to enter the field of army supplying at a time of political unrest and recurring wars. Their commercial networks across shifting political borders allowed them to guarantee supplies when goods were scarce. Moreover, they were willing and able to extend credit when the state (e.g., the Duchy of Warsaw during the Napoleonic Wars) was unable

---

83   For the additional streets see Kirszrot, *Prawa żydów*, 101. Berek Szmul moved to Orla Street briefly before his death, Samuel Marcus Posner to Nalewki Street. "Kancelaria Jana Wincentego Bandtkie," APW, syg. 41a, no. 4044/98, 120; syg. 48a, no. 4739, 178.

84   See Glenn Dynner, *Yankel's Tavern: Jews, Liquor, and Life in the Kingdom of Poland* (New York: Oxford University Press, 2013), ch. 6.

to provide immediate cash payments. Their willingness to take presumably greater risks than many fellow Christian businessmen often enabled Jewish merchants, suppliers, and bankers to prosper. Though they were not particularly sophisticated or advanced in their business methods, their mobility, occupational flexibility, and commercial networks allowed them to adapt to new branches. The example of Warsaw demonstrates that the shift into banking was also fostered by the prior expertise of Jewish entrepreneurs in financing, expertise that stemmed from their experience in army supplying and advancing payments for supplies. Their move from commerce and army supplying to banking and leasing state monopolies was rooted in earlier business ventures, and it exhibited many continuities.

CHAPTER 3

In Warsaw and Beyond: The Contribution of Hayim Zelig Slonimski to Jewish Modernization

Ela Bauer

The name Hayim Zelig Slonimski (1810–1904) is usually invoked to illustrate the effort of proponents of the Eastern European *Haskalah* (Jewish Enlightenment-based reform) to add popular scientific writing to their Hebrew literary corpus. From 1834—the year in which his first book, *Mosde Hokhmah*, was published in Vilna—until the last decade of the nineteenth century, Slonimski strove to develop a broad Jewish scientific discourse that would be accessible to as many educated Jews as possible. Several scholars have already noted Slonimski's key role in disseminating science among the Jews of Warsaw and the rest of the Kingdom of Poland.[1] However, the transnational aspect of his career, in particular his involvement in Haskalah circles throughout the Russian Empire, has not yet attracted the academic attention it merits.[2]

---

1 Mordechai Zalkin, "Scientific Literature and Cultural Transformation in Nineteenth-Century East European Jewish Society," *Aleph* 5 (2005): 249–71; Ira Robinson, "The Diffusion of Scientific Knowledge among Eastern European Jews in the Nineteenth Century: the Writing of Hayim Selig Slonimski," in Yakov Rabkin and Ira Robinson (eds.), *The Interaction of Scientific and Jewish Cultures in Modern Times* (New York, 1995), 49–65; Isaac Goldberg, "Chaim Selig Slonimski: 19th Century Popularizer of Science," in Gerson Appel (ed.), *Samuel K. Mirsky Memorial Volume: Studies in Jewish Law, Philosophy and Literature* (New York, 1970), 247–61; Jeffery C. Blutinger, "Creatures from before the Flood," *Jewish Social Studies* 16.2 (2010): 67–69.

2 Slonimski's name appears frequently in research dedicated to the Haskalah in parts of Eastern Europe. However, a close look at the research reveals a lack of in-depth discussion about his agenda and his involvement in institutions associated with Haskalah activities. See, for example, Michael Stanislawski, *Tsar Nicholas I and the Jews* (Philadelphia, PA, 1983); Eli Lederhendler, *The Road to Modern Jewish Politics* (New York and Oxford, 1989); Brian Horowitz, *Jewish Philanthropy and Enlightenment in Late Tsarist Russia* (Seattle and London, 2008). Research dedicated to the Haskalah in the Kingdom of Poland, such as Raphael Mahler's, makes no reference to Slonimski. See Raphael Mahler, *Hasidut ve'hahaskalah* (Merhavia, 1961). A more recent book mentions him, but only in regard to the controversies between Hasidic and integrationist Jews: see Marcin Wodziński, *Haskalah and Hasidism in the Kingdom of Poland: A History of Conflict* (Oxford, 2005), 170–76; and Alina Cała's earlier *Asymilacja Żydów w królestwie polskim (1864–1897)* (Warszawa, 1989), 33–49.

Slonimski's influence was more broad-based because he not only employed Hebrew, the lingua franca of the maskilim, but played key roles in two Haskalah centers: a "Russian" one that was active throughout the Tsarist Empire proper, and a "Polish" one situated mainly in Warsaw. Young Jews growing up in the tsarist empire and Kingdom of Poland alike during the second half of the nineteenth century deeply appreciated Slonimski's contribution to their intellectual development, declaring that their path to the university began with his Hebrew books and articles.[3] Even in the final decades of the nineteenth century, when Slonimski was already relatively advanced in years, he was still venerated as an authority among young educated Russian and Polish Jews.[4] The transnational nature of Slonimski's career thus unsettles certain assumptions about regional distinctions within the East European Haskalah.

Slonimski and the Diffusion of Scientific Knowledge among Eastern European Jews

Slonimski's main interest, the diffusion of scientific knowledge, placed him in an odd position within the Haskalah circles of Eastern Europe, which tended to emphasize the Humanities. His books were not the first scientific books written for the Hebrew reader—there were several books in Hebrew on mathematics, geometry and astronomy, all of which presented the sciences within the context of legal and ritual (*halakhic*) issues.[5] But Slonimski's writings reflected the programmatic importance he attached to explaining new scientific phenomena to broader Jewish audiences. This objective, as articulated in his earliest books, linked Slonimski to the aspirations of several non-Jewish scientific popularizers throughout nineteenth-century Europe.[6]

Two other recent studies contribute significantly to our understanding of the development of new Jewish elites in the Kingdom of Poland, yet mention Slonimski only in passing: see Helena Datner, *Ta i tamta strona: Żydowska inteligencja Warszawy drugiej połowy XIX wieku* (Warszawa, 2007), 38 and 224; and Agnieszka Jagodzińska, *Pomiędzy: akulturacja Żydów Warszawy w drugiej połowie XIX wieku* (Wrocław, 2008), 44.

3 Letter of Slonimski to Zvi Shapira, 7 Kislev 1880, in Hayim Reuven Rabinovitz (ed.), *Igrot Hayim Zelig Slonimski: Areshet Sefer shana l'cheker ha-sefer ha-ivri* 4 (1966), 65.

4 See, for example, Reuven Brainin, "Ezrat sofrim ozo eyza," *Ha-melits* (11/23 March 1888).

5 See, for example, Joseph Solomon Delmedigo, *Sefer elim hukot shamayim* (Amsterdam, 1629); and Eliyahu ha-Cohen Hechim, *Shvili dr'ekiya, tekunat ha-shamayim* (Prague, 1785); see also below, n. 14.

6 Slonimski, *Mosedei hakhmah* (Vilna and Horodno [Grodno], 1834); and idem, *Kochva de-shavit* (Vilna, 1835).

Slonimski's effort to explain new scientific phenomena to broader audiences began at the end of the eighteenth century. His initial explanations appeared in encyclopedias and the first popular scientific publications.[7] His *Kokhva de-shavit* provided scientific explanations on the nature of comets, while his *Mosdei hokhmah* offered readers an A to Z compendium on mathematics and science. Slonimski believed that every nineteenth-century person should possess scientific knowledge, including all Hebrew readers, as this type of information would open their eyes and help them understand the world in which they lived. It was incumbent upon all Jews, he argued, as members of human society, to understand science. He reminded his readers that scientific works had always been part of Jewish tradition, but that the various traumas endured by numerous Jewish communities over the years had caused many books to be lost. Those Hebrew scientific works that were available were, however, obsolete.[8]

Some of Slonimski's arguments were based on the eighteenth-century Hebrew work *Tekhunat ha-shamayim*, by Rafael Levi Hanover, a student of Leibnitz and correspondent with Moses Mendelssohn.[9] He was also influenced by Naftali Hertz Wessely, whose famous *Divrei shalom ve-emet* made a distinction between Jewish knowledge (*Torat ha-elohim*) and human knowledge (*Torat ha-adam*). In addition, he was influenced by Isaac Ber Levinson (Ribal), author of the foundational book of the Russian Haskalah, *Te'udah be-yisra'el* (1827).[10] As genuine Haskalah works, Slonimski's writings were not radical, nor did they place him outside the consensus of traditional Jewish society. Indeed, assorted Jewish scholars from far-flung corners of the Jewish world exhorted him to continue his work.[11]

---

7   Ruth Barton, "Just before Nature: The Purposes of Science and the Purposes of Popularization in Some English Popular Science Journals of the 1860s," *Annals of Science* 55 (1998): 3–6.
8   Ibid.
9   Rafael Levi Hanover, *Tekunat ha-shamayim* (Amsterdam, 1756).
10 On the Haskalah in the Russian Empire during the first decades of the 19th century and on Ribal and his book *Te'udah be-yisra'el*, see Michael Stanislawski, *Tsar Nicholas I*, 49–69, and Mordechai Zalkin, *Ba-alot ha-shahar* (Jerusalem, 2000), 143–51.
11 There was one significant exception to Slonimski's moderate approach. In *Ha-tzefira* (18/29 December 1891), Slonimski published an article entitled *Ma'i hanukah* in which he challenged the traditional reference to the Hanukah miracle. Following the strong responses to the article in 1893, Slonimski published a pamphlet entitled *Malshinai beseter* (Odessa, 1893), which presented the whole polemic that had developed after the publication of *Ma'i hanukah*. For more on this, see Wodziński, *Haskalah and Hasidism*,

In his early works, Slonimski highlighted the importance of writing on the sciences in Hebrew, while he later emphasized that his books were aimed at a broad readership and were not limited to elite circles. In the early generations, he explained, few had access to wisdom. More recently, however, research and wisdom had found their way into broader social strata. The eyes of the non-Jewish masses had been opened and books were being published in different languages to fill the needs of all non-Jews who sought to drink from the springs of wisdom. Yet Jews remained behind. While many possessed the talent for study, they lacked the requisite books in languages they could read.[12]

Slonimski believed it was his duty, without the aid of rabbinical authorities, to convince the traditional majority that learning new sciences would not negatively affect their faith. Perhaps this was why his later books did not contain endorsements from distinguished rabbis. Instead, they presented letters of commendation from maskilim like Nachman Krochmal and Solomon Judah Loeb Rapport (Shir) from Galicia, and Abraham Stern from Warsaw. *Toldot ha-shamayim*, published in Warsaw in 1838, even contains a letter in Polish from the director of the astronomical observatory in Warsaw. He had not actually read the book, as it was in Hebrew; nonetheless, a long conversation with Slonimski had convinced him that his scientific knowledge was impressive and very rare in Jewish society. Slonimski's desire to help the Israelites, as the Polish astronomer called them, by writing on this topic in Hebrew, was remarkable. He hoped that the book and subsequent ones would help the Israelites make strides toward modernity. The list of subscribers willing to buy Slonimski's book in advance of its publication differs from the subscription list to his previous books, in that it includes progressive Jews from Warsaw and non-Jewish Poles who could not read Hebrew but wanted to help Jews who were interested in its message.[13]

Slonimski's commitment to science only increased after his arrival in Warsaw, owing both to his marriage to Abraham Stern's daughter and the supportive, intellectual atmosphere in Warsaw. Stern, a *maskil* and prominent member of the local community, became Slonimski's patron in Warsaw.[14]

      174–76. It is important to underline that Slonimski did sometimes publish highly controversial views.

12   Slonimski, *Toldot ha-shamayim* (Warsaw, 1838).

13   Ibid.

14   In February 1844, Stern applied to the government Committee on Religion and Internal Affairs, in efforts to exempt Slonimski from the Billet tax. Among others, Stern wrote in his request that "God, Providence, sent me a son-in-law who is in agreement with me regarding moral and scientific issues." A copy of Stern's request, from February 1844,

He was a member of the Censorship Committee on Hebrew Books and Periodicals and of the Supervisory Committee on Jewish Elementary Schools. In 1830, Stern became a member of the exclusive Warsaw Society of Science.[15] He was the first Jew in the Kingdom of Poland to attempt to demonstrate to Jewish society that the study of science did not have to entail heresy or atheism.[16]

Stern's influence opened doors to the local community of Warsaw and legitimized Slonimski's scientific work. Yet the father and son-in-law held differing views about the dissemination of science. Stern argued that secular education was appropriate only for a minority of Jews, and worried that it might have a radicalizing effect on the younger generation of Jews.[17] Slonimski, on the other hand, favored diffusing secular knowledge throughout all strata of Jewish society and argued that he and others should reassure Jews that scientific knowledge was not dangerous but was completely compatible with a traditional way of life. Nevertheless, for Slonimski, whose first marriage had broken up because of his commitment to spreading scientific knowledge throughout Jewish society, being part of a family that at least approved of his scientific activity was of great significance, a source of support that was not to be taken for granted.[18] His new family's support, coupled with his new environment in Warsaw, gave Slonimski the approbation he had never received in Zabłudów (Białystok County), where he had resided from 1825 to 1838. Western European ideas had begun to reach Warsaw at the end of the 1830s and the beginning of the 1840s as a result of increased intellectual interest in the humanities and sciences and an increased desire not to lag behind Western Europe. Thanks to

---

can be found in the personal archives of Raphael Mahler 66/990, the Diaspora Research Institute Archives, Tel-Aviv University. Stern's attempt to exempt Slonimski from this tax failed. Slonimski was to receive that exemption a few years later, after Stern's death.

15 Ibid.
16 Jacob Shatzky, "Avraham Ya'akov Stern (1768–1842)," *The Joshua Starr Memorial Volume. Studies in History and Philology* (New York, 1953), 203–18.
17 Ibid.
18 We know that that there were many young Jews, such as Moses Leib Lilienblum (1843–1910) and Micha Josef Berdyczewski (1865–1921), whose first marriages ended in crisis and divorce; and that in Warsaw and in other areas of the Russian Empire, maskilim and other integrationists were related to each other. In Warsaw, Paprocki, an instructor in Jewish history at the Rabbinical Seminary, was Jakub Tugendhold's son-in-law; the maskil Moshe Tannenbaum was Hilary Nussbaum's father-in-law; and Hilary Glattstern was Samuel H. Peltyn's father-in-law. On marriage among such families in the Russian Empire, see Zalkin, *Be'alot ha-shachar*, 272–74.

this new social and intellectual ambience, Slonimski was able to step up his efforts.[19]

Around that time, progressive Jewish circles successfully initiated several educational reforms. According to the historian Jacob Shatzky, in several traditional academies (*Talmud Torahs*) the curriculum included subjects such as arithmetic and the Polish language. The number of Jewish students who studied in modern elementary schools was on the rise, as well. In 1843, the first *realgymnasium* opened in Warsaw and enrolled Jewish students from its very inception. Many progressive Jews were involved in this new wave, and those who had acquired a general education began to work as physicians and engineers. Ludwik Natanson, a leader of the community, had studied medicine and was the publisher of the first Polish medical periodical, *Tygodnik Lekarski*. He was active in public health and other social issues on behalf of the Jewish and Polish communities.[20] Matthias Rosen and Leopold Kronenberg financed the publication of the important Polish periodical *Biblioteka Warszawska*. A group of Jewish doctors founded the Polish Medical Society.

After settling in Warsaw, Slonimski did not limit himself to popular scientific writing. In the 1840s, he developed a mathematical formula for making calculations for the Hebrew calendar. He published several articles on this subject in scientific periodicals in Germany.[21] These achievements gained him recognition among scientists from all over Europe, as well as from the Tsar and the Prussian Kaiser, who awarded him stipends and prizes.[22] Slonimski's

---

19 Jacob Shatzky, *Geshikhte fun yidn in varshe*, vol. 2, 161.
20 On the Natanson family, see, for example, Itshak Shipper, "Di familye natanson," *Haynt* (21 June–4 July 1935), 142–56.
21 After these articles were published, Slonimski conducted several visits to various cities in Germany, to introduce his inventions and establish connections with local scholars. During these visits he met Friedrich Wilhelm Bassel (1784–1846), a renowned mathematician and astronomer, who was the director of the Königsberg observatory, and Carl Gustav Jacob Jacobi (1804–1851), considered one of the greatest mathematicians of his time. Following these acquaintances, Slonimski was invited to present the mathematical formula he had developed at the Academy of Sciences in Berlin. On that occasion, he met the person he considered to be the greatest scholar of the time, Alexander von Humboldt (1769–1859). On the meeting between Slonimski and Humboldt and Humboldt's influence on Slonimski, see Ela Bauer, "Ka'asher ha-maskil ha-yehudi pagash et ha-mada'an ha-germani," in Arnon Soffer et al. (eds.), *Tavniyot nofim tarbuti'im* (Haifa, 2011), 47–63.
22 In his request to exempt Slonimski from the aforementioned Billet tax, Stern wrote that as a young man, Slonimski was already known as someone with mathematical and astronomical knowledge. His achievements also gained recognition in the Russian Empire and in Prussia.

engagement with the non-Jewish scientific world distinguished him from other Jews who attempted popular scientific writing in Hebrew, while strengthening his position within progressive Jewish intellectual circles.

Despite his expanding activities, however, Slonimski remained devoted to his primary goal of promoting accessible scientific writing in Hebrew. In the 1860s, he decided to advance it by another means, a weekly Hebrew periodical named *Ha-tzefira*. It seems that Slonimski—who had consistently argued throughout the years that Jews and non-Jews living in the nineteenth century should be aware of how technology, science, and new inventions affected their lives—was himself aware of the ways in which technology, industry and transportation had changed newspapers, and grasped how a periodical could assist him in reaching a broader audience. Periodicals were accessible to a relatively wide public, were published frequently, provided the ability to update information from one issue to the next, and dealt with a range of topics, all of which could help him reach the maximum number of traditional Jews and thereby promote the cause of Polish Jewish progress.

Slonimski's aspiration to publish a scientific periodical in Hebrew coincided with the widespread phenomenon of popular science periodicals in England. Science was attaining great popularity around this time, particularly after the publication of *The Origin of Species* by Charles Darwin, a book that had increased awareness that the public must be informed of the achievements of science.[23] In addition, the establishment of *Ha-tzefira* meshed well with developments in Warsaw. Following the completion of a railroad line between Warsaw and Vienna, a new industrialization process was underway in various parts of the Kingdom of Poland. Widespread admiration for the advantages the railroad and other new inventions provided led to renewed appreciation for how science and education could facilitate the modernization of civilization and society.[24]

The greater part of the opening article of *Ha-tzefira*[25] was dedicated to the development of human knowledge, arguing that human knowledge was expanding as technological thinking led to innovations and discoveries. Understanding scientific theories and gaining an awareness of new technologies and innovations could, he hoped, facilitate modernization and social betterment. There was great similarity between this and earlier optimistic assertions appearing in Slonimski's various books, although his writing style was now much more colorful. The opening article of *Ha-tzefira* not only

---

23 Barton, "Just before Nature," 4–5.
24 Jerzy Jedlicki, *Błędne Koło 1832–1864* (Warszawa, 2008), 201.
25 Slonimski, "Petach ha-davar," *Ha-tzefira* (4 February 1862).

revisited his earlier arguments, but also mirrored ideas and comments circulated within his local non-Jewish environment.[26]

In the following years, the intellectual environment of Warsaw continued to supply an array of sources from which Slonimski could draw inspiration and tap for information for his articles in *Ha-tzefira*.[27] As he himself observed, the publication of *Ha-tzefira* fit the Polish intellectual atmosphere. Supporters of Polish Positivism in particular encouraged the popularization of scientific writing, and from 1864 to the end of the nineteenth century a vast number of scientific books and articles, in both popular daily newspapers and special periodicals, were published in Warsaw and were predominantly aimed at the broad public.[28]

As a result of the failure of the Polish revolt of 1863, the number of Polish researchers allowed to work in universities and research labs declined.[29] As a result, extra-mural science classes became a popular alternative to formal academic studies. The notion of extra-mural classes also had a popular ideological justification, for it was in line with the orientation of Polish Positivism. Supporters of Positivism considered education—particularly scientific education—important capital that could advance Polish society, and argued that scientific researchers in particular could transform Polish society.[30] Aleksander Swiętochowski and other supporters of Polish Positivism avidly disseminated such ideas by means of the Polish press. Diverse articles published in 1859 and in 1860 in *Gazeta Codzienna* hailed the power of the sciences and enlightenment to bring peace and civilization to the world, while other periodicals published in Warsaw urged respect for the work of scientists. Although wars employing weapons had failed, Polish society could gain victory by

---

26 Idem, *Ot ha-zikarin* (Berlin, 1858), 9–10, 74–75. See, for example, the quotation from *Gazeta Codzienna* 269 (1859), cited after Jedlicki, *Błędne koło*, 201.

27 Blutinger, *Creatures from before the Flood*, 70–71, shows that between 1874 and 1879 Slonimski wrote about several geological phenomena based on the works of British and French scientists. Slonimski probably knew about these works from Polish scientific writing of the time. Various positivist authors translated and adapted British studies. Slonimski also used Polish publications for his writings on Darwin's theory of evolution.

28 According to Janina Żurawicka, *Inteligencja warszawska w końcu XIX wieku* (Warszawa, 1978), 33, 793 scientific books and 606 scientific articles were published in Warsaw between 1864 and 1900.

29 Magdalena Micińska, "Inteligencja na rozdrożach, 1864–1918," in Jerzy Jedlicki (ed.), *Dzieje inteligencji polskiej do roku 1918*, vol. III (Warszawa, 2008), 15.

30 Żurawicka, *Inteligencja warszawska*, 31–35.

developing a cultural and scientific arsenal.[31] In addition, a flurry of public lectures dedicated to scientific issues ensued, while many books in the public libraries that had opened up all around Warsaw were scientific in nature.[32] The Warsaw context thus nourished the popularity of Slonimski's own science-oriented Hebrew newspaper.

The spectrum of scientific topics published in *Ha-tzefira* was wide. Under the section "News about the World and Nature" (*Yediot ha-olam ve-hateva*) there appeared articles on optics, astronomy, mechanical engineering, unusual geographic and geological phenomena, discoveries in physics, biology, chemistry, and metallurgy, and news about natural occurrences like volcanic eruptions and other geographical phenomena.[33] Diverse scientific topics, technological developments, and new inventions were presented as a single cluster. The explanations, especially those pertaining to new technological inventions such as how the telegraph or telephone worked, were quite lucid.[34]

Slonimski was careful not to offend potential readers, most of whom belonged to the traditional Jewish world yet were curious about the sciences, and could only gain exposure in Hebrew. He took their pious sensibilities into careful consideration. Many famous people, he wrote in one of his articles, had not stopped believing in God after acquiring scientific knowledge. Even Copernicus was a believer until the day he died.[35] These gestures helped Slonimski gain his readers' trust.

The scientific sections of *Ha-tzefira* were the single most important reason for the newspaper's popularity among young Jews.[36] For many young men, *Ha-tzefira* was a gateway to scientific knowledge and the bridge between the study house (*bet hamidrash*) and the non-Jewish street:

---

31   See note 29.
32   Żurawicka, *Inteligencja warszawska*, 147–255.
33   The first issue published one of Slonimski's well-known articles on the telegraph. On 17 April 1862, Slonimski produced an article on photography. On 8 May 1862, he published an article on beavers. On 15 May 1862, he published an article on light and what the eye can see. Between 24 April and 24 July 1862, S.Y. Abramovitsh (Mendele Mokher Sforim) published a series of articles on chemistry.
34   Slonimski, "Yediot ha-olam ve-ha-teva, pe'ulat ha-telofon ve-toaltau," *Ha-tzefira* (19 December 1877).
35   Idem, "Ha-tikvave-ha-hayim," *Ha-tzefira* (4 /16 April 1878).
36   See the letter of January 1864 from Slonimski to Leon Rosental, the secretary of the Society for the Promotion of Enlightenment among the Jews of Russia (OPE), in Leon Rosental (ed.), *Toldot hevrat marbei haskalah be'yisra'el be'erets rusiyah*, vol. 2 (St. Petersburg, 1886), 7.

> [...] You cannot imagine the way I felt at the age of 15, when I first saw a telegraph. I heard that through telegraph wires, one can transmit a message anywhere. For me, it's a veritable wonder, more awesome than the ten creations which God had completed by Friday night. People talked about the telegraph during the entire year, sitting by their fireplaces in their houses of study. I could understand why the telegraph made us so excited. But I was restless. I felt I had to learn the secret behind it. I didn't know how to obtain that information. And then, all of a sudden, *Ha-tzefira* appeared. I opened the first issue and in large, clear letters, in the very first article, the editor, Slonimski, explained to his readers, even to those who had learned only a small portion of the Talmud, how the telegraph works. Yes, *Ha-tzefira* was a rich resource for me. I loved science and I loved that periodical, which was responsible for my acceptance into the Medical Academy in St Petersburg.[37]

As Slonimski's influence on Jewish society, and on its youth in particular, transcended the boundaries of Warsaw, he was able to extend his influence to the far reaches of the Russian Empire.

Slonimski and Russian Haskalah Circles

Slonimski began his Haskalah activities several years after the publication of the Hebrew tract *Te'udah be-yisra'el*, by Yitzhak Ber Levinson (Ribal).[38] However, it would be wrong to include him among the first generation of maskilim in the Russian Empire. Not only was he younger than Levinson (Ribal), Gintsburg, Lebensohn and others, but as he himself wrote later on in his life, at the time he published his first books he had not taken part in theoretical discussions about the definition of the Eastern European Haskalah:

> I did not speak about the Haskalah or what the Haskalah was, its goals and aims. My objective was to spread wisdom and knowledge among people who were part of the religious world, *Bet Midrash* and Yeshiva students, who knew nothing beyond rabbinical literature and Halakha (Jewish ritual law). I wanted to open their eyes and let them find their

---

37 *Sefer ha-yovel shel ha-tzefira*, 63–65.
38 On the Haskalah in the Russian Empire in the first decades of the 19th century and on Ribal and his book *Teu'dah be-yisra'el*, see Stanislawski, *Tsar Nicholas I*, 49–69; and Mordechai Zalkin, *Ba-alot ha-shahar*, 143–51.

way to springs of wisdom published in non-Jewish languages. I believed that after drinking from those springs, the Haskalah would be part of their world and they would understand its meaning and purpose.[39]

The writings of maskilim who were active during the first half of the nineteenth century, in contrast, focused more on subjects like literature and philosophy, with a special interest in nurturing the Hebrew language. Slonimski's writing centered predominantly around the sciences, including mathematics, geometry and astronomy, not the humanities. But as a pioneer of scientific writing in Hebrew he still contributed immensely to the early development of modern Hebrew writing—even if this was a secondary goal.

Slonimski's association with Russian Haskalah circles began only in the 1860s, a period when a new generation of maskilim was coming into its own.[40] Eli Lederhendler identifies several institutional loci of Russian Haskalah between the 1850s and the 1870s: the crown schools and the rabbinical seminaries in Vilna and Zhitomir, the *Society for Promoting Enlightenment among Jews in Russia* (OPE), and the Haskalah press.[41] During the second half of the nineteenth century, Slonimski was affiliated, albeit in different ways, with such institutions, first through his own newspaper, *Ha-tzefira*. In 1863, he was appointed censor of Hebrew books in Zhitomir and was named inspector of the governmental rabbinical seminary.[42] He served as inspector for twelve years, until the Russian authorities closed such seminaries down. The position had been previously held by Ya'akov Eichenbaum (1796–1861), an early poet of the Russian Haskalah who was also a well-known mathematician, which may explain why Slonimski, as a mathematician, was appointed his successor. The two inspectors were also similar in their trans-regional mobility. While Eichenbaum was born in Zamość (Kingdom of Poland) and moved to Russian cities such as Uman, Odessa and eventually Zhitomir, Slonimski had left the Russian territories for Warsaw, returning only after several decades. It is possible that Slonimski's reputation as someone who kept his political opinions to himself and who was, moreover, not native to the Kingdom of Poland helped his candidacy, for he could more easily qualify for positions outside of the kingdom. Nor did the Polish revolutionary events in Warsaw at the beginning of the 1860s interfere with his nomination.

---

39   Slonimski, "Shalmi toda," *Ha-tzefira* (26 February/9 March 1880).
40   Stanislawski, *Tsar Nicholas I*, 108.
41   Lederhendler, *Road to Modern Jewish Politics*, 109–33.
42   Slonimski, "Et te'asef ha-tzefira," *Ha-tzefira* (12/25 July 1862).

Slonimski was inspector during a time of vociferous Jewish public discontent with those who served as state rabbis, i.e. the very posts that the Zhitomir seminary was ostensibly training its students to fill.[43] Even Haskalah circles were critical of such seminaries.[44] Nevertheless, Slonimski continued to display his loyalty to the Haskalah agenda throughout his twelve years in Zhitomir. This loyalty may be gleaned from the following episode: in 1868, Eliezer Zweifel, at the time a Talmud teacher in the rabbinical seminar in Zhitomir, published *Shalom al yisra'el*, the first revisionist, sympathetic approach to Hasidism by a maskil.[45] The book's publication led Slonimski to publish the following response in *Ha-melits*:

> No doubt, many words will be written against this popular book. What led Zweifel to go against the very nature and tenor of the Haskalah? As for me, it is not my way to involve myself in different quarrels, but I find it necessary to mention that the author's arguments reflect his own views only. He does not represent the views of our institution.[46]

Only after the seminary's closure and his return to Warsaw did Slonimski admit publicly that there was no way the seminary could train rabbis who would be acceptable to the majority of Jewish society; and that most of the students at the seminary were, at any rate, not interested in becoming rabbis. According to Mikhail Morgulis, most students were merely eager to acquire secular knowledge[47]—something which was of course of great interest to Slonimski as well. He and his wife were thus involved in diverse extracurricular activities unrelated to the seminary's formal curriculum.[48] Despite his criticism of the seminary, however, Slonimski thanked the Russian authorities for their

---

43 Azriel Shohet, "Yachas ha-tsibur el ha-nichei batei ha-midrash le-rabanim," in Immanuel Etkes (ed.), *Ha-dat ve'ha-hayim* (Jerusalem, 1993), 256.
44 Shmuel Feiner, *Milhemet tarbut: tenu'at ha-haskalah ha-yehudit ba-me'ah ha-tshaesreh* (Jerusalem, 2010), 251–254.
45 Eliezer Zweifel, *Shalom al yisra'el*, ed. Abraham Rubinstein (Jerusalem, 1972).
46 Slonimski, "Zhitomir," *Ha-melits* (18/30 September 1868).
47 Quote in Brian Horowitz, *Empire Jews: Jewish Nationalism and Acculturation in 19th- and Early 20th-Century Russia* (Bloomington, 2009), 159.
48 At a Purim celebration in 1863, students at the seminar (including Avrom Goldfaden) performed the Yiddish play, *Serkele*, written by the Yiddish poet and dramatist Shloyme Ettinger. Sara Slonimski brought the play to Zhitomir. For additional information about extra-curricular activities conducted by the non-Jewish teachers, see ibid.

efforts and support of the seminaries in both Vilna and Zhitomir after they were closed down.[49]

Slonimski's affiliation with the controversial seminary did not mar his reputation as a moderate intellectual who acted in concert with traditional Jewish society. Nor, even, did his nomination as censor of Hebrew publications in Zhitomir. Slonimski believed that as a censor he had an obligation to promote the Haskalah agenda and remain loyal to the Russian authorities. In this sense, he was similar to other censors who served in that position throughout the nineteenth century. Until the dissolution of Tsarist Russia, the position of the Hebrew censor depended not only on the statutes or the loyalty of the censor to the authorities, but hinged as well on the censor's views, preferences and commitment to reforming Jewish society. Many of the censors were considered a burden on the Jewish press and Jewish book publishing.[50] On several occasions, censors demanded that Jewish newspaper editors and publishers of Hebrew books even change historical and geographical facts that could be construed as disloyal to the Russian authorities.[51] Slonimski, thanks to his brief experience as the editor of a Hebrew periodical, understood the absurdity of some of these demands. He felt that even if authors' views diverged from his own he should not prevent their books from being published so long as they did not express rejection of censorship or disloyalty to the authorities.[52]

Many censors were known to support the integration of Jews into the surrounding population.[53] Slonimski, too, demanded adherence to state laws and support for new educational reforms: to learn the state language and sciences, which he regarded as an obligation for all members of civil society and a prerequisite for lifting the curtain dividing Jews from the rest of the population.[54] Thus, Slonimski differed from other Hebrew censors more in tone than in agenda. As a censor, as well as a writer and editor, Slonimski almost never took a tone that might place him outside the consensus of Jewish society. Perhaps

---

49   Slonimski, "Al batei sefer ve-hinuch," *Ha-tzefira* (23 May/4 June 1878).
50   Dmitrii Arkad'evich Eliashev, "A Note on the Jewish Press and Censorship during the First Russian Revolution," in Stefani Hoffman & Ezra Mendelsohn (eds.), *The Revolution of 1905 and Russia's Jews* (Philadelphia, 2008), 49.
51   Evidence on this type of dialogue can be found in Nahum Sokolov, "Ha-tzefira ve-ha-mevakrim mita'am," in G. Kressel (ed.), *Be-mar'ot ha-keshet* (Jerusalem, 1960), 207–37. *Inter alia*, Sokolow described how one of the censors was furious at him because in his book, *Mitsukei erets*, an adaptation of an English book, Sokolow wrote that Siberia was unknown to Russians.
52   *Ha-melits* (18 [30] September 1868).
53   Eliashev, *A Note on the Jewish Press*, 50.
54   Slonimski, "Divrei shalom ve-emet," *Ha-tzefira* (3 July 1862).

this is why his name was rarely included among Jewish censors when they were mentioned in a negative context.

The fact that Slonimski was nominated as a Russian Jewish censor after spending some years in Warsaw was not exceptional. There were others who had crossed political boundaries, a prominent example being Wolf Tugendhold, who was born in Kraków and appointed to the Censorship Committee in Vilna. Nor were censors the only Jewish intellectuals who found themselves traversing the Russian and Polish borders. After Slonimski was appointed to the post in Zhitomir, he asked the poet Judah Leib Gordon to move to Warsaw and become editor of *Ha-tzefira*.[55] But it does seem that, although Slonimski lived in Warsaw from the late 1830s to 1862, he was never truly considered a Polish Jew. The fact that at a time of conflict between the Polish people and the Russian authorities he had received an appointment that demanded loyalty to the latter seems to confirm this sense of foreignness. It seems that even some Russian maskilim did not consider him a Polish Jew, for he joined the *Society for Promoting Enlightenment among Jews in Russia* (OPE) a short time after his arrival in Zhitomir.

Slonimski and the Society for Promoting Enlightenment among Jews in Russia (OPE)

On December 17 1863, the first meeting of the Society for Promoting Enlightenment among Jews in Russia (OPE) took place. The 21 people invited to attend were considered the elite of the Russian maskilim.[56] Slonimski was part of that group, and had been a member of its board right from the society's conception.[57] He had not abandoned what he believed to be his primary goal: to disseminate popular Hebrew scientific writing in newspaper format. As he was now the censor of Hebrew publications, he was not allowed to apply for a license to publish a Hebrew periodical. He had hoped that OPE would apply for the license on his behalf, but its board turned him down.[58]

---

55 Letter of J. Judah Leib Gordon to Zev Kaplan, 3 June 1862, in Yitzchak Yaacov Weissberg (ed.), *Igrot Yehudah Leib Gordon* (Warsaw, 1894), 76–77. Gordon turned the position down, not because it was in Warsaw, but because the salary Slonimski offered him was insufficient.

56 Horowitz, *Empire Jews*, 117.

57 See the minutes of the first meeting, 8 October 1863, in *Toldot hevrat marbei haskalah*, vol. I, 4.

58 Minutes of 28 April 1865, ibid., vol. I, 20; and letter from the Society to Slonimski, March 1865, ibid, vol. II, 15. Further information about Slonimski's negotiations with the Society for the Promotion of Enlightenment can be found ibid, vol. I, 4–22 and vol. II, 6–40.

Nevertheless, Slonimski continued his engagement with the Society. As there was no consensus about its priorities or mission, Slonimski, like others in the Society, was able to remain a member despite his differences with other members.[59] Moreover, the fact that OPE's activities fell into several categories rather than pursuing a single ideological direction helped Slonimski forge his own path.[60] He believed that the mission he had taken upon himself to expose Eastern European Jews to modernity by means of scientific knowledge, whether through periodicals or Hebrew books, could be part of OPE's agenda. Indeed, other members of the OPE board, including Rosenthal, who served as the Society's secretary, respected Slonimski's contribution to this mission, to which he had now devoted himself over the span of 30 years.[61] Although the organization had not helped him publish a scientific Hebrew newspaper, Slonimski maintained his connection with the OPE after he returned to Warsaw and for many years hence.

When Slonimski had begun writing in the 1830s, the maskilim in Russia were still considered a minority among Russian Jewry. They were not yet regarded as a coherent intellectual or social group, and were limited in their ability to propagate their views.[62] Only during the period between the 1830s and the beginning of the 1860s did the maskilim in Russia develop into a well-coordinated movement.[63] This was what allowed Slonimski to integrate into the new Russian Haskalah sphere in Zhitomir. There, as in Warsaw, Slonimski continued to be interested solely in scientific issues. Nevertheless, the years spent in Warsaw, between 1838 and 1862, when he consolidated his position as a central figure in the emergent scientific writing, helped him consolidate his position in the Haskalah and bridge two generations of maskilim in Tsarist Russia.

Slonimski and Warsaw

Before he left Warsaw for Zhitomir in 1862, Slonimski's engagement in local Jewish life had been decidedly marginal. Apart from his role in the 1857 attempt by a group of Jewish intellectuals to obtain a license for a periodical that would be published simultaneously in Polish and in Hebrew, there were

---

59   Horowitz, *Jewish Philanthropy*, 37.
60   Ibid.
61   Letter from Slonimski to Rosenthal, in *Toldot hevrat marbei haskalah*, vol. II, 192.
62   Stanislawski, *Tsar Nicholas I*, 57.
63   Ibid., 108.

no indications of his involvement in Jewish public life in Warsaw.[64] The fact that *Ha-tzefira* stopped appearing a short time before the outbreak of the conflict in 1863, a time when both the Polish and Jewish streets in Warsaw were already stormy, might signal Slonimski's involvement in the revolutionary events.[65] But Slonimski had no interest in political affairs and was always very cautious in managing his relations with the Russian authorities in Warsaw, who forbade the publication of political articles or commentaries on the events of 1862–3.[66] Slonimski's appointments as inspector of the governmental rabbinical seminary and censor of Hebrew books in Zhitomir confirm the sense that *Ha-tzefira* did not cease publication as a result of the events preceding the January Uprising of 1863 or Slonimski's involvement with local revolutionary events.[67]

In September 1875, after a short period in which *Ha-tzefira* was published in Berlin (Slonimski could not at that point obtain a license to publish his newspaper in Warsaw), he announced the return of *Ha-tzefira* to Warsaw, which was better suited to the publication of his newspaper.[68] Although *Ha-tzefira* readers came from a variety of locales, Slonimski believed that his newspaper should be part of the Polish Jewish public arena. Following the return of the newspaper to Warsaw, it shifted its focus onto daily life in Warsaw, its local Jewish community, leaders, wealthy intellectuals and religious leaders.[69] *Ha-tzefira* covered important events like the opening of the Great Synagogue on

---

64   The attempt was denied by the Russian authorities. On this attempt, see Marian Fuks, *Prasa żydowska w Warszawie, 1823–1939* (Warszawa, 1979), 99–100.

65   Fuks argues that although *Ha-tzefira* did not cover the preparations for the uprising of January 1863, and did not mirror the stormy atmosphere of Warsaw during the period preceding the uprising, there was a link between the two events. See ibid., 105–6.

66   In one of his early essays, dedicated to the history of the Hebrew press, Samuel Leib Citron argues that the Russian authorities' censorship policy in Warsaw did not allow the publication of political articles or commentary on the events of 1862–3. This policy, argues Citron, fit in with Slonimski's approach and lack of interest in anything not related to science and technology. See Samuel Leib Citron, "Reshimot al toldot ha-itonut ha-ivrit," *Ha-olam* (14 December 1928).

67   After all, *Jutrzenka*, another Jewish periodical published in Warsaw at the time, was closed on October 1863 and its editor, Daniel Neufeld (1814–1874), was exiled to Siberia.

68   *Ha-tzefira* (1 September 1875).

69   Examples of items published in *Ha-tzefira* in the late 1870s include the opening of a new trade school financed by the convert Leopold Kronenberg (16/28 September 1875); the final exam held at the orphanage directed by Hilary Nussbaum (30 September/12 October 1875); Mathias Bersohn's Judaica collection (10/22 December 1875); elections to the board of the Warsaw community administration (28 September/10 October 1877); and reforms in Talmud Torah schools in Warsaw (20 September/4 October 1878).

Tłomackie Street with great pride, and displayed illustrations.[70] However, Slonimski did not personally write about Warsaw. Other members of *Ha-tzefira*'s editorial board, such as Hayim Yisrael Zagordski, covered the city and reported on events and developments there, while the editorial board encouraged correspondents from cities and communities in other Polish regions to send in reports and even critiques.[71]

Links between the newspaper and the city intensified only after 1880.[72] Upon his return to Warsaw in 1874, Slonimski's involvement in the local public Jewish arena did not change dramatically. From the way in which connections between *Ha-tzefira* and Warsaw were strengthened, however, we can assume that Slonimski was no longer on the margins of local society. This can be deduced from Slonimski's involvement with the establishment of the Jewish Public Library near the Great Synagogue (*Wielka Synagoga*) on Tłomackie Street. Slonimski was engaged in this project along with the bibliophile and writer Eigacy Bernstein and the Synagogue's rabbi and preacher, Dr. Izaak Cylkow. It was an interesting coalition. Cylkow was primarily interested in religious philosophy, Bernstein in Jewish ethnography, and Slonimski in popular science in the Hebrew language. Thanks to the efforts of these three, the library became a unique institution.[73] For many young people, it served as a gateway to the modern world. The involvement of Slonimski in its establishment, in addition to his position as editor of *Ha-tzefira*, expanded the horizons of Warsaw Jews and connected them to other locales. These institutions provided opportunities for Jews to transcend the narrow, local Jewish arena.

Slonimski's journalistic activities transcended Warsaw and the local Jewish community. Through his scientific writing, Slonimski was able to approach Jews who lived relatively far away. At the same time, his modest involvement in the local public arena does not mean that the city and its intellectual environment did not influence him. Warsaw provided a supportive and nurturing base for his mission, disseminating the sciences in Jewish society. Members of Jewish intellectual circles there valued Slonimski not only for his local involvement but for the recognition and reputation he had gained beyond Warsaw.[74]

---

70 See *Ha-tzefira* (4/10 October 1878) and (18 February 1879).
71 *Ha-tzefira* (5/17 May 1876), (16/28 July 1876).
72 After Sokolow joined the editorial board of *Ha-tzefira* at the beginning of the 1880s, the newspaper's slant changed and its involvement in the city's life and in Polish Jewry's public life increased.
73 Nahum Sokolow, "Ha-tzofeh le-veit yisra'el," *Ha-tzefira* (1/13 June, 1890).
74 Hilary Nussbaum, "C.Z. Slonimski," *Izraelita* (13/25 April 1884).

At the same time, Slonimski's renown created tension between his involvement in local Haskalah circles in Warsaw and his project to modernize Jewish society in territories further eastward. As mentioned earlier, Slonimski's decision to settle in Warsaw was based on his acceptance by the maskilim and integrationists of Warsaw in the 1830s. Aside from Abraham Stern, there were integrationists such as Jakub Tugendhold, Abraham Buchner, Abraham Paprocki and Antoni Eisenbaum, whose activities were linked to various government institutions.[75] According to Shatzky, not all of them had good relations with Slonimski. Yet, despite some personal disagreements, Slonimski's agenda did not clash with their program.[76] The mission that Slonimski had taken upon himself was in line with all those who had undertaken the mission of disseminating universal values within Jewish society. All were in agreement that Jews should be loyal to the state and the monarch, and that there was a need to integrate non-traditional subjects into Jewish education.[77]

Their differences were primarily over the issue of language. While Slonimski agreed with the Haskalah imperative that Jews needed to know other languages, in particular the state language, his own Haskalah writing, for practical rather than ideological reasons, was in Hebrew. This set him apart from members of the younger progressive circles, who also wrote in Polish. We know that Slonimski interacted socially with some. Mathias Rosen provided him with financial assistance when he needed it.[78] Slonimski's willingness to join Jakub Rotwand, Hilary Nussbaum and Jakub Eisenberg's group, as well as his attempt to obtain a license in 1857 for a periodical that would be published simultaneously in Polish and in Hebrew, also suggest that Slonimski had good personal and professional connections with some. But he did not fit the profile of the collective identity of the maskilim and progressive Jews of Warsaw. His name did not appear on the list of people involved in local cultural or philanthropic activities.[79] Various studies that examine the development of progressive synagogues in Warsaw, such as the one on Tłomackie Street, or on Daniłowiczowska Street, do not mention Sloniniski's involvement. It seems that local progressive

---

75 More on the involvement of these maskilim in such institutions can be found in Wodziński, *Haskalah and Hasidism*, 40–45.
76 Jacob Shatzky, *Geshikhte fun yidn in varshe*, vol. II, 126.
77 For more about the ideology of Polish maskilim, see Wodziński, *Haskalah and Hasidism*, 48–51.
78 Nussbaum, "Slonimski."
79 In Jacob Shatzky, *Geshikhte fun yidn in varshe*, vol. II, 123–32, in the sections on Jewish cultural activity; on the involvement of Warsaw Jewry in Polish cultural life, ibid., 161–169; and on Jewish literary activity, 284–87. Slonimski is not mentioned at all.

religious developments did not attract him. As he was only interested in scientific writing, his relationship with the more diverse literary republic of writers remained limited.[80] Yet because his Haskalah work was aimed not only at Warsaw, but also at a relatively broad Jewish public, in addition to the fact that Warsaw was an important Hebrew literary center that was relatively more open to the publication of non-religious Hebrew books, all made Warsaw an auspicious place for him.

In *Ha-tzefira*, Slonimski did engage some topics unrelated to the sciences. In one of the first issues, he declared that Jews should be good citizens and integrate into the societies in which they lived, particularly on Polish territory.[81] From 1875 to the end of the 1880s, Slonimski participated in public discussions on modern Jewish education. Following arguments that he had previously used in introductions to his books, in 1870 he stressed that there was no contradiction between acquiring a modern education and sustaining traditional Jewish beliefs.[82] As former inspector of the governmental rabbinical seminary, he was of the opinion that the training of rabbis should include non-traditional topics.[83]

Several years later, Slonimski spoke out against rabbis who served in Polish communities, differentiating between them and rabbis from the Lithuanian territory, for whom he had much greater appreciation. He hoped that the non-Jewish authorities would soon decide on radical reforms that would include changes in the way rabbis in the Polish areas were selected.[84] These remarks were similar to criticism voiced by various maskilim in the Russian and Polish territories.

---

80   We know that while in Zhitomir, Slonimski established contact with Abramovitsh (Mendele Mokher Sforim). Slonimski and Abramovitsh had a mutual interest in developing scientific writing in Hebrew. Slonimski had a high regard for Abramovitsh's book, because he appreciated the fact that Abramovitsh had not used only one source for his book but had integrated several books. After Abramovitsh began to pursue other literary directions, the connection between them was lost, as Slonimski had little interest in literature. See Letter from Slonimski to Abramovitsh, June 1864, in *Toldot hevrat marbei haskalah*, vol. 11, 41. He had some professional connections with Yosef Shmuel Fuenn (1818–1891), the editor of *Ha-karmel*, and with Salomon Buber (1827–1906).
81   Slonimski, "Divrei shalom ve-emet," see above, fn. 54.
82   Idem, "Al batei sefer ve-hinuch," see above, fn. 49.
83   Idem, "Al ma'amad ha-rabanim," *Ha-tzefira* (19 April 1877); idem, "Al batei sefer," see above, fn. 49; idem, "Al davar aseifat ha-rabanim," *Ha-tzefira* (11 March 1897); idem, "Ha-tikva ve-ha-hayim," see above, fn. 35.
84   Slonimski, *Malshinai beseter*, see above, fn. 11.

Conclusion

Slonimski's impact beyond the boundaries of Warsaw was confirmed when the Hebrew literary republic celebrated the fiftieth anniversary of his literary work:

> Fifty years have elapsed. The Haskalah is more widespread. Today, our sons are much more educated. But who encouraged them? We know that Slonimski's books woke the young people up and led them to their goal. His books were eyes to hundreds of students who listened to his voice and Torah from a distance.[85]

Thus, if the spectrum of topics about which Slonimski wrote was somewhat limited, the range of his influence was wide. Already during his lifetime, various intellectuals were aware of the impact his writing had on young Jews throughout Eastern Europe.

As this chapter has argued, although Slonimski was considered part of the local Warsaw Haskalah and other progressive circles, particularly during the last decades of the nineteenth century, he was also recognized as an advocate for modernity outside Warsaw.

His dual role found further expression in the way local and non-local Jews marked his 70th birthday in March 1880. The OPE decided that, in honor of Slonimski's birthday, it would give a scholarship in his name to a Jewish student of mathematics or engineering at the University of St. Petersburg.[86] Numerous telegrams and greeting cards arrived at Slonimski's home in Warsaw, from colleagues, members of the Haskalah republic from different areas, as well as from others who introduced themselves as his students.[87] Some had been his students in Zhitomir.[88] Others regarded Slonimski as their teacher through his writings. Of all the greetings he received on his birthday, those that pleased him most were from people who declared that their path to the university began with his books.[89] In a letter of gratitude, Slonimski drew attention to his unique contribution: he had written books and articles that had brought

---

85 "Hayim Zelig Slonimski," *Ha-asif* 2 (1885).
86 *Ha-tzefira* (16 March 1880).
87 "Divrei toda ve-halel," ibid. Among them were Tzvi Rabinowicz, who over the years contributed to scientific writing in Hebrew, Alexander Tzederbaum, his competitor, and writers such as Judah Leib Gordon.
88 Slonimski to Herman Sapira, 7 Kislev 1880, letter no. 12, Rabinovitz (ed.), *Igrot* (1966).
89 Slonimski, *Ha-tzefira* (9 March 1880).

about change, supplying *bet midrash* students with knowledge and tools for their future university studies.

At the same time, many of those who read Slonimski's books and articles were not archetypal auto-didactic maskilim, but belonged to the generation of young, educated Jews who were already styling themselves as an intelligentsia. Slonimski was thus a major inspiration for the first generation of Jewish intelligentsia. On the map of Jewish modernization in Eastern Europe, we can place Slonimski between the pre-intelligentsia generation and the generation of the first Jewish intelligentsia. He himself did not belong to the generation that came of age in Warsaw between 1840 and 1860, but his activism contributed much to its development, both in Warsaw and throughout the Russian Empire, by connecting the Jewish street with the world beyond.

CHAPTER 4

The Garment of Torah: Clothing Decrees and the Warsaw Career of the First Gerer *Rebbe*

Glenn Dynner

In the late 1850s, while researching the Hasidic movement for his planned history of the Jews, the Polish writer M.P. Sawicki decided to pay a visit to Rabbi Isaac Meir Alter, the future "Gerer *rebbe*," who at the time resided in central Warsaw. Sawicki had heard a good deal about Hasidim, followers of "charlatan, miracle-working, neo-prophets." In the Kingdom of Poland, he informed his readers, their capital was the town of Kotzk, home to Alter's master, Rabbi Menahem Mendel. Tens of thousands of Jews were said to continually stream towards Kotzk bearing gifts for Rabbi Menahem Mendel, who spent most of his time reading the Zohar and smoking his pipe in an attempt to scare off demons. Sawicki heard that on every Sabbath eve the wealthiest Jews would sit around the rabbi's table, receive his blessing, and then dive towards his plate to grab the fish and bread he had just blessed.[1]

But Sawicki wanted to learn about the Hasidim first-hand, and without having to travel as far as Kotzk. So he decided to pay a visit to Alter, the famous disciple and likely successor, in Warsaw. Sawicki arrived at Alter's residence at 1015 Krochmalna Street and took a seat in the dirty, litter-filled reception room, where an unkempt woman was cooking near a group of young men ("philosophers") with extremely long side-locks, until at long last he was conducted towards the Rabbi. Along the way, a group of fifteen or so traditionally-clad Jews stood around making absurd grimaces [probably praying]; in the next room bound and unbound pages written apparently in Hebrew were strewn across a long table. Suddenly there stood before him "an Israelite of advanced years with a gray beard, a tall frame, quick and penetrating eyes, a handsome face, and a solemn, meditative bearing" smoking a long pipe, surrounded by several young attendants. It was none other than the famous Rabbi Isaac Meir

---

[1] M.P. Sawicki, *Żydzi: ich dzieje ze względu na stan obecny Polski mieszkańców wyznania Mojżeszowego* (Warsaw: Nakładem Księgarni J. Błaszkowskiego, 1865), 336. Many thanks to Levi Mendelow, Shaul Stampfer, and Gershon Bacon for their help at various stages of preparation of this chapter, as well as the National Endowment for Humanities Senior Scholar fellowship at the Center for Jewish History for vital support.

Alter himself, "revered by one hundred thousand Hasidim" though not yet crowned as *rebbe*.²

When asked what he desired Sawicki replied, "until now no one who has written on the Hasidic sect has spared it curses and censure whereas I, a writer about Jews and Hasidism who wishes to carefully examine the topic and do it justice, beseech Pan Rabbi to send me a disciple who might accurately explain everything." Upon receiving Alter's assent (in German), Sawicki was led out. On his way, he inquired about the unbound books on the table and was told that Alter was the sole publisher of Hasidic books in Warsaw which, Sawicki was surprised to learn, was his main source of income. Several days later, Sawicki was visited by three of Alter's followers. Nothing the Hasidic emissaries said during the two hour interview seemed at all fanatical to Sawicki; in fact, he found them to be profound thinkers and ethicists.³

This episode provides a window onto Alter's leadership style, which is not at all what we might expect from the founder of a Hasidic dynasty that has come to be associated with ultraorthodox insularity in our own day. Rather than ejecting the curious outsider, Alter seized the opportunity to explain Hasidism to a Polish readership by means of his most worldly and articulate followers. This accommodationist style was to characterize Gerer Hasidism down to the Holocaust, manifested *inter alia* in its modern modes of political organization and communication, its sponsorship of the political party Agudat Yisrael and the Beis Yaakov school system for girls, and its publication of newspapers like *Dos yidishe vort, Der yid*, and *Dos yidishe togblat*.⁴

But accommodation to modernity had its limits; and some of Alter's tactics had clearly become a source of embarrassment to Gerer Hasidim by the interwar period. While Gerer court historians could craft chronological accounts of their movement and its leaders so rich in detail as to resemble products of modern historiography, the finest example being Abraham Issachar Benjamin Alter's *Meir eyene ha-golah* (Warsaw, 1932), their yearning for a more heroically militant past tended to overwhelm their dedication to the historian's craft when it came to their dynasty's progenitor. In their hands, R. Isaac Meir Alter was transfigured into a passionate, defiant personality ready to endure

---

2   Ibid., 337–8.
3   Ibid., 338–9.
4   See Gershon Bacon, *The Politics of Tradition: Agudat Yisrael in Poland, 1916–1939* (Jerusalem: Magnes, 1996). For recollections of the formation of these modern institutions, see Yaakov Rosenheim, *Zikhronot* (Bnei Brak: Netzah, 1979).

imprisonment and embrace martyrdom rather than succumb to government attempts to impose modernity upon his sacred community.[5]

This tendency towards hagiographical distortion is most glaring in Gerer reconstructions of Alter's career in the 1840s and 1850s, a period best known for the attempted governmental reforms of traditional Jewish dress known as the "clothing decrees." Although Alter certainly played a key role in mitigating the clothing decrees, contemporaneous documentary sources suggest a personality much more like that encountered by Sawicki. The current chapter accordingly seeks to recast Isaac Meir Alter's Warsaw career—as well as those of his traditionalist colleagues—as characterized more by selective accommodation and restrained protest than by militancy.

Hasidism in the Capital City

One might expect Warsaw Jewry to have followed a course similar to that of the Jewish communities in Russian cities like Odessa and St. Petersburg, where a direct line may be drawn between urbanization, wealth, and acculturation.[6] But Polish cities suggest a strikingly different model: new urban Jewish centers with entrenched religious and secular-oriented subcultures in which economic prosperity did not overwhelmingly favor one cultural group over another.[7] Warsaw's thriving communities of Hasidim, Mitnaggdim, integrationists, and, eventually, representatives of the new Jewish politics (Zionists, Socialists, and Diaspora Nationalists) coexisted in close proximity. Hasidim and non-Hasidim shared local political responsibilities almost every year, and sometimes cooperated in resisting or mitigating governmental decrees. In Polish cities, the watchword was accommodation.

This striking growth of Polish Hasidism in the capital was due in great part to the patronage of Polish Hasidic leaders (*tzaddikim*), including Alter, by

---

5 A great deal of detail, however distorted, is also to be found in Yoets Kim Kadish, *Si'ah sarfe kodesh* (5 vols.; Piotrków Trybunalski, 1923).

6 On Odessa Jewry see Steven Zipperstein, *The Jews of Odessa: a cultural history, 1794–1881* (Stanford, CA: Stanford University Press, 1985); on St. Petersburg Jewry see Benjamin Nathans, *Beyond the Pale: the Jewish encounter with late imperial Russia* (Berkeley: University of California Press, 2002); on Kiev see Natan Meir, *Kiev—Jewish Metropolis: A History, 1859–1914* (Bloomington, IN: Indiana University Press, 2010).

7 On the diversity of Jewish culture in Łódź, including a prominent Hasidic subculture and prominent Hasidic entrepreneurs, see Jacek Walicki, *Synagogi i domy modlitwy w Łodzi* (Łódź: Druk, 2000).

several of the most prominent members of the Warsaw Jewish mercantile elite. Defying the presumptive correlation between wealth and assimilation, entrepreneurs like Berek and Temerel Sonnenberg-Bergson ensured Hasidism's economic viability and successfully lobbied government officials to uphold the kingdom's constitutional guarantees of religious tolerance, all the while retaining their traditional Jewish attire instead of adopting the Polish bourgeoisie's sartorial markers.[8] In 1827, just three years after their victorious lobbying effort, Alter requested official sanction for his Warsaw prayer houses (*shtiblekh*) on 1027 and 1057 Grzybowska Street and 959 Targowa Street, each becoming a hub within an emerging network of Hasidic prayer houses in the capital.[9]

It is difficult to quantify Warsaw's Hasidic presence during the second half of the nineteenth century.[10] Jacob Shatzky's claim that two-thirds of the city's 300 prayer houses were Hasidic by 1880, a figure invoked uncritically in several contemporary studies, is quite dubious.[11] Eleonora Bergman's data yield a total of only 167 Warsaw prayer houses in 1869, a number that dwindled to 117

---

8 See Glenn Dynner, *Men of Silk: The Hasidic Conquest of Polish Jewish Society* (New York: Oxford University Press, 2006), esp. chapters 1 and 3; and François Guesnet, "Chasydzki klal-tuer wobec metropolii i nowoczesności: Joel Wegmeister z Warszawy, 1837–1919," in *Żydzi Warszawy: Materiały konferencji w 100. rocznicę urodzin Emanuela Ringelbluma* (ed. Eleonora Bergman and Olga Zienkiewicz; Warsaw: ŻIH 2000), 41–57. On Hasidic urbanicity, see Dynner, "Hasidism and Habitat," in idem., *Holy Dissent: Jewish and Christian Mystics in Eastern Europe* (Detroit, MI: Wayne State University Press, 2011), 104–30. On the cultural dimension of the bourgeoisie, see Pierre Bourdieu, *Distinction: A Social Critique of the Judgment of Taste* (Cambridge, MA: Harvard University Press, 1984), esp. chapters 3 and 7.

9 Printed in Ignacy Schiper, *Żydzi Królestwa Polskiego w dobie powstania listopadowego* (Warsaw, 1932), 28.

10 For a good summary of the scholarly debate on the quantitative spread of Polish Hasidism in the first half of the nineteenth century, see Antony Polonsky, *Jews in Poland and Russia*, II: 296–7. For more, see Dynner, "How Many Hasidim Were There Really in Congress Poland? A Response to Marcin Wodziński," *Gal-Ed: On the History & Culture of Polish Jewry* 20 (2005): 91–104. For an analysis that favors lower estimates, see Marcin Wodziński, "How Many *Hasidim* were there in Congress Poland? On the Demographics of the Hasidic Movement in Poland during the First Half of the Nineteenth Century,' *Gal-Ed* 19 (2004): 13–49. For a rejoinder see my review essay, "On the Borders of Haskalah: *Hasidism and Haskalah in the Kingdom of Poland* (London: Littman, 2005), by Marcin Wodziński; and *Ba'alot ha-shahar*, by Mordehai Zalkin (Jerusalem: Magnes, 2000)", *Kwartalnik Historii Żydów* 222.2 [in Polish]; English translation available at https://www.academia.edu/6352771/_Transl.Haskalah_Review_Wodzinski_Zalkin.

11 Shatzky, in *Geshikhte fun yidn in varshe*, III: 364 cites Milkh, who makes no such claim. On the repeated use of Shatzky's flawed data by contemporary historians, see Dynner, "Hasidism and Habitat," 109, no. 28.

by 1910.[12] At the same time, memoirs provide an impression of thriving Hasidic enclaves that became only more so over the course of the nineteenth century.[13]

Warsaw's hospitality to tradition-oriented subcultures was to a great extent an unintended consequence of the imposition of residential restrictions in 1809 and, in an expanded form, in 1821, resulting in a Jewish Quarter (*rewir*) in the northwestern portion of the city.[14] The restrictions contained an exemption feature for wealthy and acculturated Jews that was to prove deeply consequential: Warsaw Jews who possessed 60,000 złotys, rid themselves of their beards, *peyos* (sidelocks), and traditional Jewish attire, enrolled their children in public schools, and fit a desired professional profile were eligible for permission to live and work on restricted streets. This exemption feature, intended to encourage integration, seems to rather have had the effect of sifting the most prominent acculturated Jews out of the Jewish Quarter while leaving behind a more traditional, heavily Hasidic mass of Jews willing to renounce the privilege of residing on lucrative restricted streets. By the 1840s, the period of the clothing decrees, the great majority of Warsaw Jewry, including its deliberately non-bourgeois upper middle class, was under the sway of a consciously "traditionalist" leadership.[15]

---

12 Eleonora Bergman, *"Nie masz bóżniczy powszechnej": synagogi i domy modlitwy w Warszawie od końca XVII do początku XXI wieku* (Warsaw: DiG, 2007), 136–57 and 91.

13 Ya'akov Milkh described Franciscan Street in the 1880s as a setting where "every Hasidic *shtibl* in Warsaw" coexisted, including Kotzk, Ger, Grodzisk, Biala, Warka, Radzymin, Neushtadt, and "even Trisk". A passer-by could hear any Hasidic melody or see any Hasidic dance. Ya'akov Milkh, *Oytobiagrafishe skitzen* (New York, 1946), 81–2. On Franciscan Street twenty years earlier, see Yehezkel Kotik, *Meine zikhroynes* (Warsaw, 1913), 71–3.

14 On Jewish quarters, see *Yankel's Tavern*, and Archiwum Główne Akt Dawnych (AGAD), Komisya Rządowa Spraw Wewnętrznych (KRSW) 188, fol. 96–7. Over the next decade, Jewish Quarters were established or reinstated (based on earlier privileges) in 31 towns and cities. The towns of Maków and Wschowa do not seem to have been able to reinstate their Jewish Quarters after 1821.

15 On residential restrictions in the Duchy of Warsaw and the Kingdom of Poland, see Dynner, *Yankel's Tavern: Jews, Liquor and Life in the Kingdom of Poland* (New York: Oxford University Press, 2013), ch. 3; idem., "Hasidism and Habitat;" and idem., "Jewish Quarters: The Economics of Residential Segregation in the Kingdom of Poland," in Rebecca Kobrin and Adam Teller, eds., *Purchasing Power* (Forthcoming, University of Pennsylvania Press). On "traditionalism," see Jacob Katz, "Orthodoxy in Perspective," *Studies in Contemporary Jewry* 2 (1986): 4.

The Clothing Decrees

The clothing decrees were part of a series of social engineering initiatives introduced by the tsar's viceroy, Prince Ivan Paskevich, in the 1840s when, a decade after the suppression of a major Polish uprising against the tsar (1830–1), political conditions in the kingdom now felt stable enough to begin experimenting again with government-imposed integration. The decade saw momentous Jewish reform initiatives—military conscription (1843), agricultural inducements (1843), education reform (1844), and a ban on rural Jewish tavern-keeping (1844), in addition to the clothing decrees. Alter emerged as a major leader of Polish Jewry during this critical time alongside prominent traditionalists like Chief Rabbi of Warsaw Hayyim Dawidzohn, Chief Rabbi of Praga Szaia Muszkat, the entrepreneur Solomon Markus Posner, as well as the declining Hasidic leader R. Isaac Kalish of Warka (who passed away in the midst of the clothing decrees affair, in 1848).[16] These leaders proved able to galvanize mass Jewish discontent and neutralize initiatives they felt threatened the distinctive Jewish way of life, notwithstanding the efforts of maskilim and other Jewish integrationists.[17]

What was at stake in the clothing decree episode? Clothing might seem superficial, or at least something that conceals as much as it reveals. But recent works on semiotics—the symbolic meaning of language, gestures, and so on—reveal clothing as a vital strand within the "webs of significance" we all weave.[18] Historians of colonial India have been particularly keyed-in to the symbolic power of clothing, thanks to Mahatma Gandhi's very public adoption of the home-spun *khadi* and loincloth. These deliberate and widely advertised moves signaled Gandhi's rejection of western forms, his solidarity with the peasantry, and his refusal to consent to the British regime's co-opting of educated Indian elites, many of whom had become, in his view, collaborators.[19]

16　On the decrees of the 1840s, see *Yankel's Tavern*, chapters 2 and 6. For a detailed account of R. Isaac of Warka's public role that argues for his predominant influence, see Marcin Wodziński, *Hasidism and Politics: The Kingdom of Poland, 1815–1864* (Oxford and Portland, OR: Littman Library of Jewish Civilization, 2013), 178–98.

17　The flip-side of this story, failure of integration, constitutes the main thread of Antony Polonsky's three-volume synthesis, *The Jews in Poland and Russia* (Oxford and Portland, OR: Littman Library of Jewish Civilization, 2010–12).

18　Clifford Geertz, "Thick Description: Towards an Interpretive Theory of Culture," in idem, *The Interpretation of Cultures: Selected Essays* (New York: Basic Books), 3–30.

19　Robert J.C. Young, *Post-colonialism: An Historical Introduction* (New York: Oxford University Press, 2006), 328.

Gandhi was not the first to embrace this mode of subaltern defiance. Many ordinary Indians regarded the adoption of European clothing as a violation of caste and a cause of ritual impurity, and sometimes socially ostracized native Indians who adopted it. But Gandhi's reversion to traditional Indian garb after having earned a law degree in England wearing quite proper British costume particularly enraged the British; all the more so as he began promoting his subversive gesture among his brethren. The British regime responded by firing government employees who wore traditional attire and fining or physically beating others who did so. According to Gandhi, these actions only exposed British moral and cultural inferiority: the British were attempting to repress those who respected themselves and their nation and who did not wish to conceal their distinctive identity. Gandhi later went so far as to deem the *khadi* "sacred cloth."[20]

Similarly, though in a different context, Eastern Europe's unemancipated Jews usually wore "a distinguishing dress," in the words of one foreign visitor to Warsaw in 1800, imbued it with religious and moral significance, and tended to frown upon any blatant mimicry of the dominant culture's fashions.[21] The eighteenth-century moralist Tzvi Hirsch Kaidanover complained, for instance, that certain "licentious" Jewish women were known to "walk about in clothing like that worn by gentile women" so that one could no longer "tell a Jewish woman from a gentile woman;" and that certain "licentious" Jewish men were prone to not only "walk about in clothes made according to gentile styles, but cause further evil by shaving their beards."[22] Representatives

---

20   Emma Tarlo, *Clothing Matters: Dress and Identity in India* (Chicago: University of Chicago Press, 1996), 44, 84, 87.
21   For a description of Warsaw Jewry, see Nathaniel William Wraxall, *Memoirs of the courts of Berlin, Dresden, Warsaw, and Vienna, in the years 1777, 1778, and 1779*, 2 vols. (London, 1800), II: 8–9. Similarly, Robert Johnston remarked that the Jews of Dubrovna (Vitebsk District, present-day Belarus) "are all dressed alike, in long tunics of black silk, with a broad silken sash tied round the waist, on the head they wear a small velvet cap and over it a huge one of fur." See Robert Johnston, *Travels Through Part of the Russian Empire and the Country of Poland: Along the Southern Shores of the Baltic* (London, 1815), 376. This description suggests a town inhabited predominately by Hasidim. Compare Gershon Hundert, "From the Perspective of Progress: Travelers and Foreigners on Jews in Poland and Lithuania in the Eighteenth and Early Nineteenth Centuries," in David Assaf and Ada Rapoport-Albert (eds.), *Let the Old Make Way for the New: Studies in the Social and Cultural History of Eastern European Jewry Presented to Immanuel Etkes*, 2 vols. (Jerusalem: Zalman Shazar, 2009), II: 115–36; esp. 121. Hundert likely means to refer to the 1845 legislation there.
22   Tzevi Hirsch Kaidanover, *Kav ha-yashar* (Frankfurt/Main, 1705), ch. 82. On the importance of beards for European and Levantine Jews, see Elliot Horowitz, "The Early Eighteenth

of institutions of Jewish self-government within Poland-Lithuania reiterated the prohibition against "mimicking gentiles" in their dress and re-emphasized the importance of visible differentiation.[23] By the mid-nineteenth century, increasing cases of sartorial transgression cropped up in rabbinical responsa, and rabbis worried over the possible ritual ramifications.[24] The memoirist Ezekiel Kotik was nearly disowned by his parents when they discovered that he wore his trousers over his boots in the "German style," which Kotik dismissed as an "example of fanaticism." But the memoirist Pauline Wengeroff, who had adopted Russian fashions herself, interpreted such strong reactions more empathically: "after all, the entire people would have to atone for the sin of the individual."[25]

Jews who voluntarily adopted sartorial changes did so for several reasons: they had internalized the dominant culture's discomfort with traditional Jewish styles, they hoped to obtain exemptions from residential and other restrictions, or they simply desired to integrate socially into the Polish bourgeoisie. Russian maskilim like Wolf Tugendhold and Samuel Joseph Fuenn were convinced that "the first source of estrangement and hostility between the Jews and the Christians of our land is the difference in dress," and waged a veritable campaign to have earlier clothing bans (1804 and 1835) enforced so as to "remove this barrier" to integration. In 1843, a vocal coterie of such Russian maskilim went so far as to present a petition to the tsar that pronounced traditional Jewish attire "the first obstacle to the enlightenment of the Jewish people" and

---

Century Confronts the Beard: Kabbalah and Jewish Self-Fashioning," *Jewish History* 8.1–2 (1994): 95–115. On mimicry of dominant elites by subalterns, see Homi Bhabha, *The Location of Culture* (New York: Routledge, 1994), ch. 4.

23 These prohibitions were often interwoven with sumptuary legislation. See Shmuel Arthur Cygielman, *Jewish Autonomy in Poland and Lithuania until 1648 (5408)* (Jerusalem, 1997), 95–6. On such laws in early modern Poznań, see Anna Michałowska-Mycielska, *The Jewish Community: Authority and Social Control in Poznań and Swarzędz, 1650–1793* (Wrocław: Wydawnictwo Uniwersytetu Wrocławskiego, 2008), 175–6 and 181.

24 In 1857, for example, a Jewish community had purchased yeast for their *hallot* (Sabbath loaves) in Stanisławów from an "evil" Jew who was not only lax in dietary matters but "wears gentile clothing and whose wife goes about with her hair uncovered." Should one believe his claim that, when he had left his tavern in gentile hands and traveled to Tysmienice over Passover, he had sold off his leavened products in the ritually prescribed manner, the rabbis wondered? See Yosef Shaul ben Aryeh Leibush Nathanson, *Sho'el u-meshiv: mahadora tanina* (Lemberg, 1890), part IV, no. 10. See also cases discussed below by R. Shlomo Kluger and R. Menachem Mendel Schneersohn, the "Tzemakh Tzeddek."

25 Ezekiel Kotik, *Mayn zikhroynes* (Remembrances), tr. by Lucas Bruyn, chapter 10, available at http://www.onforeignsoil.com/kotik.htm (last consulted on May 23, 2014); Pauline Wengeroff, *Rememberings: The World of a Russian Jewish Woman* (tr. Henny Wenkart; ed. Bernard Cooperman; Potomac, MD: University Press of Maryland, 2000), 67.

requested its abolition. Wearing distinctive garb was not, in any case, a Jewish religious requirement, they argued, and was thus quite dispensable.²⁶

This was to elide—intentionally or not—the function of custom and precedent in Jewish ritual law (*halakha*). Sartorial differentiation and outward markers of religiosity had long obtained the force of law in Ashkenazic Jewish society, as had prohibitions against outwardly resembling non-Jewish elites.²⁷ Debates were mainly confined to the question of where exactly to position the adoption of gentile fashions on the spectrum of transgression—did it inhabit the category of outright idolatry (*hukotehem*), softer idolatry ("Amorite ways"), or the slightly less serious licentiousness (*pritzut*)? Joseph Karo's *Shulkhan Aruh*, the preeminent sixteenth-century legal code, declared—based on Moses Maimonides' medieval code *Mishneh Torah*—that "one must not wear clothing that is unique to [gentiles]," adding that nor should one "grow a forelock on his head like the forelocks on *their* heads nor shave the sides and leave hair in the middle, nor shave the hair bare from ear to ear leaving a ponytail."²⁸ The Polish authority R. Moses Issleres ("Remu," 1520–72), who repurposed Karo's code for Ashkenazic use, emphasized that a Jew must deliberately "differentiate from them in dress and other practices" while avoiding any fashion "adopted by them as a result of their licentiousness." In Poland-Lithuania, he elaborated, this applied to the penchant among nobles for brazenly wearing red—even if such a fashion did not contain a trace of their ancestors' "Amorite ways."²⁹

---

26 Eli Lederhendler, *The Road to Modern Politics: Political Tradition and Political Reconstruction in the Jewish Community of Tsarist Russia* (New York: Oxford University Press, 1989), 97–8; Eugene Avrutin, "Jewish Legibility: Documentation Practices and Reform During the Reign of Nicholas I," *Jewish Social Studies* 11.2 (2005): 151. Polish Jewish integrationists would try out the same logic on their readership, stressing the opposition of Isserles and other earlier authorities to the practice of female head-shaving. See J.G., "Zwyczaj golenia głów przez mężatki żydowskie, uważany ze stanowiska halachicznego," *Izraelita* 8 (1871), 82–3. For the Hungarian case and attitudes towards traditional dress, see especially Michael Silber, "The Emergence of Ultra-Orthodoxy: the Invention of a Tradition," in *The Uses of Tradition: Jewish Continuity since Emancipation* (ed., Jack Wertheimer; New York-Jerusalem: JTS, distributed by Harvard University Press, 1992), 23–84.

27 For the rabbinical injunction to opt for martyrdom rather than yield to a religiously-motivated royal decree that coerces even minor sartorial alterations, like changing the color of one's shoe straps, see BT Sanhedrin 74a–b. See also Bhabha, *The Location of Culture*, ch. 4.

28 Yosef Karo, *Shulkhan Aruh im kol ha-mefarshim*, "Yore de'ah," 178: Laws of Gentiles (2 vols.; reprint Jerusalem, 1956), vol. 2. See also Maimonides, *Mishneh Torah*, vol. 1 ([New York]: Grossman, 1953), "Laws of Idol Worshippers," ch. 11, 96.

29 Moses Isserles on Karo, *Shulkhan Aruh im kol ha-mefarshim*, "Yore de'ah," 178. Isserles invokes the moderate 15th-century Italian authority R. Joseph ben Solomon Colon Trabotto ("Maharik," 1420–1480/84), who held that one must merely refrain from deliberately

R. David ha-levi Segal (the "TaZ," 1586–1667) argued, similarly, that it did not matter whether it was "this or that" gentile hairstyle; the prohibition applied to any distinctly gentile hairstyles like the long hairstyles and Mohawk-like *blorit* worn by "soldiers in many lands," for the fundamental principle was "that Israel differentiate from [gentiles]."[30]

In other words, while a distinctively Jewish appearance might imply a symbolic rejection of the dominant society's supposed values, such as "idolatry" or "licentiousness," it was more fundamentally a performance of difference.[31] Maskilim like Fuenn and Tugenhold thus correctly discerned an underlying separatist impetus, even if they overestimated its dispensability.[32]

---

imitating gentile dress. Joseph ben Solomon Colon Trabotto (Maharik), *Sefer she'elot u-teshuvot Maharik* (Jerusalem, 1973), 48–9 [95–6]. Colon's discussion revolves around the wearing of the Cappa gown by Jewish doctors, which he argues is acceptable. Isserles also made allowances for Jewish doctors, courtiers, and so on. R. Shabbatai ben Meir HaKohen ("Shakh," 1621–1662) added an additional reason for proscribing the color red: in contrast to black, it was not "the way of modesty." See Shabbatai ben Meir HaKohen, *Siftei ha-kohen, Shulkhan Aruh im kol hamefarshim*, "Yore de'ah," 178. On the category "Amorite ways," which connoted more of a soft idolatry, see Beth Berkowitz, *Defining Jewish Difference: From Antiquity to the Present* (Cambridge: Cambridge University Press, 2012), 96–100; 146–8. On Colon, see 177–80; on Isserles, see 187–8. The book's discussion about contemporary orthodox debates over the adaptation of gentile dress, despite some jarring misconceptions about Polish Jewish life (e.g. "the Jewish villages" of Poland), is also illuminating. See 214–19.

30   See TaZ, on Karo, *Shulkhan Aruh im kol ha-mefarshim*, "Yore de'ah," 178. The *blorit* was a hairstyle associated with pagans who would grow the back long and then offer it to the gods. See Berkowitz, *Defining Jewish Difference*, 102 and 120–1.

31   Recent attempts to trace traditional Polish Jewish garb back to the costume of the sixteenth century nobility are quite suspect, particularly in light of Isserles contemporaneous repudiation. For such theories, see Eric Silverman, *A Cultural History of Jewish Dress* (London: Bloomsbury, 2013), 120–23; and R. Straus, "The Jewish hat as an aspect of social history," *Jewish Social Studies* 4 (1942): 59–72. Straus argues that the *shtreimel* was not a "specifically Jewish hat" in the seventeenth century (71).

32   There is an almost uncanny parallel tension in contemporary Islamic society over the wearing of the veil by women. In response to the argument by Egyptian intellectuals that "veiling is not so much a divine injunction as it is a continuation of regional customs... that has mistakenly become enshrined as a religious edict," Saba Mahmood's respondant retorts that those secular intellectuals ignore "how the practice of veiling is an integral part of an entire manner of existence through which one learns to cultivate the virtue of modesty in all aspects of one's life." A Muslim politician goes even further, asking "why should we not take pride in the symbols that distinguish us from others [like the veil]? See Saba Mahmood's *Politics of Piety: The Islamic Revival and the Feminist Subject* (Princeton, NJ: Princeton University Press, 2005), 51–2. Many thanks to Kristin Zahra Sands for recommending this work.

FIGURE 4.6   A Warsaw Jew and his Wife (*1846*). *By Leon Hollaenderski.*

Jewish sartorial differentiation was compatible with a pre-modern ethos that condoned and sometimes even required visible distinction among estates, social classes, and residents of different locales. Eighteenth-century criticisms by non-Jewish observers, appearing in Polish satires and Sejm (Polish Diet) resolutions, usually targeted the perceived opulence of Jewish attire rather than its distinctiveness per se. When critics did attack the foreignness of Jewish attire, it was often on economic grounds—luxurious fabrics like silk, satin, and velvet were imported from countries like France to the detriment of Polish textile manufacturers, they claimed.[33] But sartorial differentiation was not compatible with a modernizing ethos of homogeneity.[34] By the nineteenth century, Polish reformers were increasingly charging that Jewish clothing and hairstyles produced and perpetuated difference, which in the eyes of budding Polish nationalists and absolutist officials threatened to undermine social harmony. Traditional Jewish attire was now deemed clannish and visibly repugnant, while Jewish hairstyles were said to encourage the spread of the scalp infection known as *koltun*.[35] Sartorial change became a key condition for obtaining exemptions from legal disabilities, as we have seen in the case of residential restrictions.

Thus, it would be wrong to place sole blame on the Russian maskilic authors of the 1843 petition for the tragicomic affair that followed. In fact, the decision to ban Jewish garb had already been made twice, in 1804 and in 1835, and a decision to vigorously enforce the ban was made in 1841 as a result of deliberations by a non-Jewish "Jewish Committee," which associated Jewish attire with insularity and an aversion to civility, and which probably did not need much convincing by maskilim.

In 1844, the tsar took the first decisive step towards enforcement, decreeing a tax on Jewish clothing. In April, 1845, he announced an all-out ban on Jewish clothing in the Russian Empire, scheduled to take effect in 1850. Until then,

---

33 Emanuel Ringelblum, "Yidishe malbushim in poylin sof 18 y'h," *Fun noentn ovor* V (1938): 17–18; R. Żebrowski, "Zagadnienie stroju żydowskiego w dobie sejmu czteroletniego: projekt reformy," *Biuletyn Żydowskiego Instytutu Historycznego* 131–2 (1984): 31–47. As late as 1824, authorities in the "free city" of Kraków still made an economic argument: Jews should be made to stop wearing silk in order to "help revive local industry" by wearing clothes made within the country. See Adam Penkalla, "The Socio-Cultural Integration of the Jewish Population in the Province of Radom, 1815–1862," *Polin* 3 (2004): 221.

34 For an insightful contrast between pre-modern and modern or nationalist societies with respect to differentiation and homogeneity, see Ernest Gellner, *Nations and Nationalism* (Ithaca, NY: Cornell University Press, 2008), e.g. 13 and 105.

35 Few native Poles were likely to share the opinion of the traveler Harro Harring, who on beholding Jewish women in the Kingdom of Poland found that their "faithful adherence to their national costume serves to heighten their natural attractions." See Harro Harring, *Poland under the Dominion of Russia* (Boston, 1834), 22. For negative assessments, see Kajetan Koźmian, *Pamiętniki* (3 vols.; Wrocław, 1972), III: 22, where Jewish clothing is held responsible for spreading *koltun*; Walerian Łukasiński, *Pamiętnik* (Warsaw: PWN, 1960), 202. This was to become an issue even during the Polish Uprising of 1830–1, when Jews wished to fight for the Polish national cause yet retain their beards. See *Yankel's Tavern*, 108.

there was to be a grace period during which a Jew could retain his traditional costume by purchasing a permit (*konsens*).[36] Two months after the announcement, officials in the Kingdom of Poland began to inquire whether the tsar's Russian clothing policy also applied within his Polish kingdom, an inquiry that speaks volumes about the erosion of Polish autonomy after the suppression of the 1830–1 uprising. On November 6, 1845, Polish officials received their answer in the form of a similar decree for Jews in the kingdom.[37]

It was at this point that Alter and other prominent *tzaddikim* convened in Warsaw and composed a letter to the British philanthropist Moses Montefiore, who was planning to undertake a journey to St. Petersburg to intercede on behalf of East European Jewry. Their letter mentions "harsh decrees" in general, which may have implied the impending clothing decrees.[38] The Russian tzaddik R. Israel of Ruzhyn then sent Montefiore a more explicit letter in the beginning of 1846, protesting the "mild decree (*gezerah kalah*) aimed at changing Jewish clothing" and arguing that "wherever the authorities do this it afflicts the holy Torah."

Montefiore arrived in Warsaw on May 13, 1846. The British Consul in Warsaw, Col. Du Plat, later remarked that were Montefiore to succeed in rescinding the clothing decrees he would undoubtedly earn the blessing of the Jewish masses. However, Du Plat suspected that Jewish hopes would be disappointed.[39] In fact, Montefiore personally favored a gradual change in traditional Jewish attire: his petition to the Tsar in November explained (with little basis) that distinctive clothing had been imposed on the Jews by the Polish government three centuries earlier and that most Jews were now ready to discard it.[40] Nevertheless, Montefiore did persuade the tsar's Polish officials to delay the implementation of the grace period and concession fees for three months as "relief to the

---

36   Yisrael Klausner, "Ha-gezerah al tilboshet ha-yehudim, 1844–1850," *Gal-Ed*, 6 (1982): 15–17; Avrutin, *Jews and the Imperial State: Identification Politics in Imperial Russia* (Ithaca, NY: Cornell University Press, 2010), 39–42.

37   AGAD KRSW 6643, fol. 3. The diminishment of Polish autonomy in the Kingdom of Poland, which was not very extensive to begin with, forms a major theme in *Yankel's Tavern*.

38   Letters in A.S. Halevi, *Yimalei pi tehilatekha* (London, 1974), 6 and 10. Compare Bartal and Assaf, "Shtadlanut ve-ortodoksiyah: tzaddike polin be-mifgash im ha-zmanim ha-hadashim," in Rachel Elior, Yisrael Bartal, and Chone Shmeruk, eds., *Tzaddikim ve-anshe ma'aseh: mehkarim be-hasidut polin* (Jerusalem: Mosad Bialik, 1994), 84.

39   Letter from May 16, 1848. Printed in Stefan Kieniewicz, "Konsul brytyjski w Warszawie i Moses Montefiore," *Biuletyn Żydowskiego Instytutu Historycznego* 1–2 (1982): 165.

40   Petition from November 10, 1846. Printed in full, in Dawid Kandel, "Montefiore w Warszawie," *Biblioteka Warszawska* (1911): 89.

poor," since it was no small thing to require impoverished Jews to obtain new wardrobes.[41]

On May 22, a delegation of Hasidic and non-Hasidic traditionalists, which likely included Alter but which was led by the wealthy, non-Hasidic entrepreneur Solomon Posner, visited Montefiore. Posner gave his complete assent: according to Montefiore's secretary, he "informed Sir Moses that he would, though an old man, comply with the desire of the Government, and change the Polish for the German Costume." Montefiore could therefore be forgiven for thinking that the clothing decrees were no cause célèbre among Polish Jews.[42]

During the grace period from July 1, 1846 to January 1, 1850, Jews could purchase a permit for wearing traditional attire from the Warsaw commissioner or the mayor of the nearest town within the domain of their Synagogue Council. The price of the permit was set according to occupation—fifty rubles per year for large-scale merchants and liquor monopoly lessees; thirty rubles for smaller-scale merchants and tavernkeepers; twenty rubles for purveyors of market stalls and agents (factors); ten rubles for petty traders; five rubles for artisans, rural inhabitants, farmers, clerks, servants and laborers; and three rubles for everyone else.[43] Exempt were children under ten years of age, anyone over the age of 60 (provided they could prove their age, not always a simple matter), and of course, those who had already changed over to either Western dress or the style of Russian merchants. Proceeds from the sale of clothing permits would go to charity.[44]

"Western" dress was defined as French-style hats or field caps with no yarmulke or *peyos*, and short overcoats of wool, tweed, thick cotton, and linen with no velvet hems or belts with buttons. "Russian" attire was defined as long overcoats cut in the Russian style, long pants, Russian hairstyles, which (crucially) included beards, but explicitly not caftans, sashes, fur headdresses, yarmulkes, knee-breeches, slippers, or anything made from silk. Women were not to wear turbans, headbands, Jewish-style dresses, "colorful" shoes, or any other distinctively Jewish clothing or jewelry, and were only permitted to

---

41 Louis Loewe, ed., *Diaries of Sir Moses and Lady Montefiore* (London: Jewish Historical Society of England, 1983), 351–2. Du Plat visited Montefiore several times in Warsaw, and presented him with a copy of the Ukase stating the three-month delay.

42 Loewe, ed., *Diaries of Sir Moses*, 354–5. See also Israel Bartal, "Moses Montefiore: Nationalist or Belated Shtadlan?" *Studies in Zionism* 11.2 (1990): 118–19; and Abigail Green, *Moses Montefiore: Jewish Liberator, Imperial Hero* (Cambridge, MA: Belknap Press of Harvard University Press, 2010), 322–4.

43 AGAD KRSW 6643 fol. 74. Table reprinted in Agnieszka Jagodzińska, *Pomiędzy: akulturacja żydów warszawy w drugiej połowie XIX wieku* (Wrocław: WUW, 2008), 87.

44 KRSW 6643 fol. 3–15b; fol. 17.

wear "simple" caps or caps in German or Russian styles.⁴⁵ Subsequent decrees harped insistently on silk. While poor Jews were allowed to continue wearing silk for another two years, the rest of the Jewish population—including those who chose the Russian option—had to foreswear silk immediately. This preoccupation with silk betrays the depth of official antipathy towards members of the burgeoning Hasidic movement, whose penchant for wearing the fabric had earned them the moniker *kitajcy*, or Men of Silk.⁴⁶

Tsar Nicholas took some pains to explain his new policy. As distinctive dress was not required by the religion of the Jewish people, he stated confidently, and as distinctive dress was one of the "chief reasons their progression towards civilization has been held back," such dress must be abolished in his kingdom. He then elaborated: Jewish men must no longer wear silk, certain kinds of wool (*prunelowe*), Jewish-style long coats (*kapotas*), belts, Jewish hats, yarmulkes, short Jewish-style pants, knee-high laced shoes, beards or *peyos*. Jewish women must no longer wear turbans, headdresses, garments of a Jewish-cut, or other clothing that was distinguishably Jewish. Further decrees, composed in Polish and Yiddish and hung up in Jewish houses of worship throughout the kingdom, evinced even greater fashion interest, going into acceptable and unacceptable hats, belts, buttons, haircuts, hairstyles, pinafores, headbands, and so on.⁴⁷

Polish officials were optimistic: a Russian colleague had assured them that the implementation of similar decrees in the tsarist Empire proper had already caused "many Jews, especially in Vilna, Minsk, Bobruisk, and Ihumen to voluntarily give up their Jewish costume." In the kingdom, the project would

---

45   KRSW 6643, fol. 37–38.
46   Literally, "oriental." On this designation, see Dynner, *Men of Silk*, esp. ch. 2. See also the memoirist Abraham Gottlober's description of the costume of a young, affluent Ruzhner Hasid: "a black coat, the chest fastened with iron clasps, masculine and feminine [jewelry] 'at the side of each were wreaths' [Kings 1, 7:30] protruding from the corners of the silk material, woven work appearing on the coat like a shield around the neck and extending down the chest here and there, from the right side of the coat down to the feet (for such was the length of the coat in those days and the amount left hanging), and from the left side extending down to his loins, and a great furry black hat on his head, and a cane in his hand." Prior to the appearance of Hasidism, silk was often associated with luxury within the Jewish community; only "outstanding scholars" were allowed to wear silk in Poznań. See Michałowska-Mycielska, *The Jewish Community*, 176.
47   AGAD, KRSW 6643, fol. 35–38; 6649 s. 365–366.

be implemented through the Warsaw Synagogue Council, the kingdom's "most principal Jewish representative body." What could possibly go wrong?[48]

But the Russian option, which existed from the very start (it was not a later compromise, as some have claimed), entailed quite a loophole, since Jews who chose it could continue to wear long coats and, even more importantly, keep their beards.[49] Such an option really only made sense in a Russian context. Jewish communal representatives in the Russian Empire proper had conceived this solution themselves forty years earlier in response to articles 9 and 28 of the 1804 Statutes, which stated that any Jew who wished to be appointed a member of the magistracy or to enter the Russian interior had to wear "German" i.e., western clothing "without any distinction from other people." Jewish representatives, eager to retain their beards, had argued that it was "much more proper to go about in Russian dress on the example of [bearded] Russian merchants; in German dress, with shaved beards, they are likely to serve as an object of scorn and mockery." The rather progressive 1812 Jewish Committee in Russia had agreed, adding that "by means of permission to wear Russian clothes one could much sooner bring the understandings and the values of the Jews nearer to the understandings and values of Russians."[50] When the initiative was revisited in the 1840s, tsarist officials included the Russian merchant option in view of that reasoning. Clearly such logic did not apply to the Kingdom of Poland, however, where Russian merchants were few. But no one seemed to notice.

The Fashion Police

The confusion began almost immediately. One problem was the transnational nature of Jewish trade. In February 1845, several months before the clothing ban was extended to the kingdom, police detained and forcibly shaved the beards off of two Jewish merchants from Terespol (Kingdom of Poland) who were in Brest-Litovsk (Russian Empire proper) on business. As residents of the Kingdom of Poland, the two Jews pointed out in their petition, they were not yet subject to the ban.[51] Once the ban was implemented in the Kingdom

---

48 KRSW 6643, fol. 38. Ihumen likely refers to a small town in the Minsk Province of Belarus, known today as Cherven.
49 KRSW 6643, fol. 10–11.
50 Mikhail T. Shugarov, ed., "Doklad o Evreiakh imperatoru Aleksandru Pavlovichu," *Russkii arkhiv* 41 (February 1903), "Report about Jews to Emperor Alexander Pavlovich, 1812," Section B.5, 270. Tr. Melissa Frazier.
51 KRSW 6643 fol. 70–73.

of Poland, a similar problem emerged with respect to Jewish merchants from Kraków and throughout Galicia (Austrian Poland), where no such decree was in force.

An incident that caused Polish officials some concern and embarrassment occurred on a train from Warsaw to Kraków and involved three Galician merchants who were returning from Warsaw on business: Markus Rosenstrauch, Leibel Piarecki, and Berek Buttner, all residents of Kazimierz (a suburb of Kraków). As the train was passing through the town of Piotrków, Markus and Leibel were attracted by music coming from the dining car. Upon entering the car they encountered several uniformed railroad clerks, police, and the Police Inspector, Mikołaj Jaskiewicz. The police demanded to see Markus and Leibel's passports (which identified them as Habsburg subjects) and began to question them. Then, at Jaskiewicz's order, they produced scissors, grabbed Markus, cut off his *peyos*, and stripped him of his Jewish-style shirt and jacket. Next, they grabbed Leibel and ripped off his outer clothes. At that point, their friend Berek entered the car. As neither Leibel nor Berek had visible *peyos* (they wore their hair "in a Karaite fashion," which was long enough to cover their temples), the police at first only ripped off their shirts and jackets. But next they began to go for their beards, beginning with Markus. Now, something remarkable happened: Berek began to physically defend his friend, while certain passengers and railroad clerks began to vocally protest against the behavior of the police. Finally, at the appearance of a Habsburg inspector, the police desisted. Though Inspector Jaskiewicz was to later claim that the "fanatical" Jews had "quarreled" with him, he was reprimanded and sentenced to twenty-four hours in a military prison.[52]

Another complicating factor was widespread Jewish poverty. Could one realistically expect poorer segments of the Jewish community to simply change their wardrobes? In their petitions to authorities, certain Jews claimed that every Jew in the kingdom *would* be willing to change over to Russian garb even before the deadline, but many were in no condition to buy new clothes or permits owing to the high cost of basic necessities that year.[53] The Kalisz Synagogue Council declared the potential economic effects of an imposed change of clothing and permit requirements a "disaster for our people, especially for the lower classes, at so critical a time." The silk prohibition would be particularly devastating for poor Jews, they claimed, since while members of the "merchant class" could afford to give up silk the poor could not, for

---

52   KRSW 6647 260–76.
53   KRSW 6643 fol. 104; KRSW 6644, 44.

they would be unable to resell their silk clothes as a result of the ban.⁵⁴ The Kałuszyn Synagogue Council argued that many Jews supported themselves by extending credit and would collapse financially if they had to buy permits.⁵⁵ The Siedlice Synagogue Council drew officials' attention to the effects of current food prices and a recent flood.⁵⁶

One had to admit that the timing was inauspicious. As Jankiel Spira pointed out in his petition, Jews had just been banned from engaging in rural tavernkeeping the prior year (1844), forcing erstwhile tavernkeepers to move to towns and cities in search of a livelihood. It is difficult to determine how many such tavernkeepers there were, given the tendency of rural Polish landowners to merely install Christian "fronts" in their taverns while encouraging Jews to continue to run them furtively. But there does seem to have been significant attrition. Moreover, according to Jankiel, crops had done so poorly that year that many cattle had died and the townspeople had been forced to request a tax reduction.⁵⁷

Police harassment only exacerbated the negative economic effects. Numerous witnesses claimed that police and hired Cossacks were shaving beards off Jews who dressed even in Russian garb—Warsaw Jews who had adopted Russian garb like Israel Wein, Hersz Berenstein, Jan Wollak, Aaron Gielb, Gil Hasklow Daches, and his wife Dwojra complained of continued police harassment.⁵⁸ Though eventually neutralized by bribes to police, in the short term such harassment gave rise to an atmosphere in the capital that one Christian observer compared sardonically to an "Italian carnival," and which one Jewish observer warned was going to cause trade to collapse, since many Jews feared to even venture outside.⁵⁹

---

54   KRSW 6643 fol. 110–112.
55   KRSW 6643 fol. 195.
56   KRSW 6643 fol. 196–198.
57   KRSW 6643, fol. 107. On the eviction of rural Jewish tavernkeepers, see Dynner, *Yankel's Tavern*, ch. 2.
58   KRSW 6644, 47–8, 184.
59   Shatzky, *Geshikhte fun yidn in varshe*, II: 91. Yet François Guesnet has found evidence that the enforcement of clothing decrees and head-shaving bans (see below) was, with notable exceptions lenient thanks to police enthusiasm for bribes, and that in some places local authorities "tried to ingratiate themselves by warning Jews wearing the traditional garb ahead of inspections." See Guesnet, *Polnische Juden im 19. Jahrhundert: Lebensbedingungen, Rechtsnormen und Organisation im Wandel* (Cologne: Böhlau, 1998), esp. 198. KRSW 6644, 47–8, 184, 203–5. Jews in Siedlce, Biała, the Radomski district, Kielce, Chęcin, Łęczna, Ostrów, Opatów, Łódź, and Stawatycz made similar complaints. See KRSW 6644, 33–35; KRSW 6647, 42; KRSW 6647, 150; KRSW 6647, 237; KRSW 6647, 116;

The situation in other cities was just as dire. Two Warsaw Jewish army suppliers who were in Lublin on business, W. Miller and A. Hercman, reported that the Lublin Mayor was insisting that Jews who chose the Russian option wear elaborate Russian costume, including the Kuczerski cap with red stripes, the Kuczerski frock, and Russian-style headbands over their yarmulkes. His police were forcibly shaving off the beards of those who did not comply, going so far as to search houses for bearded Jews. Some Lublin Jews, feeling virtually unprotected by the law, had gone into hiding or left town, thus interrupting important business affairs and suffering enormous losses. Conditions were similar back in Warsaw, compelling Miller and Hercman to abandon their trade and leave the city in order to avoid having their own beards shaved. As they were the main suppliers of fuel, oil, and liquor to the army stationed in Lublin, important military deliveries had been delayed.[60]

Significantly, these examples of Jews who were determined to keep their beards and traditional attire at some personal cost and risk included wealthy, middling, poor, urban, small-town, and rural Jews alike. The broad range of petitioners illustrates how hazardous it is to generalize about Jewish responses to the clothing decrees on the basis of class or urbanicity. Rather, the reigning tendency across the spectrum was to adopt minor sartorial alterations that vaguely satisfied official dictates but preserved distinction. The Russian option did precisely that, if only the police could be reined in.[61]

In 1847, the adjutant governor of Warsaw ordered his police to desist from forcibly shaving the beards off Jews dressed in Russian garb, but some did not apparently comply.[62] In 1851, Chief rabbi of Warsaw Hayyim Dawidsohn and Praga rabbi Szaia Muszkat finally issued a stirring protest on behalf of all of the kingdom's Jews, insisting that the government abide by its own rules. Even those Jews who adopted Russian garb, they claimed, were hunted and persecuted. "If someone has a beard without offending any law, yet is exposed to shameful inspections... this is an affront to their humanity," they argued. The fact that the regime had permitted beards under certain circumstances was proof that

---

KRSW 6648, 89 and 197–8 (in this case, the petitioners had purchased concessions and demanded a refund).

60   KRSW 6647, fol. 147–9.
61   Compare Jagodzińska, *Pomiędzy: akulturacja żydów Warszawy*, 80–102, esp. 91 and 96. Jagodzińska claims that "middle class" urban Jews underwent a major sartorial transformation along modern western lines. Later, she concedes that "the majority of Jews did only what was required of them by the law and were not interested in further changes." However, these were ostensibly non-middle class urban Jews (138–9).
62   Mahler, *Divrei yemei Yisrael*, 239, incorrectly claims that this decree put an end to such harassment.

it respected the religious obligations of the Jewish people. So why were the police entitled to detain Jews who dressed according to the law and to nitpick, "finding certain buttons out of place or certain hair that hadn't been properly cut?" It was disgraceful to see numerous people being made sport of by police. Perfectly respectable Jews were being treated like criminals; and some were being "horribly beaten." Such inhumane treatment was in fact endangering peoples' health and depriving families of breadwinners, since many men felt compelled to stay at home. The very thing that Jews proudly viewed as a matter of conscience—their beards—was being treated as a desecration.[63]

Admittedly, there was genuine confusion over what "Russian garb" actually meant. As few Russian merchants were to be found in the Kingdom of Poland, the police had to be given a series of lithographs depicting figures clothed in the accepted styles. The Russian coat, for example, was supposed to be long, double-breasted, and without front pockets.[64] But no one had remembered to instruct the Jews themselves. One Jewish merchant, who had attempted to base his clothing on what he remembered seeing Russian merchants wear in Warsaw, sincerely requested a "model or drawing" of Russian attire after the Mayor had used Gendarmes and Cossacks to cut the beards off Jews who thought they were complying.[65]

In such a situation of ambiguity, most Jews made minimal "Russian" adjustments to their clothing. Officials complained that some merely reshaped and lengthened their coats and "consider this Russian attire," while others only exchanged their yarmulkes for Russian-style caps.[66] The "majority of Jews, mainly the poorer classes," even kept their yarmulkes, *peyos*, and beards and "pretend to dress in Russian garb by using a different type of cloth [than silk]" which was "practically no change at all."[67] Many were shaving off their beards and then growing them back later, officials claimed.[68]

Officials were further exasperated by individual requests for legal exemptions that employed overly creative reasoning. Mendel Mendelsohn of Lublin requested permission to continue to wear his green yarmulke on account of his "rheumatic headaches."[69] Pinkus Peterilije claimed that his doctors had ordered him to be "extremely careful to remain warm," and that he must keep

---

63   KRSW 6647, fol. 84–85.
64   KRSW 6644, 265–270; S. Yerusalimski, (no title), *Evreiskaia starina* v, 334–8.
65   KRSW 6647, 237.
66   KRSW 6646, 159 and 205.
67   KRSW 6644, 111–112.
68   KRSW 6648, 3.
69   KRSW 6647, 104.

THE GARMENT OF TORAH 111

FIGURE 4.7 *Examples of Russian Merchant Dress Presented to the Warsaw Police, 1847.*
COURTESY OF *ARCHIWUM GŁÓWNE AKT DAWNYCH* (AGAD).

his beard or risk losing his life. Pinkus had built a factory "without equal" in the entire kingdom at great personal cost, he added, reminding officials of his importance to the economy. He then leveled with them: "I am not superstitious or ignorant, and in spiritual and religious matters I do not tend to cherish extremely trivial things." He was only concerned about remaining alive, so that he could continue to take care of his wife, six children, and many employees; and his very life depended on keeping his face warm. So he needed to retain his beard and should not have to pay a fee or adopt Russian-style clothing.[70] Individual Jews who requested exemptions on account of their poverty had a significantly better chance of succeeding than those with medical excuses.[71]

Some Hasidim, emboldened by the teachings of certain *tzaddikim*, did not bother to make "Russian" alterations or seek exemptions.[72] According to the State Council, "while a significant number of younger, more civilized, and wealthier Jews accepted the attire of other inhabitants of the kingdom, many elders and members of the so-called Hasidic sect have remained in the old attire, declaring themselves ready to pay the fine for Jewish garb." In 1850, the State Council reported that most Jews had retained their beards and continued to wear the forbidden fabric, silk.[73] The next year, the mayor of Warka complained that "Jews who, being fanatics, belong to the Hasidic sect, which is for

---

70   KRSW 6644, 316–19.
71   Exemptions for impoverished Jews in 1851 amounted to 17 in the Płock district, 19 in the Warsaw district, 50 in Augustów district, 7 in the Radom district, and 7 in the Sandomierz district. KRSW 6647, 60–1.
72   Simha Bunem of Pshyskhe (Przysucha) emphasized that "our father Abraham saw the clothes of the gentiles in his area and dressed differently." Therefore, "one must be careful not to change from the clothes of his ancestors, for all holiness depends on this." See Yoatz Kim Kadish, *Si'ah sarfe kodesh* (Bnei Brak, 1989), III, 238 and parshat Hukat, 113. Isaac Meir Alter of Ger preached, surprisingly enough, that "when one changes one's clothes one also changes one's essence." See ibid., on parshat Hukat. Tzvi Elimelekh of Dinów considered it "incumbent upon a person to purposely differentiate between Israel and the other peoples in customs, and according to Jewish custom the outer clothing called *tuzlik*... is a respectable article of clothing and precious attire." Thus, a Jew leaves his external garment on when he meets respectable people, while a gentile removes it. See *Bnei yissakhar* (New York, 1990), II, Tishre, 10:7, gloss. For sartorial teachings of Galician Hasidic masters, see Avraham Simkha Bunem Mikhalzohn, *Ateret menahem* (Bilgoraj, 1910; reprint Brooklyn, 2002), 12–15; and see Yehoshua of Belz, *Or yesharim* (Ashdod, 1902), 229: "Jacob feared that if the parents resembled Esau in clothing, the children would be likely to learn other things from this and, as a result, would transgress the entire Torah." Several of these sources are cited in Amram Blau, "Gedolei he-hasidut ve-gezerat ha-malbushim," *Ha-eikhal ha-besht* 12 (1950): 86, 88, and 117.
73   KRSW 6647, 291.

the most part a supporter of fanaticism, conceal their *peyos* somewhat, but nearly all have beards and wear the old Jewish attire." The mayor recommended that the government hire Cossacks and gendarmes to "convince" these Hasidic Jews to adopt genuine Russian dress if they wanted to keep their beards.[74]

R. Isaac Meir Alter Weighs In

Leading rabbinic ritual authorities (*poskim*) reacted in varying ways to the clothing decrees. R. Solomon Kluger (1783–1869), rabbi of Brody and the major Galician *posek* of his day, was among the more extreme:

> If [government officials] decree a change of all or most clothing, so that there will be no way to distinguish Jews from gentiles, of course this is an issue of licentiousness (*pritzut*). For take a look at the majority of countries where they did this. Why did they breach the fence of the Torah to begin with? Was it not because of clothing, that they dressed like gentiles and that this caused them to circumvent our holy Torah in its essence and fundamentals?[75]

As the change of clothing was a prime catalyst of assimilation, Kluger reasoned, resistance warranted outright martyrdom. Any Jew who adopted gentile dress, whether voluntarily or coerced by government decrees aimed at effecting conversion or instituted out of pure anti-Jewish animus, was to be deemed an "apostate."[76] But R. Solomon Drimer of Sokołów, another major

---

74 KRSW 6647, 81 [adjusted grammatically]. For more testimony on Hasidic recalcitrance, see Jagodzińska, *Pomiędzy: akulturacja żydów Warszawy*, 96 and 100.

75 Shelmo ben Yehuda Kluger, *Tuv ta'am ve-da'at* (reprint New York: Grossman, 196?), fol. 75b, no. 188. It should be noted that, while Kluger did not have to contend with severe clothing restrictions in his own domain, clothing reform was, since 1844, a pre-requisite for marriage in Kraków (a "free city" still administered jointly by Russia, Prussia, and Austria that year but absorbed into the latter two years later).

76 Ibid, nos. 188 and 189. Kluger was preceded in these strong views about Jewish attire by several Galician Hasidic masters, including R. Menahem Mendel of Rymanów, R. Tzvi Elimelekh of Dinów, and R. Yehezkel Panet. See Menahem Mendel of Rymanów's letter of 1812 and decree of 1815 in Avraham Simkha Bunem Mikhalzohn, *Ateret Menahem* (Bilgoraj, 1910; reprint Brooklyn, 2002), 12–15. On the Kraków decree and the responses of additional Galician *poskim*, several of whom advised betrothed Jewish youth to emigrate in order to marry without having to change their clothing, see Amram Blau, "Gedolei he-hasidut ve-gezerat ha-malbushim," *Ha-eikhal ha-besht* 12 (1950): 122.

Galician *posek*, openly disagreed with the suggestion by "one of the famous wise men of our generation" who had advocated martyrdom, i.e., Kluger. With the Neo-orthodox in mind, he asked his readers to "take a look at the German lands, in prior and even the current generations, all of whom dress in actual gentile clothes and who have not opposed the great, wise ones who resided in the German lands in every generation and abided by the [relatively lenient] position of the Maharik."[77]

In tsarist Russia proper, where full-fledged clothing decrees had actually been implemented, rabbinic authorities were just as divided. Several did not think it necessary for the poor to spend their money on clothing permits, and simply advised everyone to "do as he thinks is right." Martyrdom was warranted only if every single article of clothing had to be changed, argued one authority; even one distinctive garment sufficed.[78] R. Menachem Mendel Schneersohn of Lubavitch (The Tzemah Tzedek, 1789–1866) enumerated several reasons for leniency, including the rather generous observation that, as many Jews had already changed over to gentile clothing, it was not truly "gentile" anymore![79] However, other Russian rabbinical authorities urged their followers to "uphold the customs of their fathers and not make any changes to their clothing, for clothing changes the inner self," thus implicitly advocating martyrdom.[80]

---

77 Solomon Drimer, *Bet shelomo*, cited in Blau, "Gedolei he-hasidut ve-gezerat ha-malbushim," 112. Drimer seems to have had German Neo-orthodoxy in mind. He was prompted to weigh in after learning that Jews were beginning to emigrate from the tsarist empire rather than embracing martyrdom to avoid "altering even their shoe straps" (BT Sanhedrin 74a–b). As noted earlier, R. Joseph ben Solomon Colon Trabotto ("Maharik," 1420–1480/84), concluded that one must only refrain from deliberately imitating gentile dress, and made allowances for doctors wearing the Cappa gown. See Joseph ben Solomon Colon Trabotto (Maharik), *Sefer she'elot u-teshuvot maharik* (Jerusalem, 1973), 48–9 [95–6].

78 Judah Leib Batlan Ziskind of Dvinsk; Meir Horowitz of Dzikov; Moshe of Kobrin; and Nehemia of Dubrowna, cited with commentary, in Blau, "Gedolei he-hasidut ve-gezerat ha-malbushim," 108–17.

79 Menachem Mendel Schneersohn, *She'alot u-teshuvot tzemah tzedek*, in *Yoreh de'ah* (reprint Brooklyn, 1994), no. 91, 156. See also Blau, "Gedolei he-hasidut ve-gezerat ha-malbushim," 107–8. Schneersohn adds briefly that "as it is a matter of Judaism (*yahadut*), public martyrdom is required," yet only apparently in reference to the precise Talmudic case of white sandal straps versus black ones.

80 R. Aaron II of Karlin and R. Isaac of Volozhin. See Blau, "Gedolei he-hasidut ve-gezerat ha-malbushim," 108–17. See also the discussion in Nehemia ben Avraham Ginzberg, *Divre nehemia*, "Yoreh de'ah," (Vilna, 1866), 314, no. 181.

From the perspective of Gerer court historians, the clothing decrees episode in the Kingdom of Poland offered R. Isaac Meir Alter an opportunity to showcase his readiness for self-sacrifice and martyrdom. According to their reconstruction of events, Alter initially approached Abraham Winawer with a request to intervene with officials, but the acculturated leader refused to help. When the year 1851 arrived and the all-out ban went into effect (no clothing permits were sold after that date), Alter joined forces with the *tzaddik* Abraham of Ciechanów in urging Jews to accept martyrdom rather than shave their beards and *peyos*. Both leaders, we are told, knew that the government's real intention was mass conversion. R. Menahem Mendel of Kotzk refused to endorse their effort and condemned all encouragements of martyrdom, but Alter refused to heed his master. Soon, at the instigation of the Maskilim, he was arrested and pressured to shave his beard while in prison, which of course he refused to do. The next day, tens of thousands of Jews allegedly converged upon the square outside the city council to protest Alter's imprisonment. Fearing a revolt, Viceroy Paskevich ordered his release. Alter quickly relocated to the town of Nowy Dwór to get out of the spotlight, and in 1851, the day before Passover (the holiday commemorating the Jews' liberation from Egyptian bondage), word went out that the clothing decrees had been cancelled.[81]

Historians have by and large accepted the Gerer account, notwithstanding the tendency of late hagiography to impose ultra-orthodox conceptions on earlier traditionalist figures, and notwithstanding its deployment of unmistakable archetypes: maskilim—a term invoked by Hasidic hagiographers to refer to any type of acculturated Jew—are cast as villains; higher government authorities are benign but misled; Hasidic leaders are, of course, heroes and martyrs.

But Alter's character and career were complex. At times, he supported Polish insurrectionary efforts against the tsar, activities which complicated his bid for the post of assistant rabbi of Warsaw.[82] Yet he eventually emerged as a premier

---

81   The fullest account appears in Alter, *Meir eyene ha-golah* (1932), 1: 121–30. See also Moshe Menahem Walden, *Ohel Yitzhak* (Piotrków and Jerusalem, 1967), 15 (8).

82   According to Hasidic hagiography, during the 1830 uprising against the tsar Alter and his master Menahem Mendel of Kotzk issued a circular urging Kotzker Hasidim to raise money for General Antoni Ostrowski, commander of the Polish revolutionary National Guard. After the suppression of the revolt both Hasidic leaders, fearing that circulars bearing their old surnames might lead to their arrest if discovered, fled to Brody (then under Habsburg rule). Menahem Mendel changed his surname from Halpern to Morgenstern, while Isaac Meir changed his from Rothenberg to Alter. See Menasshe Unger, *A Fire Burns in Kotsk* (tr. Jonathan Boyarin; Detroit, MI: Wayne State University Press, forthcoming); Eleazar Hakohen, "Etz Avot," in *Hidushe maharah* (Warsaw, 1898), 9; M. Bereban, "Geshikhte fun gerer hoyf," *Unzer ekspres* (Friday, January 13, 1933), 8;

leader of Warsaw Jewry thanks, in part, to his willingness to collaborate with "collaborators," his Jewish integrationist rivals. In 1841, he joined traditionalist leaders like the non-Hasidic Rabbi Hayyim Dawidsohn, the Hasidic leader Isaac of Warka, the non-Hasidic entrepreneur Solomon Posner, and Polish Jewish integrationists like Jacob Tugenhold, Mathias Rozen, and Abraham Winawer, in issuing an appeal to Polish Jews to engage in agriculture, which was one of the hallmarks of the regime's efforts to "normalize" its Jewish population and which, from the perspective of Jewish traditionalist leaders, was an acceptable solution to Jewish unemployment.[83]

On the other hand, Alter's accommodationism should not be exaggerated. Unlike his active support during the 1830 uprising, he prudently opted for neutrality during the 1863 uprising. While he did urge his followers to compose documents for fictitious sales of leavened food on Passover in Polish, a gesture that generated much enthusiasm among acculturated co-religionists who interpreted it to mean that he supported polonization, this was probably an attempt to uphold the legal imperative to ensure that one's gentile "buyer" understood the contract.[84] To judge by Alter's poetry, he privately opposed linguistic assimilation.[85] And while it has been suggested, without sufficient evidence, that he encouraged Jewish *heder* (traditional Jewish elementary school) teachers to employ native Poles to teach their students the Polish language, Alter was in fact outspoken in his opposition to curricular reform.[86] In an 1844 letter of appeal to Abraham Winawer, Alter pointed out the dangers of curricular changes and teaching non-Jewish languages to Jewish youth, and promised

---

Yitzhak Alfasi, *Gur* (Tel Aviv: Sinai, 1978), 88; David Kandel, "Kariera rabiniczna cadyka Icie-Majera," *Kwartalnik poświęcony badaniu przeszłości żydów w Polsce* 1/2 (1912): 131–6.

83 The appeal is printed in its entirety in Yisrael Hayyim Zagarodzki, *Di familiye davidzohn* (Warsaw, 1924), appendix XII–XX. The initiative bore modest results: by the middle of the nineteenth century there were fifty-six Jewish agricultural colonies established by Jewish or noble entrepreneurs, with an estimated 4,405 members. This does not capture the absolute number of Jews in agriculture, which had risen to 33,666 by 1852. Calculations based on estimates by Julian Bartys, "Stan ilościowy i struktura żydowskiego osadnictwa rolniczego w Królestwie Polskim w okresie przeduwłaszczeniowym," *Biuletyn ŻIH* (1962): 18–40.

84 "Wiadomości bieżące," *Jutrzenka* 3 (1863): 152.

85 See, for example, his "Shir neged riformim u-kedomeihem," printed in Yehuda Leib Levin, *Hidushe ha-rim al ha-torah* (Jerusalem, 1986), 375.

86 See Zofia Borzymińska, *Szkolnictwo żydowskie w Warszawie, 1831–1870* (Warsaw: Żydowski Instytut Historyczny, 1994) 219–20. However, the document cited there only mentions "our Rabbis". See "Nadzieje postępu," *Jutrzenka* 2 (1862): 381.

Winawer a place in heaven if he would intercede to prevent *heder* reform. Hasidic tradition credits Winawer with the rescission of the decree.[87]

Contemporaneous documentary sources contradict several key Gerer claims about the clothing decrees episode. First, it turns out, Winawer did intercede with the government in this affair, as well, though not apparently in the interest of defending tradition. In a petition from October 11, 1846, co-signed by Chief Rabbi of Warsaw Hayyim Dawidsohn and the merchant Moses Feinkind, Winawer pointed out that barely one thousand Jews had bothered to purchase clothing permits because most preferred the Russian option, which permitted beards alongside minor alterations to traditional garb. Winawer, Dawidsohn, and Feinkind complained that the Russian option surely did not help achieve the regime's objective of bringing Jewish sartorial habits closer to those of other inhabitants in the kingdom—all it had done was create a new Jewish costume![88] Their petition highlights the oddness of the emerging alliance between traditionalists and integrationists, for although the signatories unanimously opposed the Russian option their reasons seem to have differed. Winawer clearly saw the Russian loophole as an obstacle to the modernization of Jewish dress, but this was unlikely of much concern to Dawidsohn, a traditionalist. Perhaps Dawidsohn hoped that, in the absence of a Russian option, officials would allow Jews who adopted western dress to retain their beards. But whatever their respective motivations, they each agreed about the anemic response to clothing permits (confirmed in the low official figures preserved in the archives) and the widespread use of the Russian loophole, all of which undermines the notion that the price of retaining one's beard was imprisonment, let alone martyrdom.[89]

The extent to which the Russian loophole calmed even certain Hasidic leaders' concerns is reflected vividly in a letter from the future Aleksander *rebbe*, Shraga Feivel Danziger, who was at that time rabbi of Maków. The town owner had pressured Danziger to effect a mass reform of local Jewish attire, but Danziger had "circumvented the matter" by promising that he would personally see to it that all local Jews dressed in Russian style, which was "still not a considerable change." Danziger only hoped that God would "also bring salvation to the Israelites in other towns," since in Prużany and Ciechanów certain

---

87   Letter printed in *Si'ah sarfe kodesh* 1:7–8 and Alter, *Meir eyene ha-golah* (Warsaw, 1932), appendix, letter no. 4, 110.
88   AGAD, KRSW 6643, fol. 269–271.
89   In Warsaw, only 88 Jews applied for age-based exemptions; only 115 Jews who were not of exemption age purchased clothing permits. KRSW 6642, fol. 279–280.

"agents of evil have already cut the beards off of many, many of our people."[90] Jacob Aaron Yanovski, a Vurke Hasid and town rabbi (*av bet din*) of Aleksander, was even more optimistic, deeming the clothing decrees "ordained by Heaven." Thanks to the decrees, certain "perfect, God-fearing ones who walk in the ways of Torah and believe in the ways of the wise and righteous" had adopted gentile clothing themselves and could now mingle more naturally with wayward Jews and induce them to repent. Yanovski urged his pious audiences not to rebuke or ostracize fellow Jews who complied with the clothing decrees, for that would merely push them further away "as had occurred in Germany."[91]

The acceptability of the Russian option explains why, instead of passionately defying the clothing decrees, on November 7, 1849, Alter co-signed a circular with rabbis Dawidsohn and Muszkat urging Jews to immediately comply. No Jews between the ages of ten and sixty were to wear long *peyos*, *shtreymels*, *kitels* (white robes), or *kapotas*, and whoever did not comply *sinned against God*, their circular proclaimed.[92] Alter's participation in promulgating the decree was not likely under duress, as is sometimes claimed without evidence.[93] It was, rather, eminently sensible in view of a Russian loophole that preserved sartorial differentiation within a Polish context. It also forwarded Alter's political ambitions—he had been seeking official recognition as a spiritual leader in Warsaw for the past six years. If he had really been imprisoned for refusing to shave or change his attire and then freed after mass street protests, which incidentally went completely unmentioned in the Warsaw press that year, it strains credulity that the very next year, in 1852, Alter should have attained his long sought after official recognition as Warsaw's assistant rabbi "so long as he strictly abides by the Magistrate's decrees," a probable reference to the clothing decrees.[94]

90 See full letter, printed in Azriel Hayyim Zamlung, *Eser zekhiot* (Piotrków, 1931; reprint Jerusalem, 1974), 35, no. 19; and in Avraham Bromberg, *Migdolei ha-hasidut IV: admorei Aleksander* (Jerusalem, 1954), 28.

91 Yaakov Aharon Yanovski of Aleksander, *Bet yaakov* (Jerusalem, 1901), "Drashot le-erev r.h. lizkor brit," 162–3. Only occasionally do we find indications of alarm on the part of Polish rabbis. A government informer claimed that R. Aryeh Leib Hirshberg, the Rabbi of Pilica and a Kotzker Hasid, urged his congregants in 1850 to pray fervently lest the "government and monarchy ... take your children to the army, take our traditional clothing and tell us what to wear, and shave our beards." Quoted in Wodziński, *Hasidism and Politics*, 292.

92 The decree is printed in Jacob Shatzky, *Geshikhte fun yidn in varshe*, II, appendix, no. VII. For Shatzky's analysis of the clothing decrees, see II: 84–100. However, several of Shatzky's references are not possible to track down, and must be treated with caution.

93 For one instance of this claim, see Shatzky, *Geshikhte fun yidn in varshe*, II: 95.

94 Kandel, "Kariera rabiniczna cadyka Icie-Majera," 135. For the most recent endorsement of the imprisonment story, see Zvi Mark, "'The Son of David will not come until the

Nor were the clothing decrees cancelled the day before Passover or on any other day, for that matter.⁹⁵ In 1851, the grace period expired, the decrees went into full effect, and the fine for wearing traditional Jewish dress was set very high, at fifty-seven rubles. Local authorities were in some cases instructed to use force if the decrees were ignored. At the same time, enforcement proved nearly impossible. The poorest residents, who could not afford changes in clothing, certainly could not pay the exorbitant fines. Many mayors of towns and villages, moreover, proved willing (ostensibly for a price) to tip off Jewish residents and warn them to temporarily change "at least their outer clothing" whenever they learned that official inspectors were about to arrive.⁹⁶

In 1853, the government issued a more definitive set of decrees, exempting rabbis and other spiritual leaders, including Alter, and allowing certain poor Jews and Jews on their way to synagogue on Sabbaths and festivals to retain their old dress.⁹⁷ These concessions were significant; but the entire issue was soon moot in any case. The Russian style quickly came to be known in the Kingdom of Poland as the "Jewish style," an imported custom that preserved differentiation and whose alien origin was deleted from cultural memory. Winawer, Feinkind, and Dawidsohn had been right.⁹⁸

Bans on Female Head-shaving upon Marriage

Undaunted, the tsarist government set its sights on the Jewish custom of shaving off women's hair upon marriage. Interestingly enough, earlier rabbinic authorities like Maimonides, Karo, and Isserles had already prohibited the practice in the interest of preventing androgyny—"one might not be able to

---

sovereignty of Aram (Alexander, King of Russia) rules over the entire world for nine months': Messianic Hopes in Gur Hasidism," *Tarbiz* 77.2 (2008): 295–324.

95   Shatzky notes failed attempts by the Gerer Hasidic entrepreneur Birnbaum to achieve an indefinite extension of the grace period, though he did achieve a short extension. Shatzky, in *Geshikhte fun yidn in varshe*, II: 93–4.

96   On the instruction to use force and the practice of tipping off Jews by local authorities in the Radom District, see Adam Penkalla, "Socio-cultural Integration in Radom," 222. For similar behavior elsewhere, see Guesnet, *Polnische Juden im 19. Jahrhundert*, esp. 198.

97   For the full decree, in Polish and Yiddish, see KRSW 6649, 365–6. For the published Yiddish version, see Jacob Shatzky, "Tzu der geshikhte fun 'gezeyras ha-levush' in Poylin," in E. Tscherikower, ed., *Historishe shriftn* I (Warsaw, 1929): 731–2. On exemptions for spiritual leaders and poor Jews, see KRSW 6647, fol. 48, 60–1, 68, and 86.

98   On this anti-syncretic strategy in Judaism, see Berkowitz, *Defining Jewish Difference*, 145 and 214–219.

tell a man from a woman" and possibly misconstrue their ritual legal status. At least one authority felt that it "disfigured" a woman. The practice was only permitted for medical purposes in a commentary published in 1742.[99]

The transition to female head-shaving in Eastern Europe over the course of the eighteenth century is nevertheless attested to in a commentary by Dov Beirish Gottlieb (1740–1796), who appears nonplussed by Maimonides' prohibition. Perhaps Maimonides only meant to prohibit using an implement specifically used by men, i.e., a razor? Gottlieb then writes revealingly: "To the contrary, I have heard that there are *some* women who *do* shave their heads with a razor, and I know of no *posek* who forbids it." Any such prohibition, he concludes, must be strictly "local custom."[100] The main arguments in favor of the practice were that a married woman's hair might occlude her full immersion in the ritual bath and that any hairs that might stray outside of the head-covering would suggest immodesty. Bratslav Hasidic sources preserve a symbolic reasoning, as well, describing a tradition of plaiting the bride's hair, disheveling it, and then "shearing off all of the hair in order to cleanse her and completely remove all superficiality from her...." These considerations evidently outweighed earlier rabbinic concerns about androgyny.[101]

The tsar first prohibited female head-shaving in tsarist Russia proper, without explanation. In April, 1851, he was "graciously pleased to command that Jewish women be forbidden to shave their heads upon entering into marriage." The next year, a fine of five rubles was decreed for women who shaved their heads, and more severe punishments, including military conscription, for any rabbis who dared to permit or encourage it. According to government officials, Jewish women began to evade the ordinances by concealing their baldness under wigs or headdresses, a claim that finds corroboration in rabbinical sources. One rabbi reported that Jewish women had responded to the 1851

---

99 See Maimonides, *Mishneh torah*, "Idol Worshippers," ch. 12, 101, no. 10; *Shulhan arukh*, "Yoreh de'ah" (Vilna, 1876), 182:4, with Isserles' approval. However, Maimonides' prohibition against shaving a woman's head "like a man" is ambiguous. See Dov Beirish Gottlieb's commentary *Yad ha-ketanah* (Lemberg, 1800; reprint Königsberg, 1859), part 2, 278, no. 31. Yehuda Ashkenazi of Tiktin's gloss "Be'er metiv" (1742) on Karo's *Shulhan arukh*, "Yoreh de'ah," 181, permitting female head-shaving to cure a fever or cold or for "physical needs." For the disfigurement claim, see *Tzemah yehuda*, part 4, no. 19. For several of the sources cited here see, with caution, S. Ze'ev, "Toldot minhag hitgalhat le-nashim nesu'ot [ashkenaziyot]," *Or yisrael* 21 (2001): 228–30.

100 Dov Beirish Gottlieb, *Yad ha-ketanah* (Lemberg, 1800; reprint Königsberg, 1859), part 2, 278, no. 31. Emphasis mine.

101 Natan Sternharz, *Likutei halakhot* VI (Lublin, 1917), "Halakhot kidushin," end (passage concludes with several untranslatable puns).

decree by either "walking about with their hair uncovered" or, in the case of "modest" women, by wearing wigs upon their shaved heads. R. Solomon Kluger, across the border in Galicia, confirmed that in the tsarist lands "because of the decree there, women go about with their own hair." However, he was just as dismayed by the wearing of wigs, "particularly in the state of Russia, where the decree is in effect," since wigs induced licentiousness as effectively as natural hair. Nevertheless, he was inclined to be lenient, since Russian Jewish women seemed to be adopting wigs under duress.[102]

When officials became aware of the ruse, some began to subject Jewish women to humiliating inspections, several of which are recorded poignantly in the memoirs of Pauline Wengeroff and petitions by Zhitomir Jewish merchants. Police are portrayed ceremoniously ripping off women's wigs and head coverings, pouring buckets of water over their heads, imprisoning them, and forcing them to sweep the streets.[103] Similar spectacles were to occur in the Kingdom of Poland after the circulation of a new set of clothing decrees in 1853 that incorporated bans on female head-shaving, an initiative that was fervently applauded in conservative Polish periodicals.[104]

But first came attempts to forestall and mitigate the legislation. In September of 1851, a delegation of Warsaw Jews submitted a petition arguing that, while many women were ready to comply with a head-shaving prohibition, they should still be allowed to wear caps and other head coverings just as Christian women were accustomed to do. Of course, women who were recently married and "easily given to fashion appreciated the [new] law as a shield against

---

102 Kluger, *Kinat sofrim* (Lemberg, 1847), 38, no. 21 (inquiry from the Rabbi of Krzemienice); and idem, *Shanot hayyim* (Lemberg, 1857), 211, no. 317.

103 Simon Dubnow, *History of the Jews in Russia and Poland* (3 vols.; tr. I. Friedlaender; Philadelphia, PA: Jewish Publication Society, 1918), vol. 2, 144; Wengeroff, *Rememberings*, 94–6. However, Wengeroff dates the event as "summer of 1845," apparently in error. On Zhitomir, see "Persecution of Women's Headgear," *Evreiskaia starina* 8 (1915): 400–1; the document is translated in ChaeRan Y. Freeze and Jay M. Harris, eds., *Everyday Jewish Life in Imperial Russia: Select Documents (1772–1914)* (Hanover, NH: Brandeis University Press, 2013), 302–3.

104 The headshaving prohibition appears in articles 16 and 17 of a series of decrees in Polish and Yiddish circulated throughout Warsaw on June 19, 1853. See KRSW 6649, 365–6; and Shatzky, "Tzu der geshikhte fun 'gezeyras ha-levush' in poylin," 731–2. *Kurjer Warszawski* suggested that any rabbis or other spiritual leaders who violated the women's head-shaving ban should be imprisoned for two to three years and, in the event of a second infringement, recruited into the army or imprisoned for ten to twelve years. See the editorial by Fr. Hieronim Okszewski, a "teacher in the Kielce Technical High School (Szkoła Wyższa Realna w Kielcach)," in *Kurjer Warszawski* 187 (July 9, 1853).

fanaticism, and would surely let their hair grow." But exemptions should be made for the elderly and infirm, including pregnant women, because growing out their hair would endanger their health—elderly women certainly could not be expected to grow back their hair, for this would expose them to scalp infections (*koltun*) and headaches. The petitioners therefore requested that, just as beards were allowed under certain conditions, allowances be made for head-shaving. The government was actually amenable, exempting women who obtained a doctor's note.[105]

True to style, R. Isaac Meir Alter worked with other Jewish spiritual leaders to bring the new legislation within acceptable ritual legal bounds. In 1852, Alter co-signed a protest with rabbis Dawidsohn and Muszkat against the humiliating searches and the bans on wigs. At least married women should be able to wear caps that did not distinguish them as Jews and which would not count as wigs, but would only constitute a "superficial difference."[106] Alter then co-signed a lengthy petition with a larger group of Warsaw Jewish spiritual and lay leaders declaring their intention to back the government's initiative, but only under certain conditions. Jewish women must no longer be subjected to humiliating searches and should be allowed to don caps and wigs made from hair, as non-Jewish women were allowed to do.[107]

Next, Alter, Dawidsohn, Muszkat, and four other spiritual leaders co-signed a petition that explained the head-shaving custom in some depth. Upon marriage, they wrote, a Jewish woman had to submerge her entire body in a bath, and it was important that her hair not interfere. If any point of her body did not get submerged, she would be deemed unclean and thus unable to have relations with her husband. As a precaution against ritual impurity, Jewish women "from time immemorial" had cut off all their hair. In addition, they explained, for a woman to reveal her hair was considered insolent and unvirtuous in Jewish society. If the regime was, nevertheless, still unwilling to respect this Jewish custom, then Jewish women should at least be permitted to keep their hair *short* so as not to violate the "cardinal principles" of Judaism. In addition, Alter and his colleagues requested a cessation of all police inspections of women, "for words cannot express the gravity of the insult to both women and their families." In return, they promised to ensure that women would not shave their heads, and that any detractors would be punished.[108]

---

105   KRSW 6647, 285–88; S. Yerusalimski, (no title), *Evreiskaia starina* V, 334–5.
106   KRSW 6648, 5.
107   KRSW 6649, 3–8.
108   KRSW 6649, fol. 6–8. See also a similar series of complaints by the Piotrków Synagogue Council, fol. 307.

Satisfied, Alter joined Muszkat and Dov Ber Meisels, the new chief rabbi of Warsaw, in issuing yet another call to Polish Jewry to comply with official clothing restrictions in the kingdom, while explicitly warning women to cease wearing *tichels*, or traditional head coverings. A married woman could conceal her short hair, but only by means of other kinds of head-coverings.[109] Fourteen years later, the Chief Rabbi of Warsaw, Jakob Gesundheit, would sign a reiteration of these decrees.[110]

When it came to head-shaving, the custom's relatively short history and checkered ritual legal past enabled Polish and Russian rabbinic authorities more latitude than the case of clothing and beards. By re-prohibiting female head-shaving, they probably hoped to spare their communities another ordeal. One commentator charged that those rabbis who advocated female head-shaving only encouraged the more problematic practice of donning wigs. They were "shepherds without knowledge [who] did not know or understand that this prohibited custom [i.e., headshaving], while intended as a good deed and a 'fence,' caused all of the Torah to be breached and that there is 'a time for silence.'"[111] The controversy over female head-shaving continues to reverberate in contemporary ultra-orthodox society, for Hungarian rabbinic authorities have vigorously upheld the custom.[112]

Conclusion

A reconstruction of documentary sources presents Isaac Meir Alter as a scholarly, pious yet politically sophisticated leader cautiously navigating his

---

109   Issued in 1857; printed in full in the YIVO Archives, Jacob Shatzky papers, Series II, folder 58; and in *Izraelita* 13 (1871): 103. Jagodzińska apparently means this 1857 decree when referring to a decree signed "by Meisels in 1851 (*sic*)," since Meisels was not appointed Rabbi of Warsaw until 1856. See her *Pomiędzy: akulturacja*, 117.
110   *Izraelita* 13 (1871): 104; S. Yerusalimski, (no title), *Evreiskaia starina* v, 334–8.
111   Moshe ben Nahum Katzenellenbogen, *Ha-torah ve-ha-mitzvah* (Szczecin, 1865), 79, no. 30.
112   Menasseh Klein attributes the appearance of the mysterious custom to a decree of the Council of Four Lands, which I have been unable to verify. See *Mishneh ha-halakhot* part 12, no. 85. Yitzhak Yaakov Weiss, *Minhat yitzhak* (Jerusalem, 1993), part 7, no. 3, does not speculate on when it occurred, but observes that "it is said that those from the Russian countries that there was a decree there that women must grow the hair on their heads, and because the decree was enacted they reverted to the prohibitions" of the Shulhan arukh and others. Weiss, who was of Hungarian descent, emphasizes the problem of *hatzitza* (obstructions during immersion), and brings the well-known Zoharic custom of female head-shaving ("Parshat Nasso") and the well-known Hatam Sofer ("Even ha-ezer," no. 36) for support.

community's Diasporic existence within a colonized Polish entity in a way that effectively preserved outward differences. Gerer court historians of the interwar period re-imagined Alter in a way that transfigured him into a symbol of ultra-orthodox purity and defiance, most importantly by effacing his vocal support of mitigated clothing decrees from Hasidic memory and substituting a legend of conscientious objection. Their version, which has spread well beyond the Hasidic fold, making its way into the modern historiography, is refuted by documentary evidence and simple logic: Jewish leaders in the kingdom sought and found ways to maintain the desired level of sartorial differentiation. It was only rank and file Jews who suffered from police harassment and humiliation in the process.

Yet it is not this chapter's purpose to merely debunk Gerer Hasidic collective memory, let alone discredit Hasidic hagiography in general. The attempt by Gerer court historians to hypostatize individual cases of harassment, self-sacrifice, and impassioned protest into the figure of Isaac Meir Alter may not hold up to scrutiny, but their narrative does succeed in evoking the widespread anxiety and indignation that altered, for many decades, the complexion of Polish Jewish society.[113]

In the end, the colonial Russian regime's attempt to coerce Jews, an unemancipated diasporic minority, into outwardly resembling western Europeans, Russians, and possibly (but not necessarily) colonized Polish Christians seemed to only increase the Jewish community's will to preserve and re-inscribe its outer differences. It was not so much the clothing decrees themselves, riddled as they were with loopholes and exemptions, as their crude and arbitrary enforcement—the fees, fines, shavings, beatings, inspections, and so on—that made it impossible to continue to adhere to Jewish sartorial customs passively. The humiliating nature of enforcement, moreover, made the dominant society appear morally and culturally inferior, belying its supposed civilizing agenda and undermining the case for integration. The clumsy enforcement simply raised the stakes on Jewish dress.

---

113 Amos Funkenstein has observed that the historian, too, is "unwillingly a captive of his own point of view.... He may sincerely intend to tell the truth... but his eyesight and account are blurred and blocked by deep cultural, even linguistic structures that bind him to his own time and place." See Funkenstein, *Perceptions of Jewish History* (Berkeley: University of California Press, 1993), 23. Jan Vansina's calls on scholars of collective memory to "always try to check on as many sources of error and falsification as possible, while at the same time avoiding a hypercritical attitude which would end in rejecting *a priori* all testimonies whatsoever," in *Oral Tradition: A Study in Historical Methodology* (trans. H.M. Wright; Chicago: Aldine, 1965), 112. I am grateful to Jonathan Boyarin for suggesting these readings.

The entire affair ultimately played into the hands of figures like Alter, who spurned integration, acculturation, and bourgeois tastes, yet wished to remain law-abiding subjects. At the same time, Polish Jewish traditionalism did not take on the militancy of its Hungarian counterpart, which espoused secessionist "ultra-orthodoxy." Few Polish rabbinical leaders resembled R. Akiva Joseph Schlesinger (1837–1922), who (mis)interpreted the teachings of Moses Sofer ("Hatam Sofer," 1762–1839) in such a manner as to mandate female head-shaving and male sartorial uniformity while fiercely proscribing social contact with Jews who did not conform.[114] The acute moral panic evinced in Hungarian rabbinic literature would not appear in its Polish counterpart until the secular Jewish cultural awakening following the 1905 Revolution. And even then, Polish traditionalists tended to preserve the compromise solutions forged by Alter and his contemporaries. Statements in the interwar period by the then Gerer *rebbe*, Abraham Mordecai Alter, to the effect that "he who shortens his clothes shortens his spiritual life" only implied a continued rejection of the "Western" option. The Russian option had long ceased to be Russian.[115]

Another distinctive feature of the emergent Polish Jewish traditionalism was tactical. Alter's careful, coordinated campaigns marked an important stage in the evolution of Polish Jewish *shtadlanut* (political intercession) for, although it would be a stretch to identify Hasidic machinations in this period with modern Jewish politics, we do see a refinement and expansion of *shtadlanut* to include collaboration among Hasidim, non-Hasidic traditionalists, and integrationists, eventually cementing what has been sardonically termed an "unholy alliance" in communal politics.[116] The clothing decrees affair marked one of the first overtures towards Polish Jewish integrationists, who were a good deal

---

114 Akiva Schlesinger, *Lev ha-ivri* (Lemberg, 1869), esp. 67–8; Silber, "The Emergence of Ultra-Orthodoxy: the Invention of a Tradition." Jacob Katz highlights the "awareness of other Jews' rejection of tradition" in Hungarian traditionalism. See "Orthodoxy in Perspective," 4. For some preliminary comparisons between Hungarian and Polish orthodoxy, see Moshe Samet, "The Beginnings of Orthodoxy," *Modern Judaism* 8.3 (1988): 249–69. Frieda Veizel, who is writing her M.A. thesis on this topic at Sarah Lawrence College, brought Schlesinger's interpretations of the Hatam Sofer to my attention, for which I am grateful.

115 Letter from 1822 to the "Rabbi of Kirchendorf," printed in *Osef mikhtavim ve-k"k admor shelitah mi-gur* (Augustburg, 1947), 35. On the impact of the 1905 Revolution on Polish Jewish cultural change, see the latter chapters in this volume; and on social change, see Scott Ury, *Barricades and Banners: The Revolution of 1905 and the Transformation of Warsaw Jewry* (Stanford, CA: Stanford University Press, 2012).

116 For an attempt to frame Hasidic lobbying in terms of modern Jewish politics, see Wodziński, *Hasidism and Politics* (Oxford: Littman Library of Jewish Civilization, 2013), esp. 295–6. For the more restrained interpretation, see Bartal and Assaf, "Shtadlanut

less anti-Hasidic and otherwise ideologically-driven than the kingdom's isolated maskilim, and who sometimes proved willing to intervene with officials to mitigate perceived assaults on the Jewish tradition. While we have focused on Abraham Winawer's intercessions, it should also be noted that the Jewish integrationist Jacob Tugendhold intervened on Alter's behalf on several occasions, as well—once to suppress the publication of an anti-Hasidic romance, another time to counteract planned educational reforms.[117] Russian rabbinical leaders, in contrast, both lacked an equivalent loophole and had to contend with idealistic maskilim who were stronger, more numerous, and more politically assertive in the Pale than their rare counterparts in the Kingdom of Poland.[118] Alter's collaborations may not have sat well with interwar Hasidim, but they were emblematic of Jewish life in the Warsaw metropolis, where variant cultural and religious groups not only cohabitated but cooperated.[119]

The Warsaw metropolis was not, however, an ideal setting for a Hasidic court. In 1859, after Menahem Mendel of Kotzk passed away and Alter was

---

ve-ortodoksiyah." On the "unholy alliance," see Shatzky, *Geshikhte fun yidn in varshe*, III: 141.

117 Tugendhold's order to censor the anti-Hasidic manuscript in 1862, on the grounds that "a very significant portion of the Israelite people in the Kingdom and Empire, of which the vast majority are actually pious and moral," appears in "Materiyalin un notitzen," *YIVO Bleter* X (1936): 364–5. Marcus Jastrow claims that Tugendhold attempted to stymie educational reform at the prompting of Hasidim; see his letter to R. Jacob Raisin, in the Jacob Shatzky papers, YIVO archives, RG 356.

118 On Russian maskilim and their role in the affair, see Lederhendler, *Road to Modern Politics*, 97–8. On the weakness of Haskalah in the Kingdom of Poland, see Raphael Mahler, *Hasidism and the Jewish Enlightenment: Their Confrontation in Galicia and Poland in the First Half of the Nineteenth Century* (trans. Eugene Orenstain, Aaron Klein, and Jenny Machlowitz Klein; Philadelphia, PA: Jewish Publication Society, 1985): "it is as though the Haskalah bypassed this country [the Kingdom of Poland]" (203). On crucial distinction between maskilim like Abraham Stern and more radical Polish Jewish integrationists like Eisenbaum and Tugendhold, see Dynner, *Yankel's Tavern*, 169–171; and idem, "On the Borders of Haskalah."

119 There are indications that the collaborations embarrassed Alter. One Hasidic hagiographical account has him approaching a prominent acculturated Jew for help contravening an impending decree only to find him eating non-kosher food. *Si'ah sarfe kodesh*, III: 74. For a similar episode, see II: 112. Another has him agreeing to act as *sandek* (godfather) at the circumcision of the son of an acculturated Jew on a Sabbath, only to discover several Jews smoking cigarettes during the ceremony (ibid., IV: 102). Another has him being chased down by an acculturated Jew eager to shake the hand of a celebrity, which he agreed to do very reluctantly (ibid., IV: 102). On Hasidic collaboration with prominent acculturated Jews in general, see Bartal and Assaf, "Shtadlanut ve-ortodoksiyah."

crowned as *rebbe*, Warsaw police were soon perplexed by "throngs" of unkempt Hasidim pouring in from the provinces hoping to gain audience with Alter at 1015 Krochmalna Street, "a sorry sight for both us and them, and setting a bad example for our children." The report begged the government to "instruct us to expel the rabbi of these Hasids [Isaac Meir Alter], along with his throngs, to some small town; to make the Hasids apply for passports since most enter Warsaw without them; and to require them to change their old-style clothes and shave their beards." Clearly, the clothing decrees had made little headway among them.[120]

Alter responded prudently, of course. He initially moved his court to Eisengas Street, which had a sparser Jewish population, but soon relocated to Góra Kalwaria, a small town near Warsaw.[121] Góra Kalwaria was a more attractive setting for a Hasidic court anyhow, enabling better control of communal appointments, more rigid Jewish-Christian separation, and less contact with prominent acculturated Jews. At the same time, thanks to the town's close proximity to Warsaw, Alter continued to visit the capital on "state" matters, negotiating and collaborating, as was his way.[122]

---

120   AGAD CWW 1871, 306–7.
121   Ostensibly, he moved his court to shield young followers from the commercial and cosmopolitan influences of the big city: *Si'ah sarfe kodesh*, V: 33; Yitzhak Alfasi, *Gur* (Tel Aviv: Sinai, 1978), 68; Shatzky, *Geshikhte fun yidn in varshe*, III: 357. See also R. Yehudah Leib Alter of Ger, *Language of Truth: The Torah Commentary of the Sefat Emet* (trans. and commentary Arthur Green; Lincoln, NE: University of Nebraska Press, 1998), xxv; and Eleonora Bergman's dismissal of the traditional view, in "Gora Kalvariya", in Rachel Elior, Yisrael Bartal, and Chone Shmeruk, eds., *Tzaddikim ve-anshe ma'aseh*, 111, no. 2.
122   On Hasidic leaders' preference for small-town environments for their Hasidic courts, see Dynner, "Hasidism and Habitat," 104–30. On the impact of Alter's settlement on Góra Kalwarya, see Bergman, "Gora Kalvariya;" eadem, "Góra Kalwaria: The Impact of a Hasidic Cult on the Urban Landscape of a Small Polish Town," *Polin* 5 (1990): 3–23; and "Rusland," *Ha-Magid* (1866), 100.

CHAPTER 5

From Community to Metropolis: The Jews of Warsaw, 1850–1880

François Guesnet

In the course of one generation, between 1850 and 1880, the number of registered inhabitants of Warsaw more than doubled, from around 150,000 to ca 300,000.[1] In the same period of time, the number of Jews registered as inhabitants in the Polish capital grew threefold, from below 40,000 to more than 120,000.[2] It formed the largest Jewish settlement in the world, and at the time, surpassed any other Jewish community of European diasporic history. In the earlier decades of the nineteenth century, Jews originated from smaller towns and the countryside of the central Polish provinces; later, a steady influx of Jews from the Tsarist Empire added to this internal process of urbanization. As contemporary observers stated from the mid-nineteenth century, they formed an agglomeration of co-existing smaller units, defined by origin, religious persuasion, and cultural choices. Jewish and non-Jewish contemporaries alike were well aware of this extremely dynamic demographic process. Jewish observers worried about the consequences of this dynamism, realizing early on that a more traditional communal set-up of community would be subverted by the sheer number of Jews living in the capital. And in fact, the period between the middle and late nineteenth century offers a number of striking changes in the institutional fabric of the community. During this period, demographic, political and cultural changes heralded the emergence of the first Jewish metropolis, a place which "breaks the cake of custom," as Robert

---

1   For a table of the development of the Jewish population in Warsaw, see François Guesnet, *Polnische Juden im 19. Jahrhundert: Lebensbedingungen, Rechtsnormen und Organisation im Wandel* (Cologne and Vienna: Böhlau, 1998), 34 (henceforth Guesnet, *Polnische Juden*).
2   Numerous anecdotal references testify to the substantial difference between registered and unregistered inhabitants in Polish towns of the period: the actual number of inhabitants was invariably significantly higher than those registered in the official records, cf. Shatzky, *Geshikhte fun yidn in varshe*, vol. III, 115. The administrative procedure to become a registered inhabitant remained cumbersome and expensive even after the emancipation of 1861, as a local resident commented in 1902 in the Polish-language weekly *Izraelita*, adding that a third of the Jews living in Warsaw—sometimes for a long period—were not registered, cf. Guesnet, *Polnische Juden*, 42.

Park famously posited in his description of the impact of the large city on its inhabitants. At the same time, Warsaw would be the arena of true metropolitan dialectics and allow traditionalist Jewish communities to thrive, form new alliances and challenge competitors on a whole new level.[3]

Around 1850, the Jews of Warsaw constituted a young community. The first cemetery had been founded just two generations ago by Shmuel Zbytkower, a wealthy army contractor and banker, on the east bank of the Vistula river due to settlement prohibitions in the Polish capital proper.[4] From a couple of thousand Jews living in the Praga suburbs and within the noble precincts, called *jurydiki*, exempt from the capital's *privilegium de non tolerandis judaeis*, the Warsaw Jewish community grew into a significant regional center with around forty thousand registered Jewish inhabitants in 1850. The communal leadership would be securely in the hands of the *misnagdim*, the traditional rabbinical observant community. Their hegemony, though, was challenged by an ever growing hasidic community and a small, but influential group of wealthy Jews—bankers, tax farmers, army contractors and industrialists—who would attempt to adapt the precepts of the German-Jewish reform to the realities of partitioned Poland. At the end of this period, Jewish Warsaw had grown into the largest Jewish settlement in the world, functioning according to its own unique set of rules.[5] The Jews formed new types of alliances among themselves and with non-Jews, and inserted themselves into the capital's social fabric and urban landscape. During this period, political challenges of a new kind arose—with episodes like the antisemitic agitation of the journalistic polemic known as the "Jewish War" and the neo-romantic Polish-Jewish rapprochement of 1861. The January Uprising of 1863 against Russian dominion challenged the political identifications of Warsaw Jews, with individual Jews becoming highly visible agents of political contestation. Since the emancipation of 1862, Jews could settle wherever they could afford to buy or to rent, resulting in the emergence of densely populated Jewish neighbourhoods just north of the city center. Thousands, if not tens of thousands of Jews from the Pale of Settlement, know as *Litvaks*, arrived in Warsaw and found themselves

---

3   Robert E. Park: "Human Migration and the Marginal Man," *The American Journal of Sociology*, XXXIII (1928), reprinted in Richard Sennett (ed.), *Classic Essays on the Culture of Cities* (Englewood Cliffs, NJ: Prentice Hall, 1969), 131–42.
4   See Glenn Dynner, *Men of Silk. The Hasidic Conquest of Polish Jewish Society* (Oxford: Oxford University Press, 2006), especially 25–54, 89–116.
5   This administrative entity had come into being as a result of the Congress of Vienna in 1815 and therefore was also known as Congress Poland, or *Kongresówka*, in Polish.

in one of the most dynamic centers of trade and finance of the Russian Empire. After the expulsion from Moscow in 1891, many more were yet to come.[6]

In 1881, Warsaw no longer had a chief rabbinate, while its community board had been replaced by a so-called "community administration" (Pol. *Zarząd Gminy*), controlled by Jewish integrationists (pol. *postępowcy*). This façade institution had, however, no control over the most substantial needs of the vast majority of Warsaw Jewry, and a thriving, highly complex network of individual, associational, and administrative forms of support emerged. Another process culminated in 1881 as well: after numerous smaller incidents and minor riots, Catholic Poles went on a three-day rampage against their Jewish neighbors, much to the shock and dismay of the more enlightened members of the Polish and Jewish public, who had thought that the events of Southern Russia would not and could not occur in Poland.

For the first level of analysis, the transformations of Warsaw's communal institutions will be used to illustrate the profound organizational shifts in the Jewish street, revealing a movement away from a coherent community. The following section will investigate three forms of encounters within metropolitan Jewish and non-Jewish spaces. First, I propose to understand the widespread practice of Torah processions as a tool of inner-Jewish cohesion. Secondly, I will investigate the encounter of Jewish and non-Jewish masses in the streets of Warsaw as a means of collective self-assertion in the multinational metropolis. Thirdly, I will invoke the parks of Warsaw and their use by Warsaw Jews to offer some insights into the realities of urban spaces that held out the promise of openness and neutrality, but which were nonetheless defined by complex modes of in- and exclusion.

"Litvaks" and the Demographics of an Emerging Metropolis

Around 1840, the authorities of Warsaw registered 36,934 Jewish inhabitants in the capital of the Kingdom of Poland. At that moment, it was already by far the largest community in the kingdom, with four to five times more Jewish inhabitants than the second largest community, Lublin.[7] Warsaw became the main destination for the internal migrations of Jews and non-Jews in a period marked by dynamic urbanization. Jews had more reason to leave the countryside and

---

6 François Guesnet, "Migration et stéréotype: Le cas des Juifs russes au Royaume de Pologne à la fin du XIX siècle," *Cahiers du Monde russe* 41.4 (2000) 4, 505–18.
7 S. Warszawski, "Struktura społeczna i gospodarcza żydowstwa warszawskiego w 1840 roku," *Miesięcznik Żydowski* 1.2 (1930/31), 245–62, here 250.

the small towns than their non-Jewish neighbours, as they were confronted with sustained efforts by the authorities to drive Jews out of one of their main trades, namely the production and distribution of alcohol (Pol. *propinacja*).[8] Also, until the partial emancipation of 1861, the Jews of the Kingdom of Poland were not allowed to settle with twenty kilometers from the border.[9]

In contrast to the more senior Jewish communities in Poznań, Kraków, Vilna or Lemberg, going back to the earliest phases of Jewish settlement in the late medieval period, the communal self-image of Warsaw Jews was shaped by a sense of fragmentation, owing to the recent immigration of Jews from a great variety of places of origin. Thus, a letter from Warsaw to the Magdeburg-based *Israelitische Wochenschrift* read in 1874 that "we have plenty of Jews here, but not a community."[10] The most remarkable influx began in the 1860s and stemmed from the Western provinces of the Russian Empire, profoundly impacting the Jews in Warsaw and Jewish–non-Jewish relations. These immigrant Jews would later be identified as *Litvaks*, as Jews from Lithuanian territories, despite their broader range of places of origin. Their presence would inspire a whole range of images and stereotypes.[11]

Jews had started to move to the Kingdom of Poland from the Empire since the Russian suppression of the Polish uprising of 1863. The first—though not the last—Jew from Lithuanian territories to join the Warsaw Synagogue Supervisory Board would be the army contractor Ziml Epshteyn who had come to the Polish capital even earlier, in the aftermath of the November Uprising 1830.[12] Trade between the Kingdom of Poland and the Russian Empire and the need for trade representatives with intimate knowledge of

---

[8] The vast majority of Jewish households residing in the countryside would rely in their livelihoods on the production and distribution of alcohol, as well as innkeeping, see Gershon Hundert, *The Jews of Poland-Lithuania in the Eighteenth Century. A Genealogy of Modernity* (Berkeley, CA: University of California Press, 2004), 53; for a detailed analysis of the developments in the 19th century see Jürgen Hensel, "Polnische Adelsnation und jüdische Vermittler 1815–1830: Über den vergeblichen Versuch einer Judenemanzipation in einer nicht emanzipierten Gesellschaft," in *Forschungen zur Osteuropäischen Geschichte* 23 (1883), 7–227, and most recently, Glenn Dynner, *Yankel's Tavern. Jews, Liquor, and Life in the Kingdom of Poland* (Oxford: Oxford University Press, 2014), especially 82–102.

[9] Artur Eisenbach: *Z dziejów ludności żydowskiej w Polsce w XVIII i XIX wieku* (Warszawa: Państwowy Instytut Wydawniczy 1983), 142.

[10] Cited after Shatzky, *Geshikhte fun yidn in varshe*, vol. III, 122.

[11] Guesnet, "Migration et stéréotype," 507.

[12] Shatzky, *Geshikhte fun yidn in varshe*, vol. II, 86. Later *litvishe* members of the Supervisory Board would be e.g. members of the Korngold (from Kobryn) and Frumkin (from Grodno) families, ibid., vol. III, 121–22.

the Russian markets triggered their settlement in the main urban centers of Warsaw and later Łódź.[13] An additional factor was that until 1874, Jews in the Kingdom of Poland could seek exemption from the conscription to military service. Wielopolski's emancipatory legislation for the Kingdom of Poland, enacted in June 1862, abolished restrictions in matters of professional activity and settlement with very few exceptions.[14] Also, the demise of the January Uprising 1863–64 and measures implementing Russian as language of all levels of administration and the judiciary offered opportunities for people with the necessary language qualifications—in private enterprises, but also as freelance translators, authors, or clerks.[15] In the mid-1880s, a correspondent of a Russian-Jewish weekly commented that "physicians, lawyers and other representatives of so-called academic professions in large numbers go to Łódź."[16] Before the Uprising, the settlement of Jews from the Russian Empire went practically unnoticed, as the newcomers would be quickly absorbed in the large local Jewish community.[17] After the Uprising, as Russian-Jewish immigration increased and sensitivities about shifts in cultural affiliations grew, this situation changed. In the mid-1870s, the Polish-language and integrationist weekly *Izraelita* commented on the growing concerns about the newcomers:

> Those who know the reasons and the economic consequences of this immigration will refrain from claiming that it is of harm to the local entrepreneurs, or that in fact it constitutes an invasion. To the contrary, whoever is familiar with the trade relations to the [Russian] Empire will admit that the considerable increase in industrial output is due for a large measure, or even perhaps entirely, to these newcomers. Who are they? Well, go and ask any merchant or industrialist, they will tell you:

---

13 Artur Eisenbach, "Mobilność terytorialna ludności żydowskiej w Królestwie Polskim," in Witold Kula (ed.), *Społeczeństwo Królestwa Polskiego: Studia o uwarstwowieniu i ruchliwośći społecznej*, vol. 2 (Warszawa: Państwowe Wydawnictwo Naukowe, 1966), 177–316, here 287–315; Shatzky, *Geshikhte fun yidn in varshe*, vol. III, 374; Elżbieta Kaczyńska, *Społeczeństwo i gospodarka północno-wschodnich ziem Królestwa Polskiego w okresie rozkwitu kapitalizmu* (Warszawa: Rozprawy Uniwersytetu Warszawskiego, 1974), 41–43.

14 Antony Polonsky, *The Jews in Poland and Russia*, vol. 1 (Oxford and Portland, OR: Littman Library for Jewish Civilization, 2010), 299–314. For a contemporary discussion of 1863 as a turning point in the immigration of Russian Jews see "Pogadanki," *Izraelita* 37 (1879), 303.

15 The linguistic qualifications and familiarity with Russian administrative procedures were frequently cited as an important factor for the success of the Litvak settlement in the Kingdom, see "Kronika," *Izraelita* 34 (1877), 275 and "Pogadanki," ibid. 30 (1878), 249.

16 Guesnet, "Migration et stéréotype," 509.

17 Shatzky, *Geshikhte fun yidn in varshe*, vol. III, 374.

these are the salesmen who connect the [Russian] wholesale merchants and our local industrialists with the nearby and far away regions of the Empire.[18]

After slow beginnings in the mid-nineteenth century and a much more visible settlement of Jews from Russia after the January Uprising, a new stage was reached after the wave of anti-Jewish violence in the southern provinces of the Russian Empire and the ensuing hardening of Russian state policies towards the Jewish population.[19] Most notably, Jewish residence in the countryside was restricted, leading to widespread expulsions, a cap on enrollment of Jewish university students was introduced, and existing restrictions on residence were enforced with much more rigor, for example in Kiev.[20] In his memoir, the Bundist activist Avraham Kotik reflects on the fact that fear of violence and persecution prompted his parents to relocate from the Ukrainian metropolis to Warsaw in 1881—the year at the end of which, as will be discussed later, the first full scale pogrom took place in the Polish capital.[21] The most visible influx of Jews from the Russian Empire would occur after the expulsions of 20–30.000 Jews residing in Moscow, which started in April 1891.[22] Inspired by nationalist sentiments and with the intention to de-judaize the Russian capital, they ended in September 1892 with the highly symbolic closing of the

---

18 "W kwestji Żydów handlujących z Cesarstwa," *Izraelita* 39 (1876), 307. Further evidence for the intensifying settlement of entrepreneurs from Imperial Russia is the publication in 1880 of a Warsaw city guide in the Russian language geared towards businesspeople: "Z tygodnia," *Izraelita* 30 (1880), 240. So far, it has not been possible to locate a copy of this publication.

19 For a comprehensive analysis of the violence occurring in the Russian Empire, see John D. Klier, *Russians, Jews, and the Pogroms of 1881–82* (Cambridge: Cambridge University Press, 2011), passim, and Polonsky, *The Jews in Poland and Russia*, vol. 2 (2010), 3–39.

20 Benjamin Nathan: *Beyond the Pale: The Jewish Encounter with Late Imperial Russia* (Berkeley, CA: University of California Press, 2002), 257–307; Jews were expelled from Kiev several times during the 1880s, with thousands of individuals forced to leave the city at least for a certain amount of time. Although many returned soon after the expulsions, the growing precariousness of living conditions made a resettlement in a safer place in the Empire, e.g. Warsaw, a plausible strategy; Natan M. Meir, *Kiev, Jewish Metropolis: A History, 1859–1914* (Bloomington, IN: Indiana University Press 2010), 104–5.

21 Abraham Kotik, *Dos lebn fun a idishn inteligent* (New York: Farlag Toybenshlag, 1925), 26–27.

22 For the most comprehensive recent discussion of the circumstances and the implementation of the expulsions see Yvonne Kleinmann, *Neue Orte—neue Menschen: Jüdische Lebensformen in St. Petersburg und Moskau im 19. Jahrhundert* (Hamburg: Vandenhoeck & Ruprecht, 2006), 348–87.

Minor Synagogue and the expulsion of Rabbi Zalkind Minor, affiliated with this place of worship. Although no robust statistical material is available about numbers of Jews from Moscow settling in the Kingdom of Poland, anecdotal evidence suggests their high visibility in provincial centers like Zamość and Radom, and in urban centers like Łódź and above all, Warsaw. It seems quite obvious that Russian Jews established themselves at times fairly quickly on the basis of business relations developed in earlier years. *Izraelita* observed:

> In Warsaw, one now meets Jews in Russian dress and speaking Russian. More and more shops carry a sign "De Pétersbourg" or "De Moscou." Russian Jews have opened in 1891 and 1892 over one hundred shops and workshops. The newcomers have established their own associations in order to facilitate their establishment, in which they succeeded. They have successfully taken the shoe trade into their hands, and now also want to control the production of shoes.[23]

The settlement of a considerable number of Russian-Jewish businesspeople and tradesmen in the Polish capital in the 1890s enlarged a pre-existing visible sub-community of Russian Jews who had kept close ties with the Empire, and were familiar with the Russian language and administration. Culturally, they were unreceptive to the Hasidic movement, indifferent to the Polish cause, and rather unsympathetic to those local Jews who would consider Polonization a viable cultural trajectory. In their early nationalist fervor, these young student members of the Russian-Jewish community in 1884 wrote to Yehuda Leyb Levin (1844–1925), the pioneer of poetry in Modern Hebrew and early sympathizer with the *Hibat Tsion* movement:

> The miserable situation of the Jews has awoken our sympathies for the Jewish nation, whereas the local youth in Warsaw, and especially the progressives, are thoroughly indifferent to the Jewish question. They believe themselves to be Poles of Mosaic Persuasion. This is why we, Lithuanian Jews in Warsaw, have to awaken their feelings for their own people.[24]

---

23 "Kronika," *Izraelita* 12 (1893), 101. The article is in part a comment on and a translation of an article in *Novoe Vremia*, a Russian daily close to the imperial administration, with the St. Petersburg daily expressing some pride in these Russian-Jewish successes in refractory Warsaw.

24 Cited after Shatzky, *Geshikhte fun yidn in varshe*, vol. III, 375.

The establishment of Russian Jews in Warsaw after the January Uprising offered living proof of the possibility of alternative political, religious and cultural identifications. This, combined with their economic prowess, constituted an important factor in the emerging resentment against Russian Jews expressed by Hasidic and integrationist Jews alike.[25] It is outside the purview of this chapter to discuss the later, very considerable impact of the Russian-Jewish presence on Polish-Jewish relations towards the end of the century. There is little doubt, however, that their arrival contributed significantly to the emergence of a metropolitan Jewish community characterized by the presence of a variety of sub-communities demarcated by religious affiliation, geographic origin, and preferred cultural and social contexts. More significant, however, would be the fading of any functional communal authority that could claim to govern the fate of this largest Jewish community in the world.

Communal Institutions

Several factors contributed to the emergence of a structure of co-existing centers of communal power and influence: the dismantling of institutions of traditional communal leadership by the government; competing claims to leadership formulated by traditional, rabbinic elites, the Hasidic movement, and members of a new, western-oriented bourgeois elite; the abolition of the chief rabbinate, and, closely connected to these processes, the willingness of an integrationist *inteligencja* to take up central functions in a newly created "Community Administration." The so-called *Zarząd Gminy*, functioning as the equivalent of the provincial Synagogue Supervisory Boards, developed a number of institutions and agencies of its own. The metropolitan community as such however, with its innumerable schools, confraternities, charities and places of worship, would develop without any significant input or supervision

---

25 Władysław Bartoszewski and Antony Polonsky, "Introduction," in Bartoszewski and Polonsky (eds.), *The Jews in Warsaw: A History* (Oxford: Blackwell, 1991), 21; Guesnet, "Migration et stéréotype," 516–17; Peter J. Martyn: "The Undefined Town Within a Town: A History of Jewish Settlement in the Western District of Warsaw," in Bartoszewski and Polonsky (eds.), *The Jews in Warsaw*, 55–83, here 67; Stephen D. Corrsin, "Aspects of Population Change and of Acculturation in Jewish Warsaw at the end of the Nineteenth Century: The Censuses of 1882 and 1897," in Bartoszewski and Polonsky (eds.), *The Jews in Warsaw*, 212–31, here 222–23.

from the Community Administration, the latter not amounting to much more than a disconnected administrative façade.[26]

In comparison to Jewish communities of the early modern period in other parts of the European diaspora, the prerogatives of the community board (Hebr. *kahal*) in the Polish-Lithuanian commonwealth in matters of communal governance were exceptionally far-reaching, as has been frequently discussed and demonstrated in scholarship.[27] This held true for the whole of the early modern period, independent of an individual community's relative seniority: a community as recent as that in the emerging industrial centre of Łódź would feature the full range of representative communal bodies, charities and institutions, a variegated structure that would remain essentially unchallenged until the late nineteenth century.[28] Parallel to the other Jewish communities in the Kingdom of Poland, the traditional *kahal* in Warsaw would be abolished in 1822 and replaced by the so-called Synagogue Supervisory Board (Pol. *dozór bóżniczy*), introduced for this purpose in 1821.[29] This new would-be community board was a state subsidiary and accountable to the local authorities. As in most other Jewish communities in the Kingdom of Poland, the civil leadership in Warsaw belonged to the top tier of Jewish merchants and entrepreneurs. It was, however, based on a different electoral system. The Jews of Warsaw elected their community representatives by voting in their individual congregations for electoral delegates. These in turn would gather in the city hall on election day and in a first round of votes establish a list of candidates consisting of fifteen names—without any restriction on who could be named. The fifteen individuals named most often would become candidates, and from among them

---

26 The abolition of the chief rabbinate is discussed in more detail by Shaul Stampfer in his contribution to this volume.

27 For an interesting contrasting comparison of the prerogatives of the Jewish civil leadership in the medieval and early modern period, see Stefanie B. Siegmund, "Communal Leaders (rashei qahal) and the Representation of Medieval and Early Modern Jews as 'Communities'," in Jack Wertheimer (ed.), *Jewish Religious Leadership: Image and Reality*, vol. 1 (New York: JTS Publications, 2004), 333–70, as well as David Ruderman, *Early Modern Jewry: A New Cultural History* (Princeton, NJ: Princeton University Press, 2010), ch. 2, 57–98, especially 86–93.

28 In this respect, the comparison between the communities of Poznań, among the eldest in the commonwealth, and Swarzędz, founded in the 17th century, as proposed by Anna Michałowska-Mycielska: *The Jewish Community: Authority and Social Control in Poznań and Swarzędz, 1650–1793* (Wrocław: Wydawnictwo Uniwersytetu Wrocławskiego, 2008), is especially relevant.

29 See Guesnet, *Polnische Juden*, 223–29 for this legislation and further literature.

the delegates were supposed to name their top five.[30] In a second round, five candidates from among the list of fifteen with the highest number of cast votes and cast their votes. Delegates from around one hundred such congregations in Warsaw and in Praga participated in the elections—e.g. in the year 1839, representing around three quarters of the eight thousand registered families in Warsaw as a whole.[31] These were probably the most democratic local elections in the entire Russian Empire throughout the entire nineteenth century. This electoral system would guarantee a majority of *misnagdim* (adherents of a traditional rabbinical observance) and followers of various Hasidic communities, and as Jakob Shatzky pointed out, many misnagdic members of the Supervisory Board in this period had "strong streaks of enlightenment."[32] Despite the deep and lasting disagreements between these two variants of traditional Judaism, the ongoing confrontation with Russian legislation and Polish administrative regulations on taxation, dress, and attempts to regulate or restrict Jewish economic activities, members of the Warsaw Synagogue Supervisory Board tended toward selective cooperation.[33] Mirroring the situation in most other Polish communities, the Synagogue Supervisory Board in Warsaw would accept that despite the abolition of the *kahal* and all other traditional forms of religious and charitable confraternities, these associations would continue to exist and function. More than that: the outlawed confraternities would continue to provide most of the funds necessary for upholding the activities of the community board in religious, educational and charitable matters.

Of central relevance in this context was the continued activity of the Burial Society (Hebr. *hevra kadisha*). In Warsaw, the notables of the Jewish community had reacted to the formal abolition of this and other confraternities by creating the so-called "Burial Administration" (Pol. *Administracja Pogrzebowa*).[34] Its main documented income would consist in a nominal burial fee, representing however only a small fraction of its actual income. As was the case before the abolition of the *Hevra Kadisha*, the heads of the Burial Administration would impose payments from the families of deceased community members

---

30   Guesnet, *Polnische Juden*, 404–10.
31   Shatzky, *Geshikhte fun yidn in varshe*, vol. II, 53. The number of places of worship would increase through the whole of the 19th century to reach more than three hundred and eighty officially registered Jewish places of worship in 1904, see Guesnet, *Polnische Juden*, 346, and more recently Eleonore Bergman, *'Nie masz bóżniczy powszechnej.' Synagogi i domy modlitwy w Warszawie od końca XVIII do początku XX wieku* (Warszawa: DiG 2007).
32   Shatzky, ibid., 86. Shatzky's formula is "maskilish shtark farshpitst."
33   Ibid.
34   Guesnet, *Polnische Juden*, 370.

at their discretion. These funds, which still constituted the largest source of income for the Supervisory Board, would be administered independently from it, thus effectively undermining the purpose of the 1822 legislation.[35] Well into the 1840s, the official budget submitted by the Supervisory Board to the authorities would not include details about income and expenses connected to burial.[36] Similar to the traditional *hevrot kadisha* in their attempt to maintain and control religious observance, the Burial Administration in Warsaw would sanction perceived religious dissidence through discriminatory burial practices.[37] Accordingly, it would also keep control of a wide range of communal responsibilities. In the context of an official inquiry conducted in the whole of the Kingdom of Poland in 1843, prompted by revelations in Lublin about the continued activities of a *hevra kadisha*,[38] the Warsaw Synagogue Supervisory Board explained that "the [Warsaw, F.G.] Burial Administration is taking care of the burial of the dead, in itself an important religious service. Beyond that, it pursues the following charitable activities: 1) it gives clothes to the poor; 2) it funds religious schools; 3) it supports the poor with small amounts of money, with flour for Passover, and with firewood; 4) it administers a loan fund which gives out small amounts of money without interest." Its charitable tasks were thus almost identical those of the former *kahal*, except that it functioned without governmental approval and without the prerogatives of a recognized representative body of the Jewish community.[39]

The founding of the Warsaw Jewish Orphanage in 1840 reflects the emergence of a metropolitan Jewish elite. Over the years it developed a pattern of coordinated reactions to what it perceived as the most urgent needs of the ever-growing community. Following this pattern, representatives of the three most influential factions in the capital, namely the *misnagdim*, the upper echelons of the western-oriented bourgeoisie, and Hasidim would share responsibility for the task at hand. In the case of the orphanage, the task was the

---

35 In 1824, from an income of ca 23,000 złoty, the Burial Administration would cover 17,000, ibid.

36 Guesnet, *Polnische Juden*, 371.

37 Ignacy Schiper, *Żydzi Królestwa Polskiego w dobie powstania listopadowego* (Warszawa: F. Hoesick 1932), 43.

38 About the uncovering of the Burial Society in Lublin and the wide ramifications of this incident see Guesnet, *Polnische Juden*, 381–86. For a prewar discussion of the abolition of the *hevrot kadisha* see the master's thesis written under Majer Balaban's supervision by Dora Szterenkac, "Zniesienie kahałów i utworzenie dozorów bóżniczych w pierwszych latach Królestwa Polskiego" (M.A. thesis, Warsaw, n.d., preserved in the Jewish Historical Institute, Warsaw).

39 Guesnet, *Polnische Juden*, 373–74.

need to fend off Protestant missionaries' attempts to take advantage of the growing pauperization in the community by caring for Jewish orphans. Meir Berson (1801–1873), a banker, and also the head of the above mentioned Burial Administration, together with Zalman Abramson, a *misnaged*, and Meir Shahna Reykh, a Gerer *hasid*, jointly appealed to the Jews of Warsaw to fund this new institution, and in a short period of time collected a hundred thousand złoty in donations.[40] Another prominent banker, Itshak Shimon Rosen, bought the grounds on which the first building was opened in 1845, with an expansion opening in 1847. Shimon Rosen had come to Warsaw from German lands and was the father of Mathias Rosen (1804–1865), who would play a prominent role in Warsaw community politics from the 1840s onwards.[41] The founders established that the funds for the *Instytucya Dobroczynności* (Charity Institution) and its main institution, the *Dom Schronienia Starców i Sierot* (Almshouse), would come from the funds generated through burial services, from the lease on the kosher meat tax, as well as from the lease on the tax for wearing traditional Jewish garb.[42] De facto, these funds remained outside of the control of the Synagogue Supervisory Board, and thus outside of the control of the authorities.

In the case of both the Burial Administration and the Charity Institution, the trustees would represent the main denominations in the Jewish metropolis, and would fulfill their role independently from oversight of the Supervisory Board or the authorities. A major reconfiguration occured after the partial emancipation of the Jews in the Kingdom of Poland in June 1862, when the kosher meat tax was abolished and alternative sources of funding needed to be established. Among others, the almshouse would be one of the beneficiaries of public lotteries introduced in 1869, apportioning the funds to major religious charitable institutions in Warsaw, though in a manner not advantageous to the Jewish charity.[43]

Soon after the creation of the *Zarząd Gminy* in 1871, the energetic Ludwik Natanson (1822–1896) attempted to gain control of the board of trustees of the *Instytut Dobroczynności*, but failed.[44] Comparable "centrist" committees or

---

40   Shatzky, *Geshikhte fun yidn in varshe*, vol. II, 152.
41   François Guesnet: "Mathias Rosen," in Gershon Hundert (ed.), *YIVO Encyclopedia of Jews in Eastern Europe*, vol. II, 1591.
42   Shatzky, *Geshikhte fun yidn in varshe*, vol. II, 152.
43   Guesnet, *Polnische Juden*, 428.
44   Guesnet, *Polnische Juden*, 376. The review of the electoral system leading to the establishment of the *Zarząd Gminy* went hand in hand with the massive reduction of people with voting rights, from several thousand households able to vote for their electoral delegates

boards of trustees would emerge for a range of issues which the informal leading circles in the various Jewish denominations of Warsaw would consider too important to be left to the *Zarząd Gminy*. One of these was the *Erets-Yisroel-Kase*, which administered donations for the Jewish communities in the Holy Land. Among its trustees in the mid-nineteenth century would be the leader of the Gerer Hasidim, Itshak Meir Alter (1799–1866), the misnagdic head of the Synagogue Supervision Board, Moses Feinkind (1805–1869), the misnagdic and polonophile chief rabbi Dov Berush Meisels (1798–1870), as well as Jakob Gesundheit (1816–1878), the last chief rabbi of prewar Warsaw.[45]

In 1843, military conscription for Jews was introduced in the Kingdom of Poland. In contrast to the harsh cantonist system introduced by Nicolas I in Russia in 1827, which traumatized the Russian Jewish community for generations to come, Jews in the kingdom could be exempted from military service against a payment to the treasury in certain circumstances. Thus, all over the country committees would function to gather the necessary funds, which would remain legal until the introduction of compulsory military service in 1874. During this approximately thirty-year period, the Warsaw committee to redeem Jewish recruits counted among its trustees prominent misnagdic (members of the Prywes, Lothe, and Feinkind families) and Hasidic (Haskiel Bardlower) Jews, but also representatives of the bourgeois *inteligencja* (Ludwik Giwartowski).[46] An equally central task, namely visiting the sick in the Jewish hospital, would be entrusted to the confraternity *hevra bikur holim*, which enjoyed considerable communal prestige: at its yearly banquet, the members of the *hevra* would celebrate together with the medical staff, the trustees of the hospital—among them the decidedly integrationist banker Jozef Epstein—as well as representatives of the *Zarząd Gminy* and of the local rabbinate.[47] Until the so-called "unholy alliance" between hasidic and integrationist community leaders in 1871, discussed below, the rabbinate itself would be carefully balanced between *misnagdim* and sympathizers of the various hasidic communities.[48]

in their individual places of worship (see above, fn. 31) to a number in the lower hundreds, corresponding to a fraction of one percent of the adult Warsaw Jewish population, see Shatzky, *Geshikhte fun yidn in varshe*, vol. III, 116, 119, 125.

45 Shatzky, *Geshikhte fun yidn in varshe*, vol. II, 68, explains that in the mid-19th century, the average funds of this religious charity would exceed the yearly budget of the Synagogue Supervision Board.

46 Guesnet, *Polnische Juden*, 185–86. Every year, many hundred individuals donated to this committee, which had a yearly budget of up to ten thousand rubles, a quite considerable amount of money.

47 Ibid., 327.

48 Shatzky, *Geshikhte fun yidn in varshe*, vol. III, 133.

These examples of negotiation and coordination in a number of essential communal matters could be complemented with examples of *ad hoc* committees created in emergency situations like the cholera epidemic in 1892, all of which followed a similar pattern of cross-denominational cooperation.

This should however not obscure the fact that throughout the nineteenth century, and including the period under consideration in this chapter, an ongoing pattern of denominational competition became more prevalent and visible. In this competition, the *Zarząd Gminy* under Ludwik Natanson would indeed expand its activities in the last two decades of the nineteenth century, but it would never been accepted by the Jewish public as representing the community. Rather, it would be one player among several, and, because of the all too visible lack of connection to the Jewish street, not the most efficient.[49] The response to the ever growing needs of a rapidly increasing, impoverished metropolitan Jewish population through traditional religious charities as well as the *Zarząd Gminy* turned out to be less and less adequate towards the end of the century, hitting a low point in the first years of the twentieth century.[50] Several factors prevented a sustainable, efficient and adequate network of Jewish charitable organizations from emerging in the metropolis in this later stage: the overwhelming dynamic of the demographic development, the overall pauperization of the Jewish population, the slow adjustment of traditional forms of charitable work to the conditions of the modern city, the obsessively tight control of any form of associational life that discouraged charitable initiatives through extremely slow processes of approval, and the undermining of the activities of existing charities by an overbearing police supervision.[51]

Throughout the period under consideration here, the authorities would demonstrate a much more lenient attitude towards the formation of religious congregations. Furthermore, an obvious lack of political will to control the burgeoning multitude of private Jewish schools allowed such schools to satisfy the basic educational needs of the emerging, diverse Jewish metropolitan community. Although legislation concerning primary and secondary education in

---

49 Scott Ury, *Barricades and Banners. The Revolution of 1905 and the Transformation of Warsaw Jewry* (Stanford, CA: Stanford University Press 2012), 48–51.

50 Ibid., 69–74, and François Guesnet, "Thinking Globally, Acting Locally: Joel Wegmeister and Modern Hasidic Politics in Warsaw," *Quest. Issues in Contemporary Jewish History. Journal of Fondazione CDEC* 2 (October 2011) URL: www.quest-cdecjournal.it/focus.php?id=222; and idem, "Revolutionary Hinterland: Transformations of Jewish Associational Life in the Kingdom of Poland, 1904–06," in Franziska Schedewie et al. (eds.), *The Russian Revolution of 1905 in Transcultural Perspective: Identities, Peripheries, and the Flow of Ideas* (Bloomington, IN: Slavica Publishers, 2013), 105–20.

51 Guesnet, *Polnische Juden*, 247–50.

the Kingdom of Poland was highly regulated, Jewish private primary schools (Yidd. and Hebr. *heder*) were never as closely monitored as, for example, Polish ones.[52] A survey in 1891 established that around 450 male and 376 female pupils attended the ten elementary schools established and supervised by the *Zarząd Gminy*, dwarfed by the more than twenty six thousand Jewish boys and girls attending private *heder* schools in Warsaw—hence, the officially recognized administration of the largest Jewish community in the world controlled just two or three percent of elementary schooling of Jewish children. The vast majority of Jewish children were taught privately without any administrative supervision to speak of—or, in the case of the large segment of impoverished Jewish tradespeople, received no structured education at all.[53]

As has already pointed out, the opening and maintaining of synagogues and prayer houses mirrored the structure and practices of the community. Applications were made to the authorities by individuals, and independently of the Synagogue Supervisory Board.[54] Their diversity reflected the metropolitan community, and congregations often served as institutional cores for the major religious, cultural and political identifications among Warsaw Jewry. This holds true for the dozens of associational prayer houses (for an example, see below), for the numerous prayer houses of the various Hasidic communities,[55] for the synagogue founded by the small but assertive group of Jews from German lands establishing themselves during the Prussian rule 1796–1806,[56] for the so-called Polish Synagogue which in 1840 attempted to achieve the status of an independent community,[57] as well as for the considerable number of Russian-Jewish prayer houses, some of which—towards the end of the period under consideration in this chapter—would sign on to the early Zionist programme of *Hibat Tsion* (Hebr. Love of Zion).[58]

---

52 For the close supervision and oppressive regulation of Polish elementary education, especially after the January Uprising in 1863, see Ryszard Kucha, *Oświata elementarna w Królestwie Polskim w latach 1864–1914* (Lublin: Krajowa Agencja Prasowa, 1982).

53 "Kronika," *Izraelita* 19 (1891), 157. These numbers were based on official statistics, which means that the numbers of Jewish children attending schools outside the control of the *Zarząd* was probably significantly higher.

54 Guesnet, *Polnische Juden*, 397.

55 Dynner, *Men of Silk*, 89–116.

56 Jürgen Hensel, "Wie 'deutsch' war die 'fortschrittliche' jüdische Bourgeoisie im Königreich Polen?" in Hans Hecker and Walter Engel (eds.), *Symbiose und Traditionsbruch: Deutsch-jüdische Wechselbeziehungen in Ostmittel- und Südosteuropa* (Essen: Edition Klartext, 2004), 135–72.

57 Aleksander Guterman, "The Origins of the Great Synagogue in Warsaw on Tłomackie Street," in Bartoszewski and Polonsky (eds.), *The Jews in Warsaw*, 181–212.

58 *Izraelita* 1 (1885), 4.

Beyond these fixed places of worship, less perceptible and more transient expressions of Jewish religious life proceeded without significant interference from the authorities and created spaces of Jewish religious practice, some permanent, some temporary, that served to integrate the emerging metropolitan community. Among the most notable were the processions to celebrate the completion of a new Torah scroll, for one of which we have an impressive description from the Polish press:

> The association of the local water carriers has its prayer room in the Grützhändler house on Nowowiniarska Street. It celebrated the completion of a Torah scroll yesterday. At eleven o'clock in the night, around fifteen thousand Jews paraded along the Nowowiniarska and the Świętojerska Streets, went down the Nalewki, up to Franciszkańska Street and back to Nowowiniarska Street. The new Torah scroll was protected by a canopy. A dozen torch bearers preceded the parade, huge lanterns, flags and pennants accompanied it. Young men whistled in a harrowing way. Around twenty members of the association in outlandish disguise were on horseback, some of them wearing spooky masks.[59]

This lively description captures the performative impact of such a parade: the nightly spectacle with lights, noise, disguises and horses would on the one hand mark a very special moment in the existence of a rather modest association. On the other hand, the parade would also serve to underline the association's place both in the Jewish community and in urban space. The route chosen for the parade would lead around two blocks in the very heart of the Jewish neighbourhood and demonstrate the claim of the water carriers as constituting an important part of this Jewish world.

Even if the number given in the article is in all likelihood inflated, similar parades would take place in Warsaw and other towns of the Kingdom on a regular basis, without being, it seems, hampered by the authorities.[60] They are documented for the whole period under consideration here, and demonstrate

---

59   *Kurjer Warszawski* 238 (18/30 December 1873); for a later photograph of the prayer house see Bergman, 'Nie masz bóżniczy powszechnej', 263. For an earlier example of how Jewish celebrations on occasion were highly visible and public events see Dynner, *Men of Silk*, 83–85, discussing the wedding of the grand-son of the Seer of Lublin (Yaacov Yitshak Horowitz, 1745–1815) in the town of Żelechów in 1805.

60   The description of another Torah procession in 1866 in Warsaw explains that "old people and children, men and women from far away and nearby places gathered" for the occasion, see Guesnet, *Polnische Juden*, 257. More parades were reported in 1877 and 1878, see *Izraelita* 31 (1877), 245 and 32 (1877), 256, as well as ibid., 35 (1878), 281 and 47 (1878), 381.

the appetite of members of religious associations for asserting their status and place in the community publicly, ignoring the reservations repeatedly formulated by the Warsaw *Zarząd Gminy*.[61]

Less transient, but still less visible than for example a synagogue were the sabbath enclosures (*eruvin*) installed around Jewish neighbourhoods in Polish towns and cities, and also in Warsaw. Here, the attitude of the authorities seems to have been more ambivalent. Although a ministerial order in 1860 allowed for the installation of *eruvin*, it also stipulated that local authorities should take care that these enclosures would "not offend other faith communities."[62] Repeated calls to dismantle these demarcations of Jewish space point to the fact that these restrictions were not, however, enforced.[63]

From the Politics of Spectacle to the Spectacle of Politics

The formation of the metropolitan Jewish community in Warsaw was based on the extraordinary increase in the Jewish population and its growing diversity. Traditional charities as well as the state-approved communal administration attempted to cater to the needs of this rapidly growing and diversifying Jewish metropolis, and failed. One reason for the failure of Jewish communal institutions to adapt to those changing needs was the overbearing administrative and police control of public life, the consequence of the Polish patriotic aspirations of the period that culminated in the January Uprising of 1863. There is no need to repeat the often and well-told story of the short period of Polish-Jewish brotherhood in 1861, the limited but noticeable involvement of Jews in the January Uprising of 1863, this last attempt in the nineteenth century for a military reversal of Russian rule, as well as the emergence of a specifically Jewish thread in the "organic work," and its attempt to invigorate Polish society through educational reform, social policy, and an advancement of Polish economic endeavors.[64] Rather, this last section proposes to investigate

---

61 Ibid., 259.
62 Jakob Kirszrot, *Prawa Żydów w Królestwie Polskim* (Warszawa: Nakład Zarządu Warszawskiej gminy starozakonnych, 1917), 15.
63 In reaction to attacks on the *eruv* in a provincial town, the Warsaw head of police prohibited new enclosures in 1878. As these restrictive regulations were published on several occasions, the Jews of Warsaw seemingly did not fully comply, see Guesnet, *Polnische Juden*, 261.
64 A very short overview over this period in Polonsky, *The Jews in Poland and Russia*, vol. 1, 314–21, and in more detail in Magdalena Opalski and Israel Bartal: *Poles and Jews: A Failed Brotherhood* (Hanover, NH: University Press of New England, 1992), as well as the still

the role of public spaces in Warsaw in this tumultuous period as reflecting the emergence of a metropolitan Jewish community.

The so-called "Jewish War" of 1859 offers a first occasion to investigate the role of urban space and the public sphere in this period. A review of a violin recital in the *Gazeta Warszawska*, a leading Warsaw daily, triggered the affair. The author of the review claimed that the soloist, although a first class player, had only a sparse public because she was not Jewish; thus, the Jewish public had not bothered to turn up.[65] This statement then led the author to racist and antisemitic statements of the crudest kind:

> As we can see, Ms Neruda [the violon soloist, F.G.] does not have the favors of a large coterie, thought to have musical taste and certainly making claims to it. She did not have the eagle's nose, the dark tone of the skin, the black hair and other characteristics of this non-Aryan tribe—she doesn't trill the *r*, her family name doesn't end in *berg, blatt, kranc, stern* or the like. Thus there's no reason for this mysterious coalition which has garnered the whole of Europe in general, and us in particular.[66]

The lengthy reflections which followed came to the conclusion that, unfortunately, the Jews in Poland would not return to their homeland, and thus constituted a major problem for the Polish nation. A short period later, the editor of *Gazeta Warszawska*, Antoni Lesznowski, made public the fact that he had received anonymous letters challenging the concert review, emphasising the contribution of the Jews to the Polish economy, culture, and society. Lesznowski also explained that he had handed over the letters to the police for investigation. This in turn led to more accusations against him, some of

---

essential Alina Cała, *Asymilacja Żydów w Królestwie Polskim, 1864–1897: postawy, konflikty, stereotypy* (Warszawa: Państwowy Instytut Wydawniczy, 1989).

65 The balanced and most complete account of this episode is Kazimierz Bartoszewicz, *Wojna żydowska w roku 1859: początki asymilacji i antisemityzmu* (Warszawa: Gebethner i Wolff, 1917). See also Artur Eisenbach, *The Emancipation of the Jews in Poland, 1780–1870* (ed. Antony Polonsky; Oxford: Blackwell in association with the Institute of Polish-Jewish Studies, 1991), 398, 420–21; and Theodore R. Weeks, *From Assimilation to Antisemitism: the "Jewish Question" in Poland, 1850–1914* (DeKalb, IL: Northern Illinois University Press, 2006), 39–41.

66 Cited after Bartoszewicz, *Wojna żydowska*, 37–38; for a recent republication of several central texts of this episode see François Guesnet, *Der Fremde als Nachbar: Polnische Texte zur jüdischen Präsenz. Texte seit 1800* (Frankfurt am Main: Suhrkamp Verlag, 2009), 127–55, here 135–36.

which were formulated in a letter signed by members of the younger generation of Warsaw Jews who identified with the Polish cause and Polish culture. Lesznowski brought the authors to trial on charges of slander and libel, drawing further attention to the debate, which was also intensely debated in the Polish emigration in Western Europe, with Joachim Lelewel (1786–1861), among the leading liberal thinkers in the emigration, devoting a long essay to the affair. Lesznowski's decision to go before a criminal court was considered by parts of the Polish public as un-patriotic—in any case, because of the January Uprising in 1863, it was never adjudicated.[67] The most important consequence of the affair would be the fact that Polish-Jewish relations as well as Jewish cultural choices were intensely debated publicly.

This would be all the more important in the years to come, when political and cultural identifications were put on display in the context of the patriotic mobilization, the insurrectionist upheaval, but also in later years. Chief rabbi Dov Berush Meisel would very consciously involve himself in patriotic demonstrations, most famously joining the funeral of the victims of the police attack against a patriotic demonstration on March 2, 1861.[68] He also encouraged the singing of the Polish national anthem in synagogues, prompting the chief of police to inform Rabbi Meisels that, "unless he stops the singing of the national hymn in the synagogues, he will shut them up."[69]

Much less well known are later instances of Jews participating in patriotic demonstrations. Their reflection in the international press documents the relevance that contemporaries attached to these occurrences. On the occasion of the funeral of Archbishop Melchior Fiałkowski (1778–1861), a correspondent of *The Times* observed that

> the foreign Consuls, English and French, took part in the sad ceremony, and joined it on the Saxon-place; as also the Protestant and Jewish congregations, with every symptom of profound and fervent sorrow. The body of the Archbishop was carried in turns by the clergy, the peasants, artisans, Government officials, students, and Jews.[70]

---

67 *Sprawa żydowska w r. 1859, w liście do Ludwika Merzbacha*, (Merzbach: Poznań, 1860).

68 The painting by Aleksander Lesser, *The funeral of the Five Victims of the Demonstration of 2 March 1861* (1866), today on display in the National Museum in Kraków, is the iconic expression of this episode.

69 Correspondence from Kraków of 13 July, 1861, reported in *The Times* (London) (23 July, 1861). The correspondent further wrote that the head of police does not "threaten to close the Catholic churches, in which the hymn is sung, [therefore] it has been hastily inferred that the Lieutenant-General attaches less importance to the prayer of a Christian than to that of a Jew."

70 Correspondence from Warsaw of 15 October, 1861, *The Times* (London) (24 October, 1861).

FIGURE 5.8 Funeral procession of the archbishop of Warsaw, Antoni Melchior Fijałkowski (d. 5 October 1861), detail from a broadsheet by Maksymilian Fajans (1827–1890). *The funeral took place in the midst of considerable political mobilization against Russian rule. The broadsheet shows representatives of a variety of charitable, educational and cultural institutions, guilds, estates, the clergy, and representatives of foreign nations paying their last respects to the much admired archbishop. The funeral was considered a patriotic demonstration, and in its wake the Russian administration declared martial law. This detail shows "ministers and youth of the Mosaic persuasion" immediately following the coffin, with one of the students carrying a flagpole. The proximity to the coffin visualizes the strong commitment of these Jews to the national cause.*
COURTESY OF THE NATIONAL LIBRARY, WARSAW.

The remarkable lithograph of this funeral by the well-known painter and photographer Maksymilian Fajans (1827–1890), himself sympathetic to the Polish cause, highlights the prominent place of the Jewish representatives. A group of around six students is shown following directly behind the hearse with the archbishop's remains, themselves followed by a larger group of Jews headed by Dov Berush Meisels and the preacher of the so-called German synagogue on Daniłowiczowska Street, the young Dr. Markus Jastrow (1829–1903).[71] In the following years, other funerals would be highly politicized events and occasions for the public display of political discontent, as in the case of the suicide in 1880 of Ignacy Neufeld, a young Jewish student who took his life in reaction

---

71 Maksymilian Fajans, *Exportacya Zwłok nieodżałowanej pamięci Najdostojnieszego Arcybiskupa Metropolity ks. Antoniego Melchiora Fijałkowskiego zmarłego w dniu 5 października 1861 r.*, collections of the National Library Warsaw, also accessible through http://polona.pl/item/854772 (last accessed April 17, 2014). About Rabbi Jastrow, who later emigrated to the United States and became a leading figure in American Judaism, see Michał Galas, *Rabbi Marcus Jastrow and His Vision for the Reform Judaism. A Study in the History of Judaism* (Boston, MA: Academic Studies Press, 2013).

to extremely harsh reprimands for the demonstration of Polish patriotic feelings. Also in this case, the fact that the funeral crossed religious boundaries seemed to define the participating communities themselves:

> Although he belonged to an Israelitish [sic] family, the funeral procession, led by a rabbi, was attended by a throng of at least 10,000 persons, consisting of both Poles and Jews, and including some of the most prominent citizens of both nationalities and confessions.[72]

The incident was also reported in *The New York Times*, with a stronger emphasis on the political implications:

> An immense crowd of about 10,000 persons accompanied him to his final resting-place; women sobbing, and cries of "Down with the tyrant" were heard the whole way. Such a crowd has not been seen in the streets of Warsaw since 1863. The Police turned out in full force, the military being under arms the whole time in the barracks. The excitement is great and continues to increase.[73]

Of greater importance in the context of the emergence of a metropolitan Jewish community, however, would be crowds gathering for the funerals of the two most respected and admired religious authorities in the Polish capital in the period under consideration in this chapter: Yeshaya Mushkat, the rabbi and supreme judge of the Praga Jewish community, who died in 1868, and the Warsaw chief rabbi Dov Berush Meisels, who passed away in 1870. Their respective deaths would be momentous events in the history of the metropolitan community.

In the case of Mushkat, his demise would lead to the abolition of an independent *bet din* in this neighborhood, which had been the site of the first Jewish cemetery in Warsaw. It also offered an opportunity to officially incorporate the Praga *Hevra kadisha* into the Burial Administration of Warsaw and spelled the end to the semi-autonomous existence of the Praga Jewish community.[74] His

---

72 "A Popular Demonstration in Warsaw," *The Times* (London) (12 February, 1880). See also Shatzky, *Geshikhte fun yidn in varshe*, vol. III, 226.

73 "Driven to Despair by Russian Injustice," *The New York Times* (9 February, 1880).

74 Guesnet, *Polnische Juden*, 229 and 391; both Ignacy Schiper, *Przyczynki do dziejów chasydyzmu w Polsce*, ed. Zbigniew Targielski (Warszawa: Państwowe Wydawnictwo Naukowe, 1992), 67; and Shatzky, *Geshikhte fun yidn in varshe*, vol. I, 134, argued for such an exceptional status of the community in Warsaw-Praga.

funeral was attended by several thousand Warsaw Jews, the first mass funeral of many to follow. The contemporaries emphasized the exceptional number of people in attendance, bearing witness to the outstanding status of Mushkat, who could claim to have commanded respect among misnagdic and hasidic Jews alike.[75] About the funeral of Dov Ber Meisels, we read in *Der Israelit*, the lead publication of German observant Jews, published by Rabbi Lehmann:

> In accordance with strict Jewish observance, the funeral avoided any ostentation—nevertheless, it was an impressive event due to the formidable crowd it attracted. Not only the Jews of Warsaw, who form the largest community in Europe, attended the event, but many Christians from all walks of life. Meisels enjoyed the highest esteem, as a rabbi and as an individual, but also as a political personality [...] Due to his liberal outlooks and his Polish patriotism, the authorities did not trust him—and this distrust continued after his demise: The censor has forbidden to print any obituary in the local papers except for a short note about his passing away, and certainly no mentioning of the formidable funeral.[76]

These funerals seem to have been among the first public gatherings of very large numbers of Warsaw Jews in an explicitly Jewish context. The impact of such an encounter of huge Jewish crowds can hardly be overstated, as they would have provided a concrete experience of what Warsaw would be for the decades to come: the largest Jewish community in Europe, and for a considerable period of time, of the world. In the history of the community as a representative and administrative body of the Jews of Warsaw, it would be of equal relevance. Few later figures would command a cross-denominational respect comparable to that of these two leaders. Their demise would have a significant impact on the metropolitan rabbinate. Warsaw's rabbinical reach would expand to Praga, ending independent halakhic jurisdiction east of the Vistula. Furthermore, after the removal of Yaacov Gesundheit from his office as chief rabbi, the halakhic supervision in the Polish capital would rest with district rabbis who lacked authority over the whole of Warsaw. These subdivisions would be a reflection of the polycentric character of the emerging Jewish metropolis.

Torah processions, demonstrations, and funerals, which would make the presence of a large Jewish community visible, and which would insert this community into the social, cultural and political fabric of the capital, certainly

---

75 Tsevi Falk Vinaver: "Rusland," *Ha-magid* 13 (1868), 100; and Shatzky, *Geshikhte fun yidn in varshe*, vol. I, 146.

76 "Rußland," *Der Israelit* 9 (2 March, 1870), 158.

contributed to a sense of identification and belonging to this place which was Warsaw. This appropriation of the local space however also had an everyday dimension which would be based both in Jewish and in non-Jewish contexts. In order to illustrate how urban space needed to be negotiated between communities, but also between communities and the authorities, seemingly neutral urban spaces offer an appropriate perspective. More specifically, the use of urban parks, closely connected to the formation of the European metropolis as such, allow us to further understand the processes through which the Jewish community of Warsaw negotiated its place in the capital. The two most important green spaces in nineteenth-century Warsaw, the Saxonian Garden (*Ogród Saski*) and the Krasinski Park (*Park Krasińskich*), were both situated in the immediate vicinity of the Jewish quarter. The realities and complexities of using these popular venues are well reflected in a letter to the German *Der Israelit*:

> The Saxonian Garden features an establishment for mineral waters, visited by thousands of patrons during summer. The police chief orders the Jews to enter the Garden only from the rear entrance of the park, and prohibits them from walking around during the drinking cure, although this is recommended therapy. The order does not explicitly target the Jews, it is claimed, but only the traditional [Jewish] dress [...] The great majority of the Jews of Warsaw, even if they do not appreciate the generally accepted European dress, visit the Garden in appropriate, even elegant garments. These measures are dictated by the hatred of Jews alone. During the shortlived Wielopolski government [1861–62, F.G.] such narrow-minded restrictions had disappeared, yet we find them again today.[77]

Thus, multiple objectives governed the use of recreational space in central Warsaw. From the point of view of the authorities, a modern institution like an urban park was incompatible with traditional Jewish dress, and over decades conflicts would erupt around the question whether Jews in non-European dress could be admitted or not.[78] Water cures as an innovative form of healthcare, immensely popular among Jews and non-Jews alike, seemed to offer a

---

77 "Rußland und Polen," *Der Israelit* 26 (26 June, 1870), 491.
78 For the role of green urban spaces in the context of "popular autocracy" in the imperial Russian context, see Boris Anan'ich and Alexander Kobak: "St Petersburg and Green Space, 1850–2000: an introduction," in Peter Clark (ed.), *The European City and Green Space. London, Stockholm, Helsinki and St Petersburg, 1850–2000* (Farnham: Ashgate, 2006), 247–71, here 254.

counter-argument to a restrictive definition of acceptable dress, as healthcare would trump the narrow-minded argument of the chief of police.

Russian administrators did not, however, have a monopoly on narrow-mindedness. Even for integrationist Jews the presence of traditional Jews in urban parks was difficult to stomach:

> The observant middle classes, after some hesitations in the past years, also joined the event [a charitable fundraiser]. We were appalled by the boldness with which these visitors, dressed in their long garbs and accompanied by their wigwearing wives, moved through the Garden. Their loud babbling and shouting of repulsive names like Moyshe, Khaye, Gitle, with a loud voice, resonated with a hurtful echo in the hearts of the better educated patrons.[79]

Thus, the metropolitan Jewish community had to negotiate not only its own diversity, but also cultural, behavioral and religious choices with the wider community as well. Also, modern recreational spaces like urban parks would not be neutral. They would be governed and policed by the same principles as the remainder of urban space. They would, however, offer new forms of engagement and interaction. The Krasinski Park in particular would become a frequent venue for Jewish charitable events, like the above-mentioned lottery for the *Dom Schronienia*, the almshouse supported by the whole of the Jewish community.[80] The two central parks would remain venues for Jewish charitable events in the years to come, and a report about the coordinated distribution of cheap meals by competing observant and Russian-Jewish charities on the occasion of *Lag b'omer* in the year of crisis and revolution, 1905, seems to indicate that at least in the area of charitable work, these urban spaces could claim to offer neutral grounds.[81]

Finally, the places and spaces of the rapidly growing Warsaw Jewish community needed to be negotiated not only within this community and with an authoritarian administration, but also with the non-Jewish, mostly Polish community in the capital. As is well known, the first large scale pogrom took place in Warsaw at the very end of the period under consideration in this chapter, on Christmas Day 1881. It seems that already earlier, the cohabitation of Jews and non-Jews had led to outbursts of violence. In one case, Jews celebrating the Feast of Tabernacles (Hebr. *sukkot*) were attacked in their hut:

---

79 "Pogadanki," *Izraelita* 34 (1872), 274.
80 See above, fn. 43.
81 "Odgłosy," *Izraelita* 20 (1905), 230.

On the evening of Sukkot, cheery and even-minded Jewish families had sat down in their beautifully decorated huts, as a mob of around 50 Christians assaulted them and beat and kicked men, women, and children. The head of police in this 9th district angrily dismissed the complaint, claiming it to be a non-issue, as nobody had been killed [...] The very next day, uncouth youths attacked a Jewish funeral, but this time the perpetrators were arrested.[82]

It seems of relevance here that the 9th district—to the west of the Warsaw city center—was at quite a distance from the Jewish neighbourhood, and reflects the reluctance of Poles to accept Jewish settlement beyond their traditional quarters.[83]

Conclusion

The third quarter of the nineteenth century was a crucial period in the emergence of the first Jewish metropolis in European diasporic history. The first reason is demographic—not only was Warsaw the setting of the largest Jewish community in Europe, and for a number of years in the world,—but of a highly diverse community. More importantly, each subgroup would develop a strong sense of identity, contrasting its own religious and cultural choices with those of other Jews, and translating these distinctive characteristics into politics, socializing, *weltanschauung*, and, last but not least, community politics. This holds true for the Jews who came to Warsaw from German territories as well as from Lithuania or the Russian heartland, for the misnagdim and the members of the numerous hasidic communities. Jews with inclinations towards a reviewed aesthetic of dress, everyday life and religious ritual rejected the ways of old, while the period of patriotic mobilization in the 1860s witnessed the emergence of a Jewish romantic commitment to the idea of a Polish fatherland for Jews, as well.

This demographic growth and cultural diversification proved an additional factor in the unhinging of traditional forms of Jewish civil leadership. The Synagogue Supervisory Board, itself only a weakened successor of the former *kahal*, was replaced by a seemingly more efficient Community Administration;

---

82 "Rußland," *Der Israelit* 44 (1 November, 1871), 812.
83 This is also reflected in the animosities against Jews taking up residence in locations from which Jews had been excluded until the emancipation of 1862, leading to threats to houseowners letting to Jews, see "Warschau," *Der Israelit* 37 (1862), 296.

the latter however was not much more than the playground of a technocratic *inteligencja* willing to leave the very substance of Jewish communal and religious matters of charity, education and representation to a variety of self-declared spokespeople from the whole range of above-mentioned sub-communities. The rules of engagement, however, were dictated by an authoritarian occupant, who picked and chose at random which areas of the evolving metropolitan society he wished to admit and which to suppress. These difficulties notwithstanding, the Polish capital became a place where Jews would physically encounter their own community as a mass society, defining, marking and sometimes overwhelming public space. In the period under consideration, confident public events like demonstrations or funerals would become occasions for a wholly new Jewish encounter—one of a metropolitan community.

CHAPTER 6

An Unhappy Community and an Even Unhappier Rabbi

Shaul Stampfer

The story of R. Jacob Gesundheit's tenure as the rabbi of Warsaw was not a happy one. He was appointed to the position in 1870, was fired in 1873, and died in 1878. His was a short and painful rabbinical career, but well worth studying because it contributes much to our understanding of the history of the Jews in Warsaw and reflects the rapidly changing Jewish world of late nineteenth-century Eastern and East Central Europe. By the time of his appointment, the Warsaw Jewish community had already been the largest Jewish community in Eastern Europe for decades. This community was far from homogenous. It included an influential group of wealthy 'enlightened' Jews, though most of the Jews could still have been traditionalists. At the same time, many Warsaw Jews were Hasidim but they were far from being an overwhelming majority. Warsaw's Jewish community had never been homogeneous in the past, and this had not prevented the selection of a communal rabbi. However, the growing heterogeneity, which was to become characteristic of almost every major Jewish community in Eastern Europe, made communal decisions far more complex then previously—as it also did elsewhere. R. Gesundheit was one of the first public casualties of the new reality.

Fortunately for those interested in the topic, the historian Jacob Shatzky devoted a chapter of his magisterial history of Warsaw Jewry to the Warsaw rabbinate and documented the sequence of events that took place during

---

* I would not have been able to write this paper do so without the ongoing assistance and encouragement of Glenn Dynner, who put me on to the topic and informed me about the Russian sources related to the tenure of R. Gesundheit, to Binyamin Lukin who showed me where they were, to Vladimir Levin who helped me read them, to Beni Gesundheit—a direct descendent of R. Jacob for sources and encouragement, to Gershon Bacon who helped make my words more readable and to Marcin Wodziński and Agnieszka Jagodzińska who helped me track down Polish language sources that I could not find in Jerusalem. Marcin Wodziński read a draft of the paper, as well. Friends are a wonderful thing.

R. Gesundheit's short career as rabbi of Warsaw.[1] However, it was precisely Shatzky's strengths—his mastery of the details and sources related to Warsaw Jewry—that left room for those who have tried to follow in his footsteps to analyze some of the dynamics and issues of the Warsaw rabbinate that were not central to Shatzky's concerns. Here, the lessons learned from Antony Polonsky's sensitivity to structure and to context are of critical importance. Moreover, with the aid of recently discovered sources from Russian archives that were not available to Shatzky, it is possible to fill out the story of Rabbi Gesundheit's short and unhappy tenure and appreciate its significance.

• • •

To better understand the short lived career of R. Gesundheit, it is necessary to bear in mind some characteristics of the rabbinate in early modern Europe. In the Ashkenazi tradition, rabbis were elected by communities to serve as communal rabbis.[2] There were often various eligibility requirements for

---

1 Jacob Shatzky, *Geshikhte fun yidn in varshe*, III: 137–144. He was preceded by Hilary Nussbaum, *Szkice historyczne z życia Żydów w Warszawie* (Warszawa: Druk K. Kowalewskiego, 1881), 133 –136 and Azriel Natan Frenk, "Ha-rabanut be-varsha lifnim [The Rabbinate in Warsaw in the Past]," *Ha-tzefira* (3 May 1921): 2. Unless otherwise noted, the details on R. Gesundheit's tenure are based on Shatzky and the sources he cites there. Jacob (Yankev) Shatzky was a fascinating personality in his own right. See Robert Shapiro, "Shatzky, Yankev," *YIVO Encyclopedia of Jews in Eastern Europe*, 2: 1704–05. Yitshak Grünbaum wrote an article "Bor'ba za vlast' v varshavskoi evreiskoi obshchine" in *Vestnik evreiskoi obshchiny* 1.4 (1913): 3–12 and 1.5: 10–26, but I was unable to find a copy of the journal with the first half of the article. Judging by the second half, it seems that he dealt mainly with internal divisions in Warsaw Jewry at the end of the nineteenth century and not with R. Gesundheit.
2 On the rabbinate in general see Simon Schwarzfuchs, *A Concise History of the Rabbinate* (Oxford: Blackwell, 1993), passim. For the medieval and early modern rabbinate see Jacob Katz, *Tradition and Crisis* (trans. Dov Bernard Cooperman; New York: New York University Press, 1993), 65–75, 141–155, as well as Eric Zimmer's *Harmony and Discord* (New York: Yeshiva University Press, 1970), 104–131, and Salo Baron, *The Jewish Community* (Philadelphia: Jewish Publication Society, 1942), vol. 2, 123–169 and his many notes. On Eastern Europe in the early modern period, see Simha Assaf, "Lekorot ha-rabanut," *Reshumot* II (1922): 259–300 and Elhanan Reiner, "The Yeshivot of Poland and Ashkenaz During the Sixteenth and Seventeenth Centuries: Historical Developments," in *Studies in Jewish Culture in Honour of Chone Shmeruk* (ed. Israel Bartal, Ezra Mendelsohn and Chava Tumiansky; Jerusalem: The Zalman Shazar Center for Jewish History, 1993), 9–80 [Hebrew]. On the rabbinate in the Tsarist Empire see Isaac Levitats, *The Jewish Community in Russia 1772–1844* (New York: Columbia University Press, 1943), 147–172.

participating in the election process, though in all cases only males had the right to vote. Sometimes it was all of the males, sometimes it was only those males who paid taxes. Sometimes the election was direct, sometimes voters chose a group of electors who ultimately made the decision. Whatever the system, the choice reflected the 'general will' of the Jewish community. In many respects, rabbis were seen as embodying the values of the community and, as such, the selection of a rabbi was an expression of the values of a community. The rabbi's function as an embodiment of communal ideals could be even more important than a rabbi's technical abilities to interpret Jewish law or elucidate rabbinic texts.

Rabbis were employees of the Jewish community and Jewish communities tried to maintain their independence in the selection of rabbis and to ensure, at least in theory, that they were not appointed by outsiders—Jewish or non-Jewish.[3] When chosen, rabbis were not given lifetime tenure; rather their contract was contingent and renewable at regular intervals. Rabbis could thus be fired, and this sometimes happened—as was to be the case with R. Gesundheit. Such a step on the part of a Jewish community was not exceptional.

There were, of course, exceptions and variations. Simony or the purchase of a rabbinical position by rabbis or for rabbis by their relatives was not unknown. There were also cases of noble landowners who intervened in the selection of rabbis in communities located on their lands. However, until the modern period, these were individual incidents, not a matter of policy or routine. Within the Western provinces of the Russian empire, even the 'government rabbis', a post established in the 1840s, were elected by communities and not appointed—though they had to, of course, meet government criteria and be approved.[4]

While inheritance of rabbinical posts 'looks' traditional today, it is actually a modern phenomenon and can be dated among Ashkenazi Jewry to the late eighteenth century.[5] The transmission of the rabbinate of a community from

---

3 See Moshe Rosman, *The Lord's Jews: Magnate-Jewish Relations in the Polish-Lithuanian Commonwealth during the 18th Century* (Cambridge, MA: Harvard University Press, 1990), 185–205, and Adam Teller, "Rabbis Without a Function? The Polish Rabbinate and the Council of Four Lands in the 16th–18th Centuries," in *Jewish Religious Leadership: Image and Reality* (ed. J. Wertheimer; New York: Jewish Theological Seminary, 2004), vol. 1, 371–340. The avoidance of non-Jewish intervention in the appointing of rabbis was an issue in the dispute over the appointment of R. Gesundheit. See Frenk, "Ha-rabanut."

4 Azriel Shochat, *The "Crown Rabbinate" in Russia* (Haifa: Haifa University Press, 1975) [Hebrew].

5 I deal with this topic at length in "The Inheritance of the Rabbinate in Eastern Europe," ch. 14 of my book *Families, Rabbis and Education: Traditional Jewish Society in Nineteenth-Century*

father to son undermined the power or authority of the Jewish community because it took away the power to choose and made firing a rabbi much more difficult. In a sense, inheritance of a position means abdicating communal choice to fate (or divine will), in that the heir is chosen not by the members of the community, but by genetics. Therefore, the usual practice was for communities to select their rabbi.

In the early modern period, Rabbis were not the 'heads' of Jewish communities in terms of determining communal decisions or possessing the power to force members of communities to accept their decisions in issues that were not directly *halakhic*. Even in *halakhic* matters their hands were often tied. The greatest degree of power had always resided with the secular leadership, or *parnasim*, for they were the ones who administered tax collection within the Jewish community and transmitted those taxes to the rulers or government. The position of 'parnas' was unquestionably the most powerful communal position. In addition, *parnasim* could directly or indirectly hire and fire rabbis, not vice versa. Of course, rabbis still enjoyed real influence in traditional communities. They presided as the heads of rabbinical courts and, as such, they could have a significant impact on the well being—and pockets—of members of their communities.[6]

All of this began to change in the modern period. When governments began to collect taxes directly from individual Jews in the early nineteenth century, the communal institutions and the *parnasim* who ran them lost much of their power. The functions of communal leaders and communal rabbis were transformed. The concurrent increasing recourse of Jews to secular or non-Jewish courts meant that rabbis, too, lost much of their influence. At the same time, the positions continued to offer rabbis prestige and more importantly, no new positions developed to fill the leadership vacuum. Thus, perhaps paradoxically, rabbis continued to serve as representatives of the Jewish community at large and in the wake of the sharper decline in the role of *parnasim* and new responsibilities for registering births, marriages and deaths, their representative and symbolic roles became even larger than they had been.[7] Therefore, the post— and elections to the posts—of rabbi continued to be taken very seriously. The choice of rabbi was still a symbolic reflection of the values of a community— and of the relative power of different elements within the community.

Europe (London and Portland, OR: Littman Library, 2010), 302–323. For an earlier version, see my article "Inheritance of the rabbinate in Eastern Europe in the modern period—causes, factors and development over time," *Jewish History* 13.1 (1999): 35–57.

6 See Katz, *Tradition and Crisis*, 141–155.
7 See Eugene Avrutin, *Jews and the Imperial State* (Ithaca, NY: Cornell University Press, 2010).

⋯

The modern history of the Warsaw rabbinate began around 1819. The first 'chief' rabbi of Warsaw was R. Shlomo Zalman Lifshitz. Upon his death in 1839, the question of a successor arose. Already at this time, the capabilities of Isaac Meir Alter,[8] who was then a resident of Warsaw and only later the *rebbe* of Ger Hasidism, were widely recognized. However, selecting a Hasidic rabbi as the rabbi of Warsaw was not a realistic option. The invitation to serve as rabbi of Warsaw went to a non-Hasidic, very elderly resident of Warsaw—R. Haim Dawidsohn.[9] According to some reports, this was at the suggestion of R. Alter;[10] and according to others, it was the initiative of the young R. Gesundheit.[11] To everyone's surprise, Dawidsohn lived another 15 years and served all this time as rabbi of Warsaw.

When the position became vacant upon R. Dawidsohn's death in 1854, R. Alter was once again regarded as the natural candidate of the Hasidim. According to one report, some supported him while others supported none other than R. Gesundheit. According to the followers of Alter, he did not want the position, but this is not certain. What is clear is that, with the votes split, the Hasidim joined forces with the integrationists ('enlightened' or 'progressive' polonized Jews) and brought R. Dov Ber Meisels to Warsaw.[12] R. Meisels was a very pragmatic and intelligent rabbi who turned out to be a gifted politician to boot. During the years he served as rabbi of Warsaw he maintained good relations with all circles in the city. However, we should not forget that in later years, some Hasidim felt that had R. Gesundheit not appeared as a candidate, R. Alter might have been elected as Rabbi of Warsaw and not R. Meisels. Others could have felt that were it not for R. Alter's support for R. Meisels, R. Gesundheit might have been chosen. According to Hasidic sources, this caused tension between R. Gesundheit and R. Alter, and would prove highly significant.[13]

---

8   For more on Alter and on the Ger Hasidic dynasty, see Arthur Green, "Ger Hasidic Dynasty," YIVO *Encyclopedia of Jews in Eastern Europe*, 1: 582–84.
9   For more on Dawidsohn, see François Guesnet, "Dawidsohn, Ḥayim," YIVO *Encyclopedia of Jews in Eastern Europe*, 2: 395–96.
10 David Flinker, *Arim ve-imahot be-yisrael* (Jerusalem: Mossad Harav Kook, 1948), vol.3 (Varsha), 106.
11 Chaim Karlinsky, *Ha-rishon le-shoshelet brisk* (Jerusalem: Machon Yerushalayim, 1984), 244.
12 Avraham Issachar Alter, *Meir einei ha-gola* (Warsaw: Libeskind, 1932), vol. 2, 14, no. 449. See also Flinker, *Arim*, 108. In English, see François Guesnet, "Meisels, Dov Berush," YIVO *Encyclopedia of Jews in Eastern Europe*, 2: 1148.
13 Alter, *Meir*, vol. 2, 16–17, no. 455.

In 1870, R. Meisels died. It was, of course, necessary again to choose a rabbi, but now the selection process had become more complicated. In the wake of the failed Polish uprising of 1863, the Russian viceroy (*namiestnik*) General Fedor Berg announced new regulations on 29 February, 1868, bestowing broad powers on the government regarding the appointment of Jewish communal figures, including rabbis. It may not have been a blessing for the Jewish communities, but it was for the historian, because this decree meant that correspondence regarding the rabbinate went back and forth between the viceroy in Warsaw and his superiors in St. Petersburg—correspondence that was only recently discovered. It gives added insights into the hiring and firing of R. Gesundheit.

Fedor Berg[14] was to play a major role in the rabbinical career of R. Gesundheit. He was born into a Baltic German family in what is now Estonia in 1793. After studying in the University of Dorpat (now Tartu), he entered military service as a volunteer during the war with Napoleon in 1812 and spent much of his early career involved in what would be termed today geographical surveys. During the Polish uprising of 1831, he was transferred at his own request to a fighting unit and was ultimately promoted to general and given the rank of count. He was appointed commander of the Russian forces in Poland during the uprising in 1863 and, after it was crushed, he was named Russian viceroy in Poland.[15] The condition and status of Jews was not a central concern in his career as viceroy.[16] He was not known for an exceptionally warm attitude towards Jews.

---

14 The most useful biography I found is Mikhail Polievktov, "Berg, Graf Fedor Fedorovich (Fridrikh Vil'gel'm Rembert)," *Russkii biograficheskii slovar'* (ed. A.A. Polovtsov; St. Petersburg: Imperatorskoe Russkoe Istoricheskoe Obshchestvo, 1896–1918), vol. 2, 724–728. For a convenient short biography of Berg that focuses on his attitudes to the Jews, see Iulii Gessen, "Berg, Fedor Fedorovich (1793–1874), graf," *Evreiskaia entsiklopediia* (St. Petersburg: Brokgauz Efron, 1906–1913), vol. 4, cols. 203–204. It makes no mention of R. Gesundheit, however. A short (16 page) biography of Berg was published that I have not been able to see: *Le feldmaréchal Comte Berg: namiestnik dans le royaume de Pologne et commandant en chef des troupes de l'arrondissement militaire de Varsovie* (Varsovie: Imprimerie de Joseph Unger, 1872). The most recent extended discussion of Berg that I have found is Michał Ludewicz, "Urząd Namiestnika w Królestwie Polskim w latach 1815–1874" (Masters' thesis, University of Wrocław, 2010), 105–110 (despite incorrect data in the table of contents!). This, too, makes no mention of Jews or of rabbi Gesundheit.

15 There are many references to his career in Łukasz Chimiak, *Gubernatorzy rosyjscy w królestwie polskim: szkic do portretu zbiorowego* (Wrocław: Fundacja na Rzecz Nauki Polskiej, 1999).

16 The massive (over five hundred pages) unpublished biography of Fedor Berg by his relative, Boris Berg, *Fel'dmarshal Graf F.F. Berg i ego sovremenniki*, kept in the Bakhmeteff Archive of the Rare Book and Manuscript Library at Columbia University, does not refer

He opposed giving Jews equal rights in the absence of clear evidence of the Jews' positive disposition towards Christian society. At the same time, he was pragmatic. He supported requirements for Jews to modernize their clothing (see Glenn Dynner's chapter in this volume), but also called for accommodations for older Jews who were set in their ways.[17]

In seeking a replacement for R. Meisels, the Warsaw community could rely on precedents. The usual procedure was to take a rabbi who had served in a smaller community and proven his abilities—and who was ready to move on to a higher position. Thus, standard biographies of leading rabbis usually recount a sequence of moves to ever larger Jewish communities. However, now the community had to follow a different procedure. They were asked to prepare a shortlist from which the government representative would pick a rabbi. Selecting candidates was not a simple matter. As mentioned above, Warsaw Jewry was made up of Hasidim, integrationists ('enlightened' or 'progressive' polonized Jews), and non-Hasidim ('Mitnagdim'). Each had their own agenda and their own views as to what kind of individual would be an appropriate rabbi for the Warsaw Jewish community. Two of the major groups were not able to come up with a good candidate.

There was no obvious learned and authoritative Hasidic candidate available for the position. R. Isaac Meir Alter, the first Gerer *rebbe*, had died in 1866 and his interim successor had died in 1870. His heir was Rabbi Yehudah Aryeh Leib, who was to become famous as the 'Sfas Emes,' the title of his main collection of homiletic teachings; but at the time he was only 22 years old, too young for a position as rabbi of Warsaw. On the other hand, if the position went to another powerful Hasidic figure, that person might potentially challenge R. Yehudah Aryeh Leib for Hasidic preeminence and Gerer Hasidim obviously wanted to avoid this.

The integrationists also lacked a candidate. To mount a serious campaign for someone from their camp, they needed a figure that both reflected their values and could make a credible claim for recognition as a scholar of Judaica. Marcus Jastrow could have been such a candidate, but he had been forced

---

to his ties with Jews. Berg's papers are kept in the Estonian Historical Archive in Tartu. A careful check by Maarja Kivi, an archivist there, found no letters to or from R. Gesundheit or referencing Jews in general. I am extremely grateful to her for her generous help, however. Nor did Alo Sarg and Malle Salupere (both in Estonia), who both wrote on Berg, come across any such sources.

17 Iulii Gessen, "Bor'ba pravitel'stva s evreiskoi odezhdoi v Imperii i v Tsarstve Pol'skom," in *Perezhitoe: Sbornik, posviashchennyi obshchestvennoi i kul'turnoi zhizni Evreev v Rossii* (ed. S.M. Ginzburg et al.; St. Petersburg: Brokgauz Efron, 1908–10), vol. 1, pt. 2, 10–18.

to leave Warsaw in 1863 and, by 1870, was already well established as a rabbi in Philadelphia.[18] He had no chance of being able to return to Warsaw and probably no desire to do so. Izaak Cylkow, who was to be the first rabbi of the Great Synagogue on Tłomackie Street was in 1870 the preacher at the "German Synagogue" on Daniłowiczowska Street and it was a bit premature to regard him as a potential candidate for the position of rabbi of Warsaw. He was also a Polonophile, and it was highly unlikely that the Russian regime would accept a candidate who was openly sympathetic to the Polish national cause. Thus there were good reasons why there were no serious attempts by the integrationist camp to come up with a candidate of their own.

There was also a more basic problem for the integrationists. They were regarded by the Russian governmental officials in Warsaw as problematic from a political point of view and with a potential for getting involved in subversive activities. From the point of view of these officials, traditionalist Jews were more likely to hold conservative political views and to support the government side.[19]

Traditionally, Jewish communities preferred to appoint rabbis who did not have previous ties with the community. The prior rabbi of Warsaw, R. Meisels, had come to Warsaw from Krakow and, in this respect, had fit the traditional mold of rabbinic appointments. Thus it was no surprise that in 1870 many Warsaw Jews felt that that the best candidate was a non resident—the rabbi of Brest, R. Zvi Orenstein.[20] He was a well known, respected and experienced rabbi. Moreover, he was on good terms with both Hasidim and non Hasidim,

---

18   On Jastrow see Michał Galas, "Jastrow, Markus," YIVO *Encyclopedia of Jews in Eastern Europe*, 1: 819, as well as Michał Galas, *Rabin Markus Jastrow i jego wizja reformy judaizmu: Studium z dziejów judaizmu w XIX wieku* (Kraków: Austeria, 2007). An English translation of this fascinating book is now available as *Rabbi Marcus Jastrow and His Vision for the Reform of Judaism: A Study in the History of Judaism in the Nineteenth Century* (trans. Anna Tilles; Boston: Academic Studies Press, 2013).

19   See the letter of the police chief of Warsaw written November 19, 1870. It is kept in the archive of the Department of Religious Affairs of Foreign Confessions of the Ministry of Internal Affairs in the Russian state history archive (St. Petersburg) (RGIA). F. 821, op. 8, d. 548 l. 10.18. The police chief quotes General Kalikst Witkowski, the Lord Mayor of Warsaw, as presenting the view that the traditionalists are more trustworthy. See the article of Vadim Malakhov, "Pol'skoe vosstanie 1863 g. i politika vlastei po otnosheniiu k evreiam Tsarstva Pol'skogo," available here: http://mkonf.iriran.ru/papers.php?id=154. This point is developed by Marcin Wodziński in *Hasidism and Politics: The Kingdom of Poland, 1815–1864* (Oxford: Littman Library, 2013), 157–162.

20   For his biography, see Meir Wunder, *Me'orei galitsia* (Jerusalem: Machon Le-Hantsakhat Yahadut Galitsiya, 1978), vol. 1, 74–78; and Haim Gertner, "Orenstein Family," YIVO *Encyclopedia of Jews in Eastern Europe*, 2: 1288–89.

which would have been a major advantage for Warsaw Jews. Rabbi Orenstein had come to Brest from Lemberg and was a fine scholar. His only drawback, a critical one, was that he was not a Russian citizen but rather a citizen of the Austro-Hungarian Empire. Brest, of course, was in the Russian Empire; but this was not enough. Berg's instructions were that the rabbi of such a key community as Warsaw must be a Russian citizen, which automatically ruled R. Orenstein out. Only a few years later, in 1873, he was expelled from Brest and forced to go back to the Hapsburg lands on the grounds that he was a foreigner.

Other possibilities were ruled out as well. Some of the relatives of the deceased rabbi of the city, R. Meisels, could have been candidates. His son was rabbi of Siedlice and well respected; however, sons were not the first choice for take off. R. Meisel's brother in law, R. Israel Bornstein, was also problematic. Among other factors, he was not a Russian citizen. In any case, he died on June 7, 1870, so he would not have been a candidate for long.[21]

What is striking is who was missing from the list of proposed candidates. The Warsaw community looked specifically for Polish rabbis as candidates for the position and turned to other Polish communities for rabbis even when these communities were not in the Russian Empire. But the Warsaw community showed little interest in rabbis from non-Polish Jewish communities such as in Lithuania and Belorussia, even though they were also in the Tsarist Empire. R. Orenstein, R. Bernstein and R. Meisels' own son were all seen as Polish Jews and potential candidates; and their not deriving originally from the Russian-ruled Kingdom of Poland was not a central factor. In other words, the Warsaw Jewish leaders may have felt that there were no worthy candidates in the Kingdom of Poland, but the availability of many first-rate scholars in other nearby cultural/linguistic Jewish groups did not seem to interest them. This says a great deal about their sense of identity.

The Polonocentric attitude of the Warsaw community was not total. However, the exception only proved the rule. According to the Russian governmental correspondence, there was yet another potential candidate—R. Yehoshua Heschel Levine.[22] He had been a resident of Vilna and was a

---

21 For his genealogy see: http://www.ics.uci.edu/~dan/genealogy/Krakow/Families/Bornstein.html (accessed on 14.7.13).

22 Cf. GARF (State Archive of the Russian Federation) f. 109 I, ex. III, otd. 1870 MMF/793. A microfilm copy is available at the Central Archive for the History of the Jewish People in Jerusalem. I discuss Levine's career in my *Lithuanian Yeshivas of the Nineteenth Century: Creating a Tradition of Learning* (Oxford and Portland, OR: Littman Library, 2012), esp. 67–74. Levine had been a candidate for the leadership of the Volozhin yeshiva, and therefore it was a bit surprising to find his name mentioned as a potential candidate Rabbi of

highly regarded scholar and activist. Despite adhering to very conservative values, he was able to adapt modern tools for the traditionalist cause. He dressed in modern clothes and was the first to try to put out an orthodox (or proto-orthodox) newspaper. In many respects, he might have been an ideal choice. He apparently put himself up for the position but did not attract a great deal of local support.[23] His candidacy was not pursued; and what is more significant, it was not even discussed in the Warsaw Jewish periodical *Izraelita*. It seems that Levine's non-Polish background disqualified him before any serious steps were taken. Had his name not come up, it would have been possible to explain the lack of non-Polish candidates as 'accidental' or due to a lack of information about potential candidates. But since he was mentioned, it is clear that Warsaw Jews knew of non-Polish options but did not follow up on them. While not surprising, this preference underscores the deep lines dividing Jewish subgroups that had little to do with political positions.

At the end of all the internal discussion, the Jewish community presented three candidates: R. Zvi Orenstein of Brest, R. Israel Bornstein, and R. Jacob Gesundheit. The expectation was that the well known R. Orenstein would be chosen and, if not him, then R. Bornstein. Instead, the government authorities chose R. Gesundheit. This was not by chance.[24]

R. Jacob Gesundheit[25] was unquestionably a Polish Jew and a citizen of the Tsarist Empire. He was born in 1815 in Praga, a suburb of Warsaw, to a distinguished family. His father was a well-known scholar and his mother was famous for giving charity. In other words, his was also an affluent family. He excelled in Talmud study as a young man and married, as was the custom, at the age of 17. He apparently never mastered the Polish language, though he was a successful businessman. Already in 1842, before he was even 30 years old, he published the first volume of a commentary on part of the Shulhan Arukh. This is testimony both to his talents and the financial resources at his disposal. While it would be tempting to anticipate that wealth and Polonization went hand in hand among the Warsaw Jews in the mid-nineteenth century, R. Gesundheit's

---

Warsaw. This was not mentioned in any of the sources I accessed when researching his biography.

23 This is mentioned in a letter of the Lord Mayor of Warsaw, General Witkowski, to Viceroy Berg written on September 9, 1870. It is kept in the archive of the Department of Religious Affairs of Foreign Confessions of the Ministry of Internal Affairs in the Russian state history archive (St. Petersburg) (RGIA). F. 821, op. 8, d. 548 l. 7.

24 Frenk, "Ha-rabanut."

25 For a concise biography see François Guesnet, "Gesundheit, Ya'akov," *YIVO Encyclopedia of Jews in Eastern Europe*, 1: 591.

biography is a reminder that there were a number of distinct circles of wealthy individuals with distinctive characteristics and that not every affluent Jew was an integrationist. His circle was a well-off but a traditionalist one.

For many years, R. Gesundheit was an active business man, but at the same time he taught students in what he termed a 'yeshiva'. This was not an institution in the Lithuanian mode but rather a more ad hoc framework in which young scholars came regularly to listen to lessons that he gave. Quite wisely, as it appears in retrospect, he avoided rabbinical positions and preferred the life of an independent scholar and highly respected teacher. By taking that approach, he did not acquire practical experience in the give-and-take necessary to deal with a community. Nevertheless, he enjoyed a reputation as a brilliant scholar and rabbinic authority—and apparently acquired some of the charisma that came with that kind of reputation. The fact that R. Gesundheit apparently had a distinguished appearance (he was one of the first East European rabbis to be photographed) must have added to his stature.[26]

His status seems to have been generally recognized—in time he seems to have become the de facto leader of the non-Hasidic traditionalists in Warsaw. In 1854, he and R. Isaac Meir Alter were cosigners to an approbation of the rabbi of Warsaw, R. Haim Dawidsohn to a volume of the Dubno Maggid.[27] In 1856 he was among those signing a petition to the government to lift the ban on collecting money for the Jews in Palestine.[28] In 1859 he was one of nine cosigners of a proclamation regarding standards for kosher meat in Warsaw.

---

26   See Lucy S. Dawidowicz, "Pictures of the Jewish Past," *Commentary* 60.3 (October 1975): 64–68: "The Jews, like everyone else, began to have their pictures taken. The earliest of these photographs are of the high bourgeoisie ... and even some of the more prestigious big-city rabbis and communal leaders, a few of whom sat for the camera as early as the 1860's." In footnote no. 1 she adds: "A stunning photograph of Jacob Gesundheit comes to mind, taken in 1870, when he became rabbi of Warsaw. The rabbi, in a long satin robe with a velvet head covering, sits on an ornate and finely carved high-backed armchair, upholstered in deep plush. He is posed, pen in hand, at a table with a splendidly embroidered damask cloth; several tomes, *seforim*, are at his elbow. It is a photograph that bespeaks the status and prestige of Warsaw's chief rabbi and does honor to the Jewish community." On the very first Polish rabbis to be photographed and on the distribution of their photographs, see Agnieszka Jagodzińska *Pomiędzy: Akulturacja Żydów Warszawy w drugiej połowie XIX wieku* (Wrocław: Wydawnictwo Uniwersytetu Wrocławskiego, 2008), 112–115.

27   Yaakov Kranz, *Ohel yaakov* [on Numbers] (Königsberg? 1861).

28   See Marcin Wodziński, *Judaica w aktach Centralnych Władz Wyznaniowych Królestwa Polskiego Archiwum Głównego Akt Dawnych: Informator archiwalny* (Wrocław: Wydawnictwo Uniwersytetu Wrocławskiego, 2010), 68.

His name appears after that of R. Meisels (the rabbi of Warsaw), R. Isaiah Muskat (rabbi of the Praga suburb of Warsaw) and R. Alter—the Gerer rebbe.[29]

R. Gesundheit was not a Hasid and was actually known as an opponent of Hasidism. There are folkloristic reports that during an outbreak of messianic hopes in 1860 that he stood up on a *bimah* in his synagogue and swore that the Messiah would not come that year. Whether or not this happened is not as important as the fact that he seemed to have been regarded, in some circles at least, as an opponent of mystical speculations.[30] However, as is often the case, he did not fit neatly into the category of a *mitnaged*. It seems that he had warm personal ties with R. Isaac Meir Alter, the Gerer *rebbe*,[31] though apparently these ties did not extend to the *rebbe's* grandson and ultimate heir— R. Yehudah Aryeh Leib. Nonetheless, in Gerer traditions, a student of his was accused of trying to besmirch R. Isaac Meir Alter as having spoken dismissively of the Vilna Gaon.[32] R. Gesundheit's ties with the integrationists and maskilim were also not easy to classify. He did not know Polish or Russian, nor was he identified as a maskil or as a person with maskilic tendencies. However, apparently he was familiar with enlightenment literature in Hebrew.

Interestingly enough, already in 1863, someone who hid behind a pseudonym took the trouble to write a short biography of R. Gesundheit, intending to publish it in *Ha-tzefira* the Warsaw maskilic Hebrew language journal that had just begun to be published. While the identity of the author is unknown, he clearly was linked to the enlightenment movement—and to R. Gesundheit. *Ha-tzefira* temporarily ceased publication just then, but the author did not give up. Instead of submitting the biography to another journal, the author took the trouble to publish the biography in Johannisburg (Prussia) as a brochure. However, he did not explain why it was so urgent to publish the biography. The author identified himself as D.N.I S.L.I on the title page. This abbreviation or pseudonym is not known from any other sources.[33] Near the end of the

---

29   Tzvi Michelson, *Tirosh ve-yitshar* (Biłgoraj: Kronenberg, 1936), 69, no. 25.

30   See *Reshumot* I (Odessa, 1918), 387. The story was reported by Judah Elzet (Zlotnik). An almost identical text appears in Mordechai Lipson, *Di velt dertseylt* (New York: Doros, 1928), 25, no. 24, without citation of a source, but it appears to be derived from Elzet. On the messianic speculation in 1840, see Abraham Duker, "The Tarniks," in *Joshua Starr Memorial Volume* (New York: Conference On Jewish Relations, 1953), 191–201.

31   For cooperation on charities, see Avraham Issachar Alter, *Meir*, vol. 2, 83. On a joint recommendation for a book, see Yitzhak Meir Alter, *Kuntres Mikhtevei ha-Ri"M*, appended to *Sefer Ha-zekhut* (New York: Bet Hillel, 1999), 269.

32   Alter, *Meir*, vol. 1, 29, no. 109.

33   I checked in all of the standard resources and consulted with various learned individuals to no avail. One possible clue as to the authorship of the booklet lies in the Jewish

autobiography, the author commented that it was his intention to proceed with a parallel biography of R. Isaac Meir Alter, the Gerer *rebbe*, but that he needed more material. The biography merited a short review in *Jutrzenka*, the Polish language Jewish periodical not known for its interest in traditional rabbis and their lives; but the reviewer did not note the identity of the author.[34] The body of the biography, minus the explicitly maskilic introduction, was reprinted in the introduction of the 1910 edition of R. Gesundheit's book *Tiferet Yaakov* on *Hullin* (part two) as the work of a 'dear person,' but without any other information. This biography and the interest in *Ha-tzefira* suggest that R. Gesundheit had wide horizons—but not in a direction that would have attracted support for him either among Hasidim or among those Jews who called for integration in Polish culture.

The quiet and comfortable life R. Gesundheit had led changed in the wake of the unsuccessful Polish revolution of 1863. His financial situation apparently declined, though details are not known.[35] When the position of rabbi of Warsaw opened in 1870 he, or someone close to him, took steps to get him the post. It is hard to believe that an initiative could have been taken without his awareness and consent. According to A.N. Frenk, his supporters employed modern tactics. They organized a letter-writing campaign in which hundreds of letters were sent to the government.[36] These letters emphasized R. Gesundheit's well-known policy of non-involvement in the Polish political agenda (as opposed to R. Meisels), the fact that he was locally born, and his well deserved reputation as a rabbinical scholar. When R. Gesundheit was subsequently interviewed by the Russian viceroy (Berg) he emphasized that he felt that Jews must be loyal to the government.

---

tradition of *gematria*, according to which each Hebrew letter is assigned a numerical value; thus each word written in Hebrew has a both a meaning and a numerical value. The name DNI SLI has a numerical value of 164 and the word/name Gesundheit, spelled without the letter 'yud' has the same value. This was pointed out to me by Prof. Gershon Hundert. However, I am not certain how to interpret this—I find it difficult to imagine that R. Gesundheit wrote this biography himself.

34 See *Jutrzenka* 3.1 (2 January 1863): 7. I suspect that if the identity of the author were to be discovered, that information would also explain why there was a review in *Jutrzenka*. I thank Marcin Wodziński for the reference to this source.

35 According to *Israelitische Wochenschrift für die religiösen und socialen Interessen des Judenthums*, 4.35 (3 September 1873): 282, R. Gesundheit went bankrupt at least once and was under economic pressure to seek out a position that could yield him a good income. However, the article has such a negative slant that it is difficult to rely on.

36 See the description in Frenk, "Ha-rabanut."

It is very possible that Jewish dress was an issue. Since the mid-nineteenth century, the Tsarist government had long pressured the Jews in the Empire, including Congress Poland, to adopt either the Western or the Russian style of dress, and laws were enacted that required this—with punishments and fines for those who did not comply. However, it changed little on the ground. In 1869 Viceroy Berg corresponded with Tsar Alexander II on this topic. Berg was pragmatic in his implementation of the policy. Rabbis were exempted from the requirement to change dress, while Jews were also allowed on holy days to wear the traditional Jewish dress without penalty. The issue came to a head in 1870. Berg was under pressure from St. Petersburg to enforce changes in dress and he continued to delay its implementation. Skilled bureaucrat as he was, his delaying tactics were ultimately successful.[37] However, at the time when Berg was involved in the process of selecting a rabbi, the issue was still unresolved. Apparently, he asked R. Gesundheit what the response should be to a government order to cut sidelocks, trim beards and adopt western dress. The rabbi replied that such changes could be permitted. Berg, the viceroy, apparently liked what he heard. The Jewish masses, however, were less enthusiastic, and some Hasidim were concerned that the government might proceed to a general ban on Hasidism.[38]

The supporters of R. Gesundheit came largely from non-Hasidic or anti-Hasidic circles, groups that have not yet been systematically studied. Both in the Kingdom of Poland and Galicia there existed, until the Holocaust, significant populations of middle-class Jews who were neither ideological integrationists nor Hasidim but simply committed traditional Jews as in previous generations. They were often sufficiently economically well off to give their children a good Jewish education, but did not have organizational structures that gave them identity and leadership. They were 'simply' householders

---

37   See the description in Gessen, "Bor'ba pravitel'stva" (note 18 above). Hasidim apparently felt that R. Gesundheit was involved or even behind the government initiative to force Polish Jews to change their clothing style. See the short vignette of Judah Elzet (Zlotnik) in *Reshumot* I (Odessa, 1918), 387. Rabbi Samuel Munk, writing almost one hundred years later, stated that he had heard that there was a disagreement between R. Gesundheit and R. Isaac Meir Alter as to whether adopting the clothing styles of non-Jews was forbidden by Jewish law (R. Alter's position) or permitted (R. Gesundheit's position). See Samuel Munk, *Peat Sadekha* (Jerusalem: Safra, 1975), 221. See also the chapter by Glenn Dynner in this volume.

38   This is according to Frenk who was apparently reflecting 'common knowledge' in Warsaw at his time. Frenk did not have access to Berg's notes of the conversation. Even if this is not true, this claim was the basis on which many Jews in Warsaw determined their attitudes to R. Gesundheit. See Frenk, "Ha-rabanut."

(*ba'ale batim*). The 'masses' often had respect for them, but did not identify with them nor automatically follow their lead. Hence the non-Hasidic— non-integrationist element was a presence, but in a time of growing political activity and democracy or proto-democracy, not an active presence.

Many Warsaw Jews, possibly a majority, were not in R. Gesundheit's camp. The strength of Hasidism in Warsaw had increased dramatically in the previous decade as more and more Warsaw Jews were attracted to Ger Hasidism—or as more Hasidim came to the city.[39] It is difficult to measure the numerical strength of the Hasidim in Warsaw, at that time or later, but their organization and internal structure gave them more strength than mere numbers would warrant. Nor was R. Gesundheit close to the integrationist circles to which many of the rich Jews belonged. They would have preferred a rabbi with a modern education who spoke Polish but, as noted above they didn't put up a candidate—probably because they were unable to find an attractive candidate that was also a Russian citizen and who had the requisite characteristics. Moreover, the integrationists had been irritated by R. Gesundheit's open non-support of the Polish national movement and lobbied with the government to allow the community to simply dispense with the post of communal rabbi altogether, allowing each sub-group to appoint their own rabbi.[40] In short, neither the Hasidim nor the integrationists wanted R. Gesundheit to represent them or the Warsaw Jewish community.

For Berg and his superiors in St Petersburg, however, R. Gesundheit was the best, or to be more precise, the least undesirable candidate. His lack of knowledge of Polish was probably a plus in the eyes of the Russian administration, though the fact that he also did not know Russian or standard German must have been a drawback. In addition to his well-earned reputation as a rabbinic scholar, his opposition to the Polish national movement was a clear plus for the Russian officials. R. Meisels had been a vocal supporter of the Polish independence movement and one such rabbi was more than enough for them. Berg

---

39   See Bronislaw Bloch, "*Spatial Evolution of the Jews and General Population of Warsaw, 1792–1939*," in *Papers in Jewish Demography 1973: Proceedings of the demographic sessions held at the 6th World Congress of Jewish Studies* (ed. U.O. Schmelz, P. Glikson, S. della Pergola; Jerusalem: Institute of Contemporary Jewry, Hebrew University of Jerusalem, 1977). On migration to Poland, see also François Guesnet, *Polnische Juden im 19. Jahrhundert: Lebensbedingungen, Rechtsnormen und Organisation im Wandel* (Cologne and Vienna: Böhlau, 1998), 29–80.

40   Frenk, "Ha-rabanut." He writes in a footnote that Hilary Nussbaum, author of *Szkice historyczne z życia Żydów w Warszawie*, could not have written about such matters earlier because of Tsarist censorship.

wanted Gesundheit.⁴¹ Gavriel Vinaver, a wealthy Warsaw Jew, presented the formal application for his appointment in the name of the Jews of Warsaw, but this was a mere formality.⁴²

When the time came for Warsaw Jews to vote, there was only one candidate, R. Gesundheit, and he was elected for a three-year term as prescribed by the government regulations. On 13 September, 1870, he was officially installed as rabbi of Warsaw. This was not an entirely happy occasion for him. The ceremony was marred by a demonstration of young Hasidim, yet there was no counter display of support by his backers. Nor was this the end of the opposition to his appointment. Shatzky details the campaign of the Hasidim to harass R. Gesundheit. Posters were put up denigrating the rabbi who had attained his position on account of government support. Perhaps more seriously, opponents would come to R. Gesundheit with contrived *halakhic* questions and would then use his responses to attack him for being too lenient.⁴³

The appointment of R. Gesundheit to the post of rabbi was balanced out by the appointment of R. Nathan Spiegelglass (1798–1873) as head of the rabbinical court (Av Bet Din). He was a well-known scholar with Hasidic leanings who had served on the rabbinical court in Warsaw. He was not an adherent of the Gerer Hasidic court and it seems that his closest ties were or had been with the *Rebbe* of Kuznitz, R. Moses Elyokim Bri'ah Hopstein, and the dynasty founded by Ezekiel Taub of Kuzmir. However he was also on good terms with the Gerer rebbe. In short, he could serve as a representative of the Hasidic community but was not identified with a specific branch.⁴⁴ There is a report that he had seen himself as a candidate for the position, but nothing came of it.⁴⁵ Perhaps

---

41   Berg was not noted for an aversion to gifts. See Antoni Zaleski, *Towarzystwo warszawskie; listy do przyjaciółki* in "letter 5" on p. 42 of the (second) Kraków edition, published by Żupański and Heumann in 1888. I do not have a copy of the first edition at my disposal. It is of course impossible to know today if he received any financial inducements to choose R. Gesundheit but it cannot be ruled out as impossible. There may well have been differing views within the Russian regime. Malakhov wrote in his article "Pol'skoe vosstanie 1863 g." (see note 20 above) that I.V. Witkowski (!), who was the Russian-appointed Lord Mayor of Warsaw, supported the Hasidic candidate because the Hasidim posed fewer difficulties for the authorities. He cites as his source documents in the Russian State Historical Archive (RGIA) f. 821, op. 8 D. 548, L. 18. I was unable to consult this source. If it is accurate, it is necessary to conclude that despite his opinion, Berg did not change his mind.
42   See H.M. Winawer, *The Winawer Saga* (London: H.M. Winawer, 1994), 21–23.
43   See Shatzky, *Geshikhte fun yidn in varshe*, III: 140 for details.
44   See the introduction to his book *Meorot natan* published in Bilgoraj in 1910, 5.
45   See the letter of the police chief of Warsaw written November 19, 1870. It is kept in the archive of the Department of Religious Affairs of Foreign Confessions of the Ministry of

he was seen as too old, perhaps it was a matter of Hasidic politics, or perhaps he was not seen as the right person for such a representative post.

The conflict over the prestigious appointment quickly attracted the attention of Jews far beyond the municipal boundaries of Warsaw. R. Gesundheit's opponents organized a rather successful public relations campaign against him in the Jewish press abroad and tried to besmirch his reputation for integrity in business.[46] He did attract some support from unanticipated circles, but this support was not necessarily to his benefit. A short announcement of the appointment of R. Gesundheit to the position of rabbi of Warsaw, written by Aryeh Leib Cohen in Warsaw on September 21, praised the decision to recognize a local scholar and not to seek a rabbi from afar. Cohen also celebrated his appointment as a victory over the Hasidim who, as he put it, absolutely hate R. Gesundheit. What is significant is the journal in which it was published— Ha-shachar.[47] This was a *haskalah* journal published in Vienna that was well known for its strong support for modernization and radical change within the Jewish community.

Shortly after the publication of a positive article about R. Gesundheit in Ha-shachar, another article that referred to the appointment, this time in very negative terms, was published in the German Jewish periodical *Jüdische Presse: Organ für die religiösen Interessen des Judenthums*.[48] This was an orthodox journal published in Berlin, and the editor at the time was Hirsch, son of R. Esriel Hildesheimer. In other words, it was not necessarily a journal that would be expected to publish an article opposing the appointment of R. Gesundheit. The author did not identify himself, but he noted that he was a resident of Lemberg/Lvov and compared the situation of the rabbinate in Warsaw with the situation at that time in Lemberg. The author claimed that R. Gesundheit was not a serious scholar and that he was appointed only because he had found favor in the eyes of the government authorities. Most of the Jews of Warsaw, he added, were against his appointment.

The article published in the *Jüdische Presse* cannot be relied on blindly. It is not clear why the author saw Lemberg as such a positive example. The rabbi of

---

Internal Affairs in the Russian state history archive (St. Petersburg) (RGIA). F. 821, op. 8, d. 548, l. 10. While he was alive, it was unlikely that R. Shmuel Zanvil Klepfisz, another well known scholar, would have been regarded as a potential candidate.

46   Karlinsky, *Ha-rishon*, 245. Karlinsky does not cite his source.

47   The author was clearly not a rabbinical figure, though I was not able to obtain any further information as to his identity; Aryeh Leib Cohen: [untitled report] *Ha-shachar* 2.1 (1871): 12.

48   *Jüdische Presse: Organ für die religiösen Interessen des Judenthums*, 1.18 (4 November 1870): 143–144.

Lemberg at the time was R. Joseph Shaul Natanson, a conservative non-Hasidic rabbinic scholar like R. Gesundheit. Moreover, he was actually an open supporter of R. Gesundheit. The author of the article claimed that R. Gesundheit was not learned enough to be a rabbi, a somewhat dubious claim in light of his learned publications that are recognized today as works of scholarship, even if they did not introduce novel methodologies. To send such a letter from Warsaw might have been somewhat dangerous, since it was critical of government policy. Thus it might well be the case that this scurrilous letter was written by R. Gesundheit's opponents in Warsaw under the cover of a letter supposedly from Lemberg—a city in the Austro-Hungarian Empire. This still does not explain, however, why a Berlin orthodox journal would have published it; nevertheless, even without a detailed explanation it is clear that R. Gesundheit had not developed ties with German Jewish orthodoxy.

The anti-Gesundheit article was followed up by an anti-anti-Gesundheit (!) article written by Perets Smolenskin that appeared in a later issue of *Ha-shachar* that year.[49] He claimed that the opponents of R. Gesundheit had tried to derail his appointment by informing government officials that R. Gesundheit was a rebel who did not honor the law, but that this had been shown to be false. He concluded by stating that he himself had recently been in Warsaw and had found widespread support for R. Gesundheit. But all this support for R. Gesundheit in *Ha-shachar* was a mixed blessing in Warsaw. It certainly did not strengthen R. Gesundheit's position among the traditionalists; even less so among the Hasidim. The case of the Warsaw rabbinate was on its way to becoming a cause célèbre in the Jewish world.

R. Gesundheit did not respond to the Hasidic opposition by making public overtures towards them. To the contrary, he tried to replace Hasidic *shokhtim* (ritual slaughterers) with non-Hasidic ones on the grounds that the former were incompetent. The Hasidim responded in kind. Apparently, the Gerer Hasidim published pamphlets with many charges against him, including accusations that he had purchased the rabbinate and that his position was beholden to the non-Jewish government.[50]

Relations between Hasidim and R. Gesundheit worsened when, after his appointment, the government re-imposed restrictions on traditional dress.[51]

---

49 Perets Smolenskin, "Lehashiv le-enosh zidkoto," *Ha-shachar* 2.3 (1871): 122. On Smolenskin see Shmuel Feiner, "Smolenskin, Perets," YIVO *Encyclopedia of Jews in Eastern Europe*, 2: 1765–67.

50 Y. Ahisham (=Simkhe Bunem Petrushka), "Ver zenen geven di amolige hoypt-rabonim in varshe?" *Haynt* 279 (9.12.1934). About the author, see the chapter by Joanna Nalewajko-Kulikov in this volume.

51 Frenk, "Ha-rabanut."

R. Gesundheit gave this step public support. On 31 March 1871 the following announcement appeared in the Polish language Jewish newspaper *Izraelita*:[52]

> Announcement of Rabbi Jacob Gesundheit in 1871
> RABBI OF THE WARSAW DISTRICT
> Be it known to all of our co-religionists that on the basis of the supreme confirmation of the ordinance of 22 February (6 March) of this year, the Jews are obligated to wear dress that does not differ from that of other inhabitants of the Empire. All the details were published as is generally known in all the periodical press and besides that, the [Jewish] council of the Warsaw region announced it by means of printed announcements in all the synagogues and prayer rooms. Therefore, every Israelite should unconditionally comply with the ordinance and prepare accordingly in order to avoid coercive measures in response for non fulfillment of the ordinance before the deadline, i.e. March 15 (27), especially since the ordinance requiring the change of clothing does not at all violate the religious ordinances of Mosaic Law.
>
> Warsaw, 10 (22) March 1871
> Rabbi Jacob Gesundheit

It is impossible today to know if R. Gesundheit signed the announcement because he really believed what he wrote or whether he saw it as a necessary but insincere step that had been done by others in the past for ostensibly similar reasons. The Hasidim certainly did not judge him charitably, in any case. They regarded him as an official imposed on them by the government and his support or acceptance of the government decree certainly did not enhance his popularity among them.[53] The possibility that R. Gesundheit would or did use his position to favor non-Hasidic kosher slaughterers and supervisors certainly had economic implications. Finally, at least some saw R. Gesundheit's

---

52   *Izraelita* (31 March 1871): 104. The original can be downloaded here: http://polona.pl/archive_prod?uid=8008897&cid=9607413. I thank Glenn Dynner for informing me about this source and to Agnieszka Jagodzińska for helping me locate it online.

53   Already in 1849 R. Chaim Dawidsohn, R. Isaiah Mushkat and R. Israel Meir Alter and in 1857 R. Ber Meisels and the same R. Mushkat and R. Alter had publicized statements in support of obeying official demands for change of dress—even though what motivated them was probably more duress then dress. See the issue of *Izraelita* cited in the previous footnote. There is no evidence other than the announcement published in *Izraelita* to indicate that R. Gesundheit was in favor of change in Jewish dress. He certainly did not set an example by adopting western dress styles. For a discussion, see Jagodzińska, *Pomiędzy: Akulturacja Żydów Warszawy*, 117, and now, Glenn Dynner's article in this volume.

appointment as a public victory of the *mitnagdim* over the Hasidism, which disturbed them.

R. Gesundheit enlisted well known rabbis to support his *halakhic* positions regarding *shekhita*. The best known supporter of his was R. Yosef Shaul Natanson, the non-Hasidic rabbi of Lemberg. R. Gesundheit wrote to him to ask him if his *halakhic* position on *shekhita* was justified, and R. Natanson inserted at the end of the first part of a volume of responsa he published in 1873 a responsum written to R. Gesundheit. The responsum opened with a statement that the question was a simple one, but that out of respect to R. Gesundheit he would consider it. This was an oblique way of saying that those who had questioned R. Gesundheit's decision did not even understand a simple question of ritual law. At the end he wrote "I am pained very much by those who cause injury to this scholar [e.g. R. Gesundheit] for no reason, because I have known of his fine reputation for many years..."[54] A similar letter of support was written at more or less the same time by R. Azriel Arye Leib Rakowski, the rabbi of Płock.[55] Rakowski, as well, was a non-Hasidic Polish rabbi well known for his opposition to Hasidism.[56] Such support, especially coming from abroad (Lvov), did not seem to have had an impact on either Warsaw Jews or the responsible government officials. It is interesting that these rabbis did not seem to have been concerned by R. Gesundheit's public position about the new laws regarding Jewish dress.

It seems that the Hasidim not only tried to arouse popular opinion against R. Gesundheit but also took steps that were removed from the public eye.[57] Their goal was to bypass Berg and deal directly with the authorities in St. Petersburg. According to government informants, one of the key figures in these efforts was R. Shmuel Zanvil Klepfisz. He had a personal interest: as a

---

54   Yosef Shaul Natanson, *Sheelot u-tshuvot shoel u-meishiv tinyana*, part 1 (Lemberg: Salat, 1873), responsum no. 97, 78b. This responsum, along with the text of R. Gesundheit's letter to R. Natanson, was reprinted in *Moriah* V.5–6 (53–54) (1974): 7–9.

55   See Mordechai Rosenthal, *Pri Mordechai Avraham* (Warsaw: Baumritter, 1895), part 2, 20–22. This book contains a responsum written to R. Gesundheit in the fall of 1872.

56   For information on him in English see: http://www.jewishgen.org/yizkor/plock/plo026.html#Page28, accessed 15.7.13. See also Marcin Wodziński *Hasidism and Politics*, 246–247; and his *Źródła do dziejów chasydyzmu w Królestwie Polskim, 1815–1867, w zasobach polskich archiwów państwowych / Hasidism in the Kingdom of Poland, 1815–1867: Historical Sources in the Polish State Archives* (Kraków and Budapest: Austeria Publishing House and Institute for the History of Polish Jewry and Israel-Poland Relations, Tel Aviv University, 2011), 482–487 and 596–597.

57   The following description of the Hasidic initiative is based on the materials in GARF cited above.

senior *dayan* (judge), he was the obvious candidate to succeed R. Gesundheit should he have to vacate the post. Another was R. Yechiel Rotbajn (1819–1880),[58] apparently a less impressive figure (in 1854 he was recorded as a *belfer*) but a rabbinic personality nonetheless.[59] The practical side of the Hasidic struggle against R. Gesundheit was left to other figures. Among these, Isaiah Prives apparently was a central figure. He was a major merchant who invested in real estate, and he put some of his employees to work on the project. Others were Joseph Barkhan, Moshe Joseph Mendelson, Moshe Zakheim[60] and Nachum or Nathan Spiegelglass.[61]

According to the correspondence of Berg, Yosef Krell and Yeshayah Prives set to work raising funds to fight the appointment. In November 1870, they sent two representatives, Matityahu Zweigbaum and Leib Zakon, to St. Petersburg with a substantial budget (6,000 rubles) in order to 'influence' key figures to act against the appointment of R. Gesundheit. Bribery alone rarely changes positions, since a justification has to be given.[62] So it would be quite interesting to know how else they expected to convince the authorities in St. Petersburg to oppose R. Gesundheit. Unfortunately, this information is not in the archives. But what is clear is that they unintentionally infuriated Berg. He was livid at the attempt to go behind his back and undermine his authority, and he demanded that the authorities in St. Petersburg expel the Jews in question and send them back to Warsaw. Indeed, this is what took place.

At more or less the same time, the Gerer Hasidim undertook an equally unorthodox step to end R. Gesundheit's tenure. Elections were called for a new community council in 1871. Not every Jewish resident had the right to vote, but rather only those who paid a significant tax. This gave a clear advantage to the integrationists, many of whom were affluent. However, they were aware that they alone could not get enough votes to get a majority of seats on the council. After a fair amount of maneuvering, an agreement was made between the integrationists and the Hasidim. The Hasidim would ensure the integrationists a majority of seats on the council in return for their cooperation on issues that

---

58 http://www.jewishgen.org/family/rotbajn.html, accessed 15.7.13.

59 http://www.przodkowie.com/warszawa/index.php?nazw=Rotbajn&view=item, accessed 15.7.13.

60 He apparently became the rabbi of Kowel. See a short obituary in *Ha-peles* 3 (1903): 381. In 1870 he would have been in his late twenties.

61 On Spiegelglass, see Simcha Elberg, *Varsha shel ma'ala* (Bnai Brak, 1969), 84–89, 236–243, 291–302.

62 For a fascinating discussion of this, see Andrzej Chwalba, *Imperium korupcji w Rosji i w Królestwie Polskim w latach 1861–1917* (Kraków: Księgarnia Akademicka, 2006), passim. See also Marcin Wodziński, *Hasidism and Politics*, 206–212.

were of particular concern to the Hasidim. The coalition worked, and for many years the integrationists ran the Warsaw Jewish council with quiet support of the Hasidim. The fact that it was quiet was important, because the integrationists were concerned that open ties would damage their relationships with Berg and other government officials. The non-Hasidim were, of course, livid about what they termed 'The Unholy Alliance,' but their criticism could not change the reality. Both sides had similar views about R. Gesundheit, hoping to see an end of his tenure as rabbi of Warsaw, even if their reasons differed.[63]

In 1873, the community's contract with R. Gesundheit was up for renewal. Both parties of the 'unholy' alliance, the integrationists and the Hasidim, opposed an extension. The lay leaders proposed a system of rotation in which each neighborhood would have a rabbi and each month a different neighborhood rabbi would serve as the chief rabbi. This proposal effectively eliminated the position of communal rabbi and R. Gesundheit's position. The proponents of the idea were able to convince the authorities to adopt it and not to renew R. Gesundheit's appointment. The long term expectations of the two groups were, however, quite different. The Hasidim apparently hoped that they would be able to maneuver the appointment of someone from their camp as rabbi of Warsaw. However, the position remained vacant, and no one was appointed—which was exactly what the progressives had hoped for. From their point of view, it was better to have no rabbi at all than a conservative one, and so it was to be. In July of 1873, it was decided not to renew the contract of R. Gesundheit. It was kept a secret until December, when R. Gesundheit received the official announcement. While council decisions may have been kept secret, the fact that the contract of the rabbi was up for extension was common knowledge, and the communal divisions regarding the rabbi were also no secret; and the news spread quickly. According to Shatzky, this aroused such an outburst in the community that the censor forbad any discussion of it in the Jewish press.[64] This suggests that R. Gesundheit actually had a substantial group of supporters.

Not surprisingly, the press war continued long after R. Gesundheit was dismissed from his post. It was a two way street. R. Gesundheit's unexpected supporter, Perets Smolenskin, published a long report on Warsaw that included a positive description of R. Gesundheit.[65] He found the rabbi sympathetic to the need to teach young people the vernacular language. However, he felt that

---

63 On changes in the community structure, see Shatzky, *Geshikhte fun yidn in varshe*, III: 110–129.
64 Ibid., 143.
65 Perets Smolenskin, "Masa berusia," in *Ha-shachar*, 5 (1874): 152–157. On 152 he refers critically to what he regarded as R. Gesundheit's stringencies in the field of *kashrut*.

such a step could be taken only after the finances of the educational system were guaranteed. Smolenskin wrote with understanding of this position and of the problems of the rabbinic establishment. However, few of the rabbi's potential supporters were likely to have been readers of *Ha-shachar*, and he did not find vocal support in other publications.

At the same time, very negative articles appeared in the German press. A long and very critical article appeared in the Berlin orthodox weekly, *Jüdische Presse: Organ für die religiösen Interessen des Judenthums* in late August, 1873,[66] and three weeks later an equally negative article appeared in *Jüdische Volkszeitung: Wochenschrift für Freunde des Fortschritts in Gemeinde und Schule, Synagoge und Leben*, published in Leipzig.[67] Yet another anti-R. Gesundheit article appeared on 3 September, 1873, in the conservative *Israelitische Wochenschrift für die religiösen und socialen Interessen des Judenthums*.[68] R. Gesundheit's opponents were clearly well organized.

What is not clear is why the alliance of progressives and Hasidim succeeded in convincing the authorities to go ahead with the firing of R. Gesundheit, given the fact that the government had little love for either Polonophile progressives or Hasidim. At the moment there is no data that can explain this, though contemporaries offered explanations. Certain circumstantial evidence can be adduced. R. Gesundheit's major supporter was the viceroy, Fedor Berg. He was born in 1793 or 1794 and died, around the age of 80, on January 6, 1874. While there is no detailed biography of Berg that I know of, it is reasonable to assume that in the last half year of his life, when the crucial decisions regarding R. Gesundheit were being made, he was not in the best of health and could devote little energy, if he indeed wanted to, to protect his protégé. Without strong support within the government, R. Gesundheit's position was hopeless.

What is even more mysterious is why the Hasidim were so adamant in their struggle against R. Gesundheit, who had publicly honored R. Alter at his funeral despite the troubled relations between him and the Gerer Hasidim.[69] There is, moreover, no evidence that in R. Alter's lifetime he had not maintained a proper, if not warm, relationship with R. Alter. The fact that they co-signed

---

66   *Jüdische Presse: Organ für die religiösen und socialen Interessen des Judenthums*, 4.24 (29 August 1873): 273–275.

67   See for example the very negative report after R. Gesundheit was fired, in *Jüdische Volkszeitung: Wochenschrift für Freunde des Fortschritts in Gemeinde und Schule, Synagoge und Leben*, 38 (17 June 1873): 299.

68   *Israelitische Wochenschrift für die religiösen und socialen Interessen des Judenthums*, 35 (3 September 1873): 282.

69   Alter, *Meir*, vol. 2, 90–91, no. 658.

proclamations does not indicate friendship but it does suggest that there was a degree of coordination. It is not certain that there were real grounds to justify such a vehement onslaught against R. Gesundheit apart from the issue of Jewish dress. Certainly there was money involved. R. Gesundheit was opposed to a free market of kosher slaughtering. He claimed that a free market would be catastrophic for the income of veteran meat slaughterers and that this would also have a bad impact on the kosher quality of the meat. Of course, for those trying to break into the field, a very low income was better than none. It is quite likely that there were many Hasidim among those trying to 'break the cartel', and that this might justify the vehement opposition to R. Gesundheit. However, even this is not terribly convincing. Vehemence is found, I think, more when positions are being protected than in anticipation of future gain.

One factor that may have contributed to the vehemence was the internal situation of Gerer Hasidism in these years. This merits attention because they were the largest group of Hasidim in Warsaw and because the key figures in the opposition to R. Gesundheit came from their camp. The founder of the movement, Isaac Meir Alter, had died in 1866 leaving no obvious heir. He was succeeded by Chanokh Heynekh HaKohen Levin, who lived for only four more years and was in turn followed by Yehudah Aryeh Leib Alter—the young grandson of R. Yitzchak Meir. Thus, in the same year that the learned R. Gesundheit became rabbi of Warsaw, a 22-year-old was becoming the leader of the Ger Hasidim. It is not impossible, though difficult to prove, that the Hasidim had been concerned that a powerful and attractive figure serving as rabbi of Warsaw could be powerful competition for the young leader of the Gerer Hasidim. In the course of time, R. Yehudah Aryeh Leib was to prove himself as an exceptionally qualified leader, but this was still in the future. While possible, there is no hard evidence for this explanation. It may be that the Hasidism worked against R. Gesundheit simply as a matter of principle. In any case, the efforts expended in the struggle against R. Gesundheit were remarkable.

When R. Gesundheit had appeared as a candidate for the position of Warsaw rabbi in 1870, it was not in competition with R. Isaac Meir Alter, who was no longer alive. However, the memories of previous tensions may still have been there. It is not difficult to imagine that for many Hasidim, preventing his election or reelection was fit revenge for whatever he had done to R. Alter.

•••

What is certainly clear is that despite the unique characteristics of the struggle over the Warsaw rabbinate and the personality of R. Gesundheit, the outcome was not at all exceptional. In almost every major East European Jewish community at the end of the nineteenth century there was no communal rabbi—and in almost every case, the community involved saw their situation as 'special'! This elimination of the position of Rabbi of Warsaw was thus consistent with major changes in eighteenth- and nineteenth-century Jewish communal life. As long as Jewish communities were recognized by the non-Jewish authorities as bodies with a degree of autonomy that provided financial services to the authorities, it was essential that they function—and they did. The same structures that distributed the tax load and dealt with recalcitrant residents could also deal with issues as divisive as choosing a rabbi. Moreover, when the communities were responsible for tax payments, there had also been a modicum of agreement in the communities, at least among the elite, regarding the desirable qualifications of a rabbi. Despite sharp divisions, there were areas of consensus.

Concurrent with the erosion of communal authority and responsibilities, and perhaps linked to that process, the divisions between different subgroups with the community grew. There were few practical needs for a communal rabbi. For day-to-day functions, synagogue rabbis or *dayyanim* sufficed. However, it was precisely because of the symbolic role attributed to a communal rabbi as representative of the ideals of a community that led some groups to try to promote candidates from their camp, and the same reason made it so difficult in Warsaw, as in other large cities, to pick a rabbi. When it got too hard, the office was dispensed with. Thus, by the end of the nineteenth century, not only in Warsaw but also in almost every large Jewish community there were many rabbis but no recognized rabbi of the community.[70]

Why was R. Gesundheit fired and why did the Warsaw chief rabbinate end? Was it because of the new factors tied to new realities of the community, or was it the familiar and traditional constellation of the chance removal of a key supporter (Berg), power struggles by interest groups, and the poor political abilities of a rabbi who was unable to maintain a coalition? It is impossible to isolate the factors. They all had a role. A skilled politician could probably have maintained his position, but ultimately, with all possible skill, ongoing support for government figures, and even fewer internal divisions, the communal rabbinate was doomed. The divisions were too great and the function of the rabbinate was too limited. For our purposes, pointing out the factors is even more important than measuring the relative weight in this specific case.

If we don't know exactly which factor was the tipping point, it is clear that R. Gesundheit was the last rabbi of Warsaw and that his end was a sad one.

---

70   See Stampfer, *Families, Rabbis, and Education*, 277–301.

The end of the rabbinate in Warsaw may not have been unique, but some of the factors involved in its demise were. This struggle was a landmark in the use of media, in the techniques applied to influencing government bodies, and in the publicity it engendered. For perhaps the first time, a local choice of rabbi became a topic of interest not only in the region but in neighboring countries. Jewish public opinion was now a significant factor.

It was also sad in another special way. Though not widely known at the time, R. Gesundheit was a dying man during his tenure. Shortly after he was fired he died, and in retrospect, all of the effort to fire him proved superfluous. Of course, his future was at the time not at all clear. To us, in retrospect, the firing of R. Gesundheit was part of a general phenomenon that was typical in most Jewish communities of the time, an exceptional case that proved the rule but not actually an exception.

CHAPTER 7

Distributing Knowledge: Warsaw as a Center of Jewish Publishing, 1850–1914

Nathan Cohen

Up to the mid-nineteenth century, the Warsaw Jewish community did not bear many significant distinguishing characteristics, though its rapid demographic growth was certainly remarkable. From a small community of 2,519 Jews lacking any residence rights in 1754, it grew to be the largest Jewish community in Europe (337,074) up to its proportional peak during World War I, when it reached 38.1% of the whole population.[1] It was during the second half of the nineteenth century, however, that Warsaw truly emerged as central to East European Jewish life—including intellectual life. One catalyst was a tsarist decree in 1836 that closed down Jewish printing houses all over the Russian empire proper and restricted printing in Hebrew characters to certain printers in Vilna and Zhitomir. Warsaw was located outside the bounds of the prohibition and, moreover, possessed less stringent conditions of censorship. Soon, an enormous influx of Jews from the Russian empire, coupled with these other factors, transformed the city into a burgeoning center of Hebrew and Yiddish printing that included many diverse works outside the traditional corpus and canon.

While several of Warsaw's Jewish printing houses were closed down shortly after their establishment, most functioned for relatively long periods of time. Four Jewish printing houses were functioning in Warsaw in 1851, and within eight years their number doubled.[2] From the end of the 18th century and up to

---

1 Gabriela Zalewska, *Ludność żydowska w Warszawie w okresie międzywojennym* (Warsaw: Państwowe Wydawnictwo Naukowe, 1996), 16, 28–48, 53, 75; Stephen D. Corrsin, "Aspects of Population Change and of Acculturation in Jewish Warsaw at the End of the Nineteenth Century: The Censuses of 1882 and 1897," *Polin* 3 (1988): 122–141; idem, "Literacy Rates and Questions of Language, Faith and Ethnic Identity in Population Censuses in the Partitioned Polish Land and Interwar (1880s–1930s)," *Polish Review* 43 (1998): 131–160.

2 For detailed information regarding Jewish printers in Warsaw see Jacob Shatzky, *Geshikhte fun yidn in varshe*, II: 135–138; III: 251–263; Yitzkhak Kornfeld, "Le-korot hotzaat ha-sefer ha-ivri ba'ir varsha [On the history of Hebrew book publishing in Warsaw]," *Perakim* 4 (1966): 347–363. (Part of this paper is a Hebrew translation of what Shatzky wrote in *Geshikhte fun yidn in varshe*.)

1862, a total of 950 Hebrew books were printed there, of which some fifty can be defined as "maskilic books", i.e., promoting Jewish Enlightenment-based reform predominantly in Hebrew.[3] Promoters and learned Jews opened new printing houses and began distributing ever greater doses of Rabbinic, Hasidic, maskilic, and other literature in Hebrew, Yiddish, and Polish.

This state of affairs encouraged prominent secular-oriented Jewish writers from far and wide to send their manuscripts to Warsaw for publication. Such writers included Shmuel Yossef Fuen and Ayzik Meir Dik from Vilna, Sholem Yankev Abramovitch (Mendele Moykher Sforim) from Berdyczów and Żytomir, Avrom Ber Gotlober from Żytomir and elsewhere, Moyshe Arn Shatzkes from Kiev and Judah Leib Gordon from St. Petersburg.[4] Maskilim from the province would visit Warsaw frequently, either to publish their books there or to solicit subscribers for their books ("prenumerantn").[5]

Much of the demographic and cultural shift that took place in Warsaw from the second half of the century down to World War I can be attributed to the continuous influx of migrants from areas that were historically part of Lithuania and other northeastern provinces. After the 1863 uprising, these migrants already constituted the majority of new Jewish settlers in Warsaw. Local Warsaw Jews felt a certain hostility towards the newcomers, whom they derisively referred to as "Litvaks". They differed from Polish Jews in their Yiddish dialect, their knowledge of Russian language and Russian laws (they were accused of being agents of Russification); their being "misnagdim" (in contrast to the Hasidic majority of Warsaw Jews); and their involvement in politics.

Many Litvaks were learned young men who opened "Hadorim" or private schools, where they would indeed teach, among other subjects, the Russian language. Some continued their traditional religious studies, while others became involved in the new awakening of Jewish political movements. They tended to live and pray separately and generally did not socialize with local Polish Jews. From an economic perspective, Litvaks were considered wealthier than the native Jews and thus living better and running more successful

---

3 Shmuel Verses, "Ha-sifrut ha-ivrit be-polin—tekufot ve'tzi'uney derekh [Hebrew literature in Poland: periods and landmarks]," in Yisrael Bartal and Yisrael Gutman (eds.), *Kiyum vashever: yehudey polin le'doroteyhem* (Jerusalem: Shazar Center, 2001), 163.
4 Khone Shmeruk, *Prokim geshikhte fun der yidisher literatur-geshikhte* [Chapters in the history of Yiddish literature] (Tel Aviv: Y.L. Peretz farlag, 1988), 296–297.
5 Shatzky, *Geshikhte fun yidn in varshe*, III: 279–285.

businesses.⁶ It should be noted that, with the passage of time, other non-Polish or non-Hasidic settlers in Warsaw were "crowned" Litvaks, in a way quite similar to the attachment of the nickname "Daytchn" (Germans) to Maskilic and/or modern Jews who were altogether disconnected from Germany.

A few Jewish printers were known for publishing books in the Polish language. Early initiatives by Jews to publish comprehensive Polish encyclopedias were launched by the brothers Jan (1793–1859) and Teofil (1796–1876) Glucksberg (*Encyklopedia Powszechna*, 4 vols., 1831; and *Encyklopedia Obrazkowa Systematyczna*, 1835–1838). Szmul Orgelbrand (1810–1868) was the printer and publisher of the first full edition of the *Encyklopedia Powszechna* (1858–1868) as well as the printer and publisher of the first "Polish" edition of the Babylonian Talmud (1859–1864).⁷ Józef Unger was known as an art lover and patron. In the publishing arena he was known as printer of the 12-volume *General Encyclopedia of Human Knowledge* (*Encyklopedia Ogólna Wiedzy Ludzkiej*, 1872–1877).⁸ Another famous Warsaw Jewish publisher was Solomon Löwenthal, who contributed much to the Jewish community but was converted to Christianity close to his death.⁹ According to Jacob Shatzky, Jews were the printers of the best Polish calendars since 1863, as well.¹⁰ Major publishers usually maintained bookshops attached to their printing houses. Some pious Jews who could barely read Polish published Polish books, sold them, and allowed their shops to become meeting points for Polish scholars in diverse fields of knowledge. Nearly a third of all such bookshops in Warsaw belonged to Jews in

---

6   Stephen D. Corrsin, "Aspects of Population Change," 132–133; Piotr Wróbel, "Jewish Warsaw Before the First World War," *Polin* 3 (1988): 162–164; Theodore R. Weeks, "Poles, Jews and Russians, 1863–1914: The Death of the Ideal of Assimilation in the Kingdom of Poland," *Polin* 12 (1999): 252–254; Shatzky, *Geshikhte fun yidn in varshe*, III: 19–20, 66–67, 158, 215, 228, 282, 292–294.
7   Shatzky, *Geshikhte fun yidn in varshe*, II: 132–137; III: 258–262, 407–408.
8   Stanisław Arct and Eugenia Pawłowska, "Wydawcy warszawscy w latach 1878–1914," in S. Tazbir (ed.), *Z dziejów książki i bibliotek w Warszawie* (Warsaw: PIW, 1961).
9   Marianna Mlekicka, *Wydawcy książek w Warszawie w okresie zaborów* (Warsaw: Państwowe Wydawnictwo Naukowe, 1987), 163–186, provides a list of Jewish (or Jewish origin) publishers with a significant place in the print industry in Warsaw in the second half of the nineteenth century. According to Shatzky's estimate, ten out of the 56 Polish language periodicals that appeared in Warsaw in 1894 were published by Jewish printers (Shatzky, *Geshikhte fun yidn in varshe*, III: 410). For more on Jewish printers and publishers see Shatzky, II: 161–163, III: 269–277 and 217–221. See also Marian Fuks, *Żydzi w Warszawie* (Poznań: Sorus, 1992), 217–221.
10 Shatzky, *Geshikhte fun yidn in varshe*, III: 410.

the mid-nineteenth century.[11] Some specialized in old Polish prints and manuscripts—according to Shatzky, only the collection of the Warsaw University Library could compete with that of the Hasid Getzl Salcstein (1773–1841).[12] Other booksellers specialized in Judaica and attracted Jewish scholars and collectors as well.[13]

Warsaw's emergence as a nerve center of Jewish publishing began in the early 1860s, when David Slutzki (d. 1889), a Jewish scholar apparently from Leipzig, settled in the city and resumed his project of editing and publishing medieval Jewish philosophic works under the general title "Sifrei khokhmat yisrael" (Books of the wisdom of Israel). The first book in the series (R' Saadya Gaon's *Emunot vedeot*) was published in Leipzig in 1864; however, that same year three more books were published in Warsaw, another three over the following six years, and another in 1876.[14] Slutzki's project, as well as similar projects in Vilna and Odessa, was highly praised by the pioneering author S.Y. Abramovitz, who regarded them as an important step forward in republishing Hebrew philosophical works that would not provoke "the [Jewish] conservative circles,"[15] an effort no doubt helped by the rabbinical endorsements Slutzki managed to obtain for the publications.

Another prominent Hebrew publisher and printer was Yitzkhok Goldman (1812–1888), a former printer in Orgelbrand's printing house and, later, owner of a printing house that functioned for many years. Goldman was a "Litvak" who settled in Warsaw in 1837 and temporarily taught in the local Rabbinical

---

11   Mlekicka, *Wydawcy*, 133–137, counts 29 bookshops owned by Poles, 12 owned by Jews and 9 by Germans for the period between 1865 and 1918.
12   Shatzky, *Geshikhte fun yidn in varshe*, II: 164. Zaltzshteyn managed his shop for fifty years. During these years it became a meeting point for Polish writers, scientists and other scholars. In the late nineteenth century, five members of the Sacstein family kept bookstores (Shatzky, *Geshikhte fun yidn in varshe*, II: 165). For more information on booksellers and book collectors in Warsaw at the end of the nineteenth century see Ester Halpern, "Zikhroynes vegn varshever yidishe mokhrey-sforim un bikher-zamlers," YIVO *bleter* 35 (1951): 240–244.
13   Shatzky, *Geshikhte fun yidn in varshe*, II: 163–164.
14   The list of books contained Maimonides, *Shmona prakim* (1864); Yedaya ben Avraham Habardashi, *Bekhinot olam* (1864); Shlomo Ibn Gevirol, *Mivkhar ha-peninim* (1864); Maimonides, *Milot higayon* (including a commentary by Moses Mendelsohn, 1865); Yehuda Iben Tibon, *Sefer ruakh khen* (1867); Yehuda Halevi, *Sefer ha-kuzari* (1867); Bahye ben Yosef Ibn Pakuda, *Torat khovat ha-levavot* (1870); and Slutzki, *Nosafot le'sefer khovat ha-levavot* (1877). Slutzki republished Hebrew works in Warsaw already in 1860, but not in the series under discussion.
15   Sh.Y. Abramovitz, "Puk khazey may ama diber," *Ha-melits* (29 December 1865/11 January 1866 and 5/18 January 1866), 762–764, 13–14.

Seminary. Close to the 1863 uprising he promoted Jewish-Polish solidarity by writing and distributing brochures in that spirit. In the early 1870s, Goldman's printing house was considered the largest Jewish printing house in the city. According to Shatzky, Goldman sought to dominate not only Jewish printing but also the Jewish book market. He opened his own bookshop and sold the books he published there on an exclusive basis, refusing to sell them to other book sellers.[16] Goldman, a maskil himself, also printed maskilic books. But his fear of losing his traditionalist Jewish customers eventually moved him to promise the traditional establishment to refrain from printing such books.[17] In 1887 Goldman initiated the publication of a 15-volume Hebrew encyclopedia, in biweekly booklets, under the title *Ha-eshkol* (The Cluster). Goldman and his assistant Shaul Pinkhas Rabinovitz (Shefer, 1845–1910) began work on the project, but Goldman passed away before he could fulfill his wish. One of his sons published the first booklet of *Ha-eshkol* in March 1888, and in the following six months five more booklets were published (altogether 766 columns, with 2,500 entries alone between *alef* and *vav*).[18]

Jewish Lexicography in Warsaw

Earlier Hebrew lexicographic publications in Warsaw included Yitzkhak Zibenberg's Biblical dictionary *Otzar ha-shorashim ha-klali* (The General Treasure of Stems, 1846, 1847 and 1862) and Shlomo Gelblum's popular concordance, *Sefer ha-milim* (Book of Words, 1876).[19] Two pioneering lexicographic projects appeared in 1880. One of them was the initiative of Dov Ber (Bernard) Natanson (1832–1916), a Hebrew author and editor from Odessa, who chose Alexander Ginz' printing house in Warsaw to publish his *Sefer ha-milim: Hand Lexicon* (Book of Words, Hand Lexicon), a dictionary of foreign words translated into Hebrew. The dictionary explained each word's source and included non-Hebrew words from the Talmud. The other project, composed by a Jewish teacher Yossef Arye Tretzek from Ostróg, was named *Ha-meassef*

---

16   Shatzky, *Geshikhte fun yidn in varshe*, III: 255–257; see also II: 212, 262.
17   Yehuda Leyb ben Moshe Moseszohn [Smolenskin], "Masa be'rusiya" [A Journey in Russia]," *Ha-shachar* 5 (1874): 157.
18   Shimeon Brisman, *A History and Guide to Judaic Encyclopedias and Lexicons* (Cincinnati: Hebrew Union College Press, 1987), 24–26.
19   Shatzky, *Geshikhte fun yidn in varshe*, II: 129–132.

(The Collector), and constituted a similar dictionary.[20] In addition to providing the source and translation of a given word or expression, this dictionary also provided the word's original orthography. *Ha-meassef* was printed at Yitzkhok Goldman's printing house. Both authors emphasized in their prefaces the need for an auxiliary tool for young readers who had never learned foreign languages but sought to be enlightened. Eliezer ben Yehuda (1858–1922) and Yehuda Grazovski (1862–1950), both already living in the Land of Israel, published their *Full Russian-Hebrew-German Dictionary* in 1901 in the Warsaw "Tushiya" Hebrew publishing house. The same publishing house published a *Hebrew-Russian-German, Russian-Hebrew-German pocket dictionary*, composed by Grazovski and Yossef Klauzner (1874–1958), at the same time.[21]

Warsaw printing houses also contributed significantly to the Jewish bibliographical and bio-bibliographical corpus, sometimes with a discernible ideological intent. In 1864 the Warsaw proofreader and Kotzker Hasid Aharon Walden (1834–1912) published a new and updated edition of a bio-bibliographical lexicon by Rabbi Khayim Yossef David Azulay (Khida), *Shem ha-gdolim* (Names of the Great Ones, originally printed in Livorno 1774) under the title *Shem ha-gdolim hekhadash* (The New Names of the Great Ones). Walden added names and works of predominately Hasidic scholars who lived after the publication of the original lexicon, thus cleverly canonizing his movement's leaders. Another updated publication was R' Yekhiel Haylperin of Minsk's bibliographical chronicle, *Seder ha-dorot* (The Order of Generations, 1878–1882, first edition 1769), prepared by Naftali Maskil Laeytan (1829–1897), a Warsaw bookseller in his own right.

The maskil Shmuel Yosef Fuen from Vilna (1818–1891) published nine booklets of a lexicon of great Jewish scholars, *Knesset yisrael* (The Gathering of Israel, letters ALEF to YOD), at Zaks and Tzukerman's printing house between 1886 and 1890. A different lexicon, *Sefer Ha-shemot* (The Book of Names), composed by Yikhezkel Mandelshtam from Poltava, containing 2,688 biblical names, was published in 1889. There were also *Dor, dor vedorshav* (Each Generation and its Guidance), a list of 6,600 dates of death of famous Jews "since the creation of the world and until now" [1900] by Yossef Levinshteyn (1834–1927); *Sefer ha-mazkir* (The Reminder) of biblical names and places that are mentioned in the Talmud, by Moshe David Asner (1900); and *Mishpekhot sofrim* (Families

---

20   The same author published also an introduction to ancient mythology, *Mistorei ha-goyim ha-kadmonim* [The Mysteries of the Ancient Nations] (Varshe: Goldman, 1875).
21   The first was *Milon male ve'shalem russi-ivri-ashkenazi*, and the other, *Milon shel kis me'ivrit le'russit ve'ashkenazit ume'russit le'ivrit ve'ashkenazit*.

of Authors, 1903), the first part of a bio-bibliographical encyclopedia of Jewish scholars by Shalom Albek (1858–1920).

Khayim Khizkiya Medini (1833–1905), a rabbinical scholar who lived in the Land of Israel and Turkey, chose Warsaw for his monumental publication of an 18-volume Talmudic encyclopedia under the title *Sdei khemed* (Fields of Grace, between 1891 and 1911). Two non-hagiographical biographies of Hasidic leaders were published in Warsaw in 1910. The first and most comprehensive were two volumes devoted to R' Shneur Zalmen of Liady, founder of the Lubavich dynasty.[22] The other was a biography of R' Nakhman of Bratzlav, written by Hillel Zeitlin (1871–1942). The same year, Zeitlin also published a booklet on Hasidic thought. These two booklets were to be part of a series, but no further publications appeared.[23]

The preeminent Warsaw-based publishers Nahum Sokolow (1859–1936) and Yisrael Hayyim Zagorodski (1864–1931) published *Sefer zikaron le-sofrey yisrael he-khayim itanu ka-yom* (A Memorial Book for Contemporary Jewish Writers, 1889), a biographical lexicon of contemporary Jewish writers that appeared in Warsaw, included a separate list of contemporary Jewish scholars living in Jerusalem. Mathias Bersohn's (1823–1908) Polish language biographical lexicon of Polish Jewish scholars between the 16th and 18th centuries was published in 1905 under the title *Słownik biograficzny uczonych Żydów polskich XVI, XVII i XVIII wieku*.[24]

In 1900, the proverbs collector and philanthropist Yitzkhok (Ignac) Bernstein (1836–1909), famous among Poles and Jews, published a two-volume catalog with 4,761 bibliographic items from his personal collection of proverbs in all languages.[25] In 1908 he published two editions of 3,993 Yiddish proverbs.[26]

---

22   Mordekhay Tenenboym, *Ha-rav me'ladi u'mifleget khabad* [The Rabbi from Liady and the Khabad Party]. These two books were published in the framework of Ben-Avigdor's "Biblioteka gedola" (see below). The second volume contained an appendix exposing the readers to R' Shneur Zalmen's knowledge of "geometry, astronomy and studies of nature."

23   Zeitlin's booklets were: *Rabi Nakhmen me'breslav: khayav ve'torato* [R' Nakhmen from Bratzlav, his Life and Teachings] (1910), and *Ha'hasidut le'shitoteha u'zrameha* [Hasidic Systems and Schools] (1910).

24   Brisman, 144–145, 169, 178–180, 239–240, 250, 261–262, 346–347.

25   *Katalog dzieł treści przysłowiowej składających bibljotekę Ignacego Bernsteina* (2 vols.; Warszawa, 1900).

26   *Yidishe shprikhverter un rednsartn, gezamlt un derklert fun Ignac Bernstein* (Varshe, 1908). This book includes a transliteration of each entry and an explanation in German. A Yiddish edition the same year was donated as a prize to subscribers of the daily newspaper *Undzer lebn*. A first booklet of Bernstein's collection was published by Mordekhai Spektor in 1888.

Many booksellers who appealed to Jewish consumers also functioned as publishers,[27] but in much more modest proportions than the professional publishers mentioned above. They usually offered Yiddish folktales ("Maysse bikhlekh", "Khsidishe bikhlekh" and "Badkhonishe bikhlekh") composed by local authors[28] as well as free adaptations of popular world literature such as *Robinson Crusoe* (1840, 1850, 1874), *Rinaldo Rinaldini* (1865–1866) and Eugène Sue's *The Mysteries of Paris* (1865–1866). These booksellers also published calendars and letter-writing manuals (*Brivnshtellers*).

Warsaw and the Popularization of Knowledge

The state of the Jewish book trade in Warsaw was sometimes subjected to sharp criticism. A sincere, though tendentious, description from 1874 can be found in Yehuda Leyb Moseszohn's (Peretz Smolenskin's brother) *Rishmey masa* (Notes from a Trip), published in *Ha-shachar*. Moseszohn-Smolenskin condemned the absence of qualified Hebrew writers in Warsaw and what he saw as total anarchy in selecting, translating and distributing Yiddish popular books and booklets. These conditions encouraged "corrupted novels" that were in high demand by young Yiddish readers, practically destroying their literary taste and preventing their exposure to high quality literary and scientific works in Hebrew.[29] Moseszohn went so far as to claim that "in a city like Warsaw, where there are more than 90,000 Jews, there is no Hebrew writer to revive one's soul with his wisdom".[30]

Such criticism did not do justice to the Warsaw Jewish book market, which was much more varied and active than Moseszhohn was willing to admit. Among those who left their mark on the Jewish book market in the last decades of the nineteenth century were Avrom Tzukerman (1843–1892), Eliezer Yitzkhok Shapiro (1835–1915), and Yude Leyb Morgnshtern (1869–?). The first two sold both Hebrew and Yiddish books but printed mainly Hebrew books. Following the successful mode of distributing knowledge and high quality

---

27 Shatzky, *Geshikhte fun yidn in varshe*, III: 269, notes that most of the 16 Jewish booksellers in Warsaw in 1892 functioned also as publishers.
28 Shatzky, *Geshikhte fun yidn in varshe*, II: 123–138; III: 264–270, 277; Nokhem Oyslender, "Varshever mekhabrim in di 50er-60er yorn," *Bibliologisher zamlbukh* 1 (Kharkov-Minsk, 1930), 164–197.
29 Yehuda Leyb ben Moshe Moseszohn [Smolenskin], "Masa be'rusiya," *Ha-shachar* 5 (1874), 157–160.
30 Idem, 159.

literature that was popular among Polish readers—the use of low cost series of booklets ("Biblioteki" [Libraries])[31]—Shapiro published the first Hebrew "Biblioteka" (Library) under the title "Beit otzar" (Treasure House), a series of some forty children's books beginning in 1875.[32] Yude Leyb Morgnshtern opened his bookshop on Franciszkanska Street in 1851, where he published Yiddish popular books and booklets by local authors. Many of these publications were works he himself wrote under various pseudonyms. Their contents varied from melodramatic, fantastic stories and romances to Hasidic tales. Morgenshtern transformed his bookshop into a lending library, possibly the first of this kind in Jewish Warsaw.[33] Less prominent but still significant publishers and printers were Yekhiel Mikhl Halter and Levi Levin-Epstein. Halter was a traditional, learned Jew who employed pious printers in his publishing house. He used to print religious texts and Hebrew and English textbooks (such as letter-writing manuals and Hebrew grammar books). Nevertheless he did not reject literary works by Y.L. Peretz or Avrom Reizen. Levin-Epstein opened his publishing house in Warsaw in 1880, publishing mainly religious texts but also popular Yiddish literature. After he immigrated to the Land of Israel (1934), he reestablished his publishing house in Jerusalem.

A somewhat exceptional Hebrew publisher was Yisrael Borukh Hacohen Alapin (1840–1907), a Litvak who settled in Warsaw and, after a short and significant career as a publisher, became a teacher in Russian-Jewish gymnasia. In 1881, he published *Mekor ha-khayim* (The Origins of Life)—a book on biology and physics that also introduced Charles Darwin's theory of evolution to the contemporary Hebrew reader.[34] Alapin also began to print a series of booklets

---

31 Up to 1918 no less than 150 different Polish "biblioteki" were published in Warsaw and in other Polish speaking areas. Janusz Kostecki, "Ruch Wydawniczy," *Słownik literatury polskiej XX wieku* (Wrocław: Zakład Narodowy im. Ossolińskich, 1992), 975–976; Artur Jazdon, *Wielkopolskie serie wydawnicze do 1945 roku* (Poznań: UAM, 1997).

32 For more about these two bookselling publishers, see the relevant chapters in Hagit Cohen, *Be'khanuto shel mokher ha-sfarim* [At the Bookseller's Shop] (Jerusalem: Magnes, 2006).

33 Shatzky, *Geshikhte fun yidn in varshe*, II: 133; III: 269.

34 For more on Alapin see Shatzky, *Geshikhte fun yidn in varshe*, III: 250, 255. Another book that dealt with Darwin's theory of evolution is Yaakov Frenkel, *Ha-yerusha ha-tivi'it* [The Natural Heritage] (Varshe: Halter, 1899). See more about these authors and their books in Yaacov Shavit and Jehuda Reinharz, *"Ha-el ha-mada'i"—Mada populari be'ivrit b'mizrakh eyropa ba'makhatzit hashniya shel ha-mea ha-tsha-esre: beyn yeda u'temunat yekum hadasha* ["The Scientific God": Popular Sciences in Hebrew in Eastern Europe in the Second Half of the Nineteenth Century: Between Knowledge and a New Image of the Universe] (Tel Aviv: Ha-kibbutz ha-meuchad, 2011), 139–140, 163–164.

on numerous fields of science by Aharon Berenstein (1812–1884), originally published in Berlin as *Naturwissenschaftliche Volksbücher* (1855–1865). The Hebrew edition—*Yedi'ot ha-teva* (Knowledge/Studies of Nature) was published in Warsaw in twenty-one booklets between 1881 and 1886. The translator of the first two booklets was Pessakh Ruderman (1854–1887); Dovid Frishman (1860–1922) translated the remainder. The printers who followed Alapin in this project were Goldman and Ginz. High demand for the series necessitated a second edition (1891–1892) and a short adaptation into Yiddish (1891).[35]

Other scientific publications, mainly in Hebrew, were printed in Warsaw in this period (and some even earlier). Their main objective was to broadly disseminate knowledge and provide their readers with new insights without undermining their religious beliefs. A "kosher" publication of this kind was Yossef Sheynhak's (1812–1870) comprehensive work *Toldot ha-aretz* (History of the Earth, 1841–1859).[36] The work was accompanied by endorsements from rabbis, replete with references to Biblical and Talmudic sources. A traditional approach was also apparent in the astronomical booklet *Otot ha-shamayim* (Heaven's Signs, 1886), attributed to Yehudah ben Shlomo Hacohen from Toledo.[37] Additional works on astronomy and earth sciences like *Or u'meorot* (Light and Light Sources, 1894) and *Me'kadmey olam* (The World's Predecessors, 1899) by Mikhl Veber (1859–1907) provided new but often baseless insights.[38] Apart from numerous scientific and other articles in *Ha-tzefira* (see below),

---

35 On Berenstein and the Hebrew series, see Yosef Vardi, "*Yedi'ot ha-teva*—tekufon ha-mada ha-populari ha-rishon be'ivrit," [*Yedi'ot ha-teva*—The First Popular Science Periodical in Hebrew] *Qesher* 11 (1992): 107–112. The Yiddish adaptation in one volume was made by Yitzkhok Leyb Sapirshteyn. It was entitled *Natur Vissenshaft* (Natural science) and was printed at Boymritter and Gonshor's printing house. The Yiddish adaptation included mainly practical information about weather, light, motion and nutrition. A more comprehensive translation in Yiddish was published in London, 1910.

36 Yosef ben Binyamin Dov Sheynhak, *Toldot ha-aretz*, pt. 1, "Toldot ha-hayim" [History of Life] (Varshe: Bromberg, 1841), a zoological lexicon; Pt. 2, "Toldot ha-tzmakhim" [History of Plants] (Varshe: Lebenzohn, 1859), a botanical lexicon; Pt. 3, "Toldot ha-mutzakim" [History of Solids] (Varshe: Lebenzohn, 1859), a geological lexicon. It should be noted that most subscribers to Sheynhak's work were Lithuanian Jews (Sheynhak himself lived in Suwałki). See Shatzky, *Geshikhte fun yidn in varshe*, III: 296–297.

37 Yehuda ben Shlomo Hacohen Metulila, *Otot ha-shamayim* (Warsaw: Lebenzohn, 1886). According to the title page the old manuscript was prepared for printing by R' Yaacov Shapiro and R' Yosef Zvi Live.

38 Mikhl Veber, *Or u'meorot* (Varshe: Ginz, 1896); Idem, *Me'kadmey olam* (Varshe: Shuldberg, 1899). Veber used also to publish works in Yiddish (see below) and articles on scientific matters in *Ha-tzefira*. Veber's Hebrew works are defined as "bizarre" in Shavit and Reinhartz, *"Ha-el ha-mada'i,"* 81, 165–166.

Nakhum Sokolov (1860–1936) translated a book on physical geography that was published by Yitzkhok Goldman (1878).[39] Sound information intended to widen the reader's horizons was collected by Nekhemya Dov Hoffmann (1857–1928), a Litvak and maskil who lived for some time in Warsaw between his journey to the United States and his eventual immigration to South Africa (in 1889). The three books he published in Warsaw supply information on zoology, astronomy, geology, hydrology, geography and botany, combining belles-lettres with well-analyzed, reliable data.[40]

A similar book, but more popular and narrow in scope, was *Toldot ha-amtzaot ha-khadashot* (The History of New Inventions, 1887) by Moshe Yaakov Levin. According to the author's preface, he did not intend to provide the Hebrew reader with an additional book dealing with "matters of the utmost importance" as is typical of Hebrew authors, but rather intended a more practical book.[41] In Levin's book one could find the origins of useful older innovations such as in printing, banking, glass, and precious stones, as well as novel innovations like newspapers, postal stamps, fashion, family names, the calculator, the telegraph, the camera, the typewriter, electric light, and so on. Another, similar book was *Kaveret dvash, o mea she'elot u'teshuvot be'khokhmat ha-teva* (Honey Beehive, or Hundred Questions and Answers on the Wisdom of Nature, 1889) by David Horowitz (1858–1914).[42] This small volume provided answers to questions such as "Why was the earth created in a round shape?"; "Why can't plants grow on sand?"; How is a flying tower [hot-air balloon] made?"; "What is a magnet?" and "How can a telegram be sent and accepted through one wire?"

Jewish Historical Works

Several major works on Jewish history were also published in Warsaw. Eliezer Atlas (1851–1904), a Litvak from Białystok, published a yearbook for Jewish

---

39   Nakhum Sokolov, *Metzukey eretz o yesodey yediat ha-geografia ha-tivi'it* (Warsaw, 1878). The source for this book was Matthew Fontaine Maury, *The World we Live in* (New York, 1871).
40   Nekhemia Dov Hoffmann, *Maasey hakhamim* [Deeds of Wise Men] (Varshe: Unterhendler, 1884); Idem, *Maamar me'kadmey eretz* [Primordial Composition] (Varshe: Goldman, 1886); Idem, *Sipurey ha-teva* [Nature's Stories] (Varshe: Goldman, 1887). The books' subtitles declared that the author's purpose was to bring to the readers updated information that is approved by the leading scientists in the world.
41   Moshe Yaakov Levin, *Toldot ha-amtzaot ha-hadashot* (Warsaw: Goldman, 1887).
42   David ben Sholem Shakhne Halevi Horowitz, *Kaveret dvash, o mea sheelot u'teshuvot be'hokhmat ha-teva* (Varshe: Boymritter, 1889). A second edition was published in 1893.

history and literature under the title *Ha-kerem* (The Vineyard, 1887) on Goldman's press.[43] Shaul Pinkhas Rabinovich's (Shefer) Hebrew translation of Heinrich Graetz's eight-volume *History of the Jews* was first published between 1891 and 1900 in various printing houses.[44] Another attempt to translate Graetz into Hebrew at the same time was made by Eliezer David Finkel (1861–1918).[45] Zeev (Volf) Yaavetz (1847–1924) chose Warsaw as the place to publish the third (and fourth) edition of his *Jewish History* "with many additions and corrections" (1892) and four volumes of a general history "in a Jewish spirit" (1893–1894).[46]

One of the first books in Hebrew on general history to be printed in Warsaw was the pro-Russian *Toldot napoleon* (The History of Napoleon, 1849) by Fayvl Schiffer (1809–1871). A Hebrew writer who was born in Zamość, Schiffer settled in Warsaw in 1835, opened a private school and began promoting a transition to agriculture among Polish Jews.[47] In later years, Warsaw was chosen by the Society for the Promotion of Enlightenment among the Jews of Russia as the place to print and publish a comprehensive History of Russia (*Sefer divrey yemey rusia*, 1875) by the young scholar from St. Petersburg, Solomon Mandelkorn (1846–1902).[48] Warsaw was also the printing place of Mordecai

---

43   The Yearbook was given as a prize for *Ha-melitz* subscribers. It included historical research, literary critique and belles-lettres. Of the more familiar names published there were Yaakov Rayfman (1818–1895), Shlomo Mandelkorn (1846–1902) and Yaakov Halevi Lifshitz (1838–1921).

44   *Sefer divrey yemey yisrael*, 8 vols. The ninth volume was added in 1908. A first attempt to publish this Hebrew translation was made by Rabinovich at Alapin's printing house in 1888. Y.Y. Lerner (1847–1907) translated Graetz' *Geschichte der Juden* into Yiddish as *Yidishe folks geshikhte*, vols. 1–4 (Varshe: Zaks, 1898). Itzkhok Leyzer Leyzerovich (1883–1927) and Ber Karlinski (1886–1935) published a comprehensive history of the Jews in Yiddish, based on Graetz and "other sources", as *Yidishe geshikhte* (Varshe: Shimin, 1912–1913). The first three volumes of Graetz' *History* were translated into Polish by Stanisław Szenhak (1835–1913) and published in supplements between 1902 and 1913 (*Historja Żydów*), with the first full Polish translation published in 1929.

45   *Toldot ha-yehudim* [History of the Jews], vols. 4–5 (Varshe: Boymritter, 1893–1894). In 1905 Sokolov undertook a translation of his own, of which only one volume appeared: *Toldot ha-yehudim: Me'ha-et ha-kadmoniya ad ha-dorot ha-ahronim* [History of the Jews from Ancient Times until the Last Generations] (Varshe: Ha-tzefira, 1905).

46   *Divrey ha-yamim le-am bney yisrael* [History of the Jewish People] (Varshe: Shuldberg, 1892); *Divrey yemey ha-amim: katuv be'ruakh bney yisrael* [History of the Nations: Written in Jewish Spirit], 1–4, (Varshe: Shuldberg, 1893–1894).

47   Shatzky, *Geshikhte fun yidn in varshe*, II: 129, and Shmuel Feiner, *Haskalah and History: the Emergence of a Modern Jewish Historical Consciousness* (Oxford: Littman Library of Jewish Civilization, 2002), 176–177.

48   More about the book and the author see ibid., 210–211, 215–216.

Aharon Guenzburg's (1795–1846) second edition of *Yitutey rusya* (Russian Times, 1884).[49]

The history of the ancient world was also considered worthwhile reading for Hebrew readers, especially if it had a connection to the Near East. In this context *Dorot olamim* (World Generations, 1865), by Zalmen Sobel[50] and *Toldot amey ha-mizrakh ha-kadmonim* (History of the Ancient Eastern Nations, 1897) were published in Warsaw.[51] A general history for Yiddish readers was initiated at first in 1901–1902 in the form of a series of booklets by the "Ahiassaf" publishing company (see below), that combined four volumes of a comprehensive world history.[52] Further works on general history were published through the series "Folks-univerzitet" (see below). While Vilna was a center of Socialist literature, at least three booklets on the French revolution appeared in Warsaw.[53] In addition, a booklet on the history of the United States was published in 1905 and another, *The History of Religions and Religious Beliefs*, in 1911.[54]

---

49 On Guenzburg as a historian, see ibid., 176ff.

50 Ibid., only in the Hebrew version (Jerusalem: Shazar Center, 1995), 192.

51 The source for this work, of which only one booklet was published, was the French Egyptologist Gaston Maspero (1846–1916), *Histoire ancienne des peuples de l'Orient classique* (3 vols.; Paris, 1895–1897). The Zionist Avraham Ludvipol (1866–1921), living in Paris at the time, translated it into Hebrew, assisted by another Parisian Jewish scholar, Yosef Halevi (1868–1921).

52 The first volume of *Di velt-geshikhte* [World History] was edited by Jankev Dinezon (1856?–1919). It was devoted to China, India, ancient Egypt, Mesopotamia and Assyria. For the publication of the following volumes, the authors and translators Shmuel Rozenfeld (1869–1943), Dr. Yeshaye Roznberg (1871–1937) and M. Kamenetzky formed the editorial board. The second volume was devoted to Jewish history in ancient times, including in Persia and ancient Greece. The third volume dealt with ancient Greece and contemporary Jewish history, and the fourth volume was devoted to ancient Rome and to contemporary Jewish history. Before World War One, at least two editions were published (1909 and 1913).

53 *Ertzehlungen fun der frantzoyzisher revolutzye: di parizer komune* [Stories from the French Revolution: the Paris Commune] by A. Nyemanski (Alexander Zeldov, 1873–1924), (Di Velt, 1906); *Di tzesterung fun bastilye* [The destruction of the Bastille] by Philip Krantz (1858–1922), (Di Velt, 1906). Krantz was an editor and popularizer of scientific works, who immigrated to the United States in 1890. The third work devoted to the French Revolution was *Di geshikhte fun der frantzezishe revolutzye* [The history of the French Revolution] by historian Azriel Frenk (1863–1924) (Di proletarishe velt, 1907). On Frenk see François Guesnet: "Between Permeability and Isolation: Ezriel Natan Frenk as Historian of the Jews in Poland," *Polin* 24 (2012): 111–130.

54 Philip Krantz, *Geshikhte fun amerika* (Varshe [?]: Progress, 1905); Dr. M. [Mordkhe] Robinzon (trans.), *Di geshikhte fun gloybn un religyonen* (Shimins groyse velt-bibliotek, 1911).

The publication of works devoted to various aspects of non-Jewish history was a sustained project that began as a typical maskilic endeavor during the first half of the nineteenth century to expose readers to new perspectives on Jewish existence in a wider, more universal context and to encourage Jewish loyalty towards the sovereign and the law while contesting the parochialism inherent in an isolated, exclusive Jewish history.[55] At the same time, works on ancient history strove to awaken Jewish national awareness, while some Yiddish historical works aimed to arouse social consciousness and political awareness.

The Jewish Press in Warsaw in the Nineteenth Century

According to Shatzky's estimate, some fifty Hebrew "maskilic" writers lived in Warsaw in the second third of the nineteenth century.[56] Nevertheless, in a letter to *Ha-melitz*, Khayim Zelig Slonimski (1810–1904), who published some of his books in Warsaw, described the difficulties he had to overcome in order to distribute his books in and beyond Warsaw.[57] Slonimski (see chapter 4 of this volume) is best known as the founder of the first Hebrew newspaper in Poland, *Ha-tzefira* (1862, 1875–1931), a cultural enterprise that helped Jewish Warsaw become a major "producer of culture," and not only from a technical standpoint. He arrived in Warsaw as a young enlightened scholar who had already published a Hebrew book on mathematics (Vilna, 1834). In Warsaw, he published three more books and hundreds of articles on scientific and technological subjects. Thanks to Słonimski, *Ha-tzefira* served for many years as a conduit for scientific and technological knowledge in a vibrant Hebrew idiom while usually managing to avoid provoking the traditional establishment.

As Nakhum Sokolov (1860–1936) became more influential on the editorial board in the 1880s, the newspaper became more informative, national, and political. The sciences remained an important feature of the paper at this stage, but were now more a means for justifying national and political claims. In addition, belles-lettres were considered well worth publishing in newspapers during Sokolov's days. In its first years, the newspaper had barely a thousand subscribers. When it became a daily paper in 1886, it had 2,000 subscribers; and

---

55 Feiner, *Haskalah and History*, 157–203, 341–348.
56 Shatzky, *Geshikhte fun yidn in varshe*, II: 128–130.
57 Khayim Zelig Slonimski, "Amilan shel sofrim" [The toil of authors], *Ha-melitz*, 9/21 June 1866, 340–342.

by 1891 distribution had reached 10,000.[58] Yet when other Hebrew and Yiddish newspapers began to appear (in 1905–1906), *Ha-tzefira*'s distribution declined to 3,000 copies.[59]

Shortly before the establishment of *Ha-tzefira*, a Polish-language Jewish newspaper appeared in Warsaw under the title *Jutrzenka* (1861–1863), an enterprise of a group of polonizing or "assimilationist Jews" who sought to acculturate the Jewish masses to the Polish environment yet, at the same time, bring assimilated circles closer to Judaism. A few years after *Jutrzenka* ceased to appear, one of its contributors, Hilel (Hilary) Glatshtern (1827–1874), established a short-lived German newspaper in Hebrew characters, *Warshauer yudishe tzaytung* (The Warsaw Jewish Newspaper, 1867–1868) in an attempt to ease the linguistic and cultural transformation. This paper had only 150 subscribers in Warsaw and another 30 in the province and ceased to appear after the 54th issue. A new Jewish weekly in Polish, *Izraelita*, appeared in 1866. Under Sokolov's direction it extended its readership and continued to appear until 1912. These newspapers have already been subjected to a great degree of scholarly analysis.[60]

New Initiatives in Turn-of-Century Warsaw

In the 1880s and 1890s, Hebrew literature was reinforced by the appearance of new and significant publications such as Avrom Ber Gotlober's (1811–1899) *Haboker or* (Early Morning, intermittently between 1879–1886),[61] Sokolov's *He-asif* (Harvest, 1884–1888, 1894) and *Sefer Ha-shana* (Yearbook, 1900–1903, 1906), Shmuel Pinkhas Rabinovich's *Kneset yisrael* (Gathering of Israel, 1886–1888) and the "Ahiassaf" publishing company's calendar, *Luakh ahiassaf* (1893–1905).

---

58   Shatzky, *Geshikhte fun yidn in varshe*, III: 307–310. For preliminary research on *Ha-tzefira* and its editor see Oren Sofer, *Eyn lefalpel! Iton "Ha-tzefira" ve'ha-modernizatzya shel ha-siakh ha-khevrati ha-politi* [There is no place for Pilpul! The journal *Ha-tzefira* and the modernization of sociopolitical discourse] (Jerusalem: Magnes, 2007).

59   Marian Fuks, *Prasa Żydowska w Warszawie, 1823–1939* (Warsaw: Państwowe Wydawnictwo Naukowe, 1979), 298.

60   The third, fourth and fifth chapters in Fuks' book are devoted to these newspapers. See also Khone Shmeruk's review of Fuks' book: "A Pioneering Study of the Warsaw Jewish Press," *Soviet Jewish Affairs* 11.3 (1981): 35–53; Ela Bauer, *Between Poles and Jews: The Development of Nahum Sokolow's Political Thought* (Jerusalem: Hebrew University Magnes Press, 2005); and Shatzky, *Geshikhte fun yidn in varshe*, III: 314–315.

61   This attempt was probably not successful, cf. Verses, "Ha-sifrut," 169–171.

The bilingual author and editor Avrom Leyb Shalkovich (Ben Avigdor, 1866–1921) arrived and settled in Warsaw in 1891. Upon his arrival, he initiated a cheap series of 25 booklets a year of the best works of contemporary Hebrew authors, "Sifrey agora" (Penny Books). He even offered royalties to authors who would let him publish their works—a new phenomenon in the Jewish literary milieu of that time.[62] This initiative encouraged another Warsaw publisher—Shmuel Nakhum Kahanovski (1856–1926)—to publish a similar serial of 16 booklets, "Sifrey shaashuim" (Amusement Books), most of them his own works.[63] One of the participants in "Sifrey agora" was Yitzkhok Goydo (better known as B. Gorin, 1868–1925), who tried to import the new idea to his hometown, Vilna, and print a similar series in Yiddish. Only four books appeared in that series.[64]

Ben Avigdor helped establish a modern Hebrew publishing company in Warsaw, "Ahiassaf", in 1893, which soon became one of the leading Jewish publishing companies in Eastern Europe, publishing periodicals in Yiddish as well.[65] Three years later, Ben Avigdor withdrew from "Ahiassaf" and established his own publishing company, "Tushiya" (Wisdom). Among its publications was the series "Biblioteka ivrit" (Hebrew Library), consisting of more than 200 issues of belles-lettres and reference books (1898–1902). Between 1910 and 1912 "Tushiya" published a new series, "Biblioteka gedola" (Large Library), composed of 80 books. Similar series for children and adolescents were "Hanitzanim" (Sprouts), "Haprakhim" (Flowers, one hundred issues each), "Bikurim" (First Fruits, 200 hundred issues), and the children's weekly *Olam katan* (Small World, 1901–1905, 160 issues). "Tushiya" was the first Hebrew publishing company to publish Hebrew textbooks that served the Hebrew educational system for many years. Ben Avigdor also took part in the Yiddish "Folksbildung" publishing company that distributed high quality books and journals among Yiddish readers.

In 1910, Shlomo Shrebrek (1876–1944), a bilingual publisher from Vilna, bought the rights to Mendele Moykher Sforim's works and, together with the Warsaw Yiddish publisher Yankev Lidski (1868–1921), established the

---

62   On Ben Avigdor and his initiative, see Shulamit Shalhav, "Mi'kavanot le'ma'assim: perek rishon be'toldot ha-molut ha-ivrit ha-hilonit ha-modernit [From intentions to deeds: a first chapter in modern, secular Hebrew publishing]" (MA thesis, Tel Aviv University, 1994), 8–48.
63   Verses, "Hasifrut," 173–174.
64   A. Litvak, *Vos geven: etyudn un zikhroynes* [What was: writings and memoirs] (Vilna: Kletzkin, 1925), 74–75.
65   It published the *Der yid* (The Jew, 1899–1902) and *Di yidishe familye* (The Jewish Family, 1902), printed in Kraków in order to avoid censorship.

"Mendele" publishing house and printed 17 volumes of Mendele's complete works. Thanks to Shrebrek's initiative to strengthen the Jewish publishing activity in Warsaw, four Jewish publishers (in Hebrew and in Yiddish), including "Tushiya", joined forces in 1911 and created a large bilingual publishing company called "Tzentral"/"Merkaz" (Center).[66]

In 1908, Fishl Lakhover (1883–1947) established the "Ha-sifrut" (Literature) Hebrew publishing company in Warsaw and initiated the series "Biblioteka sifrut" (24 books in two years) and "Biblioteka mikra" for youth (32 booklets), in addition to the journal *Reshafim* (Sparks), edited by David Frishman (1909–1911). All of these publications were intended to encourage talented writers, enrich Hebrew literature, and widen its circle of readers. In 1911 "Ha-sifrut" joined "Tzentral"/"Merkaz".[67]

The Flourishing of Yiddish Publishing in Warsaw

During the last decades of the nineteenth century, several leading cultural activists and writers whose language of choice was Yiddish settled in Warsaw. Among them were Yitzkhok Leybush Peretz (1852–1915), Yankev Dinezon (1856?–1919), Mordkhe Spektor (1858–1925), Heshl Eplberg (1861–1927), Avrom Kotik (1868–1933) and Avrom Reyzen (1876–1953). These figures lay the groundwork for a lively and fruitful Yiddish literary center that attracted many young talents from the provinces in the following years. As early as 1887, Spektor published a literary anthology entitled *Der familiyen fraynd* (The Family Friend), followed by five volumes of *Der hoyzfraynd* (The Home Friend) between 1888 and 1896. Spektor and Eplberg separately published literary calendars that were distributed in relatively large numbers (500 to 2,000 copies each).[68] Shatzky considered these calendars a transition between the primitive, popular old

---

66 Shalhav, "Mi'kavanot le'ma'assim," 163–178; Yokhanan Pograbinski, "Le'toldot ha-molut ha-ivrit" [On the History of Hebrew Publishing], *Ha-sefer ha-ivri* 9 (1951): 39–47; Bernard Yakobovitch, "Assot ve'hafetz sefarim harbe: le'toldoteha shel hotza'ot ha-sefarim 'Tzentral'–'Merkaz' be'varsha (1911–1933) [Make and distribute many books: Towards the history of the publishing company "Tzentral"-"Merkaz" in Warsaw, 1911–1933]" (MA thesis, Tel Aviv University, 1997).

67 Pograbinski, "Le'toldot ha-molut ha-ivrit," 51–53.

68 The first calendar to appear was Eplberg's *Warshaver yudisher kalendar* (Warsaw Jewish Calendar, 1889). With the passage of time Eplberg's calendars changed their titles. See more on them and on Spector's calendars in Avrom Kirzhnitz, *Di yidishe presse in der gevezener russisher imperye (1823–1916)* [The Yiddish press in the former Russian Empire] (Moscow-Kharkov-Minsk: tzentraler felker-farayn fun pssr, 1930), items 286, 295, 296, 288.

stage of Yiddish literature and a modern, sophisticated new stage, best represented by the personality and works of Y.L. Peretz.[69]

Nevertheless, demand for Yiddish popular literature kept rising. While no local publisher proved willing to publish Peretz's works in 1886 (he settled in Warsaw in 1889), popular Yiddish literature was distributed in 10,000 to 12,000 copies each.[70] Peretz began his cultural activity in Warsaw slowly and deliberately. First he participated in a statistical and ethnographical expedition in small towns in the provinces of the Pale of Settlement. The expedition was initiated by the convert and activist against anti-Semitism, Jan Bloch. Peretz' experiences from this mission were artistically reflected in his series of reportages *Bilder fun a provintz-rayze* (Scenes from a journey through the provinces, 1891). He gave lectures (in Hebrew) at various social meetings and published a variety of periodicals in Yiddish. The first was the anthology *Di yidishe bibliotek* (The Jewish Library, 1891, 1892, 1894), where Peretz provided a platform to young and talented writers who were taking their first steps in Yiddish literature (such as Avrom Reyzen, Yeoash, Sh. Ben-Zion), and to well known writers like Dinezon and Sokolov (their first time writing in Yiddish). In 1894, Peretz published two collections of belles- lettres and essays, one in Yiddish (*Literatur un lebn* [Literature and Life]) and the other in Hebrew (*Ha-khetz* [The Arrow]). At the same time, he also published, with the assistance of his friends Spektor and Dovid Pinski (1872–1959), literary brochures known as *Yontef bletlekh* (Holyday Leaflets, 17 brochures between 1894 and 1896).

Peretz was very concerned about both the state of Jewish education (conservative, traditional versus modern) and the low standards of contemporary Yiddish theater (due to unqualified actors, poor repertoires and an ignorant audience). He tried to influence public opinion on these subjects. With the passage of time, Peretz's apartment at Cegalna St. no.1 became a pilgrimage site for Yiddish writers in Warsaw and from the provinces. Meeting him was for many an unforgettable and inspiring experience.[71]

Another prominent Yiddish editor and writer was Avrom Reyzen, who lived in Warsaw between 1899 and 1905 and was deeply involved in the local literary milieu. Reyzen initiated and edited a new and comprehensive literary anthology, *Dos tzvantzikste yorhundert* (The Twentieth Century, 1900). The anthology

---

69 Shatzky, *Geshikhte fun yidn in varshe*, III: 273.
70 Ibid., 273–277.
71 Sh. Niger, *Y.L. Peretz*, (Buenos Aires: Argentiner opteyl fun yidishn veltlekhn kultur kongres, 1952), 195ff.; Nathan Cohen, *Sefer, sofer ve'iton: merkaz ha-tarbut ha-yehudit be'varsha, 1918–1942* [Books, writers and newspapers: the Jewish Cultural Center in Warsaw, 1918–1942] (Jerusalem: Magnes Press 2003), 11–14.

contained works in prose and poetry of local authors, as well as translations, mainly of contemporary Polish writers and Yiddish publicists.[72]

Another step towards the creation of a vibrant Yiddish publishing center in Warsaw was Lazar Tzukerman's initiative to publish a series of popular adaptations and translations from foreign languages ("Tzukermans folks-bibliotek" [Tzukerman's Popular Library], 1898–1899).[73] Only four books were published in this series.[74] Shortly afterwards the first modern Yiddish publishing company was established in Warsaw in 1900 by Yankev Lidski (1868–1921). Its name, "Progress," starkly communicated its goal. Lidski himself already had some experience as a publisher in Chicago. He served as a representative of American Jewish publishers in Eastern Europe and helped radical activists smuggle illegal literature into the Russian Empire. Lidski's publishing company flourished thanks to the good quality and variety of its books and the general growth in demand for Yiddish books by a wide range of readers. In 1910 the "Ha-shachar" publishing house (1908) joined Lidski; and a year later Lidski became a partner in "Tzentral"/"Merkaz". During World War I, Lidski established a new publishing company, "Yiddish", soon the most active Yiddish publishing enterprise in Warsaw.[75]

It is no wonder, then, that as soon as Shoel Ginzberg's appeal to publish a Yiddish daily newspaper was accepted in October, 1902, he rushed from St. Petersburg to the "very center" (*hoypt-tzenter*) of Yiddish literature, Warsaw, in order to recruit local literary figures to work for his paper. Although the Warsaw Yiddish literary milieu felt that "di goyishe [un-Jewish] Petersburg" does not deserve a daily newspaper, they welcomed Ginzburg and participated in his *Der fraynd*.[76] Two years later Warsaw got its own first daily Yiddish newspaper—*Der veg* (The Way, 1905–1907) that was edited by Zvi Prylucki

---

72 Avrom Reyzin, *Epizodn fun mayn lebn* [Episodes of my life], vol. 1 (Vilna: Kletzkin, 1929), 242–260.

73 Tzukerman was a bookseller and publisher who inherited the enterprise from his father Avrom Tzukerman (1843–1892), a "Litvak" who immigrated to Warsaw and opened his bookshop in 1877. With the passage of time, he became a well known Hebrew bookseller and publisher in city.

74 *Der Koyfman fun venedig* (1898), an adaptation in prose by Meir Yankev Freid, of Shakespeare's *The Merchant of Venice*; *Di Goldmakher* (1898), an adaptation of Johann Heinrich Zschokke, *Die Goldmacherdorf*; [Meir Vankev Freid], *Kapitan Drayfuss: der farshikter oyfn tayvls inzl* [Captain Dreyfus: the one exiled to Devil's Island] (1898); *Der eviger yid* (1899), an adaptation of Eugène Sue, *Le Juif Errant*.

75 Yakobovitch, *Assot ve'hafetz sefarim harbe*, 43–47.

76 Shoel Ginzburg, *Amolike peterburg* [Old time St. Petersburg] (New York: Tziko, 1944), 190, 192.

(1862–1942). In the following year the number of daily Yiddish newspapers in Warsaw grew to five and were distributed in no less than 96,000 copies per day, while the three Hebrew daily newspapers were distributed in only 12,000 copies.[77]

The Jewish socialist intelligentsia of Warsaw had once kept their distance from Yiddish speakers and readers. But the presence of young Yiddish writers and activists and the large number of high quality new publications in Yiddish changed their attitude. One of the leading socialist activists who contributed a great deal to the advancement of Yiddish culture in Warsaw was Avrom Kotik.[78] In cooperation with the bookseller Alter Bresler (1866–1930), he established a small publishing house called "Kotiks oysgaben" (Kotik's Publications, 1895–1896), which published a series of seven booklets (with illustrations) on popular science, translated by both, as well as Dovid Pinski, under the general title "Vissnshaftlikhe folksbikher" (Popular Scientific Books).[79] His aim in publishing this kind of literature in Yiddish was to broaden the reader's horizons to include all that had to do with history and human progress.[80] An attempt to publish a similar series about ten years later was made by the "Yavne"

---

77   Nathan Cohen, "Zikhronot tzvi prilutzki: te'uda merateket le'cheker itonut yidish be'varsha" [Zvi Prylucky's memoirs as a source for the research of Yiddish journalism in Warsaw], in David Assaf et al. (eds.), *Mi-vilne li-yerushalayim: mechkarim be'toldoteihem u'be'tarbutam shel yehudey mizrakh eyropa mugashim le'profesor Shmuel Verses* [From Vilna to Jerusalem: studies in East European Jewish history and culture in honor of Professor Shmuel Werses], (Jerusalem: Magnes Press, 2002), 385–402; Fuks, *Prasa Żydowska*, 298.

78   Kotik studied pharmacology at Warsaw University and was part of the Russian speaking Jewish intelligentsia. He did a lot for the sake of Yiddish culture, though he was far from being fluent in Yiddish, as Avrom Reyzin recalled in his memoirs. See Avrom Reyzin, *Epizodn fun mayn lebn* [Episodes of my life], vol. 2 (Vilna: Kletzkin, 1929), 46–48. Kotik published his own memoirs under the title *Dos lebn fun a yidishn intelligent* [The life of a Jewish intellectual] (New York: Farlag Toybnshlag, 1925). On Yekheskel Kotik, Avrom Kotik's father, see Scott Ury's chapter in this volume.

79   The booklets were: 1. [Boris] Pavlovich, *Vi hobn mentshn gelebt mit eynike toyznt yor tzurik* [How did people live a few thousand years ago], 1895; 2. [Dimitri] Korobchevski, *Dertzeylungen vegn vilde mentshn* [Stories about wild people], 1895; 3. [Alexander Bogdanov], *Arbet un kapital* (Labor and capital], 1896; 4 and 7. Khaye Zeldes [Yitzkhok Goydo], *Vinter oventn* [Winter evenings], 1896, 1898(?); 5. [Zigmunt] Yanishevski, *Vegn luft* [About Air], 1896; 6. [Dimitri] Kudriavski, *Adam harishons doyres, oder di forhistorishe tzayt fun mentshn* [Adam's era, or the prehistory of mankind], 1896. In later years Alter Bresler tried to continue the project of translating scientific works in various types of publications.

80   As stated in the editor's preface to booklet number 2.

publishing house and Pinkhes Kantorovich (1866–1927), a translator of popular scientific works from Russian into Yiddish and Hebrew.[81]

Kotik went on with his initiatives and established the "Bildung" (Education, 1901–1904) publishing company, which provided readers with additional popular scientific works, usually translated from foreign languages, as well as belles-lettres.[82] While attacking the traditional Jewish educational system on the one hand and acculturation on the other hand, Kotik encouraged his learned colleagues to contribute to the existing inventory of high quality works in Yiddish in all genres and fields. He blamed the booksellers for distributing "American multi-volume novels" for profit, capitalizing on the readers' unsophisticated literary tastes.[83] Kotik published a list of 323 recommended Yiddish books for libraries and tried—without success—to conduct a survey of the reading preferences of Yiddish readers.[84] Alter Bresler, Kotik's partner, turned his bookshop into a lending library, one of the first of its kind in Warsaw. Isaac

---

81   For this series, the following items are documented: *Di erd* [The Earth], 1907; *Di ershte yedies fun der natur lere* [The first knowledge of nature studies], 1907; *Di ershte yedies vegn magnetism un elektritzitet* [The first knowledge of magnetism and electricity], 1907; *Elektritzitet far ale* [Electricity for All], 1908. Kantorovich published the following items in Hebrew: *Khimiya be'hayey yom yom* [Chemistry in everyday life] (2 vols.; Varshe: Sokolov, 1902–1903) and *Ha-aretz* [The Earth] (Varshe: Ha-tzefira, 1903).

82   The editors intended to publish four series of 24 booklets each, and a literary anthology, of which only ten booklets appeared: 1. A[rchibald] Geikie, *Fizishe geografye* [Physical geography], 1901; 2. S[ergey] Melgonov, *Di algemayne geshikhte: di mizrakh felker fun der alter tzayt* [General history: the nations of the ancient Near East], 1902; 3. *Abraham Lincoln: der bafrayer fun shklafn. Zayn lebn un gezelshaftlikhe arbet* [Abraham Lincoln, Liberator of the slaves: his life and social activity], 1902; 4. [Nikolay] Rubakin, *Der zeyde tzayt, oder di antviklung fun der velt: der erd un altz vos es lebt af ir* [Grandfather Time, Or the development of the World—The Earth and all that lives on it], 1901, 1904; 5. *Politishe ekonomye fun A. Bogdanov* [A. Bogdanov's political economics], 1902, 1904; 6. Lev Tolstoy, *Der koyekh fun fintzterkayt* [The power of darkness], 1904; 7. Dovid Pinski, *Drabkin, Yom Kipper: tzvey dertzeylungen* [Two stories: Drabkin and Yom Kipur], 1902; 8. Avrom Reyzin, *Skitzn* [Sketches], 1902; 9. H.D. Nomberg, *Men vekt* [Waking up], 1902; 10. Sholem Aleichem, *A mayse on an ek* [An endless story], 1902, 1904.

83   *Prospect, baygeleygt a katalog fun oysgeveylte yidishe bikher* [Brochure, including a catalog of selected Yiddish books] (Varshe: Farlag Bildung, 1902), 3–12.

84   Ibid.; At the turn of the twentieth century Jewish booksellers and publishers used to import large number of Yiddish books from the United States, both trivial popular literature, belles-lettres and popular scientific works. For more on this subject see Hagit Cohen, "The USA-Eastern Europe Yiddish book trade and the formation of an American Yiddish cultural center, 1890s–1930s," *Jews in Russia and Eastern Europe* 2(57) (2006): 52–84.

Bashevis Singer considered his first visit to Bresler's library a formative experience in his life.[85]

Similar to Polish Christian intellectuals, Jewish intellectuals demonstrated concern for (Jewish) public health. Practical instructions for personal and family hygiene and rules for keeping good health and identifying medical problems were written by Dr. Meir Gotlib (1866–?) and published by Avrom Tzukerman in a series of booklets under the title "Zayt gezunt" (Be Well, 1899–1903).[86] Another publication in Yiddish in this context was a medical encyclopedic dictionary, *Der hoyz-doktor* (The Domestic Doctor, 1895), translated and published by Mikhl Veber (mentioned above in the Hebrew context). This book was divided into numerous chapters on physiology, nutrition, sexuality and a long list of diseases.[87] Veber also published an illustrated booklet on astronomy in Yiddish.[88]

The first decade of the 20th century was characterized by a growth in both supply and demand for Yiddish literature, whether original or translated from foreign languages. Yiddish publishers and printers were, no doubt, influenced by the great success of some of the 150 Polish popular "Libraries" ("Biblioteki") published between 1840 and 1918 with the intention of distributing knowledge and bringing higher quality literature to the common people.[89] As mentioned earlier, the Hebrew "Libraries" of the 1890s were quite successful; in consequence, various Yiddish "Libraries" emerged, too. One of the first was called "Kleyne folks-bibliotek" (Small Public Library, 1904–1906), an initiative of

---

85 Isaac Bashevis Singer, *Love and Exile* (Harmondsworth: Penguin, 1986), 26–29.

86 The plan was to publish 12 booklets, but only five or six were published. The booklets were devoted to first aid, to tuberculosis, to the digestive system, to sexually transmittable diseases, and to nervous disorders. The whole series was printed in several editions as one book, entitled *Zayt gezunt* (Be well). Dr. Gotlib also translated a Polish book concerning smallpox: *Vos is pokn un vos darf men ton um tzu farhitn zikh fun pokn* [What is smallpox and what should one do in order to protect oneself from smallpox], 1902.

87 *Der Hoyz-Doktor: eytzes tzu hitn di gezunthayt un higyenishe mitlen kegn krankaytn* [The domestic doctor: advice for preserving one's health, and hygienic methods against illnesses], edited by Dr. Y[aakov?] Frenkel and translated by Mikhl Veber (Varshe: author's and translator's publication, 1895). The source for this book was Dr. Frenkel's *Shomer ha-briut* [The health's keeper] (Varsha: Halter, 1890)—a collection of articles that the author had published in *Ha-tzefira* plus various additions.

88 Mikhl Veber, *Di geheimnis fun der velt, oder a sof fun der velt, a populere astronomye* [The mysteries of the World, or The end of the world: popular astronomy] (Varshe: Lidski, 1904 and 1914).

89 Kostecki, "Ruch Wydawniczy," *Słownik literatury Polskiej XX wieku*, 975–976; Jazdon, *Wielkopolskie serie wydawnicze*.

Yankev Lidski's that sought to "provide the Jewish masses with cheap and useful books from European and Jewish literature, [in order to] refine their literary taste and to educate them at a higher level."[90] It was a series of only ten booklets of Jewish and European literature. In 1911, Lidski tried to renew the series under the title "Di folks-bibliotek" (The Public Library), but probably owing to the establishment of "Tzentral" / "Merkaz," only one booklet appeared.

In 1903, Magnus Krinsky (1863–1916), a writer and educator established in 1903 a Hebrew publishing company called "Ha-or" (The Light). In addition to Hebrew texts and children's books, it published booklets (and later books also) in Yiddish under the general title "Bikher far ale" (Books for All) from 1905 on. In the first year of its existence "Bikher far ale" published 40 booklets of Yiddish belles-lettres. Among the large variety of publications there were three booklets devoted to sexual dysfunction in the sub-series, "Farlag higiyene"(1908).[91] In 1910, "Bikher Far Ale" began to publish the series "Groysse bibliotek" (Large library). Among the 12 books it contained were a dictionary of foreign expressions, a collection of poems, and sheet music. These were given as gifts to subscribers to the new daily newspaper *Der moment*.[92] In 1907, a publishing company called "Algemayne bibliotek" (General Library) published at least 24 booklets of translated Russian stories and a Polish-Russian-Yiddish dictionary, which appeared in weekly installments.[93]

Simultaneously with the establishment of the Yiddish daily newspapers *Dos yiddishes tageblat* (The Jewish Daily) in 1906 and *Haynt* (Today) in 1908, and thanks to their editor, Shmuel Yankev Yatzkan (1874–1936), two large "Libraries" were launched: "Hoyz bibliotek" (House Library, 1906–1911) and "Familien

---

90 Cited from the back cover of Elisée Reclus, *Der hungeriker* [The hungry man] (np, 1906).
91 One of the booklets dealt with the question of birth control—a novelty in the Jewish sphere of the time: R.G. Nisse, *Kegn shvangershaft: meditzinishe eytzes un mitlen vi oystzumaydn dos shvangern un kinder-hobn* [Against pregnancy: medical advice and ways to prevent pregnancy and childbirth]. The other two books were: Dr. T. Kornik, *Higyene far umfarhayratete: vikhtike eytzes un erklerungen far yungelayt vi azoy tzu firn a reyn lebn* [Hygiene for the unmarried: important advice and explanations for young people on how to live a clean life]; Dr. M(eir) Gotlib, *Populere algemayne higyene: zeyer vikhtike eytzes vi azoy tzu firn a rikhtiks lebn un farhitn di gezunthayt* [Popular general hygiene: very important advice how to live properly and keep one's health] (Varshe: Ha-or).
92 *Fremd-verter-bukh*, tzuzamengeshtelt durkh Dr. A.B. Roznshteyn [A dictionary of foreign expressions, compiled by Dr. A.B. Roznshteyn], 1914; *Der deklamator: a literarishe zamlung far muzikalish-literarishe un familyen-oventn*, gezamlt durkh Avrom Reyzin [The performer: a literary anthology for literary-musical and family events], 1914.
93 M. Volfszohn, *Polnish-russish-yidisher verter-bukh* [Polish-Russian-Yiddish Dictionary], 1907.

bibliotek" (Family Library, 1909–1914). The first was dedicated to popular science (50 booklets), and the other included both belles-lettres (mainly works by Sholem Aleichem) and popular science (150 booklets). Around 1910 Yatzkan founded an independent publishing house called "Yehudia".[94] Among a variety of publications in Yiddish (many of which were presents for *Haynt* subscribers) and publications in Hebrew, including prayer books and Passover Hagadot, "Yehudia" launched the series "Folks-univerzitet" (Popular University, 1913–1914), which aimed to cover "all the fields of sciences" for the benefit of the knowledge-seeking reading public. Three experts were appointed to an editorial board to achieve this lofty goal.[95] During less than two years, 19 booklets (of *circa* 120 pages each) were published, presenting basic information on the natural and social sciences and general history.

In 1914 at least three other series appeared in Warsaw. The first was "Universal bibliotek" at Levin-Epstein's press, with nine booklets of literary works that included prefaces, authors' biographies, and occasionally the authors' portraits. Nine more booklets were planned but did not appear because of the outbreak of war. Another series, "Mayselekh" (Folktales), put out by a publishing house with the same name, was intended for children and contained 19 illustrated booklets with works by Peretz, Hans Christian Andersen, Edmondo De Amicis, Alexander Pushkin, and others. A third series, also intended for children, was called "Kinder velt" (Children's World). Its initiator and author of its animal stories was the educator Shloyme Hurvitz-Zalkes (1878–1960).[96]

Another notable publishing company in Warsaw that found its way to "Tzentral" / "Merkaz" was Binyomin Shimin's (1880–1942) company. In 1905, he opened a bookshop and thanks to cooperation with the "Hatzefira" press he published the Yiddish socio-political series "Tzayt bibliotek" (The Time Library, 1905–1907), with eight translations and adaptations of works by Karl Marx, Ferdinand Lassalle, August Bebel and others. From 1907, Shimin also functioned as an independent publisher. His first project as such was the publication of works of outstanding authors (both Jewish and non-Jewish) in a series called "Universal bibliotek." In 1909, he announced a subscription enterprise entitled "Shimins groyse velt-bibliotek" (Shimin's Grand World Library). During its three-year existence, it supplied subscribers with the best of Jewish

---

94 Before then he used mainly the two newspapers' names as publishers of the two "libraries".
95 The editors were the critic and cultural activist Dr. Izidor Eliashev (Baal Makhsoves) (1873–1924), the educator Dr. Tzemakh Feldshteyn (1885–1945) and the engineer Iser Yoysef Aynhorn (1871–1925).
96 Probably only one booklet appeared out of five or more that were planned: *Di rabe hun, Di veverke* [The spotted hen, The squirrel].

and world literature every other week, including various reference books (66 in all). These books were printed on good quality paper and furnished with illustrations.[97] Shimin also published a Yiddish dictionary of foreign words and phrases, composed by Ber Karlinski (1886–1935), a journalist and writer who took part in the literary adaptations of the "Velt bibliotek."[98]

Cultural Institutions

The library of the Great Synagogue on Tłomackie Street, which later became the library of the Institute for Jewish Studies, was no doubt a central cultural institution for distributing knowledge in Warsaw. The first calls for establishing a substantial Jewish library were heard already in 1860, but the idea was realized only in 1879 as part of the Warsaw Great Synagogue that had been dedicated the prior year. Five years later, the library contained 6,819 Judaica books, half of them in Hebrew, and 22 manuscripts. The library subscribed to Jewish periodical publications from around the world. Thanks to the financing of Ignacy Bernstein, it enlarged its collection of manuscripts and old prints. In 1896, the library was open six days a week and contained already more than 10,000 volumes, including incunabula, manuscripts, and some private archives. In 1904, the number of volumes increased to 14,126. Jewish publishers used to visit the library looking for interesting manuscripts or old prints to publish in new editions.[99] The idea of establishing a separate building for the Judaica library had been voiced already in 1903, but was inaugurated only in 1936. The inventory now grew to 34,000 volumes and 150 manuscripts. At that stage, according to the law, a compulsory copy of every printed Jewish book in Poland had to be sent to the library.[100]

A more popular cultural center was "Hazomir" (An Association for Hebrew Singing and Literature), established in 1906. Its first chairman was the physician and cultural activist Dr. Gershon Levin (1868–1939). A year after its establishment a "Yiddish dramatic group" was initiated within Hazomir by

---

97 Yakobovitch, *Assot ve'hafetz sefarim harbe*, 49–54 and Shimin's advertisements in his various publications.

98 B. Karliner [Ber Karlinski], *Fremd verterbukh* [Dictionary of foreign expressions], 1911.

99 Shatzky, *Geshikhte fun yidn in varshe*, III: 323–326; A[rn] Gavze, "Di yudaistishe hoyptbibliotek in varshe," *"Haynt" yoyvl-bukh (1908–1938)* [Haynt—Jubilee Book, 1908–1938] (Warsaw, 1938), 299–305.

100 N. Mayzil, "Di varshever sinagoge-bibliotek [The Warsaw Synagogue-Library]," *Haynt*, 1 July 1931, 7; A[rn] Gavze, ibid.

Y.L. Peretz and Sholem Asch. Hazomir performed in a variety of cultural events such as concerts, sing-along evenings, readings by authors, and dramatic performances and lectures in both Hebrew and Yiddish. Within a period of ten years Hazomir was defined as "a 'mood-meter' for spiritual streams that couldn't find a home in our places."[101] Hazomir's success was realized also by the establishment of a public library (1910) that functioned until the outbreak of the Second World War.

Conclusion: Warsaw in the Context of Other Jewish Cultural Centers

Following the easing of the restrictions on Jewish printing in the 1860s, three Odessa publishers regularly issued books in Hebrew characters. Within a few years, more than 100 titles in Hebrew and Yiddish had been published, most in Hebrew.[102] Odessa became a Hebrew literary center and home to leading Hebrew writers, either permanently or, more often, temporarily. Nevertheless, when Kh.N. Bialik and his colleagues Y.Kh. Ravnitzky, Sh. Ben-Zion and A.L. Levinsky founded the "Moria" publishing house, they had to cooperate with Ahiassaf in Warsaw for the first years of their existence (after which they operated independently). According to partial statistics from 1889, 38 out of the 115 Yiddish books published that year in Eastern Europe were printed in Warsaw, whereas 42 were printed in Vilna (and five in Odessa). There were no recognizable differences in the characteristic of books between both places.[103] In a more detailed statistical compilation of Yiddish publications from the year 1912, 148 out of 348 Yiddish (non religious) books were printed in Warsaw, and only 35 in Vilna (18 were printed in St. Petersburg and 12 in Odessa).

At this stage, it is quite clear that Warsaw supplied most literary works and Vilna supplied most of the political ones (regarding nonfiction, the two cities were more on par).[104] A shift in favor of Warsaw is also noticeable in the Jewish press, in both Hebrew and Yiddish. As mentioned earlier, when Shoel Ginzberg

---

101 A. Horn [Arn Einhorn?], "Der yubileum fun 'hazomir' ", *Haynt*, 16 August 1916, title page.

102 Steven J. Zipperstein, *The Jews of Odessa: a cultural history, 1794–1881* (Stanford, CA: Stanford University Press, 1985), 83–84.

103 A.K., "A reester fun ale zhargonishe bikher vos zaynen opgedrukt inem yor 5649" [A Register / List of All Yiddish Books that were Printed in the Year 1889]," *Di yudishe folks-bibliotek*, vol. 2 (Kiev, 1889), 135–139.

104 Moshe Shalit, "Statistik fun yidishn bikher-mark in yor 1912" [Statistics of the Yiddish Book-Market], *Der Pinkes* (Vilna: Kletzkin, 1913), 302–306.

received permission to publish the first Yiddish daily newspaper in Russia, he went directly to Warsaw to look for contributors to the paper. Even printing a newspaper in St. Petersburg was not an easy task.[105] Within a few years of its existence, *Der fraynd* experienced difficulties and finally, in 1909, it was moved to Warsaw. Since the first Yiddish daily newspaper appeared in Warsaw in 1905, the Polish capital exceeded centers like St. Petersburg, Odessa and even Vilna, with a constantly growing number of newspapers and other periodicals.[106]

Since the late 18th century, Jewish Berlin had served as a model for enlightened Jewish scholars in Eastern Europe. In the nineteenth century, Berlin became famous for its *Wissenschaft des Judentums*. Vilna, on the other hand, was famous among Jews as "the Jerusalem of Lithuania," owing to its world-renowned traditional scholarly prestige. It is no wonder, then, that Vilna emerged as a Haskalah center and, later, as a center for Zionist ideology and Jewish socialist activity. Vilna was, in fact, the only Jewish cultural center that could compete with Warsaw for the role of leader of the East European Jewish cultural arena, but its preeminence was never fully realized.

Jewish Warsaw in the period under discussion did not seem to have pretensions to compete with any of these highly respected centers, nor to take a leading cultural position. It was mainly owing to Warsaw's relative freedom of the press that so many Jewish printers decided to settle and to produce there. Next to that was its constantly shifting social, economic and political composition, much of which was due to the influx of Litvaks. Warsaw also attracted many young and enthusiastic Jewish cultural activists (not necessarily Litvaks), thus emerging as the preeminent conveyor of knowledge among Jews until at least the outbreak of the First World War.

---

105   Ginzburg, *Amolike peterburg*, 190–214. Under the title "Periodicals, Collections and Encyclopedias" published in St. Petersburg, Mikhail Beizer counted seven Hebrew entries (up to 1914), 13 in Yiddish, and 37 in Russian. As publishers he mentioned "Kadima" and "Ezro" but skipped other publishers, such as "Likht", "Avangard" and "Di naye bibliotek" (Mikhail Beizer, *The Jews of St. Petersburg: Excursion Through A Nobel Past*, Philadelphia and New York: The Jewish Publication Society, 1989), 277–286.

106   Shmeruk, *Prokim geshikhte*, 304–305, and "Aspects of the History of Warsaw as a Yiddish Literary Center," *Polin* 3 (1988): 140–155.

CHAPTER 8

In Kotik's Corner: Urban Culture, Bourgeois Politics and the Struggle for Jewish Civility in Turn of the Century Eastern Europe

Scott Ury

Looking out on the great turn-of-century metropolis of Warsaw, A. A. Friedman, editor of the Hebrew daily *Ha-tzofe* (The Observer), could not help but notice that the city and its residents were changing. Among the many changes unfolding before the paper's keen journalistic eye was the appearance of numerous "Jewish" cafés: coffee houses that were patronized almost exclusively by Jews. Typical of a turn-of-century daily's love-hate relationship with the modern city, the newspaper was both drawn to and repulsed by Warsaw's many sites of urban attraction and horror, including cafés.[1] Indeed, not only had "the Jews" changed the face of "the city," the city had changed the face of "the Jews":

> The number of cafés in our city has grown at an alarming rate of late and some of these institutions are even open on Shabbat. The reason for this phenomenon is the growing number of solitary people [*aneshim bodedim*] living in our city without their families. These people have much difficulty finding a place where they can go on Shabbat...[2]

This seemingly innocuous item about the changing nature of Warsaw's cityscape speaks volumes about a series of fundamental social transformations—the massive in-migration of single Jewish men to the city, noticeable changes in levels of religious observance, and the appearance of a new public

---

* Research for this article was made possible by a generous grant from the Israel Science Foundation, ISF, Grant No. 361/12.
1 On dailies as guides to the perplexities of urban living, see Peter Fritzsche, *Reading Berlin, 1900* (Cambridge, MA: Harvard University Press, 1998), 16–20. Also see Judith R. Walkowitz, *City of Dreadful Delight: Narratives of Sexual Danger in Late-Victorian London* (Chicago: University of Chicago Press, 1992). I also discuss some of these questions in Scott Ury, *Barricades and Banners: The Revolution of 1905 and the Transformation of Warsaw Jewry* (Stanford: Stanford University Press, 2012), 45–90.
2 *Ha-tzofe*, no. 498 (25 VIII/ 7 IX 1904), 849.

culture. Together, these changes altered Jewish society and culture in urban centers across turn-of-century Eastern Europe.[3] These and related developments will serve as the backdrop to this article's discussion of the emergence of Jewish coffee houses in Warsaw, vital public spaces that will serve as a rubric here for examining the Jewish encounter with and response to modernity in Eastern Europe.[4] What can the triangular relationship between coffee, Jews and the urban ideal tell us about Jewish perceptions of and responses to the very epitome of modern society, the metropolis?

For over a generation, coffee houses have stood at the center of critical theories interrogating the development of modern, liberal societies and their ostensible guarantor, the bourgeois public sphere (or, alternatively, civil society). In his now classic *The Structural Transformation of the Public Sphere*, Jürgen Habermas persuasively argues that coffee houses were part of a series of new spaces and institutions that emerged in eighteenth-century Western Europe to form a "public sphere," the bedrock of modern, western society, politics and culture that guaranteed Western Europe's path from enlightenment and democracy to cosmopolitanism and co-existence. At its core, the bourgeois public sphere was a collection of institutions—coffee houses, newspapers and theaters—that enabled the assembly of individuals and the crystallization of "the public." Its key characteristics were its open nature, rational foundations, and new spaces in which individuals could assemble to debate rationally the issues of the day and form a collective public without abandoning their individual autonomy. According to Habermas, "the bourgeois public sphere may be conceived above all as the sphere of private people come together as a public; they soon claimed the public sphere regulated from above against the public authorities themselves, to engage in a debate over the general rules governing relations in the basically privatized but publicly relevant sphere of commodity exchange and social labor. The medium of this political confrontation was peculiar and without historical precedent: the people's use of their reason."[5]

---

3   For more on Jewish public culture at the time, see: Jeffrey Veidlinger, *Jewish Public Culture in the Late Russian Empire* (Bloomington: Indiana University Press, 2009).

4   For recent studies on the connection between Jews and coffee, see Sarah Wobick-Segev, "Buying, Selling, Being, Drinking; Or, How the Coffeehouse Became a Site for the Consumption of new Jewish Modalities of Belonging," in Gideon Reuveni and Sarah Wobick-Segev (eds.), *The Economy in Jewish History: New Perspectives on the Interrelationship between Ethnicity and Economic Life* (New York: Berghahn Books, 2011), 115–134; and Robert Liberles, *Jews Welcome Coffee: Tradition and Innovation in Early Modern Germany* (Waltham, MA: Brandeis University Press, 2012).

5   Jürgen Habermas, *The Structural Transformation of the Public Sphere: An Inquiry into a Category of Bourgeois Society*, trans. Thomas Burger (Cambridge, MA: MIT Press, 1996), 27. My thanks to Derek Penslar for his insightful comments on this issue.

In addition to reconfiguring the nature of urban space and shaping the very mode of public interaction between individuals, the public sphere was also an inherently political and contestatory body, one that served as both the foundation of "the public" as well as the source of the public's confrontation with authorities. Thus, the bourgeois public sphere came to be seen not only as a key marker of modern society but also the guarantor of such leitmotifs of modernity as civil society and democracy. Ultimately, coffee houses and other central public sphere institutions came to symbolize what was widely viewed as the Western European model of modernity—one that was inherently rational, democratic, and progressive.[6]

Despite Habermas' influence, some critics contend that, notwithstanding the allure of progress that the great project of modernity offered, cracks eventually began to appear. Like the cliché regarding a Bolshevik omelet, far too many "eggs" were broken along modernity's path of progress and redemption. Some have even argued that the source of the breakdown of the great project of modernity is, in fact, embedded deep within its very essence.[7] Inspired by these and other readings of the development of modern society, I have argued elsewhere that many of these contradictions are as salient for Jews as they are for other residents of the European continent, both its western and eastern halves.[8] The following analysis further develops this discussion by highlighting the contradictions embedded deep within the Jewish encounter with the metropolis—the very hallmark of modernity—and the accompanying attempts to construct the autonomous (Jewish) self—one of modernity's chief aspirations.[9]

Located in the heart of Warsaw's Jewish district, at 31 Nalewki Street, Yehezkel Kotik's coffee house vividly illustrates many of these contradictions. Throughout this chapter, I will highlight two aspects of Kotik's coffee house that explore the dialectics of Jewish and general modernity in turn-of-century eastern Europe. On the one hand, Kotik's café was a quintessential public sphere institution. For many of Warsaw's Jewish residents, both veteran residents and

---

6 On the connection between civil society and democracy, see, for example, Michael Walzer, "The Concept of Civil Society," in Michael Walzer, ed., *Toward a Global Civil Society* (Oxford: Berghahn Books, 1995), 16, 24. See also Ernest Gellner, *Conditions of Liberty: Civil Society and Its Rivals* (London: Hamish Hamilton, 1994), 5, 53–54, and 103.

7 See, for example, Max Horkheimer and Theodor W. Adorno, *Dialectic of Enlightenment*, trans. John Cumming (New York: Continuum, 1999). For an alternative view, see Zeev Sternhell, *The Anti-Enlightenment Tradition*, trans. David Maisel (New Haven, CT: Yale University Press, 2010).

8 See Ury, *Barricades and Banners*, 261–272.

9 On modernity and the fate of the modern self, see Igal Halfin, *Terror in My Soul: Communist Autobiographies on Trial* (Cambridge, MA: Harvard University Press, 2003).

recent arrivals, his centrally-located café was a dynamic, open urban space in which Jewish individuals from a wide cross-section of Warsaw's diverse urban society and the surrounding region would congregate to debate the affairs of the day. In this and other ways, Kotik's café was typical of the many new public forums in Warsaw that encouraged debate between individuals and an attendant imagination and re-construction of an urban Jewish community. True to Habermas's model, this community of discourse would often serve as the foundation for a burgeoning collective body politic, if not a nation in the making.

At the same time, Kotik himself was a tireless communal activist who regularly used the café to advance his own particular vision of bourgeois politics, urban reform, and Jewish national regeneration. Thus, an analysis of the projects for urban renewal that Kotik promoted within his coffeehouse sheds light not only on the language and ideal of Jewish urban reform but also on his inherently ambivalent relationship to modernity and the precarious place of the individual within his visions of Jewish civility, citizenship, and self. Taken together, Kotik's quintessentially modern, urban café and his plans for urban reform expose a set of contradictions and tensions inherent in modernity itself, thereby problematizing our understanding of the Jewish encounter with and understanding of urban society, the Jewish community and the Jewish self in the modern world.[10]

In Kotik's Corner: Coffee and the Construction of the Jewish Public Sphere

As many observers have noted, the last third of the nineteenth century was a period of rapid industrial and urban growth across great parts of the Russian Empire. Although diverse factors contributed to these developments, a series of virtually new cities arose in late nineteenth-century Eastern Europe, including Łódź, Warsaw, and Odessa.[11] Like many other developments, the emergence of these new centers affected the lives of many of the Russian Empire's

---

10   For traditional views of the path of Jewish modernity, see Jacob Katz, *Tradition and Crisis: Jewish Society at the End of the Middle Ages*, trans. Bernard Dov Cooperman (New York: Schocken, 1993); Jacob Katz (ed.), *Toward Modernity: The European Jewish Model* (New Brunswick, NJ: Transaction Books, 1987); and Shmuel Feiner, *The Jewish Enlightenment*, trans. Chaya Naor (Philadelphia: University of Pennsylvania Press, 2004).

11   On the growth of cities in late imperial Russia, see Daniel R. Brower, *The Russian City between Tradition and Modernity, 1850–1900* (Berkeley: University of California Press, 1990) and Michael F. Hamm, *The City in Late Imperial Russia* (Bloomington: Indiana University Press, 1986).

five million Jewish subjects. Attracted by new economic opportunities as well as intellectual and cultural possibilities, many Jews began to migrate from provincial towns and small centers (*shtetls*) to the new metropolises.[12]

While population figures are always problematic, official statistics regarding Jewish population growth in these new centers are telling. In the decades preceding World War I and the collapse of the old regime, Odessa's Jewish population grew almost fourfold, from approximately 55,000 in 1880 to roughly 200,000 in 1914; the Jewish population of Łódź sky-rocketed from around 10,000 in 1873 to some 170,000 by the outbreak of World War I, and the number of Jews in Warsaw grew almost three-fold from 125,000 in 1881 to some 340,000 in 1914. (In each of these cases, it should be noted, the non-Jewish population grew at similar rates, and the portion of registered Jewish residents in cities like Odessa, Łódź and Warsaw hovered around one-third of the total population throughout the period.) As a result of these changes, roughly one-half of Warsaw's Jewish residents in 1897 were newcomers who had been born outside of the city. Furthermore, roughly 50% of the city's Jewish residents at the time were under the age of twenty.

The influx of a great number of young Jewish migrants to the city created a radically new social dynamic that set off intensive public debates about the nature and fate of urban society.[13] Jewish and Polish observers alike charged that many Jewish arrivals to Warsaw were foreign not only to the city, but also to Polish society and culture. Labeled and often derided as *"Litvaks"* (Jews from Lithuanian lands), Jewish migrants were said to lack both an affinity for Polish language and culture and a sense of loyalty to the burgeoning concept of "the Polish nation." As a result of these and other prejudices, Jewish newcomers were often portrayed as disruptive, foreign elements that upset the city's precarious social balance at the turn of the century city. The term *Litvaks* quickly became code for many of the problems that seemed to divide Poles and Jews in Warsaw.

Thus, the typical growing pains of urbanization were exacerbated by tensions between veteran Jewish residents and newcomers, as well as between Poles and Jews. These and related changes led many residents to begin searching for new frameworks that might lend a sense of order, structure and meaning to an increasingly chaotic urban environment. Jewish newcomers, in particular, who were frequently marginalized by both Polish and Jewish elites, as well

---

12 For more on Jewish migration to such centers see Shaul Stampfer, "Patterns of Internal Jewish Migration in the Russian Empire," in Ya'akov Ro'i (ed.), *Jews and Jewish Life in Russia and the Soviet Union* (Ilford: Frank Cass, 1995), 28–47.

13 I discuss some of these debates in Ury, *Barricades and Banners*, 45–90.

as by established Jewish communal organizations, needed new frameworks that would help them respond to many of the problems they encountered in the new, oftentimes dizzying urban arena. Soon, a series of new, ostensibly apolitical public institutions like coffee houses, lunch buffets, and other public establishments began to appear and serve as impromptu centers for urban assembly, community, and organization. Thus, Jewish coffee houses were not only an integral part of the changing cityscape but also served critical social, cultural and political functions. They provided physical arenas in which Jewish migrants and other urban residents could meet, converse, and debate as part of a coherent public.

At their core, coffee houses and similar urban institutions were markedly different from the traditional Jewish communal institutions they began to supplement, and those differences were the secret of their success. First, unlike synagogues, study houses, and other traditional Jewish communal spaces, coffee houses were commercial enterprises that lay beyond the jurisdiction of the official Jewish community and thus beyond Jewish communal supervision. In addition, their ostensibly apolitical nature enabled them to operate right under the suspicious eyes of tsarist officials, who were anxious to wield control over the empire's cities, with their increasingly unruly residents and multiple sources of unrest. While this was particularly relevant in the years surrounding the Revolution of 1905, tsarist officials remained concerned about maintaining a semblance of urban order well after the revolutionary tide subsided.[14] Lastly, the open nature of coffee houses and their storefront appeal made them particularly inviting to newer Jewish residents, who often felt shunned by established communal institutions or lost in the urban shuffle. As cities expanded and new arrivals roamed the streets in search of alternative modes of belonging, coffee houses provided an enticing forum. Migrants, activists and other random urbanites could meet there, discuss the issues of the day, and simply be, without risking arrest, imprisonment, expulsion, and worse.

Yehezkel Kotik's coffee house at 31 Nalewki Street, one of the period's best-known Jewish coffee houses, seems to fit Habermas's model of the bourgeois public sphere to a "T". Established by Kotik soon after his arrival in Warsaw from Kiev, the café quickly became a regular meeting point for a variety of Jewish intellectuals, activists and observers. Much like Habermas's theoretical public sphere, Kotik's coffee house was considered an open public space in which individuals from a variety of political and intellectual camps could

---

14   On the regime's attempts to assert order in Warsaw and neighboring regions, see Robert E. Blobaum, *Rewolucja: Russian Poland, 1904–1907* (Ithaca, NY: Cornell University Press, 1995), 260–291; Ury, *Barricades and Banners*, 91–140.

gather to debate and sometimes effectively create the affairs of the day. True to Habermas's model, impromptu meetings and open-ended discussions often helped lay the foundations for the critical transition from public assembly to urban community and from intellectual debate to political action.

Hebrew and Yiddish memoirs of journalists and cultural figures like A. Litvin, Avrom Reisen and Shlomo Shreberk recall the open, vibrant nature of the discussions and meetings that took place at 31 Nalewki Street. Again matching Habermas's theory, these discussions often revolved around published works, both newspapers and literature, and popular politics. According to the publicist Shreberk:

> One could always meet the Yiddish writers at a certain café on Nalewki street. It was a rather inexpensive establishment, and for twenty kopeks one could eat lunch for a week. Most of the patrons were, for the most part, lower class businessmen: traders, office clerks and, once in a while, a teacher. One could even find the paper *Ha-tzefira* on the table and to the best of my knowledge this was the only restaurant in which one could find the paper. People would sit there for hours and hours, they would read the paper, get to know one another, and converse. Sometimes they would do all three at the same time; even people who met for the first time in their lives in the café... They would speak about new literary works by writers, recent newspaper articles and the lives of the writers themselves such as Frishman, Sokolow, Peretz, [and] "Zionism," local matters and general affairs among the Jewish people. All of these were daily topics...[15]

Elsewhere, Shreberk notes the seemingly natural intersection of bourgeois society, secular culture and Jewish politics in Kotik's café. Here, as well, Shreberk recalls the wide variety of people who took part in the public debates that characterized the inchoate public culture developing in the café and similar public institutions.

> ... Kotik's café became the home of Warsaw's Jewish writers. All of the worker activists would also come there. One could meet the Bund leaders

---

15 Shlomo Shreberk, *Zikhronot ha-motzi le-or shlomo shreberk* (Tel Aviv: S. Shreberk, 1955), 144. Also see Avrom Reisen, *Epizoden fun mayn lebn*, vol. 1 (Vilna: B. Kletzkin, 1929), 214–216. For this and many other indispensable sources on Kotik, see: Yehezkel Kotik, *Mah she-raiti: zikhronotav shel yehezkel kotik*, ed. and trans. David Assaf (Tel Aviv: Diaspora Research Institute-Tel Aviv University, 1999), 26.

Beinush Mikhalevitch and Alter Erlich. H. D. Nomberg and Avrom Reisen were also regular guests even though Kotik had Zionist tendencies. In Kotik's café people would read new stories and poems before they were published...[16]

Initially established as part of his prosaic search for stable income in a new environment, Kotik's coffee house quickly became integral to Warsaw's new Jewish cityscape.

In many ways, the coffee house was as eclectic as its owner and as dynamic as the city itself. It served alternatively as an informal community center, a cultural venue, and political meeting site. Indeed, Kotik's café was almost never about just coffee. In fact, Kotik's café and its tireless owner seemed perfectly suited for the fluid, changing nature of Jewish society in the monstrosity of a metropolis that Warsaw had become. True to Habermas's model of the bourgeois public sphere, Kotik's café provided an open, public space where patrons could meet to discuss rationally cultural affairs, communal projects, and political activities beyond the watchful eye of Tsarist officials and traditionalist communal leaders, together forging a sense of an urban Jewish community.

Nor was discourse about the café limited to coffee culture and political memoirs. In a series of feuilletons published by Sholem Aleichem on the pages of Warsaw's phenomenally popular Yiddish daily *Haynt* in 1913, the author's literary alter ego Menakhem-Mendel is emplotted deep within the metropolis of Warsaw. Like many other Jewish residents of Paris, New York, Berlin, and other great turn of the century cities, Menakhem-Mendel roams the streets of Warsaw in apprehension and excitement, fervently searching. However, unlike Benjamin's flâneur, who thrives on the margins of urban society in a state of perpetual liminality, Sholem Aleichem's Menakhem-Mendel searches incessantly for a new home, a new center, and a new Jewish order.[17] And, like so many other Jewish urban residents, he finds this new Jewish order in the new spaces and institutions that began to appear and coalesce into a Jewish public sphere. Menakhem-Mendel's description of his new urban life to his long distance wife Shayne-Shendel bespeaks this search for belonging in an ostensibly fictionalized city:

---

16   Shreberk, *Zikhronot*, 158–159.
17   On the image of the flâneur, see Walter Benjamin, *Charles Baudelaire: A Lyric Poet in the Era of High Capitalism*, trans. Harry Zohn (London: Verson, 1985), 35–66.

> Stuffed like a barrel with news from the papers and the smoke of cigarettes, I take my walking stick and go to my milk bar to drink coffee and to converse with people. My milk bar is on Nalewki, Khaskl Kotik's place.... We sit and sit, just the two of us, Khaskl [Yehezkel] Kotik and me, over a cup of coffee and discuss our Jewish brethren...[18]

Thus, in a relatively short period of time, Kotik's café had become not only a central location for Jewish cultural and political activists in Warsaw, but also a literary symbol of how many readers, observers and other urbanites would imagine and experience modern Jewish society and culture across a host of turn-of-century cities. For Sholem Aleichem, Shlomo Shreberk, Avrom Reisen and many others, coffee houses like Yehezkel Kotik's café on Nalewki Street typified the inherently open, neutral locations in which seemingly random urban residents would meet and connect "over a cup of coffee and discuss our Jewish brethren..."

At the same time, Menahem Mendel's urban wanderings highlight a deeper tension that unsettles the seemingly natural connection between the modern city, the modern community, and the modern self. Like a *dreidel* (a Jewish top associated with the holiday of *Hanukkah*) spinning through the maddening maze of modernity, Sholem Aleichem's Menakhem-Mendel is, in a sense, suspended. Like many other Jewish urbanites, he feels a sudden rush and urge to break away and explore the rich, endless urban terrain that the modern city seemed to promise. But every time he arms himself with his walking stick—his symbol of bourgeois civility, urban defense, and male empowerment—and sets out to lose himself in the city's inherent infinity, he is drawn back into his "milk bar," "Khaskl Kotik's place." The East European city, with its ornate buildings, enticing boulevards, and seas of anonymous inhabitants promised Jewish urbanites exactly what the *Haskalah* was never able to deliver, freedom. At the same time, that same city, with its sheer size, constant motion, and new sights, sounds and smells, intimidated Jewish flâneurs and drove them towards distinctly Jewish urban spaces. From their earliest encounters, the inherent universality of the modern city and the ideal of an urban Jewish community were at odds; and the modern Jewish individual vacillated constantly between these two poles in the Polish metropole.

---

18   Sholem Aleichem, *Menahem mendel be-varshah*, trans. Aryeh Aharoni (Tel Aviv: Alef, 1977), 19–20.

Between Public Sphere and Public Reform: Urban Stains and the Struggle for Jewish Civility

In addition to being a familiar public space where Jewish urbanites could congregate and discuss the affairs of the day, Kotik's café gave the owner himself a base from which to popularize his own particular visions of urban reform, bourgeois society, and Jewish civility. Hence, Shreberk, Litvin and others all note that Kotik regularly used the coffee house to promote the different self-help organizations that he initiated in Warsaw, including Brotherly Aid (*Ahi-'ezer*), The Children of Zion (*B'nei tzion*), and others. According to Shreberk:

> I remember the first time I was in the café, the owner [Kotik] handed me a small brochure in Yiddish entitled, "Ten Commandments for the Daughters of Zion." After he saw that I knew Hebrew he gave me the same brochure in Hebrew. To more radical patrons, he would give "The Proletarian Calendar, 1907–1908," which he edited, as well as the brochure, "The Jewish Deputy."[19]

Kotik's coffee house thus played another critical role in turn-of-century Warsaw: the promotion of projects for urban reform and the rehabilitation of Warsaw's Jewish residents and its Jewish community.

As many scholars have noted, Jewish communities in Eastern Europe had a long history of communal organization and philanthropy.[20] These projects included both community-wide endeavors run by the official Jewish community and those organized by local societies and informal groups.[21] Thus, the established Jewish community in Warsaw (*gmina*), recognized and

---

19 Shreberk, *Zikhronot*, 158–159. Shreberk is probably referring to the bilingual pamphlet published by Kotik in 1899 entitled *'Aseret ha-dibrot le-benei tsion*. See below, note 35. Also note Litvin's description of how Kotik would peddle his organizational literature. A. Litvin (Shmuel Leib Hurwitz), "Yehezkel Kotik," *Yudishe neshomes*, vol. 4 (New York: Folksbildung, 1917), 2–3, 7 and 9.

20 On Jewish charity and philanthropy in Warsaw and other regions, see Jacob Shatzky, *Geshikhte fun yidn in varshe*, II: 139–160 and 175–192; III: 110–129 and 172–191; Isaac Levitats, *The Jewish Community in Russia, 1844–1917* (Jerusalem: Posner, 1981), 69–84 and 163–179; and Brian Horowitz, *Jewish Philanthropy and Enlightenment in Late Tsarist Russia* (Seattle: University of Washington Press, 2008).

21 For more on Jewish charities and philanthropy at the time, see Rainer Liedtke, *Jewish Welfare in Hamburg and Manchester, c. 1850–1914* (Oxford: Clarendon, 1998); and Derek J. Penslar, "Philanthropy, the 'Social Question' and Jewish Identity in Imperial Germany," *Leo Baeck Institute Year Book*, 38 (1993), 51–73.

regulated by Tsarist authorities, administered a series of charitable, religious and educational projects that included a Jewish hospital, Jewish orphanages and other institutions.[22] Nevertheless, the size and scope of the urban environment severely strained communal resources and left many Jews in Warsaw, in particular newcomers who felt shunned or disenfranchised by established communal institutions, overexposed and vulnerable.[23] These developments encouraged increasing numbers of individuals to create and take part in societies and organizations based outside of the official Jewish community.

A new arrival from Kiev and the owner of a popular coffee house in the heart of Warsaw's Jewish district, Kotik was particularly well-suited to respond to the pressing needs of Warsaw's Jewish residents and visitors. Thus, Kotik initiated several self-help organizations that were dedicated to reforming urban Jewish society and rehabilitating individual Jewish urbanites. For example, Kotik founded an organization designed to create a communal synagogue and provide assistance to local Jews (*Ahi-'ezer*), a body dedicated to the reform of Jewish youth (*B'nei tzion*), and other projects. Various sources regarding these organizations not only offer fascinating insights into Kotik's own interpretation of the Jewish urban condition, but also many of the inherent tensions in reigning visions of modern Jewish society and selfhood.

Kotik's role as both café owner and a crusader for urban reform demonstrates how a public sphere institution like the coffee house could serve as the foundation for larger projects aimed at the reconstruction of Jewish society and the rehabilitation of the Jewish individual.[24] As I have noted elsewhere in regard to the development of modern Jewish politics, the dual transition from public debate to a discourse of action, and from urban society to Jewish community, represents a critical turning point in the Jewish encounter with and response to modernity.[25] Thus, unlike other interpretations that often emphasize a symbiotic if not inherently positive relationship between Jews and modernity, Kotik's various projects for urban reform and the rehabilitation of the individual reveal a deeply ambivalent, problematic, if not dialectical,

---

22 On these and related institutions, see Shatzky, *Geshikhte fun yidn in varshe*, III: 110–129 and 172–191.

23 François Guesnet, *Polnische Juden im 19. Jahrhundert* (Cologne: Böhlau, 1998), 161–176 and 438–446.

24 On the precarious fate of the individual within the context of various reform projects, see Michel Foucault, *Discipline and Punish: The Birth of the Prison*, trans. Alan Sheridan (New York: Vintage Books, 1995); Foucault, *Madness and Civilization: A History of Insanity in the Age of Reason*, trans. Richard Howard (New York: Vintage, 1973); and, Halfin, *Terror in My Soul*.

25 Ury, *Barricades and Banners*, 172–213.

relationship between modernity and many of its key symbols like the city and the modern (Jewish) self.²⁶

Like many other observers of turn-of-century cities, Yehezkel Kotik felt that the urban environment was in dreadful disarray and desperate need of repair. His conviction that the city was a dangerous and corrupting environment and that the Jewish community and individual were its potential victims unsettles some of the more traditional renditions of that encounter. The brochure that he published in 1896 promoting the construction of a synagogue that would both facilitate urban reform and provide assistance to its members reflects his abiding fear that an imminent crisis threatened the urban Jewish community and the lives of hundreds of thousands of Jewish urbanites. Anticipating sociologist Georg Simmel's canonical critique of modern life, Kotik's writings depict Warsaw's Jewish residents as drowning in a sea of anonymity.²⁷ The introduction to his brochure for the self-help organization *Ahi-'ezer* (Brotherly Aid) contended that a pervasive sense of alienation threatened any and all sense of community in Warsaw and, in turn, in other turn of the century cities.²⁸ For Kotik, a nineteenth century that was once full of optimism and hope had come to a screeching halt, necessitating a re-evaluation of modernity and its impact on urban Jewish society. The café owner-cum-reformer observes:

> There are here, right now, some two-hundred thousand of our fellow children of Israel who are strangers unto one another [*muzarim heme ish le-ahiv*], they are like a large forest, with many trees, all of which plant roots in the earth, and none of which are connected to the other; everyone worries only about himself, and no one looks out for his neighbor ...

---

26 See, for example Katz, *Tradition and Crisis*; and Feiner, *The Jewish Enlightenment*. On the search for the modern Jewish self, see Marcus Moseley, *Being for Myself Alone: Origins of Jewish Autobiography* (Stanford, CA: Stanford University Press, 2006), 387–480; and Kenneth B. Moss, *Jewish Renaissance in Revolutionary Russia* (Cambridge, MA: Harvard University Press, 2009), 173–216.

27 For prevailing interpretations of urban society at the time, see Georg Simmel, "The Metropolis and Mental Life," and "The Stranger," in *The Sociology of Georg Simmel*, ed. and trans. Kurt H. Wolff (Glencoe, IL: Free Press, 1964), 409–424 and 402–408, respectively.

28 On alienation as a leitmotif of modernity, see Hannah Arendt, *The Origins of Totalitarianism* (New York: Harcourt, Brace Jovanovich, 1973), 305–326 and 474–479; George L. Mosse, *Masses and Man: Nationalist and Fascist Perceptions of Reality* (New York: Howard Fertig, 1980), 33, 75 and 230; and Pheng Cheah, *Spectral Nationality: Passages of Freedom from Kant to Postcolonial Literatures of Liberation* (New York: Columbia University Press, 2003), 166 and 243.

there is no love or solidarity between us, each person takes care of only himself... and the only thing that remains between us is hatred and jealousy and a division between the hearts.[29]

At first glance, his solution to the impending collapse of urban Jewish society seems to be a rather traditional one. According to Kotik, the seasoned communal activist (*klal tuer*), the answer to these and other troubles that beset hundreds of thousands of Jews in Warsaw could be found in one of the oldest of Jewish institutions, the synagogue. His brochure detailing the by-laws and goals of *Ahi-'ezer* points to the synagogue as the remedy for what seemed to be the most pressing of all modern, urban ailments: the impending atomization, and potential dissolution, of the urban Jewish community.[30]

However, while there were many synagogues and prayer houses in Warsaw at the time, none were really equipped to resolve the twin crises of urbanization and communal disintegration. In fact, the large number of small, Hasidic prayer houses that dominated Warsaw's cityscape actually divided Jewish urban society further. Indeed, as many of those who operated these prayer houses were, according to Kotik, motivated by narrow self-interests, these prayer houses ultimately endangered an already precarious community. In this, as in other cases, Kotik voiced charges similar to those aired by both maskilic critics and antisemitic observers regarding the state of Jewish religious practice and urban society, which suffered from a chronic lack of decorum, an ingrained aversion to beauty, and an irrepressible desire for financial gain. According to Kotik, the very institution that was supposed to serve as the foundation of Jewish society was rotten to the core:

> Unfortunately, in Warsaw, the great city of God, our eyes shutter at the sights as the holy mission of the synagogue, and there are many, and the small prayer houses, whose numbers rise into the hundreds, that have become private businesses in the hands of simple people from among the masses who do not differentiate between the holy and the profane and between that which is tainted and that which is pure... These people undertake all sorts of unspeakable and strange acts that ultimately

---

29 Yehezkel Kotik, *Hatsa'at hukei ahi 'ezer* (Warsaw, 1896), 4.

30 Kotik, *Hatsa'at hukei ahi 'ezer*, 4–5. "Our wise men, of blessed memory, who knew our state of dispersion and the division between the hearts that prevailed among us suggested a way to fix this problem; and this tool became a fortress to organize our society under one roof... this is none other than the synagogue, the house for public prayer; this, in fact, is the best medicine for the disease of division and disquiet that continues to this day..."

> humiliate us in the eyes of our neighbors, including in many cases where they rent spaces that are to be used to create houses of God which lie near the trash gate or the local outhouse, places that cannot be used for residence...[31]

Instead, influenced by reigning conceptions of bourgeois urban civility exemplified by Jewish communities in cities like St. Petersburg, Berlin and Budapest, Kotik called for the creation of a "great, expansive synagogue."[32] Such an institution would not only resolve the growing sense of alienation and division among Jews but would also return a sense of decorum and dignity to the people meant to serve as a "light unto nations." Ultimately, a large, communal synagogue would ameliorate pervasive fears of urban chaos and accompanying anxieties regarding the decline of Jewish society and resolve many of the problems that plagued Jews in the metropolis. Kotik's comments reflect his own transitional role between maskilic ideals, bourgeois values and national politics.

> And thus wake and awake all those according to his own desire and ability to work and strive toward creating a communal synagogue in which all of our estranged brothers can congregate, especially those that have arrived from the four corners of Russia for their business needs and livelihood... New residents will join with veterans who came earlier or with members of the older generation who live here; the synagogue will include all of the advantages that we yearn for, so that we can achieve the coveted and elevated goal of supporting one another, spiritually and financially... and thus we will become productive and honest people and we will also be well received in the eyes of the government.[33]

Ahi-'ezer and its synagogue proposal were, like other self-help projects, thus conceived not only to reform the nature and image of urban Jewish society, but to transform individual Jewish urbanites from potential embarrassments to model citizens.

---

31 Kotik, *Hatsa'at hukei ahi 'ezer*, 5–6.
32 On debates regarding the construction of the Choral Synagogue in St. Petersburg, see Benjamin Nathans, *Beyond the Pale: The Jewish Encounter with Late Imperial Russia* (Berkeley: University of California Press, 2002), 153–164. On the Great Synagogue in Budapest, see Rudolf Klein, *The Great Synagogue of Budapest* (Budapest: Terc, 2008).
33 Kotik, *Hatsa'at hukei ahi 'ezer*, 8.

This mixture of anxiety and ambivalence regarding the city and the nature of urban Jewish society was not limited to *Ahi-'ezer* and designs for institutional, communal and, ultimately, individual reform. Another reform project proposed by Kotik, *"Aseret ha-dibrot li-vene tzion"* (Ten Commandments for the Children of Zion), advocated a similar mix of maskilic ideals, bourgeois norms, and national values as the key to rehabilitating the Jewish urbanite and the urban Jewish community.[34] Like *Ahi-'ezer*, this educational project repeatedly combined the goals of individual rehabilitation and communal reform within a larger framework of urban reform and social engineering. Here, in particular, the goal was the reform of the Jewish individual. Thus, the brochure's introduction emphasizes the need to "educate them [*b'nei tzion*] from the smallest to the oldest, whether they are among the poor or among the rich, with a good and honest education so that they will be industrious [*harutzim*] and happy [*mausharim*] and bring pride to their parents and their people."[35] Throughout, Kotik expressed the hope that proper education, social reform, and communal cohesion would lead to both individual and collective happiness, if not redemption.

True to the Haskalah spirit that informed so many of Kotik's designs for urban reform, the rehabilitation of Warsaw's Jews was to be founded on a detailed program of popular re-education.[36] Like many other latter-day maskilim who turned to modern reform projects and modern Jewish politics, Kotik was a firm believer in the ability of educational institutions to improve and regenerate both urban society and the modern individual. However, here too, these designs often exposed deep tensions between the reformer's goals and the obstinate object of reform, Warsaw's Jewish residents. Like much of the Haskalah agenda he inherited and the bourgeois platform he advocated,

---

34   On other reform projects see Lee Shai Weissbach, "The Jewish Elite and the Children of the Poor: Jewish Apprenticeship Programs in Nineteenth-Century France," *AJS Review* (1987), 123–147.

35   Kotik, *'Aseret ha-dibrot li-vene tsion* (Warsaw, 1899), cover page, 1. On social engineering in twentieth-century Eastern Europe, see Stephen Kotkin, *Magnetic Mountain: Stalinism as Civilization* (Berkeley: University of California Press, 1995).

36   Kotik, *'Aseret ha-dibrot li-vene tsion*, 13–14. "And all this we cannot achieve if we do not fix and improve the state of education, which is the one and only foundation and institution that can guarantee the people's happiness and well-being; only education can change our status for the better; without proper and improved education all the efforts to improve and enhance our situation will be completely and totally wasted endeavors." For more on Jewish education at the time, see, for example, Shaul Stampfer, *Families, Rabbis and Education: Traditional Jewish Society in Nineteenth-Century Eastern Europe* (Oxford: Littman, 2010), 145–210.

a key imperative was that Warsaw Jews become respectable and productive members of urban society.³⁷ Accordingly, Jews had to learn to behave as "respectable guests." As in many other cases, Kotik's drive for reforming individual behavior was rooted in the belief that many Jews in Warsaw behaved inappropriately and that their actions embarrassed and even threatened the city's other Jewish residents. Time and again, Kotik's calls for reform were rooted in a palpable fear regarding what Polish Varsovians thought of their Jewish neighbors.

Ultimately, a proper education would teach Jewish urbanites civility and thus ensure peaceful relations between Jews and their neighbors. Kotik's comments seamlessly passed from institutional and religious reform to individual behavior and, ultimately, consciousness:

> We should implant in the hearts of the children of Israel the knowledge that they are 'guests' and not 'landlords'... They will always be considered as guests in the eyes of their neighbors; and thus, they should teach their children the ways and the rules of the guest and instruct them to how to behave among those citizens who are the 'landlords.' And these are the ways of the guest: when you enter a strange person's house you should behave with more manners and civility than the homeowner himself, when you sit at the table you should sit straight up and eat with your hands and feet aligned and balanced; all of your movements should be measured and polite...³⁸

But chronic lack of decorum was not the only factor that threatened urban Jewish society. With his keen eye focused on the urban environment, Kotik also noted the abysmal living conditions that characterized many Jewish neighbor-

---

37 Note Kotik's demand that Jews undertake so-called productive professions. Kotik, 'Aseret ha-dibrot li-vene tsion, 28. "We must continue and undertake all of those things which the rabbis commanded us and which are pertinent to the people's existence and happiness. And they said: 'A person should always teach his son crafts, and anyone who does not teach his son crafts it is as if he taught him how to stray.'"

38 Kotik, 'Aseret ha-dibrot li-vene tsion, 37–38 and 41–42. For similar comments regarding the need for Jews to behave appropriately in eighteenth century Prague see Ezekiel Landau, "Sermon for the Sabbath Preceding Passover, (1782, Prague)," in Marc Saperstein (ed.), Jewish Preaching, 1200–1800: An Anthology (New Haven: Yale University Press, 1989), 362 and 363. "We should act respectfully toward inhabitants of this kingdom" because "it is their own land, while we are only guests. A sense of submissiveness is good when it comes from within." My thanks to Michael K. Silber for bringing this and many other sources to my attention.

hoods. Here, as well, he was torn between his admiration of Warsaw's Jews and his disgust with their behavior, a disgust that he was no longer able contain.

Commenting on the pressing need for "cleanliness and purity" in the city's Jewish areas, Kotik writes: "It is known that our brethren, the Children of Israel, are far from being clean and pure. It is more than enough to look at the storefronts and shops that sell food and goods that belong to Jews and those that belong to non-Jews to see that the difference between the state of the former and those of the latter are as clear as day and night."[39] However, while he was alarmed at the lack of "cleanliness and purity" that characterized urban Jewish society, the source of these conditions could ultimately be corrected. Thus, he rails against "the pressures and the paucity [that] have forced us to sit in dark corners and tiny alleys, in places with trash and mud, filth and the like, until, over the years, we lost our sense of cleanliness and purity."[40] Here too, addressing the "trash and mud" and the "filth" that colored Jewish neighborhoods and shops was intended not only to improve the Jews' living conditions, but also to deflect potential criticism and animosity.[41] True to his faith in liberal, reform politics, both of these social ills—the Jews' lack of cleanliness and the non-Jews' potential animosity—could be ameliorated by addressing the connection between "cleanliness and purity."

Kotik's concerns regarding the Jews' chronic inability to act appropriately is echoed in his comments on "impudence." Here, as well, impudence not only represented a gross violation of bourgeois codes of civility, but endangered Jewish society itself. In fact, Kotik considered impudence to be "the biggest evil of them all, one that has been with us from time immemorial and because of which has fallen upon us many troubles and woes and is still a stumbling block and a hurdle in each and every path of our lives..."[42] As in other cases, key markers of bourgeois civility and society such as rational discourse and good manners would ensure social reform and the health, happiness and future of the city's Jews. Again tying together urban reform, individual behavior, and collective redemption, Kotik notes:

> If we desire the happiness of our people, we will instruct our children to respect their elders, the wise men and the learned. If a younger

---

39 Kotik, ʿAseret ha-dibrot li-vene tsion, 60.
40 Ibid., 61.
41 Note Kotik's concern that: "those who hate use and persecute us are not interested in knowing the reasons for the lack of cleanliness that is prevalent among us," ibid.
42 Ibid., 73–74. For similar comments regarding Jewish arrogance in Prague, see Ezekiel Landau, "Sermon for the Sabbath Preceding Passover," 363 and 364.

person hears something from a learned one with which he disagrees, he will not dismiss the person and will not humiliate him in a rude manner, but will ask his elder or teacher if such matters are, indeed, correct... And, if a person can prove to his friend that his opinion is correct, if we have, indeed, taught them how to speak wisely and explain their view to their peers—what could be better and more pleasant.[43]

Like many other urbanites in turn-of-the-century Eastern Europe, Yehezkel Kotik was caught in-between. Though a widely-recognized figure in Warsaw's Jewish cityscape, he remained a newcomer who felt removed from the Jewish community's established, Polonized elite. Nor was he part of the growing number of seemingly superfluous urban Jews who roamed the city's streets. Thus, he was repeatedly shocked by much of what he saw around him. His simultaneous familiarity and fear inspired various designs for Jewish urban reform that liberally integrated maskilic ideals, bourgeois values, and national norms.

Kotik's repeated warnings regarding the potential dangers of poor citizenship reflected a much wider anxiety over the nature of urban Jewish society at the turn of the century. While these and other points echo Haskalah debates over the improvement of "the Jews" and the need for proper relations with their non-Jewish neighbors, Kotik was determined to reform urban Jewish society. Thus, in addition to divisions and discord among Jews, he worried that "the Jews" were indeed an unclean, immoral, and greedy people whose repeated displays of rude and insolent behavior disrupted the delicate urban ecology. Such flaws had to be identified and rectified before they brought disaster to Jews in Warsaw and, perhaps, throughout Eastern Europe. Once implemented, Kotik's programs for re-education and social reform would ensure that Warsaw's Jews become civil, productive members of urban society who would conform to the reigning urban social norms. In this and other ways, Kotik's call to reform Warsaw's Jewish residents was grounded in a discourse that was deeply ambivalent about the state and fate of urban Jewish society and the modern Jewish individual.

Conclusion: Kotik, Coffee and the Contradictions of Jewish Modernity

Yehezkel Kotik, his coffee house, and his various reform projects tell us much about the Jewish encounter with the modern world that cities like Warsaw

---

43 Kotik, 'Aseret ha-dibrot li-vene tsion, 95–97.

engendered. On the one hand, Kotik and his coffee shop at 31 Nalewki served as a stabilizing influence in a time of massive upheaval and displacement. As seemingly random Jews met, conversed and befriended other Jewish residents of the city, the city's universalism was repeatedly challenged—if not subverted—by the allure and sense of Jewish familiarity. Thanks to their open, neutral status, coffee houses like Kotik's quickly became integral parts of a growing, distinctly Jewish public sphere in Warsaw. Ultimately, this new public forum not only lent a much-needed sense of order and stability to the inherently chaotic urban arena, but promoted public debate between seemingly random urban residents and helped forge a sense of community among the many strangers who were very often lost in the metropolis. As Sholem Aleichem's alter-ego Menakhem Mendel noted: "My milk bar is on Nalewki Street, Khaskl (Yehezkel) Kotik's place... We sit and sit, just the two of us, Khaskl Kotik and me, over a cup of coffee and discuss our Jewish brethren."[44] Thus, Kotik's coffee house became a Jewish oasis in an urban jungle.

From his café on Nalewki Street, Kotik also fulfilled another classic urban role, that of flâneur. His multiple roles as migrant, observer, and communal organizer (*klal tuer*) familiarized Kotik with the darker side of Warsaw's urban Jewish society, including its poverty-stricken immigrants, instances of filth, displays of rude behavior, and growing tension between the city's guests (Jews) and hosts (Poles). In response to his exposure to such a wide cross-section, Kotik created and implemented a series of projects that were designed to domesticate, rehabilitate and transform Jewish urbanites from potential embarrassments into paragons of urban civility. Through institutions, frameworks, and projects that could overcome the many problems associated with urban life, educate Jewish residents, and come to the aid of a new Jewish underclass, Kotik could, perhaps, save the Jews of Warsaw from themselves. However, in order to effect this transition, Kotik would first have to rescue Warsaw's Jews from the most deadly and carcinogenic of all modern diseases, the city itself.

Taken together, Kotik's repeated efforts to use modern means of organization, education and reform to restructure urban Jewish society reflect his own ambivalence towards the city, urban society, and the modern world. In this and countless other cases, it was the role of the Jewish reformer—the self-anointed prophet of Jewish decay and regeneration—to lead the Jewish urban masses out of their state of darkness and into the light of modernity. Ultimately, proper reform projects would save the Jews of Warsaw from their sorry state and their many weaknesses. They would also help avert an imminent clash with the Jews' neighbors, who were quickly losing patience with their guests,

---

44   Sholem Aleichem, *Menahem mendel be-varshah*, 19–20.

for among the veritable sea of modern maladies produced by the city (and *de facto* modernity) was intolerance and hate. Thus, many of these reform projects were concerned not only with the city's Jews but with relations between Jews and Poles in the contested capital city of Warsaw.

Lastly, Kotik's coffee house and his reform initiatives expose many of the fundamental contradictions embedded deep within the very project of modernity. As Shreberk, Litvin and others noted, it was in his coffee house at 31 Nalewki where Kotik would push his brochures and promote his reform projects among unsuspecting patrons. Moreover, it was at that very moment that the coffee house—one of the foundations of the bourgeois public sphere—was used to advance plans for large-scale urban reform and individual rehabilitation that the course of modernity would pass from one of rational debate between individuals to impassioned pleas for subduing base desires and re-shaping individuals in the name of infinitely higher ideals, like collective rehabilitation, communal cohesion, and, ultimately, (Jewish) national redemption. Thus, Yehezkel Kotik, his coffee house and his visions of bourgeois civility not only provide a window onto the lives of everyday Jews in turn-of-century Warsaw, but also onto the crooked path of modernity among Jews, Poles and other residents of Warsaw and the rest of Eastern Europe for the remainder of the twentieth century.

CHAPTER 9

Hope and Fear: Y.L. Peretz and the Dialectics of Diaspora Nationalism, 1905–12

Michael C. Steinlauf

Let us begin by comparing two epitaphs: Sholem Aleichem's and Y.L. Peretz's. Sholem Aleichem wrote his own in 1905; it is inscribed on his tombstone in the Workmen's Circle section of the Mt. Carmel Cemetery in Queens.

Do ligt a yid a posheter	Here lies a simple Jew
Geshribn yidish-taytsh far vayber	Wrote in Yiddish for women
Un farn prostn folk hot er	And for simple folk
Geven a humorist, a shrayber.	He was a humorist, a writer.
Dos gantse lebn oysgelakht	He laughed at all of life
Geshlogn mit der velt kapores	Told the world where to get off
Di gantse velt hot gut gemakht	Made the whole world feel good
Un er—oy vey—geven af tsores.	But he—oh dear—had troubles.
Un dafke demlt ven der oylem hot	And just in fact when the audience
Gelakht, geklatsht un flegt zikh freyen	Laughed and clapped and had a fine time
Hot er gekrent—dos veyst nor got—	He'd get ill—as only God knows
Besod, az keyner zol nit zen.[1]	Secretly—so no one should see.

Peretz's epitaph is inscribed on the inside of the cupola of the elaborate *ohel* (mausoleum) erected in the Warsaw Jewish cemetery on the tenth anniversary of his death. Buried beside Peretz are the writers Sh. Anski and Yankev Dinezon. The words of the epitaph were taken from Peretz's play, *Di goldene keyt* (The Golden Chain), about four generations of a Hasidic family. The expression *di goldene keyt* quickly became a trope for the old/new Jewish culture that Peretz and his disciples were shaping, linking the creations of talmudic genius with

---

1 Dan Miron, *A Traveler Disguised: A Study in the Rise of Modern Yiddish Fiction in the Nineteenth Century* (New York: Schocken, 1973), 83. All translations from Yiddish are my own.

those of modern Jewish art. In Act 1, as his terrified Hasidim look on, the patriarch Reb Shloyme at his *tish* (ritual table) refuses to perform *havdole*, the ceremony marking the return of normal time after the Sabbath. Reb Shloyme, in other words, attempts to force redemption, thereby risking the destruction of the world. In the final act, Shloyme's descendent Yoynesn is left doubting his power to lead, to maintain the golden chain unbroken. But it is the words of Reb Shloyme that were inscribed on Peretz's *ohel*:

Azoy geyen mir,	So we go,
Zingendik un tantsndik ...	Singing and dancing...
Mir groyse, groyse yidn,	We big big Jews,
Shabes-yontevdike yidn,	shabbes-holiday Jews,
Di neshomes flakern!	Our souls blaze!
Far undz volkn shpaltn zikh!	Clouds part before us!
Himlen praln di toyrn oyf!	The heavens burst their gates!
In onen-hakoved shvimen mir arayn	Into the Cloud of Glory we swim
Tsum kise-hakoved-tsu!	Right up to the Throne of Glory!
Un mir betn nisht	And we don't ask
Un mir betlen nisht	And we don't beg
Groyse shtoltse yidn zenen mir—	Big proud Jews are we
Mir zogn im:	We tell Him:
Lenger vartn nisht gekont!	Couldn't wait any longer!
Shir hashirim zingen mir,	We sing the Song of Songs
Zingendik, tantsndik geyen mir![2]	Singing, dancing we go!

The ironies are extraordinary. Sholem Aleichem, the self-described *kleyn mentshele* (little man) who liked to make people laugh, rests in an out-of-the-way corner of New York. But his creation, Tevye, has permanently rooted himself in Jewish and world culture. Peretz, the supremely public man who situated himself at the prophetic center of modern Yiddish culture of which he made maximum demands, lies today under a crumbling monument in the vast, ruined Warsaw Jewish cemetery. Briefly reconfigured during and immediately after the Holocaust as the comforter of his people in the face of incomprehensible catastrophe,[3] Peretz today is, like his *ohel*, nearly completely forgotten.

---

2 In this article I rely on Peretz's texts as published in the Yiddish press and note their republication in the widely available CYCO edition of his works, *Ale verk*, 11 vols (New York: CYCO, 1947–48). The text here is taken from Peretz's *ohel*; it is slightly different in *Ale verk*, vol. 6, 127.

3 Anita Norich, *Discovering Exile: Yiddish and Jewish American Culture During the Holocaust* (Stanford, CA: Stanford University Press, 2008).

But a hundred years ago in the Yiddish-speaking world, Peretz's stature could not be easily exaggerated. From his apartment in Warsaw, Peretz oversaw, for a quarter of a century, each new stage in the development of modern Yiddish culture. As millions of Jews left Eastern Europe for the Americas, Western Europe and Palestine, Peretz remained in the Warsaw center, the avatar of a cultural nationalism rooted in the Eastern European diaspora. There is a vast literature about Peretz, much of it by pilgrims to his legendary address at Ceglana 1, from which they then went forth to build the Yiddishlands of the world. We have a mass of memoirs and literary essays, most of them hagiographic. But we lack the most basic documentation of Peretz's life and work, even a single reliable biography or bibliography. At best we have what Yiddish writers called *materyaln tsu* (materials toward) a biography or bibliography. The various editions of Peretz's so-called complete works are anything but, and the dating of works, where it exists, is guesswork. Too often, we don't know what the man known as the father of modern Yiddish literature wrote first, second, and third.[4] One significant book in English about Peretz has appeared in the past decades, Ruth Wisse's small volume, *I. L. Peretz and the Making of Modern Jewish Culture*.[5] The book, however, is marred by its author's rather merciless Zionist agenda, which causes her to conclude with the following judgment of a Jewish national culture that dared to live without an army: "The schoolchildren of Vilna and of all Poland were murdered with the words of Peretz on their lips."[6] The present essay focuses on Peretz as a theorist and activist of a diaspora nation that indeed hoped to live without an army.

The notion that Jews, above all in Eastern Europe, could be seen as a nationality, that their homeland was wherever they lived in large and compact communities, became increasingly popular towards the end of the nineteenth century. It developed in a world where numerous other groups were using the discourse of nationality to define themselves, albeit for the non-Jewish groups, the homeland tended to be geographically contiguous. The principles of Jewish diaspora nationalism were first formulated by the historian Simon Dubnow in a series of articles published in the Russian Jewish journal *Voskhod* beginning in 1897.[7] This happened to be the year of the first Zionist congress in

---

4 While the texts in vol. 13 of the Farlag Yidish edition, *Ale verk* (New York, 1920), seem to be identical to those in the CYCO edition, their sequence is only correct in the Farlag Yidish edition. I am indebted to Professor Simon Rabinovitch of Boston University for this observation.
5 Seattle: University of Washington Press, 1991.
6 Wisse, *Peretz*, 109.
7 In English, see Simon Dubnow, *Nationalism and History: Essays on Old and New Judaism*, ed. Koppel S. Pinson (Philadelphia: Jewish Publication Society, 1958), 73–241.

Basel and the founding of the Jewish socialist Bund in Vilna. Dubnow's historical writings had focused on the importance of Jewish communal organizations (*kehillas, khevres*) in premodern Jewish life, on their ability to facilitate a high degree of communal autonomy for centuries within the Polish-Lithuanian Commonwealth. The Jews were *de facto* a nationality, Dubnow now declared, and he developed the political consequences of this idea under the conditions of modernity. He argued that Jews needed to strengthen the internal structure of their communal institutions, which had been weakened after a century of rule by tsars and kaisers, even as they fought for representation within a future multinational state. By the first decade of the twentieth century, the Bund had adopted much of Dubnow's program but only within the context of socialism while skirting the politically incorrect word "nationalism." In subsequent years, the Folkspartey (Folkist Party) adopted Dubnow's program *in toto*, and even Polish Zionists of the interwar period advocated a struggle for Jewish national rights while the nation remained dispersed.

For Peretz, it was the cultural imperatives of diaspora nationalism that were of ultimate interest. Nevertheless, in the course of the turbulent first decades of the twentieth century, Peretz found himself drawn into a host of political struggles. The first of these came amidst the Revolution of 1905–06, when Peretz, then in his early fifties, had reached the peak of his influence.

∙ ∙ ∙

On January 22, 1905, in St. Petersburg, a demonstration of over a hundred thousand workers and their families was set upon by the police. This event, which became known as Bloody Sunday, triggered escalating protests throughout the empire that climaxed in a general strike in October. On October 30, Nicholas II issued the so-called October Manifesto that granted civil liberties and established a representative parliament, the Duma, thereby turning the empire into something approximating a constitutional monarchy. The Manifesto was a great victory for liberal forces, but over the next several weeks, as revolutionaries organized a soviet in St. Petersburg and an armed uprising in Moscow, the counter-revolutionary right represented by the Black Hundreds fomented a wave of violence which included the worst pogroms in Russian history. In the three months following the Manifesto, over three thousand Jews were murdered and tens of thousands injured in over six hundred pogroms.[8] With few

---

8   Shlomo Lambroza, "The Pogroms of 1903–1906," in John D. Klier and Shlomo Lambroza (eds.), *Pogroms: Anti-Jewish Violence in Modern Russian History* (Cambridge: Cambridge University Press, 1992), 226–32.

exceptions, the police and army stood by or, occasionally, participated in the violence. Simultaneously, the government declared martial law. Over the following months and years, much of what had been promised in the Manifesto was gradually undermined.[9]

Der veg (The way), the first Yiddish daily in Warsaw and only the second in the Russian Empire, began to appear in August 1905, published by Tzevi Hirsh Prilutski, with Peretz as a contributing editor.[10] The government had long refused to permit a daily press in Yiddish. Permission to publish *Der veg* and the numerous other dailies that followed, along with the gradual lifting of the ban against Yiddish theater, were major victories and led quickly to the flowering of a mass Jewish culture based in Warsaw. Hundreds of thousands of Jews became theater-goers and newspaper readers nearly overnight. Traditional and secular, rich and poor, newspaper readers and theater-goers began to constitute a new kind of community. They found it increasingly natural to think of themselves, using the discourse of modern nationality, as *dos yidishe folk*—the Jewish people or nation. It was a nation in practice, if not yet in theory.

From its first day of publication, *Der veg* brought news of the revolution to this audience. Coverage widened when the October Manifesto abolished press censorship. There were daily dispatches from St. Petersburg, Moscow and the far corners of the empire. The focus of the paper, however, was Congress Poland. Here mass political organizations replaced the old conspiratorial elites of the Polish gentry and the modern Polish national movement was born. Even more important were workers and their parties rooted in the large industrial centers. For the first time, the ideologies of nationalism and socialism, previously confined to drawing rooms and garrets, swept up great numbers of ordinary people. In Warsaw and Łódź, the Polish Socialists and Social Democrats, the

---

9 On the revolution in Poland, see Robert E. Blobaum, *Rewolucja: Russian Poland, 1904–1907* (Ithaca, NY: Cornell University Press, 1995). On Polish-Jewish relations see also Frank Golczewski, *Polnische-Jüdische Beziehungen, 1881–1922* (Wiesbaden: Steiner, 1981); and Stephen D. Corrsin, *Warsaw before the First World War: Poles and Jews in the Third City of the Russian Empire, 1880–1914* (Boulder, Col.: East European Monographs, distributed by Columbia University Press, 1989).

10 *Der veg* was preceded only by *Der fraynd*, published first in St. Petersburg in 1903 but from 1909 in Warsaw. On *Der veg* and early Yiddish newspapers in the Russian Empire, see Sarah Abrevaya Stein, *Making Jews Modern: The Yiddish and Ladino Press in the Russian and Ottoman Empires* (Bloomington, Ind.: Indiana University Press, 2004). See also David Fishman, "The Politics of Yiddish in Tsarist Russia," in Jacob Neusner, Ernest S. Frerichs, Nahum M. Sarna (eds.), *From Ancient Israel to Modern Judaism, Intellect in Quest of Understanding: Essays in Honor of Marvin Fox* (Atlanta, Ga.: Scholars Press, 1989), vol. 4, 155–71.

Bund and other parties organized nearly non-stop strikes, factory occupations and uprisings, along with a wave of worker violence against the underworld, especially brothels.[11] The pages of *Der veg* report daily robberies, shootings and bombings in the streets of Warsaw. After the pogroms exploded, the paper published days of dispatches from special correspondents in Odessa, Gomel, Białystok, Siedlce and other cities.

Der veg sought to educate its readers to make sense of the moment as well as to popularize the work of Jewish writers. There were articles on the Paris Commune and revolutions in Mexico and Cuba. After the October Manifesto, the paper published a supplement that included photographs of parliaments throughout the world. The paper featured ads for Yiddish theater, in banner headlines on the front page, as well as theater reviews. It attracted literary contributors from the elite of established and rising Yiddish and Hebrew writers, including, in addition to Peretz himself, Sholem Aleichem, Sholem-Yankev Abramovitsh, Sholem Asch, Itshe-Mayer Weissenberg, H.D. Nomberg, Bal Makhshoves, Avrom Rayzn, Yente Serdatski, Mark Arnshteyn, Rubin Braynin and Dovid Frishman. *Der veg* published their works both daily and in special supplements.

In the course of nine months, from August 1905 to May 1906, under his own name and under the pseudonyms Dr. Shtitser and Lutsifer, Peretz published some fifty texts in *Der veg*. These writings span the entire range of his creativity. There are stories and one-act plays; poetry, in verse and in prose; translations; literary and theater criticism. The largest category is that of essays, some journalistic, others polemical and philosophical, the genre known as *publitsistik* in Yiddish letters. Peretz had worked with the early workers' movement when he edited *Yontev bletlekh* with Dovid Pinski in the 1890s, and later worked with Zionists as a contributor to the pioneering periodical *Der yid*.[12] His support for both ideologies was conditional, however, subject to his abiding skepticism and tempered by the daily realities of Jewish Warsaw. But in 1905, socialism and nationalism sprang from theory to praxis. Today, a century later, knowing what would come of all this, for good and for evil, it is an effort to imagine days when, amidst the violence, anything seemed possible, above all the dreams of

---

11   Edward J. Bristow, *Prostitution and Prejudice: The Jewish Fight Against White Slavery, 1870–1939* (New York: Schocken, 1983), 58–62. In addition to Bristow's sources (58; the Yiddish titles, unfortunately, have been "germanized"), see "Pogrom," *Prawda* (Warsaw) 21 (May 21, 1905).

12   On *Der yid*, see Ruth R. Wisse, "Not the 'Pintele Yid' but the Full-fledged Jew," *Prooftexts* 15.1 (January 1995), 33–61.

the new ideologues, when, to paraphrase Peretz, men felt they could be eagles. To put it another way, Reb Shloyme's *tish* was now in the streets.

Peretz used every means and every genre at his disposal to realize the new potentials. He leaped at the opportunity, first of all, to use the new daily press to bring modern literature to its readers. One of the first issues of *Der veg* announced a series of translations by Peretz from world literature. Over the following months these included works by the Polish writer Feliks Brodowski, the Dutch writers Multatuli and Herman Heijermans, as well as Lafcadio Hearn and Oscar Wilde. Awed by the work of Bialik, Peretz translated his prophetic poems "In the City of Slaughter" [*Be-ir ha-harega* (1904) as "Masa nemirov"] and *Scroll of Fire* [*Megillat ha-Esh* (1905) as "Fayerdike megile"] soon after their Hebrew publication.[13] As numerous Yiddish theater companies began to perform in Warsaw, Peretz wrote theater criticism, publishing a flurry of reviews in which he denounced the popular theater of so-called *purimshpilers* as trash that lowered the aesthetic and moral standards of its audiences.[14] He weighed a handful of new dramas by Mark Arnshteyn, Jacob Gordin, Dovid Pinski, Sholem Aleichem and Maxim Gorki, and argued for the creation of a Yiddish theater that would incarnate the loftiest aspirations of a Jewish national culture. Peretz's disciples Noyekh Prilutski and Mark Arnshteyn began to write regular theater criticism.

Peretz continued to publish fiction. He published only four stories in *Der veg*, but they are central in his canon.[15] Varied in subject matter and theme, they demonstrate the futility of approaching his work, as advocated by some Yiddish critics, through a chronology of themes or styles. "Mishnes hasidim" (Hasidic Teachings) is probably Peretz's most highly developed story of Hasidic rapture, a disciple's account of his master. "On mazl" (Unlucky) is a devastating tale of the destruction of a young woman through an arranged marriage, as told by her coarse, unaware but well-meaning father. In "Mayses" (Stories), a lonely young Jew in the big city maintains a tenuous relationship with a wary young Polish seamstress through storytelling. "Hisgayles oder di mayse fun tsignbok" (Revelation, or The Story of the Billygoat) is a story that Peretz chose to publish

---

13 "Masa nemirov," in *Der veg* 18 (1906), 30; "Fayerdike megile," ibid., 52, 59, 64, 69, 70 (1906). See also *Ale verk*, vol. 1, 255–67; "Fayerdike megile" was apparently not reprinted.

14 See Michael C. Steinlauf, "Fear of Purim: Y. L. Peretz and the Canonization of Yiddish Theater," *Jewish Social Studies*, 1.3 (1993), 44–65.

15 "Hisgayles oder di mayse fun tsignbok," *Der veg* 1 (1905), literary supplement; "On mazl," ibid., 9 (1906); "Mishnes hasidim," ibid., 31 (1906); "Mayses," ibid., 73 (1906), Passover supplement. Reprinted in *Ale verk*, respectively, vol. 4, 202–08; vol. 3, 290–95; vol. 4, 179–86; vol. 3, 462–77.

on the first pages of the literary supplement that accompanied the first issue of *Der veg*. It is a tale within a tale, told by the *tzaddik* Reb Nakhmanke as a way of explaining his sadness. It concerns a billygoat with magical horns that each night secretly extend to heaven for news of the coming of the Messiah. During hard times, the billygoat pulls gems out of heaven and hurls them into the marketplace to provide a livelihood for the townsfolk. But struck by the beauty of his horns, Jews begin to approach the billygoat for pieces from which to make snuffboxes, and gradually his access to heaven is lost. Critics have read this story as a parable of the artist, which doubtless it is, but it is also something else to which we will return.

In the weeks prior to the October Manifesto, most of Peretz's *publitsistik* consisted of attacks on the Jewish assimilationists of *Izraelita*, the Polish-language Jewish monthly that had been appearing in Warsaw for forty years.[16] Not only ideology but political power was at stake here, for it was assimilationists who, with the quiet partnership of Ger and other Hasidic dynasties, controlled the Warsaw *kehilla* and resisted the national stands of Peretz and his colleagues at *Der veg*. It was also a class issue, for the *kehilla* leadership, as Peretz pointed out, isolated itself from the lives of the Jewish masses. It was, finally, a personal issue as well, for throughout his years in Warsaw Peretz worked for the Warsaw *kehilla*, in whose offices he was known as Leon and was often treated contemptuously. "We have long been convinced," writes Peretz, "that the assimilationist program is *not* a program for the people, but an egoistic program for a few big money-bag-privilege and concession-holders".[17]

After the Manifesto and with the dawning of parliamentary politics, Peretz turned directly to Poles. In an essay entitled "'Yidish' in Poyln",[18] he predicted that Poles would win cultural autonomy, because "peoples that live, that don't sell their souls for a pot of lentils, *derlebn nakhes* [attain satisfaction]." They would not insist on political and economic autonomy, Peretz predicts, because Congress Poland needed the link to Russian markets, without which it would resemble impoverished Austrian Galicia, where "one has long been able to wear old Polish costumes but no one can afford them."[19] In this new world, however, "What will happen with 'Yiddish'?" demands Peretz. "That is the question!" And he proceeds to analyze the platforms of all the Polish political

---

16   "Levaye," *Der veg* 24 (1905); "Keyn yidishe kishke kon men nit shatsn," ibid., 28 (1905); these texts were apparently not reprinted.

17   Ibid., 28 (1905).

18   Ibid., 81–82 (1905); apparently not reprinted. The word *yidish* appears in quotation marks, suggesting the contemporary transition to this word from the earlier term *zhargon*.

19   Since 1867, the inhabitants of the Austrian Empire had enjoyed full civil rights.

parties, from right to left, finding them all seriously wanting. *"Dos zelbe golus, nor gants liberal* [The same exile, though nice and liberal]"[20] is Peretz's reaction to the Progressive Democrats, for example, who announced that publicly-funded Polish schools would be open to Jews—though Jewish schools should not receive government support. While in the aftermath of the revolution, Poles did not gain all that Peretz thought they would, his analysis of their position on Yiddish accurately predicted the obstacles that would complicate Jewish attempts to gain state support for Jewish culture in the Second Polish Republic of the interwar years.

There is foreboding throughout Peretz's writings at this time, and not just those concerning Poles and Jews. Wandering through streets filled with demonstrators of every persuasion, resounding with frequent cries of *"Jedność* [Unity],"* Peretz cannot muster the trust to believe in it all: "A new day, you say— you believe, but I don't! Do you have the right to demand faith from me?"[21] His disquiet emerges full blown in his poetry. "Don't go with me, true and golden child. Sad is the lonely wanderer's road" is the refrain of a prose poem published before Rosh Hashanah, a month before the October Manifesto.[22] The wanderer's road leads him through horrors, nights filled with lost souls seeking redemption and wrathful fallen angels, days when "through the ash of those burnt up, through the dust of those never brought to their graves, an angry red sun glares." This is not the only place where Peretz's visions seem premonitions of the Holocaust. Yet he begs forgiveness of the child for what he has planted in its heart. In the following day's *Der veg*, on the eve of Rosh Hashanah, appears "To the New Year", another poem about innocence and experience, this time a dialogue.[23] A young woman, modishly weak-willed, solicits New Year's wishes from her older interlocutor. He at first demurs, explaining that he can scarcely imagine her future. When she insists, he responds with three wishes. The first is that she tell a smith to stop forging plowshares and make crowbars and hammers instead because "there are so many gates to smash." The second is that she no longer play kittenishly with the sea but wrestle with it as with a lion. The third is that she learn to dance among swords. Terrified, the young woman recoils, whereupon her interlocutor offers "a lighter wish," that she "love the

---

20 See also "Der tog," *Der veg*, 74 (1905).
21 "Der tog," *Ale verk*, vol. 9, 73. I have been unable to identify the original source, but the lines were apparently written just after the October Manifesto. This text as a whole (70–99) is a potpourri of passages from articles, some of which were first published in *Der veg*. The Farlag Yiddish edition includes the identical text (vol. 12, 296–324).
22 "Gey nisht mit mir," *Der veg*, 38 (1905); reprinted in *Ale verk*, vol. 3, 439–42.
23 "Tsum nayem yor," *Der veg* 39 (1905); reprinted in *Ale verk*, vol. 3, 480–83.

morning, the radiance of the new day. Lay to rest the sweet poison of the dying evening and live for tomorrow when new life awakens [...] It will carry you away, child!" The speaker concludes, ambiguously: "Is this also beyond your strength?" Two poems in two days, fearing action and counseling action, acting and apologizing for acting. Should it surprise us that shortly after, in the first issue of *Der veg* for 1906, Peretz chose to publish a bit of Kohelet (Ecclesiastes)? *Hevel havolim* (Vanity of vanities) sounds like this in Peretz's Yiddish:

Narish, narish! Alts iz narish!	Foolish, foolish! All is foolish!
Men vet di velt fun flek nisht rirn!	One will not move the world from stain!
Umzist dos alts, vos s'iz geshen,	In vain all that has occurred
Vi dos vos vet amol pasirn[.]²⁴	As that which will still happen[.]

Doubting his own strength and the very value of acting, Peretz nevertheless stepped fully into the political. Published in early January 1906, "Oyf a miting" chronicles his venture onto the dangerous evening streets and to a socialist gathering.²⁵ The piece is signed Lutsifer, one of Peretz's scoffing alter egos. He listens to a speaker invoke a litany of capitalist crimes and dubs it the *toykhekhe*, the chapter of curses from the Bible.²⁶ When the speaker concludes, "But now your day has arrived! You will be the judges ... And you will judge ... measure for measure!", Peretz responds, "It sounds like the trumpets over the walls of Jericho," and asks, "Is the day really so near?" "Moscow is quiet now," he reflects, "the barricades are smashed ... the 'guilty' and 'innocent' blood is covered with clean, innocent snow." In a word, though some may be unaware of it as yet, the revolution is waning. "Does the audience believe the speaker?" Peretz wonders. And he notices, among the workers, many non-workers, whom he identifies as mice fleeing a sinking ship. There are the trendy writers, "not those who quietly weave ideas for future times, but those who work *by day* and *for the day*! Retail salesmen ... second or third hand ... These are incarnations [*gilgulim*] of those who always serve the present ... who once demonstrated black on white that God's own hand had created the herd, and the dog to guard the herd, and the shepherd to shear it. Or: lords, serfs and the police in their midst." Also present are representatives of the bourgeoisie [*balebatim*] with "silly faces and silly staring eyes.... Only yesterday [...] they took every demand for higher

---

24   "Hevel havolim," *Der veg* 1 (1906); Peretz's translation of the entire Kohelet appears in *Ale verk*, vol. 10, 161–236.
25   "Oyf a miting," *Der veg* 89 (1905); reprinted in *Ale verk*, vol. 9, 65–69.
26   Leviticus 26: 14–25.

wages as insolence, for a shorter work-day as shameless crime, and believed all workers to be simple thieves whom they searched each time they [...] left the factory." Now they cry bravo, beat their breasts, and fill the collection plates as on Yom Kippur "for the jailed, the wounded, for the families of the fallen, for the exiled and—for weapons!" Even the clergy [*di shvartse*] have come, who yesterday blessed the oppressors. Walking home, Peretz edges past a drunken Cossack by offering him a cigarette.

Ten days later, abandoning the persona of Lutsifer, Peretz addresses the workers' movement directly. Amidst the flux of counter-revolutionary violence, liberal hopes, and declining revolutionary prospects, Peretz embraces the workers' movement and simultaneously challenges it. The result is an extraordinary text entitled "Hofnung un shrek" (Hope and fear).[27] "My heart is with you," he begins. "My eye can't have its fill of your flaming banner, my ear doesn't tire of your mighty song. Man should eat his fill and have light... And he should be free, and able to shape his own life and labor [...] When you march on old Sodom to tear it down, my soul goes with you; and the certainty that you *must* triumph fills and warms and intoxicates me like old wine..."

"And yet I fear you. I fear the oppressed who triumph, they can themselves become oppressors [...] Do they not say among you that humanity must march like an army and that you will play the tune along the way? But humanity is not an army. The strong go in front, the more passionate feel more deeply, the proud grow taller [...] Will you not spread your wings over mediocrity? Will you not armor indifference and protect the gray, identically shorn herd? [...] As victors, *you* can become the bureaucracy. [...Y]ou will be preoccupied with regulating... how strongly and how often the human pulse may beat, how far the human eye may see, how much the ear may take in, and what dreams the longing heart may dream [...] There will be no empty stomachs, but souls will hunger [...and] the eagle, the human spirit, will stand with clipped wings by the trough beside the cow and the ox [...J]ustice [...] will abandon you, and you will not notice it [...] And you will build prisons for those who [point to] the abyss into which you are sinking. [...] I want, I hope for your victory, but I fear and tremble for your victory. You are my hope, you are my fear." No other of Peretz's writings, to my knowledge, better deserves to be called prophetic.

In the weeks after this reckoning with revolutionary socialism, Peretz published a series of three articles entitled "Heymishe zakhn."[28] These texts are

---

27 "Hofnung un shrek," *Der veg* 5 (1906); reprinted in *Ale verk*, vol. 9, 101–03.
28 "Heymishe zakhn," *Der veg* 11, 15, 24 (1906); fragments of the last two of these texts may be found in "Der tog," in *Ale verk*, vol. 9, 86–88.

an attempt to formulate his own credo. The expression *heymishe zakhn* means both domestic things and things that are snug, cosy and warm. The latter meaning here is entirely ironic.

The first article begins with a vision of the End of Days in which God judges the nations in the Valley of Yehoshafat. Among the nations stand the Jews, the only people without its own soul (and, adds God, not much of a body either). The Jews are divided into classes, though it is difficult to distinguish among them, and into parties, which are only identifiable by their banners. Standing on the side are groups of nervous "*ibermentshen*" (supermen), those who might be leaders, to each of which God asks: "What have you done for the soul of your people?" Each group confesses it had no time to "spin the soul of our people" and each receives an appropriate punishment. Revolutionaries, for example, who were caught up in "red flaming days," in seconds that "flew asunder like lightning," are turned into fireflies that die each day with the setting sun. Pampered, well-educated young ladies who raced from one lecture or meeting to another are turned into a swarm of butterflies.

The second article is a manifesto of diaspora nationalism, unique in Peretz's writings. Addressed to socialists, it weaves their own language with that of biblical prophecy: "My people has been chosen for shame and derision, for wounds and woe, for blows and pain [...] The reddest of banners has been thrust into its hand with the cry: Go! Further and further, with all liberators, all fighters for the future, all the destroyers of Sodom... But you will not rest with them... The earth will burn under your feet [...] As long as blood is spilled, a desire suppressed, a wing clipped, it will be your wing, your desire, your blood. You will be the very last to be freed, when man is freed from the earth! When out of human worms human eagles rise [...] Don't pride yourself on your red banner, it is just the weak reflection of the bloody banner in the hand of the chosen people! [...] I go with my people. The glint of its banner ignites my soul and I call: Jews of all lands and peoples, unite... Long and perilous is the road—hold together!" Here—and elsewhere as well, as we will see—Peretz reaches out of conventional secular discourse towards the language of religion.

The last article plunges back into the fallen world. It is subtitled "*Tandet*," a word that denotes cheap, shoddy goods, and speaks in the name of the Jewish masses: "What is the world? An antechamber to the next one. Here one passes through, there one remains. To work here? To love here? To think of tomorrow and the day after here? Let millionaires build marble mausoleums to themselves; for us poor, a flimsy headboard is enough. And one lives just to get by (*abi vayter*), just to survive (*ibertsukumen*). On the eve of a holiday one sighs: the holiday's over already! [...] Childhood is a prelude to marriage, and on the wedding day the groom dons a shroud, bride and groom fast and confess their sins [...]. Two little flowers of exile (*golus-blimelekh*) sprout in the Jewish heart: *abi vayter, abi iberkumen*. [...] *Tandet*. Everything is *tandet*: life, trade, work. Without love, without certainty, without today, and later—trembling shadows, trembling and clutching. [...] Piety and good deeds (*tsidkes umaysim-toyvim*), party activism, politics—half a flicker, a quarter flicker, a wisp, a thread ... the community of Israel (*Kneses Yisroel*) sits and patches and darns. [...] The old 'chosen ones' (*yekhide-sgule*), the few dead, fossilized Cedars of Lebanon look down on our little grasses and sigh: these are our grandchildren!"

We are rather far from Reb Shloyme. And we are also rather far from any of the many attempts during Peretz's lifetime and after to distill a simple message from his writings. What, at least at this moment, is Peretz's countervision, his response to the creeds that surround him?

Both socialism and Zionism posited a movement that was fully redemptive. One could aspire to a post-revolutionary world, classless and just, or to a so-called normal life lived in one's ancestral land. One way or another, the future would not resemble the present; it would differ from it absolutely. What was the guarantee? Some combination of human will and historical necessity. But also something else, working underneath this human time and its possibilities, or perhaps beyond it. It was redemptive time, or better, redemptive teleology, that guaranteed the outcome of human struggles. It would take extraordinary sacrifices, the individual might not live to see it, it could take generations, but *it* would come to pass. Despite the impassioned denials of its contemporary champions, there was a touch of something beyond the human in such thinking.

But Peretz rejected this teleology. He rejected all guarantees. Summoned to believe, his belief falters even as he attempts it. His eyes cannot tire of the red banner but the possibility of its triumph fills him with foreboding. It could turn into its opposite. And what sort of triumph would even the steadiest stream of Jewish settlers to the Land of Israel entail? Could it possibly transform the situation of the Jewish masses in Eastern Europe, or elsewhere in the world for that matter?

Peretz's vision, in contrast, is mired in immanence. The Bundists' favorite word was *do*, here, which produced the abstract noun *doikeyt* (hereness), meaning one's energy was to be directed here, to the daily struggles of the working masses, and not there, *dort*, toward some bourgeois Zionist dream. But Bundists nevertheless maintained a teleological link to something that was as *dort*, in its own way, as the Zionist dream, namely, the promise of a just world. In contrast, Peretz's commitment to *doikeyt* was absolute. What was *do*?

It was everyday Jews—*yidn fun a gants yor*[29]—in *golus*, exile. One dreams of leaping out of *golus*, and sometimes one leaps. But when one leaped, there was no guarantee, either for the individual or the nation. One leaped in full awareness of the probable consequences, which are failure. And yet one leaped. One leaped because the alternative was *tandet*, spiritual death.

Peretz was hardly the only diaspora nationalist in Eastern Europe. But more than Simon Dubnow and even Sh. Anski, he seems to have grasped the tragic core of *golus*.[30] One can rise. One must rise. The expression *oyb nisht hekher* (if not higher), the title of Peretz's celebrated story,[31] just like *di goldene keyt*, escaped its context and became an exhortation to several generations of Yiddish-speaking Jews: Go higher than that! Aspire! Create! Liberate! One rises, and perhaps one is also pushed a bit, or tugged, by redemption. "Like every generation that preceded us," reflected Walter Benjamin in the 1930s, inching from Marx toward the God of history, "we have been endowed with a *weak* Messianic power."[32] But one pays the price. *Golus* exacts a toll.

And here we can return to Reb Nakhmanke's billygoat with its magical horns in the story Peretz published in the first issue of the first daily Yiddish paper in Warsaw. The billygoat's horns stretch to heaven each night for news of the Messiah; they also physically nourish an entire community. But the townspeople grow too familiar with the billygoat. And they love putting snuff into their noses. Because they love the tickle and the sneeze, the magical horns are gradually chopped into snuffboxes, into the detritus of *golus*. This is the story that the holy Reb Nakhmanke chooses in order to channel the cosmic sadness that has overcome him. Perhaps the celebrated lines of Peretz's disciple Sh. Anski, with which his play *The Dybbuk* begins and ends, may be usefully recalled: "Why oh why/ Did the soul descend/ From the highest heights/ Into the lowest depths?/ The falling contains/ the rising within it…"[33] And the rising,

---

29 Literally, Jews of a whole year, that is, Jews who are Jews not just on special days but every day.

30 On Dubnow, see also Sophie Dubnow-Erlich, *The Life and Work of S. M. Dubnov: Diaspora Nationalism and Jewish History* (Bloomington, Ind.: Indiana University Press, 1991), and David H. Weinberg, *Between Tradition and Modernity: Haim Zhitlowski, Simon Dubnow, Ahad Ha-Am, and the Shaping of Modern Jewish Identity* (New York and London: Holmes and Meier, 1996), 145–216. On Anski, see Gabriella Safran, *Wandering Soul*: The Dybbuk's Creator, S. An-sky (Cambridge, Mass.: Harvard University Press, 2010).

31 "Oyb nisht hekher," in *Ale verk*, vol. 4, 98–102.

32 Walter Benjamin, "Theses on the Philosophy of History," in idem, *Illuminations: Essays and Reflections* (New York: Schocken, 1969), 254, emphasis in the original.

33 Sh. Anski, *Der dibek: Dramatishe legende in 4 aktn*, in Hyman Bass (ed.), *Di yidishe drame fun 20stn yorhundert* (New York: Congress for Jewish Culture, 1977), 9, 60.

need one add, contains the falling. *Am olam*—the world people, the eternal people—is also the eternally dying people. This is a conception that makes us squirm, and doubly: as children of the *all-rightniks*, those Jewish-American lovers of success who denied they were in *golus*, and as children of *shereshapleytim*, survivors of the worst-case *golus* of the Holocaust. That squirming may be the most important reason that Peretz has been forgotten. But as the alternatives play themselves out and one telos after another bites the dust, Peretz's arduous vision, conjuring transcendence despite itself and affirming all the possibilities of *golus*, may well speak ever more powerfully to us.

• • •

In the years following the revolution, its gains proved flimsy. The Left was driven back underground, into factionalism and exile. Parliamentary politics, one of the chief promises of the newly granted constitution, was undermined by successive tsarist decrees. Voting to the newly created Duma was increasingly weighted toward property owners and professionals; factory workers were largely disenfranchised.[34] Nevertheless, opportunities for political organizing, however guarded, improved. With the Left in disarray, the chief beneficiaries of the new conditions were the National Democrats, the right wing of Polish nationalism. The Endecja advocated what it called "integral nationalism," whereby membership in the Polish national community was narrowly defined as ethnic Polish descent and the profession of Roman Catholicism. Tapping into the popular language of Social Darwinism, Endeks argued that a modern national existence demanded "national egoism" in a merciless struggle for survival against other peoples, above all the Jews. Before the revolution, the Polish Positivists had preached a more inclusive national vision which welcomed the participation of Jews committed to the Polish cause. But during the revolution, with the emergence of Jewish nationalism, albeit still only potentially, as a political force, even leaders of this faction turned sharply against the Jews. What could these Jews want, they asked, if not a Judaeo-Polonia, a Jewish state on Polish soil? Meanwhile, even as the new Yiddish press preached the struggle for Jewish national interests, Jewish political behavior was still largely quiescent, controlled by the assimilationist officials of the Warsaw *kehilla* with their silent partner, the powerful Hasidic leadership, representing the ever-cautious merchants and shopkeepers of Warsaw.

Parallel to such politics, and transcending it in daily importance, the new cultural initiatives unleashed by the revolution now became permanent

---

34 See Corrsin, *Warsaw before the First World War*, 84–89.

features of Warsaw life, both on the Polish and the Jewish street. Peretz seized on the new opportunities. He worked extensively for the Yiddish press as contributor and editor, he helped create Yiddish schools, and he founded a key institution, the musical-literary society Hazomir, which attracted a generation of young Jews eager to become activists for Yiddish. By 1908 at the Czernowitz Conference, when Yiddish was declared "a national language of the Jewish people," Peretz was ready to identify the Jewish nation with the speakers of Yiddish: "One Jewish people. Its language is—Yiddish. And in this language we wish to gather our treasure, create our culture, further wake our soul, and unite culturally throughout all lands and in all times."[35] But Peretz's doubts, though often veiled, were never far off. Several months earlier, he published in a Vilna paper "A Letter" to an anonymous figure who sees only roses, who avoids the mean streets, the hospital and the slaughterhouse, who, Peretz concludes, "has seen the sea, but not its storm ... nor the broken ship on the sea. You are fortunate, but I, I don't envy you."[36] Most importantly, it was precisely at this time that Peretz was working and reworking his magisterial drama, *Night at the Old Marketplace*, in which messianism suffers a crushing—though perhaps not final—defeat.[37]

In a series of articles in the Warsaw Yiddish daily *Der fraynd* that appeared from March 1 to May 11, 1911, Peretz presented his vision of the past and future of the Jewish people in a form more fully developed than any he had attempted since the revolutionary days of 1906. As Ruth Wisse has pointed out, this is not a well-argued essay.[38] Peretz's characteristic style, marked by rapid shifts between thoughts with dashes and dots marking the swings, is here taken to an extreme. The essay is angry, filled with ironic outbursts against most of the political and cultural alternatives current in the Jewish world. Indeed, Peretz entitled the series *Vegn, vos firn op fun yidishkayt*, which I translate as "Paths that Divert from Yiddishkayt," retaining untranslated the problematic word that is the subject of the entire essay. Wisse, indeed, faults the essay for being little more than "a monument to [Peretz's] own intellectual and artistic anxiety."[39] But turmoil, contradiction and, indeed, anxiety are precisely what

---

35   "Tshernovitser shprakh-konferents," in Nakhmen Mayzil (ed.), *Briv un redes fun Y. L. Peretz* (New York: IKUF, 1944), 373. A shorter version of this talk is in *Ale verk*, vol. 11, 293–96.

36   "A briv," *Di naye tsayt* 4 (1908); also in *Ale verk*, vol. 9, 115.

37   In a subsequent study, I will argue against Chone Shmeruk's characterization of the play as an unrelieved "vision of despair." See his *Peretses yiesh-vizye* (New York: YIVO, 1971).

38   Wisse, *Peretz*, 99.

39   Ibid.

distinguishes Peretz's thinking, and in this case well reflects the world around him, littered with the dregs of revolutionary dreams.

Peretz begins with an easy target, Jewish converts. He adopts what he calls "the loftiest national perspective," from which what irks him is "not the *number* of the renegades, but [...] the *ease*, more—[...] the *frivolity* of conversion." No Marranos or Spinozas or Heines here: "We are dealing with *trifles*: in those circles where the least bit of earthly pleasure appears, they jump over Yiddishkayt as over a straw...It's no longer a tragedy, no longer a drama, in these circles it's become a comedy, a farce!"[40] Peretz continues in a similar vein to attack what he calls the "modern person" who "has no life, only moments. He therefore has no character, no will, but caprices and 'willfulness'...."[41] The art he creates "isn't real art, it isn't true, it can't live, it's a game, a way to pass the time! [...] There is no green sky, no purple peach, and geese have no more than two feet..."[42] He has words for Reform Judaism: "Dead forms are sliced, and not a drop of blood appears, no groan is heard!...Perhaps a Shekhina grumbles in a ruin somewhere—who hears her?"[43] And also for Zionism: "Your home is open, tomorrow I'll give it to you! And when tomorrow came and the door was still barred, some abandoned us, their hope of rescue gone...Or: What you do *among strangers* is built on water, built on sand, for the wind to scatter...Discouraged, one seeks foreign cultures, foreign goods[.]"[44]

Peretz's greatest antagonist by far, however, to whom he devoted nearly half of the thirteen articles in the series, was the journalist and religious philosopher Hillel Zeitlin (1871–1942). Born into a Lubavitcher Hasidic family in Belarus, Zeitlin followed a characteristic path of his generation into secularism: Haskalah, modern Hebrew letters, and Zionism. Relatively early in life, however, he reconfigured Jewish nationalism with a religious base rooted in personal piety and practice. This was a highly unusual stance for a writer of his time and place. In 1906 he moved to Warsaw and began to publish prolifically in the Hebrew and Yiddish press on a host of political, social and cultural issues. Beginning in the Yiddish daily *Haynt* in 1908 and continuing in *Der*

---

40 "Di gefar," *Der fraynd* 40 (1911), 2; reprinted in *Ale verk*, vol. 9, 160–62. For the correct sequence of articles in *Vegn*, see vol. 13, 44–88 in the Farlag Yidish edition of Peretz's works.

41 "'Modern'—a maymer hamusger," *Der fraynd* 49 (1911), 3; reprinted in *Ale verk*, vol. 9, 160–62.

42 "Di moderne gefar (tsveyte un letste helft 'maymer hamusger')," *Der fraynd* 52 (1911); also in *Ale verk*, 169–70.

43 "Kekhol hagoyim," *Der fraynd* 84 (1911) and in *Ale verk*, vol. 9, 182. In popular and mystical lore, Shekhina, seen as female, is God's earthly emanation.

44 "Nokh vegn," in *Der fraynd* 90 (1911); and in *Ale verk*, vol. 9, 189.

moment in 1910–11, Zeitlin published a series of articles entitled *Brivelekh tsu der yidisher yugnt* (Letters to Jewish youth).[45]

The "letters" are rooted in classical Jewish texts, but Zeitlin takes these texts into non-traditional contexts. The first several letters, for example, are framed by Zeitlin's reading of the celebrated passage in Rebbe Nakhman's "Tale of the Seven Beggars" about the spring that flows from the top of a mountain and the heart of the world that stands opposite the spring and longs for it.[46] The heart of the world, Zeitlin explains, is "the extraordinary human beings who feel all the suffering of the world, the suffering of humanity." And the spring is "the highest of the high, the deepest of the deep [...] that which we can't name with one name but know that it's the only thing we can strive for." Buddha, Tolstoy, Moses, as well as the Jewish people [*Folk Yisroel*] are examples of such hearts.[47] In subsequent articles, Zeitlin focuses directly on the Pentateuch. He insists that the laws of Torah are as eternal as the laws of nature. But he reads them through the rationalist commentary of Ibn Ezra, Yehuda Ha-Levi, and Maimonides as well as what he terms the "generally accepted comparative method of the sciences." The meaning of the *mitzvot*, he explains, should be understood in new ways in new historical periods.[48]

Concurrently with the "Letters to Youth," Zeitlin also published "An Open Letter to Warsaw Hasidim" in which he urges repudiation of the assimilationist leadership of the Warsaw *kehilla*.[49] Jews who believe in the Torah, he argues, dare not turn the *kehilla* over to Jews who lead their children to conversion, who do nothing to combat Jewish poverty or fight for Jewish rights. He compares the rule of the Dicksteins and Natansons[50]—Peretz's perennial *bêtes noires*—to that of Herod in the era of the Second Temple, and concludes: "Too long have the Jews of Poland sung *mayufes* [abased themselves...] Does the Shekhina no longer dwell among Jews?"

---

45   The first series was published in *Haynt* 233, October 17, 1908–26, January 30, 1909. The second series, entitled *Naye brivelekh tsu der yidisher yugnt*, appeared in *Der moment* 14, December 14, 1910–66, March 31, 1911.

46   There are many translations; see for example, *Yenne Velt: The Great Works of Jewish Fantasy and Occult*, trans. Joachim Neugroschel (New York: Stonehill Publishing, 1976), 336–38.

47   *Der moment* 14 (1910).

48   *Der moment* 48 (1911). *Mitzvot* are the "good deeds" prescribed by Jewish law.

49   "An ofene briv tsu varshever hasidim," *Der moment* 28, 31 (1911).

50   Samuel Dickstein (1851–1939), a leading assimilationist, was an official of the Warsaw *kehilla* in charge of the educational and statistical departments from 1885–1918. Several generations of the large Natanson family, bankers and merchants, were pillars of the Warsaw *kehilla* from the second half of the nineteenth century until World War I.

Given the congruence of some of these views with Peretz's own, Peretz's response to Zeitlin is surprisingly ferocious. "Back to *kheyder*, recite Psalms, study Torah... Yank back yesterday," begins Peretz's assault. He calls Zeitlin the Prophet of Yesterday and accuses him of preaching nothing more than "Khumesh mit Rashi," Pentateuch with the commentary of Rashi, the curriculum of the *kheyder*, the traditional elementary school. He chastises him for knowing nothing of Saadiyah Gaon or Maimonides.[51] "The Khumesh (not your Khumesh) speaks of life! Life demands movement, development, progress, changing what is around us through spirit and will—but you insist on *standing still*. And so the living God, encased in one historical moment stuck within the next, is transformed into a dead idol, earlier forms of relationship between man and God, into idol worship—and you call this 'Yiddishkayt'!"[52] The disparity between this characterization of Zeitlin and what he actually wrote is so great that one is tempted to question whether Peretz actually read him.

On his side, in his "Open Letter to Y. L. Peretz," Zeitlin claims to have read only one of Peretz's articles and that only by chance.[53] But his response to Peretz's attack is revealing. Peretz had cited approvingly a well known statement attributed to Zeitlin that "Peretz has a heaven, but there's no God in heaven." "The first half of the sentence is certainly a compliment," Peretz writes, "and I bow with an amiable, brotherly smile. Better late than never. As for the second half of the sentence—*that I affirm unequivocally*. Indeed, I don't even know where to seek Him—Before the world—as its Creator? After the world—emerging from it?"[54] But in his letter to Peretz, Zeitlin reminds him of his actual words: "Peretz's heavens are only a word, a noise, a hue—no God resides in them." Peretz, Zeitlin explains, has neither heaven nor God. "It is not a question of atheism here," Zeitlin continues, "but of artistic nihilism." Zeitlin, in other words, accuses Peretz precisely of the frivolousness that Peretz attributes to the so-called modern artist. Peretz's theological musings are irrelevant, says Zeitlin. The question is simpler: "Do you, Romantic, Hasid, Poet of Hasidismus, have God in your heart?" If Peretz understood that Yiddishkayt can be neither internal nor external, reactionary nor progressive, he "would grasp that there is no other Yiddishkayt but Khumesh with Rashi (understood, certainly, as not just Rashi but *everything* that illuminates and explains the eternal holy laws)."

---

51   *Der fraynd* 57, 58, 68, 73 (1911); also in *Ale verk*, vol. 9, 190–92, 172–74, 193–96, 174–77.
52   "Ver iz shuldik," *Der fraynd* 73 (1911); also in *Ale verk*, vol. 9, 174–75; emphasis in the original.
53   "An ofener briv tsu Y. L. Peretz," *Der moment* 72 (1911).
54   "Der ershter veg," *Der fraynd* 68 (1911); also in *Ale verk*, vol. 9, 193; emphasis in the original.

And he concludes by taunting Peretz with a line from a Hasidic song: "Akh you old *misnagid*, time already to repent."[55]

Neither Peretz nor his literary contemporaries were prepared to accept or even conceive of a Torah-centered perspective on the issues of the day. Yet as he jousts with Zeitlin, Peretz is drawn into explicit God-talk. Peretz's God, however, exists only as a being in time. "He must always be *passing!*" declares Peretz. "At the moment of ecstasy and revelation He appears and is seen *from behind*... Whoever sees His face cannot live—he has lived to see everything! To live is only to seek! And He must be distant, so that man may never reach Him. [...] Not in what *was*, which has *passed*, not in what is, which is passing, is God to be found. 'I will be that which I will be.' God is in what's next, in the eternal *future*, in *eternity*. Seeking Him must be eternal!"[56]

It is in history—and not in Torah—that Peretz discovers Yiddishkayt. But what sort of vision finally emerges? In an era of escalating exclusivist nationalisms throughout Europe, when Polish nationalists had declared political war on the Jews, Peretz replies in kind. The result upsets our twenty-first century sensibilities: "Jews and gentiles stand opposed, Jewish blood and gentile blood... For Jewish blood, which in its religious form is *monotheistic*, in its philosophical form *monistic*, cannot mix with any other blood. A higher worldview cannot surrender to the lower, and must struggle for its right to create its own world-culture."[57] And he presents a triumphalist mythology of Jewish history:

> Nomadic blood, a family of wanderers in the wilderness. In its blood—rectitude, justice. And its God, who wanders with it, is the same, and therefore not made of wood or stone, but a moving, living God. A lofty conception of God, a free and open conception of the world, without borders, without differences... And when it abandons the wilderness to wander other lands, it cannot mix with the inhabitants. They repel each other and the people lives apart, and finally escapes coercion and oppression to seek a separate land... The land conquered, the familial God

---

55 Zeitlin, "An ofener briv"; emphasis in the original. The term *misnagid* refers to a rationalist opponent of Hasidism.

56 "Der ershter veg," *Der fraynd* 68 (1911): and in *Ale verk*, vol. 9, 195–96. Peretz cites the famous biblical verse *Ehyeh asher ehyeh* (Exodus 3:14) which is more usually translated as "I am that I am." But here the future tense is clearly what Peretz intended.

57 "Nokh vegn," *Der fraynd* 90 (1911): and in *Ale verk*, vol. 9, 188; emphasis in the original.

becomes the God of the chosen [people][58] in its chosen land. It wanders no more, and raises its temple in the land. [...] A small people, a separate state—a state of priests and a holy people ... After a time it fell. [...] The people becomes a world-people, its God, who does not abandon it and suffers exile with it—a God of the world ... And the world, the entire field of exile, becomes an arena of struggle between the one God and the many gods ... God will triumph![59]

Peretz ends his essay with the following passage, widely celebrated in Peretz's time, but rarely read in context.

A Jewish *life* must blossom anew. The Bible as its seed must be carried to the people; Jewish folk symbols and legends, their energy restored, will serve as dew and rain! The field will revive, the people will revive, awake to suffer for the truth with steadfast faith in victory.

We must raise the banner of *Jewish* renaissance. The banner of Messiah, of world-judgment and world-liberation—of a future free humanity!

This is the mission of the eternal people, the world-people, and it must be the mission of Jewish life, the Jewish home, the Jewish school, the Jewish theater, the Jewish book, and everything that is Jewish.[60]

For several generations, Peretz was canonized as the father of a secular Jewish culture. But here again, a preliminary reading of Peretz's writings in the context of his times problematizes this identification and suggests the complex relationship in his thinking between religious and secular elements. More generally, it raises a question that is rather contemporary: What exactly do we mean by Jewish secularism? Moreover, Peretz's combative, triumphalist discourse also calls into question our assumptions about "good" and "bad" nationalism.

⋯

Scarcely a year after his polemic with Zeitlin, Peretz leaped into heated political activism during elections to the Fourth Duma, scheduled for October 1912.[61]

---

58 The CYCO edition has the word *God* here; the Farlag Yiddish edition has the correct word *people*.
59 "Di farfremdete inteligents," *Der fraynd* 96; and in *Ale verk*, vol. 9, 197.
60 Ibid.; also in *Ale verk*, vol. 9, 200.
61 See Corrsin, *Warsaw before the First World War*, 89–101.

Elections were indirect. First, eligible voters in various curiae (official constituencies) voted for party lists of electors and then the latter chose the actual delegates. Warsaw was entitled to two, but beginning in the previous election, one of these was required to represent the small Russian curia. That left one delegate to represent both Poles and Jews. Since the last election five years previously, under the influence of the Yiddish press and the increasing Jew-baiting of the National Democrats, more Jews had registered to vote, particularly in the so-called general curia, representing upper and middle class voters. In August 1912, the government announced that 55 percent of eligible voters in the general curia were Jews. This news stunned Polish leaders; earlier that year Warsaw's population had been estimated as 57 percent Polish and 36 percent Jewish. In the ensuing turmoil, two competing Polish candidates emerged. Roman Dmowski, leader of the National Democrats, refused all cooperation with Jews, whom he accused of making war on Poles. Jan Kucharzewski, advanced by liberal Polish groups and Jewish assimilationists, made contradictory statements about the "Jewish question" that alienated Jewish voters. When it became clear that Jews would not support Kucharzewski, Polish liberals and Jewish assimilationists urged Jews not to antagonize Poles, not to provoke pogroms, and abstain from voting at all.

Peretz, who ran as an elector on the Jewish list, insisted that Jews absolutely had to vote. In a rare transcribed talk, delivered about two weeks before the choosing of new electors, Peretz begins by judging those heretofore involved in elections: "It is a tragi-comedy that until now at least, the Jewish election campaign in Warsaw has been led either by those who don't believe in Jewish life in diaspora [*in der fremd*], who look at Jewish life *in golus* through dark glasses [i.e., Zionists], and, on the other side, the assimilationists, who don't believe in their own right to exist [...]. There's also another group of electors. These are the old conservatives, who trail after the assimilationists, and when they demand it, spit on the Duma! There can be vital Jewish questions [*yidishe lebns-fragn*] before the Duma, from the Pale of Settlement to Beilis, but if the assimilationists demand it, it's no use [*farfaln*]: the Hasidic top hat spits on the Duma."[62]

---

62 "Oyf a farval-farzamlung," in *Briv un redes fun Y. L. Peretz*, 387. A version of this talk can also be found in *Ale verk*, vol. 11, 305–10. According to Mayzil, the speech originally appeared in *Haynt*, October 1, 1912. Shmuel Yatskan, the editor of *Haynt*, had termed the campaign a tragedy. In typical fashion, Peretz corrected him by calling it a tragi-comedy. At the time of this talk, Mendel Beilis had been sitting in a Kiev prison for over a year awaiting trial for ritual murder. The trial was not to begin for another year; Beilis was ultimately acquitted.

Peretz continues, in a voice that recalls his evocation of the Jewish masses in the article *"Tandet"* of 1906: "These were the leaders; the Jew, the simple Jew who builds right here [*oyfn ort*] and who wants to hold his own right here, he said nothing, he is not organized and is without a will. [But] everything is supposedly done in his name. I myself want to speak in the name of the simple Jew, who wants above all to hold his own where he is, who knows quite definitely and clearly that life is struggle and he struggles for his life... Had he been organized, it would not have come to a tragi-comedy. Obtaining a majority, in politics a majority is—law."[63]

"Will they beat us?" asks Peretz, and replies: "I don't know. The *Kurier Warszawski* [liberal Polish daily] assures us that it lacks the instincts for beating. The Leftists say they will not permit beating. The officials say: 'There will be no beating!' But if there is beating, gentlemen, they beat those who are bent over, who let themselves be beaten... The courtly times [*riter-tsayt*] and their morals, the times of Don Quixote, are over. Those lying down are beaten and only those—but antisemitism, the refined kind that doesn't hit, grabs the food out of one's mouth."[64]

But it's not really about antisemitism, argues Peretz, but rather the changing economic and social relations of modern times. "When relations changed, the [Polish] people became different. The entire Polish press against us is not a question of love and hate, love and revenge! We are definitely more liked, at least less hated, than the 'faithless Jew' [*żyd niewierny*] of the past, in the economically best of times. What's changed is this: So long as Poles asked us to pity them, to weep for the *golus* of the Polish Shekhina, to protest (quietly at home, loudly abroad) against oppression, they gladly permitted us the title of *Pole*. Wail, Jew! Cry with us! You also have ears in Europe, and what's the harm? Lament [*zog kines*] our *golus* too!"[65]

But now, the assimilationists act as if nothing has changed. "Why are they silent, why haven't they revealed the secret that the golden times of kindness and love are over? That [the *szlachta* (gentry)] want to eat? Why do they still want to convince us that it's the fault of the Zionists, the Litvaks, and Yatskan,

---

63 *Briv un redes fun Y. L. Peretz*, 387–88.
64 Ibid., 388–89.
65 Ibid., 390. Peretz is parodying the narrative of Polish-Jewish "reconciliation"—shaped by Polish positivists and Jewish assimilationists—in the aftermath of the 1863 Uprising. See Magdalena Opalski and Israel Bartal, *Poles and Jews: A Failed Brotherhood* (Hanover, NH, and London: Brandeis University Press, 1992).

and that without them we'd have a paradise [*gan-eydn*]? Why haven't they told us the truth, that the *szlachta* have become shopkeepers?"⁶⁶

Peretz concludes by imagining Kucharzewski strolling through the hallowed streets of Warsaw's Old City, past sites that were once off limit to Jews. "But while Kucharzewski wants to recall the shades of the past, it is we who drive Warsaw ever further, and on new paths. And if Kucharzewski [presumably scandalized] heard a Jew in the Old City ask: 'What's the price of a cubit of earth?,' I heard gentiles [*goyim*] asking: 'Where is there a cabaret here? Where is there a brothel [*freylekh heyzl*]?'"

"We want to vote!" ended Peretz, to a sustained ovation.⁶⁷

On October 15, 1912, in the voting for electors, Dmowski was eliminated and the Jewish list scored a clear victory. On November 7–8, after several rounds of voting, the Jewish electors swung their support from a Jewish to a Polish candidate. This was Eugeniusz Jagiełło, a little- known socialist who was the only Polish candidate who pledged to support equal rights for Jews. For the first time, Jews manifested their political clout as Jews. Most of the Polish press, including its liberal wing, was outraged, and anointed Jagiełło a Jewish delegate who did not represent Poles. Dmowski and the National Democrats responded by declaring a boycott of Jewish enterprises, publicized through their newly created mass-circulation tabloid, *Gazeta Poranna 2 grosze* [Two penny morning paper].⁶⁸ This was the first skirmish in a war that was to continue, to the increasing disadvantage of Jews, throughout the interwar period in independent Poland.⁶⁹

Through these many conflicts, Peretz emerges as a far different figure from the Peretz of the hagiographies. Neither prophet nor all-knowing father nor comforter of his people, Peretz aspired to the highest ideals but was ultimately rooted in the fallenness, the funkiness of the everyday, that is, in the reality of *golus*. I began this essay by citing the inscription on Peretz's *ohel*, the words of

---

66   Ibid., 391. The term "Litvak" is used here to designate Russian-speaking Jews who settled in increasing numbers in Warsaw at the turn of the century; Yatskan, the editor of *Haynt*, was himself a Litvak; see also the article about *Haynt* by Joanna Nalewajko-Kulikov in this volume.

67   Ibid., 393–94.

68   By the end of 1912, *Gazeta Poranna* had achieved the "unheard of" daily circulation of 40,000 copies; see Corrsin, *Warsaw before the First World War*, 102.

69   From May 1912 to June 1913, a period that spanned the Duma elections and the subsequent boycott, Peretz produced a series of nearly fifty columns for *Haynt* entitled *In mayn vinkele* [In my corner]. The sequence of texts in the Farlag Yidish edition is far preferable to that in the CYCO. A study of these texts in the context of their turbulent times will be the subject of subsequent research.

the *tzaddik* Reb Shloyme from the first act of Peretz's play *Di goldene keyt*. I will close with Peretz's poem "Mayn muze" (My muse), written near the beginning of his career:

Nisht keyn bliml iz mayn muze,	My muse is not a flower,
Oyf der vize vakst zi nisht;	She doesn't grow on lawns;
Nisht keyn shmeterling, vos zukht	No butterfly that seeks
Ale blumen oyf un kusht!	All the flowers out to kiss!
Nisht keyn nakhtigal mayn muze,	Not a nightingale my muse,
Hot keyn treln, hot keyn zise...	She has no trills or sweetness...
S'iz a yidene an alte,	She's an old Jewess,
An ayngeshrumpene, a miyese;	Shriveled and ugly;
An agune mit yesoymim	An abandoned wife with orphans
Un farshpreyte oyf der velt;	Spread out across the world;
Un an evyente a groyse	A down-and-out pauper
Un zi shrayt nor, un zi shelt...[70]	And she only yells and curses...

Peretz, it seems, may be found somewhere between Reb Shloyme and this muse.

---

70 See *Ale verk*, vol. 1, 28; this edition gives the date of the poem as 1891.

CHAPTER 10

"Di Haynt-mishpokhe": Study for a Group Picture

Joanna Nalewajko-Kulikov

The post-1905 period in the Tsarist Empire witnessed a flourishing Jewish press, especially in Yiddish, the Jewish vernacular. Although the first Yiddish daily, *Der fraynd*, was allowed to appear in St. Petersburg in 1903,[1] it was the 1905 revolution that led to the softening of restrictions that helped give rise to most Yiddish newspapers. In 1907, according to Dmitrii Eliashevich, eleven Yiddish journals and newspapers were published (in addition to six Hebrew periodicals).[2] While those associated with political parties disappeared relatively soon, the more apolitical organs virtually blossomed. Two great Yiddish dailies that became integral to the history of Polish Jewry were *Haynt* (established in 1908) and *Der moment* (established in 1910). Both continued to be published until the fateful year of 1939.

For many years, historians paid relatively little attention to the history of the Yiddish press even if they made recourse to it as a historical source.[3] The majority of discussions of its history were confined to the memoirs of former journalists and contributors.[4] This situation has begun to improve thanks to

---

1 On *Der Fraynd*, see Saul Ginzburg, *Amolike peterburg* (Tsiko: New York, 1944), 184–236, and Sarah Abrevaya Stein, *Making Jews modern: the Yiddish and Ladino press in the Russian and Ottoman Empires* (Bloomington, IN: Indiana University Press, 2004), passim. On changes in the censorship policy regarding the Jewish press, see Dmitrii A. Eliashevich, *Pravitel'stvennaia politika i evreiskaia pechat' v Rossii, 1797–1917: ocherki istorii tsenzury* (St. Petersburg and Jerusalem: Gesharim—Mosty kul'tury, 1999), passim.

2 Dmitrii Elyashevich, *A Note on the Jewish Press and Censorship during the First Russian Revolution*, in *The Revolution of 1905 and Russia's Jews*, ed. Stefani Hoffman and Ezra Mendelsohn (Philadelphia: University of Pennsylvania Press, 2008), 51.

3 An exception was Marian Fuks, *Prasa żydowska w Warszawie 1823–1939* (Warszawa: Państwowe Wydawnictwo Naukowe, 1979)—a book that has all advantages and disadvantages of a pioneering study. For detailed reviews see Chone Shmeruk, "A pioneering study of the Warsaw Jewish Press," *Soviet Jewish Affairs* 11.3 (1981): 35–53; and Andrzej Notkowski, "O działalności wydawniczej Żydów warszawskich w XIX i XX wieku," *Przegląd Historyczny* 72.4 (1981): 723–746. It should be emphasized, however, that, as far as I know, no other historian set himself such an ambitious task as Fuks did, so his study remains until today, in many ways, the only point of reference.

4 See, for example, the anthology *Di yidishe prese vos iz geven*, ed. Dovid Flinker, Mordekhai Tsanin, and Sholem Rozenfeld (Tel Aviv: Veltfarband fun di yidishe zhurnalistn, 1975). This

recent research by Nathan Cohen, Sarah Abrevaya Stein and, most recently, Kalman Weiser.[5] Yet so far, there has been no sociological or historical study devoted to Yiddish journalists as a group.[6]

FIGURE 10.9   The Watchmaker, *by Yehudah Pen, 1914. From the Archives of the YIVO Institute for Jewish Research, New York.*
COURTESY OF YIVO.

  book also had an earlier Hebrew edition: *Itonut yehudit she-haita*, ed. Yehuda Gothelf (Tel Aviv: Ha-igud ha-olami shel ha-itonaim ha-yehudim, 1973).
5 Nathan Cohen, "'An ugly and repulsive idler' or a talented and seasoned editor: S.Y. Yatzkan and the beginnings of the popular Yiddish press in Warsaw," *Jews in Russia and Eastern Europe* 1–2 (2005): 28–53; idem, "'Shund' and the tabloids: Jewish popular reading in interwar Poland," *Polin* 16 (2003): 189–211; idem, "The Yiddish press and Yiddish literature: a fertile but complex relationship," *Modern Judaism* 28.2 (2008): 148–172; idem, "The Yiddish press as distributor of literature," in *The Multiple Voices of Modern Yiddish Literature*, ed. Shlomo Berger (Amsterdam: Menasseh ben Israel Institute, 2007), 7–29; idem, "Zikhronot Tsevi Prilutski: teudah merateket le-heker itonut yidish be-varsha," in *Mi-vilne li-yerushalayim: mechkarim be'toldoteihem u'be'tarbutam shel yehudey mizrakh eyropa mugashim le'profesor Shmuel Verses*, ed. David Assaf et al. (Jerusalem: The Hebrew University Magnes Press, 2002), 385–402; Stein, *Making Jews Modern*; Kalman Weiser, *Jewish People, Yiddish Nation: Noah Prylucki and the Folkists In Poland* (Toronto: University of Toronto Press, 2010).
6 An article by Marian Fuks, despite a title promising a more comprehensive treatment of the subject, contains only three biographical sketches on Maurycy Orzech, Simkhe Pietrushka

Haynt makes a particularly interesting case study for a number of reasons. First, during the 31-year period of its existence it passed from being a tabloid, labeled contemptuously "yellow press," to a well-respected informative daily. Second, despite its Zionist sympathies (and not just sympathies—after 1919 *Haynt* was an official organ of the Zionist Organization in Poland), its main readership was the Jewish middle class. Third, its editors seemed to have honed to perfection the Jewish intelligentsia's sense of mission while, nevertheless, managing to sustain a successful newspaper business.

The peak years for *Haynt* were those preceding the First World War, when circulation reached 100,000 copies. This was something that was never repeated (in the 1930s the print-run was 25,000–35,000 copies).[7] Yet throughout its life, *Haynt* boasted an impressive list of collaborators, starting with Hillel Zeitlin, David Frischman, Hersh Dovid Nomberg, Y.L. Peretz and ending with Azriel Carlebach, Zusman Segalovich and Nachmen Mayzil. The paper serialized novels by the most renowned Yiddish authors, from Sholem Aleichem to Israel Joshua Singer. In addition, it generated and engaged in discussions about all aspects of Jewish life and attempted to influence the lives of readers, including calling on them to boycott German products in the 1930s.[8]

In this chapter, I endeavor to reconstruct and analyze the life itineraries of the highly influential paper's staff members and contributors. Drawing upon the only existing monograph on *Haynt*, by Chaim Finkelstein,[9] in addition to data from other reference works and published memoirs, one accumulates a list of 160 *Haynt* contributors, from full-time editors and journalists to its more occasional authors. Some of them went down in the annals of Jewish history, like Yiddish authors Sholem Asch and Y.L. Peretz or the leader of the Zionist movement in interwar Poland, Yitzhak Grünbaum. Others were simple proofreaders, night-editors, reporters, or correspondents from various towns and shtetlekh who lived in relative obscurity.

---

and Tsvi and Noyekh Prilutsky, see M. Fuks, "Dziennikarze prasy żydowskiej w Polsce," *Kwartalnik Historii Prasy Polskiej* 24.3 (1985): 35–52. Daria Nałęcz's study on journalists in interwar Poland focuses predominantly on the Polish journalists. See *Zawód dziennikarza w Polsce 1918–1939* (Warszawa-Łódź: Państwowe Wydawnictwo Naukowe, 1982).

7   Andrzej Paczkowski, *Prasa codzienna Warszawy w latach 1918–1939* (Warszawa: Państwowy Instytut Wydawniczy, 1983), 245.

8   For a short outline of the newspaper's history see Joanna Nalewajko-Kulikov, "'Hajnt' (1908–1939)," in *Studia z dziejów prasy żydowskiej na ziemiach polskich (XIX–XX w.)*, ed. J. Nalewajko-Kulikov with G.P. Bąbiak and A.J. Cieślikowa (Warszawa: Neriton and Instytut Historii PAN, 2012), 61–75.

9   Chaim Finkelstein, *Haynt—a tsaytung bay yidn* (Tel Aviv: Farlag Perets, 1978).

"Generations" of Contributors

As mentioned earlier, in the history of the daily one can distinguish four distinct periods of development. Three groups of contributors (if we take as the main determinant the beginning of their collaboration with the *Haynt*) spanned these four periods.

The first group includes those who began to contribute to *Haynt* before the fall of the Russian Empire—or, in most cases, even before the First World War. The five "Founding Fathers" of *Haynt* were Shmuel Yankev Yatskan, Avrom Goldberg, Aron Gavze and the Finkelshteyn brothers, Noyekh and Nehemia. The first group also includes those who are today commonly associated not with the *Haynt* but with its ideological opponent, *Der moment*—Hillel Zeitlin and Hersh Dovid Nomberg are just two examples—because, while they also contributed to *Haynt* in the period before the First World War, they definitely ceased after 1918, remaining loyal to *Der moment* until 1939.

Most of the editors and journalists who worked for *Haynt* in the very first period of its existence were born in the 1870s and 80s. They often contributed (before or simultaneously) to the Hebrew and Russian-Jewish press. Some switched languages only after the Revolution of 1905. Generally speaking, this was the first generation of Yiddish-speaking intellectuals to discover that publishing in mass-circulation Yiddish press allowed them to better reach *a prostn folksmentsh* (a simple man). For this reason, the modern Yiddish press became an attractive means of communication for writers like Y.L. Peretz or Hillel Zeitlin, as well.

The largest group of contributors consisted of those who joined the *Haynt* staff after Poland regained its independence in 1918. Some had worked previously for the Zionist *Dos yudishe folk* and became *Haynt* contributors when both newspapers merged in 1920. This shift had two momentous consequences: geographical, because some of the previous contributors remained within the borders of what was to become eventually the USSR—and political, because it was Yitzhak Grünbaum who took over *Haynt* and influenced its political profile.

The last group of contributors consisted of those who joined the *Haynt* staff in the 1930s, or more precisely, after 1932, another turning point in the newspaper's history. After 1932, *Haynt* was run by a cooperative of employees called "Alt-nay", headed by Chaim Finkelstein. It was truly a generational change, for those who took power in the editorial office had come of age in independent Poland. Similar changes could be observed in the Polish press.[10] In addition,

---

10   Nałęcz, *Zawód dziennikarza*, 103–104.

some of the older contributors passed away, while Grünbaum left Poland for Palestine that year.

From this very quick overview, one might ask whether we can dare to create a single group picture of what *Haynt* staff members, as implied by the title of Chaim Finkelstein's memoirs, called *Di haynt-mishpokhe* (the *Haynt* family)?[11] Did these diverse generations of contributors share any common patterns, such as family background or education? Did they have anything in common apart from happening to contribute to the same newspaper? In other words, is it really possible to create a group picture of such a significant part of the Jewish intelligentsia? For a possible answer to this question, it is necessary to survey sample biographies of five core staff members—those most often associated with *Haynt*.

From the Russian Empire into the Large World

Shmuel Yankev Yatskan[12] was born in 1874 in Vobol'niki (Lithuanian: Vabalninkas) in Lithuania.[13] Later on, he would say that whenever he wrote anything, be it an article or a tiny item, he had the simple Jews from Vobol'niki before his eyes—the primary recipients of his Yiddish newspaper. He received a traditional education at a yeshiva in Ponevezh and left with a rabbinical ordination in 1892. He claimed to be able to speak several languages, but Chaim Finkelstein remembered that "No matter whether he spoke Russian, Polish,

---

11   The term "Haynt-mishpokhe" is used by Chaim Finkelstein in titles of two chapters of his book on *Haynt*, namely Chapter 8 (146) and Chapter 9 (158) as well as in Berl Kuczer's memoirs (B. Kuczer, *Geven amol varshe...Zikhroynes*, Paris: [no publisher given] 1955, 103. Unfortunately, neither of them gave its origins; it seems, however, to be a slogan used among the newspaper's staff. Both Finkelstein and Kuczer used it as an equivalent of the word "team" or "staff".

12   His last name is also sometimes spelled in English as Jackan.

13   Finkelstein, *Haynt*, 27–38; Boris Kotlerman, "Yatskan, Shmuel Yankev," in *YIVO Encyclopedia of Jews in Eastern Europe*, 2: 2046–47; "Yatskan, Shmuel Yankev" [no author given], in *Leksikon fun der nayer yidisher literatur* (hereafter: LNYL), ed. Efraim Oyerbakh, Yitskhok Kharlash and Moyshe Shtarkman (New York: Congress for Jewish Culture, 1961), vol. 4, 211–213; Zalmen Reisen, *Leksikon fun der yidisher literatur, prese un filologie* (Vilnius: B. Kletskin Farlag, 1929) (hereafter: Reisen, *Leksikon*), vol. 1, 1231–1234; Melekh Ravitsh, *Mayn leksikon*, vol. 2 (Montreal, 1947), 124–126. The title page says it was "published by a committee in Montreal."

German, French, English, it sounded like Yiddish, and with a characteristic Litvish '*sin*'[14] at that."[15]

Instead of becoming a rabbi, Yatskan moved to St. Petersburg and began to contribute to the Hebrew press, first to *Ha-melitz* and later (probably once he moved to Warsaw in 1902) to *Ha-tzefira*. He became involved in the Zionist movement and, after the revolution of 1905, began to publish a series of cheap Yiddish newspapers: starting with a humoristic weekly *Di Bin*, then a cheap daily *Yidishes tageblat*, and, finally, the more serious *Dos yidishes vokhenblat*. In 1908, together with Noyekh Finkelshteyn, his brother Nehemia, Avrom Goldberg and Aron Gavze (the last two were his colleagues from the *Ha-tzefira* times) he founded *Haynt*. It was neither the first Yiddish daily in the Russian Empire, nor even in Warsaw, but it boasted a number of features which had been common in the European press since the mid-nineteenth century yet were absent in Jewish press: it provided extensive coverage of the latest political news, developed a network of local correspondents, sent representatives to report on all the important events, and included serialized novels.[16] All of this was Yatskan's vision, and it made him adored by some and hated by others.[17]

Another thing that made Yatskan controversial was his Litvak origins. He was considered "a typical representative of Litvaks in Warsaw."[18] As such, he seemed to be the favorite "negative example" of various Polish authors and journalists—both those who were openly anti-Semitic and those who may have had nothing against Jews but who feared that the development of a "jargon" press would draw Yiddish-speaking Jews away from the Polish language and culture and impede the acculturation process. Yatskan even made it into contemporaneous Polish literature—Artur Gruszecki's novel *Litwackie mrowie* depicts him through a certain "Juda Salomonowicz Sudorow," founder of the first Yiddish daily in Warsaw.[19]

---

14   In northeastern Yiddish (Litvish Yiddish), spoken by Litvaks, the consonant "shin" is pronounced as "sin".
15   Finkelstein, *Haynt*, 37.
16   An analysis of one of these novels, which were often written by A.L. Jakubowicz, can be found in Chone Shmeruk, "Te'udah nedirah le-toldotejha shel ha-sifrut ha-lo-kanonit be-yidish," *Ha-sifrut* 32 (June 1982): 13–33.
17   For more on contradictory opinions about Yatskan and his role, see Cohen, "An ugly and repulsive idler," 39–53.
18   Ravitsh, *Mayn leksikon*, vol. 2, 124.
19   A. Gruszecki, *Litwackie mrowie* (Warszawa: Gebethner i Wolff, 1911), 215, 217. I am grateful to Grzegorz Krzywiec who located this book for me. For more on Gruszecki's novel see François Guesnet, "'Wir müssen Warschau unbedingt russisch machen': Die Mythologisierung der russisch-jüdischen Zuwanderung ins Königreich Polen zu Beginn

After *Haynt* merged with *Dos yudishe folk* on January 1, 1920, Yatskan had to resign from his post of editor-in-chief. This was done at the explicit demand of Yitzhak Grünbaum, who later explained in his memoirs that "it was difficult to hope for a harmonious collaboration" between both of them.[20] Yatskan left for the States and returned to Poland one year later as a sales representative of the Manischewitz company. Having had little success selling their matzot in Poland, he left again, this time for Paris, where he founded, in 1926, a Yiddish daily *Parizer haynt*.[21] While it attracted some attention, it did not get as popular a reception as Yatskan had expected; so he returned to Warsaw and founded, in 1929, a Polish-language daily *Ostatnie Wiadomości*, a paper whose covert goal was to draw away Polish audiences from those Polish newspapers he considered anti-Semitic. *Ostatnie Wiadomości* was a mild success, but Yatskan, with all his intuition about what an average Jewish reader wanted, had no flair for business. He eventually had to sell the newspaper. He died in 1936 in Paris, but was buried in Warsaw.

Menachem Kipnis, a cantor's son, was born in 1878 in Ushomir, Volhynia (contemporary Ukraine).[22] Orphaned early, he lived with his elder brother (also a cantor) and received a traditional education. He began to perform at an early age in local synagogues and throughout the Pale of Settlement (save for a three years' break, owing to a vocal injury). In 1902, he entered the Warsaw Conservatory of Music and joined the Warsaw Opera as the first tenor. During the First World War, Kipnis and his pupil (and later wife), Zimra Seligfeld, gave a number of concerts of Yiddish folk songs in Poland and all over Europe, gaining huge popularity.

---

unseres Jahrhunderts am Beispiel eines polnischen Trivialromans," in *Geschichtliche Mythen in den Literaturen und Kulturen Ostmittel- und Südosteuropas*, ed. Eva Behring et al. (Stuttgart: Franz Steiner, 1999), 99–116.

20   Yitzhak Grünbaum, "Zikhroynes vegn 'haynt'," in *Di yidishe prese vos iz geven*, 19.

21   On the *Parizer haynt* see Aline Benain and Audrey Kichelewski, "'Parizer Haynt' et 'Naïe Presse', les itinéraires paradoxaux de deux quotidiens parisiens en langue yiddish," *Archives Juives* 36.1 (2003): 52–69.

22   Finkelstein, *Haynt*, 220–223; Natan Meir, "Kipnis, Menakhem," in *YIVO Encyclopedia of Jews in Eastern Europe*, 1: 897–898; Haim Bar-Dayan, "Kipnis, Menahem," in *Encyclopaedia Judaica*, ed. Michael Berenbaum and Fred Skolnik, 2nd ed., vol. 12 (Detroit, MI: Macmillan Reference USA, 2007), 179–180.; Ravitsh, *Mayn leksikon*, vol. 1 (Montreal, 1945), 230–232; Isachar Fater, *Muzyka żydowska w Polsce w okresie międzywojennym* (Warszawa: Rytm, 1997), 141–146; Reisen, *Leksikon*, vol. 3, 645–649; Itzik Nakhmen Gottesman, *Defining the Yiddish Nation: the Jewish Folklorists of Poland* (Detroit, MI: Wayne State University Press, 2003), 56–66.

From 1907, Kipnis contributed articles on music to the Hebrew and Yiddish press and soon became a regular contributor to *Haynt*. Apart from learned pieces on music and musicians and several concert reviews, he published humorous feuilletons that were adored by readers, especially those that featured a character named "Pan Mecenas," a stupid Polish anti-Semite. He collected Yiddish folk songs and folk stories and published them in anthologies. Shortly before the outbreak of the war he co-organized a Jewish symphonic orchestra that hired Jewish musicians who had been fired from other orchestras. He was an active member of various cultural associations dedicated to preserving and popularizing Jewish folk music, he photographed Jewish daily life and characteristic Jewish types, and he was famous for his collections of antiques (specializing in clocks and canes). As Itzik Nakhmen Gottesman has noted, "His recommendations could make or break the career of a cantor. His ethnographic articles combined all of his fieldwork talents: photography, an ability to transcribe songs with musical notation, and a lucid ethnographic writing style."[23]

Kipnis continued to collect folk-related materials in the Warsaw Ghetto, where he died of a cerebral hemorrhage in 1942. The Ringelblum Archive staff made efforts to incorporate his papers into their collections, but his widow did not agree. When she herself was deported to Treblinka, all traces of Kipnis's materials were lost.

Avrom (Abraham) Goldberg was born in 1881 in Brest-Litovsk (now Brest in Belarus).[24] His father, Aron Noyekh, was a maskil, a member of Hovevei zion, and a Hebrew teacher and poet. One of his brothers, Menachem, later known as Menachem Boraisha, was to become a leading figure in the Yiddish literary life in the United States.

Goldberg received a traditional Jewish and general education, studying first with his father, then in a Talmud-Torah, and then as an external student in Odessa (we can assume that he passed some sort of exit exam without actually attending the school on a regular basis). At the turn of the century, he contributed to a number of periodicals, including *Ha-melitz* and *Ha-tzefira* but also to the Russian-Jewish *Voskhod* and *Rech'*, an organ of the Constitutional-Democratic Party. In 1902, he became a technical employee at *Ha-tzofe*; and in

---

23   Gottesman, *Defining the Yiddish nation*, 56.
24   Finkelstein, *Haynt*, 38–42; Getzel Kressel and Jerold C. Frakes, Goldberg, Abraham," in *Encyclopaedia Judaica*, 2nd ed., vol. 7, 689–690; Khayim Leyb Fuks, "Goldberg, Avraham," in LNYL, vol. 2, 43; Reisen, *Leksikon*, vol. 1, 477–479; Y. Zineman, *In gerangl*, Paris: [no publisher given]), 1952, 114–119; Ravitsh, *Mayn leksikon*, vol. 2, 107–109.

1905, he began to write in Yiddish. As one of the "Founding Fathers" of *Haynt*, Goldberg served for many years as its actual editor (especially after Grünbaum took it over), although formally he was only secretary of the editorial board. According to Jacob Zineman, a historian of Zionism, it was Goldberg who really made *Haynt* both Zionist and great.[25] As a representative of *Haynt*, Goldberg made the acquaintance of European intellectuals like Martin Buber. In 1912, he conducted and published a series of interviews with leading Russian intellectuals like Maxim Gorki on the Jewish question in Russia. He urged them to protest the Beilis trial.

Involved early in the Zionist movement (as a young man he spent a year on a kibbutz in Polesie), Goldberg served on the Central Committee of the Zionist Organization in Poland and was one of the founders of the Shul-kult school network. He belonged to Yitzhak Grünbaum's close circle of friends; no wonder that during the Sejm elections in 1922 he supported the idea of the National Minorities Bloc,[26] and later the Al ha-mishmar faction of the Zionist Organization.[27]

Nearly everyone who met Goldberg would later stress his devotion to both *Haynt* and Zionism. He is remembered as being very demanding towards Yiddish journalists and authors, but a natural born editor. However, as Yitshak Grünbaum noted, "Goldberg did not see the newspaper as a school for beginners, he did not deal with proofreading or editing their articles, notices and stories, he did not teach nor show how to become a good journalist (...). He was in the newspaper like an army commandant. (...). And yet in his writing he was not a fighting man."[28] He died in 1933 in Warsaw. His two sons, Beniamin

---

25   Zineman, *In gerangl*, 114.
26   The National Minorities Bloc was created in 1922 at the initiative of Yitshak Grünbaum as a coalition of ethnic minorities in Poland in the parliamentary elections. It was the second largest party in the 1922 Sejm and had a considerable influence on the choice of the first Polish president, Gabriel Narutowicz, supporting him against a candidate of the National Democracy (Endecja). As the result of an aggressive propaganda campaign against the Left and the National Minorities Bloc, Narutowicz was assassinated just a few days after taking office, on 16 December 1922.
27   The Zionist Organization in Poland was created in 1916 as a branch of the World Zionist Organization. It was the most powerful Zionist party in interwar Poland and its members were referred to as General Zionists. It had two factions: more radical Al ha-Mishmar, led by Yitshak Grünbaum and Apolinary Hartglas, and more moderate Et Livnot, dominated by Jewish politicians from Galicia, such as Yeshaye (Ozjasz) Thon. Although *Haynt* sympathized with Al ha-Mishmar, its columns were open for other Zionist politicians as well and one of its more important contributions was Y. Thon.
28   Yitzhak Grünbaum, *Fun mayn dor* (Tel Aviv: Makor, 1959), 323–324.

(known as Jerzy Borejsza) and Józef (known as Józef Różański), both active in the interwar Communist movement, went down in the annals of twentieth-century Poland.[29]

Simkhe Bunem Pietrushka (Petrushka, Pietruszka) was born in 1893.[30] His father was a Vurker (Warka) Hasid who named his son Simkhe Bunem after the Vurker Rebbe Simkhe Bunem Kalish (1851–1907), although Pietrushka went only by his first name, Simkhe. He received a traditional education and was an outstanding Talmudic scholar with a great memory. An autodidact, he learned several languages (Polish, Russian, German and English), translated from them into Yiddish, and read widely on mathematics, astronomy, geography, history and philosophy. As a young man he would spend whole days in the reading room of the Great Synagogue of Warsaw, reading one book after another. Later on he would help to prepare a large bibliographic catalogue for the Warsaw University Library. And when HIAS hired him in 1920, he would, among other feats, publish a Spanish-Yiddish dictionary for them—although, according to Ber Kuczer, Pietrushka knew no Spanish before.[31]

At the age of 19, Pietrushka started to contribute to the Yiddish press. During the First World War, he wrote anti-Zionist articles for Orthodox newspapers; but in 1924 he actually made a kind of 'aliyah' and started to work as a correspondent for *Haynt*. His political volte-faces were frequent since, as Chaim Finkelstein put it: "He was an opportunist and paid no attention to whom he served and who paid him."[32] In the 1920s, he co-founded at least two ephemeral periodicals, published under the aegis of *Haynt: Der emigrant* and *Handels-tsaytung*. But his sensationalist correspondences sent from Eretz Israel caused such a stir among the readers that *Haynt* ceased publishing them. In 1927, Pietrushka left Palestine for New York, where he intended to publish an American version of *Haynt*; but as nothing came of the plan he returned to Warsaw. Back in Warsaw, he co-founded *Velt-shpigel*, an illustrated Yiddish

---

29   Both of them survived the war in the USSR and took high posts upon returning to Poland. Jerzy Borejsza became involved in re-organizing Polish culture after the war—among others, he founded the leading publishing house "Czytelnik". Józef Różański, on the contrary, worked for the Ministry of Public Security where he gained notoriety as one of the most brutal functionaries. For more information, especially on Jerzy Borejsza, see Eryk Krasucki, *Międzynarodowy komunista: Jerzy Borejsza—biografia polityczna* (Warszawa: Państwowe Wydawnictwo Naukowe, 2009).

30   Finkelstein, *Haynt*, 174–180; Fuks, *Dziennikarze*, 40–45; Reisen, *Leksikon*, vol. 2, 902–904.

31   Ber Kuczer, "Sh. Y. Yatskan—'haynt' un 'hayntige nayes'," in *Di yidishe prese vos iz geven*, 70.

32   Finkelstein, *Haynt*, 176.

weekly, and in 1929 became an editor in *Hayntige nayes*, a sensational afternoon tabloid (both published by the *Haynt* press empire).

Shortly before the outbreak of the Second World War, Pietrushka left Poland and settled first in New York City and later in Montreal. He published a Yiddish folk encyclopedia in two volumes and a Yiddish translation of *Mishnayot* with commentaries. In 1945, the Jewish Theological Seminary of America awarded him an honorary doctorate for his religious publications. He died in 1950, in Montreal.

Moshe Kleinbaum-Sneh was born in 1909 in Radzyń Podlaski.[33] He thus belonged to a generation who had been brought up reading *Haynt*: "I remember that when I was still a boy in a shtetl, I would wait everyday for the hour when *Haynt* was to arrive by train from Warsaw, and how I really devoured every line of our Yiddish newspaper."[34]

Kleinbaum attended a high school and got his MD from Warsaw University in 1935. Already as a student he was involved in Zionist activities. He was a fervent supporter of Grünbaum, so fervent in fact that he was nicknamed "Kleingrünbaum."[35] When Grünbaum made aliyah, the Haynt staff invited Kleinbaum to be their permanent contributor and, shortly later, made him the newspaper's political editor.

In addition to his journalistic activities, Kleinbaum held various important posts in the Zionist Organization in Poland. As such, in the summer of 1939 he participated in the Zionist congress in Geneva. He came back to Warsaw on the last plane and was called up as an army doctor. After the defeat of Poland, he escaped with his family to Vilnius and from there he reached Palestine in 1940.

In Palestine Kleinbaum made an ideological volte-face. Though right after his arrival he joined the Haganah and headed its command until 1946, two years later he co-founded Mapam (United Workers' Party), and a few years later joined the Israeli Communist Party and served as one of its Knesset deputies until 1965. After the Six Day War, bitterly disappointed with the anti-Israeli campaign of the Soviet authorities, he promoted negotiations between Israel and the Arab countries. He died in 1972 in Israel.

---

33   Ibid., 182–184; Emanuel Melzer, "Sneh, Moshe," in YIVO *Encyclopedia of Jews in Eastern Europe*, 1: 904–905.
34   Moshe Sneh, "'Haynt'—a nekhtn on a morgn," in *Di yidishe prese vos iz geven*, 54.
35   Finkelstein, *Haynt*, 182.

Recognizable Patterns

Certain features of these five sample biographies typified the community of *Haynt* journalists and contributors. This allows us to cautiously discern some common characteristics of this circle.

Age. Most of these journalists were born during the last three decades of the nineteenth century. Even Chaim Finkelstein, commonly associated with the "younger generation," was born in 1899. There might be two explanations for this generational profile. One, that the next generation of Yiddish journalists had simply no time to attain popular acclaim—they were still too young to be recognized by readers or to influence them before the outbreak of the Second World War. But another explanation might be that the golden days of Yiddish press were, regardless of the upcoming Holocaust, drawing slowly to an end, since the younger generation increasingly attended Polish schools and slowly but inevitably preferred Polish (or Hebrew) to Yiddish. As Chone Shmeruk noted: "The great achievements of Yiddish literature, theater, and press in Poland could not secure the future of the language in the face of processes over which this cultural system had no control."[36]

Gender. All core staff members and most contributors were men. While a few women, mostly associated with the Zionist circles, contributed to the *Haynt*, some of whom, like Puah Rakovsky,[37] attained significant popularity, no woman belonged to the editorial staff. This situation seems to have been a holdover from nineteenth-century journalism, where women contributed to periodicals but not dailies (it changed in Germany at the end of the century)[38] and were not appointed full-time editors. According to Daria Nałęcz, in interwar Poland only about 6% of active journalists were women, who served as translators, proofreaders, and authors of serialized novels but who hardly ever worked as full-time editors.[39] Taking into account the belatedness of the Yiddish press relative to the European press in other languages,

---

36   Chone Shmeruk, "Hebrew-Yiddish-Polish: A Trilingual Jewish Culture," in *The Jews of Poland Between Two World Wars*, ed. Yisrael Gutman et al. (Hanover, NH, and London: University Press of New England, 1989), 310.

37   For more on Puah Rakovsky see her autobiography, *My Life as a Radical Jewish Woman: Memoirs of a Zionist Feminist in Poland*, ed. with an introduction by Paula E. Hyman (Bloomington and Indianapolis: Indiana University Press, 2002); Paula E. Hyman, "Discovering Puah Rakovsky," *Nashim* 7 (2004): 95–115.

38   Jörg Requate, *Journalismus als Beruf. Entstehung und Entwicklung des Journalistenberufs im 19. Jahrhundert: Deutschland im internationalen Vergleich* (Göttingen: Vandenhoeck & Ruprecht, 1995), 196.

39   Nałęcz, *Zawód dziennikarza*, 116–117.

it seems understandable that it should have taken Jewish women longer to attain employment as journalists and editors. The few women who contributed to *Haynt* were professionally active elsewhere, such as Esther Mangel, who was vice-president of the Zionist Organization in Poland and vice-president of the Women's International Zionist Organization, or Rachel Shteyn, a member of the Warsaw City Council.

Family and social background. Almost all the contributors came from traditional milieus. Quite a few were brought up in Hasidic homes—apart from Pietrushka, it was also true of Ben Tsiyon Ginsberg, the leading correspondent from Galicia (Lviv); Moyshe Gros-Zimmerman, a correspondent from Vienna; Dovid Klaynlerer, a correspondent from Italy; Yosef Shimen Goldshteyn (known as Der Lustiger Pesimist), and others. Some were scions of rabbinical families. Aron Yitshok Grodzenski, a correspondent from Vilnius, was a nephew of the famous Talmudic scholar Chaim Ozer Grodzenski. Michał Hager, a correspondent from Będzin (Bendin) was the son of the local rabbi Menachem Hager. Maskilic families, like Avrom Goldberg's, seem less represented, though one should note Mateusz Mieses, whose family belonged to that milieu, and Shmuel Yankev Imber, a son of Shemaryahu Imber (a maskil Zionist author) and a nephew of Naftali Herz Imber (who wrote "Hatikvah"). There would likely have been more contributors of maskilic origins if *Haynt* had not been published in Yiddish and destined for a mass audience.

Geography. It is impossible to draw any definitive conclusions about the geographical origins of employees and contributors, given that in many cases places of birth are not listed. In the relatively few cases where such information is available, the number of contributors seems to be divided more or less equally between the Kingdom of Poland and the Pale of Settlement. In the Kingdom of Poland, we find such hometowns as Kutno (Sholem Asch), Lublin (Gershon Levin), Łódź (Aron Alperin and Yosef Shimen Goldshteyn), Sieradz (Hersh-Leyb Zhitnitski), Warsaw (Yankev-Kopl Dua, Moyshe Bunim Yustman, Ephraim Kaganovski) and Zamość (I.L. Perets). The Pale of Settlement is represented by Białystok (Puah Rakovsky, Zusman Segalovich), Daugai (Ben Tsiyon Katz), Kėdainiai (Aron Einhorn), Karma (Hillel Zeitlin), and Slutsk (Zalmen Vendroff). A few contributors came from Galicia, including Rava-Ruska (Ben Tsiyon Ginsberg), Boryslav (Moshe Gros-Zimmerman) and Ozerna (Shmuel Yankev Imber). This distribution of places of origin coincides more or less with the range of the readership, which was concentrated in the Kingdom of Poland and Pale of Settlement before 1914 and appeared in Galicia only after 1918.

At least four of the five "Founding Fathers" were Litvaks, which explains how certain Polish critics from the first decade of the twentieth century concluded that the Yiddish press was a "Litvak conspiracy." The role of Litvaks in creating a modern Yiddish press seems, on the other hand, to be underestimated by scholars. Many Litvaks came to the Kingdom of Poland from the Pale and the internal Russian provinces for a number of reasons, mostly economic.[40] The emerging Yiddish press gave journalists and authors of Litvak origin one more reason to settle in Poland. As the writer Avrom Reisen (himself from Minsk) put it in his memoirs:

> Kiev, which was somewhat of a center of Yiddish literature in the 1890s; Odessa, in which Mendele himself, I.Y. Linetsky, Ahad ha-Am, Y. Ch. Ravnitsky and a very young Bialik lived and wrote; even Vilnius, Jerusalem of the North, with outstanding figures of Yiddish literature, like Isaac Meir Dick and others (...)—all of them became overshadowed by a new light that rose in Warsaw. No wonder that every young talent from the aforementioned centers was attracted to Warsaw, and Warsaw became the heart of the Yiddish literature.[41]

This was no less true of the Yiddish press. Even *Der fraynd*, based initially in Petersburg, was moved to Warsaw in 1909 in an attempt to reach a broader and less assimilated audience.[42] For Yatzkan and his circle, it must have been obvious that if they wanted to succeed in the newspaper field they had to base it in Warsaw.

Education. Employees and contributors of *Haynt* definitely followed two patterns discernible in the biographies of many members of Jewish intelligentsia at the turn of the century. Practically all received a traditional religious education in a *heder*. Some then went to a secular (usually Russian) school, which introduced them to the world of non-Jewish studies, while others continued to study in yeshivas yet discovered the sciences, European literature, history, and philosophy themselves, usually by reading any available books on those topics. Simkhe Pietrushka, mentioned above, is a good example of this; but so is one of *Haynt*'s most famous contributors, Sholem Asch. Asch, who began to read secular literature at the age of 15–16, learned the rudiments of German thanks to Moses Mendelssohn's edition of the Psalms, and then proceeded to Schiller, Goethe and Heine.

---

40 For more on Litvak immigration into the Kingdom of Poland see François Guesnet, "Migration et stéréotype: le cas des Juifs russes au Royaume de Pologne à la fin du XIXe siècle," *Cahiers du Monde Russe* 41.4 (2000): 505–518.
41 Avrom Reisen, *Epizodn fun mayn lebn*, vol. 2 (Vilnius: B. Kletskin Farlag, 1929), 145.
42 Stein, *Making Jews modern*, 51.

Many continued their studies at the university level, either in Poland (Warsaw, Vilnius, Lemberg) or abroad (Berlin, Vienna, Leipzig, Bern, Paris). Among the most popular faculties were law, medicine, economics, and philosophy. To give a few more examples: Aron Einhorn studied in Lithuanian yeshivas until he was 17, then passed his gymnasium exams extramurally and left for Paris to study at the Sorbonne. Mordechai Grinfeder, after studying in a yeshiva, went to Hochschule für die Wissenschaft des Judentums in Berlin. Shmuel Yankev Imber graduated from Polish gymnasiums in Złoczów and Tarnopol, began to study German and Oriental studies at Lemberg University before the war, and finished his studies with a PhD at the Jagiellonian University in Cracow after the war. Lastly, Itshok Eliezer Leyzerovitsh, *Haynt*'s correspondent from the Beilis trial, began to study medicine in Leipzig in the middle of his journalism career.

Taking into account the relatively high percentage of those who studied in a German-speaking environment, it would be interesting to explore the possible influence of the German and German-Jewish press on the development of the Yiddish press in Poland. A network of highly-developed German universities attracted many students from the Russian Empire, including many Jews. In 1886, the percentage of Jewish students at German universities was seven times their percentage in the German population; while by 1909, nine percent of German professors were Jewish—something that Jewish students from the Russian Empire could only dream about.[43] Studying in Germany gave one access to all kinds of German and German-Jewish publications, the latter having appeared at the end of the nineteenth century with the foundation of both *Im Deutschen Reich* (the monthly magazine of the Centralverein Deutscher Staatsbürger Jüdischen Glaubens) and *Jüdische Rundschau* (the official organ of the Zionist Organization for Germany from 1896) resulting in "a new era in the field of German Jewish journalism: the era of the political newspapers."[44] Next to these two leading periodicals, there existed an ocean of smaller bulletins published by Jewish youth groups of all political and religious orientations, constituting a Jewish response to the growth of nationalism and anti-Semitism in Germany. How much the 'Ostjuden' benefited from it is an

---

43 Lisa Swartout, "Facing Antisemitism: Jewish Students at German Universities, 1890–1914," *Leipziger Beiträge zur jüdischen Geschichte und Kultur* 2 (2004), 149–165, here 152–155. For more on students from the Russian Empire in Germany see Claudie Weill, *Étudiants russes en Allemagne, 1900–1914: quand la Russie frappait aux portes de l'Europe* (Paris: L'Harmattan, 1996).

44 Margaret T. Edelheim-Muehsam, "The Jewish Press in Germany," *Leo Baeck Institute Yearbook* 1 (1956), 163–176, here 168.

open question, but the German-Jewish press probably served as their model for what a modern Jewish press should look like and constitute.

Languages. The very fact of being born in the second half of the nineteenth century or the beginning of the twentieth century in multinational, multicultural and multilingual Eastern Europe meant that *Haynt* staff members and contributors were polyglots (as were many in their world). We can safely assume that, having received a traditional religious education, all of them had more or less mastered Hebrew. In fact, many of them, like Hillel Zeitlin and Sholem Asch, published their first works in Hebrew, which was relatively common for Yiddish authors at the turn of the century. Their maternal languages differed—while in many cases it was Yiddish, it sometimes also happened that their native language was Russian or Polish. Alternatively, one could learn Yiddish at home and Polish, Russian, Ukrainian and/or other languages "by osmosis" or (especially in the case of Russian) at school. The most common foreign languages mastered were, of course, German and French, although some knew more exotic languages for the region—one of the first contributors, Eliezer Dovid Finkel, knew Latin, Greek, some Japanese, and some Arabic.

Publishing a newspaper in Yiddish or contributing to such a newspaper, both before and after 1918, was a political as well as cultural choice. Some contributors, like Apolinary Hartglas, learned Yiddish precisely for the publishing field. However, these political choices did not always correlate with personal choices, regarding the education of their children and choice of language(s) spoken at home. I would risk a hypothesis (based more on intuition than on sources) that most *Haynt* contributors considered Yiddish to be a language of today—but not a language of tomorrow. The fact is that in 1933 the "Alt-nay" cooperative decided to publish a Polish-language weekly *Opinia*, which published selected materials from *Haynt* translated into Polish.[45] At the same time (in 1932, to be precise), they also launched a Hebrew weekly *Ba-derech*. Contents of each issue of *Opinia* and *Ba-derech*, as well as their advertisements, were published in *Haynt*, usually on its front page (respectively in Polish and Hebrew, although at the beginning there were also Yiddish advertisements for *Opinia*); but while the first one reached a circulation of around 25,000 copies, the latter did not attract the expected audience and was closed down in 1937. It is characteristic that, faced with the rapidly growing linguistic acculturation of the younger generation, *Haynt* did not issue a call to re-Yiddishize them, but rather offered them a summary of its contents—all in Polish.

---

45   For more on *Opinia* see Katrin Steffen, *Jüdische Polonität: Ethnizität und Nation im Spiegel der polnischsprachigen jüdischen Presse 1918–1939* (Göttingen: Vandenhoeck & Ruprecht, 2004), passim.

War itineraries. The five sample biographies reflect a sad truth: among those who were alive in Poland on September 1st, 1939, usually only those who left Warsaw had a chance of survival. Some of them, like Kleinbaum-Sneh, Apolinary Hartglas or Zusman Segalovitsh, managed to reach Palestine. Several others escaped to the East and survived the war in the Soviet Union, such as Ephraim Kaganovski, Bernard Singer, Aron Tsofnas or Yosef Shimen Goldshteyn. After the war, they were repatriated to Poland but left shortly afterwards, mostly for Israel. It is still unknown how many contributors survived the war in Poland—so far this can be said only of the historian Philip Friedman. Among those who remained in Poland, most perished in the Warsaw ghetto (at least 17 people). Among them were Aron Gavze, Nechemia Finkelshteyn and Aron Einhorn, active till the very end organizing relief for their fellow journalists.

Conclusions

A group picture of Yiddish journalists associated with the leading Yiddish daily is far from complete. But so is the history of the *Haynt* and of the Yiddish press in general. The Holocaust cut its history short at a moment when there was still so much to do. It destroyed practically all the overlapping circles—editors, journalists, readers; and this world was never to be reconstructed. While the Yiddish press continued after the Holocaust all over the world, never again would it have such influence over readers' minds as it had before 1939.

Haynt, together with several other Yiddish periodicals, served as a gateway for Jewish modernization and a meeting point for both first- and second-generation Jewish intelligentsia. As Avrom Goldberg wrote in his article for the *Haynt* jubilee-book in 1928: "We approached the Jewish press, Jewish journalism not only as a source of income, as a profession (...) but as a measure that helps us to realize our lifelong ideal."[46] The newspaper's editors displayed a number of features characteristic of an intelligentsia: liberal professions (journalism), adequate levels of education, creating and promoting new cultural values and, above all, a self-perception of being an intellectual elite, in this case of the Jewish nation.[47] On the other hand, for those who, unlike Goldberg, came from Hasidic milieus and had no models for writing careers in their

---

46 Avrom Goldberg, "Di entshtehung un der veg fun 'haynt'," in *Haynt yubiley-bukh* (Varshe, 1928), 3 [no publisher given but it was published by *Haynt*].

47 For more on the definition of Jewish intelligentsia in the second half of the 19th century see Helena Datner, *Ta i tamta strona: Żydowska inteligencja Warszawy drugiej połowy XIX wieku* (Warszawa: Żydowski Instytut Historyczny, 2007).

neighborhood, contributing to *Haynt* (often the result of reading *Haynt* in the first place) might have been a way to realize more modest ambitions: to see one's name in print, to find an additional source of income, and to become a part of a larger and more attractive world.

However, the confrontation between older and younger contributors did not resolve itself smoothly. Reorganizing *Haynt* into "Alt-nay" was a result of a longtime conflict between the editorial staff and the Finkelstein brothers, who were the formal owners of the newspaper. After a six-week strike of the entire staff (journalists, administration and printing house), the employees had won. At this stage of archival research, it is difficult to say who was right in the conflict: the employees who, according to Chaim Finkelstein, were not paid on time,[48] or the owners. In 1933, shortly after Goldberg's death, Nechemia Finkelshteyn wrote ironically to Goldberg's brother, the famous Yiddish author Menachem Boraisha (based in the United States), about the cooperative consisting of 'proletarians' as opposed to old-time 'bourgeois' like himself.[49] Apart from economic reasons, the conflict might have had something to do with different visions of what *Haynt* was supposed to be. The vision of the 'Founding Fathers' was realized around 1905, and their generation still belonged very much to the nineteenth century. They could definitely count as a success the fact that the newspaper they had created was still appearing twenty years later. And as Yiddish mass-circulation press (including *Haynt*) was invented and run mostly by Litvaks, its success is testimony to the deep influence of Litvaks on Polish Jewry in interwar Poland. In fact, Litvaks had become part of the fabric of Polish Jewry. But their audience was growing older with them.

The *Haynt-mishpokhe* was dispersed all over the world, but we could say that its real end was met in the Warsaw ghetto, as mentioned earlier. The recently published war correspondence of Chaim Finkelstein (who spent the war in New York) with his family in the Warsaw ghetto is proof of the respect and confidence he had in two leading *Haynt* personalities, Nechemia Finkelshteyn and Aron Gavze. They consistently informed him about his family's condition, and he often reminded his wife that she could count on them if she needed help.[50] As often happens, in the shadow of extreme danger old-time conflicts

---

48   Chaim Finkelstein gives his account of the conflict in: Finkelstein, *Haynt*, in *Fun noentn over*, [no editors given] vol. 2 (New York: Congress for Jewish Culture, 1956), 113, 115–121.
49   YIVO Archives, RG 641, Files of Menachem Boraisha, Box 1, Folder 17.11, Letter of Nechemia Finkelshteyn to Menachem Boraisha dated 29.11.1933, no pagination.
50   *...Tęsknota nachodzi nas jak ciężka choroba...Korespondencja wojenna rodziny Finkelsztejnów*, ed. Ewa Koźmińska-Frejlak (Warszawa: Stowarzyszenie Centrum Badań nad Zagładą Żydów, 2012), passim.

and differences became forgotten while longtime ties become crucial, therefore fully justifying calling the *Haynt* team a family (*mishpokhe*).

It was not only the vision that was dying with the older and younger generations in the Warsaw ghetto. The world of the Jewish intelligentsia, as a transnational and multilingual group, was drawing to an end, as well. Those who had chosen Palestine (and, consequently, Israel) gave birth to a Hebrew-speaking Israeli intelligentsia. Those who had chosen the United States gave birth to an American Jewish intelligentsia. Those who survived the Holocaust in such countries as France, Poland and the Soviet Union either eventually passed away without leaving successors or assimilated linguistically. The story of *Haynt* is thus a closed chapter now. As Moshe Kleinbaum-Sneh put it in the title of his memoirs on *Haynt*, it was a yesterday with no tomorrow, *a nekhtn on a morgn*.

CHAPTER 11

A Warsaw Story: Polish-Jewish Relations during the First World War

Robert Blobaum

This essay is about an accelerated downhill slide in Polish-Jewish relations in Warsaw that is part of a larger central and east European story about the deterioration of Christian-Jewish relations at the turn of the twentieth century. During the First World War, the image of the speculating and profiteering Jew became widespread in central Europe especially during the second half of the war, when food and other shortages became the norm. That image became prominent in the front-line town of Freiburg, for example, and was disseminated through the caricatures of the Munich-based *Simplicissimus*.[1] In Berlin, not only were Jewish middlemen blamed for profiteering, but the very idea of profit became characterized as unpatriotic; though rising anti-Semitism in wartime Berlin also owed much to an influx of Jewish refugees.[2] In Vienna, where conditions most closely approximated those in Warsaw, the food profiteer was likewise depicted as stereotypically male and Jewish. Jews were also choice targets there for rumors about internal enemies, while tens of thousands of Jewish refugees from Galicia fed wartime "expulsion fantasies" that would actually become law in September 1919.[3]

---

1 Roger Chickering, *The Great War and Urban Life in Germany: Freiburg, 1914–1918* (Cambridge: Cambridge University Press, 2007), 498; Jean-Louis Robert, "The Image of the Profiteer," in Jay Winter and Jean-Louis Robert (eds.), *Capital Cities at War: Paris, London, Berlin, 1914–1919*, vol. 1 (Cambridge: Cambridge University Press, 1997), 131.

2 Belinda J. Davis, *Home Fires Burning: Food, Politics and Everyday Life in World War I Berlin* (Chapel Hill, NC: University of North Carolina Press, 2000), 73.

3 Maureen Healy, *Vienna and the Fall of the Habsburg Empire: Total War and Everyday Life in World War I* (Cambridge: Cambridge University Press, 2004), 67, 86, and 306. As in Warsaw, the presence of a large number of Jewish refugees in Vienna and the significance of welfare work among them led to a perceptible shift in Jewish political culture that transformed Zionism into a popular movement but also raised suspicions of Jewish loyalty among the Viennese Christian population; see David Rechter, *The Jews of Vienna and the First World War* (London: The Littman Library of Jewish Civilization, 2001), 83–84. About the Jewish experience in central and eastern Europe more generally, see Frank Schuster, *Zwischen allen Fronten: Osteuropäische Juden während des Ersten Weltkrieges (1914–1919)* (Cologne: Böhlau Verlag,

Exaggerated notions of illegitimate Jewish wealth, excessive influence, overpopulation, and disproportionate political clout, already common in central and eastern Europe before the war, now found "confirmation." Responsibility for the unprecedented social and economic catastrophe of wartime was rather easily transferred onto Christian Europe's eternal "other." The war, its deprivations, and the long-term damages it inflicted on economies and societies helped produce the virulent strain of anti-Semitism that would spread through much of Europe in the interwar years.

In Warsaw, the period immediately preceding the First World War had already witnessed a rapid deterioration in Polish-Jewish relations, marked by increasingly intense economic competition and political conflict that reshaped old ethno-religious stereotypes and gave rise to new ones. Polish-Jewish disputes over representation in the projected but as yet unrealized bodies of municipal government, Jewish refusals to support Polish national candidates in elections to the Russian State Duma, and Polish boycotts of Jewish commerce and trade were still fresh memories when war broke out in the summer of 1914.[4] Although there was tentative and partial unity between Poles and Jews at the very outset of the war such solidarity would give way soon enough to renewed conflict, amplified by the ever-increasing hardships brought on by Europe's first total war.

In the following pages, I seek to explore themes that transcended Warsaw's periods of Russian rule and German occupation, despite the dramatically different attitudes of these regimes toward the Jewish population. The actions of the Russian army, to be sure, were largely responsible for the large Jewish refugee presence in the city in 1915 and 1916, one of the main sources of Polish-Jewish tensions. By contrast, the principal goal of the German occupational regime was to maintain stability, which required a balancing act between Poles and Jews in Warsaw and which many Poles interpreted as serving Jewish interests. The existential crisis of wartime, however, would do more than the presence of either Russians or Germans to define Polish-Jewish relations, which

---

2004). For the Polish Kingdom specifically, see Konrad Zieliński, *Stosunki polsko-żydowskie na ziemiach Królestwa Polskiego w czasie pierwszej wojny światowej* (Lublin: Wydawnictwo Uniwersytetu Marii Curie-Skłodowskiej, 2005).

4 On Polish-Jewish relations in Warsaw on the very eve of the war, see Robert Blobaum, "The Politics of Antisemitism in Fin-de-Siècle Warsaw," *The Journal of Modern History* 73.2 (2001), 275–306. For a longer perspective, see Magdalena Opalski and Israel Bartal, *Poles and Jews: A Failed Brotherhood* (Hanover, NH: Brandeis University Press, 1992) and Theodore R. Weeks, *From Assimilation to Antisemitism: The "Jewish Question" in Poland, 1850–1914* (Dekalb, IL: Northern Illinois University Press, 2006).

reached the breaking point on two occasions—at the time of Russian evacuation in the summer of 1915 and as Polish forces took control of the city from the Germans in November 1918. In fact, it is difficult to find anything that was not contested between Warsaw's Poles and Jews during the war, including spare change. Yet despite the heightened tensions, inter-communal violence was, remarkably enough, usually avoided. The absence of outright rupture, anticlimactic and consequently unexplored, also requires our attention.

•••

For Warsaw's Jews, the first weeks of the war were already fraught with fears of a pogrom brought on by Russian army commanders, who both believed and encouraged rumors of wholesale Jewish espionage on behalf of the Central Powers.[5] The widespread belief that Jews constituted an "unreliable element" that posed a security risk to Russian troops was reflected in the instructions to the Warsaw Superintendent of Police to suspend the issuing of passports to Warsaw Jews and to provide information about any Jews from Warsaw who were currently abroad. Shortly thereafter, drunken soldiers from the 86th infantry regiment stationed in Warsaw began to beat Jews whom they encountered at random. In early September, the rumored appearance of an article in the Yiddish-language *Der moment*, which supposedly contained information on how Jews in Warsaw should greet German troops, provoked a police investigation into Jewish attitudes. Although no such article had ever appeared, these and other, similar rumors heightened fears of impending violence within the Warsaw Jewish community.[6]

Meanwhile, the outbreak of the war was accompanied by panic-buying, immediate price increases, a run on local banks, and the hoarding of coin as a hedge against inflation of paper banknotes. Combined with the behavior of the Russian army, the association of Jews with coin-hoarding—which would eventually figure in one-fifth of the reports of anti-Jewish violence in the

---

5 For a more extended discussion of the Russian army's treatment of Jews in the western part of the empire during the war years, see Daniel Graf, "Military Rule behind the Russian Front, 1914–1917," *Jahrbücher für Geschichte Osteuropas* 22 (1974), 390–411 and Eric Lohr, "The Russian Army and the Jews: Mass Deportation, Hostages and Violence during World War I," *The Russian Review* 60 (July 2001), 404–419.

6 Archiwum Państwowe m. st. Warszawy (APW), Zarząd Oberpolicmajstra Warszawskiego (ZOW) 1116. *Der moment*, along with *Haynt*, were the two major Yiddish dailies published in Warsaw before the First World War. During the war, they would become closely associated with Folkist and Zionist political factions, respectively; see Michael Steinlauf, "The Polish-Jewish Daily Press," *Polin: A Journal of Polish-Jewish Studies* 2 (1987), 219–245, 220, 228.

Polish Kingdom during the first year of the war[7]—alarmed even the National Democrats (Endecja), who shared Jewish fears of major disorders in the city. *Gazeta Poranna 2 grosze*, which had begun publication in 1912 in order to promote the Endecja-led anti-Jewish boycott, warned: "All manifestations of physical violence toward Jews we regard as harmful, above all for Polish society, and beneath our national dignity."[8]

Perhaps because the Endecja, the most powerful political organization in Warsaw, was able to moderate its anti-Jewish stance, Poles and Jews were able to set aside their differences during the immediate outbreak of the war and advance of German forces on Warsaw.[9] With mobilization, Polish and Jewish families congregated at mustering points for reservists in Warsaw, where they shared their common concerns.[10] The mass circulation press in Warsaw, whether Polish or Yiddish-language, received with enthusiasm the August 14 proclamation of Grand Duke Nikolai Nikolaevich, Russian commander-in-chief and uncle of the tsar, which promised to reunite Poland under the scepter of the Romanovs.[11] Once the Russian authorities permitted it, Jewish day laborers joined Poles for work on field fortifications as the front moved closer to Warsaw in September.[12] As the first wave of refugees began to arrive in Warsaw from the western provinces of the Polish Kingdom, particularly from the area around Kalisz, little heed was paid publicly to their religion or ethnicity, although around half of them were Jewish.[13] Then in October, as Russian defensive lines held against the German assault, thanksgiving prayer services were held in both St. John's Cathedral and the Great Synagogue on Tłomackie

---

7   Eric Lohr, *Nationalizing the Russian Empire: The Campaign Against Enemy Aliens during World War I* (Cambridge, MA: Harvard University Press, 2003), 148.
8   "Szkodliwe odruchy," *Gazeta Poranna 2 grosze* 235 (26 August 1914), 1.
9   There had always been a certain political instrumentality to the Endecja's anti-Jewish politics; for more on the ideological evolution of exclusionary Polish nationalism before the First World War, see Brian Porter, *When Nationalism Began to Hate: Imagining Politics in Nineteenth-Century Poland* (New York: Oxford University Press, 2000).
10 Zieliński, *Stosunki polsko-żydowskie*, 102.
11 "Żydzi a odezwa do polaków," *Kurjer Warszawski* 227 (18 August 1914, aft. ed.), 2.
12 "Żydzi do fortec," *Nowa Gazeta* 421 (11 September 1914, morn. ed.), 1. According to the Warsaw Superintendent of Police, local Jews were doing everything at this time to deflect suspicion that they were siding with the enemy, which also included participation in the creation of infirmaries for the wounded returning from the front and volunteering to work in the ambulance service and as nurses; APW, ZOW 1116.
13 Franciszek Herbst, "Działalność społeczna i samorządowa," in Krzysztof Dunin-Wąsowicz (ed.), *Warszawa w pamiętnikach pierwszej wojny światowej* (Warsaw: Państwowe Instytut Wydawniczy, 1971), 287–288.

Street, the main symbolic reference points for the Roman Catholic and Jewish communities in Warsaw.[14]

Even in this period of relative calm, however, tensions lurked just below the surface. Although the pro-Russian Endecja, recalling the urban violence of the 1905 revolution, may have feared mass disorders in Warsaw, it nevertheless suspected that Jewish claims of loyalty to the tsarist authorities were insincere.[15] Nor did it take long for public assistance to become a bone of contention. To be sure, the officially sanctioned Warsaw Citizens Committee (known locally as the KO), which was formed immediately upon the outbreak of the war by the city's notables and would assume control over a wide range of social welfare activities, received an early offer of cooperation from representatives of all Jewish philanthropic societies in the city.[16] Already in the war's first month, however, the Polish conservative daily *Kurjer Warszawski* would claim that lists submitted to the KO containing the names of individuals needing assistance in Jewish neighborhoods had been deliberately falsified, the first of many charges of fraud related to the provision of wartime public assistance to the Jewish community.[17] Jews, for their part, complained immediately and directly to the Committee about the spread of these and other false rumors.[18]

Access to the KO's employment agencies became another early source of wartime Polish-Jewish conflict. With unemployment spreading throughout

---

14 "Nabożeństwo dziękczynne," *Kurjer Warszawski* 292 (22 October 1914, aft. ed.), 3; "Komitet Synagogi na Tłomackiem," *Nowa Gazeta* 550 (25 Oct. 1914, morn. ed), 4. At the beginning of the war, the Great Synagogue built in 1878 could still be considered a bastion of Warsaw's assimilated Jewish elite. By the end of the war, however, the Synagogue's congregation had changed into a much more inclusive community whose representatives were more democratic and nationally-minded; see Alexander Guterman, "The Congregation of the Great Synagogue in Warsaw: Its Changing Social Composition and Ideological Affiliations," *Polin: Studies in Polish Jewry* 13 (1998), 112–126.

15 "Umizgi," *Gazeta Poranna 2 grosze* 229, (20 August 1914), 1.

16 APW, Komitet Obywatelski m. Warszawy (KOMW) 1, protocol no. 8 of 8 August 1914. Three of the original fifteen members of the Warsaw Citizens Committee—Mieczysław Pfeiffer, Henryk Konic, and Józef Natanson—were from the assimilated Jewish elite, leading *Haynt* to express its dissatisfaction that no Jewish activists "who actually live among Jews" were selected to serve on the KO; Zieliński, *Stosunki polsko-żydowskie*, 172.

17 "Akcja ratunkowa," *Kurjer Warszawski* 231 (22 August 1914), 2. A month later, the Polish nationalist press would come to consider Jews a "real plague" on the stores of the KO; Jewish women supposedly brought children to these stores by the "bunches" to haul away "bagfuls" of purchased salt; "Sklepy Komitetu Obywatelskiego," *Gazeta Poranna 2 grosze* 262 (22 September 1914), 1.

18 APW, KOMW 1, protocol no. 9 of 8 August 1914.

the city already during the war's first month, Christian workers began to expel their Jewish counterparts from the KO's labor offices. To maintain peace, a separate office for day workers was established in the Jewish community.[19] Perhaps the most alarming development before October resulted from the war's immediate effect on landlord-tenant relations, particularly in the form of disputes over unpaid rent, which raised renewed fears of potential anti-Jewish disturbances. Although the publication of a special appeal was thought to be "premature," the KO agreed to work with building superintendents and its own district instructors to calm Polish opinion.[20]

Ironically, the turning back of the German attack on Warsaw proved devastating for the Jews. The association of Jews with Germans, as already noted, was reflected in the spy scare of the war's first months, to which Russian officials and army officers, more than Polish opinion, initially gave greater credence.[21] As German forces were temporarily rolled back through small towns like Skierniewice and Rawa later that fall, observers would note that the front line of battle had seemingly crossed the middle of their Jewish districts, from which the Russian army then expelled entire populations, forcing tens of thousands to seek refuge in Warsaw.[22] These forcible expulsions of Jews from the immediate front zone toward the interior involved a handful of communities before January 1915, after which time a more systematic policy of coordinated mass expulsions of Jews began in earnest.[23] Even though Jewish behavior in Warsaw remained loyal and beyond political reproach, many Warsaw Jews

---

19 Ibid., protocol no. 31 of 26 August 1914.
20 Ibid., protocol no. 32 of 27 August 1914. Despite the relatively high proportion of Jewish ownership of rental properties, the long-standing impression that Jews dominated the real estate market in Warsaw is a false one. According to Konrad Zieliński, Jews comprised roughly one-third of all owners of real estate in Warsaw before the war, a percentage slightly lower than the Jewish proportion of the city's population; Zieliński, *Stosunki polsko-żydowskie*, 33.
21 At times, these rumors of Jewish spying came from far afield. The Chief of the Volhynia Provincial Gendarmes, for example, reported receiving information that Warsaw Jewish spies were providing the Germans with information on Russian troop locations on maps that were sealed in bottles and then allowed to float down the Vistula from where they were retrieved by the enemy; APW, ZOW 1116.
22 Stanisław Dzikowski, *Rok wojny w Warszawie: Notatki* (Kraków: Centralne Biuro Wydawnictw N.K.N., 1916), 30–33. The Russian army's actions at the end of October had also reportedly led to an influx of 4000 refugees from Grodzisk alone, who were followed by hundreds more from Mława; see "Żydzi bezdomni," *Nowa Gazeta* 509 (30 October 1914, aft. ed.), 2.
23 Graf, *Military Rule*, 398.

now sought additional insurance by changing their German-sounding names to Slavic ones.[24] Jewish leaders also became justifiably alarmed, first by the idea and then by the reality of state confiscations of property from Warsaw's ethnic Germans, viewing the violation of property rights on the basis of ethnicity as a slippery slope that could easily extend to the Jewish community.[25]

Indeed, though the Russian army's actions against persons and property were initially aimed at citizens and subjects of enemy states, they were subsequently extended to Russian subjects—Germans, Jews, Muslims and others—who were easily conflated into the category of "enemy aliens."[26] In particular, the association of Jews with the German enemy and the ill-treatment of Jews on Warsaw's periphery by the Russian army would over time become a self-fulfilling prophesy, as stories of the experiences of the refugees generated negative attitudes within Warsaw's Jewish community toward the cause of Russian arms. In the spring of 1915, Russian Army headquarters and the Warsaw Governor-General coordinated the mass expulsion of Jews from some forty towns in the vicinity of Warsaw, affecting roughly 100,000 individuals, 80,000 of whom appeared in the city shortly thereafter.[27] In early March, the Warsaw Governor had announced that all letters and correspondence in Yiddish would be destroyed because of the difficulties that language posed for Russian censorship.[28] A couple of weeks before the German takeover of the city in the summer of 1915, the Russian authorities banned the publication of all Yiddish- and Hebrew-language periodicals in the Polish Kingdom, the most important of which were located in Warsaw, including the mass circulation dailies *Haynt, Der moment*, and *Ha-tzefira*.[29]

The final weeks of Russian rule in Warsaw were accompanied by a sharp rise in anti-Jewish pronouncements and actions among the local Polish population. By the time the Russians began to prepare their evacuation of the city in the summer of 1915, Polish-Jewish relations had deteriorated to the point that the already notorious anti-Semite Andrzej Niemojewski, whom even

---

24 "O zmianę nazwiska," *Nowa Gazeta* 576 (10 December 1914, morn. ed.), 2.
25 In November 1914 the state began to entertain the idea of confiscating the city's "German" gasworks, with its assets of approximately 1 million rubles in cash, certificates and bonds, which were then indeed sequestered before the winter holidays; "Konfiskaty," *Nowa Gazeta* 541 (18 November 1914, aft. ed.), 2; "Sekwester Zakładów Gazowych," *Nowa Gazeta* 600 (24 December 1914, morn. ed.), 2.
26 Lohr, *Nationalizing the Russian Empire*, 1.
27 Lohr, *The Russian Army*, 409–410.
28 "Żydowskie listy," *Gazeta Poranna 2 grosze* 62 (3 March 1915), 3.
29 *Kurjer Warszawski* 197(19 July 1915, spec. ed.), 3; "Zawieszenie gazet," *Nowa Gazeta* 322a (19 July 1915), 2; Zieliński, *Stosunki polsko-żydowskie*, 116.

Kurjer Warszawski criticized for his "one-sidedness" and "demagogic treatment of serious questions," was greeted with "thunderous applause" from an overflowing audience at the Museum of Agriculture and Industry when he spoke of Jewish sins against Polish national dignity.[30] Ethnic-based animosity had also taken a cultural turn in the Polish Catholic and nationalist campaign over the content of films playing in Warsaw's cinemas. The Yiddish and Hebrew newspapers were attacked when they opposed proposals to place controls on movie houses, described by the Polish press as "hotbeds of moral depravity" for showing what were then wildly popular Russian crime and erotic-genre films. To Polish Catholic protests against "the systematic poisoning of society by the cinemas," the Jewish press (according to *Kurjer Warszawski*), concerned as it supposedly was for profit over morality, had screamed "Hands off! This is our business and nobody is allowed to touch it."[31] The Warsaw Citizens Committee, for its part, considered the application of coercive measures against the Jewish-owned movie houses, and would have done so had not the German occupation of the city brought an end to the showing of Russian films.

Meanwhile, the Russian retreat from the Warsaw military region coincided with new expulsions that took on the character of outright pogroms in which soldiers and the local Christian population joined in the looting and seizure of Jewish property.[32] In Warsaw itself, sudden and steep inflation caused by panic-buying, goods shortages, and hoarding of coin reminiscent of the war's first weeks again led to a channeling of popular anger onto Jews. Although acts of collective violence were ultimately avoided inside the city's contemporaneous borders, local Poles did join soldiers in the looting of Jewish stores in the nearby suburbs of Czyste and Błonie. Even on Warsaw's immediate periphery, however, such incidents were not as widespread as elsewhere in the Polish Kingdom.[33]

---

30 "Odczyt Niemojewskiego," *Kurjer Warszawski* 160 (12 June 1915), 4–5.

31 "W sprawie kinematografów," *Kurjer Warszawski* 174 (26 June 1915, aft. ed.), 4. During the course of the Russian evacuation and despite increasing desperate economic conditions, twenty-five cinemas continued to operate in Warsaw as eager audiences devoured the Russian films, see Krzysztof Dunin-Wąsowicz, *Warszawa w czasie pierwszej wojny światowej* (Warsaw: Państwowe Instytut Wydawniczy, 1974), 222.

32 Lohr, *The Russian Army*, 415. In the front zones, the army tolerated the participation of soldiers in the plundering and rape of Jews, while local Poles gathered outside with carts to haul off their share of the remaining loot. The Warsaw Governor-General himself expressed the concern that "especially if soldiers participated," the local population could not be controlled; see also Lohr, *Nationalizing the Russian Empire*, 17.

33 Zieliński, *Stosunki polsko-żydwoskie*, 132.

Having suffered considerably more from the "various repressions" of the tsarist authorities, as one historian put it, Warsaw's Jews were bound to express far greater sympathy than Poles towards the arriving Germans.[34] Unlike the Poles, who had mixed feelings about the Russian evacuation and the arrival of new occupiers, most Jews greeted the end of Russian rule with open relief, a natural response to the terror they had experienced in the war's first year in Warsaw, a frontline city. According to a German officer's letter published in *Der Lodzer Zeitung* and later quoted in *Gazeta Poranna 2 grosze*: "The Jewish population greeted us by removing their caps and with joyful shouts."[35] Though such reports of Jewish enthusiasm for the German entrance into Warsaw may be exaggerated, they nevertheless reveal a division in attitudes toward the Germans that would become an important factor in the intensification of mutual animosities and recriminations in Polish-Jewish relations.

For their part, the Germans made it clear from the beginning that the public aggravation of ethnic tensions would not be tolerated.[36] In his first meeting with editors of Warsaw's local dailies and weeklies, the new German press director Georg Cleinow called for a complete suspension of Polish-Jewish hostilities in print as well as in social and public spheres.[37] One visible consequence was a change on the masthead of *Gazeta Poranna 2 grosze*, which under the Russians still contained the slogan "Don't Buy from Jews." This would disappear and be replaced by the milder message: "We accept advertisements from Christian firms only." While the antisemitic daily was forced to become more circumspect, it found other ways of expressing itself—for example, in reporting on any and all Jewish nationalist and Zionist attacks that appeared in *Der moment* or *Haynt* on the Warsaw assimilationists and the community administrative board that they, together with the Orthodox Jewish leadership, still dominated.[38]

---

34 Dunin-Wąsowicz, *Warszawa*, 22.

35 "Niemcy w Warszawie," *Gazeta Poranna 2 grosze* 224 (15 August 1915), 1.

36 On the wartime policies of the imperial German state toward the Jews in both the Kaiserreich and in the occupied territories, see the classic study of Egmont Zechlin, *Die deutsche Politik und die Juden im Ersten Weltkrieg* (Göttingen: Vandenhoeck u. Ruprecht, 1969). On the formulation of early German occupation policy toward Warsaw in particular, see Marta Polsakiewicz, "Spezifika deutscher Besatzungspolitik in Warschau 1914–1916," *Zeitschrift für Ostmitteleuropa-Forschung* 58.4 (2009), 501–537.

37 Aleksander Kraushar, *Warszawa podczas okupacji niemieckiej 1915–1918: Notatki naocznego świadka* (Lwów: Wydawnictwo Zakładu Narodowego im. Ossolińskich, 1921), 16–17.

38 To cite but a couple of examples of this kind of reporting, see "O interesy żydowskie," *Gazeta Poranna 2 grosze* 222 (13 August 1915), 1–2 and "O przedstawicielstwo żydów," *Gazeta Poranna 2 grosze* 329 (29 November 1915), 3.

The Germans would ultimately discover that calming Polish-Jewish relations in the aftermath of the Russian evacuation was easier said than done. Indeed, within a few months of the establishment of the German occupation zone in the Polish Kingdom, the newly appointed Warsaw Governor-General Hans von Beseler reported to the Kaiser that "the political future of the country" required a solution to the "difficult and complicated Jewish question."[39] Beseler had already witnessed disputes over the Citizens Guard, a militia formed under the Warsaw Citizens Committee to preserve order in the city following the Russian evacuation until it could be replaced by a regular police force. Staffed primarily by young male participants in Polish sporting organizations, which in turn had been strongly influenced by the National Democrats, it is not hard to imagine the consternation aroused by the militia's appearance in the Jewish community. In September, Jewish newspaper editors sent a memorial to the authorities citing thirty-five serious incidents of violations of the law and discrimination against Jews by the Citizens Guard in the second half of August alone.[40] By the same token, Jewish participation in the Citizens Guard, particularly in Polish residential areas, was practically non-existent.[41]

Thus, once the German occupation authorities established themselves in Warsaw, they seemed determined to perform a balancing act between Poles and Jews as a means of maintaining the peace. The affinity of Yiddish to German would naturally lead to the employment of Jews as interpreters and to their recruitment as office personnel in the occupation administration, which immediately aroused the ire of Warsaw's Poles.[42] According to Alexander Kraushar, himself from an assimilated family unfamiliar with Yiddish, the tax offices in the occupation administration were occupied "mainly by persons of

---

39   Archiwum Glowny Akt Dawnych (AGAD), Cesarsko-Niemieckie Generał-Gubernatorstwa w Warszawie (CNGGW) 1, Report of General Hans von Beseler of 23 October 1915.

40   Zieliński, *Stosunki polsko-żydowskie*, 228. On the very day of its official "coming out" during the Russian evacuation, the Citizens Guard was forced to respond to charges of anti-Jewish discrimination; see "Straż Obywatelska," *Nowa Gazeta* 336 (27 July 1915, morn. ed.), 2. A commission subsequently created under the city administration to investigate these charges determined, after some nine months had passed, that they could not be verified; "Skarga redaktorów żargonowskich," *Gazeta Poranna 2 grosze* 134 (15 May 1916), 3.

41   For more on this issue, see the memoir of Mieczysław Jankowski, a member of the Citizens Guard stationed in the Jewish quarter; Mieczysław Jankowski, "Pierwsze dni okupacji niemieckiej," *Warszawa w pamiętnikach*, 140–141. Even after the Citizens Guard was transformed into a regular police force under the city administration, Jews constituted a mere five percent of its total personnel; "Z Rady Miejskiej," *Nowa Gazeta* 339 (13 August 1917, aft. ed.), 1–2.

42   Jankowski, *Pierwsze dni*, 140; see also Zieliński, *Stosunki polsko-żydowskie*, 229–230.

Litvak descent."[43] The reliance of the occupation authorities on experienced Jewish merchants to procure grain, livestock, and metals meant that, although state monopolies were universal, contracts for the sale of regulated goods went primarily to Jews.[44] At the same time, the Germans entrusted Polish-dominated institutions—the Warsaw Citizens Committee, its presidium and its sections, as well as their successors in a reorganized city administration—with the essentials of municipal government, local law enforcement, and the distribution of basic provisions, all of which became arenas of conflict with Jews, who felt woefully underrepresented and victims of on-going discrimination.[45] Perhaps the best evidence of German efforts to maintain a sense of fair play between Warsaw's Poles and Jews occurred on the eve of the Easter and Passover holidays in 1917, at which time they announced a 25% reduction in flour rations. In their announcement, the German authorities were careful to note that the new norms were designed to insure that in the distribution of flour for the making of matzo, "the Christian population will not find itself in a situation worse than the Jewish population."[46]

Despite such German attempts to occupy a middle ground, most Poles believed that Jews were served by the "new order." In fact, the popularity of the Germans among Jews was never uniform—for example, both assimilationists like Kraushar and Orthodox Jews, at least initially and for different reasons, were extremely skeptical and cautious in their approach to the "Jewish" enunciations of the new authorities. For the duration of the German occupation, Jewish positions can only be characterized as complex and dynamic. The Folkists, led in Warsaw by Noah Pryłucki and Samuel Hirszhorn, were the first to respond to German overtures, followed eventually by the Orthodox whom the Germans during the second year of the occupation empowered and helped to mobilize through the creation of the *Agudas Ho-ortodoksim*, the precursor to *Agudat Israel*, which would come to play an important role in interwar

---

43 Kraushar, *Warszawa podczas okupacji niemieckiej*, 29.
44 Zieliński, *Stosunki polsko-żydowskie*, 222, 233.
45 Although the KO was expanded to include three additional Jewish members during the course of the Russian evacuation, bringing the total number to six, a petition signed by Jewish intellectuals was presented to the community board in March 1916 which called for the dramatic expansion of Jewish representation on the KO. According to *Der moment* (as reported in *Gazeta Poranna 2 grosze*), Jews were entitled to 20 places on the 60-member KO, given that they accounted for around 40% of Warsaw's population at that time; "Przedstawicielstwo żydów," *Gazeta Poranna 2 grosze* 75 (15 March 1916), 2.
46 "Mąka," *Nowa Gazeta* 127 (16 March 1917, morn. ed.), 3.

Poland.⁴⁷ The latter development signified, however, that the Germans would henceforth treat Jews as a religious rather than a national minority in Poland, which deeply disappointed the Folkists because it ran counter to the basis of their entire political program. It similarly led their Zionist rivals to distance themselves from the policies of the occupier and to identify themselves increasingly with the British, particularly after the Balfour Declaration. Led by Yitshak Grünbaum, Apolinary Hartglas, and Moshe Körner, the Zionists openly began to express support for an independent Poland that would grant Jews equal political rights.⁴⁸

Thus, when historians like Ezra Mendelsohn refer to the German occupation as a "new era of political freedom for Polish Jewry," they are referring primarily to the opportunities afforded for mass political mobilization, which for Warsaw's Jews marked a fundamental transformation in the local political culture and institutions.⁴⁹ Otherwise, aside from a few Jewish merchants who profited from state contracts with the occupation regime, Jews' hopes in the German presence were turned into disappointments by the restrictions on commerce and a general economic collapse.

Nevertheless, the entire Jewish population came to be perceived by many on the Polish side as supporters of the Germans and Austrians, just as they had been seen as supporters of tsarist Russia before the First World War (and of the Soviet Union after it). As the war continued and a divided Polish opinion came to view support for the Central Powers with increased hostility,

---

47   Guterman, *Congregation*, 121–122. The role of German rabbis in the fashioning of modern political formations among the Orthodox community in the Polish Kingdom is emphasized by Matthias Morgernstern, *From Frankfurt to Jerusalem: Isaac Breuer and the History of the Secessionist Dispute in Modern Jewish Orthodoxy* (Leiden: Brill Studies in European Judaism, 2002), 65–74. On the significance of local actors, see François Guesnet, "Thinking Globally, Acting Locally: Joel Wegmeister and Modern Hasidic Politics in Warsaw," *Quest. Issues in Contemporary Jewish History*, 2 (October 2011), available online at http://www.quest-cdecjournal.it/focus.php?id=222#e. See also Tobias Grill, "The Politicisation of Traditional Polish Jewry: Orthodox German Rabbis and the Founding of *Agudas Ho-Ortodoksim* and *Dos yidishe vort* in Gouvernement-General Warsaw, 1916–1918," *East European Jewish Affairs* 39.2 (August 2009), 227–247. On the larger history of *Agudat Israel*, see Gershon Bacon, *The Politics of Tradition: Agudat Yisrael in Poland, 1916–1939* (Jerusalem: Magnes Press, 1996).

48   Zieliński, *Stosunki polsko-żydowskie*, 199–201.

49   Ezra Mendelsohn, *Zionism in Poland: The Formative Years, 1915–1926* (New Haven: Yale University Press, 1981), ix, 37–38, 41–43. According to Mendelsohn, "1915 ushered in a new era of political freedom for Polish Jewry: the German occupation made possible the organization of mass political parties, and the Zionists, like their ideological opponents, took full advantage of this opportunity."

a significant number of the city's Poles would come to see Jews as allies of anti-Polish forces, "enemy aliens" from within, made worse by the deteriorating economic situation for which Poles held Jews, as much as they did Germans, responsible.

•••

Warsaw's wartime economic crisis began under Russian rule, however, and as inflationary pressures mounted in the fall of 1914 the accusation in the Polish nationalist press of Jewish price-gouging would quickly become a constant refrain. There followed demands for the imposition of controls to contain the "exploitation" and "profiteering" of wholesale merchants of soap, candles, soda and other articles whose prices were deemed "excessive."[50] These thinly disguised attacks on Jewish commerce became even more transparent once controls were imposed and newspapers like *Kurjer Warszawski* published the names and addresses of principally Jewish storeowners who had been fined or jailed for violating price regulations.[51] Rumors of Jewish hoarding became particularly intense in February 1915, when Russian police—as a prelude to future requisitioning—inspected commercial stores and stocks in Warsaw's 4th, 7th, 8th, and 15th precincts, where they reportedly found "an enormous amount of supplies" belonging "mainly to Jews," "speculators" who were holding on to goods and then selling the "last batch" for markups of 300 to 400%. Meanwhile, advertisements appearing in Jewish newspapers for "Dąbrowa coal"—that is, coal from a region that had been taken by the Germans seven months earlier—provided further evidence for Polish nationalists of Jewish profiteering.[52] This would lead to calls from the otherwise "liberal" Polish weekly *Tygodnik Ilustrowany* for an intensification of the struggle against speculation, which in its words "should have a prophylactic character, one conducted with severity and ruthlessness by all state and social actors."[53]

As winter turned to spring in 1915, speculative purchasing of flour by Jewish bakers was blamed for the rising prices of baked goods, leading to a proposal by the Provisions Section of the Warsaw Citizens Committee for a distribution scheme by which bakers in the city's Jewish community would receive a

---

50 "Wyzysk hurtowników," *Kurjer Warszawski* 281 (11 October 1914), 5.
51 "Ponad taksa," *Kurjer Warszawski* 313 (12 November 1914, morn. ed.), 3 and 323 (22 November 1914), 2.
52 "Rewizje w składach," *Kurjer Warszawski* 41 (10 February 1915, morn. ed.), 5 and "Spekulacja," *Kurjer Warszawski* 42 (11 February 1915, aft. ed.), 2.
53 "Spekulacya," *Tygodnik Ilustrowany* 9 (27 February 1915), 316.

maximum 35% of the flour based on the Jewish proportion of the city's population.[54] Even so, *Gazeta Poranna 2 grosze* accused the Citizens Committee of giving away flour to Jewish bakers, a charge that had no basis in fact but nevertheless pressured the Committee into making a public denial.[55] From the other end, the Committee was accused by the liberal Russian paper *Severniia Zapiski* of refusing to sell basic goods and commodities to Warsaw's Jews, the first of many claims of discrimination fostered by the segregation of public welfare and social assistance programs in the city on the basis of religious affiliation.[56] In response to this charge, the Committee's Provisions Section published a communiqué in which it maintained that there were no restrictions on sales based on religion or nationality, but that there were restrictions against large purchases, the aim of which was to stockpile goods for the purposes of speculation. Restricting purchases to one-time sales were justified, in its opinion, in order to feed a population already living from hand to mouth.[57]

Inflation would rapidly accelerate during the German occupation, accompanied by renewed charges against Jewish speculators, especially following the introduction of rationing at the beginning of 1916. With rations came black markets, which would become rampant in Warsaw by the second half of the following year. These "bacilli of speculation" were in almost every instance in the possession of the "skullcaps" and "sidelocks," according to *Gazeta Poranna*.[58] Nine months later, the daily was holding Jewish speculators responsible for the high cost of shoes by hoarding supplies that were eventually uncovered by the city militia.[59] *Der moment*, perhaps to counter such attacks, blamed Polish farmers for holding back butter from the market to drive up prices in the hungry winter of 1916–1917.[60]

---

54   APW KOMW 2, Presidium protocol no. 66 of 16 April 1915.
55   Ibid., protocol no. 82 of 31 May 1915.
56   Ibid., Presidium protocol no. 86 of 11 June 1915. Jewish assimilationists were particularly frustrated with the segregation of public assistance during wartime and blamed it for the sad state of Polish-Jewish relations; see the discussion of an article published in the renewed weekly *Izraelita* by Józef Wasercug in "Z prasy," *Nowa Gazeta* 142 (29 March 1915, aft. ed.), 2.
57   "Sklepy komitetowe," *Kurjer Warszawski* 168 (19 June 1915, aft. ed.), 4–5. In support of its argument that segregation was not synonymous with discrimination, the Section also published statistics which showed that 33.38% of the total value of purchases at KO stores had been made by Jews, who also constituted 31.65% of the stores' clientele.
58   "O bakcyle spekulacji," *Gazeta Poranna 2 grosze* 237 (30 August 1917), 3.
59   "Dlaczego buty są drogie," *Gazeta Poranna 2 grosze* 93 (7 April 1918), 3.
60   As quoted in the article "Spekulacya masłem," *Nowa Gazeta* 558 (5 December 1916), 2.

Jews were also blamed for the high price of meat, starting in the spring of 1915. Although Jews claimed that despite high meat prices, no profits were being made and that every day someone was going out of business,[61] Polish newspapers like *Kurjer Warszawski* remained skeptical. In particular, the daily cited the disappearance of 300 head of cattle from the stockyards, not one of which had made its way to local butchers, as evidence of a "conspiracy of speculators" when, in fact, the cattle had been requisitioned by the Russian army.[62] Against the backdrop of such accusations, the Warsaw Citizens Committee at the end of May met with a delegation of Christian butchers that presented it with an eight-point plan for the regulation of meat prices, the final point of which called for the suspension of kosher slaughtering by means of emergency regulations.[63] For its part *Kurjer Warszawski* called upon the Committee to serve as the "middleman" between meat producers and consumers, which in effect would drive Jews from the meat trade.[64] Indeed, in the first half of June, the KO decided to purchase one hundred head of cattle on a weekly basis, justifying its action by claiming that it was designed to curtail the profits of speculators.[65]

The Germans, after they took control of the city, had a different idea of controlling inflation by establishing a meat monopoly and contracting it with the Jewish merchant Liman Rozenberg. This led to all kinds of Polish protests and petitions demanded that the monopoly be entrusted to Christian butchers serving the majority of Warsaw's population and, failing that, be placed in the hands of the Polish-dominated city administration. Eventually, a consortium consisting of ten Christian and ten Jewish butchers was formed under the city administration to serve as an intermediary between Rozenberg, who retained exclusive rights under the Germans to bring cattle into Warsaw, and local butchers. Rozenberg's temporary arrest in January 1916 on fabricated criminal charges would lead to the awarding of the meat monopoly to the Frankowski Brothers firm, a solution which temporarily satisfied both Polish nationalist

---

61 "Drożyzna mięsa," *Kurjer Warszawski* 142 (25 May 1915, spec. ed.), 5.
62 "Sprawa mięsna," *Kurjer Warszawski* 144 (27 May 1915, morn. ed.), 3. For its part, *Gazeta Poranna 2 grosze* questioned why "only Jews" had the right to transport livestock to Warsaw; "Sprawa mięsna, część I," *Gazeta Poranna 2 grosze* 147 (29 May 1915), 1.
63 "Drożyzna mięsa," *Kurjer Warszawski* 147 (30 May 1915, Sunday ed.), 3.
64 "Błędne koło," *Kurjer Warszawski* 149 (1 June 1915, aft. ed.), 2. According to Bina Garncarska, the development of specific "Jewish trades," including the meat trade, was a late nineteenth-century development; Bina Garncarska, "The Material and Social Situation of the Jewish Population of Warsaw between 1862 and 1914," *Gal-Ed: On the History of the Jews of Poland* 1 (1973), xvi.
65 "Mięso dla Warszawy," *Kurjer Warszawski* 158 (10 June 1915, morn. ed.), 3.

opinion and commercial interests.⁶⁶ The supply and politics of meat, however, would remain a sore point in Polish-Jewish relations for the remainder of the war, as Christian butchers protested the proportional distribution of monopolized meat and Jews decried the purchase by Polish consumers of kosher meat.⁶⁷

As can be seen in the case of meat, charges of Jewish hoarding, speculation, profiteering and exploitation during the hardship of wartime quickly became an extension of the prewar nationalist agenda of reducing the Jewish presence in commerce and trade, the unfulfilled goal of the 1912–1914 boycott. The attack on Jewish commerce in the city took forms other than those already mentioned. Under the pretense of defending Warsaw's seamstresses, who were being "mercilessly exploited" from dawn to dusk for 20–25 kopecks per day, *Kurjer Warszawski* called upon the Warsaw Citizens Committee to eliminate Jewish middlemen and establish its own shops.⁶⁸ When the Russians began to evacuate Warsaw at the end of June 1915, and the city again experienced a shortage of coin with which to make change, the conservative daily condemned the practice of some storekeepers of issuing IOUs instead of spare change as a Jewish "trick" to compel customers to return to their stores for their next purchase. The issuing of IOUs among Polish trolley conductors and sausagemakers, however, failed to elicit such commentary.⁶⁹ Then, as the Russians prepared their final departure from the city at the end of July 1915 and presumably with the public interest as the only necessary consideration, Polish nationalists called upon the KO to confiscate goods in the hands of Jewish merchants who were said to be keeping basic provisions from the market in order to drive up prices.⁷⁰

As already noted, access to public assistance, not to mention representation on those bodies delivering it, was another issue that divided Poles and Jews in Warsaw during the First World War. The fact that Jews indeed comprised

---

66 The subject of the meat monopoly and the German contract with Rozenberg became a regular feature of *Gazeta Poranna 2 grosze*; for a sampling see "Monopol na mięso," 324 (24 November 1915), 1; "O monopol na mięso," 326 (26 November 1915), 1; "Monopol mięsny," 328 (28 November 1915), 2; "Monopol mięsny," 338 (8 December, 1915), 2; "Sprawa mięsna," 352 (22 December 1915), 1; and "Monopoly mięsny," 4 (4 January 1916), 2. For the award of the monopoly to the Frankowski Brothers, see "Monopol mięsny," *Kurier Warszawski* 39 (6 February 1916, aft. ed.), 7.

67 "Zmiany w sprzedaży mięsa," *Kurjer Warszawski* 186 (7 July 1916, aft. ed.), 3; "Co mogą jeść chrześcijanie," *Gazeta Poranna 2 grosze* 287 (19 October 1917), 3.

68 "Wyzysk szwaczek," *Kurjer Warszawski* 14 (14 January 1915, morn. ed.), 2.

69 "Drobne," *Kurjer Warszawski* 178 (30 June 1915, morn. ed.), 3, "Z powodu brak drobnych," *Kurjer Warszawski* 180 (2 July 1915, morn. ed.), 2 and "'Kombinacyjki' na tle 'drobnych',"*Kurjer Warszawski* 181 (3 July 1915, aft. ed.), 3.

70 "Z chwili," *Nowa Gazeta* 341(29 July 1915, aft. ed.), 1.

a relatively small percentage of the industrial labor force and were therefore largely unaffected by the widespread unemployment and underemployment that immediately struck Warsaw's factories, gave rise to the belief already at the war's outset that Jews were better able to weather the wartime economic crisis.[71] As the war continued, the number of Jewish "businesses" actually multiplied, which in the minds of Poles offered evidence of Jewish "prosperity." In reality, the existence of these "firms" was the result of the ever-worsening economic situation, the collapse of larger Jewish enterprises, and the resort to panhandling as a survival strategy.[72] Nonetheless, Poles believed that Jews were better able to adjust to inflation and speculation as owners of stores and shops simply by raising prices.[73] Finally, the Polish press, which was quick to publish news of external assistance to Warsaw's Jewish community, whether from Russia and later the United States, fostered the belief that Jews were well supported by philanthropy from abroad.[74] All of these factors contributed to the notion that Jews were materially better off than Poles and therefore less deserving of assistance offered through public institutions, first through the non-governmental organization of the Warsaw Citizens Committee, and subsequently the agencies of the Warsaw city administration.[75]

As the war continued and the economic crisis deepened, however, even newspapers like *Kurjer Warszawski* were forced to recognize signs of the Jewish population's impoverishment, while Jewish relief workers spoke even more dramatically of the "pauperization of the entire Jewish population."[76] This development helped to transform Zionism into a movement of great popular

---

71 According to the 1897 census, the percentage of wage-earners among Jews was 30,6%, compared to 61,3% among Christians; Garncarska, *The Material and Social Situation*, xiii. This was reflected in the structure of unemployment visible already in the war's first weeks; "Giełdy pracy," *Kurjer Warszawski* 256 (6 September 1914, aft. ed), 3.

72 Zieliński, *Stosunki polsko-żydowski*, 223.

73 This view can also be found among Polish historians; see, for example, Dunin-Wąsowicz, *Warszawa*, 119–121.

74 On support from the Jewish "Committee" in Petrograd, for example, see the following articles published in *Gazeta Poranna 2 grosze*: "Помос за жудów," 359 (30 December 1914), 3 and "Pieniądze z Rosji za żydów," 152 (6 June 1917), 3.

75 At the end of 1915, in response to requests to the ко from the "Ezra" society, the chief philanthropic organization of the Warsaw Jewish community, for additional funding of its public kitchens, *Gazeta Poranna* called for Jewish organizations to turn over all donated funds, "including one million rubles from America," to the Warsaw Citizens Committee; "Memoriał żydowski," *Gazeta Poranna 2 grosze* 344 (14 December 1915), 2. For more on "Ezra," see Guesnet, *Thinking Globally, Acting Locally*.

76 To be sure, the daily found evidence of this impoverishment in the decline of "lavish" spending on Jewish weddings; "Bez wesel," *Kurjer Warszawski* 195 (17 July 1915, aft. ed.), 3.

appeal in Warsaw, particularly as it gained the upper hand during the years of the German occupation over the distribution of welfare in the Jewish community, whose administrative board in turn became more assertive in making Jewish claims to a greater share in funding for public kitchens and refugee shelters, as well as in demanding equal access to basic provisions.[77]

In an effort to balance the competing claims of Poles and Jews, the Warsaw Citizens Committee decided already in October 1914 to distribute coupons to its ever-growing number of public kitchens in proportion to Polish and Jewish shares of the city's population.[78] Later, it voted to subsidize three to four public kitchens run by the "Ezra" Society by paying for 1500 of a total of 5500 daily meals.[79] In November, it also voted a subvention to a Commission on Jewish Refugees created by the Jewish community and which operated separately from the KO's own Refugee Section.[80] At approximately the same time, it determined that 30% of donated clothing collected in Petrograd for beleaguered Warsaw in the aftermath of the recently lifted German siege would be distributed to the Jewish poor.[81]

The Citizens Committee's decisions would be criticized by nationalists on both sides—by Poles as excessive relief provided at the expense of the Christian population, by Jews as inadequate in comparison with that provided to Roman Catholics.[82] These claims were frequently accompanied by accusations and counter-accusations of fraud and corruption, especially from, but not limited

---

[77] Mendelsohn, *Zionism*, 41–43. The growing strength of Zionism was already evident in the last months of Russian rule and was reflected in demands for the use of Yiddish and Hebrew in providing education to Jewish refugee children, which in turn led Warsaw assimilationists to warn of the "fatal consequences" for both Poles and Jews that would accompany the spread of "separatism" among the Jewish masses; "Listy do Redakcyi," in *Nowa Gazeta* 151 (3 April 1915, morn. ed.), 1.

[78] APW, KOMW 1, protocol no. 78 of 23 October 1914.

[79] Ibid., protocol no. 100 of 3 December 1914 and no. 103 of 12 December 1914.

[80] Ibid., protocol no. 94 of 21 November 1914.

[81] Ibid., protocol no. 98 of 28 November 1914.

[82] In the summer of 1916, *Gazeta Poranna* complained that even though Jews had important resources from a variety of sources at their disposal, including a recent 186,000 rubles from America, "they never cease to demand and receive large sums for their needs from the city administration" which "proves that the Jewish community is more privileged from a monetary standpoint and that the city administration is too quick to extend credits to the Jewish community, while simultaneously rejecting the necessary and positive requests of Christian institutions—and sentencing them to inactivity as a result of insufficient funds; "Na dobie," *Gazeta Poranna 2 grosze* 178 (29 June 1916), 2.

to, the Polish side, which often found "evidence" in the Yiddish daily press of wrongdoing in the administration of the Warsaw Jewish community. Following the introduction of rationing for bread and flour in January 1916, charges of counterfeiting ration or public kitchen coupons, and the registration of "dead souls" to receive additional coupons, became frequent.[83]

Especially when coupled with disputes over access to public assistance, the high number of Jewish refugees in the city, particularly in 1915 and 1916, became a major area of contention in Polish-Jewish relations while Warsaw still remained under Russian rule and for the first months thereafter. While exact numbers are difficult to come by, it would appear that the Jewish refugee population in the city reached 80 to 90 thousand by mid-April 1915, of whom less than half received public support from Jewish community institutions assisted with limited funding by the Warsaw Citizens Committee. For example, of the 46,000 ruble income reported by the KO's Jewish Refugee Section from all sources for 1914, only 7,000 rubles were provided directly from the KO, the rest coming from private donations and the contributions of Jewish philanthropic institutions.[84] Almost immediately, however, the Jewish press found itself refuting claims from its Polish nationalist counterparts, and particularly *Gazeta poranna 2 grosze*, that Jewish refugees in Warsaw had become a burden on institutions supported almost entirely by the Christian population—this at the very beginning of Warsaw's refugee crisis. According to radical Polish nationalists, these Jewish refugees "prefer[red] to wait out the ugly times in Warsaw" at the expense of Poles.[85]

By spring, the Polish press published increasingly dire reports of the "enormous influx" of Jews into Warsaw from the provinces, a situation that *Kurjer Warszawski* described as "alarming," citing an article published in the nationalist *Dzień* that inflated the number of Jewish refugees to 200,000. These Jews, moreover, had reportedly refused offers to resettle in Vilna or Minsk—to which *Kurjer* responded that they should be forced to go to other cities of the Empire "whether they liked it or not," especially since they were "making life difficult for the permanent residents of Warsaw." Worse still, according to oft-repeated warnings of the Polish press, the malnourished and poorly dressed Jewish

---

83   "Fałszywe bony na chleb," *Kurjer Warszawski* 18 (18 January 1916, morn. ed.), 3; "Martwe dusze," *Gazeta Poranna 2 grosze* 66 (6 March 1916), 2; "7 obiadów dla jednej osoby," *Gazeta Poranna 2 grosze* 55 (24 February 1917), 3.
84   APW, KOMW 2, protocol no. 116 of 16 January 1915.
85   "Fałszywe i szkodliwe informacye," *Nowa Gazeta* 507 (29 October 1914, aft. ed.), 2.

refugees could "easily provoke numerous epidemics" among the city's population and the Russian army.[86]

Thus, sanitary conditions among the mainly Jewish refugees and general public health concerns were cited as reasons for their forcible resettlement. For more radical Polish nationalists, the danger to public health came not only from refugees, but more generally from the streets inhabited by the Jewish poor. Dzika, Franciszkańska, Nalewki and Muranowska, they argued, were "the source of every possible kind of epidemic" and where "the eyes of all members of sanitary commissions" should turn their gaze. "It is necessary in the general interest to resettle part of this impoverished crowd to other localities," claimed *Gazeta Poranna 2 grosze*. "In addition to the many healthy people in the city, there are hundreds of wounded soldiers who would be most threatened by the outbreak of an epidemic." Small wonder that Stanisław Kempner would sarcastically refer in *Nowa Gazeta* to such "public health" demands for the resettlement of Jews, whether refugee or resident, as "airing out Warsaw."[87]

In mid-April 1915, a group of Jewish community leaders and physicians signed a memorial directed to the City President, arguing that the planned evacuation of tens of thousands of Jewish refugees for "sanitary reasons" was completely unjustifiable, because Warsaw was well organized and equipped to deal with the appearance of infectious diseases, whereas far more dangerous sanitary conditions in the provinces were precisely of the kind that could lead to spread of epidemics.[88] Nonetheless, poor sanitary conditions were cited as the main reason for the closing of eight Jewish refugee shelters in early May and the transfer of several hundreds of their inhabitants to Otwock, Falenica, Józefów, Świder and Płudy, where they would later be observed "living like wild animals," struggling to survive by stealing produce from the gardens of local residents.[89]

---

86 "Napływ żydów," *Kurjer Warszawski* 41 (10 February 1915, aft. ed.), 4; "Bezdomni żydzi," *Kurjer Warszawski* 53 (22 February 1915, morn. ed.), 4; "Napływ żydów bezdomnych do Warszawy," *Kurjer Warszawski* 67 (8 March 1915), 5.

87 "Rozsadnik epidemii," *Gazeta Poranna 2 grosze* 84 (25 March 1915), 2; "Ewakuacja czy 'pogrom'," *Gazeta Poranna 2 grosze* 85 (26 March 1915), 1.

88 "Warszawska gmina starozakonnych," *Nowa Gazeta* 176 (19 April 1915, aft. ed.), 2. For the Polish perspective on the memorial, see "Bezdomni żydzi," *Kurjer Warszawski* 107(19 April 1915, aft. ed.), 5.

89 *Kurjer Warszawski* 130 (12 May 1915, aft. ed.). 4. For a description of conditions prevailing among the refugees on the Vistula's east bank a couple months following their evacuation from Warsaw, see Dzikowski, *Rok wojny w Warszawie*, 46.

These refugees were merely replaced by new arrivals in the final month of Russian rule, which brought more human traffic into and out of Warsaw.[90] Following the Russian evacuation, there were concerted efforts between the German authorities, the Jewish refugee assistance organization in Warsaw, and provincial committees to return refugees to their homes. By November, the number of "homeless Jews" receiving public assistance in the amount of 20 kopecks per day had been substantially reduced to some 7,000, although according to *Gazeta Poranna* there was still a "significant number" of Jews from other parts of Poland, whose presence in the city was fueling inflation.[91] Renewed fighting in early 1916 would lead to the arrival of new waves of Jewish refugees into Warsaw, particularly from the Austrian occupation zone to the east of the city. According to *Gazeta Poranna*, although Warsaw's total population had declined by 100,000 by March 1916, the number of Jews in the city had increased by 200,000–300,000.[92] These much inflated numbers were again rapidly reduced, so that by the summer of 1916 *Gazeta Poranna* had merely 4,000 Jewish refugees to concern itself with as a "burden" on "Polish institutions."[93]

The waning of the Jewish refugee crisis coincided with the contentious issue of Jewish representation in a new Warsaw city council, once such an institution became possible. The Spring of 1915 had brought with it the Russian promise of the establishment of urban self-governing institutions in the Polish Kingdom, including and especially Warsaw, which the assimilationist and liberal daily *Nowa Gazeta* conceded "must understandably be Polish," so long as they were "democratic" and "accessible to all."[94] Though such promises remained unrealized by the time of the Russian evacuation of the city, Warsaw municipal elections were held in the summer of 1916 under the supervision of the German occupation authorities. In anticipation of such elections, representatives of the KO met in several extraordinary sessions in April to write and vote on an electoral ordinance. Of these, the most extended and divisive deliberations occurred during the session of 16 April. Piotr Dziewiecki, who would later become president of the city, argued for a set quota or percentage for Jewish participation, to prevent Jews from capturing a majority. Prince

---

90 "Nowi bezdomni," *Gazeta Poranna 2 grosze* 195 (16 July 1915), 2.
91 "Bezdomni żydzi," *Gazeta Poranna 2 grosze* 324 (24 November 1915), 2.
92 "Ewakuacja bezdomnych żydów," *Gazeta Poranna 2 grosze* 62 (2 March 1916), 3.
93 "Ewakuacja bezdomnych," *Nowa Gazeta* 568 (12 December 1916), 4. As late as October 1917, Polish nationalists were still complaining that only 1228 persons had been evacuated by the Jewish community from Warsaw over the previous six months; "Nie chcą wyjeżdżać," *Gazeta Poranna 2 grosze* 288 (20 October 1917), 2.
94 "Samorząd," *Nowa Gazeta* 160 (9 April 1915, aft. ed.), 1.

Zdzisław Lubomirski, installed as city president by the Germans the previous summer, argued that the "Polish character" of the council had to be preserved by all means, despite whatever bad impression this might leave externally. These motions to restrict Jewish participation through quota restrictions were defeated, however, by a vote of 15–8, with one abstention.[95]

Nonetheless, the Jewish Election Committee, which now contained a Zionist majority, agreed to accept a deal with the main Polish parties that gave Jews 15 of 75 total seats from the first five electoral curiae representing various elements of the propertied classes. Jewish leaders accepted the deal to keep the peace in Warsaw, despite the fact that the percentage of Jewish population was much greater than reflected in the number of allotted seats. This decision was challenged, however, when the opposition Folkist party, which had been demanding 35% of the council seats in accordance with the Jewish share of the population, broke with the Jewish Election Committee to gain an additional four mandates in the sixth curia representing non-propertied male voters (the Bund gained one seat as well). On the Polish side, the National Democrats and their allies won a plurality of the vote (40%) in elections in which only 36,781 out of 80,000 eligible voters participated.[96] Even though Jews would remain underrepresented on the city council as a consequence of the pre-election bargaining, *Gazeta Poranna 2 grosze* chose to interpret the results as a "victory" of "extreme nationalism" among Jews.[97]

In the event, the Warsaw city council became one of the main arenas where Polish-Jewish conflicts played out for the remainder of the war. As a sign of things to come, the first session of the council was set for a Saturday, causing the Folkists to petition the authorities with a request to move it to the following Monday to preserve the Sabbath.[98] When the council actually met at its first session, the four Folkists, as a sign of protest, remained in their seats as the rest of the delegates rose to their feet to hail "Long Live Poland!" *Haynt*, representing the Zionists, quickly condemned the Folkists' demonstrative political behavior as "scandalous irresponsibility."[99] Thereafter conflicts erupted over the language of instruction in Jewish schools and the accessibility of Jews to public elementary schools more generally; the introduction of a general Sunday holiday as a day of rest in Warsaw; subsidies for the establishment and maintenance of public kitchens; the ban on entrance to public parks and

---

95 APW, KOMW 6, protocol no.290b of the extraordinary session of the KO of 16 April 1916.
96 Mendelsohn, *Zionism*, 49–53; Dunin-Wąsowicz, *Warszawa*, 146.
97 "Zwycięstwo," *Gazeta Poranna 2 grosze* 196 (17 July 1916), 2.
98 "Zachowanie szabasu," *Gazeta Poranna 2 grosze* 199 (20 July 1916), 3.
99 As reported in the article "Pierwszy krok...," *Kurjer Warszawski* 205 (26 July 1916, aft. ed.), 2.

gardens to individuals not dressed in "proper European attire," and on-going disputes with the city police who, among other things, arrested and "disinfected" bearded Orthodox and Hasidic males en route to and from prayer houses for violating public health codes.[100]

By the end of 1916, *Nowa Gazeta* lamented that the "Jewish question" had come to dominate the meetings of the City Council and that it, in turn, was dominated by "demagogues on both sides," while voices of the "democratic camps" remained silent.[101] Shortly thereafter, the Zionists withdrew from the bloc of Jewish Councilmen to join and compete with the Folkists in opposition to the remaining factions of assimilationists, Orthodox, and non-party representatives. Without the Zionists, the effectiveness of the assimilationists and their ability to act as a "buffer" between more radical Polish and Jewish positions was seriously undermined and would be reflected in their crushing defeat in community board elections in the middle of 1917. There followed the sale of *Nowa Gazeta*, which *Der moment* celebrated as "the end of Jewish assimilation in Poland ... even on paper."[102] Meanwhile, Folkists and Zionists crossed verbal swords with Dr. Konrad Ilski from the Endecja, who on one occasion before the Warsaw City Council reportedly said that "the Jewish district is full of fences, thieves, and dealers in human flesh."[103] Ilski would later be nominated to the position of the Director of the City Provisions Department, which met with the protests of practically all Jewish councilmen, especially after Ilski vowed "to act everywhere against the enemies of Polishness."[104] Such exchanges often paralyzed sessions of the council, causing one delegate to complain: "In the morning, the Jewish question. In the afternoon, the Jewish question. In the evening again the Jewish question."[105]

• • •

Meanwhile, the city's economy had reached the point of collapse. Rationing, inflation and the black market had become the order of the day, hunger was turning into starvation, and fear of epidemics had been replaced by their

---

100 For a sampling of these disputes, see "Przeciw święceniu niedzieli," *Nowa Gazeta* 555a (4 December 1916, special morning supplement), 2; "Ubranie europejskie," *Nowa Gazeta* 559 (6 December 1916, morn. ed.), 2, "O hygiene kąpielową," *Nowa Gazeta* 102 (27 February 1917, aft. ed.), 2.

101 "Nastroje w Radzie miejskiej,"*Nowa Gazeta* 572 (14 December 1916, aft. ed.), 2.

102 As quoted in the article "Nowa Gazeta," *Gazeta Poranna 2 grosze* 227 (9 October 1917), 2.

103 "Mowa r. Ilskiego w żargonówkach," *Gazeta Poranna 2 grosze* 188 (12 July 1917), 3.

104 "Ilskowstręt," *Gazeta Poranna 2 grosze* 34 (4 February 1918), 3.

105 "Z Rady Miejskiej," *Nowa Gazeta* 339 (13 July 1917, aft. ed.), 1–2.

reality. The Warsaw city administration was barely able to pay its own workers, let alone provide relief to the mass of the city's poor and unemployed.[106] By the summer of 1918, Warsaw's inhabitants faced a real existential catastrophe, one revealed in the dramatic multiplication of mortality rates.[107]

The city's wartime demographic catastrophe requires further exploration. Over twenty-five years ago, Warsaw historian Krzysztof Dunin-Wąsowicz argued that during the war Warsaw's Poles indeed had it worse than its Jews in that the decline in the birth rate was more dramatic among Christians and the increase in the mortality rate was lower among Jews.[108] Although Dunin provided little evidence for such a conclusion, data published in *Nowa Gazeta* at least partially bear him out. During the week of March 18–24, 1917, some 462 birth certificates were issued, 288 to Jews. During this same period, there were 405 registered deaths of Christians, compared to 248 deaths of Jews.[109] Data from a few months later, although they reflect a more rapidly deteriorating situation among the Jewish population, still generally indicate lower birth if not a higher mortality rates among Christians. For the week of July 8–14, 1917, there were 124 registered births of Christian children, compared to 146 for Jews, and 338 registered deaths of Christians and 255 of Jews.[110]

Such differences cannot be explained in terms of higher living standards, better nutrition, or relative resistance to disease—especially since Warsaw's Jews, over 25% of them dependent on public assistance, were particularly susceptible to typhus and tuberculosis, the two great catastrophic illnesses of the war. Higher marriage rates among Jews, family structures peculiar to the non-industrial employment of Jews, different cultures of child care, and different patterns of out-migration—factors that explain demographic differences among Warsaw's Jewish and Polish populations before the war—are of similar importance in understanding the magnification of such differences during the war. For example, the death rate for Jews in the Polish Kingdom in 1908 was 14.50 per thousand, compared to 22.20 per thousand among Christians.[111]

---

106 See the memoir by Franciszek Herbst, "Działalność społeczna i samorządowa," in Dunin-Wąsowicz (ed.), *Warszawa w pamiętnikach*, 322–325 for a description of Warsaw's financially-starved city government and its struggle to provide assistance to its own employees.

107 According to Jerzy Holzer and Jan Molenda, the death rate in Warsaw, not counting infant mortality, tripled between 1914 and 1917; see Jerzy Holzer and Jan Molenda, *Polska w pierwszej wojnie światowej* (Warsaw: Wiedza Powszechna, 1963), 123.

108 Dunin-Wąsowicz, *Warszawa*, 88–91.

109 "Miasto w cyfrach," *Nowa Gazeta* 188 (19 April 1917, aft. ed.), 2.

110 "Ze statystyki miejskiej," *Nowa Gazeta* 382 (6 August 1917, morn. ed.), 2.

111 Zieliński, *Stosunki polsko-żydowski*, 31.

According to Piotr Wróbel, one of the factors influencing Jewish mortality rates was the fact that Jewish women in Warsaw rarely worked in factories far removed from their homes, resulting in better infant and child care.[112]

Regardless of the actual situation yet more important to our purposes here, the nationalist Polish press was keen to report such statistical information and to create its own reality around it. *Gazeta Poranna 2 grosze*, for example, attributed the miniscule natural growth of the Jewish population in Warsaw to a general well-being, or *dobrobyt*, among Jews. More absurdly, the newspaper argued that "a huge percentage of Jews have avoided the army.... And now they are fathering children in *dobrobyt*."[113]

In June 1918, German occupation authorities began to receive reports of pogrom agitation in Warsaw, where the Endecja—no longer deterred by the strictures of the German occupation regime on anti-Jewish propaganda—was openly calling for a boycott of Jewish trade and commerce. By October, Jews—perceived as better off by most Poles—were becoming frequent targets of physical attacks and robberies. Fighting actually broke out between Poles and Jews in one of Warsaw's market areas, as well as at the newly reopened Warsaw University, where Jewish students who had expressed their willingness to work for Polish independence were told to go to Palestine. As the occupation regime melted away in the first weeks of November, there were instances of attacks on Jewish pedestrians by newly minted Polish soldiers who threatened them with weapons and beatings, and shouted "traitors" and "collaborators" at them.[114]

All of this begs the question—if Polish-Jewish relations in Warsaw had deteriorated to such an extent, why no pogrom in November of 1918 as would occur, for example, in Lwów? After all, Warsaw's economic freefall, its skyrocketing inflation, its crisis of industrial employment, its catastrophic shortages of food and fuels, the acute vulnerability of its inhabitants to disease, and its ever mounting social tensions created an environment no less combustible than that prevailing in Lwów. Yet in Lwów's case, three days of rioting, looting and mayhem from November 22 to 24, 1918, would lead to the murder of dozens of Jews and the wounding of several hundreds more, not to mention the victimization of several thousands who suffered material losses from the destruction. As William Hagen points out, the visceral nature of the pogrom violence in Lwów and the apocalyptic mindset of many of its perpetrators were

---

112   Piotr Wróbel, "Jewish Warsaw before the First World War," *Polin: A Journal of Polish-Jewish Studies* 3 (1988), 165.
113   "Danina krwi a żydzi," *Gazeta Poranna 2 grosze* 33 (8 February 1918), 2.
114   Mendelsohn, *Zionism*, 88; Zieliński, *Stosunki polsko-żydowskie*, 404.

unprecedented, at least until the Second World War when such scenes were played out on a larger scale in places like Jedwabne.[115]

Certainly, the struggle for hegemony in Lwów between Poles and Ukrainians in the vacuum left by the final collapse of Austrian authority, and the failed attempt of Jews to have both sides respect their neutrality in the conflict, created a situation quite unlike that prevailing in Warsaw, where Polish hegemony was never contested by a third party. However, a more fundamental difference is that, unlike Lwów, which had been the scene of actual military conflict during the war as control of the city passed back and forth between Austrian and Russian armies and then between Polish and Ukrainian forces, Warsaw never experienced such fighting within its borders. Sure enough, control of Warsaw had passed from Russian to German hands in August 1915, and between German and Polish hands in the second week of November 1918, but the transfer of authority had occurred in both instances almost peacefully, accompanied far more by negotiation than by military action. Prior to November 1918, exceptional violence against Lwow's Jews during the war had already occurred, courtesy of the Russian army, which in a sense legitimized and encouraged future acts of brutality against the Jewish community.[116] The Russian army in the Polish Kingdom, as we have seen, behaved similarly, but outside rather than inside the city limits of Warsaw.

The inhabitants of Lwów, in other words, had become desensitized toward a kind of brutalizing violence in a way that Warsaw's residents had not, despite the existence of a pogrom atmosphere there. Though tensions ran high in Warsaw, and Polish-Jewish relations had likely never been so distressed, assaults on Jews remained individual rather than collective acts. Piłsudski's ability to establish his authority without challenge in Warsaw in November 1918, and to negotiate the peaceful evacuation of German forces from the city, in other words, may have spared the city considerable interethnic violence. Had German forces put up resistance to a Polish takeover or to their own disarmament, which was not inconceivable, Warsaw's Jews may well have experienced a Lwów-style pogrom. Fortunately, both Poles and Jews in Warsaw were spared the test.

---

115   William W. Hagen, "The Moral Economy of Popular Violence: The Pogrom in Lwów, November 1918," in Robert Blobaum (ed.), *Antisemitism and Its Opponents in Modern Poland* (Ithaca, NY: Cornell University Press, 2005), 124–147.

116   For a more general discussion of wartime violence against Jews in and around Lwów, see Alexander Victor Prusin, *Nationalizing a Borderland: War, Ethnicity, and Anti-Jewish Violence in East Galicia, 1914–1920* (Tuscaloosa, AL: University of Alabama Press, 2005).

MAP 11.1 "The Polish Republic in the Interwar Period, ca. 1930s." From the Archives of the YIVO Institute for Jewish Research, New York.
COURTESY OF YIVO.

CHAPTER 12

The Capital of "Yiddishland"?

Kalman Weiser

"Where is the Jewish center now?" the literary critic Shmuel Niger queried rhetorically in the New York daily *Forverts* in November, 1919. Over the course of generations, the experience of autocratic tsarist rule and the interplay of such currents as Hasidism, Haskalah, socialism, and nationalism, however tempestuous, had forged a common culture and identity among Jews throughout the Russian Empire. Prior to 1914, each region of the empire had contributed its own unique portion to the shaping of a larger whole, manifested in the prewar flowering of modern Hebrew and Yiddish literatures. But as a result of the war, "Russia's great and powerful center has fallen to pieces. Only remnants endure—in Ukraine, in Poland, in Lithuania, and so on. The remnants are large and significant (above all in Poland and Ukraine); but it doesn't compare with what once was in [the Russian Empire]."[1]

The question posed by Niger may have struck some of his readers as trivial, perhaps even decadent, given the circumstances. Not only had the Great War wrought death, destruction, and dislocation on an apocalyptic scale, but hunger continued to ravage the impoverished civilian population and, as military forces continued to dispute the fate of state boundaries and individual cities, a pogrom wave on an unprecedented scale was resulting in tens of thousands of Jewish casualties, especially in Ukraine.

Niger himself had only recently fled Soviet-occupied Vilna after the Polish invasion and had narrowly evaded death. Yet for Niger, the fracturing of Russian Jewry after the collapse of the tsarist empire posed as much a threat to Jewish collective survival as famine and violence. What remained to unite Jews? For Niger, the answer was clear: not religion, but language and literature. Like other Yiddishists, he saw cultivating the modern Yiddish literary language and its literature as vital for the coherence and continuity of East European Jewish culture across new political and linguistic boundaries.

The war's immediate aftermath was a time of both great anxiety and profound hope for those who were concerned about the future of secular Yiddish culture and Diasporic Jewish nationhood. Not only had the three "classic" writers—Mendele, Sholem Aleichem, and I.L. Peretz—all died during the war,

---

[1] Shmuel Niger, "Vu iz itst der idisher tsenter?," *Forverts* (6 December 1919).

depriving Yiddish letters of its undisputed leaders, but the very "homeland" of Yiddish culture—the Pale of Settlement and Congress Poland—seemed to vanish overnight. Former subjects of the tsar were now divided into citizens of the newly independent Baltic States, the Soviet Union, and a reconstituted Poland that absorbed the former Habsburg province of Galicia, possessor of its own distinctive traditions. In addition, another historically distinct region, *Lite*—the territory of the former Duchy of Lithuania within the pre-nineteenth century Polish-Lithuanian Commonwealth—was now divided among mutually hostile countries. The desperate pursuit of survival in such extraordinarily trying times and the process of adaptation to radically new societies, many of which made greater demands—and offered greater opportunities—for cultural integration than the Old Order had, could spell the very demise of secular Yiddish culture and the concept of Jewish nationhood. Mass emigration to North America and other areas had already triggered such fears before the war.

On the other hand, the traumas and chaos of war had both necessitated and facilitated the creation of a wide array of cultural and benevolent institutions, including elementary and vocational schools that functioned in Yiddish, to serve the needs of refugees and the many other war-stricken Jews. The Yiddish press, which had come into its own only since the lifting of tsarist restrictions around the time of the 1905 Revolution, expanded and shed much of its provincial character during the German occupation of Poland and Lithuania.[2] Furthermore, dreams of national cultural autonomy, a goal fostered in the preceding decade by Jewish political parties of virtually all stripes, seemed feasible for the first time. Yiddish, already a global language since the nineteenth century, thanks to overseas immigration, was now a bearer of transnational culture more than ever; and collaboration between Eastern Europe and the burgeoning Yiddish cultural mecca in New York City, interrupted by the war, could now be resumed.

Niger's proposed solution was the creation of literary institutions such as publishing houses, journals, and literary funds, as well as cultural ones such as universities, libraries, and museums, to serve the entirety of the Yiddish Diaspora. But with each Jewish community now functioning independently and in a new context, and with the envisioned transnational institutions as yet desiderata, a singular cultural center was still very much needed to help bring together diverse and often conflicting influences and tendencies in order to unify a Jewish cultural consciousness. "Which among them, with its own forces," he asked of the Jewish communities of Poland, Lithuania, Ukraine, and

---

2   Zosa Szajkowski, "The Struggle for Yiddish during World War I," *Leo Baeck Institute Year Book* IX (1964): 131–158.

the United States, "will be able to create a life that will have a central, that is, a general national importance?"³

Niger was not alone in engaging in what writer I.J. Singer derided as "the passionate and fundamentally abstract quarrel in the small literary world about to whom hegemony belongs: New York, Moscow or Warsaw?"⁴ Indeed, the search for a world center for Yiddish, which pitted rival cities and countries against each other, was a preoccupation in Yiddish cultural circles throughout the interwar period.

Regular reporting in the Yiddish press in interwar Poland and elsewhere about the condition of Yiddish language and culture across the globe had helped popularize the concept of "Yiddishland" in lieu of a contiguous territory under a single regime.⁵ Eastern Europe, above all the territory of the former tsarist empire, was heralded as the historic home and heartland of the modern Yiddish language. But "Yiddishland," the linguistic embodiment of the Eastern European Jewish Diaspora, was said to consist of territories—or, in the perception of some, colonies—not only throughout Europe but in the Americas, South Africa, and Palestine.

This conceit was affirmed, in the eyes of Yiddishists, by the willingness of the international PEN Club to only accord membership to Yiddish literature alone among the world's stateless languages. The Yiddish philologist and Folkist leader Noah Prylucki wryly remarked in 1931 that:

> We Jews cannot come to the world with colonial exhibitions to show how we conquered lands and people and how we exploited them. We have no air squadrons to send to international flight competitions, which, in the end, have as their purpose preparing for new wars. On the economic front we are sprinkled in the general economic organism. We can claim a place in the community of peoples only through cultural creation. Proof of this is that in the federation of PEN clubs, which are built on the territorial principle, an exception was made for us. The Yiddish language is recognized as our territory and on this basis we were accepted into this federation as an equal member.⁶

---

3   Niger, "Vu iz itst der idisher tsenter?"
4   Y.Y. Zinger, "Vegn di varshever shriftn," *Literarishe bleter* 5 (4 February 1927): 83.
5   The origins of the term "Yiddishland" are unclear. For a discussion of the term and its conceptual evolution, see Jeffrey Shandler, *Adventures in Yiddishland: Postvernacular Language & Culture* (Berkeley, CA: UCLA Press, 2006), 33–4, 210 n9.
6   Cited in, M. K-ski, "Di yoyvl-fayerung fun Noyekh Prilutski," *Der moment* 106 (8 May 1931).

If Yiddish itself was, in Prylucki's words, an "anarchic republic,"[7] a surrogate for a politically and culturally sovereign nation state, then it was in need of a capital and ministries. More importantly, a secular cultural capital that transcended political boundaries would serve, at least in the minds of Yiddishists, not only as a symbol and focal point—a secular Zion—to preserve the cultural cohesion of a scattered people; it would also serve as a model and inspiration for further developments in the Yiddish nation-building enterprise and a source of pride for members of that nation. Perhaps most important of all, it would serve the needs of uprooted writers and disoriented intellectuals, both of whom were notorious for their fractiousness yet desperate for a sense of community and uniformly fearful of losing their audience to a growing tide of linguistic assimilation, economic ruin, and mere indifference.

The Contest

Given the pride of place accorded to "Vilna Yiddish" in contemporary Yiddishist mythology, one might expect Niger to have nominated Vilna, a city renowned for its centuries-old Jewish presence and a major center of pre-WWI Jewish publishing activity. But its political future was now violently contested by multiple parties, as Niger had witnessed personally. In the early 1920s, when Yiddish-writing intellectuals concentrated in world capitals, the Yiddish publishing centers of Warsaw, New York, Berlin, and Moscow were all seen as more likely contenders for cultural leadership, even hegemony, than a Vilna divorced from Russia, thrust to the economic and political margins of a newly independent Poland, and cut off from its provincial hinterland in Lithuania, an autonomous country that lacked diplomatic relations with Poland. Indeed, as a result of this reconfiguration, Vilna was now conspicuously absent from discussions in the press about the center of Yiddish culture.[8]

Warsaw, in contrast, capital of a newly Independent Poland and home to the largest Jewish community in Europe, was indisputably the "metropolis" of the Yiddish press, literature, and theatre by World War I.[9] Although it saw its Jewish population rise already in the nineteenth century, by the decades immediately preceding the war Warsaw had become home to a burgeoning and variegated creative scene concentrated around the legendary I.L. Peretz

---

7 YIVO, *Der alveltlekher tsuzamenfor fun yidishn visnshaftlekhn institut* (Vilna: YIVO, 1936), 37.

8 N. Vaynig, "Semafor: vilne," *Literarishe bleter* 45 (4 November 1932): 718.

9 On Warsaw's emergence as a literary center, see Khone [Chone] Shmeruk, *Prokim fun der yidisher literatur-geshikhte* (Jerusalem: The Hebrew University, 1988), 292–308.

and his project to develop a modern Jewish culture in Yiddish (see the chapter by Michael Steinlauf in this volume).[10] Warsaw's polyglot Jewish publishing industry drew talents from across the Russian Empire; and the Warsaw Jewish press, which grew by leaps and bounds after the 1905 Russian Revolution, was read throughout the Polish provinces and beyond.[11]

Berlin, though not yet a major center of Yiddish culture or Yiddish-speaking Jewry prior to the war, also had a Yiddish cultural scene that benefited from an influx of refugee intellectuals and literati arriving in flight from pogroms, civil war, and famine from the former Pale. For a short period, between 1922 and 1924, Berlin ranked second only to Warsaw in the total number of Yiddish titles.[12] The German capital, already a refuge for much of the Russian intelligentsia, offered opportunities for inexpensive but high quality publications due to the hyperinflation of the early 1920s, in addition to a dynamic intellectual and cultural scene. Leading members of the "Kiev group" of Yiddish writers such as Der Nister, Dovid Bergelson, Dovid Hofshteyn, Peretz Markish, Leyb Kvitko, and Moyshe Kulbak—the future kernel of Soviet Yiddish literature—settled there for a time. They were in the company of important Hebrew writers, Russian Jewish artists, and such scholars as Simon Dubnow and future YIVO stalwarts Elias Tcherikover, Max Weinreich, and Nokhem Shtif. However, most of these intellectuals found themselves there reluctantly. Indeed, they were frequently ostracized by their colleagues in Eastern Europe "... as traitors to their heritage and especially to their responsibility as protectors and perpetuators of Yiddish culture in the face of the perils which confronted it."[13] Within a few years, many eagerly returned to Eastern Europe to pursue opportunities or moved on, particularly to Palestine or the Americas.

---

10 Antony Polonsky, "Warsaw," YIVO Encyclopedia of the Jews in Eastern Europe, 2: 1993–96.
11 Kalman Weiser, "A Tale of Two Pryluckis: on the origins of the Warsaw Yiddish Press," Gal-Ed 22 (2010): 89–107.
12 On Yiddish publishing in Berlin and the brief period of Yiddish culture efflorescence there, see Gennady Estraikh and Mikhail Krutikov (eds.), Yiddish in Weimar Berlin: at the Crossroads of Diaspora Politics and Culture (London: Modern Humanities Research Association, 2010), passim; and Delphine Bechtel, "Babylon or Jerusalem: Berlin as center of Jewish modernism in the 1920s," in Dagmar C.G. Lorenz and Gabriele Weinberger (eds.), Insiders and Outsiders: Jewish and Gentile Culture in Germany and Austria (Detroit, MI: Wayne State University Press, 1994), 116–23.
13 Glenn Levine, "Yiddish publishing in Berlin and the crisis in Eastern European Jewish culture 1919–1924," Leo Baeck Institute Year Book 42 (1997): 92.

In his 1926 essay "Three Centers," Dovid Bergelson, in a reversal of his previously negative position about Soviet Yiddish culture, argued that only in the progressive USSR did Yiddish literature and culture have opportunities for broader development. In Poland, in contrast, Jewish culture remained too much oriented toward religion and Zionism. Polish publishers, responding to market forces, produced stultifying literature, cheap in both price and quality, for the mass of Yiddish readers. Meanwhile, in the USA, assimilatory forces would simply prove too irresistible to enable the survival of Yiddish culture there over the long term.[14]

For a time, Moscow seemed a promising site for the realization of Bergelson's vision. Its Jewish population, which was relatively small prior to the Revolution, rose rapidly in the first half of the 1930s, in part due to the arrival of aspiring writers, publishers, intellectuals, and performers. Bolshevik authorities were in need of Yiddish literati and were therefore willing to hire non-communists and erstwhile political opponents to produce publications. The city was home to the Jewish section of the Association of Proletarian writers and the Moscow State Yiddish Theatre, making it the center of Soviet Jewish social and cultural activity. With local universities providing instruction in Yiddish language, literature and history, as well as training teachers, it also became the largest center of Yiddish vocational and educational institutions. However, though the city saw itself as the center of the Soviet literary world, many writers chose not to stay. Displeased with submitting their talents to the immediate ideological needs of the regime and seeking an audience that could only be found in the larger Jewish population centers of the former Pale, many preferred Kiev, Kharkov, and Minsk to the Soviet capital.[15]

Indeed, Kiev was the more natural choice as a Soviet center. It was home to a small but daring modernist Yiddish literary scene linked to Vilna in the years prior to 1917. It also functioned as headquarters for the *Kultur-lige*'s intensive Yiddish educational and publishing activity during the brief period of Ukrainian independence. Since Kiev had served as the capital then, it was not suitable to the Bolshevik authorities as the capital of Soviet Ukraine. Instead,

---

14   Dovid Bergelson, "Dray tsentren," *In shpan* 1 (April 1926): 84–96.
15   Gennady Estraikh, *In Harness: Yiddish Writers' Romance with Communism* (Syracuse, NY: Syracuse University Press, 2004), 37–64; Kenneth Moss, "Printing and Publishing after 1800," YIVO *Encyclopedia of Jews in Eastern Europe*, 2: 1460–67, here 1467; Leonid Preisman, "Moscow," YIVO *Encyclopedia of Jews in Eastern Europe*, 2: 1203–4.

the honour went to Kharkov. Together with Minsk in Belarus, Kiev served as the locus for the construction of a proletarian Soviet Yiddish culture.[16]

However, as Yiddish cultural institutions in the Soviet and non-Soviet realms grew increasingly estranged from, if not actively hostile to each other over the course of the decade, it became clear for those outside the communist camp that a "western" capital was necessary. New York was not treated seriously as a contender by many in Europe, despite the presence of a large number of European literary and theatrical talents as well as press circulations among a Yiddish readership that eclipsed that of any European city. New York lacked long standing Jewish cultural traditions, and was seen as losing its Jewish youth rapidly and irretrievably to English-language culture. The American Yiddish language itself was, moreover, inundated with "barbarisms" derived from the local vernacular that would not be understood in Europe.[17] Some Americans, among them Joseph Opatoshu and H. Leyvik, did argue that, to the contrary, the Polish Yiddish literary scene lacked the "energy and collectivism" of its American counterpart. Yet most Yiddish writers living in New York City themselves saw Poland as the true home of Yiddish and, drawn by the lure of enthusiastic audiences, spent extended periods there.[18]

By the late 1920s, discussions in the Polish Yiddish press narrowed the search and stoked a rivalry between "Polish" Warsaw and "Litvak" Vilna, a rivalry that seemed an echo of earlier debates pitting Vilna and Odessa in a contest over leadership of Hebrew letters.[19] Each city had both its champions and detractors who contributed what were at times highly artificial, tendentious and

---

16 Gennady Estraikh, "From Yehupets Jargonists to Kiev Modernists: The Rise of a Yiddish Literary Centre, 1880s–1914," *East European Jewish Affairs* 30.1 (2000): 22, 32–4; Kenneth Moss, "Bringing Culture to the Nation: Hebraism, Yiddishism, and the dilemmas of Jewish cultural formation in Russia and Ukraine, 1917–1919," *Jewish History* 22 (2008): 263–294, esp. 265; Hillel Kazovsky, "Kultur-lige," YIVO *Encyclopedia of the Jews in Eastern Europe*, 1: 953–4.

17 Y.Y. Zinger, "Farzeenishn," *Literarishe bleter* 25–26 (31 October 1924): 3; B. Smolyar, "A brenendike frage fun der gantser yidisher kultur: vet take yidish als shprakh untergeyn in amerike?," *Literarishe bleter* 38 (23 January 1925): 3; Yud-Beyz, "A shmues mit d'r Iser Ginzburg," *Literarishe bleter* 120 (20 August 1926): 547.

18 Mikhail Krutikov, "Yiddish Literature after 1800," YIVO *Encyclopedia of Jews in Eastern Europe*, 2: 2069; Nakhmen Mayzil, *Geven a mol lebn* (Buenos Aires: Tsentral farband fun poylishe yidn in argentine), 227–36.

19 I thank Dan Miron for this insight. On this rivalry, see his *Bodedim be-moadam: Le-diukana shel ha-republika ha-sifrutit ha-'ivrit ba-tehilat ha-me'a ha'esrim* (Tel Aviv: Am Over, 1987), 334–81; and Schachar M. Pinsker, *Literary Passports: The Making of Modernist Hebrew Fiction in Europe* (Stanford, CA: Stanford University Press, 2011), 39–53.

emotionally-colored analyses of the state of Yiddish language and culture based on a combination of statistical and anecdotal evidence to publications spanning the intellectual and political spectrum.

The popular contest, rather than providing objective analyses of the relative condition of Yiddish culture in each city, drew up a cognitive map of Yiddishland with Poland as its leading constituent and charted the progress of the Yiddishist movement as a whole. An examination of this rivalry not only contributes to our understanding of the development and deployment of regional stereotypes among Yiddish-speaking Jews. It also offers a window onto the preoccupations, hopes and anxieties of those engaged in building secular Yiddish culture at a time that, not only in retrospect but in the eyes of many contemporaries, represented both its apex and the beginning of its decline.

Vilna

Despite the influx of thousands of refugees from the surrounding area into the city, the Jewish population of Vilna declined significantly during World War I, a result of famine, disease, forced labour, and emigration.[20] As if to compensate for Vilna's uncertain future by celebrating and thus preserving its storied past, Vilna patriots began a campaign on its behalf during the German occupation. Moyshe Kulbak's iconic poem about Vilna as a locus of both traditional religious and modern secular Jewish currents is but one example of a vast array of literary, commemorative, and popular academic works attempting to chronicle its history, honor its unique character, and otherwise lay claim to its broader cultural-historical relevance.[21] In the interwar period, Vilna's Yiddishist intelligentsia built upon the pre-existing reputation of their beloved city as the "Jerusalem of Lithuania" by proclaiming it the most Yiddish city in the world. "Vilna" Yiddish dialect—in truth, the speech of its intellectual

---

20 Mordechai Zalkin, "Vilnius," YIVO *Encyclopedia of the Jews in Eastern Europe*, 2: 1972–75, esp. 1975.

21 Samuel Kassow, "The uniqueness of Jewish Vilna," in Larisa Lempertiene (ed.), *Vilniaus žydų intelektualinis gyvenimas iki antrojo pasaulinio karo; tarptautinės mokslinės konferencijos medžiaga* [*Vilnius Jewish Intellectual Life before World War Two: International Scientific Conference*], 16–17.09.2003 (Vilnius: Mokslo aidai, 2004), 147–61; Cecile Kuznitz, "On the Jewish street: Yiddish culture and the urban landscape in interwar Vilna," *Studies in Jewish Civilization* 9 (1998): 65–92. Hirsh Abramovitsh, "Retsenzyes: Yidishe vilne in bild un vort, kinstlerisher almanakh," *Literarishe bleter* 46 (20 March 1925): 6.

class—already enjoyed superregional prestige as the "best" Yiddish by the early twentieth century.[22]

Despite its relatively small size relative to newer Jewish metropolises like Lodz, Warsaw, and Odessa, Vilna had possessed a continuous Jewish population since the sixteenth century and had been a leading site of pre-war Jewish journalistic publishing activity, in Yiddish and Hebrew, since the nineteenth century. Vilna publishing houses such as the Widow and Brothers Romm, Matz, and, later, B.A. Kletzkin, published both traditional and modern fare, much of it in service of the *Haskalah* and the Jewish nationalist and socialist movements which took firm root there earlier than in the Kingdom of Poland.[23] Kletzkin's penchant for paying considerable honoraria to writers, a practice pioneered by Sholem Aleichem in Kiev, helped to establish the city's reputation for "literary" production. This contrasted with the allegedly more "commercial" interests of Warsaw publishers, who published much *shund-literatur,* i.e. literature that appealed to less discerning local audiences in the nineteenth century.[24] Although Vilna, too, published its share of cheap literature (both in price and quality, e.g. the works of its son, I.M. Dick), the city's association with higher calibre writing was strengthened by the socialist press' willingness in Vilna to print *belle-lettres,* regardless of its ideological content, for the edification of workers.[25]

On a practical level, Vilna's Jewish intelligentsia found that its decades-old Russian cultural orientation was a liability once that city was no longer under tsarist rule. Commenting on Vilna Jewry's esteem for Russian early in the twentieth century, one observer sarcastically quipped "when you walk in the streets of Vilna and hear how Jews struggle to speak nothing less than a broken Russian, you might think the Jews of Vilna, the source of the real pure Lithuanian Yiddish, hate their language, which they no longer speak amongst themselves, with their own wives, when no one hears them, because it is a disgrace to speak the *tsimes*-language even in front of the maid."[26] Indeed, few

---

22 On the prestige of Vilna dialect, see Dovid Katz, "The religious prestige of the Gaon and the secular prestige of Lithuanian Yiddish," in Izraelis Lempertas (ed.), *The Gaon of Vilnius and the Annals of Jewish Culture* (Vilnius: Vilnius University Publishing House, 1998), 187–199.

23 Kenneth Moss, "Printing and Publishing after 1800"; Zalkin, "Vilnius," 1975–6.

24 Ewa Geller, "The Jews of Warsaw as Speech Community: Homage to Warsaw Yiddish," in Eleonora Bergman and Olga Zienkiewicz (eds.), *Żydzi Warszawy: materiały konferencji w 100. rocznicę urodzin Emanuela Ringelbluma (21 listopada 1900–7 marca 1944)* (Warsaw: Żydowski Instytut Historyczny, 2000), 111–128, esp. 122.

25 Estraikh, "From Yehupets Jargonists to Kiev Modernists," 31.

26 Izraeli, "Zhargon bay dem vilner oylem," *Di tsayt* 28 (6 [19] March 1906): 3.

children of the Jewish intelligentsia and middle class in the early twentieth century were completely ignorant of Yiddish, even if their knowledge may have been limited to "encounters with the chicken seller who came into the kitchen or grandparents who spoke it 'so the children won't hear.' "[27] And those who became engaged in the socialist movement, of which Vilna was an important organizational and journalistic center, were obliged to learn Yiddish in order to reach a mass audience.

Much of Vilna's Jewish intelligentsia came to embrace a demonstratively pro-Yiddish stance during World War I and continued to do so throughout the interwar period, even if, as elsewhere in the former tsarist empire, its members continued to speak Russian in private.[28] This strategy was conditioned by a combination of factors: their lack of identification with Polish culture and the Polish nationalist cause (despite Vilna's eventual re-incorporation into independent Poland), their distinctive Jewish nationalist aspirations, and their desire to maintain a relatively neutral position in the conflict between Poles, Lithuanians, Belarusians, and Russians over control of the city and its environs.[29]

An important prestige factor for Vilna was the presence of YIVO, the Jewish Scientific Institute, which Yiddishists considered the crowning achievement of their movement: it was the university, national library, and language academy of Yiddishland, and *the* address for Yiddishism. Members of YIVO's tight-knit administration in Vilna were all active in the various social, cultural, and philanthropic organizations functioning in and on behalf of Yiddish. In contrast with Warsaw, which drew talents from the Polish provinces and beyond, Vilna's population was remarkably homogenous—mainly *Litvaks* from neighbouring shtetls and cities in the region.[30] The marked loyalty to Yiddish and social cohesiveness allegedly exhibited (at least vis-à-vis non-Jews) by all inhabitants despite class, political and religious differences made Vilna "the most Yiddish city" in the world.[31] Dr. Tsemach Szabad, a Russified doctor committed to caring

---

27 M. Vaynraykh, "Unzer yidishe shprakh nokh der milkhome vet shoyn oykh nit zayn di zelbe vi biz itst," *Forverts* (28 December 1941): 4.
28 Moss, "Bringing Culture to the Nation," 278–9.
29 Kalman Weiser, "The Jewel in the Yiddish Crown: Who Will Occupy the Chair in Yiddish at the University of Vilnius?" *Polin* 24 (2011): 225–7.
30 Avraham Nowersztern, "Shir halel, shir kina: dimuya shel vilna ba-shirat yidish bein shetei milhamot ha-'olam," in David Assaf et al. (eds.), *Mi-vilna le-yerushalayim: Mehkarim be-toldoteihem u've'tarbutam shel yehudei mizrah eiropa mugashim li-Profesor Shemu'el Verses* (Jerusalem: Magnes Press, 2002), 485–511, esp. 492.
31 Arcadius Kahan, "Vilna: The Sociocultural Anatomy of a Jewish community in interwar Poland," in his *Essays in Jewish Social and Economic History* (Chicago: University of

for the city's indigent and a community activist who headed the Vilna branch of the Diaspora Nationalist Folksparty, was thus hailed as the "most Vilnish personality." His "return" to Yiddish and adoption of Yiddishism was not difficult, according to fellow Folkist Noah Prylucki, because "unlike in Poland, the distance here between *folksmasn* and intelligentsia is not great; one could be linguistically assimilated and still maintain the mentality and characteristics of the *folksmasn*."[32] In Vilna, more than anywhere else in Yiddishland, according to linguist and Vilna patriot Max Weinreich, the children of the intelligentsia were teaching their linguistically assimilated parents Yiddish and accommodating the language to modern life. And the Yiddish they were teaching them was literary Yiddish as fostered by Yiddishist institutions, not regional dialect.[33]

Jewish schools whose language of instruction had been Russian prior to WWI now taught in Yiddish or Hebrew, and a remarkable array of both religious and secular cultural institutions were created for the city's mere 50–60,000 Jews. In the interwar period, those institutions included Poland's only Yiddish teachers' seminary (active until 1931) and the Real-gimnazyia, one of four Yiddish language high schools remaining in Poland in the late 1930s and the only one to be accredited, if only for a time, on the same level as a Polish state school.[34] Nakhmen Mayzil, holding up Yiddishist activity in Vilna as a model, noted with satisfaction in 1927 that "in Vilna, a deep, more serious restructuring of life's conditions is occurring. The same secondary school, the same school director, the same teacher—once in Russian, now Yiddish. Mothers learned Russian and Russian culture in the same schools where daughters now study in Yiddish in a Jewish atmosphere."[35] There seemed to be a complete turnaround.

As elsewhere in the *kresy*, the multiethnic eastern borderlands of Poland where no local nationality predominated culturally, Jews identified strongly here as Jews by nationality regardless of their language preference. Indeed, like many of their non-Jewish neighbours, in fact, Vilna Jewry possessed a strong sense of regionalism and viewed their city as neither Russian nor Polish. Attendance in secular schools in Jewish languages—both Yiddish and

Chicago Press, 1986), 149–160. Mayzil, "Vilne meynt es ernst!" *Literarishe bleter* 25 (24 June 1927): 474–5.

32 Noyekh Prilutski, "D'r Tsemakh Shabad," *Moment* 23 (27 January 1935): 3.
33 On the changing nature of Vilna Yiddish in the interwar period, see Max Weinreich, "Harbe ivre," *Yidishe shprakh* 1.4 (May–June 1941): 107–8; and his "Di yidishe klal-shprakh in der tsveyter helft tsvontsikstn yorhundert," *Yidishe shprakh* XXX (1971): 17–18.
34 Shimon Frost, *Schooling as a Socio-Political Expression* (Jerusalem: Magnes Press, 1998), 39, 134–135.
35 Nakhmen Mayzil, "Vilne meynt es ernst!" *Literarishe bleter* 25 (24 June 1927): 474–5.

Hebrew—was proportionately and numerically higher here than in "Polish" Warsaw.[36]

Warsaw

In Warsaw, the Yiddish schools' perceived association with political parties—above all the anti-clerical, anti-Zionist, Bund—as well as their lower (or, in some cases, lack of) sympathy for Hebrew and religiosity, made them unpopular with impoverished and more traditional parents.[37] Moreover, in Warsaw, home to countless Hasidic courts, Yiddishist ideology (though not the Yiddish language itself) faced the opposition of a well-organized Orthodox movement, particularly that of the Gerer rebbe and the Agudat Yisrael.[38] Finally, the city's polonized Jewish plutocracy, which since the mid-nineteenth century stood at a great remove from its Yiddish-speaking petite bourgeoisie, proletariat, and wealthy traditionalists, most commonly viewed itself as Jewish by religion but Polish by nationality. Its members had little positive to say about Yiddish, usually viewing it as an embarrassing emblem of medieval separatism and primitiveness. The influential Polish literary journal *Wiadomości Literackie*, the voice of the elite of polonized Jewish intellectuals, voiced a similarly negative view of Yiddish literature.[39] Such views were, of course, hardly unique to Warsaw. But polonizing forces were weaker in Vilna.[40]

Vilna was held up as an inspiration for Warsaw.[41] "Vilna takes it [Yiddish culture] seriously," wrote Nakhmen Mayzil, the Warsaw-based editor of Poland's

---

36   For statistics for 1934–5, see Khaym Shloyme Kazdan, *Di geshikhte fun yidishn shulvezn in umophengikn poyln* (Mexico City: Gezelshaft "kultur un hilf", 1947), 189.

37   For impressions concerning differences between Warsaw and Vilna Yiddish schools, see Avrom Golomb, *A halber yorhundert yidishe dertsiung* (Rio de Janeiro: Farlag "Monte Skopus", 1958), 121–136.

38   On the activity of the Agudah, see Gershon Bacon, *The Politics of Tradition: Agudat Yisrael in Poland, 1916–1939* (Jerusalem: Magnes Press, 1996). On Orthodox attitudes toward Yiddish in Poland, see Kalman Weiser, "The 'Orthodox' Orthography of Solomon Birnbaum," *Studies in Contemporary Jewry* 20 (2004): 275–95.

39   Eugenia Prokop-Janiec, *Polish-Jewish Literature in the Interwar Years* (Syracuse, NY: Syracuse University Press), 58 and 74.

40   Czesław Miłosz, *Native Realm: A Search for Self-Definition* (New York: Ferrar, Strauss and Giroux, 1968), 98.

41   See, for example, "Fun vokh tsu vokh: vilne un varshe," *Literarishe bleter* 137 (1926): 853; Yankev Vigodski, "Di badaytung fun der yidisher vilne far di poylishe yidn," *Literarishe bleter* 45 (1932): 716.

leading Yiddish cultural and intellectual journal *Literarishe bleter*.[42] Each struggle for the rights and recognition of Yiddish or the Yiddish school, even when resulting in failure, was lauded as a model of dogged accomplishment in the face of meager resources and in an environment hostile to Jewish and, more specifically, Yiddishist aspirations.[43] Warsaw, it was pointed out, even owed its major Yiddish cultural institutions—above all, the press and schools—to the organizational and leadership élan of Vilna-oriented "Litvaks."[44] Although the subject of petty resentments among Polish Jews for their cultural foreignness and economic successes, Litvak migrants to Warsaw fostered modern ideologies like nationalism and socialism among a Polish Jewry, whose intelligentsia and plutocracy had been inclined toward ideological, not just practical, Polonization since before World War I. Not only were the founding editors of the major Warsaw dailies *Haynt* and *Moment* mainly Litvaks (see chapter by Joanna Nalewajko-Kulikov in this volume), but there was also a clear division in labor between journalists and fiction writers in *Der veg*, Warsaw's first Yiddish daily, between Jews from *Lite* and Ukraine (in the former role) and Polish Jews (in the latter).[45] "Litvaks" alone, it was argued, possessed the organizational skills needed to found institutions of modern Jewish culture.[46]

In its bustling heyday, Yiddish Warsaw was frequently criticized not only by visitors but by its own denizens for its shortcomings vis-à-vis Vilna. It was a brash parvenu, a cauldron of turmoil lacking in both physical and cultural rootedness. Its Yiddish was deemed sloppy and was consequently neglected, notwithstanding notable exceptions, by the budding field of Yiddish

---

42   Nakhmen Mayzil, "Vilne meynt es ernst!"
43   See, for example, Y.Y. Zinger, "Vilne," *Literarishe bleter* 94 (19 February 1926): 125; Yoysef Tshernikhov, "Vilne—a pozitsye," *Literarishe bleter* 45 (1932): 716–7; M. Shur. "Dos yidishe shul-vezn in vilne," *Literarishe bleter* 45 (1932): 719.
44   Strictly speaking, the term "Litvaks" denotes in Yiddish Jews from regions of the northeastern Pale of Settlement, the territory of *Lite* in the former Polish-Lithuanian Commonwealth. But it was indiscriminately applied to all Jewish migrants in Congress Poland originating in the Pale of Settlement from the late nineteenth century on, thus lumping together true Litvaks and Ukrainian Jews, cf. Stephen Corrsin, *Warsaw before the First World War: Poles and Jews in the Third City of the Russian Empire, 1880–1914* (Boulder, CO: East European Monographs, 1989), 34.
45   Noyekh Prilutski, "Lazar Kahan," *Literarishe bleter* 2 (9 January 1931): 27; Shmuel Niger, "Vu iz itst der yidisher tsenter?"; on the Litvaks' role in the *Haynt*, see also the contribution of Joanna Nalewajko-Kulikov in this volume.
46   Niger, *ibid*; Yitskhok Kanter, "Farvos iz azoy farshpreyt dos litvishe yidish?" *Haynt* 36 (10 February 1939).

philology.[47] In contrast with storied Vilna, the city was mainly to find its literary commemoration after the Holocaust, and much of it is disparaging.[48] According to I.J. Singer, who spent much of his life in Warsaw prior to his emigration to the United States, "Vilna took all the good that Russia had to offer: simplicity, openness, respect for a person, struggle, commitment to principles. Work for the sake of the collective. Warsaw took nihilism, laziness, despair, non-punctuality."[49]

In the press, Yiddish Warsaw was routinely equated with the stereotypical passionate but intellectually undisciplined Hasid, while Vilna was personified by the staid, rationalist anti-Hasid (*Mitnaged*). Even critics of Vilna typically attributed its flaws to the nefarious influence of Warsaw, Poland's political, cultural, and economic capital that reputedly embodied haste, cheap commercialism, and political factiousness alongside such positive traits as enthusiasm and creativity. Writer A. Golomb described Warsaw's bad influence on Vilna as follows:

> This is, in certain aspects, the Warsaw press, theatre, the cultural-societal events in general and social-political life in general. If you look objectively, you see that ideas do not compete here but camps, not worldviews but Hasidic courts, the Kotzker with the Belzer, excuse me, the "Medemianer" and the "Borokhovianer." The goal is not to clarify an issue or view but to destroy an opponent. The type of Shmaye the Hero, who tears the shtreimel from the rabbi and thinks this makes him victorious over his opponent, has become the dominant type in our social organizations.
>
> No longer do people read and discuss. They praise parties and denounce opponents as Hasidim do their rebbes.
>
> When Vilna led a separate cultural and societal life, the two sides balanced each other. Now that Vilna is weakened and its societal life submissive, our cultural movement has a one-sided character, 'a second-rate (*tandet*) character.'
>
> Vilna imitates Warsaw but what is organic and natural in Warsaw is pitiful and clumsy in Vilna.[50]

---

47 Geller, *Jews of Warsaw*, 114–6.
48 Shmuel Rozhanski, "Di role fun varshe in der yidisher literatur," in his *Varshe in der yidisher literatur* (Buenos Aires: Literatur-gezelshaft baym yivo, 1979), 5–18.
49 Y.Y. Zinger, "Vilne."
50 A. Golomb, "Dos poylishe varshe un di litvishe vilne," *Literarishe bleter* 22 (1 June 1924): 419–20.

Shmuel Niger's brother, the writer and long-time Vilna resident Daniel Tsharni, also captured the contrasting popular images of the two cities:

> You only have to arrive in Warsaw from the Vilna direction to feel just how big city-overloaded Warsaw is. Just coming down from the train station, you get the impression that the city might explode any minute from being too overloaded. I haven't seen such a strong but unregulated movement in any single capital city in Europe...
>
> This perhaps explains the permanent "civil war" between various workers' parties, between Zionists and Orthodox, between Hasidim of one rebbe and of another, the civil war that has really no justification because the entire energy and passion for struggle is used not along race and class lines but rather in the narrow confines between the Nalewki and Tłomacka [streets], and couldn't bring more harm.
>
> Infighting, instead of combating Jewish poverty and lack of rights. Such is Warsaw Jewish society life, press, and literature. "They don't make, they produce, not struggle but tear at each other, not breath but pant." This is the impression Warsaw made on me after not seeing it for twenty years. Being in Warsaw, you begin to long even more for the modest, famished Vilna.[51]

Vilna's growing poverty, relative geographic seclusion, and provincial character in the 1920s and 30s in comparison with that of much larger Warsaw, with its over 300,000 Jews, were transformed into virtues, proof of the intensity of its commitment to Jewish nationalism and cultural continuity and its resistance to the lures of "assimilation" that prevailed in the former Congress Poland and even more so in Galicia, where Polonization among modernizing Jews was most advanced in the nineteenth century.[52]

This optimistic construction was supposedly affirmed by Vilna's designation as the seat of the Yiddish branch of the international PEN club, despite Warsaw's being the home of the prominent Jewish Writers and Journalists Association (popularly known by its address, Tłomackie 13) and the publication of 83 Yiddish periodicals, in comparison with Vilna's 8, in the years 1919–39. Indeed, according to Joanna Lysek's appraisal, Vilna's literary scene in actuality suffered from an inferiority complex vis-à-vis that of Warsaw, which it felt

---

51 Daniel Tsharni, "Vilne-varshe," *Der vilner tog* 135 (13 June 1930): 2.
52 On beginnings of Polonization among Jews in Galicia, see Ezra Mendelsohn, "Jewish assimilation in Lvov: the case of Wilhelm Feldman," *Slavic Review* 28 (1969): 577–90.

ignored its achievements. This sense of indignation spurred it on.[53] In order to remain competitive with the Polish capital, Vilna patriots called attention to their own literary institutions, such as Rudnicki's café, home to local writers and intellectuals, and, of course, *Yung Vilne*.[54] Rather than a spontaneous development, however, the literary debut of this collection of talented young writers, as well as its very name, was orchestrated and supported by the older generation of Yiddishist intelligentsia, above all Zalmen Reyzen, in its campaign to promote the city. This sponsorship contrasted markedly with the lack of support received by Yiddish avant-garde groupings elsewhere in interwar Poland, such as *Yung yidish, Ringen, Khalyastre,* and *Albatros*, each of which adopted a defiant posture vis-à-vis prior Yiddish literary currents.[55]

From a quantitative standpoint, of course, Warsaw's importance as a center of Yiddish cultural activity could not be contested: the size and diversity of its publications dwarfed those of Vilna, the total number of students enrolled in its Jewish schools (although not Yiddishist ones) was higher, and the extent of its theatre scene was much greater. The latter even came to include, in 1917, the acclaimed *Vilner-trupe*, so named because it originated in Vilna and, contrary to the accepted practice of using Ukrainian Yiddish in theatrical productions, employed "Literary" Yiddish pronunciation. Needless to say, the Warsaw region and Warsaw proper also came to produce Yiddish journalists and literary talents of its own. Those journalists who were especially popular knew how to write about modern topics in a language appreciated by Warsaw's largely petit-bourgeois, Hasidic readership.

Despite those achievements, however, Warsaw was frequently criticized for lacking commitment to Yiddishist ideals and communal solidarity.[56] Articles regularly took stock of a variety of indicators—newspaper and periodical circulations proportionate to Warsaw's Jewish population,[57] interest in spelling reform,[58] school enrollments, census language data,[59] name-giving

---

53 Joanna Lisek, "Między Warszawą a Wilnem: Kontakty Środowisk Literackich w Okresie Międzywojennym," *Studia Judaica* 9.1 (17) (2006): 69–70, 80–81.
54 A.Y. Grodzenski, "Di 'literarishe' vilne (tsveyter briv)," *Literarishe bleter* 35 (1925): 5.
55 Justin D. Cammy, "Tsevorfene bleter: The Emergence of Yung Vilne," *Polin* 14 (2001): 174–7.
56 E.g. Z. Reyzen, "A kultur-pozitsye," *Literarishe bleter* 10 (9 March 1928), 200.
57 Nakhmen Mayzil, "Leyent men in varshe yidish," *Haynt* 10 (11 January 1935): 7, 22; and (25 January 1935): 7.
58 E.g. A. Golomb, "Forzikhtik mit dem yidishn vort," *Literarishe bleter* 26 (26 June 1931): 493–4.
59 E.g. Sh. Niger, "Undzer yugnt in poyln," *Literarishe bleter* 10 (9 March 1932): 200; Sh. L. Shnayderman, "Toyte tsifern," *Literarishe bleter* 17 (22 April 1932): 271–2.

practices,⁶⁰ commercial and communal signage⁶¹—to take the "pulse" of Yiddish in Warsaw. Commentators frequently used their findings to chastise Warsaw residents for irresponsibly neglecting or abandoning Yiddish and endangering Jewish national interests by presenting a linguistically-divided front to the Polish government.

A number of guilty parties were tried on the pages of the Warsaw Yiddish press for promoting Polish as a language of both high culture and everyday use by Jewish youth and the "jargonization" of the written word—an insult to the proud achievement of a standardized language—with a mixture of unruly Germanisms and Polonisms.⁶² While the ideologically motivated Assimilationist movement that inspired the tiny secularizing elite of Warsaw Jewry prior to WWI was no longer relevant, so-called practical or forced "assimilation" due to economic and social exigencies had become a serious concern. The majority of Jewish children attended state or private Jewish schools whose language of instruction was Polish. Preference for reading and speaking Polish understandably increased with one's level of secular education in that language as well as the increased availability of many varieties of Polish books.⁶³ The prestige of Polish, the official language of the state and the medium of a highly attractive literature, was undeniable. The best efforts of local Yiddishists aside, Yiddish suffered from association with the poorest and most religious segments of the Jewish population—those very segments least inclined to support Yiddishism either ideologically or financially.

Whereas Vilna's Jewish intellectuals were praised for their trend *away* from Russian and *towards* Yiddish, what Polish Jewish intellectual or even Yiddish writer, it was asked, actually raised his child in Yiddish or sent him to a Yiddish school? As I.B. Singer would later recall, "there was an unwritten law among the wives of Yiddish writers and of the great number of so-called Yiddishists that their children should be raised to speak the Polish language."⁶⁴ Peretz himself, the dean of literary Warsaw prior to his death in 1915, was accused of

---

60   E.g. Noyekh Prilutski, "Pan Knobelman un di yidishe nemen," *Moment* 273 (30 December 1915): 3.
61   Nakhmen Mayzil, "Yidishe shildn," *Literarishe bleter* 132 (12 November 1926): 747–8; M. Gelenberg, "Yidish oyf di varshever gasn," *Literarishe bleter* 19 (9 May, 1930): 346–7.
62   Shmuel Vinter, "Vegn der farpoylishung fun yidish," *Der vilner tog* 242 (23 October 1936): 2; Gelenberg, *ibid*. Noyekh Prilutski, "Zhargonizurung fun yidish," *Yidish far ale* 1 (March 1938): 3–8; Arn Tseytlin, "Prese-yidish," *Yidish far ale* 1 (March 1938): 8–12.
63   Ellen Deborah Kellman, "Dos yidishe bukh alarmirt: Towards the history of Yiddish Reading in Inter-war Poland," *Polin* 16 (2003): 226.
64   Isaac Bashevis Singer, *Love and Exile: An Autobiographical Trilogy* (Garden City, NY: Doubleday & Company, 1984), 187.

setting a poor example, speaking Russian or Polish as soon as he descended from a literary podium: "If the *rebbe* may, we may too, all the more so." Berating Yiddish writers themselves, who "instead of Yiddishizing, have an assimilationist effect," A. Almi, a former Warsaw resident who had immigrated to the United States, lamented in 1928:

> What about the children of Yiddish writers? Better not to speak of Mendele's children [of which his eldest son converted to Christianity]. Peretz' son is a fervent assimilationist. Sholem Asch's son is an accomplished English-language writer for whom Yiddish is foreign. Whose fault is this? Of the older generation of Yiddish writers, I can think of only two whose children write in Yiddish: [the "Litvaks"] Tsevi Prylucki and Hillel Zeitlin.[65]

Above all, Warsaw Jews, like those in Lodz and the cities of Galicia were found guilty of the sin of "shmendrikism"—being embarrassed to speak Yiddish in public and preferring Polish (in student colonies abroad, as well!), even if spoken poorly, despite—or perhaps because of—the elusive acceptance for Jews in Polish gentile society. While affecting all classes, including the proletariat,[66] "shmendrikism" was attributed in particular to the social climbing petite bourgeoisie, especially its women.[67] Indeed, women—the "Sabinas and Reginas" (alternately, "Sabinas and Balbinas"—names taken from popular stories in the Yiddish press)[68] as they were lambasted—bore the brunt of the blame as mothers who refused to speak Yiddish with their children out of shame or in order to prevent them from acquiring a socially stigmatizing Yiddish accent that would close doors to higher education and the professions in an increasingly antisemitic climate.[69] These charges were hardly new and, while exaggerated and gendered, exonerating fathers of any responsibility, they owed something to the greater willingness among traditionalists, including Hasidim, to expose women to gentile languages and culture.[70]

---

65   A. Almi, "Verter un maysim," *Literarishe bleter* 36 (7 September 1928): 699–700.
66   Y. Rabinovitsh, "Dos antloyfn fun yidishn loshn!," *Vokhnshrift* 27 (2 October 1931): 4.
67   Reyzen, "A kultur-pozitsye."
68   B. Yeushzon, "Nash psheglondizm," *Haynt* 54 (4 March 1926): 3.
69   For attitudes among polonized and polonizing Jewish youth toward Yiddish, see Anna Landau-Czajka, *Syn będzie Lech: asymilacja Żydów w Polsce międzywojennej* (Warsaw: Wydawnictwo Neriton, Instytut Historii PAN, 2006), 224–9.
70   On the inroads of the Polish language among strictly religious girls, a phenomenon noted before the interwar period in predominately Hasidic Galicia and Congress Poland, see Gershon Bacon, "La société juive dans le royaume de la Pologne du Congrès (1860–1914),"

With the exception of *Izraelita*, whose readership consisted of members of small circles of Assimilationists and which was both ideologically and linguistically foreign to the vast majority of Warsaw Jews, little existed in the way of a Polish-language press, let alone literature, directed at a specifically Jewish audience prior to the interwar period. While Jewish readers and contributors to the "progressive" Polish press (often under pseudonyms) were certainly not admired, they were not as singled out for opprobrium as readers and contributors to such "Shmendrik-tribunes" as the Jewish women's weekly *Ewa* and the Zionist daily *Nasz Przegląd*, perceived as direct competitors. In the eyes of those Yiddish journalists who did not contribute to it, the Polish-Jewish press that emerged in the interwar period to meet the needs of a rapidly growing class of linguistically polonized and polonizing Jews who still identified with Jewish nationalism was neither Polish nor Jewish. Its writers and editors, they claimed, clad in "top hats and white gloves," were ignorant representatives— like German Jews—of de-ethnicized (and hence, inauthentic), tasteless "synagogue Judaism" rather than folksy *Yidishkeyt*. They failed to appreciate Hebrew and Yiddish writers and impressed their ignorant female readers with superficial scribbling that betrayed an ignorance of Jewish history, culture, and national interests. Consequently, they had little of value to contribute to Jews and were hardly qualified to present Jewish perspectives to a non-Jewish audience and improve Polish-Jewish relations—the only legitimate purpose of a Polish-Jewish press.[71]

Needless to say, such condescending, misogynistic, and inaccurate evaluations of these newspapers smacked as much of jealousy for readers' attention as anxiety for Yiddish writers' livelihoods. The Polish-Jewish press drew away not only readers, but advertisers too, both Polish and Jewish, not to mention a sense of cultural relevance.[72] Vilna, lacking a Polish-Jewish daily, thus compared favourably on this score as well.

To read much of the interwar Yiddish press is to gain the impression that Yiddish was headed toward extinction in all major cities in Yiddishland, in Eastern Europe and beyond. But this was always with the exception of Vilna.

---

in Shmuel Trigano (ed.), *La Société juive à travers l'histoire*, vol. 1 (Paris: Fayard, 1992), 647, 656; Moyshe Prager, "Dos yidishe togblat," in *Yidishe prese in varshe*, vol. 2: *Fun noentn over* (New York: Congress for Jewish Culture, 1956), 488–489.

71 Z. Reyzen, "A kultur-pozitsye"; Yehoshue Perle, "Poylish-yidish," *Literarishe bleter* 1 (1 January 1938): 4–5.

72 "Der tsushtand fun der prese in poyln: A shmues mit Bernard Zinger," *Literarishe bleter* 51 (16 December 1932): 812–14. On the Polish-Jewish press and literature, see Michael Steinlauf, "The Polish Jewish Daily Press," *Polin* 2 (1987): 219–245.

Neither indifference nor opposition to Yiddishist ideology among a segment of Vilna's population, such as Hebraists and the Orthodox, nor the spread of Polonization among its youth or declining rates of attendance in Yiddish schools by the 1930s, compromised the images of Vilna as a Yiddish lighthouse or citadel.[73] The intensive activity of Vilna's secular Yiddish sector was the yardstick by which all else was measured.

Not all Warsaw Yiddishists agreed with all the paeans to Vilna at the expense of Warsaw, however, even if they did recognize Vilna "as first among equals," as Noah Prylucki put it, thanks to the presence of YIVO there.[74] Many resented being constantly thrown on the defensive. The poet Kadia Molodowski denounced the tendency "to negate Warsaw" in the Yiddish press. In refuting A. Almi's assertions that Warsaw, his home 20 years prior, had lost its pre-war character as an intimate literary center, Molodowski retorted that such intimacy was impossible in a city of Warsaw's size. Factionalization was inevitable among the numerous schools, libraries, and literary and cultural associations that had mushroomed in Warsaw since WWI. But this was evidence not of the decline of Yiddish culture, but its growth and diversification.[75] Nakhmen Mayzil, for his part, insisted that circulation and library statistics attesting to the sorry state of Warsaw's Yiddish readership were misleading: they failed to account for the numerous additional pairs of eyes that read a Yiddish publication or the enthusiastic audiences at Yiddish lectures and performances even among those who most commonly read or spoke Polish, not to mention

---

73   In the words of the Polish poet Czesław Miłosz, who spent his school years in Vilna ignorant of Jewish culture, "If familiarity with Jewish literature, which would have removed many prejudices, was practically nonexistent, the progressive and Leftist intellectuals of Jewish origin must share a serious part of the blame... Their journals carried on campaigns for 'conscious motherhood' and sexual freedom. But they were unwilling to take an interest in Yiddish literature or to translate it into Polish because they saw it as provincial and inferior, a leftover from the ghetto, the very mention of which was a tactless blunder." On the changing nature of Vilna Yiddish in the interwar period, see Max Weinreich, "Harbe ivre," and his "Di yidishe klal-shprakh in der tsveyter helft tsvontsikstn yorhundert." For information on school attendance, see Gershon Bacon, "National Revival: Ongoing Acculturation—Jewish Education in Interwar Poland," *Simon Dubnow Institut Jahrbuch* I (2008): 71–92; Nathan Cohen, "The Jews of Independent Poland: Linguistic and Cultural Changes," in Ernest Krausz and Gitta Tulea (eds.), *Starting the Twenty-First Century: Sociological Reflections and Challenges* (New Brunswick, NJ: Transaction Publishers, 2002), 161–73; Tsemakh Shabad, "Vegn dem natsional-kulturelrn matsev fun di yidn in vilne," *Literarishe bleter* 49 (8 December 1933): 785–6.

74   Noyekh Prilutski, "D'r Tsemakh Shabad."

75   Kadye Molodovski, "Vegn der mode tsu 'farneynen' varshe," *Literarishe bleter* 44 (3 November 1933): 693–4.

Hebrew.[76] The historian Ignacy Schiper suggested at a YIVO conference in 1935 that Vilna could accomplish much on the academic front precisely because it was so quiet, unlike Warsaw, the "center of Jewish and Polish social institutions." Vilna's very stillness of life and lack of distractions, according to this logic, provided ideal conditions for research.[77] Others offered a similar backhanded compliment: Vilna Jewry's ghetto-like character and its provincialism, in contrast with the cosmopolitan nature of Warsaw, preserved it from the temptations of world culture.[78]

While a fanatical hostility towards Vilna and Litvaks of the type exhibited by the combative writer I.M. Weissenberg was hardly typical, some Warsaw Yiddishists expressed clear dissatisfaction with Vilna's hegemony, especially concerning the operations of YIVO. The flagship institution's affiliates outside of Vilna sometimes protested against what they saw as its Vilna-centric research agenda, its refusal to accord a more active role to other centers, which it certainly relied upon for fundraising, and its refusal to even inform members outside of Vilna of important decisions. Nakhmen Mayzil argued, at a YIVO conference in 1935, that "Vilna must not become like the Land of Israel that all of the Jews of the world must work for it."[79] An embittered Noah Prylucki complained of the lack of encouragement of research about other communities, the cozy familiarity among YIVO's Vilna stalwarts, and the rude reception accorded initiatives emanating from other quarters.[80]

Max Weinreich and his colleagues in Vilna—many of whom knew each other well from their university days in St. Petersburg[81]—for their part actively attempted to keep Warsaw away from a more active role in managing YIVO's affairs. This was out of a desire to preserve YIVO's ostensibly supra-party Yiddishist commitment from the "revolution" sought by the more politicized, left-wing Warsaw activists, especially Bundists, who argued that Yiddishist cultural work that was not directly connected to class politics was essentially

76 Nakhmen Mayzil, "Vi halt es mit yidish in varshe?" *Literarishe bleter* 18 (3 May 1935): 280–1; idem, "Vi halt es mit yidish in varshe? II." *Literarishe bleter* 29 (10 May 1935): 297–8; idem, "Leyent men in varshe yidish?" *Haynt* 22 (25 January 1935): 7.
77 YIVO, *Der alveltlekher tsuzamenfor fun yidishn visnshaftlekhn institute* (1936), 35.
78 A. Almi, "Varshe, vilne, nyu-york," *Literarishe bleter* 1 (5 January 1934): 3–4.
79 Cecile Kuznitz, "The Origins of Yiddish Scholarship and the YIVO Institute for Jewish Research," (Unpublished PhD dissertation, Stanford University, 2000), 147 n. 135.
80 Weiser, "The Jewel in the Yiddish Crown," 242; YIVO, *Der alveltlekher tsuzamenfor fun yidishn visnshaftlekhn institut* (1936), 69.
81 See Yudl Mark, "Di ershte yorn fun yivo," *Di tsukunft* XXXI.4 (April 1975): 130–6.

meaningless.⁸² In some cases, personal conflicts with Warsaw colleagues (e.g. Prylucki) led to the latters' exclusion from decision-making.⁸³

A number of voices also opposed the widespread notion that "Literary Yiddish" was identical with Lithuanian Yiddish, and that there was something inherently inferior about "kopote-peyesdik," i.e. Hasidic, Polish Yiddish.⁸⁴ In actuality, the grammar of Literary Yiddish is based chiefly on that of Polish and Ukrainian Yiddish, while it employs a pronunciation most similar to that of the Vilna secular intelligentsia. Literary pronunciation was "purified" of lower prestige sounds characteristic of Lithuanian Yiddish. It thus lacks the collective features known as *sabesdiker losn* ("sabbath language," a play on *shabesdiker loshn*), i.e. the seeming inability to distinguish between sibilants in the pairs /s/ and /š/, /z/ and /ž/, and /ts/ and /č/, and the characteristic *Litvish* /ey/ where other dialects have /oy/, e.g. Literary "toyre" instead of *Litvish* "teyre." As Gennady Estraikh observes of Vilna Yiddishist intellectuals, "Many of them were, like [Ber] Borokhov, Yiddishist neophytes and either learned to speak Yiddish or returned to it after long years of speaking Russian, Polish, or German. As a result, the Vilna intellectuals' 'high' Yiddish rarely sounded like any of the dialects, including 'low' Warsaw Yiddish."⁸⁵

In any case, Literary Yiddish was associated with modern secular movements by World War I. It made inroads not only among the students of the secular Yiddish *Tsisho* schools in all dialect territories but among the girls in the religious *Beys-yankev* schools of Congress Poland, as well. Children increasingly proved diglossic, speaking an approximation of literary Yiddish in the classroom and a Warsaw dialect or a mixture of both outside the classroom.⁸⁶ Purists disdained hypercorrections in speech and signage based on often incorrect assumptions about Literary Yiddish, as well as the notion that Polish Yiddish pronunciation and vocabulary, commonly associated with provincialism and Hasidic life, was somehow unfit for higher cultural functions. A few self-proclaimed democrats, in contrast, rejected what they saw as the propagation of *Litvish* norms in the standardization of Yiddish by an elitist YIVO and

---

82   Kuznitz, "The Origins of Yiddish Scholarship," 208–9.
83   Zelig Kalmanowicz wrote concerning Prylucki to Naftali Feinerman, head of the American Division of YIVO, in late 1939, "He is a personal disgrace and unpleasant—a danger to the YIVO executive," letter from Kalmanowicz to Feinerman, 9 November 1939, YIVO Archives RG 100A, box 24.
84   Y. Rabinovitsh, 'Dos antloyfn fun yidishn loshn!" *Vokhnshrift* 27 (2 October 1931): 4.
85   Estraikh, *In Harness*, 23.
86   Note Berliner, "Vegn litvishn dialekt in kongres-poyln," *Beys yankev-zhurnal* 8.71–2 (1931): 42; Yoysef Teper, "Di yidishe kulturshprakh in ire problemen," *Literarishe bleter* 43 (25 November 1938): 713.

proposed alternate standards for pronunciation and spelling to better reflect the southern dialects of the vast majority of Yiddish-speakers.[87]

Warsaw patriots saw a tendency toward both types of "assimilation"—Polonization, on the one hand, and Litvishization, on the other—as evidence of Warsaw Jewry's shameful lack of pride and self-respect.[88] They found themselves confronted with two distinct menaces to the vibrancy and uniqueness of Warsaw's Yiddish cultural scene. The first, Polonization, represented the failure of Yiddishism to win converts to its project of building an all-encompassing modern culture for Jews chiefly, if not exclusively, in Yiddish. The second, ironically, was a product of its successes—the spread of a standardized language which drew on all dialects and undermined regional distinctiveness by means of schools, political parties, and the press.

Despite a clear trend towards Polonization in the interwar period, the vast majority of Jews in both Warsaw and Vilna continued to speak Yiddish as their dominant language, even if they were not committed to Yiddishism or were unaware of its cultural and academic achievements and aspirations. Yiddishist evaluations of each city relied heavily on accomplishments in the "three pillars" of modern Yiddish culture—the school movement, the literary language, and the press and literature—and had typically little regard for the religious, especially Hasidic, sector of Polish Jewry that did not share its aspirations. The "polysystem" described by Khone [Chone] Shmeruk—the use of Hebrew, Yiddish, and Polish in different contexts and for complementary functions by virtually all Jews in interwar Poland—was understandably filtered out by most observers in the Yiddish press or denounced as a betrayal of the goal of national monolingualism.[89]

Naturally, Warsaw Yiddish speech was every bit as linguistically innovative, expressive, and colourful as that of Vilna, especially when one did not limit one's gaze to the self-consciously secular Yiddishist sector. A positive evaluation of Warsaw Yiddish has come, however, chiefly *after* the Holocaust.[90] As in

---

87   On competing "schools" of Yiddish standardization, see Mordkhe Schaechter, "Der oyftu fun dem yivo: Roshey-prokimdike obzervatsyes un sakhaklen tsu a yoyvl-date," *Yidishe shprakh* XLVI (1973): 211–6.

88   Kanter, "Farvos iz azoy farshpreyt dos litvishe yidish?".

89   Chone Shmeruk, "Hebrew-Yiddish-Polish: A Trilingual Jewish Culture," in Yisrael Gutman et al. (eds.), *The Jews of Poland between Two World Wars* (Hanover, NH: University Press of New England, 1989), 285–311.

90   See, for example, Yitshok Varshavski, "Ot azoy zaynen geven varshever yidn," *Forverts* (9 July 1944): 3.

the case of Vilna, Warsaw's alleged shortcomings have been reinterpreted as virtues through the prism of nostalgia. Indeed, some reflections penned not long after the destruction of Warsaw Jewry praise the city for the very internal diversity and energy for which it was previously denigrated, or for its style, rootedness, and tradition, the very qualities which it was most often denied prior to the war.[91]

Conclusion

In retrospect, Yiddishists in Warsaw and Vilna jointly and consciously created a Yiddishist myth about Vilna—one which built upon the pre-existing mystique surrounding the "Jerusalem of Lithuania" and the prestige of its Lithuanian dialect. If the search for a capital city of a culture, cautiously on the ascendant during the uncertain aftermath of World War I, first characterized the contest for cultural hegemony, a heightened sense of anxiety gave it a new coloration by the 1930s. Concern about the future of Yiddishland helped to encourage the propagation of the Vilna myth as Yiddishists sought a bastion not simply for the Yiddish language and its literature but for a youth that would perpetuate the cultural institutions they had struggled to create. If not the most Yiddish city—a title that perhaps Warsaw or New York deserved based on the scale of their Yiddish-speaking populations, publications, and theatre alone—Vilna was certainly the city most dedicated to the project of Yiddishism.

A. Almi confirmed this tendency to pessimism in 1934 by claiming, albeit with a measure of avowed exaggeration, that if cities had competed for cultural hegemony in Jewish life a decade earlier, they now competed for the dubious honour of "who was going under more and faster." Youth in Vilna's Jewish quarters, other observers noted, were hardly immune to the spread of Polish.[92] As pessimism mounted, commentators everywhere in Yiddishland expressed the hope that it was "better" elsewhere. Not only did America look to Poland, and Warsaw to Vilna, but "[W]hen a Warsaw writer succumbed to pessimism and

---

91 See, for example, Mayzil, *Geven a mol a lebn*, 313; Yitshokh Varshavski, "Yede yidishe gas in varshe—a shtot far zikh," *Forverts* (2 July 1944): 4; The uniqueness of pre-war Jewish life in Warsaw is the subject of Avrom Teytlboym, *Varshever heyf* (Buenos Aires: Tsentralfarband fun poylishe yidn in Argentine, 1947).

92 Sh. Lev, "Di yidishe vilne," *Literarishe bleter* 28 (12 July 1935): 448–9.

began to think that Yiddish was dying..."[93] By late 1939, even Max Weinreich fretted over Polonization. He looked to Vilna, as the capital of independent Lithuania and a city where assimilationist pressures were less intense than in interwar Poland, for a future site of secular cultural creativity in Yiddish.[94]

---

93 Yitshok Varshavski, "Itsike montreal dermont on der amoliger vilne," *Forverts* (31 December 1946): 3–4.
94 Weiser, "The Jewel in the Yiddish Crown," 242.

CHAPTER 13

The Kultur-Lige in Warsaw: A Stopover in the Yiddishists' Journey between Kiev and Paris

Gennady Estraikh

The Kiev League

Hebraism and Yiddishism were cultural constituents of political movements with competing Jewish nation-building models. Hebraism became the linguistic platform for advocates of the ingathering (or "return") of all dispersed Jewish groups to their historical homeland, the Land of Israel, an ideology famously known as Zionism. Yiddishism, in contrast, tended to find followers among those activists who believed in a national awakening through the modernization of Jews within east and east central Europe without such an ingathering. While national territory was the key element in some varieties of Yiddishist constructs, the majority believed that Jews would ultimately thrive in the Diaspora among other tolerant, egalitarian peoples. According to these ideologues of Diasporic Yiddishism, the nascent modern Jewish nation of workers, peasants, intellectuals and (in non-socialist visions) entrepreneurs and their centuries-long Ashkenazic tradition should be made to blossom on the stump of an allegedly decaying religious and economically "non-productive" Jewry. Modern, "productive" Jews would grow together into a modern nation by means of two key agents: a highly developed Yiddish culture and language; and a network of local, regional, national, and pan-Diasporic organizations.

Yiddishism was born predominantly in the political and ideological ferment of Russian—more specifically, Lithuanian, Belarusian, and Ukrainian—Jewry, known collectively in Poland as *Litvaks*.[1] Yiddishist circles, most notably in such cities as Vilna and Kiev, challenged the *nusekh varshe* ("Warsaw brand"), which they associated with pandering to the little-educated masses, and sought to advance their *nusekh vilne* ("Vilna brand") of a sophisticated, future-oriented

---

[1] According to the Lithuanian scholar Aušra Paulauskienė, "the new imperial term—'Russian' Jew—marks mostly a territorial affiliation, while the 'Lithuanian Jew' or 'Litvak' is firstly a cultural term," cf. her *Lost and Found: The Discovery of Lithuania in American Fiction* (Amsterdam: Rodopi, 2007), 19. This should not be confused with the term's contemporary usage for describing non-Hasidic, ultra-orthodox Jews.

culture.[2] Leaving aside the tendency of advocates of the "Vilna brand" to, ironically enough, venerate the Warsaw-based guru of modern Yiddish literature, I.L. Peretz, the two competing brands can be seen as reflecting a larger, still relatively unexplored Polish-Litvak cultural clash.[3] Warsaw emerged as a main site of this clash, thanks to the well-known Litvak "invasion" of the city. Yet as this chapter will show, a creative product of the Litvak migration was the Warsaw Kultur-Lige (Culture League), a new organization aimed at nourishing a nation-defining Yiddish culture.

Vilna is often seen as the "capital" of Yiddishism, or "the most Yiddishist city in the world" (see Kalman Weiser's chapter in this volume).[4] The city really did assume this role, at least part-time, at the end of the 19th century and, even more so, in the first three decades of the 20th century. In imperial Russia, however, highly consequential developments often took place in Warsaw, Kiev, Odessa,[5] or in the actual capital, St. Petersburg—the latter being the main gravitational center for Russian Jewish politics, where all-Russian Jewish civil-society organizations had been emerging since the 1860s. In 1910, Jacob Lestschinsky, then considered the most serious social economist in the Zionist Socialist Workers' Party (which encouraged emigration with the ultimate goal of building a modern Yiddish-speaking socialist state), was happy to detect components of a "Jewish government" there, whose "departments" had

---

2   Various aspects of Yiddishism are analyzed, in particular, in Joshua A. Fishman, *Ideology, Society and Language: The Odyssey of Nathan Birnbaum* (Ann Arbor, MI: Karoma Publishers, 1987); Emanuel Goldsmith, *Modern Yiddish Culture: The Story of the Yiddish Language Movement* (New York: Fordham University Press, 1997); Itzik N. Gottesman, *Defining the Yiddish Nation: The Jewish Folklorists in Poland* (Detroit, MI: Wayne State University Press, 2003); David E. Fishman, *The Rise of Modern Yiddish Culture* (Pittsburgh, PA: University of Pittsburgh Press, 2005). For the Vilna-Kiev Yiddishist "axis," see Gennady Estraikh, *In Harness: Yiddish Writers' Romance with Communism* (Syracuse, NY: Syracuse University Press, 2005), 17–26.

3   The Israeli historian Eli Lederhendler wrote about "two separate Jewries" who lived on the territory of the Polish Commonwealth for a century before the advent of Russian rule—see his "Did Russian Jewry Exist prior to 1917?" in Yaacov Ro'i (ed.), *Jews and Jewish Life in Russia and the Soviet Union* (Portland, OR: Frank Cass, 1995), 15–27, here 17. For an overview of some sources describing the Polish-versus-Litvak relations, see Gennady Estraikh, "Di litvakes un andere yidn," *Forverts* (25 July 2008): 12–13; idem, "Varshe—a yidisher shmeltstop," *Forverts* (15 September 2009): 12–13.

4   See also Dina Abramowicz, "My Father's Life and Work," in Hirsz Abramowicz, *Profiles of a Lost World: Memoirs of East European Jewish Life before World War II* (Detroit, MI: Wayne State University Press, 1999), 31.

5   Andrew Noble Moss, "World War I and the Remaking of Jewish Vilna, 1914–1918," (unpublished PhD dissertation, Stanford University, 2010), 125.

been formed by various philanthropic organizations.⁶ Lestschinsky and those like him especially appreciated the quasi-state role of the Petersburg-centered Jewish apparatus because it dovetailed with Simon Dubnow's scheme of Diaspora Jewish autonomy.⁷

Constituents of Jewish civil society, such as various charities and savings-and-loan associations, contributed significantly to the status of Yiddish, which increasingly functioned as an institutional language. In addition, Yiddishism had taken root among various denominations of Jewish Socialists, notably in the Zionist Socialist Party and the Bund.⁸ But the structural building of a modern Yiddish cultural medium might have remained ineffective were it not for the convincing success of its literature, whose three main writers, Mendele Moykher Sforim, Sholem Aleichem and I.L. Peretz, were pronounced "Classic" only a few years after their deaths in 1915–1917.⁹

Yet for all that, a coordinated, strong Yiddishist movement never fully materialized. An attempt to consolidate the ranks of Yiddish enthusiasts by convening an international conference in the Austro-Hungarian town of Czernowitz (today Chernivtsi in Ukraine) in August 1908 did not yield tangible results. The Bureau formed to realize the conference's resolutions "was closed even before it could be opened."¹⁰ Establishing an organized movement seemed particularly urgent after the break-up of the imperial Russian Pale of Jewish Settlement. Ironically, the same Jewish intellectuals who had once condemned the Pale now grieved over its post-1917 disintegration, realizing that the segmentation of the centuries-old Jewish habitat made any Diasporic nation-building project more problematic. In March 1917, the transformation of imperial Russia into a republic triggered discussions about the structure of the incipient multinational state. The provisional government proposed cultural-personal autonomy as a way of solving the national question in Russia, while various national

---

6   Jacob Lestschinsky, "Profesyon-froyen-shule af dem Vilner tsuzamenfor," *Der shtral* (21 January 1910): 2.
7   See David E. Fishman, *The Rise of Modern Yiddish Culture*, 67–71.
8   Brian Horowitz, "Victory from Defeat: 1905 and the Society for the Promotion of Enlightenment among the Jews of Russia," in Stefani Hoffman and Ezra Mendelsohn (eds.), *The Revolution of 1905 and Russia's Jews* (Philadelphia: University Of Pennsylvania Press, 2008), 85–95; Gennady Estraikh, "Yiddish in Imperial Russia's Civil Society," in Eugene Avrutin and Harriet Murav (eds.), *Jews in the East European Borderlands*: Daily Life, Violence, and Memory (Brighton, MA: Academic Studies Press, 2012), 50–66.
9   Benjamin Harshav, *The Polyphony of Jewish Culture* (Stanford, CA: Stanford University Press, 2007), 12–13.
10 Joshua Fishman, "Was the Original Czernowitz Conference of 1908 a Success?" *Jews and Slavs* 22 (2010): 18.

movements demanded either a federative reconstruction of the former empire or its breakup into a number of independent states. Jewish ideologues usually favoured the latter, federative option, with some forms of autonomy for the Jewish population.

Various configurations of Jewish autonomy in the new, post-imperial Russia were discussed by leading journalists of the New York Yiddish daily *Forverts* (Forward), the preeminent American Jewish working class newspaper. The Bundist Moyshe Olgin (Novomiski), for example, an acclaimed expert on Russian politics and culture, contended that an independent body rather than a governmental organization had to assume responsibility for running Jewish educational and cultural institutions.[11] In 1918, Jacob Lestschinsky published a pamphlet in Warsaw entitled *Our National Demands*, picturing a post-imperial Russian federation whose society entitled citizens to become members of ethnic communal bodies with representatives who would participate in all decision-making and executive institutions of the state. Reflecting the assumption that religious sentiments would atrophy in a modern egalitarian world, Lestschinsky envisioned an essentially secular Russian Jewish community governed by a democratically elected assembly that controlled the cultural domain of national life—educational networks, publishing, libraries, theatres and museums.[12] In Kiev that same year, the Jewish socialist Ben-Adir (Abraham Rosin) described—in his programmatic treatise *Our Language Problem*—a world brotherhood of nations that included Jews as a well-organized national collective with a highly developed Yiddish culture.[13]

In other words, after the collapse of Imperial Russia the idea of Jewish extra-territorial autonomy was in the air. Shmuel Niger (Charney), then the towering figure among Vilna Yiddishists, declared at the beginning of 1919, when Vilna's state affiliation remained opaque, that Yiddish culture would suffer in either extreme in Lithuania's relations with Russia: full amalgamation or full independence.[14] He wrote this following the establishment in Vilna of the Kultur-Lige, modelled on the league founded the previous year, in April 1918, in Kiev. Earlier, the Central Rada, the governing institution of the Ukrainian People's Republic, had officially declared extra-territorial (effectively, cultural)

---

11   M. Olgin, "Tsu vos darfn di yidn fun rusland natsionale rekht?" *Forverts* (29 March 1917): 4. See also Tsivion (Ben-Zion Hoffman), "Di natsionale frage in dem frayen rusland," *Forverts* (15 April 1917): 2.

12   Jacob Lestschinsky, *Undzere natsionale foderungen* (Warsaw: Tsukunft, 1918).

13   Ben-Adir, *Undzer shprakh-problem* (Kiev: Kultur-Lige, 1918).

14   Shmuel Niger, "Lite un Rusland," *Di vokh: a vokhnshrift far literatur un kunst* (17 January 1919): 57–59; (8 February 1919): 112–15.

autonomy for Ukraine's Jews, thus creating a brief, incandescent moment in Jewish history. The initiative to create the Kiev-based Kultur-Lige belonged to a friend of Niger, Zelig Melamed, who became the "nerve and engineer" of the new organization.[15] In all probability, his own initiative followed the example of the League of Russian Culture, founded in June 1917 by a group of liberal intellectuals.[16] This chapter follows the Kultur-Lige's next transplant, however awkward, into Warsaw as a result of its suppression by the new Soviet regime.

The Kiev Kultur-Lige had emerged as an outgrowth of the Ministry for Jewish Affairs in the Ukrainian government and later depended on the support of the Ukrainian and sometimes Soviet government. Private fundraising in the war-ridden country could not have secured the league's existence, especially as its ideas of secular, Diasporic Yiddish-speaking nationhood appealed only to a minority of the Jewish population. During the 1917 elections to the All-Russian Constituent Assembly and 1918 elections to the provisional Jewish National Assembly, Zionist and religious parties outpolled both Yiddishist socialists and liberals.[17] Yet it was not in the spirit of the time and place to abide by the popular will, particularly the will of non-proletarian masses. The socialists insisted that they understood the law of history better and therefore had the right to facilitate its implementation, while circles that did not belong to the so-called "revolutionary democracy," no matter how numerous, would have to satisfy themselves with the status of a helpless minority.[18] This type of cultural force-feeding was considered legitimate because the masses were "national [i.e. non-Zionist and non-assimilationist], whether they want[ed] it or not, whether they recognize[d] it or not."[19]

The Soviet authorities began to sponsor the Kultur-Lige as early as 1919, though the Bolsheviks made it clear that they were only ready to support Yiddish cultural institutions, not structures of cultural autonomy. In January,

---

15 Shmuel Niger, "Kultur-lige," *Di vokh: a vokhnshrift far literatur un kunst* (8 January 1919): 23–25; Zelig Melamed, "Bergelson der gezelshaftler," *Literarishe bleter* (13 September 1929): 728; Khaim Kazdan, *Fun heyder un "shkoles" biz tsisho: dos ruslendishe yidntum in geranglfar shul, shprakh, kultur* (Mexico: Shlomo Mendelzon Fond, 1956), 436.

16 See, e.g., Richard Pipes, *Struve: Liberal on the Right, 1905–1944* (Cambridge, MA: Harvard University Press, 1980), 235–36.

17 Solomon I. Goldelman, *Jewish National Autonomy in Ukraine, 1917–1920* (Chicago: Ukrainian Research and Information Institute, 1968), 79; L.M. Spirin, *Rossiia 1917 god: iz istorii bor'by politicheskikh partii* (Moscow: Mysl', 1987), 273–328; Oliver H. Radkey, *Russia Goes to the Polls: The Elections to the All-Russian Constituent Assembly, 1917* (Ithaca, NY, and London: Cornell University Press, 1990), 19, 152–53.

18 Goldelman, *Jewish National Autonomy in Ukraine*, 57.

19 *Kultur-lige: ershtes zamlheft* (Warsaw, April 1921), 2.

1920, Anatoly Lunacharsky, the People's Commissar (Minister) of Education in Lenin's government, allocated a subsidy for the Kultur-Lige, but cautioned that it was a temporary measure pending a decision that would define the role of the organization. Some activists tried to secure the league's survival as part of the Soviet state-run educational and cultural system for all ethnic groups. But on 16 September, 1920, the fate of the league was sealed when a meeting of Jewish culture activists welcomed the decision to Bolshevize it, stressing that, under the specific conditions of Ukraine, the organization needed protection from all kinds of erstwhile non-Bolshevik socialists and nationalist bourgeois intellectuals. In December, 1921, an attempt was made to re-register the Kultur-Lige as a pan-Soviet organization with headquarters in Moscow and "chief committees" in Kiev and Minsk. But it was a stillborn project, since Lenin considered cultural-national autonomy "absolutely impermissible" and demanded that education and the majority of other domains of cultural activity be put under the direct control of the overall state apparatus.[20] The harnessing of the Kultur-Lige was part of the general Soviet destruction of civil-society institutions and the elimination of political and legal conditions for an autonomous civil society.[21] As a result, while many constituents of the Kultur-Lige survived in the Soviet environment, the league itself was soon dissolved.[22]

The league's transformation into a communist-controlled organization undermined its principal aspiration: to be supra-political. The pre-Soviet "political harmony" (the reality was, of course, more complex) could only be achieved in a favourable ideological climate: the three Jewish political groupings

20   *Kultur-lige: byuleten num.* 2 (Kiev: Tsentral-komitet fun Kultur-Lige, June-July 1920), 1–6, 31; Abraham Abchuk, *Etyudn un materyaln tsu der geshikhte fun der yidisher literatur-bavegung in fssr, 1917–1927* (Kharkiv: Literatur un kunst, 1934), 18; David Bergelson, "A geshikhte vegn Lenin, vos iz nokh nit dertseylt gevorn," *Frayhayt* (19 January 1929): 7; Vladimir Lenin, "'Cultural-National' Autonomy," in idem, *Collected Works*, vol. 19 (Moscow: Progress Publishers, 1977), 503–7; Estraikh, *In Harness*, 53; Kenneth B. Moss, *Jewish Renaissance in the Russian Revolution* (Cambridge, MA: Harvard University Press, 2009), 229.

21   Ruben Apressyan, "Civil Society and Civil Participation," in William Gay and T.A. Alekseeva (eds.), *Democracy and the Quest for Justice: Russian and American Perspectives* (Amsterdam: Rodopi, 2004), 110.

22   See, in particular, S.M. Shevchenko, "Orhanizatsiia navchal'no-vykhovnoï roboty v kyïvs'komu doslidnomu evreiskomu ditbudynku," *Pedahohichna osvita: teoriia i praktyka* 2 (2009): 59–65; Gennady Estraikh, "The Yidish Kultur-Lige," in Irena R. Makaryk and Virlana Tkacz (eds.), *Modernism in Kyiv: Jubilant Experimentation* (Toronto: Toronto University Press, 2010), 197–217. In February 1922, the Kultur-Lige's Central Organizational Bureau still existed in Moscow and even signed an appeal to international Jewry which appeared in the Soviet press: "Spravedlivoe trebovanie," *Izvestiia* (26 February 1922): 1.

that played prominent roles in post-revolutionary Ukraine—the Fareynikte (United Jewish Socialist Workers Party, which incorporated the Zionist Socialist Party), the liberal, Dubnowian Folkspartey (People's Party) and the Poale Tzion (Labor Zionist Party)—shared the overarching goal of building a modern Jewish nation, even if they differed on many details of both the nation-building process and its ultimate purpose. Some Bundists, too, participated in cultural projects; for instance, A. Litvak (Khaim-Yankev Helfand), a member of the Bund's central committee, was a leading figure in the organization. The bloody turmoil of the civil war left a very limited space for interparty ideological confrontations. In the Soviet environment, however, the league's struggle to remain above the political fray rapidly came to nothing.[23]

Meanwhile, as a punishment for its "nationalism" during the independence period, Kiev lost its status as the Ukrainian capital. Yiddish literati flocked either to the Soviet capital, Moscow, or to Kharkov, which obtained the status of Soviet Ukraine's capital, while many activists of the Kultur-Lige chose to leave the country and replant their organization elsewhere. The league had never, in any case, shaped itself as an exclusively Ukrainian organization. Its constitution, ratified on 15 January, 1918, defined the "whole territory of the Russian Republic" as the domain of the league's activities. The authors of the 1918 pamphlet *The Main Aims of the Kultur-Lige* mentioned Ukraine as merely *the place* where they, a group of enthusiasts, had less than nine months earlier happened to decide to establish the new Jewish cultural network's headquarters.[24]

The Warsaw Transplant

On 15 July, 1921, the *Forverts* published an article by Tsivion, who at that time was travelling in Europe. In his dispatch sent from Warsaw, Tsivion wrote:

> Every person who is more or less interested in Jewish life in Ukraine, Belorussia, Poland, Lithuania and Latvia, certainly has heard about the Jewish Kultur-Lige. [...] The Kultur-Lige was established in April 1918 and, in a rather short period of time, spread its activity over the whole territory of Ukraine. The Kultur-Lige had concentrated around itself a

---

23 See, in particular, Moss, *Jewish Renaissance*, 259–60.
24 *Di grunt-oyfgabn fun der "kultur-lige"* (Kiev: n.p., 1918); Mikhailo Rybakov (ed.), *Pravda istoriï: diial'nist' evreis'koï kul'turno-prosvitnyts'koï orhanizatsiï "Kul'turna liha" u Kyievi (1918–1925)* (Kiev: Kyi, 2001), 15.

whole range of strong groups of Jewish radical intelligentsia, who sought to organize the Jewish masses and develop Yiddish culture. [...]

Unfortunately, I did not have a chance to see the work of the Kultur-Lige in Ukraine first hand. I learned about the organization only from a number of written and published reports, as well as thanks to personal communications with central figures of the Kultur-Lige whom I met in Warsaw.[25]

Indeed, Warsaw was now the only place to host an organized group of the Kultur-Lige's high-ranking activists, i.e., those who regarded themselves as the core of the organization. They arrived virtually penniless, though rumours circulated that the group was loaded with "barrels of gold."[26] (This tale could be an echo of the earlier, German army's, evacuation from Kiev, at the beginning of 1919, when a small group of Jewish entrepreneurs relocated to Germany with portions of their wealth.)[27] The memoirs of a member of the group, the editor, publisher and literary critic Nakhman Mayzel (also spelled as Nachman Maisel, 1887–1966), provide us with a list of the newly-arrived Kultur-Lige activists:

> Our group, the Executive Bureau of the Kultur-Lige, included Dr. Moyshe Zilberfarb, the former minister [of Jewish affairs] in Ukraine; A. Litvak, the well-known Bundist writer, theoretician and speaker; Joseph Lestschinsky [Jacob Lestschinsky's brother], or J. Khmurner, as he later called himself in the Polish Bundist movement; Zelig Melamed, the energetic, stubborn champion of Yiddish; Kh[aim] Zh. Kazdan, the well-known educator, and I.[28]

Like other intellectual cohorts in the waves of the "Litvak invasion" these activists were sometimes perceived as people who culturally colonized Warsaw, the most populous European Jewish urban center and a place that offered both a less totalized political environment and highly developed infrastructure for publishing, considered "almost the world capital of Yiddish culture."[29] Warsaw

---

25   Tsivion, "Der yidisher kultur-lig in Eyrope," *Forverts* (15 July 1921): 3.
26   Ibid., 25.
27   Cf. A. Vol'skii, "Russkie evrei v Germanii," *Evreiskaia tribuna* (9 September 1921): 3.
28   Nakhman Mayzel, *Geven amol a lebn* (Buenos Aires: Tsentral-farband fun poylishe yidn, 1951), 19.
29   Adam Pomorski, "Pochemu ne priamo?," *Novaia Pol'sha* 12 (2010): 20–28, esp. 20.

was not only the main Jewish publishing hub in Eastern Europe; it also outsourced printing operations to American authors.[30]

The "Litvak colonization" of Warsaw had become especially noticeable during the 1880s, and the influx only increased in the 1890s following the expulsion of Jews from Moscow.[31] Warsaw Jews dubbed as Litvaks any Jews who spoke a different, non-Warsovian kind of Yiddish, though Jews from Lithuania and Belorussia bore the brunt of ridicule and even hatred. The Warsaw-born Yiddish journalist A. Almi (Elias Chaim Sheps) compared the Warsaw Jews' stigmatization of Litvaks to the Poles' denigration of the Jews.[32] A Warsaw Jewish dweller would quip that "a litvak iz a halber goy" ("a Litvak is a half-gentile") or "ot geyen tsvey yidn un a litvak" ("two Jews and a Litvak are walking along here").[33] Israel Joshua Singer, a Yiddish novelist and Warsaw correspondent of the *Forverts*, reported that a Polish Hasidic rebbe had suggested that a Jew baptize his daughter rather than to allow her to marry a Litvak. Singer similarly reported that some Polish Jews did not even hide their Schadenfreude when they spoke about the pogrom in the Litvak-populated town of Białystok in the summer of 1906.[34] According to the journalist and historian Azriel Natan Frenk, the term "Litwak" was invoked in the Polish press around 1907 as a euphemism for the "bad Jewish migrant."[35]

Activists of the Kultur-Lige no doubt knew that the local Jewish population would not welcome them with outstretched arms. Yet they also recognized prime indicators of a successful migration to Warsaw. At the end of the day, virtually the entire infrastructure of the Warsaw-based Yiddish press and publishing industry had been developed thanks to several generations of

---

30 Hagit Cohen, "The USA-Eastern Europe Yiddish Book Trade and the Formation of an American Yiddish Cultural Center, 1890s–1930s," *Jews in Russia and Eastern Europe* 57 (2006): 53.

31 See, e.g., Stephen D. Corrsin, "Language Use in Culture and Political Change in Pre-1914 Warsaw: Poles, Jews, and Russification," *The Slavonic and East European Review* 68.1 (1990): 84; David Assaf, "'Life as It Was'—Yekhezkel Kotik and His Memoirs," in Yekhezkel Kotik, *Journey to a Nineteenth-Century Shtetl* (Detroit, MI: Wayne State University Press, 2002), 30.

32 A. Almi, *Momentn fun a lebn: zikhroynes, bilder un epizodn* (Buenos-Aires: Tsentralfarband fun Poylishe Yidn in Argentine, 1948), 182–83.

33 A gevezener rusisher professor [A former Russian professor], "Di litvishe yidn," *Di mizrekh-yidn* (Berlin and Warsaw: Misrach, 1916), 112–13; Max Weinreich, "Galitsianer lakhn fun litvakes, litvakes fun galitsianer," *Forverts* (11 January 1930): 6.

34 G. Kiper [I.J. Singer], "Poylishe yidn, galitsianer un litvakes mishn zikh itst oys in di poylishe shtet," *Forverts* (10 October 1929): 3.

35 Azriel Natan Frenk, "Litvakes," *Dos yidishe folk* (7 February 1918): 7–8.

people born somewhere east of Warsaw.³⁶ To a large extent, Jewish nationalism in its various forms had also been imported to Warsaw by non-Polish Jews, who tended to acculturate into Russian society without assimilating, whereas acculturation into Polish society seemed to make Jews more prone to assimilation. Contemporary observers explained this phenomenon by differentiating the two cultural environments: "Russian Jews" lived, in fact, on outskirts of the empire and were mainly surrounded by local ethnic groups (such as Ukrainians and Lithuanians); therefore Russian culture had obtained a predominately abstract, universal, "bookish" quality that remained detached from Russia and Russians proper. In Poland, on the other hand, Jews were predominantly surrounded by native Poles, many of whom were well-educated, which made the impact of Polish culture more direct, demanding, and "seductive."³⁷ According to Shmuel Niger, "If a Jew has been brought up in the environment of Polish culture, often only in the Polish language, he becomes a Pole."³⁸

For all that, Warsaw was considered the only suitable venue for the headquarters of such an ambitious project as the Kultur-Lige. Apart from the sheer size of its Jewish population and its highly developed cultural infrastructure, the city had the attraction of being the capital of a newly independent country, a country which had also incorporated territories previously considered Ukrainian or Lithuanian, and where chapters of the Kultur-Lige had developed within the Kiev orbit. In addition, on 28 June 1919, Polish leaders signed the so-called Little Treaty of Versailles and thus committed the Second Polish Republic to the protection of national minorities. Also known as the "Minorities Treaty," the agreement promised that its

> nationals who belong to racial, religious, or linguistic minorities shall enjoy in law and in fact the same treatment and security as the Polish nationals. In particular, they shall have an equal right to establish, manage, and control at their own expense charitable, religious, and social institutions, schools, and other educational establishments, with the right to use their own language and to exercise their religion freely therein.³⁹

---

36   Chone Shmeruk, *Prokim fun der yidisher literatur-geshikhte* (Tel Aviv: Y.L. Peretz Farlag, 1988), 306–7.

37   A. Litvin, "Polyakn, litvakes un poylishe yidn," *Forverts* (21 February 1910): 2; Frenk, "Litvakes," 8.

38   Shmuel Niger, "Vu iz itst der yidisher tsenter?," *Forverts* (6 December 1919): 12.

39   Miriam Eisenstein, *Jewish Schools in Poland, 1919–39: Their Philosophy and Development* (New York: King's Crown Press, 1950), 1–2.

Nevertheless, the Kiev activists found themselves in a very hostile political environment controlled by several competing parties with no appetite for cooperation. Mayzel recalled:

> We had the aim, the intent to unite around the Kultur-Lige in Poland socialist, democratic and general public circles. However, it was next to impossible to achieve such a thing at that time. It was hard to bring together, under the same roof and around the same table, [even] labor representatives of the Folkspartey. It was also not easy to bring together representatives of labor parties, especially as the Bund always insisted that its hegemony in leadership was a prerequisite of participation, whereas the right Poale Tzion kept its distance from us. In the meantime, the Fareynikte and the recently established left Poale Tzion did welcome us and were ready to work in the organizational committee. So, we found ourselves between more than two fires [...].[40]

Although Warsaw seemed the best available locale for the league's transplant, it was to remain an imperfect option.

In April 1921, the first Warsaw conference of the Kultur-Lige (in fact, a gathering of representatives of about thirty already existing local branches) stated in its resolutions its object of "facilitating construction of socialist Yiddish culture for the working masses." At the same time, such people as Mayzel resisted attempts to turn their organization into an agitprop of a particular socialist party. Mayzel's type of intelligentsia sought to develop cultural activities also among the non-proletarian, middle class elements of the Jewish masses, elevating them culturally to its own level. A similar conceptual divide was characteristic of the Soviet Yiddish cultural milieu, in which some former activists of the Kultur-Lige intended to target all strata of the Jewish population but remained—paradoxically—an elitist group, since in that bigger pool they sought an audience that was receptive to highbrow cultural products.[41] Mayzel and his friends regarded themselves as custodians of I.L. Peretz's traditions, which—they contended—had declined in Peretz's own Warsaw. Moreover, Mayzel would argue that in Warsaw Peretz remained a lonely figure, with no close friendships with local intellectuals. In Peretz's vein, the activists of the Kultur-Lige sought to preserve the "golden chain" of Jewish culture, shaking off

---

40 Mayzel, *Geven amol a lebn*, 20.
41 Ibid., 23; Estraikh, *In Harness*, 114.

the ancient dust while, at the same time, absorbing nutrients of Jewish tradition and history.[42]

To overcome its image as a task force that had landed in Warsaw on a mission of ideological-cultural colonization, the Kiev activists sought an organizational umbrella that could legitimize the league's transplant into Poland. The first congress of Jewish educators, convened in June 1921, would have made the perfect forum for establishing a pan-Polish Kultur-Lige. However, the Bund, whose delegates did not have a majority, boycotted any league-related resolutions. The official argument, spelled out by the Bund leaders Beinish Michalewicz and Henryk Ehrlich, was based on their reluctance to turn the congress of educators into a congress of cultural activists. In reality, however, the Bundists simply realized that the governing body of the new organization would have a composition that reflected the delegates' diverse party affiliations, while the Bund sought hegemony over this important cultural network. As Khaim Kazdan, the secretary of the Kiev Kultur-Lige who soon jumped onto the Polish Bundist bandwagon, wrote in his memoirs, "history would show that such an organization as the Kultur-Lige could not be established by force, against the will of the strongest Jewish workers party."[43]

The Kultur-Lige activists then faced the choice either to form an elitist group of Yiddish culture-builders or to join one of the organized political currents. Those who did not want to join any political group focused on developing a Yiddish publishing house. As a result, two publishing houses, completely independent of one another, operated under the same name—one of them, in Kiev, became the main producer of Yiddish books in the Soviet Union; the other, a Warsaw-based eponymous publishing house, sought to continue the traditions of the pre-Soviet Kultur-Lige. However, in Poland, where local Yiddish cultural and educational institutions were so thoroughly controlled by politicians with entrenched interests, it was exceedingly hard to preserve the "apolitical spirit" of pre-Soviet Kiev.[44] Even more importantly, in Poland the Kultur-Lige could not obtain state funding and thus depended on party sponsorship, which of course entailed loyalty to a political current.

---

42   Nakhman Mayzel, *Y. L. Perets: zayn lebn un shafn* (New York: IKUF, 1945), 156; idem, *Geven amol a lebn*, 27–28, 42–43; Ellen Kellman, "Dos yidishe bukh alarmirt! Towards the History of Yiddish Reading in Inter-War Poland," *Polin* 16 (2003): 213–41, esp. 222.

43   Khaim Kazdan, *Di geshikhte fun yidishn shulvezn in umophengikn Poyln* (Mexico: Kultur un hilf, 1947), 101.

44   Abraham Golomb, *A halber yorhundert yidishe dertsiung* (Rio de Janeiro: Monte Skopus, 1957), 122–27.

Organizations attempting to model themselves on the Kiev Kultur-Lige in other locales, such as Kaunas, Paris, Amsterdam, Detroit, and Berlin, faced similar problems. As a result, none of the Yiddish leagues would achieve the Kiev prototype's scope of activities and supra-political status. For instance, from 1919 Kaunas had a Kultur-Lige that from the very beginning functioned as a proletarian, communist-leaning organization, and as such it was closed down by the authorities.[45] Although Berlin was a stronghold of Russian Jewish emigration, the city did not boast strong Bundist or other Jewish political groupings interested in the developing of cultural activities in Yiddish. As a result, the Berlin-based league, too, failed to become viable.[46] The Parisian league, established in 1922, initially united representatives of various political currents who would assemble in a café in the Latin Quarter. Unlike its Berlin counterpart, it did succeed in developing itself into an active organization with affiliations in towns throughout France. Ultimately, however, the French Kultur-Lige became an arena for political intrigues and manoeuvrings until the "red faction" attained, in 1925, full Communist dominance, turning it into an affiliate of the *Main-d'œuvre immigrée*, a trade unionist organization composed of immigrant workers.[47] As Marc Chagall (who had been associated with the Kultur-Lige during his Moscow stint) complained in 1925, writing from Paris to his friend, the American Yiddish novelist Joseph Opatoshu, "various *Kultur-lige* people want us to be close to the people, the workers, and wherever else!"[48]

In November 1922, the Warsaw journal *Kultur* (Culture), published by the "elitist group," featured Moyshe Zilberfarb's article entitled "On Individual or Party Foundations?" Zilbefarb honed in on the Polish Jewish cultural landscape:

> In recent years, the Jewish labor institutions in Poland have been developed exclusively along party lines. Everything belonged to the parties—trade unions, workers' cooperatives, evening classes, schools, workers' clubs, and workers' soup kitchen. It is not merely some links with this or that party. Rather, it means full dominance of one of the parties—from the personnel to the ideological direction. The moment a new party

---

45 Unpublished Yiddish memoirs of the former Kaunas activist David Tomback, preserved in the YIVO Archive (New York), RG 454, box 1, 10.

46 "Berliner 'kultur-lige'," *Undzer bavegung* 5 (1923): 12.

47 M. Liro, "Di geshikhte fun der kultur-lige," in *10 yor kultur lige* (Paris: Kultur-Lige, 1932), 3–11; Lynda Khayat, "Les étudiants juifs étrangers à Strasbourg au tournant des années trente," *Archives Juives* 38.2 (2005): 12.

48 Benjamin Harshav, *Marc Chagall and His Times: A Documentary Narrative* (Stanford, CA: Stanford University Press, 2004), 337.

appears as a separate cohort in the labor movement, it has to build a parallel network of labor institutions, such as kitchens and schools, cooperatives and libraries, which turn essentially into outposts of the party.[49]

Six decades later, the Israeli historian Ezra Mendelsohn described Jewish parties in Poland as substitutes for both "the decaying home" and a state that was not "serving this particular group the way it should." Hence "one gets the kind of party that is also an entire world, with its schools, its cultural institutions, its recreational institutions, and so forth and so on."[50] As a result, very little apolitical space was left in Poland for cultural activities sponsored by an organization that aspired to be trans-partisan and even trans-national.

Still, the publishing house Kultur-Lige started out as a struggling independent body and managed to find a niche in Warsaw's already overcrowded Jewish publishing market. The city boasted several well-established publishers, including the syndicate Tsentral (Central), created by four publishers in 1911; the "Brothers Levin-Epshtein" that moved its office from Ukraine to Warsaw in 1885; and the Yehudiya publishing house founded in 1912. In the early 1920s, Warsaw publishers produced several hundred religious and secular Jewish books annually. In addition, books appeared in other towns in Poland. Boris Kletzkin, based in Vilna, had been publishing middle-brow and high-brow literature since 1910. The Kultur-Lige elbowed its way into this highly populated terrain, positioning itself as a pan-Diasporic publisher of high-quality literature. It printed two poetic volumes by the poet Peretz Markish, who had moved from Ukraine to Warsaw; the first book by Israel Joshua Singer, a recent returnee from Russia; and books by two New York-based writers—the poet H. Leivik and the novelist Joseph Opatoshu. *In Poylishe velder* (In Polish Woods), Opatoshu's 1921 novel, became a bestseller—the Kultur-Lige released it in 1922 with a print-run of 3,500, and produced 10 more editions within two years. In November 1922, the American writer Peretz Hirschbein, who like Opatoshu contributed to the New York daily *Der tog* (Day), signed an agreement with the Kultur-Lige to publish his oeuvre. Hirschbein invested his own money in the venture, paying the publisher by means of commissions from the sales in Poland and the United States.[51]

---

49   Moyshe Zilberfarb, "Af personale oder parteyishe yesoydes?," *Kultur* (November 1922).
50   Ezra Mendelsohn, *The Jews of East Central Europe between the World Wars* (Bloomington: Indiana University Press, 1983), 212.
51   Nakhman Mayzel, *Yoysef Opatoshu* (Warsaw: Literarishe bleter, 1937), 64; Mayzel, *Geven amol a lebn*, 37–39, 48–51; Estraikh, *In Harness*, 19–20; Cohen, "The USA-Eastern Europe Yiddish Book Trade and the Formation of an American Yiddish Cultural Center," 69.

FIGURE 13.11　Erd-vey (*Earth-woe*), by Israel Joshua Singer (Warsaw: Kultur-lige, 1922). From the Archives of the YIVO Institute for Jewish Research, New York.
COURTESY OF YIVO.

According to the September 1922 memorandum written by the Kultur-Lige for the American Joint Jewish Distribution Committee, the league—whose activities began "with no funds on hand except a loan of 1,000,000 Marks [hyperinflated *marka polska*] obtained from friends"—managed to get 50,000,000 Marks from the sale of its books. About 70 percent of this income had been earned in Poland, while the United States (10 percent), Romania (10 percent) and Ukraine (4 percent) were the most significant foreign markets. Books were sold also in Germany, Latvia, Argentina, Brazil, Lithuania, France, England, Estonia, Belgium, South Africa, and "the Far East" (meaning, most probably, Harbin).[52]

Ultimately, however, all efforts to have a stable, non-party affiliated organization fell through in an environment beset by ideological factionalism. In 1924, it became clear that the Kultur-Lige was at the end of its rope. Its journal, *Bikher-velt* (World of Books), which appeared in Kiev from January to August 1919 and was re-launched in Warsaw in January, 1922, had to be phased out after April, 1924. (From April 1928 to August 1929, it re-emerged as a Bundist-controlled monthly.) Its replacement, the highbrow weekly *Literarishe bleter* (Literary Pages), was produced in Boris Kletzkin's publishing house rather than as an organ of the Kultur-Lige. In the eighth issue of the *Literarishe bleter*, dated 27 June 1924, an article by the leading left Poale Tzionist Zerubavel (Yakov Vitkin) was quite revealingly entitled "Concerning the Question of Liquidation of the Organization Kultur-Lige." Zerubavel laid the entire blame on the Bund and its unwillingness to tolerate parity with other Jewish political currents. By 1924, Mayzel and Melamed remained the only non-Bundist members of the executive. They left the organization when the Kultur-Lige ceased to function as an independent organization.

While remaining officially unaffiliated with any party, the league had effectively become an outpost of the Bund.[53] As a Bund-controlled publishing house, it continued to print hundreds of titles, with the bestselling Yiddish novelist and playwright Sholem Asch as its leading author. In 1928, it published 67 books and journals. Under the directorship of Chaim Wasser, a member of the Bund's central committee, the Kultur-Lige became one of the largest publication projects in Poland. Thousands of dollars worth of books, including

---

52 "Publishing House Kultur League, Warsaw," 27 September 1922. The Archive of the American Joint Jewish Distribution Committee, item 333115, 1–5, here 2 and 3.

53 Ellen Kellman, "The (Brief) Afterlife of the (*umparteyishe*) Kultur-Lige in Interwar Poland," *Jews and Slavs* 22 (2003): 114.

teaching material for Yiddish secular schools, would be sold to American distributors.[54]

In 1931, Abraham Cahan, editor of the New York *Forverts*, accused the Kultur-Lige of producing "translations of Bolshevik writers." This was an exaggeration. Although several books by Soviet authors, including Ilya Ehrenburg, did appear under the Kultur-Lige imprint, Cahan's remark simply reflected his and his circle's negative stance towards the Polish Bund, which—according to Cahan—"was closer to Communism than to Socialism."[55] Indeed, on some political scales, including the right-wing socialist scale of Menshevik and Menshevik-leaning socialists, both the Polish Bund and its cultural organizations were ideologically quite close to Moscow, though the Bund and the Jewish Communists always remained rivals.

In addition to its publishing house, libraries formed one of the most significant constituents of the Kultur-Lige in Poland. In the 1930s, Herman (Hersh) Kruk, who in 1920 changed his ideological affiliation from Communism to Bundism, played a central role in the league. In 1930, he was appointed director of the Warsaw library, named after the prominent Bundist Bronisław Grosser. That same year, this largest of all Jewish libraries in the city and most important of all workers' libraries in the country was now run by the Kultur-Lige. Kruk and his colleagues employed modern librarianship and coordinated some 400 (i.e., about a half of all) Jewish libraries in towns around the country. Although in 1931, during the census of the Polish population, 79 per cent of Jews named Yiddish as their mother tongue, the Warsaw library revealed a dwindling interest in Yiddish books among its readers. Initially, until 1931, its collection did not include books in Polish; but by the 1930s it was compelled to establish a Polish collection because the younger generation increasingly shunned Yiddish books and authors. Polish and Yiddish translations of books by Jules Verne, rather than works by Yiddish authors, were popular among the library's readers.[56]

---

54 Cohen, *The USA-Eastern Europe Yiddish Book Trade*, 72.

55 S. Kan, "Ab. Kahan vegn 'Kultur-Lige' un 'Vokhnshrift'," *Vokhnshrift far Literatur, Kunst un Kultur*, 6 November 1931, 5; *Ab. Kahan un der "Bund" in Poyln* (New York: Bundisher Klub, 1932), 11. See also Jack Jacobs, *On Socialists and "The Jewish Question" after Marx* (New York: New York University Press, 1992), 28–29.

56 Aleksandra Bilewicz and Stefania Walasek (eds.), *Rola mniejszości narodowych w kulturze i oświacie polskiej w latach 1700–1939* (Wrocław: Wydawnictwo Uniwersytetu Wrocławskiego, 1998), 258–59; David H. Stam (ed.), *International Dictionary of Library Histories*, vol. 1 (Chicago and London: Fitzroy Dearborn, 2001), 181; Nathan Cohen, "The Jews of Independent Poland—Linguistic and Cultural Changes," in Ernst Krausz and Gitta Tulea (eds.), *Starting the Twenty-First Century: Sociological Reflections and Challenges*

Political and cultural education of the masses played an important role in the activities of each party. Thus, when the Kultur-Lige had been monopolized by the Bund, the left Poale Tzion launched its educational arm, Ovntkursn far arbeter (Evening Courses for Workers).[57] In November 1925, the Bund used the framework of the Kultur-Lige to establish its *Folks-universitet* (People's University), which evolved into a vibrant cultural institution. Its lectures and literary galas, conveniently held in evenings and on weekends, were attended by hundreds of people. Separate classes targeted illiterate adults or those who sought to improve their general education. (Among those who joined the Bund were hard-up people with little or no education—porters, butchers, street vendors and simply poorly-qualified workers.)[58] Summer camping and tourism, including trips to France, Italy and Germany, also became domains of the Kultur-Lige's activities. The Kultur-Lige would encourage people to go to theatres and cinemas by getting quantity discounts and distributing cheaper tickets. In 1929, the avant-garde Yiddish Theatre Studio, led by Michael Weichert, was established at the Kultur-Lige. Despite the severe economic problems of the period, the league remained active through the 1930s, even playing a role in local and national elections.[59]

The Fate of the Kultur-Lige: The World Yiddish Cultural Congress

In 1932, Mayzel summed up the experience of establishing the Kultur-Lige in Poland:

> Once, ten or eleven years ago, the slogan was tossed around about creating a united worldwide Yiddish cultural organization (at that time it was associated with the popular and catchy name of the Kultur-Lige). Leagues appeared in a number of places, but they did not have any central governing body, nor had they any well-defined program or clear-cut

---

(New Brunswick, NJ: Transaction Publishers, 2002), 166; Markus Kirchhoff, *Häuser des Buches: Bilder jüdischer Bibliotheken* (Leipzig: Reclam, 2002), 41–43. Yiddish translations or adaptations of Jules Verne's books began to appear from the end of the 19th century. Many of them were produced by the Warsaw publisher A. Gitlin.

57   Bina Garntzarska-Kadari, *Di linke poyle-tsion in poyln biz der tsveyter velt-milkhome* (Tel Aviv: Y.L. Peretz Farlag, 1995), 299.
58   Bernard Goldstein, *20 yor in varshever bund, 1919–1939* (New York: Unser Tsait, 1960), 187.
59   P. Kozhets, "Iz istorii bor'by za narodnyi front v Pol'she," *Voprosy istorii* 7 (1962): 83; Gertrud Pickhan, *"Gegen den Strom": Der allgemeine jüdische Arbeiterbund "Bund" in Polen 1918–1939* (Munich: Deutsche Verlags-Anstalt, 2001), 230–35.

purpose. Therefore they either declined or took a peculiar character and form. At that time, Jewish life was still unstable, everything remained very turbulent, people did not know which balance of power would prevail between various Jewish parties, groupings and movements. All the energy was wasted in political bargaining and bickering and in attempts to secure as much influence as possible in governing bodies [of various organizations]—as it happened in Warsaw and Vilna, where the Kultur-Lige tried to establish its centers.[60]

Indeed, Yiddishism, in its "pure," non-partisan forms, could survive and even prosper in relatively narrow intellectual circles and their organizations, such as the Yiddish Scientific Institute (YIVO) and the Yiddish chapter of the International PEN Club. However, it failed to develop into a properly organized mass movement even in such a populous Jewish center as Warsaw. Seeds of the Yiddish language's decline could be detected even during its heyday in the 1910s: while many intellectuals embraced the language of the masses, the masses proper regarded Yiddish as a language of little worth.[61]

In the 1920s and 1930s, many "pure" Yiddishists moved over to the Communist camp. Thus, a pro-Soviet newspaper, *Fraynd* (Friend), was launched in Warsaw in April 1934 under the management of Boris Kletzkin, one of the best-known and most respected members of the Yiddish publishing world.[62] Soviet Communism's international character and initial, unprecedented support of Yiddish culture convinced many people that the Soviet Union and pro-Soviet circles in other countries offered the best ideological environment for realizing Jewish national and cultural aspirations. Peretz Hirschbein, who spent about a year in the Soviet Union in 1928–29, believed that the new Communist country could attract hundreds of thousands of Jewish emigrants from Poland.

Jacob Lestschinsky, who like Hirschbein did not belong to the Communist movement, offered three reasons for why Poland could not match Moscow's political stance towards Jews and, as a result, had a less attractive image. First, Poland did not have territories for colonization and could not even contemplate projects like Birobidzhan, the area in the Far East of Russia allocated for a Soviet Jewish territorial unit (from May 1934—the Jewish Autonomous Region). Second, while tens of thousands of Soviet Jews had replaced the

---

60 Nakhman Mayzel, *Af undzer kultur-front: problemen fun literatur un kultur-shafn* (Varshe: Literarishe bleter, 1936), 223–24.
61 A. Litvin, "Yidish, yidish, yidish: der kurs fun mame-loshn heybt zikh in rusland," *Forverts* (2 July 1910): 5.
62 Estraikh, *In Harness*, 66.

pre-revolutionary white-collar cadre, independent Poland did not have such a dearth of educated people and thus lacked similar opportunities. Third, rapid industrialization in the Soviet Union created jobs for Jews there, whereas the Polish economy was beset by chronic unemployment. Moreover, the Soviet government sought to transform its Jewish population for the better, whereas the Polish government merely hoped that its Jewish population would emigrate.[63]

The Kultur-Lige ideology found a new incarnation in the World Yiddish Cultural Congress (YKUF), whose formation in September 1937 in Paris was inspired by the grandiose international Congress in Defense of Culture, convened in Paris in June 1935. It reflected the modus operandi adopted by various anti-fascist ideological currents, Communist and non-Communist, which had collaborated during the Popular Front period. In this climate of cooperation, an international group of intellectuals who came to Vilna in August, 1935, to participate in the congress of YIVO announced the founding of a movement called the Yiddish Culture Front, which sought to protect Yiddish culture. In fact, YIVO did not support the initiative and supporters of the campaign had to find a time and venue outside the conference—they assembled late in the evening in a Vilna cafe. Mayzel and Chagall, the writers Yehushe Perle and Alter Kacyzne, and the historians Emanuel Ringelblum and Raphael Mahler were among the few dozen intellectuals who put their signatures on the new movement's manifesto. The founders sought to protect their culture not only from Fascism, but also from other factors contributing to the erosion of the Yiddish environment. They were worried, for instance, that in addition to the "big cultures," Lithuanian and Latvian culture had begun to distract the younger Jewish generation from Yiddish. An increasing number of young literati created works in those languages, which previously were not in competition with Yiddish.[64]

A congress of the new movement could not be convened in Poland, where it was seen as a Communist ploy (the Communist Party operated underground), and its members had to disguise their activities as a campaign to celebrate the centenary of the "grandfather" of modern Yiddish literature Mendele Moykher Sforim (1836–1917). The Yiddish Culture Front met resistance from the Bund, which as in the early days of the Warsaw Kultur-Lige, kept a wary eye on any initiative that could undermine its role as main custodian of secular Yiddish culture. In addition, the notion of a world-wide, supra-class Jewish nation

---

63   Gennady Estraikh, "From 'Green Fields' to 'Red Fields': Peretz Hirschbein's Soviet Sojourn, 1928–1929," *Jews in Russia and Eastern Europe* 56 (2006): 60–81, esp. 76; idem, "Jacob Lestschinsky: A Yiddish Dreamer and Social Scientist," *Science in Context* 20.2 (2007): 215–37, esp. 229.

64   Mayzel, *Af undzer kultur-front*, 168–69; idem, *Geven amol a lebn*, 372–80.

jarred the Bund ideologists' Marxist sensitivities to what they saw as "nationalist" constructs.[65] As a result, Paris seemed much better suited for a Yiddish cultural congress, especially as the Jewish organizations that had established their European or central headquarters in Berlin after World War I had moved to Paris in 1933. Significantly, Jewish Communists, who supported the Yiddish Culture Front as part of the Popular Front's paradigm, had a stronger organization (including the press) in Paris than did the Bund.[66]

In May, 1937, Mayzel went to Paris as a delegate to the 15th congress of the International PEN Club. While in Paris, he also took part in a meeting at the studio of the famous sculptor Naum (Nahum) Aronson. Among the guests were Isaac Nakhman Steinberg, a Yiddish delegate from London (in 1917–18, Steinberg, a member of the Socialist Revolutionary Party, was the People's Commissar of Justice in Lenin's government), and Moyshe Shalit, a representative of the Vilna-based Yiddish Writers and Journalists Association, which enthusiastically supported the idea of convening a world conference for discussing the situation in Yiddish culture. Shalit had a high opinion of Paris, the "community of about one hundred thousand Jewish dwellers, with a constant influx of Jewish intellectual and proletarian youth, in the world city of Paris, in the heart of Europe, at the time of cataclysms in surrounding countries."[67] The gathering at the art master's studio proclaimed themselves the initiators of a Yiddish Culture Front in France, which aimed first of all to organize a world congress of Yiddish intellectuals. The front itself emerged in September 1937, under the chairmanship of Aronson. The main organizer of the congress was

---

65   Mayzel, *Geven amol a lebn*, 378; Haim Zhitlovski, *Undzer nayer kultur-viln: vos vil der ykuf?* (New York: YKUF, 1941), 26; Matthew Hoffman, "From Czernowitz to Paris: The International Yiddish Culture Congress of 1937," in Kalman Weiser and Joshua A. Fogel (eds.), *Czernowitz at 100: The First Yiddish Language Conference in Historical Perspective* (Lanham, MD: Lexington Books, 2010), 153.

66   See Renée Poznanski, *Jews in France during World War II* (Hanover, NH: University Press of New England, 2001), 10; Aline Benain and Audrey Kichelewski, "*Parizer Haynt* et *Naïe Presse*, les itinéraires paradoxaux de deux quotidiens parisiens en langue yiddish," *Archives Juives* 36.1 (2003): 52–69.

67   Moyshe Shalit, "Di naye yidishe gaystike kolonye in Paris," *Literarishe bleter* (15 June 1934): 375. See also Moyshe Shalit, "Ideologisher moment," in Moyshe Shalit (ed.), *Almanakh fun yidishn literatn- un zhurnalistn-fareyn in vilna* (Vilna: n.p., 1938), 12; Mikhail Krutikov, "Isaac Nahman Steinberg: From Anti-Communist Revolutionary to Anti-Zionist Territorialist," Jews in Eastern Europe 1–2 (1999): 5–24; Hirsz Abramowicz, *Profiles of a Lost World: Memoirs of East European Jewish Life before World War II* (Detroit, MI: Wayne State University Press, 1999), 321–26.

the Yiddish playwright and journalist Chaim (Henri) Sloves, a Białystok-born enthusiast of the Bolshevik revolution, who settled in France in 1926.[68]

The congress took place in Paris on 17–21 September, 1937, with 104 delegates representing 677 organizations and institutions from Austria, Argentine, Belgium, Brazil, Britain, Canada, Cuba, Czechoslovakia, Denmark, France, Holland, Italy, Latvia, Lithuania, Mexico, Palestine, Poland, Romania, Switzerland, South Africa, United States, and Uruguay. The American delegation represented 452 organizations and institutions, which had participated in the American Culture Congress, 27–28 August; the Polish delegation: 72 organizations and institutions; the French delegation: 35. In the Soviet climate of purges, however, the Soviet party leadership did not allow a would-be delegation of five Yiddish luminaries—David Bergelson, Itsik Fefer, Izi Kharik, Moyshe Litvakov and Solomon Mikhoels—to take part in the World Yiddish Cultural Congress.[69]

"Yiddishland" became the catchword of the congress. Joseph Opatoshu stated that "[a]s a result of the historic development, 'Ashkenaz' has become an ideological rather than a geographic notion, it's become 'Yiddishland.'" Daniel Charney, the younger brother of Shmuel Niger and a well-known Yiddish litterateur in his own right, argued that the time had come to establish a "central address for so-called Yiddishland."[70] It was a "land" populated by *progressive* people who regarded themselves part of a worldwide Yiddish-speaking *nation* (rather than religious group), united by one culture and language.[71] The delegates and, generally, many activists, saw Paris as the only logical center for this virtual Yiddishland and its World Yiddish Cultural Association.

However, during the remaining years leading up to World War II, Paris did not evolve into the new Yiddish intellectual capital, although the YKUF's headquarters were located in the city. Similar to Weimar Berlin,[72] the French capital could function at best as a crossroads between the real centers of "Yiddishland," where several oases of the Kultur-Lige ideology endured on the eve and in the aftermath of World War II. The strongest of them was the New York-based

---

68   Mayzel, *Geven amol a lebn*, 380–81. See also Annette Aronowicz, "Haim Sloves, the Jewish People, and a Jewish Communist's Allegiances," *Jewish Social Studies* 9.1 (2002): 95–142.

69   Materials of the congress came out in *Ershter alveltlekher yidisher kultur-kongres* (New York: IKUF, 1937). See also Gennady Estraikh, *In Harness*, 99–100.

70   *Ershter alveltlekher yidisher kultur-kongres*, 26, 33. See also Hoffman, *From Czernowitz to Paris*, 157.

71   Zhitlowski, *Undzer nayer kultur-viln*, 12.

72   Cf. Gennady Estraikh and Mikhail Krutikov (eds.), *Yiddish in Weimar Berlin: At the Crossroads of Diaspora Politics and Culture* (Oxford: Legenda, 2010).

YKUF, with Nakhman Mayzel as one of its central figures. According to Isaac Bashevis Singer, Mayzel "had for years flitted between socialism and communism before becoming a full-fledged communist."[73] In reality, Mayzel was a fellow traveller whose mild pro-Sovietism began to evaporate in the 1950s.[74]

A new international network of organizations, infused with the spirit of the Kultur-Lige traditions, emerged after the Holocaust. The American YKUF and similar bodies in such countries as Canada, Argentina, and France gravitated to Poland, to her promising *nusekh poyln* in the shape of Jewish cultural autonomy. The Warsaw-based Yiddish publishing house Yidish Bukh issued co-editions with the YKUF and the Paris-based imprint Oysnay (Anew). Chaim Sloves's plays were performed in Warsaw by the State Polish Yiddish Theatre.[75] Still, the YKUF and its sister organizations remained on the margins of Jewish life because Yiddish and its secular culture "were not transmitted beyond one or two generations. Uprooted from its native soils, Yiddish culture did not transplant well with the immigrants who bore it."[76] All of these organizations were scorned by the Jewish mainstream as stooges of Moscow; and they became almost irrelevant following the anti-Jewish campaign in Poland in 1968, which brought to an end the period of *nusekh poyln* and the hopes of the left-wing Yiddishists. By that time, in any case, their constituency had already shrunk under the impact of the de-sanctification of Stalin, when revelations about his repression and terror moved many erstwhile Soviet sympathizers to change their ideological orientation.[77]

In 1964, that is, even before the terminal decline of Warsaw's post-Holocaust Yiddish center, Mayzel settled in Israel, hardly the proper place for a committed Yiddishist. In fact, a number of Yiddishist activists, including the social scientist Jacob Lestschinsky and the linguist Yudel Mark, moved from the United

---

73 Isaac Bashevis Singer, *Love and Exile: An Autobiographical Trilogy* (New York: Farrar, Straus and Giroux, 1986), 50.
74 Gennady Estraikh, *Yiddish in the Cold War* (Oxford: Legenda, 2008), 18.
75 Annette Aronowicz, "Homens Mapole: Hope in the Intermediate Postwar Period," *The Jewish Quarterly Review* 98.3 (2008): 355–88; Joanna Nalewajko-Kulikov, "The Last Yiddish Books Printed in Poland: Outline of the Activities of Yidish Bukh Publishing House," in Elvira Grözinger and Magdalena Ruta (eds.), *Under the Red Banner: Yiddish Culture in the Communist Countries in the Postwar Era* (Wiesbaden: Otto Harrassowitz, 2008), 118.
76 Zvi Gitelman, "The Decline of the Diaspora Jewish Nation: Boundaries, Content, and Jewish Identity," *Jewish Social Studies* 4.2 (1998): 112–32, here 122.
77 Gennady Estraikh, "Metamorphoses of *Morgn-frayhayt*," in Gennady Estraikh and Mikhail Krutikov (eds.), *Yiddish and the Left* (Oxford: Legenda, 2001), 144–66; see also Leszek W. Głuchowski and Antony Polonsky (eds.), *1968: Forty Years After*, Polin. *Studies in Polish Jewry* 21 (Oxford: The Littman Library of Jewish Civilization, 2009).

States to Israel in the 1950s through the 1970s. By that time, the Diasporic national landscape, where the Peretzian (and Kultur-Ligean) "golden chain" continued to be preserved, had become almost invisible, its organization populated predominantly by elderly people with old loyalties.[78] They, like other secular ideologues, had to a certain extent failed; they were not destined to realize the dream of a Diasporic Jewish nation with a contents-rich form of Yiddish culture.

---

78   See, e.g, Estraikh, "Jacob Lestschinsky," 233.

CHAPTER 14

Enduring Prestige, Eroded Authority: The Warsaw Rabbinate in the Interwar Period

Gershon Bacon

Introduction: The Nineteenth-Century Heritage and the Historical Narrative

The accepted narrative of the history of Warsaw Jewry portrays the abolition of the office of chief rabbi after Jacob Gesundheit's removal from office in 1873 as the turning point for the worse for the stature of the rabbinate in the Polish capital. Placing authority in the hands of a rabbinical council instead of a chief rabbi was seen as practically guaranteeing the weakness of the city's rabbinate from then on, which was not highly regarded by the leadership of the community.[1]

In the mid-nineteenth century, it is asserted, the rabbi of Warsaw could speak authoritatively in the name of Warsaw Jewry, and, in many ways, in the name of Polish Jewry as a whole. Typical in this regard are the words of Jacob Shatzky, referring to the late 1850s:

> ... after the 'Jewish War' the executive of the *kehilla* [communal council] was comprised mostly of 'enlightened' Jews. They looked upon Meisels as not just a rabbi, but as a representative of the great *kehilla*... The tales about the contacts with Polish officialdom and the respect shown him as a 'genuine Polish rabbi' quickly spread among the Jewish homes of Warsaw. In him was seen a leader, a guide, just as the archbishop was seen among Catholics... Meisels became the intercessor for the people. From all sides people turned to him for help. The *kehilla*, thanks to its chief rabbi, became the representative of the entire Jewish population in Poland.[2]

---

1 Jacob Shatzky, *Geshikhte fun yidn in varshe*, III: 149.
2 Ibid., II: 229, 231.

In Shatzky's view, it was the authoritative personality of Dov Berish Meisels that conferred prestige on the Warsaw community leadership rather than vice versa.

Due to his position and to his personality, the chief rabbi of Warsaw was a national figure. With a long career in the business world, he made his way easily through the corridors of wealth and power in the capital. His participation in the momentous events leading up to and including the January Uprising of 1863 earned him a place in the pantheon of fighters for Polish independence and as an icon of Polish-Jewish cooperation.[3] As we shall demonstrate, in the interwar period, the situation and status of the communal rabbinate in the capital were quite different from the supposed golden age half a century earlier.

The Warsaw Rabbinate in the Second Half of the 19th Century: A Golden Age, but with Shadows

While focusing on the interwar period, the present paper will attempt to revise the narrative on the Warsaw rabbinate from several perspectives. Despite Shatzky's disparagement of the rabbinical council as little more than a mouthpiece of the *kehilla* lay leadership whose proclamations served the interests of that leadership or of the Russian authorities,[4] at least until the early twentieth century, the Warsaw rabbinate could and did make its collective voice heard as a spiritual authority on communal issues, including those beyond the borders of the city. To cite one random example, during the 1892 cholera epidemic, the rabbinical council of Warsaw published an appeal to all rabbis and heads of Jewish communities of Poland to put an end to time-honored customs engaged in by Jews to ward off plagues, such as marriages of orphans or people with physical deformities in cemeteries ("Black Weddings"),[5] or street processions. Though their intentions may be proper and honorable, the very public nature of these customs, the rabbis feared, could lead to misunderstanding on

---

3   On the image and reality of Meisels' political activity as reflected in Polish and Jewish literature, see Magdalena Opalski and Israel Bartal, *Poles and Jews: A Failed Brotherhood* (Hanover, NH, and London: Brandeis University Press, 1992).

4   Shatzky, *Geshikhte fun yidn in varshe*, III: 148.

5   On this custom, see Hanna Węgrzynek, "Shvartze khasene: black weddings among Polish Jews," in Glenn Dynner (ed.), *Holy Dissent: Jewish and Christian Mystics in Eastern Europe* (Detroit, MI: Wayne State University Press, 2011), 55–68; Tsevi Friedhaber, "Hatunot magefa be're'i ha-sifrut ve'ha-itonut ha-ivrit," *Dappim le'mehkar ha-sifrut* 7 (1991): 305–316. Thanks to Glenn Dynner and Uriel Gellman for these references.

the part of non-Jews and hence a *hillul hashem*, a desecration of the Divine name. They had already led to difficulties and arguments, "... and who knows, they could lead to danger to the Jewish people?"[6] What is crucial here is the fact that the rabbis expected their directive, issued by the major rabbinic figures of the capital, to be obeyed by the rabbis and communal leaders of other communities.

On the other hand, the supposed golden age of rabbinical authority under chief rabbis was not lacking in major challenges to the rabbi's office. Before his move to Warsaw, the aforementioned scholarly, wealthy and socially well-connected Dov Berish Meisels nevertheless spent almost his entire rabbinic career in Kraków under a cloud, challenged by half of the community and openly opposed by another rabbi, Shaul Landau, who opened a competing rabbinical court in the city.[7] The three stormy years of his successor Jacob Gesundheit's term as chief rabbi witnessed numerous examples of lack of deference on the part of Hasidic and *kehilla* leaders towards the rabbi, until the forming of what Jacob Shatzky famously termed an "unholy alliance" between Hasidim and assimilationists to engineer his dismissal, ultimately resulting in the liquidation of the office of chief rabbi of Warsaw.[8]

Nor was the situation of the rabbinate in other locales necessarily better. Several rabbis who joined the rabbinical council in Warsaw in the late nineteenth and early twentieth centuries and who served into the interwar period were certainly attracted by the "pull" of the prestige of the capital and its rabbinate, but no less by the "push" of communal disputes, denunciations to the authorities and lack of deference they experienced as rabbis of smaller communities. Two examples demonstrate this point. The son of the venerable Warsaw rabbi Abraham Tzvi Perlmutter composed a 150-page Yiddish biography of his illustrious father to, of course, honor his father, but in his introduction to the volume he tells his readers that the book is more a lengthy answer to the question he was often asked: why did he go into the business world and leave Poland for Antwerp, rather than follow in the footsteps of his father

---

6 *Ha-tzefira* (26 October 1892): 2.
7 Moshe Kamelhar, *Rabbi dov ber meisels: gadol batorah, medinai ve'lohem* (Jerusalem: Mossad Harav Kook, 1970), 20. For a nicely nuanced and balanced portrayal of the image and the reality of Meisels' tenure as rabbi of Kraków, see the discussion of Haim Gertner in his *Ha-rav ve'ha-ir ha-gedolah: ha-rabbanut be'galitsiya u'mifgasha im ha-moderna, 1815–1867* (Jerusalem: Merkaz Zalman Shazar, 2013), 244–263.
8 Jacob Shatzky, *Geshikhte fun yidn in varshe*, III: 141.

into the rabbinate?[9] The book catalogs the abuse and persecution suffered by his father at practically every stage of his career, beginning with his pulpit in Raciąż, when local Hasidim objected to his taking private lessons in the Russian language from a Jewish student tutor. They threw stones at the rabbi's windows.[10] Nor was his almost thirty year tenure on the rabbinical council of Warsaw free of strife, whether from rabbinical colleagues, political opponents (Perlmutter served as a deputy in the Constituent Sejm elected in 1919) or from lay people. His son lamented the fate of a man "who bothered no one, and yet was persecuted by all, starting with the Hasidic tailor and ending with the Mitnagdic [anti-Hasidic] shoemaker."[11] The suffering of the rabbi and his family extended even to fights over his burial plot and alleged insults to the sons after their father's death, part of a struggle to get the family to release the official ledgers for recording births, deaths and marriages.

Rabbi Tzvi Yehezkel Mikhlzohn was involved in a series of disputes in his rabbinical posts in Krasnobród and Płońsk. On a visit to Karlsbad right before the outbreak of World War I, he was interned there for several months as an enemy alien. Finally able to return to his post in Płońsk after the German conquest of most of Poland and after the community received permission to bring him back, he found himself confronted by a renewed series of contentions, denunciations and quarrels, including the arrest of some of the community's leaders for almost four months due to denunciations to the authorities. As a result, after several years and with a certain amount of hesitation on his part about moving to a large city, he accepted an invitation to join the Warsaw rabbinical council, especially since it came from his relative Heshel Farbstein, president of the Mizrahi religious Zionist organization of Poland and later president of the *kehilla* council of Warsaw.[12] He took up his post in Warsaw in the fall of 1921,

---

9   Moshe Perlmutter, *Ha-rav R' Avraham Tzvi Perlmutter: zayn leben un shafn* (Antwerp, 1933), 9. For a short biographical sketch on Perlmutter, see Gershon Bacon, "Perlmutter, Avraham Tsevi," in *Yivo Encyclopedia of Jews in Eastern Europe* 2: 1344–45.

10   Perlmutter, *Ha-rav*, 35–37.

11   Perlmutter, *Ha-rav*, 8.

12   Tzvi Yehezkel Mikhlzohn, *Petah ha-bayit*, introduction to his *Bet yehezkel* (Piotrków, 1924), 18, available at www.hebrewbooks.org/69 (last accessed 3 February 2012); a slightly different version of the events given in *Har ha-bayit*, introduction to his *Pinot ha-bayit* (Piotrków, 1925), 30, available at www.hebrewbooks.org/374 (last accessed 3 February 2012). See also Nahman Shemen, *Di biografiye fun a varshever rov* (Montreal: Der Keneder Adler 1948), 15–16. On Mikhlzohn, see also Geulah Bat-Yehudah, "Mikhlzohn, Tzvi Yehezkel," in Yitzhak Raphael (ed.), *Entziklopedia shel ha-tziyonut ha-datit* (Jerusalem: Mossad Harav Kook, 1965), vol. 3, cols. 399–409; Penina Meizlish, *Rabbanim she'nispu*

serving the community with distinction both as an official rabbi and as chairman of numerous voluntary organizations. In the Warsaw ghetto, Mikhlzohn, the eldest of the serving rabbis, commanded special respect and continued his work as part of the rabbinical council until his deportation and death in Treblinka, presumably in 1942.[13]

Thus the presence of a chief rabbi did not guarantee rabbinical authority, nor did the absence of the office automatically signify any diminishing of the rabbinate's religious authority in a community, including Warsaw. Many factors were at work, leading to either deference or the lack thereof. Nor should we forgot perennial issues that could and did weaken the rabbinate in a community, such "traditional" disputes as over the right of sons or favorite students to "inherit" the office of a deceased rabbi, between Hasidim and Mitnagdim, or among various Hasidic groups over the rabbinic office.[14]

Transition: Politics and the Politicization of Orthodoxy Jewry in Poland

The major transition in Polish Jewry, however, that would affect the status of the rabbinate in Warsaw and elsewhere was the development of mass politics. This process would touch on the lives of orthodox and secular Jews alike. The process of politicization of Polish Hasidim and Mitnagdim, as well as of Polish-Russian Jewry in general, goes back to the events of the late nineteenth and early twentieth centuries, including the early appearance of underground or semi-legal party politics, the rise of Zionism and Bundism, the participation of citizens in the events of the Revolution of 1905, and the first experiences of the subjects of the Russian Empire with parliamentary politics in the wake of the Revolution of 1905 in the elections to the Imperial Dumas. Two recent doctoral dissertations have attempted to map out this process in the

---

ba'shoah, alphabetical entry on Mikhlzohn, available at http://horabis.blogspot.co.il/ (last accessed 18 March 2013).

13 See Adam Czerniaków, *Yoman ghetto varsha* (2nd ed.; Jerusalem: Yad Vashem, 1970), 176; Hillel Seidman, *Yoman ghetto varsha* (New York: Di iddishe vokh, 1957), 61–62, 341–343.

14 On the ongoing, chronic problems of the rabbinate in Eastern Europe, see Shaul Stampfer, "The missing rabbis of Eastern Europe," in *Families, Rabbis and Education: Traditional Jewish Society in Nineteenth-Century Eastern Europe* (London: Littman Library, 2010), 277–301; idem, "The Inheritance of the Rabbinate in Eastern Europe in modern times—causes, factors and development over time," *Jewish History* 13.1 (1999): 35–57 [revised edition in *Families, Rabbis and Education*, 302–323].

cases of the two key Polish cities of Warsaw and Łódź,[15] while a third examines the development of party politics among the Jews of the Russian Empire as a whole.[16] We are witness to the development of what Habermas famously characterized as the public sphere among the Jews in the cities and towns of Poland. Orthodox Jews and Hasidic Jews do not figure prominently in sources from the time or in retrospective accounts as major agents or participants in this process. Many political activists regarded them as hopelessly retrograde and an obstacle to the freedom of the "masses", even though they comprised a large portion of those masses. If we seek them out, however, there are enough signs that they, too, were affected by the politicization of the "Jewish street", though the Hasidic shtibl was substituted for the cafés and parks of the young socialists and Zionists as a gathering point,[17] and the orthodox press made its first abortive steps relatively late. As Ezra Mendelsohn put it:

> orthodox Jewish politics could take root only if the local Orthodox leaders were prepared to enter the modern political arena, a step many regarded with great trepidation. The core area of Orthodox Jewish politics, therefore, was located in those regions of Eastern Europe where the traditional Jewish Orthodox elite was prepared to co-opt the ways of modern politics and to organize the God-fearing masses in order to combat the Jewish heretics—nationalists and integrationists—and all their works.[18]

It was the desire to bring to the public square the voice of what they claimed was the silent majority of orthodox Jews that led prominent rabbis in the Russian Empire to establish the short-lived Kenesset Yisrael party in 1907–1908,

---

15 Scott Ury, "Red Banner, Blue Star: Radical Politics, Democratic Institutions and Collective Identity among Jews in Warsaw, 1904–1907" (unpublished Ph.D. dissertation, Hebrew University, 2006), which has recently been published under the title *Barricades and Banners: The Revolution of 1905 and the Transformation of Warsaw Jewry* (Stanford, CA: Stanford University Press, 2012); Yedida Sharona Kanfer, "Łódź: Industry, Religion, and Nationalism in Russian Poland, 1880–1914" (unpublished Ph.D. dissertation, Yale University, 2011). My thanks to both scholars for sharing their work and their research findings with me.

16 Vladimir Levin, "Ha-politika ha-yehudit ba-imperiya ha-russit be-'idan ha-reaktsiya, 1907–1914" (unpublished Ph.D. dissertation, Hebrew University, 2007).

17 Ury, *Red Banner, Blue Star*, 148 [= *Barricades and Banners*, 325–326, note 22], notes, however, that some orthodox Jews did find ways to go to cafés on the Sabbath and holidays by pre-paying for their drinks, and thus were not completely isolated from the café society.

18 Ezra Mendelsohn, *On Modern Jewish Politics* (New York: Oxford University Press, 1993), 51.

the first orthodox party in the empire, which can be seen as one of the precursors of Agudat Yisrael, a party that exists to this day.[19]

This was not, however, the first foray of rabbis into general politics in Eastern Europe. Besides the aforementioned activities of Dov Berish Meisels during the revolutionary upheavals of the early 1860s, there were other precedents for rabbis and communal leaders attempting to enlist the masses of orthodox Jews to defend their interests in the political sphere from perceived threats from secular Jews or governmental programs. In the Hungarian lands we are witness to the development of what would be called the Ultra-Orthodox group, which formulated its own organizational and ideological agenda for the preservation of Jewish tradition.[20] In the Austrian-ruled formerly Polish region of Galicia there arose in the late 1870s the Mahzikei ha-dat party to assert orthodox claims to communal leadership and to influence and counter efforts by liberal Jews. Rabbi Shimon Sofer of Kraków was elected to parliament, one of four rabbis who ran in the elections on the Mahzikei ha-dat list. As opposed to his liberal Jewish rivals, Sofer aligned himself with conservative Polish Catholics in the Austrian parliament, an alliance that Rachel Manekin has termed a "new covenant."[21]

By the end of World War I, there already existed practically the entire spectrum of political movements that were active in the interwar period. This included orthodox movements, but, what is more important for the present discussion, new types of orthodox communal and political activists who took on the task of representing orthodox interests in the public sector. One such new leadership type was the so-called "klal-tuer", the doer for the public, the

---

19   On Kenesset Yisrael, see Vladimir Levin, "Kenesset yisrael: ha-miflaga ha-politit ha-ortodoksit ha-rishona ba-imperiya ha-russit," *Zion* 76 (2011): 29–62. On the early development of orthodox politics in Poland leading to the founding of Agudat Yisrael, see Gershon Bacon, *The Politics of Tradition: Agudat Yisrael in Poland, 1916–1939* (Jerusalem: Magnes Press, 1996), 22–46.

20   See Michael Silber, "The Emergence of Ultra-Orthodoxy: The Invention of a Tradition," in Jack Wertheimer (ed.), *The Uses of Tradition: Jewish Continuity in the Modern Era* (New York and Jerusalem: Jewish Theological Seminary, 1992), 23–84.

21   Rachel Manekin, "Ha-berit ha-hadasha: yehudim ortodoksim ve'katolim polanim be'galitsiya, 1879–1883," *Zion* 64 (1999): 157–186; idem, "Politika ve'ortodoksiya: ha-mikreh shel galitsiya," in Yosef Salmon et al. (eds.), *Ortodoksiya yehudit: hebetim hadashim* (Jerusalem: Magnes Press, 2006), 447–469. For a short survey of the Mahzikei ha-dat organization, see Rachel Manekin, "Makhzikey ha-das," *Yivo Encyclopedia of Jews in Eastern Europe*, 1: 1119–1120.

subject of a recent pioneering study,[22] who may have been acting at the behest of a rabbinic or Hasidic religious leader, but who became a leader in his own right. Politics had made clear inroads to the orthodox community, and the communal rabbi, even of a major community, was but one of many members of a greatly expanded leadership cadre.

Nor was the communal rabbinate itself immune to the process of politicization and the new mass politics. One clear beginning point for such involvement was in the course of the elections for a new chief rabbi of Łódź, after Warsaw the second largest Jewish community in Poland, following the death of the long-serving chief rabbi Eliyahu Hayyim Meisel in 1912. In this campaign we can see the inroads of democratic politics and methods into communal matters, even if the existing election laws still limited the franchise to male taxpayers to the *kehilla*. In Łódź at the time, this translated into an electorate of several thousand, and the rabbinical election was the subject of intense debate in the Jewish daily press, which had just begun to appear in the city. The election campaign for chief rabbi was in many ways the debut of this aspect of the Jewish public sphere in the city.

Elections were held in October 1912, the same month as elections to the Fourth Duma. In the terminology bandied about in the course of the campaign, the 'traditional' rabbi Eliezer Treistmann (known as the Radomer) defeated the 'enlightened' rabbi Lifshitz (the Kalisher). Following an appeal to the authorities claiming election fraud, the results were declared invalid, with a second round scheduled for August 1913.

The contest became an all-Russian affair as all kinds of elements tried to intervene and influence the voting public in the city. The Gerer *Rebbe* led the core of the group supporting Treistmann. Ger merchants had already been sharing power with assimilationists on the community board, with a "power-sharing agreement" similar to the arrangement in Warsaw, putting religious affairs in the hands of the Hasidim. Now the Gerer turned to assimilationists for support for their rabbinical candidate, and would ultimately prevail. The Lifshitz camp eventually became a motley coalition of other Hasidim (especially the

---

22 François Guesnet, "Thinking globally, acting locally: Joel Wegmeister and Modern Hasidic Politics in Warsaw," *Quest. Issues in Contemporary Jewish History* 2 (October 2011), available at http://www.quest-cdecjournal.it/focus.php?id=222 (last accessed 6 February 2012). For an earlier Polish version of this article see idem., "Chasydzki klal-tuer wobec metropolii i nowoczesności: Joel Wegmeister z Warszawy (1837–1919)," in *Żydzi Warszawy* (Warszawa: Żydowski Instytut Historyczny, 2000), 41–57.

Alexander Hasidim, the rivals of the Gerer Hasidim), secular Jews, and religious Zionists.[23]

According to the memoirs of Pinhas Minc, later a Communist activist but at the time a clerk in the local Jewish community, the atmosphere during the elections had its own special "political" style:

> The *gmine* [communal council] became one of the most important tools in the struggle, since there was housed the list of voters and the *gmine* bureaucracy knew many ways to contribute to the victory of one side or the other, besides the fact that *gmine* became the ground for negotiations between the sides and the *gmine* building became highly animated during the election period. From early in the morning until late at night it swarmed and seethed with people: Gerer, Alexander, Sochaczower Hasidim, all kinds of Lithuanian Jews and plain respectable people. They held meetings and negotiated with each other. Suddenly it became quiet, completely quiet: people prayed the afternoon service in public in the hall of the *kehilla*, in each corner a different *minyan* . . . For 15–20 minutes it was quiet, but once they went through the silent devotion, they began to talk among themselves and to seethe, and this was not just the older Jews, but also the young scholars supported by in-laws and the Hasidic young men.[24]

This rabbinical election campaign, then, was one of the first clear instances of party politics making its way into the rabbinic world in Poland, and the process would but deepen in subsequent decades.

For orthodox Jews in Poland, the entry into politics was a slow and hesitant process, with many reversals of direction, often with no clear program or ideology apart from following the directives or direction of the *rebbe* or fighting Zionists and secularists. Even in the interwar period there would still be elements in the Hasidic community in Poland and other countries who believed that the rabbi and the community possessed adequate means to curb undesirable manifestations without requiring the modern tools of organizations, press and political parties.[25] Nevertheless, politics had made inroads on the "Jewish street", even its orthodox precincts. The old communal elites of secular

---

23 Kanfer, *Łódź*, 337–338.
24 Pinhas Minc (Alexanderer), *Lodzsh in mayn zikorn* (Buenos Aires: Yidbukh, 1958), 214.
25 Gershon Bacon, "Prolonged erosion, organization and reinforcement: reflections on Orthodox Jewry in Congress Poland (to 1914)," in Yisrael Gutman (ed.) *Major Changes within the Jewish People in the wake of the Holocaust* (Jerusalem: Yad Vashem, 1996), 82.

business leaders and a few orthodox *gvirim* may not yet have been supplanted, but political movements and alternative leadership elites had already made their appearance in communal and parliamentary elections. The communal rabbi had a new series of competitors for public standing and status.

The Interwar Period: New Challenges, Old Struggles, Residual Prestige

When we enter the interwar period, the decline in the status of the rabbinate intensifies, due to external factors and to competition from other organizations and institutions in the Jewish community, and also due to internal weaknesses within the institution of the rabbinate itself. As in the previous period, the causes for the decline in the authority of the Warsaw rabbinate in particular should be sought not in the presence or absence of a chief rabbi, but in the political and social changes occurring in Polish Jewry in the twentieth century, and more particularly in the interwar period, most of them related to the ongoing process of politicization of most aspects of life of the community. With the establishment of a more democratic communal governing body, the old rules of Jewish communal politics changed drastically, affecting all aspects of the life of the community, including the selection and status of the communal rabbis. It would be helpful to factor into our discussion the processes of modernization and secularization of Polish Jewry, surely present but as yet unmeasured and not quantified. Whatever their extent, they were surely expanding, and for at least part of the community in Warsaw and elsewhere religion and religious leadership were less important.[26]

Politics made its voice heard in the appointment of Rabbis Meisels and Gesundheit in the mid-nineteenth century, and certainly had a major role in the dismissal of the latter, or in the Łódź rabbinical elections on the eve of World War I, but this cannot be compared to the infiltration of politics and political parties into every phase of Polish Jewish life. Inevitably, this major change in the life of the community left its imprint on the rabbinate as well—

---

26 For an early twentieth century incident illustrating some aspects of these phenomena, see Gershon Bacon, "Kefiya datit, hofesh bitui ve'zehut yehudit modernit: Y.L. Peretz, Shalom Asch ve'shaaruryat ha-mila be'varsha, 1908," in David Assaf et al. (eds.), *Mi-vilna li-yerushalayim* (Jerusalem: Magnes, 2002), 167–185; for a pioneering attempt to characterize and quantify one marker of secularization, namely the decline in observance of *kashrut*, see Asaf Kaniel, "Bein hilonim, masorti'im ve'ortodoksim: shemirat mitzvot be'rei ha-hitmodedut im 'gezeirat ha-kashrut', 1937–1939," *Gal-Ed* 22 (2010): 75–106.

from the nomination of candidates for local rabbinical posts who now were often sponsored by political parties, to their confirmation by the elected *kehilla* council members (as opposed to a vote of all the [male] tax-paying members of the community, as had been the practice in the past), to their ability to function as rabbis vis-à-vis other centers of power in the community.

Despite the acknowledged scholarly and personal attainments of the various members of the Warsaw rabbinical council, as individuals and as a collective body they had to compete with a number of newer centers of authority in Polish Jewry, each one of them in differing ways eroding the prestige and the fields of activity of the Warsaw rabbinate. On most issues of public import, including ones with a clear connection to religion, the once influential voice of the Warsaw rabbinate was often lost among the now numerous centers of power and influence in the Jewish community located in the capital. Four such centers are of particular importance in this regard:

1. *Sejm deputies and other elected officials*

    In previous generations (and the biographies of Rabbis Meisels, Perlmutter and others attest to this), rabbis acted as *shtadlanim*, or intercessors with the authorities. The rabbis of the capital, along with members of the Warsaw Jewish plutocracy and some Hasidic leaders, were the de facto spokesmen for Polish Jewry.[27] Not surprisingly, in interwar Poland, both on the national level and on the local level, either the Sejm deputy or city councilman was the elected representative and spokesman of Polish Jewry, and became the address for individual Jews or Jewish communities with grievances. As visions of national autonomy and legislative initiatives by the Jewish representatives went nowhere in the generally hostile political climate of interwar Poland, they found themselves spending much of their time and effort dealing with grievances of individuals or communities wronged by bureaucratic discrimination and arbitrary rulings.[28] Parliamentary deputies had the ability to submit interpellations at question time, to which the ministers involved were obliged to respond, and they could turn directly to local, regional or national officials. Ezra Mendelsohn notes that in 1919 Zionist deputies were so busy with intercessions that they often missed sessions of the

---

[27] On Meisels' two predecessors as chief rabbi of Warsaw, Shlomo Zalman Lifshitz and Hayyim Dawidsohn, see Avraham Bromberg, *Mi-gedolei ha-hasidut, Sefer 15—Rishonei ha-rabbanim be'varsha* (Jerusalem: Makhon le-hasidut, 1959).

[28] See Moshe Landau, *Miut leumi lohem: maavak yehudei polin 1918–1928* (Jerusalem: Merkaz Zalman Shazar, 1986), 21–22.

Sejm.²⁹ City councilmen dealt with day-to-day problems of discrimination, and, on occasion, issues of physical security and anti-Jewish violence. Despite all the talk of the "new" Jewish politics of pride and struggle for national and civic rights, there was still much need in reborn Poland for the intercessor of old, even if the new politicians regarded this part of their job with reservation and some distaste.

In orthodox circles, however, the *shtadlan* enjoyed a more positive reputation, especially in light of the rather pessimistic outlook for major achievements on the legislative front. As it happened, many of the orthodox deputies elected to the Sejm and Senate of Poland were rabbis, and their electorate regarded their role as a combination of rabbi and politician. A biographer of Rabbi Aron Lewin of Rzeszów noted that his formal work in the Sejm constituted only a small part of his job. People came to him for help and advice on all kinds of matters. His patriarchal appearance and fluent Polish made a great impression on government bureaucrats.³⁰

The symbolic import of rabbi-politicians was particularly noteworthy in the case of Rabbi Perlmutter of Warsaw, elected to the Constituent Sejm in 1919, and, as a younger contemporary of the legendary Dov Berish Meisels, a living embodiment of orthodox involvement in the Polish national struggle. He and his colleagues from Agudat Yisrael tempered their criticisms of government policies toward Jews with ringing affirmations of the wondrous rebirth of the Polish state.³¹ On those occasions when Perlmutter's political actions came under severe criticism on the part of Zionist deputies or the press, his defenders stressed that his effectiveness as a *shtadlan* for individuals in distress far outweighed a few legislative faux pas.³² The fact remains, though, that Perlmutter and his rabbinical colleagues who served in the parliament were now just part of a much larger group of elected *shtadlanim*. Perlmutter was a member of the rabbinical council of Warsaw, but it appears that his newer title as Sejm deputy is what empowered him to serve as an intercessor on the

---

29　Ezra Mendelsohn, *Zionism in Poland: the Formative Years, 1915–1926* (New Haven: Yale University Press, 1981), 233.

30　*Eleh ezkerah* (New York: Research Institute of Religious Jewry, 1956), vol. 1, 48.

31　See Perlmutter's speech in the Sejm on February 24 1919—*Sprawozdanie Stenograficzne Sejmu Ustawodawczego*, February 24, 1919, col. 183; on the symbolic importance of his appearance in the Sejm, see Bacon, *Politics of Tradition*, 231, 241, 245–246.

32　*Der yid* (Warsaw) (February 17 1922): 5.

national level. The new Jewish politics offered new leadership opportunities and political roles for rabbis, but the communal rabbinate as an institution in general, and the Warsaw rabbinate in particular, were overshadowed.[33]

2. *Religious political parties and the rabbinical bodies attached to them*

Many, if not most of the rabbis serving on Warsaw's rabbinical council in the interwar period were beholden for their appointments to political parties. What is more, the rabbis of the capital acknowledged and accepted the authority of the rabbinical bodies attached to these parties. This held true not only for Agudat Yisrael, whose candidates made up most of the new appointments to the Warsaw rabbinate, but also for the Mizrahi party, responsible for a smaller number of rabbis appointed. Rabbis on the Warsaw rabbinical board were under the authority of the Aguda's so-called Council of Torah Sages, and some of them were even members of that supreme rabbinical body. A prime example is Rabbi Yaakov Meir Biderman, who had close familial ties with the Alter family of the Gerer Hasidic dynasty (son-in-law, brother-in-law, father-in-law, grandfather of various *rebbes*) and who was a member of Agudat Yisrael and its international Council of Torah Sages. After some twenty years in the capital, functioning unofficially as a rabbi and adviser, he gave in to the pressure of party officials and accepted an appointment to the Warsaw rabbinical council, part of the campaign by the Aguda-led Warsaw *kehilla* to fill longstanding vacancies in the communal rabbinate.[34] This was a clear indication that in the interwar period ultimate rabbinical authority lay elsewhere, and not in the Warsaw rabbinate.

3. *"Super rabbis"*

Rabbis whose spiritual authority reached beyond the borders of any single community or even the borders of Poland (e.g. the Hafetz Hayyim [Rabbi Yisrael Meir Kagan], the Gerer *Rebbe* [Rabbi Abraham Mordecai Alter], Rabbi Hayyim Ozer Grodziński) enjoyed a prestige that dwarfed that of the rabbis of Warsaw. Such rabbinical figures had existed in previous generations in Eastern Europe, the most notable among them being

---

33 On the fuzzy boundaries between the rabbinic office and political life in the interwar period and the variations of combinations of the two, see Gershon Bacon, "Rabbis and Politics, Rabbis in Politics: Different Models within Interwar Polish Jewry," *Yivo Annual* 20 (1991): 39–59.

34 *Eleh toldot yaakov* (Jerusalem: Yad Aryeh, 1995), 39, 47, 71, 75.

Rabbi Yitzhak Elhanan Spektor of Kovno, who died in 1896.[35] In the interwar period, however, the rabbis now gave their imprimatur to a political apparatus and exemplified the then developing doctrine of *Da'at torah*, which claimed ultimate authority for central rabbinic sages in matters religious and secular alike.[36] In an earlier article, we also termed such rabbis integrative or integrative-active leaders, depending on the degree of their involvement in ongoing partisan political affairs.[37] The example of Rabbi Hayyim Ozer Grodziński of Vilna demonstrates how the lack of a chief rabbi (in the case of Vilna from the late eighteenth century onward) did not preclude having a rabbi with a less grandiose title (in his case, being one of the members of the local rabbinical court) who nevertheless exercised tremendous local, national, and even international rabbinic influence.[38] His prestige and world-class standing persisted even after his defeat by Yitzhak Rubinstein in the 1928 election for chief rabbi of Vilna, an election imposed on the community by Polish authorities.[39]

In an incident that has taken on almost mythic proportions in orthodox historiography, when a delegation of leading rabbinic figures came to Warsaw in late 1930 to forestall a governmental attempt to impose demands for secular education for teachers in the traditional *kheyder*, it was this type of "super-rabbi" figure who took the lead and made the appeal, and not the rabbis of the capital. The elderly Hafetz Hayyim convened an emergency consultation of rabbis and Hasidic *rebbe*s in Warsaw to formulate an appropriate response to the perceived threat. Retrospective accounts of this meeting called it "the greatest assemblage of sages in Poland since the days of the Council of the Four Lands."[40] Around the

---

35 On Spektor, see the biography written by his longtime secretary and aide Yaakov Halevi Lifshitz, *Toledot Yitzhak* (Warsaw, 1896).

36 On this doctrine, see G. Bacon, *Politics of Tradition*, 50–57. For a brief survey, see Gershon Bacon, "Daas Toyre," *Yivo Encyclopedia of Jews in Eastern Europe*, 1: 387.

37 G. Bacon, "Rabbis and Politics, Rabbis in Politics," 42–48.

38 On R. Hayyim Ozer Grodziński, see Gershon Bacon and Yitzhak Hershkowitz, "Ha-rav hayyim ozer grodziński: av-tipus shel 'gadol' ba-meah ha-esrim," in Benjamin Brown and Nissim Leon (eds.), *Ha-gedolim: ishim she'itzvu et pnei ha-yahadut ha-haredit* (Jerusalem: Van Leer Institute, in press).

39 On this incident and its implications, see Gershon Bacon, "Rubinstein vs. Grodziński: The Dispute over the Vilnius Rabbinate and the Religious Realignment of Vilnius Jewry, 1928–1932," in Izraelis Lampertas (ed.), *The Gaon of Vilnius and the Annals of Jewish Culture* (Vilnius: Vilnius University Publishing House, 1998), 295–304.

40 Aharon Sorasky, *Or elhanan* (Los Angeles, 1978), vol. 2, 66. The gathering of rabbis in Warsaw and the subsequent delegation to the Polish premier occupy a prominent place

table sat representatives of the spiritual leadership of Polish Jewry: the Hafetz Hayyim, the Gerer *Rebbe* and his rivals the Alexander and Belzer *rebbe*s, Rabbis Elhanan Wasserman and Aharon Kotler from the Lithuanian yeshivot, and many more representatives of the Hasidic and yeshiva world. After much deliberation, it was decided that a delegation consisting of the Hafetz Hayyim, and the three aforementioned Hasidic *rebbe*s would present their case to the Polish premier Bartel. In all of these dramatic events taking place in the capital, the rabbis of the capital played an insignificant role. In the interwar period, and in historical memory for that matter, the spiritual leadership of Polish Jewry lay elsewhere.

4. *Rabbinical associations and other voluntary groups*

In the interwar period there existed numerous voluntary associations that registered their views on religious issues and attempted to influence Jewish public opinion on matters that in other eras were considered the bailiwick of the local communal rabbi or the rabbis of Warsaw. Most prominent among them was the Union of Polish Rabbis (Agudat ha-rabbanim), founded in 1921 and based in Warsaw. With approximately 1000 members, including members of Agudat yisrael, Mizrahi and nonpartisan rabbis, it was considered in many circles the spokesman for the Jewish religion in Poland, and the Polish government sought its opinions on any issue involving Judaism. Members of the executive committee of the Union were: Rabbi Menahem Mendel Alter of Pabianice (president), and his deputies Yitzhak Meir Kanal and Meir Warszawiak (both from Warsaw), and Rabbi Dov Ber of Ozarków. The secretary was Rabbi Reuven Neifeld of Nowy Dwór and the treasurer, Rabbi Shlomo David Kahana of Warsaw.[41] Though we can readily see that rabbis from Warsaw were among the leaders of the organization, it is not at all clear that they set the tone for its operation. Again, the presence in the capital of a major

---

in rabbinic mythology of the interwar era. See, e.g., A. Sorasky, *Toldot ha-hinukh ha-torati* (Bnei Brak: Or ha-hayyim, 1967), 68–70; M.M. Yoshor, *Ha-hafetz hayyim* (3 vols.; Tel Aviv: Netzah, 1958–1961), vol. 2, 567; idem, *Saint and Sage* (New York, 1937), 88–89; Yisrael Klapholz, *Admorei belz* (4 vols.; Israel, 1976), vol. 4, 228–229. Not surprisingly, each volume emphasizes the role of its subject in this major event. For contemporary reports on the conference and the delegation, see *Der moment*, 5 February 1930, 2; 6 February 1930, 2, and also in articles published by the Jewish Telegraphic Agency (JTA), e.g. "Noted Chassidic Rabbi presides over rabbinical conference," 2 February 1930; "Ask 10 year respite in law that rabbis know Polish," 7 February 1930; "Orthodox rabbis of Poland oppose government's plan of Jewish religious council," 5 February 1930; all available at http://archive.jta.org (last accessed 17 March 2013).

41 Avraham Levinson, *Toldot yehudei varsha* (Tel Aviv: Am Oved, 1953), 348–349.

rabbinic organization diluted any potential influence on wider communal affairs on the part of the Warsaw rabbinate, which was now but one voice among many. To cite but one instance, the Union of Orthodox Rabbis of the United States and Canada solicited letters of protest against proposed reforms of Jewish marital law designed to prevent cases of so-called "chained women" (*agunot*), and the protest letter signed by the rabbinical board of Warsaw was one letter of many (appearing after letters from the rabbis of Petah Tikva and Kishinev, and right before a letter from the rabbis of Turkey), with the letter from the Union of Polish Rabbis given a much more prominent place.[42]

In a similar vein, there existed in Warsaw, as in other cities in Poland, any number of organizations devoted to promoting Sabbath observance or family purity laws. The aforementioned Rabbi Tzvi Yehezkel Mikhlzohn was the founder and director of several such organizations and the editor of the annual published by the Association of Polish Rabbis, but his stature as a member of the Warsaw rabbinate does not appear to be the major factor in his activities or their success.

Thus, the rabbis of the capital were now but one voice of many on communal issues, with limited power of their own, and were far from the most influential. Politicians, including religious politicians, became their competitors in the Jewish public square. The rabbis of Warsaw may have had a seat of honor at the table of power in the community, but not necessarily a seat of power. Polish law specified that the local rabbi was an ex officio member of the *kehilla* executive and should attend its meetings (a similar demand by R. Jacob Gesundheit in the nineteenth century was rejected by the *kehilla* leadership, and was a factor in his dismissal).[43] In the files of the interrogation of Moshe Schorr by Soviet authorities after his arrest, Schorr mentions that he, as one of the Warsaw rabbis, attended *gmina* (*kehilla*) executive meetings on a rotating basis.[44] But the presence of the rabbis does not attest to any real impact on the deliberations. In my own experience of going over hundreds of press reports of *kehilla*

---

42   *Ledor aharon* (Brooklyn: Agudat ha-rabbanim, 1937), 70. Available online at http://www.hebrewbooks.org/7512 (last accessed 17 March 2013).

43   Alexander Guterman, *Kehillat varsha bein shtei milhamot ha-olam. Otonomia leumit be'khavlei ha-hok ve'ha-metziut, 1917–1939* (Tel Aviv: Tel Aviv University, 1997), 319–320; Shatzky, *Geshikhte fun yidn in varshe*, vol. 3, 142.

44   Michael Beizer and Israel Bartal, "The Case of Moses Schorr: Rabbi, Scholar, and Social Activist," *Polin* 21 (2009): 448.

meetings in the interwar period, I cannot recall a single instance where a comment of the rabbi in attendance was recorded.

But besides the competition offered by party politics, the growing influence of politics and the politicians in the interwar period started changing the rabbinate itself. While most of the members of the Warsaw rabbinical council were born in the 1860s and 1870s, some of those appointed in the 1930s were products of a younger generation, a generation of rabbis whose involvement in partisan politics was less a repellent compromise with modernity than something taken as a given of Polish Jewish life. Some of the rabbis could definitely be considered party activists in their own right. But this carried a price, as a party label penetrated the chambers of the rabbinical council of Warsaw. Many of the members of the Warsaw rabbinate were in effect compromised, and came under criticism, for their own involvement in communal political life before and during their tenure as rabbis. As mentioned before, several of the rabbis were members of Aguda's Council of Torah Sages, a spiritual body but one that stood at the apex of a partisan organization.

One of the relatively young members of the council, Rabbi Menahem Ziemba, illustrates the complexity of the issue. An extremely creative and original Talmudic thinker and scholar of renown, he was by turns a businessman, Aguda party activist, Aguda's representative from the Praga district on the *kehilla* council, and only relatively late in the game, in the mid-1930s, was he appointed to the rabbinical council of Warsaw.[45] Only ten years separated the violent demonstrations against the building of a dormitory for mostly secular Jewish university students close by the synagogue courtyard area of Praga, to a large extent organized and led by Ziemba, in which the *kehilla* headquarters were effectively wrecked,[46] and his assuming the post of communal rabbi. In the wake of the riots surrounding the student dormitory, we see one of the few cases where the rabbinate of the city did exert its moral authority as a neutral arbiter, convening a meeting of orthodox elected officials, Hasidic laymen, members of the rabbinate, and Praga residents opposed to the students'

---

45 For biographical details, see *Eleh ezkerah* (New York, 1957), vol. 2, 38–51. For concise biographical information and bibliographical references on most of Warsaw's rabbis in the interwar period, see Penina Meizlish, *Rabbanim she'nispu ba-shoah* (2nd ed., 2007), available online only at http://horabis.blogspot.com (last accessed 18 March 2013).

46 See report on the event in *Haynt* (26 November 1923). The struggle over the student dormitory was considered one of the flash points in the relations between orthodox and secular Jews in the capital. See Alexander Guterman, *Kehillat varsha*, 150–151. See also the extended study of the incident by Rafał Żebrowski, "Budowa domu akademickiego w Warszawie i jej miejsce w dziejach warszawskiej gminy wyznaniowej," *Kwartalnik Historii Żydów* 216 (2005): 467–480.

house. At this meeting it was decided to raise money for an alternative location for the dormitory, and a committee was set up for that purpose.[47] Here we can see the rabbinate, fearing a deepening rift between secular and religious Jews, serving to calm emotions and working for compromise, but that same meeting illustrates where the true centers of power in the orthodox community now resided.

Another example of a younger generation rabbi who joined the Warsaw rabbinical council was Shimshon Stockhammer. In addition to his rabbinic erudition, he had made a name for himself as a writer and journalist for Aguda publications. For young men such as him, party involvement was a natural thing.[48] How would their presence have affected the rabbinate in the long run? Due to his tragic end and that of all of his colleagues on the council in the Holocaust save one, this can be no more than an issue for speculation. By all indications, though, the encounter of the rabbinate with politics had serious effects, with parties running their candidates for the rabbinical office, and with the partisan label opening up the rabbis to criticism and occasional violence on the part of political opponents, and the usually fractious relations between parties on kehilla councils making the election of any rabbi a difficult matter.

The most blatant example of the problematic status of the Warsaw rabbinate in the interwar period came in the wake of the laws limiting Jewish ritual slaughter in the mid-1930s. The Polish legislation may have been designed to limit Jewish influence on the meat trade in the country, but it was perceived as an assault on the Jewish religious tradition when, as in other countries, the legal limitations on *shehita* were given the allegedly humanitarian justification of preventing cruelty to animals caused by an inhumane method of slaughter. If we look to see how the political and propaganda campaign in defense of *shehita* was carried out, the voice of the Warsaw rabbinate was only a minor one among many. What is worse, the rabbinate proved impotent in the face of brazen violations of the *kashrut* laws by butchers and wholesalers alike. At this crucial time, the rabbinate's supervision of *kashrut* was almost paralyzed by rivalries within the rabbinical council itself, with one rabbi, Hayyim Posner, claiming for himself the prerogative of being personally in charge of the matter without involving his colleagues. For several months, no one could be absolutely certain of the *kashrut* of meat purchased in any butcher shop in Warsaw, to such an extent that some pious Jews refrained from eating meat altogether. According to contemporary newspaper accounts, it was only the

---

47   *Haynt* (10 December 1923).
48   On Stockhammer see Hillel Seidman, *Ishim she'hikarti* (Jerusalem: Mossad Harav Kook, 1970), 497–501; *Eleh ezkerah* (New York, 1963), vol. 5, 316–320.

personal intervention of the Gerer *Rebbe* that broke the stalemate among the Warsaw rabbis over the supervision of ritual slaughter and brought some partial semblance of order to a market plagued by fraudulent practices.[49] Even after some order had been restored, however, fraudulent practices continued on a wide scale in Warsaw and other cities, and once more the Gerer *Rebbe* intervened, this time organizing groups of volunteer *kashrut* supervisors who would attest to the kosher status of butcher shops and restaurants, a clear vote of no-confidence in the abilities of the Warsaw rabbinate.[50] Again, we see that in the capital, ultimate religious authority lay elsewhere.

The rabbinate was weakened further by longstanding factors surrounding rabbinical appointments to office that were not lacking in interwar Poland: family connections and family rivalries among various Hasidic groups or between Hasidim and Mitnagdim, in addition to the political rivalries between Agudat Yisrael, Mizrahi and so-called "non-party" orthodox groups. The relatively long period of vacancies on the rabbinical board of Warsaw testifies to these inner tensions as well as to issues of communal priorities and the difficulties of communal finances. Even under the leadership of Agudat Yisrael, it took almost five years until a first attempt was made to fill these vacancies, which meant that for many years a Jewish community of over 350,000 had less than a dozen official rabbis.[51] Despite these inherent difficulties, it should be noted that on the daily, individual level, the members of the rabbinical council of Warsaw carried out their difficult task, dealing almost daily with any number of knotty *halakhic* problems, family disputes, registration of life cycle events, and more.[52]

It should also be recalled that since the mid-nineteenth century and through the interwar period, any number of unofficial rabbis, the so-called

---

49   Kaniel, "Bein hilonim, masorti'im ve'ortodoksim," 92. A wandering photographer working for *Life Magazine* photographed a *kashrut* certificate hanging in the window of a Warsaw butcher shop, reproduced at http://images.google.com/hosted/life/fc778823d458b4d1.html (last accessed 30 January 2012).
50   Ibid., 99–100.
51   Guterman, *Kehillat varsha*, 319; Seidman, *Ishim she'hikarti*, 499; Gabriela Zalewska, *Ludność żydowska w Warszawie w okresie międzywojennym* (Warszawa: Wydawnictwo Naukowe PWN, 1996), 53.
52   For a description of the mandated official activities of the rabbinate in Warsaw, see Guterman, *Kehillat varsha*, 396. For a listing of the 21 official rabbis of the capital in 1937, see *Głos Gminy Żydowskiej*, yr. 1, no. 1 (July 1937), 14–15. Available online at http://ebuw.uw.edu.pl/dlibra/doccontent?id=2676 (last accessed 12 May 2011). A similar list, but omitting for some reason the name of Rabbi Posner, appears in David Flinker, *Varsha* [volume 3 in the series *Arim ve'imahot be'yisrael*] (Jerusalem: Mossad Harav Kook, 1947/1948), 160. For an example of the ongoing work of the rabbinate, see *Ha-tzefira*, 11 March 1921, 6.

vinkl-rabbonim ["corner rabbis"], who set up operations in the large apartment blocks of the crowded Jewish quarters of the city, also met the day-to-day needs of religious and non-religious Jews alike in the capital. This function was made famous by Isaac Bashevis Singer in his collections entitled *In My Father's Court*[53] and *More Stories from My Father's Court*.[54] These rabbis and the many Hasidic *rebbe*s of lesser renown who made their homes in the capital provided services that the understaffed official rabbinical council could not.[55]

While most of this article has chronicled the lamentable state of the Warsaw rabbinate, this is not the whole picture. The stature of the Warsaw rabbinate may not have been what it once was, but the office held a residual prestige that was not inconsiderable. The powerful symbolism of the election of Rabbi Perlmutter to the Constituent Sejm of resurrected Poland, a living link to Dov Berish Meisels and the heroic age of Polish-Jewish amity, was lost on no one. Within the Jewish community, there was enough remaining luster to the office to literally bring crowds into the streets and meeting halls when new and controversial rabbinical appointments were being considered. Contending forces in the community saw the rabbinate as at least one avenue for the remaking of the community in its image or for promoting alternative versions of Jewish identity. Even before World War I, the election platform of the Jewish National Club for the 1907 *kehilla* elections called for an improvement in rabbis' salaries and for the appointment of a chief rabbi.[56] Subsequent platforms of the Zionists and neo-assimilationists called for improving religious services for the populace, for strengthening the rabbinate and for setting up a rabbinical seminary. Calls for renewing the office of chief rabbi of Warsaw would surface on several other occasions in later years.

The most notable incident illustrating the residual prestige attached to membership in the Warsaw rabbinate was the fierce polemic ignited by the appointment of Samuel Abraham Poznański to the rabbinical council in 1921, an incident we have treated at length elsewhere.[57] The nomination of

---

53   Isaac Bashevis Singer, *In My Father's Court* (New York: New American Library, 1966).
54   Isaac Bashevis Singer, *More Stories from My Father's Court* (New York: Farrar, Straus and Giroux, 2000).
55   Flinker, *Varsha*, 159; Guterman, *Kehillat varsha*, 260.
56   Guterman, *Kehillat varsha*, 34.
57   Gershon Bacon, "The Poznański affair of 1921: Kehillah politics and the internal political realignment of Polish Jewry," *Studies in Contemporary Jewry* 4 (1988): 135–143. For a differing view of some aspects of this event, see Rafał Żebrowski, "Modernizacja czy próba podziału gminy?—Batalia o mianowanie postępowego rabina w Warszawie," *Kwartalnik Historii Żydów* 2 (2006): 153–166.

Poznański, the rabbi of the progressive Tłomackie Street Great Synagogue and a noted scholar and Zionist leader, was a calculated act by a rump community governing board in office since 1912, elected under old laws, whose mandate had long since dissipated and who expected to be unseated once more democratic community elections would be held. At that time, Warsaw was treated to the unusual sight of elderly and young Hasidim demonstrating against the decision of the *kehilla* board.[58] There was a fear that this was but a first step in a plot to restore the abolished office of chief rabbi with Poznański as the candidate of Zionists, assimilationists and government officialdom. The claim was made that the rabbi of the Tłomackie Street synagogue was not an appropriate candidate, since his beliefs were not sufficiently orthodox and he was known to extend his hand to women. Threats of mass resignation by existing members of the rabbinical council did not dissuade the *kehilla* leadership from its decision, and on his deathbed Poznański received his official letter of appointment to the rabbinical council.[59] In the eyes of many, the Great Synagogue of the capital was a representative, flagship institution, and it was only fitting that its rabbi be awarded similar recognition and status. In that sense, the existence of a rabbinical council rather than a chief rabbi gave an opportunity for representation of various groups in the religious community of Warsaw, including the so-called progressives, who were represented by Poznański and by his successor Moshe Schorr.

Interestingly enough, with all the controversy at home regarding reviving the office of chief rabbi of Warsaw, from the (admittedly mistaken) perspective of the outside world at least, Warsaw still had a chief rabbi in the person of the rabbi of the Great Synagogue. A search of representative media in the interwar period, such as the *American Jewish Year Book*, the London *Jewish Chronicle*, or the dispatches of the Jewish Telegraphic Agency reveals that Moses Schorr was routinely referred to as Warsaw's chief rabbi.[60] In one case, Schorr was even called chief rabbi of Poland.[61]

---

58 See *Ha-tzefira* (14 March 1921): 4; (15 March 1921): 4; (21 March 1921): 4.
59 See *Haynt* (11 March 1921; 17 March 1921; 21 March 1921); letter of 11 November 1921, letter no. 3773/905, S. Poznański archive, National Library (Jerusalem), *4°1180, file 9.
60 *American Jewish Year Book* (38): 334; *Jewish Chronicle* (London) (14 September 1928): 32–33; (4 March 1938): 17; (27 October 1939): 10–11; JTA dispatches, e.g. "Institute of Judaistic Studies opens in Warsaw," 21 February 1928; "Polish Senate passes bill granting government wide powers," 22 June 1936; "Schorr refused to leave Poland, citing duty to Jews," 8 October 1939, all available at http://archive.jta.org (all above last accessed 18 March 2013).
61 *American Jewish Year Book* (40): 277.

In the 1930s, attempts by the Aguda-led *kehilla* leadership to appoint new rabbis to fill longstanding vacancies on the council reawakened the polemics over the rabbinate of the capital. It is a sad commentary on the situation at the time that the noted columnist Moshe Justman, who wrote under the pseudonym B. Jeushzohn, opened his column on the rabbinate with a remark that his readers might be wondering why he was devoting space to the issue of the Warsaw rabbinate, when the community was facing so many more urgent issues.[62] His take on the matter was that the fights over the rabbinate demonstrated to the Jewish public the bankruptcy of the present *kehilla* leadership under Aguda's aegis. His polemical stance belies the intimation of his own views in that same column—namely that the rabbinical post in Warsaw did have stature and importance, but the community leadership was betraying its trust. The article also illustrates the view that the entry of party politics into the sphere of the rabbinate irreparably damaged the latter.

Politics also played a central role in the last abortive attempt to renew the chief rabbinate of Warsaw. From 1935 onward, Agudat Yisrael made repeated efforts to appoint its former Sejm deputy, Rabbi Aron Lewin of Rzeszów, to the post. Again we see the elements of our complex story converging. The often outspoken Lewin had been deprived of his chance at re-election to the Sejm by a new restrictive constitution and new election laws.[63] Despite his rabbinic erudition, publications and proven talents, he was unable to make the transition back to the "regular" rabbinate after being politically identified for so many years, especially to the long vacant post of chief rabbi of the capital.

With its unique aspects, the story of the Warsaw rabbinate in the interwar period is part of a larger story of evident decline. It has been noted that with the death of Rabbi Kornitzer of Kraków in 1934, almost none of the major communities of Poland had chief rabbis.[64] Until recently at least, most historians of the period gave scant attention to the rabbinate, since it represented for them the strictly religious side of the *kehilla*, and their interest was to present a narrative of growing national consciousness. For that purpose, the political side of *kehilla* life was central. But even for the newer groups on the so-called "Jewish street" the rabbinate had symbolic significance, in Warsaw above all. The combination of old-style rivalries between Hasidic groups and the new politics proved to be volatile whenever a new rabbi had to be appointed. In

---

62 *Haynt* (3 December 1934): 4.
63 *Dos yiddishe togblat* (15 August 1935): 1; *Haynt* (28 August 1935): 6; G. Bacon, *Politics of Tradition*, 276–277.
64 Joseph Marcus, *Social and Political History of the Jews in Poland, 1919–1939* (Berlin-New York-Amsterdam: Mouton Publishers, 1983), 333.

the end, the rabbinate proved not to be the most felicitous avenue for pursuing modernization, but it is still worthy of our consideration. Changing concepts of the function of the rabbi, and controversies over the candidates for the rabbinate offer us a useful window onto the social transformations occurring in the Polish Jewish community.

CHAPTER 15

From Galicia to Warsaw: Interwar Historians of Polish Jewry

Natalia Aleksiun

Recalling Poland in the aftermath of the First World War, the distinguished Yiddish poet and journalist Melech Ravitch, a native of Galicia (born Zekharye Khone Bergner, in Radymno, near Jarosław), observed:

> Soon after the First World War, when Galicia was united with Poland, Jewish Galician youth flocked to Warsaw, Białystok and even Wilno [Vilna]. Galicia had always had an excess of educated Jews. [...] With one sweep, they infiltrated the important positions. [...] They were quiet and polite, but would conquer stronghold after stronghold.[1]

Although colored by a slight disdain for Jews from Congress Poland and Lithuania and a good dose of hyperbole, Ravitch's remarks pointed to an important but lesser known phenomenon in the aftermath of the First World War. Reminiscent of the more familiar "Litvak invasion" of prior decades (see previous chapters in this volume), Galician Jewish intelligentsia gravitated toward urban centers of the former Russian partition of Poland, especially to the capital of the newly resurrected Polish Republic, drawn in by professional and educational opportunities. Thanks to their education in Polish gymnasia and universities, Galician Jews took leading positions "as teachers in state schools for Jewish children, Jewish secondary schools, and administrators in various Jewish institutions."[2] University-trained Galician Jews not only "conquered" Jewish institutions in Warsaw as educators, teachers, and journalists, but also

---

1 Israel Kahan, *Sefer buchach: matsevet zikaron le'kehila k'dosha* (Tel Aviv: Am Oved, 1956), 227. Ravitch, born in 1893, settled in Warsaw in 1921, where he belonged to the literary group *Di khaliastre*. From 1924 to 1934 he served as secretary of the Jewish PEN Club (Association of Jewish Writers and Journalists) at Tłomackie 13 in Warsaw. In 1924, he co-founded the journal *Literarishe bleter*.
2 Samuel D. Kassow, *Who Will Write Our History? Rediscovering a Hidden Archive from the Warsaw Ghetto* (Bloomington, IN: Indiana University Press, 2007), 19.

played a crucial role in creating them. This Galician Jewish network included major historians dedicated to researching the history of Jews in Polish lands.

Since Warsaw emerged as the new political, cultural and intellectual center of Polish Jewry, the city proved especially attractive to Galician intellectuals because it offered them positions in Jewish institutions and opportunities to teach and preach Polish Jewish history. It is these historians and their contribution to the emergence of Polish Jewish historiography, first in Galicia and then in Warsaw, that this paper highlights. This is not to say that they were the only ones who exerted considerable influence, or that Warsaw was the only center of Jewish history writing at the time. But Galician historians were particularly well-positioned to fill the vacuum that had existed in Congress Poland. While the Russian authorities had closed down Warsaw University to allow its reopening as a Russified Imperial University, Polish universities in Cracow and Lwów had flourished. The prior absence of formal academic institutions encouraging the study of Polish history, combined with the prior lack of an open academic environment in the last decades of the 19th century, encouraged a veritable "Galician flood" into the field of Polish Jewish history.

The historians who became the beacons of Polish Jewish historiography—Mojżesz Schorr (1874–1941), Majer Bałaban (1877–1942), and Ignacy Schiper (1884–1943)—arrived in Warsaw to assume academic, communal and political positions. Schorr, who taught at Lwów University from 1896 to 1922, moved from Lwów to Warsaw, where he became the preacher at the Tłomackie Great Synagogue. In 1925, he was invited to teach at Warsaw University. Bałaban moved first to Częstochowa to head its Jewish *Gymnasium*, and in 1922, to Warsaw to run the new rabbinical school, *Tachkemoni*, associated with the Mizrachi religious Zionist movement. Schiper moved to Warsaw around 1919 to carry out his political and academic activities. A leading member of *Poalei Tzion* in Warsaw, he served as a representative in the Polish Parliament until 1927. He then became director of the Jewish Academic Center in Warsaw (*Żydowski Dom Akademicki*), reopened that year in a newly established building with a conference room and a dormitory for male Jewish students. Employment opportunities in the Jewish secondary schools in the capital of the Second Polish Republic attracted Galician graduates of the University of Vienna such as Raphael Mahler (1899–1977), who earned a doctorate in 1922 and began teaching Polish and Jewish history, among other topics, at the Gymnasium for Boys of the Ascola Association in Warsaw in 1924.[3]

---

3 Askola (Prywatne Gimnazjum i Liceum Towarzystwa "Askola" nr 102, ul. Tłomackie 11)—a private Jewish highschool, founded in 1916 in Warsaw by Zvi Zvulun Weinberg (1884–1971), and Shmuel Weinberg (1888–1938), with funds inherited from their father. Zvi Zvulun served

By the first half of the 1920s, the arrival in Warsaw of Bałaban, Schorr, and Schiper proved instrumental in creating a new center with an institutional framework necessary for scholarly work and the popularization of historical research. Their presence served to further attract Jewish students of history arriving from Galicia, such as Emanuel Ringelblum (1900–1944), Artur Eisenbach (1906–1992) and Dawid Wurm (1909–1941). Although far from uniform, their shared Galician roots influenced their focal historical conceptions, views on the purpose of Polish Jewish history, choice of subjects, and methodological approaches. Thus, this Galician cohort contributed to building the body of scholarship and the emergent model of "Jewish Polishness" emanating from Warsaw despite an atmosphere of rising antisemitism.[4]

Polish Academic Framework

The emergence of Warsaw as a meeting place for many of the leading scholars of Polish Jewish history and their students followed the general shift away from academic centers in former Galicia. Since the second half of the nineteenth century, the universities in Cracow and Lwów had produced Polish intellectuals and served as centers of Polish historical scholarship. Warsaw lacked a formal Polish academic infrastructure due to Tsarist repressions in the aftermath of the January 1863 uprising. Poland's newly regained independence opened the possibility for rebuilding the university in the capital.[5]

---

as teacher and headmaster, while Shmuel was headmaster of the Jewish teachers' seminary. While the language of instruction was Polish, Hebrew and Jewish subjects formed a significant part of the curriculum. Two separate graduation certificates were issued by the school, one in general studies, another in Jewish and Hebrew studies. See "Dr. Shmuel Weinberg" and "Zvi Zvulun Weinberg," in David Tidhar, *Entsiklopedyah la'halutsey ha-yishuv uvonav: d'muyot u'temunot*, vol. 15 (1966), 4660, 4697; Nurith Gertz, *El ma she'namog* (Tel Aviv: Am Oved, 1997), 139–140; Krzysztof Oktabiński, "Szkoły na Muranowie," in *Stacja Muranów*, online: http://www.stacjamuranow.art.pl/o_dzielnicy/szkoly_na_muranowie (accessed April 28, 2013); Anna Mieszkowska, "Gwidon Borucki: Wspomnienie (2.09.1912–31.12.2009)," in *Gazeta Wyborcza: Warszawa*, 08.02.2010, online: http://warszawa.gazeta.pl/warszawa/1,72581,7540799,Gwidon_Borucki.html (accessed April 28, 2013).

4 See Katrin Steffen, *Jüdische Polonität: Ethnizität und Nation im Spiegel der polnischsprachigen jüdischen Presse, 1918–1939* (Göttingen: Vandenhoeck & Ruprecht, 2004).

5 See *Dzieje Uniwersytetu Warszawskiego 1915–1939*, ed. Andrzej Garlicki (Warsaw: Państwowe Wydawnictwo Naukowe, 1982), 13–52; Tadeusz Manteuffel, *Uniwersytet Warszawski w latach 1915/16–1934/35: Kronika* (Warsaw, 1936).

The establishment of new university-level history seminars required recruiting scholars from among faculty of the Jagiellonian University in Cracow and Lwów University, most notably Jan Karol Kochanowski (1869–1949), who became a professor of history at Warsaw University in 1919, and Bronisław Dembiński (1858–1939), who taught in Warsaw from 1916 to 1923. Departments of Humanities at Cracow and Lwów University continued to train Polish historians in the Second Polish Republic, but their approach to Polish Jewish history changed.

At the turn of the nineteenth century, studying at universities in Lwów, Cracow and Vienna enabled Schorr, Bałaban, and Schiper to pioneer the study of Polish Jewish history. Leading faculty members such as Tadeusz Wojciechowski (1838–1919), Ludwik Finkel (1858–1930) and Szymon Askenazy (1866–1935) encouraged students interested in writing about legal, social and political aspects of the Jewish past in the Polish Kingdom and the Polish-Lithuanian Commonwealth.[6] However, Finkel retired in 1918 while Askenazy left for Warsaw and then for a diplomatic position in the League of Nations in 1920. Faculty members subscribing fully to traditions of integrationist historical writing, which stressed the exceptional treatment of Jews in Poland, the essential hospitality of the Poles, and Jewish sharing in Poland's fortunes over the centuries, found themselves marginalized and increasingly disillusioned.[7] Even more so, attitudes toward Jewish history held by new members of the faculty in Lwów encouraged the shift. The most striking case in point was the highly successful and influential seminar ran by Franciszek Bujak at Lwów University, with its cutting edge focus on local studies and social and economic history. His students took little interest in the Jewish aspects of Polish social

---

6 See Natalia Aleksiun, "Polish Jewish Historians before 1918: Configuring the Liberal East European Jewish Intelligentsia," *East European Jewish Affairs* 2 (Winter 2004): 41–54.

7 See Piotr J. Wróbel, "Szymon Askenazy (1865–1935)," in *Nation and History: Polish Historians from the Enlightenment to the Second World War*, ed. Peter Brock, John Stanley and Piotr J. Wróbel (Toronto: University of Toronto Press, 2006) 234–236; Katarzyna Błachowska, "Ludwik Finkel (1858–1930)," in *Złota księga historiografii lwowskiej XIX i XX wieku*, ed. Jerzy Maternicki and Leonid Zaszkilniak (Rzeszów: Wydawnictwo Uniwersytetu Rzeszowskiego, 2007), 303. See "Aneks prac doktorskich" in Joanna Pisulińska, "Doktoraty historyczne na Uniwersytecie Jana Kazimierza, 1918–1939," in *Wielokulturowe środowisko historyczne Lwowa w XIX i XX w.*, ed. Jerzy Maternicki and Leonid Zaszkilniak, vol. 1 (Rzeszów: Wydawnictwo Uniwersytetu Rzeszowskiego, 2004), 241–249. For the situation in Cracow, see Archiwum UJ (Archives of the Jagiellonian University, henceforth AUJ), Księga Dyplomów Magisterskich UJ. On the Jewish students at the Jagiellonian University, see Mariusz Kulczykowski, *Żydzi—studenci Uniwersytetu Jagiellońskiego w Drugiej Rzeczypospolitej, 1918–1939* (Cracow: Polska Akademia Umiejętności, 2004).

and economic history. The absence of studies in Jewish history as part of the research agenda on Polish economic history reflected Bujak's own notions about the Jews as constituting an alien, criminal and harmful element throughout Poland's history, allegedly conspiring against the interests of the country that had granted them refuge and unprecedented freedom.[8] In the aftermath of the First World War, Lwów University, renamed Jan Kazimierz University in November, 1919, and the Jagiellonian University in Cracow, remained important centers of Polish historiographies, and Jewish students continued to study history there. However, Departments of Humanities no longer produced major scholars of Polish Jewish history.

In contrast, Warsaw University had offered a viable alternative since the early 1920s and attracted Jewish students from the former Congress Kingdom of Poland, Galicia, and the Borderlands (*Kresy*). Several members of the faculty in the Department of Humanities, and after 1930 its Institute of History, supported research projects on the history of Polish Jews. Without a doubt, Marceli Handelsman (1882–1945) not only preserved a liberal atmosphere at the Department, but also created conditions conducive to research in the history of religious and ethnic minorities in Polish lands. Motivated by concepts of an open Polish identity based on the traditions of the multiethnic Polish Commonwealth under the Jagiellonian dynasty, he encouraged his Jewish students to carry out research about Polish Jewish history and invited them to present it at his seminars—regular study groups for advanced students where they discussed assigned materials and research projects.[9] Handelsman served as academic advisor to students such as Jacob Shatzky, who defended his doctoral dissertation about the Jewish question in Congress Poland under Russian Viceroy prince Paskevich before leaving Poland in 1922,[10] and Emanuel Ringelblum, who attended a variety of Handelsman's lectures and seminars

---

8   Joanna Pisulińska, "Doktoraty historyczne na Uniwersytecie Jana Kazimierza 1918–1939," in *Wielokulturowe środowisko historyczne Lwowa w XIX i XX w.*, ed. Maternicki, (Rzeszów 2004), 1: 241–249.

9   See Mieczysław B. Biskupski, "Marceli Handelsman (1882–1945)," in *Nation and History*, 353–385; Józef Dutkiewicz, "Seminarium Marcelego Handelsmana w świetle jego papierów," *Zeszyty Naukowe Uniwersytetu Łódzkiego: Nauki Humanistyczno-Społeczne*, 1.34 (1984): 145, 150–151, 155.

10 Alexander Hafftka identified it as "Kwestja żydowska w Królestwie Polskim za czasów Paskiewicza, 1831–1861"; see his "Życie i twórczość Dr. Jakóba Szackiego," in *Jakób Szacki: In Memoriam (Yacov shatzky: tsum ondenk)*, ed. Philip Friedman, Aleksander Hertz and Joseph L. Lichten (New York, 1957), 16. I found the draft of his dissertation entitled: "Oświata żydowska i polityka oświatowa wobec Żydów w dobie paskiewiczowskiej (1832–1862)" in the Central Archives for the History of the Jewish People, Jerusalem (henceforth CAHJP), Jacob Shatzky Collection P 9, folder 4.

and in 1927 earned his doctoral degree based on his dissertation "Jews in Warsaw from the earliest times until 1527".[11] He also wrote letters of recommendation on behalf of Raphael Mahler and supported the formal nostrification of his Viennese diploma in 1927.[12]

Other faculty members at Warsaw University, especially Władysław Tokarz and Stanisław Arnold—Handelsman's first doctoral student—encouraged theses and dissertations devoted to the history of Polish Jewry.[13] Apart from Arnold, Ringelblum listened to lectures by Jan Karol Kochanowski and Oskar Halecki.[14] Thanks to Handelsman, Kochanowski, Arnold and Tokarz, Warsaw University offered a relatively hospitable place for students interested in researching the past of the Jewish community in the Polish lands. None of these scholars who excelled in research on Polish and general history, however, took a particular interest in researching Polish Jewish history. They published merely a handful of articles touching on Jewish topics, based on Polish sources.[15] Until 1928, the Department did not include in its curriculum a single seminar or lecture devoted exclusively to Jewish history.[16]

---

11 See Ringelblum's student record, Archiwum Uniwersytetu Warszawskiego (henceforth AUW, Archives of Warsaw University), RP 9070.

12 See the Archives of the Goldstein-Goren Diaspora Research Center, Tel Aviv University (henceforth DRC), Mahler Collection P 66, folder 4, certificate of the nostrification of Mahler's diploma by Warsaw University on December 13, 1927 in the letter from M. Handelsman—the Dean of the Department of Humanities, dated December 15, 1927, nr 376/27. See also Handelsman's letter of recommendation for Mahler to the director of the Main Archives (Archiwum Główne [Akt Dawnych], dated December 5, 1926 asking him to assist Mahler in his work on the subject "Jewish economic relations in Mazovia in the sixteenth century," DRC, P 66, f. 3.

13 See Raphael Mahler, "Hug ha-historionim ha-tseirim be'varsha," in Bela Mandelsberg-Schildkraut, *Mekhkarim le'toldot yehudei lublin* (Tel Aviv, 1965), 30. See the letter signed by Prof. Stanisław Arnold, September 14, 1935, AUW, RP, Nr. albumu 38205, 30.

14 Andrzej Nieuważny says that Tokarz "in his youth passed through an endek phase" but "was free of any anti-Semitic prejudices. The *numerus clausus* had no place in his classroom. Many Jewish students, such as the communist fellow-traveller Maksymilian Meloch [...] participated in his seminar." See his "Wacław Tokarz (1873–1937)," in *Nation and History*, 260–279, here 275.

15 See for example Władysław Tokarz, "Miscellanea: Z dziejów sprawy żydowskiej za Księstwa Warszawskiego," *Kwartalnik Historyczny* XVI (1902): 262–276.

16 General student study groups formed at various departments of Polish universities to assist members' intellectual pursuits, tended to exclude Jewish students and to remove those who were already members, see Andrzej Pilch, *"Rzeczpospolita Akademicka": Studenci i polityka 1918–1933* (Cracow: Księgarnia Akademicka, 1997), 187. The Historians' Circle at Warsaw University was relatively more liberal. However, the group took little interest in Polish Jewish history.

Organizing Jewish Research within Polish Academia: The Historians' Circle in Warsaw

Jewish students at the University sought to organize independent study groups that would compensate for what they saw as holes in their academic training. Young historians from Galicia played an important role in organizing a study group devoted to Jewish history and proposing its agenda. In 1923, Emanuel Ringelblum organized the Seminar far Yidisher Geshikhte (or as it was rendered in Polish—Akademickie Seminarium Historii Żydów) at the Jewish Academic Home in Warsaw (Żydowska Strzecha Akademicka w Warszawie). This university-level seminar provided a venue for exchanging ideas and presenting their work on Polish Jewish history.[17] The seminar brought together over thirty young men and women.[18] Students stemming from Galicia featured prominently among the seminar's members. Apart from its leaders, Ringelblum and Mahler, they included Israel Ostersetzer (1904–1942), Józef Kermisz (1906–2005), Eliezer Feldman (1903–?), Mojżesz Krämer (1913–?), Falik Haffner (1908–1942?), and Artur Eisenbach.[19] To provide the training that these history students perceived as missing from university classrooms—research methods and questions, Jewish sources and scholarly literature in the field of Polish Jewish history—the group relied on the expertise of Schiper and Bałaban.

Following the establishment of YIVO (*Yidisher visnshaftlekher institut*, Yiddish Scientific Institute) in 1925 in Wilno, with the *Historishe sektzye* (historical section) run by Elias Tcherikower in Berlin, Ringelblum declared his group's readiness to collaborate with YIVO. The group of young Jewish historians in Warsaw became its historical branch, focusing on Polish Jewish history.[20] In the fall of 1926, the leadership of the Institute created a historical commission in Wilno, where Ringelblum had temporarily settled, independently of

---

17   In his account of the first three years of activities in the seminar in Polish Jewish history, Ringelblum mentioned short-lived attempts of organizing a group with similar goals. See Emanuel Ringelblum, "Dray yor seminar far yidisher geshikhte (1923–1926)," *Yunger historiker* 1 (1926): 7.

18   See "Fun der redaktsye," *Bleter far geshikhte* 3 (1934): 3.

19   Mahler listed the following historians as the earliest core members of the seminar: Lipman Comber, Eliezer Feldman, Hava-Joheved Warszawska, Ester Tenenbaum, Bela Mandelsberg. See Mahler, "Hug ha-historionim," 31. Ringelblum enrolled at the Department of Philosophy in the fall of 1920, see Archives of Warsaw University, RP 12349; Ringelblum, ibid., 9070. See Eliezer Feldman's student file AUW, RP 17140.

20   Mahler, "Hug ha-historionim," 32.

Tcherikower.[21] The seminar ceased to meet for discussions between around 1929 and 1933, at which point it reconvened again under the name of *Historiker krayz* (Historians' Circle).[22]

Despite the lack of an organized, authoritative body to lead Jewish scholarship in Poland, Ringelblum imagined systematic, collective work carried out under the auspices of the seminar, an indispensable addition to formal university training. He encouraged more students to undertake research projects on Jewish and especially Polish Jewish history.[23] Although a few studied law, the vast majority of members received university training in history at Warsaw University, where they studied with Kochanowski, Handelsman, and after 1927, Tokarz, Arnold and Bałaban.[24] On the eve of the Second World War, at least a third of the Historians' Circle's members held doctoral degrees, and the majority wrote their dissertations on Jewish subjects, attesting to the opportunities available at Warsaw University.[25]

---

21 E. Ringelblum to Historical Section, March 1, 1926, RG 82, folder 2401. See Cecile Esther Kuznitz, *YIVO and the Making of Modern Jewish Culture: Scholarship for the Yiddish Nation* (New York, Cambridge University Press, 2014), 88.

22 Mahler, "Hug ha-historionim," 32. The Historians Circle and Historical Committee were formally run as two different bodies, although the membership overlapped. A report on the circle's activity presented at a meeting of the Committee's Presidium (attended by Eisenbach, Hafner, Trunk, Linder, Comber and Ringelblum) in April 1938, for example, lists the circle's activities for April and May consisting of three lectures, one by Bałaban about the bibliography for the history of the Jews in Poland, his pet project, another by [Maksymilian?] Meloch about current research on the peasant question in the 19th century, indicating the inclusion of Polish history in the circle's activities. See "Protokol fun der zitsung fun prezidyum fun der historisher komisye, varshe, 29-ter April, 1938," *YIVO bleter* 46 (1980): 302, document 11.

23 Mahler, "Hug ha-historionim," 9–10. See also Jacov Berman, "Di oyfgabn fun der historisher sektsye fun yidishn visnshaftlekhn institut," *Yunger Historiker* 1 (1926): 19.

24 Ringelblum and Józef Kermisz were Marceli Handelsman's students, Emanuel Feldman worked under the supervision of Jan Karol Kochanowski, Mojżesz Krämer was Stanisław Arnold's student and Falik Haffner worked with Majer Bałaban.

25 Raphael Mahler and Philip (Filip) Friedman held doctoral degrees from Vienna University. Ringelblum, Ostersetzer, Mandelsberg, Lota Wegmeister, Celina Mendelsohn, Lipman Comber, Szmuel Szymkiewicz, Mojżesz (Mosze) Krämer and Kermisz graduated at Warsaw. Kermisz received his PhD in 1937 for a dissertation written under Handelsman about Lublin and the surrounding district 1788–1794. Szymkiewicz, who was Arnold's student, received his PhD from Warsaw University in 1938; it was published in 1959. See Samuel Szymkiewicz, *Warszawa na przełomie XVIII i XIX w. w świetle pomiarów i spisów* (Warsaw: PWN, 1959).

The students who organized the seminar concluded that studying under leading Polish historians sympathetic to the inclusion of Jewish history in the Polish narrative, combined with knowledge of Jewish languages brought from home, had to be supplemented with specialized training to prepare future historians of Polish Jewry for independent research.[26] Therefore, they raised the bar for the professional training required of a historian of Polish Jewry, with Schorr, Bałaban and Schiper as shining examples for the importance of this measure. They envisioned Jewish history in general, and Polish Jewish history in particular, as a field of scholarly pursuit and a profession in its own right, requiring rigorous university-style training.

These young historians created a Yiddish journal to publish their research called, appropriately enough, *Yunger historiker*, which was renamed *Bleter far geshikhte* after two issues. In the first volume, in July 1926, the editors expressed their aspirations to create a periodical "for Jewish history in the Jewish language."[27] They also published their research in the YIVO journals (*YIVO bleter, Historishe shriftn*) and in scholarly journals in Polish (*Miesięcznik Żydowski, Kwartalnik Historyczny, Przegląd Historyczny*) and Hebrew (*Zion*), as well as in the local Jewish press in Poland and abroad. Although the members of the seminar took an interest in all aspects of Jewish history, they focused on Jewish history in the Polish lands, in particular. As the editors of the third volume of the group's journal explained in 1934, their focus resulted from "technical-scholarly factors," since the archives available to them in Poland held materials linked to Poland, while the field of Polish Jewish history had been less developed.[28]

Most importantly, the research carried out under the auspices of the seminar had great relevance for the contemporary Polish Jewish community. Apart from creating a venue for discussions and building an academic curriculum for aspiring professional Jewish historians, the seminar's founders hoped to promote a national Jewish agenda by struggling against "inertia" and "passivity" among Jewish university students. Ringelblum envisioned discussions about Jewish history entering university classrooms as students presented their research on Jewish history to future Polish teachers, a chance to finally dispel misrepresentations and lies about contemporary Jewish society and the Jewish past. This process, he hoped, would eventually improve Polish-Jewish

---

26 E[manuel] R[ingelblum], "Drai yor seminar far idisher geshikhte (1923–1926)," *Yunger historiker* 1 (1926): 11.

27 "Fun der redaktsye," *Yunger historiker* 1 (1926): 6.

28 "Fun der redaktsye," *Bleter far geshikhte* 3 (1934): 4.

relations.²⁹ Therefore, the members of the seminar believed that they "perfom[ed] a task of immense social significance [gezelshaftlekhe arbet], a task whose goal is not just to know the Jewish past, but also to lay the foundation for the struggle that the Jewish nation of Poland is waging for its national and social liberation."³⁰ While for Schorr, Bałaban and Schiper their role of teaching a Polish audience about the Jews was implicitly a political statement about the place of the Jewish community in the Polish state, the young members of the seminar explicitly described Polish Jewish history as an intellectually sophisticated weapon in the fight for Jewish rights.

The hopes about Polish Jewish history becoming an educational tool leading to a lasting improvement in Polish-Jewish relations depended on the field remaining a part of the Polish academic milieu at the university seminars and beyond. Only by maintaining contacts with future Polish high school teachers, publishing in professional Polish journals, and speaking at seminars and conferences did the young historians have the opportunity to carry out their national mission vis-à-vis Polish audiences.

The relationship between the Warsaw seminar and the Historical Section of YIVO was complex and reflected varied trajectories in the development of a historiographic approach to Jewish history. Although members of the Warsaw seminar greeted the founding of the YIVO Institute warmly, with Ringelblum and Mahler emerging as early supporters, their backgrounds and research agendas differed.³¹ The group in Berlin relied on a cohort of self-taught scholars, while the seminar in Warsaw boasted university students and graduates.³² Moreover, the former envisioned the focus of its work in broad terms: the social, political, and cultural history of Jews in Yiddish speaking Eastern Europe in the sixteenth through nineteenth centuries, especially contemporary history just before the First World War.³³ On the other hand, the young

---

29   Ringelblum, "Drai yor seminar far idisher geshikhte (1923–1926)," 10.
30   Ibid., as cited in Kassow, *Who Will Write Our History?*, 60.
31   See Mahler, "Hug ha-historionim," 31; Kuznitz, *YIVO and the Making of Modern Jewish Culture*, 87–89.
32   See David E. Fishman, *The Rise of Modern Yiddish Culture* (Pittsburgh: University of Pittsburgh Press, 2005), 127–128.
33   Historical research carried out under the auspices of YIVO followed the ideas formulated by Shtif in a memorandum written in the fall of 1924—one of the institute's founders who believed the historical section of the Institute should concentrate on the experiences of Ashkenazic Jewry. See Kuznitz, *YIVO and the Making of Modern Jewish Culture*, 47. At a founding meeting in October 1925, Tcherikower sketched out its future activities as surveying and describing archival sources, publishing a volume on Jewish history with original sources and archival material, compiling bibliographies, and holding public lectures.

historians in Warsaw concentrated, more narrowly, on pre-WWI *Polish* Jewish history, which might have been to some extent a function of the Galician roots of many of its most active members. In December 1926, Ringelblum proposed creating an autonomous body to deal solely with the history of Polish Jews. YIVO's Organizational Committee recognized these different approaches, agreeing to create a Wilno-based commission for Polish Jewish history, while the Historical Section retained responsibility for work on all other countries.[34] When Ringelblum returned to Warsaw it became a Warsaw-based commission. Special guidelines formulated in 1929 described the relationship between the Seminar and the section.[35] In the same year the renamed Warsaw Historical Commission proposed a journal of its own, devoted to Polish-Jewish history, and reiterated its plan in the face of opposition from the YIVO leadership.[36]

The profile of the Warsaw group can be linked to its largely Galician roots and the development of a professional historical academic field in the Galician universities, carried over to Poland's capital. YIVO attempted to speak in the name of the entire Jewish people, while the Warsaw historians affiliated with it concerned themselves with the affairs of the Polish Jewish community alone.[37] With their training in Polish educational institutions and their immersion in Polish historical discourse, Warsaw Jewish historians were prone to frame East European Jewish history in a Polish context. For historians writing Polish Jewish history, all Polish Jewish history proved relevant, even "a very distant past," as Ringelblum declared when discussing the first three years of the seminar's activities.[38] Indeed, the four volumes published by the Warsaw historians

---

He singled out research on such topics as Jews in revolutionary and workers' movements in Europe. See "Die ershte zitsung fun der historisher sektsye bay dem yidishn visnshaftlekhn institut, shabat October 31 [1925] in ovent," *YIVO bleter: Journal of the YIVO Institute for Jewish Research* XLVI (1980): 291–293. Kuznitz, *YIVO and the Making of Modern Jewish Culture*, 85–87, and "Arbets-program fun der historisher sektsye," [undated (1929)], YIVO, RG 82, folder 2237.

34   Minutes of meeting of the Organizational Committee, December 22, 1926, YIVO, RG 1.1, folder 2. See also Kuznitz, *YIVO and the Making of Modern Jewish Culture*, 88–89.

35   Protocol no 2 of the Historical Section, November 21, 1929, YIVO, RG 82, folder 2238; minutes of meeting of the Warsaw Historical Commission, December 5, 1929, YIVO, RG 82, folder 2243.

36   Minutes of meeting of the Warsaw Historical Commission, November 18, 1929, RG 82, folder 2243; letter to members of the Central Board and of the scholarly sections, December 5, 1929, YIVO, RG 1.1, folder 8. See also Kuznitz, *YIVO and the Making of Modern Jewish Culture*, 88–89.

37   Kuznitz, *YIVO and the Making of Modern Jewish Culture*, 112–119.

38   See ibid., 191–192.

in 1926, 1929, 1933 and 1938 contained only a handful of articles discussing general issues of Jewish history, while the majority dealt with Polish Jewish history from the Middle Ages until the second half of the nineteenth century.[39] The history of Polish Jewry was relevant not only for the Jewish community in Poland, the editors of the third volume of its journal argued in 1934, but also for the Jewish people in general, since "the majority of Jews in the entire world stems from the lands of Old Poland."[40]

Formal Academic Frameworks: The Institute of Jewish Studies and Bałaban's Seminar at Warsaw University

While Jewish students of history organized an informal group with loose membership to regularly present their research on Polish Jewish history, the Jewish intelligentsia discussed the need for formal academic training for Jewish historians, by including Jewish history in a university curriculum. Educated at Polish academic institutions, Schorr and Bałaban supported the idea of including the study of Jewish history and culture at Polish universities. As early as 1919, Schorr argued that while Jews in Poland did not demand their own institutions of higher education, given the size of the Jewish community in Poland and the number of Jewish students "it is only fair [słusznie] that Jews should insist on the creation of special chairs of Hebrew language and literature at already existing universities and separately for Jewish history."[41]

---

39 See Ester Tenenbaum, "Der varshever birgertum un di yidn in der II-ter helft fun XVIII-tn y[or]h[undert]," *Yunger historiker* 1(1926): 41–57; Bela Mandelsberg, "Materialn tsu der geshikhte fun ekonomishn un rekhtlekhn matsev fun di lubliner yidn in XVII-tn yorhundert," ibid., 81–89; Bella Mandelsberg, "Lubliner yidishe hantverker un di shtot tsekh," *Yunger historiker* 2(1929): 54–66; Raphael Mahler, "Statistik fun yidn in der lubliner voyevodtstve in di yorn 1754–65," ibid.: 67–108. See D. Goldberg-Feldman "Der handel fun di poyzner yidn in der ershter helft funem XVII y[or]h[undert]," *Bleter far geshikhte* 3 (1934): 51–57; Eliezer Feldman, "Di eltste yediyes vegn yidn in poylishe shtet in XIV–XVI yorh[undert].," ibid.: 59–73. See also Mojżesz Krämer, "Der onteyl fun yidishe baley meluches in di kristlekhe tsekhn in amolikn poyln," *Bleter far geshikhte* 4 (1938): 3–32; Shiye Trunk, "Di rekhtlekhe lage fun di yidn in plotsk in XVI y.h. (a fragment fun a historisher monografie vegn plotsker-yidn)," ibid.: 89–107.

40 *Bleter far geshikhte*, 3 (1934): 4.

41 "Przemówienie Prof. Uniw. dra Mojżesza Schorra, III dzień obrad (4 lutego 1919)," in *W sprawie polsko-żydowskiej: przebieg ankiety odbytej w dniach 2,3,4, 9 i 16 lutego 1919 we Lwowie tudzież wnioski Komisyi wydelegowanej przez Tymczasowy Komitet Rządzący uchwałą z 1. stycznia 1919* (Lwów: Komisyja Rządząca we Lwowie, 1919), 102.

Jewish historians from Galicia played a crucial role in establishing institutions that they envisioned as formal frameworks for academic research on the history of Polish Jewry. For example, they featured prominently among the founding members of the Society for the Advancement of Judaic Studies in Poland (Towarzystwo Krzewienia Nauk Judaistycznych w Polsce), created in Warsaw in 1925. According to its charter, the Society strove "with the permission of the right authorities in Warsaw or in another city of the Polish State to found and direct a higher institute of Judaic studies and related disciplines and to promote Judaic studies among the wider spheres of the Jewish population in Poland."[42] In line with this agenda, Schorr and Bałaban envisioned and organized the Institute of Jewish Studies (*Instytut Nauk Judaistycznych*) in Warsaw, which opened in 1927. Schorr became the first rector of the Institute and presided over it from 1927 until 1930 and again in 1933–1934. Bałaban began teaching classes in Jewish history during the Institute's first academic year 1927/28, and served as its rector during five academic years: 1930–1933 and 1934–1936. The next rector until 1938 was another Jewish scholar from Galicia, Abraham Weiss (1895–1970), who held a doctoral degree from the University of Vienna and who moved to Warsaw in order to teach Talmud at the State Seminary for the Teachers of Mosaic Faith since 1923. Last but not least, the last rector of the Institute, Menachem (Edmund) Stein (1893–1942) also stemmed from Galicia. Izrael Ostersetzer Schiper and Filip Friedman also taught classes there.[43] Many of the Galician intellectuals, especially those who founded and taught at the Institute of Jewish studies in Warsaw, belonged to the leadership of *B'nai B'rith*, and covered a substantial part of the Institute's annual budget.[44]

---

42   See paragraph 2, Statut Towarzystwa Krzewienia Nauk Judaistycznych w Polsce, in CAHJP, Gelber Collection P83, G560.

43   See Israel M. Biderman, *Mayer Balaban: Historian of Polish Jewry. His Influence on the Younger Generation of Jewish Historians* (New York: Dr. I.M. Biderman Book Committee, 1976), 76–77; "Powstanie Instytutu Nauk Judaistycznych," in *Sprawozdanie Instytutu Nauk Judaistycznych w Warszawie za lata akademickie 1927/28 i 1929/30* (Warsaw, 1929) [henceforth *Sprawozdanie Instytutu*], VII; Arieh Tartakover, "Ha-machon le'mada'ei yahadut be'varsha," in Louis Ginzberg and Abraham Weiss (eds.), *Studies in Memory of Moses Schorr* (New York, 1944), 163–176; S. Shevah Eden, "Ha-machon le-mada'ei ha-yahadut," in *Entsiklopedia shel galuyot: sifrei zikaron le-artsot ha-gola ve-adoteyha, sidrat polin*, ed. I. Grunbaum, vol. 6: *Varshe*, part B (Jerusalem and Tel Aviv, 1959), 323–330.

44   See the budgets in AAN, collection Stowarzyszenie Humanitarne "Braterstwo B'nei B'rith" w Warszawie (henceforth B'nei B'rith), files 8 and 9. Bałaban joined on the day it was founded in 1922, Schorr joined the branch in Warsaw in December 1923. *Książka adresowa członków Żyd. Stow. Humanitarnego "B'ne B'rith" w Polsce* (Cracow: Drukarnia Grafia, 1926); *Warszawa Braterstwo od 1922*, 65–73 in AAN, B'nei B'rith, file 12. Among the members of

The faculty wanted this center of Jewish scholarship to achieve a status comparable to that of a university.⁴⁵ The Institute's close link to Warsaw University, requiring that all its students attend classes at the university and receive a master's degree before their graduation, reinforced its academic agenda.⁴⁶ Students took classes on a wide variety of subjects ranging from Biblical and Talmudic literature, ritual codices, Midrash, philosophy, Hebrew and Aramaic grammar, to literature, pedagogy, apologetics, homiletics, linguistics, folklore, sociology and Eretz Israel studies (palestynografia).⁴⁷

Jewish ancient, mediaeval and early modern history including its political, cultural and economic aspects formed the core of the Institute's program of study for future rabbis, teachers and social workers.⁴⁸ Although the Institute sought to educate teachers of the Mosaic faith (Judaism), Hebrew language and literature for secondary schools, and to train rabbis conversant with the methods of modern research, its founders also envisioned it as an institution for training scholars of Polish Jewish history, since "the history of Jews in Poland awaits its researchers; in our archives there are untouched sources, histories of Jewish communities that have not been properly elaborated, [and] the same is true about other subjects in the field of Jewish history in this land."⁴⁹ Bałaban and Schiper's work also proved important in that respect. Their lectures and

---

Warsaw branch there were also Dr. Mojżesz Alter, Abraham Weiss, and Edmund Stein, ibid., 1–5. Schiper was a candidate for B'nei B'rith Braterstwo in November 1937. In 1935 Ostersetzer, Weiss and Stein were all members of the Warsaw branch, see ibid., file 13.

45 Eden, "Ha-machon," 330; Israel Ostersetzer, "Instytut Nauk Judaistycznych w Warszawie: z cyklu 'Wyższe Żyd. Instytuty Naukowe w Polsce'," *Miesięcznik Żydowski* 1 (1931): 273. See also Maria Dold, " 'A Matter of National and Civic Honor': Majer Balaban and the Institute of Jewish Studies in Warsaw," *East European Jewish Affairs* 2 (Winter 2004), 55–72, here 56.

46 Biderman, *Mayer Balaban*, 77.

47 See "Wykaz obowiązkowych wykładów i ćwiczeń seminaryjnych: I do egzaminu przejściowego," and "Wykaz obowiązkowych wykładów i ćwiczeń seminaryjnych: II do egzaminu końcowego" in *Sprawozdanie Instytutu*, LXIII–LXIV.

48 The curriculum designed for all students at the Institute discussed in detail the knowledge expected of its graduates. Before the final oral exams, while rabbinical candidates and future teachers of Mosaic faith could choose history as the topic for one of their essays, future teachers of Judaic subjects were obligated to write an essay in Jewish history. See "Porządek studiów w Instytucie Nauk Judaistycznych w Warszawie," *Sprawozdanie Instytutu*, in ibid., LVIII. See also the subjects for the final oral examinations of rabbis and teachers, social workers: ibid., LIX–LXI.

49 Majer Bałaban, "Wiedza żydowska i jej uczelnie w Polsce," in *Instytut Nauk Judaistycznych w Warszawie* (Warsaw, 1927), 35. See also the assessment of the field of Polish Jewish history in the inaugural lecture delivered by Schorr on February 19, 1928, Mojżesz Schorr, "Stan i potrzeby wiedzy żydowskiej w dobie obecnej," *Sprawozdanie Instytutu*, XX.

seminars on the political, cultural and economic history of the Jews from the Middle Ages to the second half of the nineteenth century, methodology and statistics, constituted a central part of the curriculum.

The establishment of an independent institution of Jewish learning, which enjoyed official state recognition and a formal link to a university, contributed to another kind of breakthrough. It led to the formal inclusion of Polish Jewish history in the university program, as Majer Bałaban opened a formal seminar of Polish Jewish history at Warsaw University.[50] In the fall of 1928, Bałaban obtained a lectureship in Jewish history at Warsaw University's History Department, first as an Assistant Professor, and, beginning in 1936, as an Associate Professor.[51] Bałaban joined the faculty at the time when Handelsman served as Dean of the Division of Humanities.[52] The History Department at the university emerged as actively seeking to including minority histories as part of Polish historical narratives. A year after Bałaban's appointment, a leading Ukrainian historian, Myron Korduba, received an invitation to assume a position in Ukrainian history at Warsaw University, and his inaugural lecture in 1929 was published in *Przegląd Historyczny* on Handelsman's initiative.[53] By appointing a Ukrainian historian to teach Ukrainian history and a Jewish scholar to offer courses and seminars in Jewish history, both focusing on Polish lands, Handelsman

---

50 Archiwum Akt Nowych, Ministerstwo Wyznań Religijnych i Oświecenia Publicznego, Majer Bałaban, *Curriculum vitae*, 13. Maria Dold, "'A Matter of National and Civic Honor'", 56. After 1933 Bałaban also held a professorship at the Wolna Wszechnica Polska.

51 Bałaban, *Curriculum vitae*, 13. In his curriculum vitae, Bałaban stated he had convened a seminar in Jewish history and culture since 1930. He might have had in mind a history seminar and not other forms of teaching. In student files, his lectures in Jewish history appear in the 1928/1929 academic year. In the fall semester he taught "Introduction to the general history of the Jews," "A survey of Jewish history," "History of the Jewish organization in Poland," see AUW, RP, Liczba alb. 28145: Szaja Friszman. See also Hillel Seidman, *Ishim she-hikarti; demuyot me-'avar karov be-mizrah eropah*, (Jerusalem: Mosad Rav Kok, 1970), 228; Biderman, *Mayer Balaban*, 77. Dold suggests that "for Bałaban, senior in the field of Polish-Jewish historiography, teaching at the Institute was the summit of his career as a historian. [...] Bałaban's advancement appears to have been connected to his prominent position at the Institute of Jewish Studies, even in years of vehement anti-Jewish campaigns in the higher educational system," see her "A Matter of National and Civic Honor," 56. He had held a professorship at the Wolna Wszechnica Polska since 1933.

52 1927–9 and 1931–4, head of the Department of General History.

53 See Wasyl Pedycz, "Myron Korduba (1876–1971)," in *Złota księga historiografii lwowskiej XIX i XX wieku*, 462.

championed an inclusive multiethnic vision of Polish history, and by extension—a Polish culture and identity not based exclusively on religion or ethnicity.

Bałaban's seminar attracted numerous Jewish students. Galician Jews appear to have been prominent but far from a majority, as many also came from Warsaw, Łódź, Białystok and various other communities in the former Congress Poland and in the Borderlands.[54] Thus, the seminar served as a forum for the young generation of future Jewish historians, which included a considerable Galician contingent.

Bałaban's joint appointments at Warsaw University, the Polish Open University (*Wolna Wszechnica Polska*), and the Institute of Jewish Studies carried tremendous significance, enabling Jewish students to receive academic training in Jewish history and, potentially, recognition of Polish Jewish history within Polish academia.[55] The Warsaw branch of *B'nai B'rith* celebrated its member's appointment at the university, stressing its importance for Jewish scholarship.[56] Schorr praised the fact that at Warsaw University Bałaban "aroused respect for our past among non-Jews."[57] Bałaban's student, Marek Bosak, ascribed "national significance" to Bałaban's appointment at Warsaw University, where "new adepts of the [field] of the history of Jews in Poland have the opportunity to set their passion for historicizing free in the national-Jewish atmosphere, in harmony with their national attitude."[58] Even Ringelblum, who disapproved of the Institute as a "reactionary institution" because it ignored Yiddish and Yiddish literature and did not take a critical approach to the Bible,

---

54 Among his Galician students were from Cracow: Marek Bosak and Teofila Mahler (both born in Cracow in 1912) and Leon Bauminger (born in 1913); Abraham Jakub Getter (b. 1912 in Tarnobrzeg), Hersz Glejzer (b. 1909 in Drohobycz), Mechel Lisser (b. in 1908 in Horodenka), Hillel Seidman (b. in Buczacz in 1907), Dawid Wurm (b. 1909 in Brody), Chaim Simcha Babad (b. in 1907 in Zniesienie near Lwów), Falek Haffner (b. 1908 in Lwów). The list published in Bałaban's festschrift is not complete and includes 60 names but lacks such Bałaban's students as Hillel Seidman and Falik Hafner. See "Prace magisterskie pisane w seminarium his. żyd. Profesora Bałabana, które będą drukowane w części drugiej Księgi Jubileuszowej," in *Księga Jubileuszowa dla uczczenia sześćdziesięciolecia profesora Majera Bałabana* (Warsaw, 1938), 102–104.

55 See Filip Friedman, "Prof. Majer Bałaban (w 30-lecie pracy naukowej)," *Miesięcznik Żydowski* 4 (1933): 345.

56 See the protocol from the closed meeting on September 17, 1928, AAN, B'nei B'rith, file 3, 4.

57 Protokóły zebrań zamkniętych Stow[arzyszenia] Humanitarnego Braterstwo B'nei-B'rith w Warszawie, March 11, 1933, AAN, B'nei B'rith, file 3, 270.

58 M. Bosak, "Prof. Dr. Majer Bałaban (Nowy Dziennik z dnia 20 II 1937)," in *Księga Jubileuszowa... Bałabana*, 77.

admitted that it was the only institution of higher education where the country's youth could pursue Jewish studies.[59]

Indeed, Bałaban's joint appointments were exceptional not only in the context of Polish academia, but also worldwide. With no comparable chair in any European university, his position could only be compared to Salo Baron's chair in the History and Literature of the Jewish People at Columbia University (December 1928) and to the Institute of Jewish Studies in Jerusalem inaugurated in 1924, which became part of the newly established faculty of humanities at the Hebrew University in 1928.[60] Furthermore, and uniquely, Bałaban's appointment at Warsaw University was specifically in Polish Jewish history. Bałaban envisioned his seminar as an important center for training the next generation of Polish Jewish historians and as a center which would allow him to guide students in researching local Jewish history in Polish lands.

Bałaban saw his success at Warsaw University as the first opening for academic positions in Jewish history, and hoped that others could follow. Speaking at the Congress of Polish historians in 1930, he argued that Polish Jewish history was a branch of Polish scholarship and needed centralized management to train scholars in Poland and abroad. He envisioned creating chairs in Jewish history or Polish Jewish history in at least two centers with rich archives, where a new cadre of scholars could be relied upon, or rather assigning the task to the Institute of Jewish Studies itself, either by securing substantial financial assistance from the Polish state or even nationalizing it.[61]

Conclusions

In the aftermath of the First World War, Galician Jewish historians played a leading role in turning Warsaw into a vibrant center of Jewish historiography.

---

59   Ringelblum, "Sylwetki," in idem, *Kronika getta warszawskiego wrzesień 1939–styczeń 1943*, ed. Artur Eisenbach, translated from Yiddish by Adam Rutkowski (Warsaw: Czytelnik, 1983), 557.

60   Robert Liberles, *Salo Wittmayer Baron: Architect of Jewish History* (New York: New York University Press, 1995), 58, 81; David Engel, "Sefer nolad: min ha-hitkatfut beyn Filip Friedman v'Shalom (Salo) Baron, 1927–1928," *Gal-Ed* 21 (2008): 141. Moreover, there was a fundamental difference between Bałaban's chair in Warsaw and Baron's appointment in New York: the former was at a publicly funded state university, the latter an endowed position at a private university.

61   Bałaban, "Zadania historiografji Żydów," in *Pamiętnik V Powszechnego Zjazdu Historyków Polskich w Warszawie 28 listopada do 4 grudnia 1930 r.*, vol. 1. *Referaty* (Lwów: Polskie Towarzystwo Historyczne, 1930), 118.

Bałaban, Schorr, Schiper, Ringelblum, Mahler and other Jewish intellectuals debated about priorities and organized new institutions in order to form a cadre of professional historians, to continue their work, and to expand the scope of the field. These formal and informal institutions allowed young Jews to study and research various aspects of Jewish history in Eastern Europe in general and of Polish Jewish history in particular. Bałaban, Schipper, and Schorr assisted Jewish students at Warsaw University before and after the openings of the Institute of Jewish Studies and Bałaban's university seminar. Ringelblum and Mahler organized a forum for Jewish students who wanted to pursue research in Polish Jewish history, not just with a discussion group but with its own journal.

Galician Jews who helped organize Jewish academic institutions and forums in Warsaw saw them as important platforms for all Jews in the Second Polish Republic. The Institute of Jewish Studies, Historical Committee and Bałaban's University Seminar all aspired to represent and serve the entire Polish Jewish community, as non-partisan, apolitical institutions where Polish Jews came together to engage in research.[62] The founders of the Institute described this vision in perhaps the strongest terms when they called its opening an important development "for the glory of Polish Jewry,"[63] and declared that having its own center of scholarship was "a matter of national and civic honor."[64]

Following the model that crystallized in Galicia in the period of Polish autonomy there, Galician Jews in Warsaw stressed that the national Jewish historical enterprise required university training and thus strove to make Polish Jewish history a legitimate and useful professional field of academic inquiry. They insisted on great attention to sources, both primary and secondary. Both Bałaban and Ringelblum saw the role of historians of Polish Jewry as scholars and educators of both the Jewish and the general public. They thus imported ideas about the role of Polish Jewish history as an essential part of both Polish and Jewish historiography, as articulated in the Galician context before the First World War, to Warsaw.

Their experiences in building Polish Jewish historiography and making it relevant for the community whose past they studied also offer a perspective on the role of Jewish historians and historiography after the Holocaust in the

---

62 Prof. Dr. Moshe Schorr, "Di yidishe visenshaft un dos yidish bukh in poylen," in *Haynt: Haynt Yubilei Bukh 1908–1928: Yubilei Numer* (Warsaw: Hajnt, 1928), 96.

63 M. Schorr, "Stan i potrzeby wiedzy żydowskiej w dobie dzisiejszej" (inaugural lecture delivered at the opening of the Institute, February 19, 1928)," in *Sprawozdanie Instytutu*, XXI.

64 Inaugural speech by Dr. Markus Braude, ibid., IX, where he described creating Polish Jewry's own Institute of Jewish Studies as a task "of national and civic honor."

new centers of historical scholarship, mainly the U.S. and Israel. Studies exploring the works and views of Bałaban, Schiper, Ringelblum and others began to appear in Yiddish, Hebrew and English within a few years after the Holocaust, marking a process of interpretation and reformulation in which surviving historians and a new generation of scholars sought to explore interwar historiographical ideas. A series of short overviews of the historiographical activity in interwar years also appeared in the first decade after the holocaust, introducing to English- and Hebrew-reading audiences the main themes and projects of past scholarship and laying the foundation for new scholarly work, while still relating to and polemicizing with interpretations from that period.

To what extent, then, did ideas about the place of the Jews in Polish history formulated in interwar Poland become integrated into the study of Jewish history, in particular the Jewish Diaspora? One influential idea was famously presented by Salo Baron, another historian from Galicia who moved to the U.S. before the war and who advocated writing Jews into the local narrative. In a 1927 article, Baron deplored the "lachrymose theory of history" and called for a rethinking of the paradigm that portrayed the medieval and early modern periods as exclusively times of Jewish suffering. His caution against overstating cases of violence despite much longer periods of co-existence and integration[65] was shared by his fellow Galician historians, who chose to focus on the life, rather than the death, of Jewish communities. This is also echoed in Balaban's reaction to the violence in the university—isolated cases should not be allowed to overwhelm the bigger picture of co-existence.[66] There certainly seems to be an affinity between later concepts of history writing and the interwar model. How other elements of the historiographical practice developed in Poland fared in the post-Holocaust world remains a topic in need of investigation.

Much of the research carried out in interwar Poland in Polish and Yiddish became "lost" because of the language barrier. This is particularly true with the theses of Warsaw University students, only a small number of which was ever published before or after the war. Most remain in the archives of Warsaw University and the Jewish Historical Institute. In addition, only recently was Bałaban's monumental *History of the Jews in Cracow* published in Hebrew. However, the work of Jewish historians from the 1920s and 1930s is increasingly utilized by specialists, especially in the case of local studies, since many of the

---

65 On the interpretation of this call see David Engel, "Crisis and Lachrymosity: On Salo Baron, Neobaronianism, and the Study of Modern European Jewish history," *Jewish History* 20 (2006): 243–264.

66 Interestingly Baron did not study the Holocaust as part of his scholarly agenda. He was however called as expert witness at the Eichmann trial.

archives and original communal records were destroyed in the Holocaust.[67] Last but not least, Antony Polonsky has recently taken up the interwar idea of writing a grand synthesis of Polish Jewish history based on detailed local studies, producing a fresh interpretation of the history of the Jews in Polish lands.[68]

---

67   See, for example, Gershon D. Hundert, *Jews in a Polish Private Town: The Case of Opatów in the Eighteenth Century* (Baltimore MD: Johns Hopkins University Press, 1992).

68   Antony Polonsky, *The Jews in Poland and Russia*, vol. I: *1350 to 1881*, vol. II: *1881–1914*, and vol. III: *1914 to 2008* (Oxford and Portland OR: Littman Library of Jewish Civilization, 2010–2012).

CHAPTER 16

Negotiating Jewish Nationalism in Interwar Warsaw

Kenneth B. Moss

The memoir literature on Jewish life in interwar Warsaw reveals a peculiar ambiguity. Some memoirs present Warsaw as the center of a newly intense interwar Jewish nationalism. Moyshe Zonshayn describes Nalewki Street as the heart of a Jewish national "kingdom," where the Jewish national council sought to shape the fate of a putative Jewish nation, where every "national holiday" brought forth grand Jewish national processions, and where every soccer game between ethnically Jewish and ethnically Catholic-Polish teams was a nationalistically-framed event.[1] Another memoir by the Łomża Zionist activist Yisroel Levinsky represents Warsaw as a site of "historic" Zionist achievement, as when he recalls with evident pride his participation "in the historic national conference in Warsaw for the Jewish National Fund, when [Menahem] Ussishkin, the president of the fund, [demanded of] the Jews of Poland a levy [....] [towards] the half million pounds sterling [...] needed for the redemption of 100,000 new dunams of land" in Palestine.[2]

Conversely, other memoirs of interwar Warsaw register little Jewish nationalism there or maintain that Jewish nationalism in Warsaw was notably weak by contemporary standards. Indeed, this perspective can sometimes be found in the very same memoirs that elsewhere trumpet the city's significance in the annals of Jewish nationalism. The aforementioned memoir by Zonshayn, for example, describes certain streets in the city's Jewish neighborhood as almost wholly socialist in terms of their public political culture, and pinpoints other sites in the city—like the marriage-halls on Franciszkańska street—that served as stages for manifestations of a robust Hasidic subculture.[3] The Yiddishist

---

* The research for this chapter was conducted with the support of a Charles A. Ryskamp Research Fellowship from the American Council of Learned Societies. Thanks to Glenn Dynner, François Guesnet, and Marci Shore for their editorial comments, to David Engel and Shaul Stampfer for their encouragement, and to my friend and Polish tutor, Dr. Zbigniew Janowski, for his help with some of the Polish-language sources.

1 Moyshe Zonshayn, *Yidish-varshe* (Buenos-Ayres: Tsentral-farband fun poylishe yidn in argentine, 1954), 23–24.
2 Yisrael Levinsky, *Kotsim u-frachim* (Tel Aviv: Irgun 'ole lomzah be-yisrael, 1963), 99.
3 Zonshayn, *Yidish-varshe*, 40, 41–44. Franciszkańska was already a hub of Hasidism in Warsaw as early as the 1880s; see Glenn Dynner, "Hasidism and Habitat: Managing the Jewish-Christian

Nakhmen Mayzl was appalled by the absence of Yiddish-language signage in Warsaw by contrast with the much smaller Vilna.[4] And to the recollections of Yisroel Levinsky, one might counterpose the recollections of another Zionist activist, Shlomo Onikovsky, a member of the He-halutz Zionist youth pioneer movement in Warsaw in the 1930s, who remembered that "[m]ost of the Jewish population in Warsaw related to our path with indifference."[5]

Such contradictory assessments by contemporaries of popular engagement with Jewish nationalism—primarily but not only Zionism—were not peculiar to Warsaw, but rather characterize the contemporary record on Polish Jewish political culture as a whole: it is no accident that Ezra Mendelsohn began his classic 1989 essay on "Jewish Politics in Interwar Poland" with just such a counterposing of contradictory reports by Zionist emissaries regarding their reception by the Polish Jewish public in the early 1930s.[6] As Mendelsohn did in that essay, this chapter attempts to point a way beyond seeming contradiction by drawing together a range of primary sources and scholarly treatments that begin to trace a suitably complex portrait of the place(s) of Jewish nationalism in interwar Warsaw Jewish political culture.

This chapter begins by suggesting Warsaw's special place in the topography of interwar Jewish nationalism as the premiere center, alongside the young city of Tel Aviv, of organized and visible Jewish nationalism, particularly but not exclusively Zionism. It then turns to the seemingly contradictory evidence of the relative weakness of Jewish nationalism in general and Zionism in particular in Warsaw, suggesting some particular local sociological and spatial factors that blunted the attractiveness of Jewish nationalism as an option while lending special credibility to various alternatives to it—assimilationist, pietistic, and revolutionary alike. Finally, the essay turns to the much less well-explored topic of how Zionism actually functioned on a day-to-day level in Warsaw from the late 1920s through the late 1930s, and suggests that it possessed two very different, perhaps even largely unrelated dimensions. On the one hand, Zionism

---

Encounter in the Kingdom of Poland," in idem (ed.), *Holy Dissent: Jewish and Christian Mystics in Eastern Europe* (Detroit: Wayne State University Press, 2011), 110.

4 Kalman Weiser, *Jewish People, Yiddish Nation* (Toronto: University of Toronto Press, 2011), 225; on Jewish cultural display in public space in Vilna, see Cecile Kuznitz, "On the Jewish Street: Yiddish Culture and the Urban Landscape in Interwar Vilna," in Leonard J. Greenspoon (ed.), *Yiddish Language and Culture: Then and Now* (Studies in Jewish Civilization 9; Omaha, NE: Creighton University Press, 1998), 65–92.

5 Shlomo Onikovsky, "Hishtatafnu be-feulat behirot" in Sarah Segal and Aryeh Pyalkov (eds.), *Be-shadmot grokhov* (Kibbutz Lohamei ha-Getaot: Beit Lohamei ha-Getaot, 1976), 278.

6 In Yisrael Gutman et al. (eds.), *The Jews of Poland Between Two World Wars* (Hanover, NH: University Press of New England, 1989), 9–10.

(and to a much lesser extent, other nationalist movements) persisted as a distinct, self-contained, and fairly small subculture (or several subcultures). But a range of other, largely unexplored phenomena suggest that Zionism also functioned as a special sort of political horizon for many Warsaw Jews who stood well outside Zionist circles. Assaying an argument largely absent from the historiography, the third part of the chapter suggests how interwar Warsaw had become a site of increasingly underdetermined or fluid relations to Jewish nationalism and Zionism—a center for *negotiating* Jewish nationhood.

Before turning to this discussion, a few statistics will help map the terrain and, conversely, help delineate some of the ambiguities of Warsaw Jewry's relationship to Jewish nationalism. In the 1922 Sejm elections, some 80–95% of the Jewish vote went to two lists framed in Jewish-national terms, the National Minorities' Bloc (where Zionists were the dominant Jewish partner) and the Folkists; in Warsaw, the percentage of the Jewish vote accorded those two lists together was the slightly smaller but comparable 74.5%. Granted, both nationally and even moreso in Warsaw, a substantial percentage of the 50.2% of the Jewish vote that went to the Minorities Bloc actually came from supporters of the religious and broadly non- to anti-nationalist Agudes yisroel party, which briefly affiliated with it for electoral purposes, and therefore it seems clear that some substantial element among the voters for the Minorities Bloc in Warsaw were in fact *not* nationalists by any definition. Nevertheless, it seems clear that well over half of Jewish voters in 1922 were ready to support a Zionist or robustly diaspora-nationalist list.[7] Fourteen years later, in the 1936 local elections to the

---

7 Shlomo Netser, *Ma'avak yehudei polin al zekhuyotehem ha-ezrahiot ve-ha-le'umiot (1918–1922)* (Tel Aviv: Universitat Tel-Aviv, 1980), 313; Ludwik Hass, *Wybory Warszawskie 1918–1926* (Warszawa: Państwowe Wydawnictwo Naukowe, 1972), 144–45; Antony Polonsky, *The Jews in Poland and Russia*, v. III: *1914–2008* (Oxford: The Littman Library of Jewish Civilization, 2012), 115–17. Note that Netser's statistics for the 1922 elections suggest a dramatic gap between support for Jewish nationalist parties in Warsaw on the one hand and the nation-wide results on the other, but this is because he compares the nation-wide Jewish vote for the Minorities' Bloc (80–95%) with the Warsaw vote for the Minorities Bloc (50–55%) *alone*, without noting that in Warsaw, a further 23% voted Folkist; cf. Hass, *Wybory*, 145. From the standpoint of our question, namely readiness of Warsaw Jewish voters to support expressly Jewish nationalist parties, these two numbers should be combined albeit after trying to deduct, however roughly, the Agudah element within the vote for the Minorities Bloc. As for how one does that latter division, I am not sure, but the results for the Warsaw City Council elections and the 1928 Sejm elections seem to suggest rough parity if not somewhat greater Zionist strength than Agudah strength. See Polonsky, *Jews in Poland*, 117. At any rate, what emerges is a meaningful but not dramatic difference between Jewish political readiness to support expressly nationalist options in Poland-wide as opposed to in Warsaw. On the difficulty of measuring

Jewish community boards or *kehiles*—elections which were taken to represent a terrific rebuke to Jewish nationalist politics (as well as Orthodox politics)—Zionist and Folkist lists in Warsaw received 32% of the seats, as against roughly 34% Poland-wide excluding Warsaw.[8] When, in 1931, Poland's Zionists called on Polish Jewry to declare Hebrew to be their mother tongue as a symbolic assertion of Zionist commitment, the national percentage of those Jews who "obeyed the command of the Zionist movement," as Ezra Mendelsohn puts it, was a mere 7.8%. In Warsaw, the percentage of Jews who claimed Hebrew as a mother tongue was only 5.7% (19,180 Jewish census respondents out of a total of 336,140).[9]

Leaving aside for the moment the usual questions regarding the nature of nationalism as political *identity*, what these statistics offer, first, is a rough measure of the number of Jews in Warsaw who were willing to *identify with* Jewish nationalism at one moment or another, in particular political settings and contexts.[10] Second, comparing the electoral statistics to the census statistics offers a preliminary sense of the range of nationalist identification, from 5.7% of the city's Jewish population who appear to have been fully committed Zionists to a much larger population about which all one can say at this juncture is that it was sometimes willing to vote for parties that defined Jews in nationalist terms. Strikingly, this latter, passively nationalist population was many times larger than the first even at the low point of the 1936 Sejm elections.

Concretely these statistics, combined with well-established historical generalizations about Jewish nationalism in interwar Poland, suggest the following. First, Jewish nationalism under any definition was proportionally weaker in interwar Warsaw than in many other Polish Jewish locales. Certainly, there were other Jewish centers where Jewish nationalists wielded far more moral authority than in Warsaw—for example, a full 39.8% of the Jews in Kraków gave Hebrew as their native language in the 1931 census in direct response to the exhortations of local Jewish nationalist leaders.[11] Second, however, Jewish

---

Zionist electoral strength specifically in Warsaw, see Isaac Guterman, *Kehilat varshah ben shete milhamot ha-'olam: otonomyah le'umit be-khavle ha-hok ve'ha-metsi'ut* (Tel Aviv: Universitat Tel Aviv,1997), 201.

8 Antony Polonsky, "The Bund in Polish Political Life, 1935–1939," in Ada Rapoport-Albert and Steven J. Zipperstein (eds.), *Jewish History: Essays in Honour of Chimen Abramsky* (London: Peter Halban, 1988), 562, 564.

9 Ezra Mendelsohn, *The Jews of East Central Europe Between the World Wars* (Bloomington: Indiana University Press, 1983), 30.

10 On this critical distinction: Rogers Brubaker, *Ethnicity without Groups* (Cambridge, MA: Harvard University Press, 2004), 41–42.

11 Sean Martin, *Jewish Life in Cracow 1918–1939* (London: Vallentine Mitchell, 2004), 51.

nationalist identification in Warsaw was not really much weaker than the Poland-wide average. Third, Warsaw was home to a proportionally smaller core of committed Zionists than was the case in many other Polish towns, but the raw number of such committed Zionists was not negligible. Fourth, a large number of Warsaw Jews throughout the 1920s and into the 1930s were willing to vote nationalist. Fifth, this number declined substantially over time—but support for Jewish nationalist politics in interwar Warsaw always remained substantially higher than it had been in pre-war (or pre-1905) Warsaw. Sixth, these statistics fit the portrait of interwar Polish Jewish political culture painted by Antony Polonsky and Ezra Mendelsohn, among others, as one marked by high plasticity: vote-splitting, high responsiveness to changes in the political situation, and a tendency to pick and choose the moments of national self-identification.

Taken together, these preliminary indications should be understood not as straightforward information but as guides to the questions to be asked about Jewish nationalism in Warsaw. It is one of this chapter's core contentions that Jewish nationalism in interwar Poland is best understood not solely or even primarily in terms of a stable political identity and a program that one accepted or rejected (though there were some who did fully accept or fully reject Jewish nationalist programs), but in terms of an ongoing negotiation by many Jews with the idea that Jews were—or were compelled to be—a separate nation, and with the various political and cultural prerogatives and imperatives bound up in that idea.[12] This negotiation was rendered increasingly unavoidable for Polish Jews in the interwar period by domestic, regional, and global factors alike.

Domestically, as of 1918, Jews found themselves in a Polish nation-state in which ideologies and discourses of the nation colored virtually the whole of political life, albeit in varying and conflict-ridden ways, and within which large parts of Polish political society had a fraught relationship to citizens who were not ethnic Poles. Historians of Poland are sometimes keen (for admirable political reasons and with some empirical grounds no doubt) to apply the term "nationalism" only to the integral ethnonationalism of the Endek right; when treating the evidently powerful orientation toward the nation as a value in other parts of the Polish political spectrum, historians will sometimes seek an alternative term like "patriotic."[13] But other historiography rightly underscores

---

12   My current book project, *The Unchosen People: the East European Jewish Political Imagination in the Age of the Nation-State, 1918–1939*, will develop the argument sketched here.

13   Insistence on the importance of this distinction seems to have been the central dimension of Szymon Rudnicki's impassioned critique of the conference paper out of which

the point that the valorization of the nation as an end, as an organizing principle of everyday life, and as something that demanded definition, cultivation, and political representation loomed large in political life across most of the interwar Polish political spectrum, however real the differences between the "zoological" ethnonationalism of the Endeks and the complex mix of national Romanticism, republican and federalist ideals, noblesse-oblige, and tolerant but hierarchical attitudes toward ethnic minorities to be found on the center-left.[14] Questions of the nation—its openness or closure, its values, its needs, and its condition—were not merely matters of discrete debate, but inflected any number of political questions—as Jerzy Tomaszewski puts it, "[e]conomic, political, and social problems of the Second Republic were closely linked

the current essay has developed; suggestively, Rudnicki frames his many years of research on the interwar Polish right as writing the history of the "national camp" in idem, *Równi, ale niezupełnie* (Warszawa: Biblioteka Midrasza, 2008), 7, and describes Roman Dmowski as "leader of the Polish national movement" (implying that the constituent elements of Piłsudski's Sanacja government and the mainstream PPS were in no way national movements?) in idem, "Jews in Poland between the Two World Wars," *Shofar* 29.3 (2011): 8. Cf. Joseph Rothschild's classic survey in *East Central Europe between the Two World Wars* (Seattle: University of Washington, 1974), which defines both the PPS and "the Pilsudskists" as "two unimpeachably patriotic movements of the left"; compare his larger point on ibid, 11–12, which rather differently treats nationalism in much larger compass as an organizing principle of the East European successor states' relationship to ethnic minorities.

14　Here, I find very useful Eva Plach, *The Clash of Moral Nations: Cultural Politics in Piłsudski's Poland, 1926–1935* (Athens, OH: Ohio University Press, 2006), 8, which demonstrates how the struggle between the right and the center-left associated with the Sanacja involved a *shared* concern with "symbols and definitions of Polishness and Poland." Cf. Jerzy Jedlicki, "Polish Concepts of Native Culture," in Ivo Banac and Katherine Verdery (eds.), *National Character and National Ideology in Interwar Eastern Europe* (New Haven: Yale Center for International and Area Studies, 1995), 1–22, which at times draws the aforementioned distinction between the "nationalistic" ideals of the right and the opposing "romantic-historical" ideals of "Piłsudski's camp" (12, 20) (as well as discerning a third "folk-enhancing image [...] adopted by one current of the peasant movement" (21) but generally draws attention to the shared armature of investment in the Polish nation and national culture as an ideal and a core political value that framed both. See especially his concluding remarks on 22. Andrzej Chojnowski similarly reserves the term "nationalist camp" for the right while at the same time amply demonstrating that there is no way to understand Piłsudski and the Sanacja regime without recognizing their investment in Romantic ideals of a Polish nation needing to be both awakened and forged and to be educated to national greatness not least through service to the nation-state. See idem, "Polish National Character, the Sanacja Camp, and the National Democracy" in Banac and Verdery, *National Character and National Ideology*, 33–35.

with national differences and sometimes conflicts."[15] Furthermore, however one uses and delimits the term "Polish nationalism," there seems to be broad consensus that the more exclusionary, ethnically-defined, anti-Jewish variant gained ever-greater purchase in Polish political culture over the course of the interwar period.[16] Finally, though historians certainly debate the particulars of how Jews were framed within the discourse of the Polish nation (a discourse in which Jews themselves were of course also sometimes participants), it seems clear that Jews loomed as an especially serious problem in the political imagination of substantial swaths of the Polish polity—and were well aware of that fact.[17]

These local dimensions of what we might call 'the nation as political horizon' were reinforced by regional and global ones. The post-war international system was one in which privilege, access, and rights were substantially defined by ethnonational concepts and claims.[18] Moreover, from a global perspective, the Jewish situation was defined ever more fully by the entire ensemble of nationalist projects ranging from extrusionary ethnonationalist projects by state-owning majorities throughout Eastern and Central Europe[19] to the claims of

---

15 Jerzy Tomaszewski, *Rzeczpospolita wielu narodów* (Warszawa: Czytelnik, 1985), 10.

16 Compare Rothschild's summary comment that "rightist ideology permeated Polish society ever more deeply" (idem, *East Central Europe*, 38) with Timothy Snyder's view that "Polish nationalism took a turn from the confidence of the 1920s to the fear of the 1930s, shifting from the ambitions of state building to worries of powerful neighbors and internal enemies [...]" in Snyder, *Sketches from a Secret War* (New Haven, CN: Yale University Press, 2005), 63.

17 Beyond the extensive literature focusing on this question with particular attention to the Polish secular nationalist right, Brian Porter-Szücs' recent study demonstrates the somewhat different but equally potent—and increasingly overlapping—significance of "the Jewish question" in interwar Polish Catholic religious thought. Idem, *Faith and Fatherland: Catholicism, Modernity, and Poland* (Oxford: Oxford University Press, 2011), 272–314.

18 See Carole Fink, *Defending the Rights of Others* (Cambridge: Cambridge University Press, 2004).

19 Katherine Verdery offers an especially apt summation of the general regional situation in its international context, which she applies not least to interwar Poland: "The redrawn map of Eastern Europe and state independence for most East European nationalities made it both imperative and possible to sharpen and modify the definition of 'the nation' or 'people' so as to suit new realities. With the apparent end of ceaseless imperial expansions and annexations, East Europeans could begin to talk much more seriously about 'sacred soil' and to define a national identity within clearly fixed borders. The period marks a special phase in the development of national ideologies in that it was the only period in which most East Europeans had relatively free rein to create their own independent voice

Zionism, which were increasingly concretized by the political, cultural, social, and economic ascendency of the Zionist-dominated Yishuv in Palestine.

As the political capital, Warsaw served as a prime stage on which all of the many burning political questions confronting Poland played out in multiple settings, from the Sejm to the streets. The very fact that the capital of the restored Polish state was more than one-third Jewish was framed as a Polish national question,[20] and some of the most dramatic events in the city's political life, like the bitter conflict in Warsaw's press and its streets over the election of Gabriel Narutowicz to the presidency in 1922, linked the fate of the nation to the Jewish question.[21] Not coincidentally, Warsaw became a site of precocious nationally framed conflict between Jews and Poles already before the First World War, and the war itself intensified these conflicts—and their national framing—tremendously.[22] Yet at the same time, specific sociological features of Warsaw Jewry served to blunt the nationalizing effects on Jews of such an uneven nationally-framed conflict, as we shall see. What interests me in this chapter particularly is how Warsaw as a setting affected or reflected the Polish Jewish negotiation with nationhood.

A note on how the present chapter addresses the dynamics of change over time, that is, the significant variations and perhaps deeper changes in Jewish political sensibilities visible over the course of the interwar period, is apposite here. In tension with much of the historiography on interwar Polish Jewish politics, which tends to foreground the impact on Jewish politics of major events

---

[....]." Verdery goes on to echo and generalize Tomaszewski's insight: "The new societal elites who sought to define national character in this period in Eastern European history were struggling with a number of problems simultaneously in seeking to adjust to the new post-war realities of their countries [....] Many of the participants perceived the problems and argued over their solutions in the idiom of national identity." Katherine Verdery, "Introduction," in *National Character and National Ideology in Interwar Eastern Europe*, xx, xxii.

20   Thus, right-wing Polish nationalists could identify Warsaw as inadequately Polish-national and its Polish culture as permeated by Jewishness. See Plach, *The Clash of Moral Nations*, 71.

21   Piotr J. Wróbel, "The Rise and Fall of Parliamentary Democracy in Interwar Poland," in M.B.B. Biskupski, James S. Pula, and Piotr J. Wróbel (eds.), *The Origins of Modern Polish Democracy* (Athens: Ohio University Press, 2010), 133–34.

22   On the distinctly national framing of Polish-Jewish tensions in pre-war Warsaw, see the typically masterful synthesis in Antony Polonsky, *The Jews in Poland and Russia*, v. 2, *1881 to 1914* (Oxford: The Littman Library of Jewish Civilization, 2010), 95, 103–12. Regarding the war years, Piotr Wróbel notes several sites of Polish-Jewish ethnic violence in Warsaw in the last days of the war in idem, "World War One: A Turning Point in the History of Polish Jewry," in Jacques Kornberg (ed.), *The Golden Age and Beyond: Polish-Jewish History* (Toronto: University of Toronto Press, 1997), 46.

in Polish high politics, the approach of this paper is a synchronic one that subordinates attention to those changes to a more spatial and sociological account of nationalism in Warsaw. The rationale for this is twofold. Synthetically, the goal of this chapter is to identify durable or cumulative structural features that made Warsaw a distinct *kind* of center for national interest (or disinterest). Analytically, a core argument of the chapter is that there was an underappreciated general openness to Jewish nationalism and especially Zionism as an option among Warsaw Jews that, while no doubt subject to swelling and contraction in terms of numbers, seems always to have remained substantial enough (even in the late 1930s) that it is worth studying synchronically.

The justification for this approach will become clear in the course of the chapter. Here, it bears noting, simply, that while Warsaw was in many ways exceptional relative to other interwar Polish settings in the relative strengths of Jewish nationalist, anti-nationalist, and counter-nationalist commitments there, it does not seem to have been exceptional in the *timing* of the changing salience of these commitments, which one might crudely delineate as: strong nationalization during World War I for the bulk of the community alongside a countervailing upswing in Polish nationalism among polonized Jews; growing skepticism about acceptance in Poland as members of the political nation in the early 1920s coinciding with growing openness to Jewish nationalism and especially Zionism, culminating in the 'Grabski aliyah' of 1924–25; substantial revival of Jewish Polish-incorporationist hopes with Pilsudski's coup in 1926, bolstered by a first collapse of Zionist enthusiasm; the beginnings of a return to growing doubt about acceptance in Poland as early as 1928–1929, coinciding with growing openness to Jewish nationalism once again (albeit mixed with the growing power of revolutionary alternatives) which reached a high point between 1931–1934 in the context of a more general emigrationist fever and the reopening of Palestine to Jewish immigration; and finally the 1936–39 collapse of incorporationist hopes and the (relative) eclipse of Zionist and other Jewish nationalist political choices in favor of revolutionary options or options that involved demonstrative resistance and counter-nationalist politics.

One last preliminary point remains to be made regarding the relationship between the terms Jewish nationalism and Zionism in this chapter. Jewish nationalism in Warsaw, as in Poland as a whole, was not exclusively a matter of identification with Zionist ideals and institutions. Even if one defines Jewish nationalism narrowly in terms of supporting a particular political movement (which would be a conceptual error of the first order),[23] congruence between

---

23   See my *Jewish Renaissance in the Russian Revolution* (Cambridge, MA: Harvard University Press, 2009), introduction. See also Robert Blobaum's chapter in this volume.

Jewish nationalism and Zionism was even less complete in Warsaw than elsewhere in Poland, at least in the early 1920s, because of major local efflorescence of the diaspora-nationalist Folks-Partey.[24]

Nevertheless, by any reasonable definition of Jewish nationalism, much Jewish nationalist expression in interwar Poland took place in relation to Zionism. Indeed, one of the points to be developed in this chapter is that this is even more the case than we tend to think: several sections of the discussion that follows will adduce evidence of serious engagement by large numbers of non-Zionists in Warsaw with the Zionist project. Consequently, the approach taken in this chapter to "nationalism" is consciously eclectic: where appropriate, it focuses on Jewish nationalist self-identification in general or, conversely, on Zionism and engagement with Zionism in particular.

Warsaw as a Public Stage for Jewish Nationalism

What was it about Jewish nationalism in Warsaw that so impressed observers like Zonshayn and Levinsky? Texts like theirs serve to remind us that simply by dint of its size and its role as Poland's political and cultural capital, Warsaw concentrated an unparalleled range of Jewish nationalist institutions and provided a space of unequalled significance for making Jewish nationalism *visible and public*.

Thus, first, as a set of organizations, as an ideology with concrete forms of verbal and visual self-expression, and as a political culture with its own symbol-systems and practices, Jewish nationalism was arguably more visible in interwar Warsaw than in any other Jewish city to that point other than Tel Aviv. Most obviously, Jewish nationalism in Warsaw had *an address*, or many addresses, in the sense of declaredly nationalist organizations thickly clustered on the city's main Jewish streets. Alongside the prayer houses and communal organizations that long predated the interwar period, formally nationalist organizations occupied a central place on virtually every significant street.[25] With its exclusively charitable and religious organizations, the kehillah/gmina complex on Grzybowska remained a redoubt of the old 19th century assimilationist-Orthodox alliance. But on Graniczna-Twarda, the Nozhik *shul* and Serdiner *shul* were now abutted by the central branches of the General

---

24 On which see now Kalman Weiser, *Jewish People, Yiddish Nation*, 171–211.
25 See the terrific map of Jewish institutions ca. 1938 prepared by Eleonora Bergman, Ursula Fuks, and Olga Zienkiewicz, attached to Antony Polonsky, "Warsaw," in YIVO *Encyclopedia of Jews in Eastern Europe*, 2: 1998–99.

Zionist Organization of Poland, the offices of the Tarbut Hebraist educational stream, and the Jewish *Krajoznawstwo* or *Landkentenish* Society (ZTK). Further up Graniczna, the offices of the Women's International Zionist Organization were located amidst a cluster of organizations devoted to Jewish medical care and care for orphans, offering a nationalist gloss on a classic and classically gendered communal function. Continuing northward, one encountered, at the very beginning of Nalewki, the popular Maccabi sports association and the Union of Hebrew School Teachers in Poland. Zamenhofa and smaller streets to the west were dominated by offices of the Bund and the Agudah, but at the end of the street stood the offices of the pro-Zionist *Nasz Przegląd*, and in the early 1930s, the Zionist youth-pioneering movement He-halutz relocated its central offices from a preparatory kibbutz on the outskirts of the city (Kibbutz Grokhov, to which we will return) to Gęsia street, right around the corner from the competing Bundist youth organization Tsukunft.

Second, Jewish nationalism in Warsaw had a personal and much recognized *face*. Before 1914, and certainly before 1905, active Jewish nationalism was largely the pursuit of insurgent youth intellectuals and *polu-inteligenti* on the one hand and a coterie of middle-class Zionists on the other, most of whom seem to have been relative newcomers to Warsaw and indeed Congress Poland ("Litvaks," in the parlance of the time). These seem to have long remained outsiders to both Warsaw's polonized Jewish middle class and its traditionalist-Hasidic majority-cum-plurality.[26] With the exception of the protean Jewish national tribune Y.L. Peretz and perhaps Nahum Sokolow, pre-1914 Warsaw apparently did not boast a Jewish nationalist figure recognizable to large numbers of local Jews. But in the interwar period, the memoir literature suggests, figures like the Zionist leader Yitzhok Grinboym or the Folkist leader Noyekh Prilutsky commanded tremendous popular recognition on the streets of Warsaw, as did a host of Jewish journalists, writers, and publicists.[27] Jewish nationalist political leaders like the insurgent maximalist Zionist Vladimir Jabotinsky were accorded attention far beyond the circles of their committed

---

[26] This is an admittedly impressionistic account based on Shatzky, *Di geshikhte fun yidn in varshe*, III: 373ff; François Guesnet, "Chanukah and its Function in the Invention of a Jewish-Heroic Tradition in Early Zionism, 1880–1900," in Michael Berkowitz (ed.), *Nationalism, Zionism, and Ethnic Mobilization of the Jews in 1900 and Beyond* (Leiden: Brill, 2004), 240; Puah Rakovsky, *My Life as a Radical Jewish Woman*, transl. Paula Hyman (Bloomington: Indiana University Press, 2002), 58–60; Scott Ury, "The Generation of 1905 and the Politics of Despair," in Stefani Hoffman and Ezra Mendelsohn (eds.), *The Revolution of 1905 and Russia's Jews* (Philadelphia: University of Pennsylvania, 2008), 96–110.

[27] Zonshayn, *Yidish-varshe*, 27; Weiser, *Jewish People*, xii.

FIGURE 16.12 "*A General Electoral Bloc.*" Der sheygets (*The Delinquent*), Warsaw, 8 October 1930. Cartoon satirizing the not unusual situation of Jewish political parties entering into uneasy alliances in order to form parliamentary blocs. Here, the parties are shown beating each other mercilessly. (*Left to right*) Agudas Yisroel, Zionist, Mizraḥi, Folkist, Artisan, Merchant. Archives of the YIVO Institute for Jewish Research, New York. Courtesy of YIVO.

followers. The *Moment* journalist Yitzhok Borenshteyn gives the following revealing account of Jabotinsky's popular reception in Warsaw in the mid-1930s: "Leave aside the Revisionists, the Betar youth [....]; also among simple Jews there were quite a few who saw in Jabotinsky the Jewish genius [....]. No one had as much ability as Jabotinsky to attract a packed audience of 4,000 in the humid Warsaw *cyrk* on a hot summer Sabbath day."[28]

Finally, Jewish nationalism had a fitful but substantial presence on Warsaw's streets. This was true, first, of various forms of demonstrative Jewish national

---

28 Yitshok Borenshteyn, *Varshe fun nekhtn* (Sao Paolo, [s. n.], 1967), 69.

self-identification in the broad sense. The memoirist Zonshayn recalls that "on a national holiday or a traditional holiday [*folks-yontef*], [...] thousands of Jewish athletes in their uniforms" would gather on Nalewki in front of the Maccabi and the Bundist Morgnshtern building. Zonshayn recalls similar demonstrative excitement on Nalewki when Jewish sports teams would compete in matches against ethnic-Polish teams.[29] On a less festive note, in the 1930s Warsaw's streets saw intense nationally-framed protests against anti-Semitic policies in Poland and British policies in Palestine, as in the mass protests against the Sejm's attack on kosher slaughter.

Concomitantly, Warsaw offered a national stage for Zionist demonstrations. In November 1927, on the tenth anniversary celebration of the Balfour Declaration, masses of celebrants organized according to party, professional, and philanthropic membership marched down the main arteries of the Jewish quarter, led by an orchestra. The Zionist *Haynt* claimed "more than 20,000" participated; and even accounting for exaggeration, it was evidently an impressive "manifestation."[30] Warsaw also saw more spontaneous demonstrations of public engagement in the Zionist project. One such demonstration took place in the immediate wake of the bloody attacks against Jewish communities in Palestine in August 1929. According to one eyewitness, the socialist-Zionist activist Eliahu Dobkin, initial news of the events (complete with vastly inflated reports of death and destruction) produced widespread shock and even panic among Warsaw Jews. Appalled by the panic and rumor-mongering, Dobkin was nonetheless pleasantly surprised by two other features of the reaction. First, he noted, wide swaths of Warsaw Jewry demonstrated deep concern over the events and spontaneous support for the embattled Jewish community in Palestine; this was evident in a spontaneous closure of Jewish shops in the city during mass demonstrations, in which even "Jews who keep their shops open even on Yom Kippur shut them in Warsaw." Second, according to Dobkin, a gathering of Warsaw Jews on Orla Street to accompany a group of emigrants to the train-station turned into a "grand demonstration" of "some 10,000 people."[31]

None of the foregoing phenomena can be taken in any straightforward sense as evidence of an especially powerful Jewish nationalist and Zionist sensibility in Warsaw proportionally speaking, nor do they in any way contradict

---

29 Zonshayn, *Yidish-varshe*, 23.
30 "Di nekhtige grandieze balfour-demonstratsye iber di varshever gasen," *Haynt*, 14 November 1927; "Di hayntige demonstratsye iber di varsheveryudishe gasen lekoved der balfour-deklaratsye," *Moment*, 13 November 1927.
31 Eliyahu Dobkin to Eliyahu, Frumkin, and Halpern, 5 September 1929, Collection of the Vaadat Hu"l ha-Kibuts ha-Meuhad, 2–12/2/4, Arkhion Yad Tabenkin, Ramat Efal, Israel.

the long-standing historical wisdom that Jewish nationalist sentiment was proportionally stronger and perhaps also more deeply and intensely held in many other parts of Jewish Poland than in Warsaw. What the foregoing does suggest is that Warsaw provided a unique *kind* of setting for Jewish nationalist expression: by dint of the size of its Jewish population and the concentration of Jewish organizations in the city (within the larger context of the especially marked politicization of interwar Polish Jewry along national lines relative to other major Jewish populations in the period),[32] it served as a site for a more public, institutionalized, and visible Jewish nationalism than could be found almost anywhere else in the interwar Jewish world.[33]

Here we should note a different but related aspect of Warsaw's significance in shaping attitudes toward Jewish nationalism: the particular role of experiences in Warsaw in affirming nationalist identification not on the part of local Jews, but Jewish visitors from the provinces. Warsaw played host to a regular succession of large-scale meetings of all-Poland Zionist and other Jewish nationalist organizations which brought numerous Jews across Poland to the capital for a few days. Thus, November 1928 saw a meeting of the Jewish National Fund in Poland that brought 420 delegates from 200 communities

---

32 The general factors making for the political mobilization of interwar Polish Jewry along national lines, among others, are sketched above. What should be noted here in relation to the particular argument in this section is a more narrow point, namely, that while, globally speaking, there were several other great Jewish urban centers on the same scale as Warsaw or even considerably greater in this period—most obviously New York City and the great Soviet Jewish centers—Warsaw was the only Jewish urban center of such scale that was located in a country where Jews possessed considerable freedom of public expression but where their political situation was insistently and passionately framed in relation to questions of nationhood (Polish and Jewish both). New York City certainly boasted the potential for large-scale Jewish political mobilization on a scale far greater even than Warsaw and indeed saw major public demonstrations of Jewish national consciousness such as the incredible participation of some 125,000 New York Jews in the 1917 elections to the American Jewish Congress, many of whom voted Zionist. See Jonathan Frankel, *Prophecy and Politics: Socialism, Nationalism, and the Russian Jews, 1862–1917* (Cambridge: Cambridge University Press, 1981), 536–37. But such nationalist mobilizations were more intermittent than in Warsaw for the simple reason that questions of American Jewish political integration were neither as fraught nor as consistently framed in terms of ethnonational identity and conflict as in Poland. My thanks to the editors for posing the question of this comparison.

33 Of course, for the same reasons, Warsaw could and did serve as a public stage of special significance for the other Polish Jewish political movements as well, a point to which I will return below.

and drew a large local audience.³⁴ The aforementioned memoirs of the Zionist activist Levinsky offer a suggestive example of what such a meeting might have meant to participants. A kind of elder statesman of Hebraist and Zionist activity in interwar Łomża, elected several times as the Łomża delegate to Zionist meetings in Warsaw, Levinsky's recollections of the city are entirely dominated by the drama of participation in grand state-wide Zionist events like the aforementioned conference. His experience of Warsaw was one that bespoke—however accurately—Polish Zionism's nation-wide strength and mass appeal. Other contemporary sources bear this out. In an article dealing with the early 1928 meeting, the Warsaw correspondent for *Davar* expressed doubt that the meeting would energize Warsaw's lackluster "local activists" but expressed certainty that it would make a deep impression on the delegates from the provincial towns.³⁵

Spaces and Sociologies of Jewish Non-nationalism in Warsaw

But what then are we to make of the many indications of Jewish nationalism's *weakness* in Warsaw? Certainly, numerous sources sound that discordant note, too. When the veteran Zionist activist Alter Druyanov came from Palestine on a six-month visit to Poland in 1931–1932, he was disappointed by what he found in Warsaw: the city's general Zionists consumed by infighting over non-issues and a marked drop in the amount donated to the National Fund.³⁶ Just as interesting are accounts of Jewish life in interwar Warsaw that suggest the intermittent character or even absence of Jewish nationalism as an ideological option that at least demanded attention. Thus, Eliezer Hirshauge's memoir of leaving Warsaw's Hasidic world to join the city's underground anarchist movement between 1928 and 1939 registers the ideological importance of the *Polish* national question for his generation in various ways, but simply does not register any presence of Jewish nationalist ideology for him and his peers—not even as an enemy against whom it was necessary to fight. He presents himself as part of a generation of interwar Warsaw Hasidic youth who turned from Hasidic orthodoxy to anarchism out of a mix of specifically religious crisis and vague but heartfelt social discontent—all without any trace of the Zionist or national turn that many other memoirs of leaving traditional Judaism in

---

34 "Mikhtav be-polin," *Davar*, 27 November 1928.
35 Levinsky, *Kotsim*, 99; "Mikhtav be-polin," *Davar*, 27 November 1928.
36 Alter Druyanov, *Tsionut be-polaniah* (Tel Aviv: Masadah, 1932–1933), 85–96.

Eastern Europe would lead us to expect.[37] Although neither of these sources can be taken at face value, there are simply too many others that echo these accounts of Jewish nationalism's weakness in Warsaw to ignore, and the historical consensus accords with this. So rather than worrying about the reality of these representations, we can turn directly to reconstructing some of the sociological and spatial factors in Warsaw that blunted the attractiveness or relevance of Jewish nationalism as an option and lent power to various alternatives.

First, for all the anti-Semitism and Polish-Jewish tension in interwar Warsaw, the city remained the preeminent place in Poland (alongside Lwów and Kraków) where being nationally Polish continued to be a life-project for substantial numbers of Jews, and *becoming* part of the Polish nation continued to seem an attractive possibility for others. It seems clear that for obvious sociological reasons, Warsaw boasted both a much higher number of fully polonized young people than almost anywhere else with the possible exception of the Galician cities.[38] Of course, at this stage in the historiography of Polish Jewish life, it hardly bears repeating that linguistic and cultural Polonization did not necessarily connote an embrace of Polishness as national identity, and that indeed this equation became less and less self-evident as the interwar period wore on. But this higher number provided the demographic potential for a far more substantial assimilationist sub-culture than could be imagined in Poland's smaller towns. Equally importantly, Warsaw provided an especially well-developed twofold social and institutional framework to sustain such assimilationist ideals. First, some substantial portion of polonized Jews in interwar Warsaw had been born and raised in an environment unique to Warsaw, Lwów, and few other major Polish cities: a well-established, multi-generationally rooted, and ramified community of fully polonized and deeply assimilationist families for whom full integration into Polish nationhood politically, culturally, and spiritually was the most cherished goal—if not for

---

37   Eliezer Hirshauge, *Troym un farvirklekhung: zikhroynes-fartseykhenungen un bamerkungen vegn der anarkhistisher bavegung in poyln* (Tel Aviv: Zohar, 1953).

38   For a multipronged comparison of assimilation in Warsaw, Kraków and Lwów, and Poland's smaller towns, see Anna Landau-Czajka, *Syn będzie Lech: Asymilacja Żydów w Polsce Międzywojennej* (Warszawa: Wydawnictwo Neriton, 2006), 92, 104, 107–15, esp. 110–13. It should be noted that Czajka-Landau's study, while the most far-reaching and sociologically acute synthetic study of Polish Jewish Polonization and assimilation in the interwar period, is only intermittently attentive to the specifics of interwar assimilation in Warsaw, i.e. does not make the question of the city's local specifics a focus of her study.

themselves, then for their children or grandchildren.[39] Thus, not only did individual assimilationist families imbue a new generation of young Jewish Poles with a (liberal) version of Polish nationalism, but an entire community with its own *habitus* and communal values of " 'Polishness,' 'good manners,' and 'civilized behavior' " provided a supportive framework in which its offspring and (perhaps) newcomers to Polish culture could affirm these values even in the face of rising extrusionist anti-semitism and pointed doubt about the possibility of Jewish-Polish fusion.[40]

Second, Warsaw also provided the resources and sheer population density to sustain a fairly thick array of secondary institutions (youth and scouting organizations, a publishing house, student groups) formally committed to the idea that Jews were or should strive to be full-fledged participants in Polish nationhood. These latter institutions provided a home for relative social newcomers to assimilationism as an ideal, that is, individuals who adopted Polish national identity not as a result of upbringing but due to the influence of the interwar environment—perhaps, as Joseph Lichten suggests, due particularly to the influence of "[t]he Polish schools [that] raised them all in the spirit of Polish patriotism."[41]

The question of how many such newly minted assimilationists there were in interwar Poland—and in a larger sense, of whether assimilationism as an ideal was moribund, on the rise, or something in between—is a question that has periodically spurred sharp debate among scholars and about which much more remains to be written. But it does seem clear that even for Jews who were newcomers to Polishness as an aspiration, interwar Warsaw continued to afford opportunities—or at least the appearance of such opportunities—for more substantial modes of incorporation into Polish-national cultural life than

---

39 On the generational and also gendered dimensions of this, see Landau-Czajka, *Syn bedzie Lech*, 176–93; regarding Warsaw, she notes the continued efforts of wealthier Jewish families in the city to educate their daughters in the style of the nobility, complete with governesses, painting lessons, French, and music training; idem, 185.

40 Celia Stopnick Heller, "Poles of Jewish Background—the Case of Assimilation without Integration in Interwar Poland," in Joshua A. Fishman (ed.), *Shtudyes vegn yidn in poyln 1919–1939/Studies on Polish Jewry 1919–1939* (New York: YIVO Institute for Jewish Research, 1974), 266–70.

41 Joseph Lichten, "Jewish assimilation in Poland," in Chimen Abramsky et al. (eds.), *The Jews in Poland* (Oxford: Basil Blackwell, 1986), 119. Landau-Czajka's findings on the sources of first-generation assimilation in the 1920s and 1930s support this argument regarding the continuing and decisive ideological and cultural impact of Polish "schooling and reading" among Jewish children from non-polonized backgrounds: eadem, *Syn będzie Lech*, 155–56, 172–73.

could be imagined elsewhere. Warsaw was the obvious place for Jews to try to make a career in the metropolitan (hence not "Jewish" and sometimes presumptively "Polish") arts and sciences—and of course numerous musicians, artists, and architects of Jewish background did.[42] As the center of Polish arts and letters, it was also a gathering point for Polish writers, poets, critics, and scholars of Jewish descent whose very participation in the nationalistically valorized project of Polish literature involved an especially intense (though by no means straightforward) relationship to national-cultural Polishness.[43]

Of course, these Polish-using writers and intellectuals negotiated multiple relations to Polishness (itself a contested set of concepts and allegiances, it hardly need be said). Thus, the interwar period's processes of acculturation without assimilation saw a growing subculture (also Warsaw-centered) of Polish-language Jewish writers who specifically insisted on a *Jewish* national identity. More to the point, many of those cultural figures who continued to aspire to unhyphenated Polishness turned toward Communism and other revolutionary eschatologies that promised transcendence of the entire intolerable situation.[44] But as Celia Heller notes and Marci Shore demonstrates, those who joined Warsaw's world of Polish arts and letters may have had much more actual social contact and even intimacy with "members of the Polish intellectual and artistic community even if they were increasingly excluded from its formal organizations."[45]

For those who did not aim to become shapers of Polish culture but did aspire to attain and affirm a Polish national identity, Warsaw offered the aforementioned array of institutions that maintained the ideal and hope of full-fledged national fusion, like the Żagiew and Związek Akademickiej Młodzieży Zjednoczeniowej (ZAMZ) associations for assimilationist students. No doubt thanks to its large Jewish student population in the universities,[46] Warsaw was

---

42 Marian Fuks, *Żydzi w Warszawie: życie codzienne, wydarzenia, ludzie* (Poznań: Sorus, 1992), 342–48.

43 Marci Shore, *Caviar and Ashes* (New Haven, CN: Yale University Press, 2006); Joanna Michlic, "The Culture of Ethno-Nationalism and the Identity of Jews in Inter-War Poland: Some Responses to 'the Aces of Purebred Race,'" in Richard I. Cohen, Jonathan Frankel, and Stefani Hoffman (eds.), *Insiders and Outsiders: Dilemmas of East European Jewry* (Oxford: Littman Library of Jewish Civilization, 2010), 135–37.

44 On the first group, see Eugenia Prokop-Janiec, *Polish Jewish Literature in the Interwar Years* (Syracuse, NY: Syracuse University Press, 2003); on the second and their elective affinity to Communism, see Shore, *Caviar*, passim.

45 Heller, "Poles of Jewish Background," 266.

46 Although many—indeed, most—Polish Jewish university students were not assimilationist, roughly a third of the university students (taken as a single population across major

home to "the most active and largest branch" of the latter association.[47] Joseph Lichten reports that "at one of the Warsaw chapter meetings [of ZAMZ] there were upwards of 400 members," and that the organization offered a range of services including political discussions, the Wiedza organization for education about Polish culture, financial aid for needy students who adhered to assimiliationist goals, and summer retreats.[48] Warsaw also became a center for an evolving socialist wing, aligned with the PPS, within this assimilationist youth.[49] The meetings and journals of these organizations served as sites for vigorous critiques of Zionism, contact with sympathetic ethnic Poles, and affirmations of these circles' status as an "avant-garde of Jewish-Polish solidarity."[50] More generally, some sources (though not all) suggest that parts of Polish society in Warsaw remained more open to fully integrating individual polonized Jews into their civic organizations than even other sites of large-scale and precocious Polonization, like Kraków and Lwów.[51] In sum, it seems that insofar as aspirations to full-fledged Polishness remained possible in the eyes of interwar Jews, Warsaw contained far greater demographic, institutional, and social resources among both long-standing Jewish residents and aspiring newcomers than almost anywhere else.

Another factor to consider in this light, linked more to the specifically economic and career opportunities of the capital city than to any ideological formation of Polishness, is how Warsaw may have sustained a distinctive culture of Jewish *personal* aspiration toward upward mobility. More than any provincial town, Warsaw seems to have projected a sense of the possibilities open to a person of talent, despite anti-Semitism. Yisrael Oppenheim suggests that this sense that individual advancement was possible in Warsaw, regardless of the general Jewish condition, was one of the reasons that He-halutz was relatively weak in Warsaw in comparison to its popularity among declassed young Jews in smaller towns.[52] Although this aspiration to advancement in "the big city" had nothing to do necessarily with embracing Polishness as a national identity,

---

urban centers) who gave their religion as Jewish did not identify themselves as Jewish by nationality in the early 1930s. Andrzej Pilch, *Studencki Ruch Polityczny w Polsce w Latach 1932–1939* (Warszawa: Państwowe Wydawnictwo Naukowe, 1972), 145.

47 Miri Freilich, "Irgun ha-mitbolelim 'Zjednoczenie' be-polin," *Gal-Ed* 14 (1995): 103.
48 Ibid., and Lichten, "Jewish assimilation in Poland," 119.
49 Freilich, "Irgun ha-mitbolelim 'Zjednoczenie'," 100–3.
50 Ibid., 102.
51 Stanisław Krzesicki, cited in Landau-Czajka, *Syn będzie Lech*, 111. But Landau-Czajka also cites sources that stress exclusion rather than inclusion: see ibid., 105.
52 Yisrael Oppenheim, *Tenuat he-halutz be-polin (1917–1929)* (Jerusalem: Magnes Press, 1982), 453.

we may presume that on the whole it would have weighed against a choice of an active Jewish nationalist "exit" and made for a greater openness to assimilationist and integrationist ideals.

Second, and perhaps a more effective counterforce to Jewish nationalism, were the revolutionary socialist subcultures in interwar Jewish Warsaw, whether Bundist, Communist, anarchist, or PPS-affiliated.[53] In the course of the interwar period, these movements built "alternative cultures" on the model of the 19th-century German socialists—self-contained worlds of movement-framed association. For our purposes, what is significant is how these alternative cultures worked to actively counter Jewish nationalism. It is true, of course, that both the Bundists and the Communists accepted certain dimensions of Jewish national sensibility. But both movements, as well as the anarchists, sharply rejected political nationalism. both Polish and Jewish.[54] In the memoirs of one Yoynesn Grinboym we find a perfect embodiment of this dual anti-nationalism: a polonized youth who had started out in the left-Zionist Ha-shomer ha-tsair movement, he became active in an underground Communist organization among Jewish high-school students that fought both Jewish and Polish nationalism. In 1928, his organization helped disrupt the mandated participation of Jewish students in Warsaw's grand celebration of the state's 10th anniversary of Pilsudski. Barring the exits of a Warsaw Jewish girls' school, the organizers lectured the young girls against Pilsudski's "fascism" and Poland's anti-Soviet stance; and the only specifically Jewish issue mentioned was the numerus clausus.[55]

Furthermore, the sheer size and institutional ramification that these sorts of revolutionary subcultures could attain in Warsaw allowed revolutionaries to give *substance* to their promise of a world beyond nationalism. Unlike in

---

53 Oppenheim suggests that the flip-side of the promise of economic advancement in the more developed capitalist economy of Warsaw was, naturally, the greater purchase of socialist critiques of capitalism there. Ibid. Ezra Mendelsohn notes that *Zionism* too in Warsaw was particularly and disproportionately open to socialist currents, which supports this as-yet undeveloped social-historical account. Ezra Mendelsohn, *Zionism in Poland: The Formative Years 1915–1926* (New Haven, CN: Yale University Press, 1981), 284, 290–91.

54 Yosef Gorni, *Converging Alternatives* (New York: SUNY Press, 2006), 85–114, 141–74; Polonsky, "The Bund in Polish Political Life," 553–54; Jaff Schatz, *The Generation: The Rise and Fall of the Jewish Communists of Poland* (Berkeley: University of California Press, 1991), 101, 125–27.

55 Yoynesn Grinboym, "Mayne zikhroynes vegn der varshever yidisher yugnt," in *Pinkes varshe* (Buenos-Aires: Landslayt-farayn fun varshe un umgegnt in argentine and IKUF, 1955), 449–50.

a smaller town, these ideologies could represent themselves in Warsaw not as mere utopianism, but as realities in the making. Jack Jacobs' recent study *Bundist Counterculture in Interwar Poland* identifies several distinct sites of visible Bundist culture in the city that, taken together, comprised precisely what his well-chosen titular term suggests: a full-fledged counterculture in which individuals could find daily affirmation of their insurgent visions. In particular, Warsaw was home to Poland's largest branch of the Bund's youth movement Tsukunft, which hovered between 800 and 1500 members throughout the 1920s and early 1930s. Similar numbers and a similarly disproportionate size relative to other centers seem to have characterized the Warsaw branch of the Bund's Morgnshtern sports-club.[56] And the Bund could call impressive numbers of supporters into the streets: in 1928, the city hosted a funeral procession for Bundist leader Beynish Mikhalevitsh which the Warsaw correspondent for the socialist-Zionist Palestinian Jewish paper *Davar* described as being on a scale never seen before in Warsaw Jewish life.[57] The profound impression of Bundist strength that these Warsaw manifestations made on observers is thrown into sharper relief still when we recall that in these same years, the Bund remained weak on the national level.[58]

Third, Warsaw remained a center of organized orthodox and specifically Hasidic opposition to Jewish nationalism in its organized and declaredly modern forms. Unfortunately, the paucity of properly social-historical research on orthodox Jewry in Warsaw renders it impossible at this stage to offer a full account of the way such opposition or blunting might have operated (or, conversely, proven porous) at the *everyday* level: we need to know much more about the inner workings and boundedness of the community (or, more likely, communities), the degree of social control exerted by various orthodox and Hasidic leaders in the city, and what various degrees of orthodoxy really entailed. Even the raw numerical strength of observant Jews in the city is unclear—a recent piece of innovative work by Asaf Kaniel on consumption of kosher meat suggests that by the late 1930s, 25% of the Warsaw Jewish population remained committed to the observance of this decisive practice,[59] but there is little reason to assume that that data can tell us how many Warsaw

---

56 Jack Jacobs, *Bundist Counterculture in Interwar Poland* (Syracuse, NY: Syracuse University Press, 2006), 17, 60, 115 n. 42.
57 "Mikhtav be-polin," *Davar*, 27 November 1928 (see above, n. 35).
58 My thanks to the editors for noting this last point.
59 Asaf Kaniel, "Bein hilonim, masortiim ve-ortodoksim: shmirat mitzvoth be-re'i ha-hitmodedut 'im 'gezerat ha-kashrut,' 1937–1939," *Gal-Ed* 22 (2010): 95, 105–6.

Jews adhered to the ideological anti-nationalism that characterized much (though not all) pre-war orthodox Jewish political-religious thought.[60]

Still, scholarly and primary sources on the political and intellectual history of Orthodox leadership strata in interwar Warsaw allow for some preliminary account of at least several sites of Orthodox dissent or insulation from the claims of Jewish nationalism there. The newly emergent traditionalist political party Agudes yisroel (Agudat Israel), which hewed a complicated relationship to Jewish nationalism and Zionism in practice but remained publicly opposed to Jewish political nationalism,[61] was a dominant force in the Jewish communal political sphere of interwar Warsaw.[62] There it negotiated a variety of relationships with the local Jewish nationalist political movements, but also proved able to confront them with a successful, new brand of religious mass politics. A bitter 1921 campaign against the appointment of a non-orthodox rabbi to the Warsaw rabbinate marked the beginnings of a new kind of orthodox mass politics in Warsaw in which, as Gershon Bacon puts it, the Agudah "took its protests to the synagogues, study houses, and streets of Warsaw;" the culmination was an unprecedented mass demonstration of fifteen to twenty thousand Hasidim in front of the Gmina building.[63] Two years later, another angry crowd, whipped up by Agudah activists under the leadership of the influential Ger Hasidic scholar-rabbi-political leader Menachem Zemba, stormed the Gmina building, smashed furniture, and defaced portraits to protest the

---

60   Ehud Luz, *Parallels Meet* (Philadelphia, PA: Jewish Publication Society, 1988); Joseph Goldstein, "The Beginnings of the Zionist Movement in Congress Poland: the Victory of the Hasidim over the Zionists?" *Polin* 5 (1990): 114–30.

61   Here too, there is scholarly disagreement and uncertainty, born both of the fact that Agudah leaders and spokesmen articulated a variety of views about nationalism and Zionism—ranging from total ideologically ramified rejection on one extreme to partial adoption of the terms of modern nationalism on the other—and of the fact that it is not clear whether neutral or positive Agudah uses of nationalist terminology should be seen as "identification with those nationalist perspectives, [...] a practical outlook on which way the wind was blowing on the 'Jewish street,' or merely lip service." See Gershon Bacon, "Ha-yahadut ha-ortodoksit be-polin ve-rusiah, 1850–1939" in Yisrael Bartal and Yisrael Gutman (eds.), *Kiyyum ve-shever: yehudei polin le-doroteihem*, vol. 2: *Hevrah, tarbut, le'umiut* (Jerusalem: Merkaz Zalman Shazar, 2001), 480; and see Yosef Fund, *Pirud o hishtatfut: agudah yisrael mul ha-tsionut u-medinat yisrael* (Jerusalem: Magnes, 1999), 22–30, 79, 92–102.

62   Bacon, "Ha-yahadut," 470.

63   Gershon C. Bacon, "The Poznanski Affair of 1921: Kehillah Politics and the Internal Political Realignment of Polish Jewry," in Jonathan Frankel et al. (eds.), *The Jews and the European Crisis, 1914–1921* (Studies in Contemporary Jewry 4; New York: Oxford University Press, 1988), 139.

community council's plans to build a dormitory for Warsaw Jewish university students—"a house of debauchery"—on community land claimed by the Orthodox for religious uses.[64]

Over time, Warsaw's Orthodox elements found less visible but more effective modes of political organization rooted in the robust network of religious and educational institutions developed by that sector of the community. In his account of the hotly contested Warsaw Jewish communal elections of 1931, Alexander Guterman notes that while the Zionists addressed their political efforts to public spaces like packed auditoria, the Agudah forces felt less need to arrange such public meetings because they had established lines of communication with "their voters" in " 'heders,' study-houses, and the educational and charitable institutions under their aegis."[65]

In turn, Guterman's insight points us toward an as-yet not fully reconstructed spatial and institutional sociology both of Orthodox political power in Jewish Warsaw and of the ways in which Warsaw Orthodoxy developed specific institutional and cultural means to protect its normatively most important element—men who were able to study—from the attractions of other ways of thinking like Jewish nationalism. A first step toward reconstructing this sociology can be taken on the basis of the acute memoir-cum-historical essays of Avraham Zemba.[66] Nephew of the aforementioned Menachem Zemba, Avraham was an activist in Warsaw Hasidic social, religious, and political life throughout the interwar years who devoted himself in particular to the ideological mobilization and monitoring of Hasidic young men. Zemba's participant-observer essays suggest that one of the key bulwarks of Orthodoxy and Orthodox resistance to secular nationalist ideals in interwar Warsaw was a barely visible (because informal) but massive network of Hasidic *shtiblekh*— unofficial houses of prayer and study linked to particular Hasidic groups—in which, by his account, thousands of Hasidic men devoted themselves to full-time study in their late adolescence and ongoing part-time study thereafter.[67]

---

64 Michal Majewski, "Budowa Żydowskiego Domu Akademickiego w Warszawie," in August Grabski and Artur Markowski (eds.), *Narody i Polityka: Studia ofiarowane Profesorowi Jerzemu Tomaszewskiemu* (Warszawa: ŻIH and Instytut Historyczny UW, 2010), 95.

65 Guterman, *Kehilat varshah*, 284–85.

66 Ha-rav Avraham Zemba, " 'Shtiblakh' be-varshah," and " 'Metivta' be-varshah" in Shmuel Mirski (ed.), *Mosadot torah be-eiropah be-binyanam u-ve-hurbanam* (New York: Hotsaat Ogen, 1956), 355–61 and 363–80. I owe these references to Shaul Stampfer's important essay "Hasidic Yeshivas in Interwar Poland," in idem, *Families, Rabbis, and Education* (Oxford and Portland, OR: Littman Library of Jewish Civilization, 2010), 252–74.

67 Though Zemba acknowledges that no hard data exists about these *shtiblekh* (because they were not officially licensed etc. by state, municipality, or, it seems, the Jewish

Located both throughout Warsaw's main Jewish neighborhood (Zemba names sites from Nalewki, Zamenhofa, and Franciszkańska down to Twarda and Pańska) and in other districts of the city from Praga to Wola, Mokotów, and Ochota, these *shtiblekh* in Zemba's telling allowed for especially effective forms of organizational and ideological mobilization among Hasidic young men in the face of what Zemba acknowledges to have been an ideological crisis among Hasidic youth across Poland. Tracing this crisis to the First World War, Zemba recalls that both "socialism with its promises of happiness tomorrow" and "the secular-nationalist groups" buoyed by the Balfour Declaration cut a wide swath among Orthodox young people, who joined in the general "drunkenness from the wealth of new ideas and hopes" and began to defect from the strict frameworks of Hasidic traditionalism.[68] As Shaul Stampfer has observed in a groundbreaking article, one of the most visible effects of this crisis was the sudden proliferation of Hasidic yeshivot (formal institutions of Talmudic study) in Poland immediately following the First World War: as challenges to traditional religious commitment rose to crisis levels, parents could no longer rely on older patterns of study in the local study house and instead eagerly sought educational institutions where young men would be insulated from the secular world.[69] But in Zemba's telling, Warsaw's network of *shtiblekh* proved even more effective than these yeshivot.

One signal difference to which Zemba accords special import was the fact that whereas students eventually left the yeshivot and had to make a new life for themselves elsewhere, there was no such interruption in the intellectual and social life of Hasidic young men in Warsaw, who could continue regular and even daily study in their chosen *shtibl* even after entering the working world. By the same token, each *shtibl* concentrated both young men studying full-time and older male members of the traditionalist community who served as models, guides, and perhaps monitors for the younger students in their transition to adulthood and the dangers of the workaday world.

More generally, Warsaw's *shtiblekh* were not Hasidic in name only, but served in Zemba's telling as sites for vigorous reinforcement of each particular

---

community structure), he contends that they numbered in the "thousands" and ranged in size from a few students to much larger concentrations like the "three hundred" who studied in the Gerer *shtibl* on Nalewki. As a point of comparison, he also contends that the number of students in such unrecognized study houses substantially outweighed the number of students in Warsaw's growing network of formally recognized institutions for advanced religious education. Zemba, "'Shtiblakh,'" 359, 355.

68 Ibid, 364.
69 Stampfer, "Hasidic Yeshivas."

Hasidic subculture. Alongside the standard Talmud study, Hasidic books both classic and recent, from the *Kedushat levi* to the Gerer *Sfat emet* or the Aleksander *Yismakh yisrael* were a central part of the curriculum that enjoyed, in Zemba's view, "a tremendous influence" on the piety of the young men in the *shtiblekh*.[70] The Hasidic practice of fairly regular pilgrimage to one's *rebbe* not only ensured that individual students would regularly reaffirm their ties to the *edah,* but also shaped the culture and calendar of the *shtiblekh*: preparation for such pilgrimages became an important focus of everyday life and group consciousness in the *shtiblekh* virtually year-round.[71]

It was in this context of intense daily piety and mutual reinforcement that Warsaw's *shtiblekh* functioned, according to Zemba, as especially important sites for Orthodox political mobilization against secular groups and ideas. Taken collectively, these *shtiblekh* produced a committed and intellectually acute Orthodox activist intelligentsia in Warsaw of incomparable size: "[...] year after year, these Warsaw *shtiblekh* would turn out hundreds of Torah youth, pious and God-fearing, armed with the weapon of the Torah, Hasidic enthusiasm, and a deep Hasidic worldview, ready for the trials/temptations of life in all their forms."[72] More particularly, young men affiliated with the *shtiblekh* played a special role in Orthodox political mobilization in the city, serving in Zemba's words as a pillar of "the political struggle that Orthodoxy conducted [...] in those days of great struggle for the souls of the voters, when the question arose, who will represent the half-million Jews of Warsaw in the Polish Sejm, pious Jews or freethinkers? Or who will rule over Warsaw's community boards [...]?"[73]

At the same time, *shtibl*-educated youth also played a special role in the ongoing everyday cultural-political struggle to shield Warsaw's Orthodox youth from the seductions of non-traditional values. Given the virtually unchallenged normative value accorded by interwar Polish Orthodoxy to the sorts of religious knowledge and scholarly ability to which study in the *shtiblekh* provided access, graduates of the *shtiblekh* naturally claimed positions of authority among the broad circles of Orthodox Jewish young people who did not have access to such an education, not least for reasons of economic necessity. Zemba notes that activists from the *shtiblekh* made special efforts to serve as teachers and mentors among the working young people who joined the Agudes yisroel

---

70   Zemba, "'Shtiblakh,'" 358, 356.
71   Ibid., 357–58.
72   Ibid., 358.
73   Ibid., 358–59.

youth movement "Tseirei agudes yisroel."⁷⁴ That they did so "according to the recommendation of Agudes Yisroel's council of *rebbeim*" suggests a degree of centralized coordination across the many individual *shtiblekh*.⁷⁵ In serving as mentors and teachers, who might present a lesson in "Talmud, ethical teachings, and Hasidism" at evening or Sabbath meetings, these *shtibl*-trained activists also functioned as ideological monitors: "[....] They kept an eye on those young people who would devote themselves too fully to politics and thus forget the true purpose for which such Orthodox institutions had been created. In the last years before the *Shoah*, the study house regulars created a special section within Tseirei agudes yisroel that fought with elements in the organization that devoted their entire attention to politics [...]."⁷⁶ Zemba lists some dozen individuals from a half dozen *shtiblekh* who emerged as especially important "leaders and orators" with great "psychological and pedagogical talents who were able to influence and attract great masses of youth."⁷⁷

The political-cultural significance of Warsaw's *shtiblekh*, taken both individually and as a network, was linked in turn to a larger process whereby the dangers to Orthodoxy presented by city life were increasingly outweighed by the benefits of demographic size and concentration of Orthodox Jews and Orthodox institutions that the capital could provide. Zemba's memoiristic essays echo the widely attested view that in the era of the First World War, socialist and secular nationalist ideas penetrated even the smallest and most insular Jewish towns so dramatically that the advantages of small-town life for the reproduction of religious orthodoxy (not least communal monitoring and sanction) evaporated. Just as this development convinced Hasidic parents to approve of sending their kids away to yeshivot, where they would be surrounded (it was hoped) by the like-minded, it also convinced them that the small town was no better than the big city and maybe worse, Zemba suggests—and Warsaw already boasted a great concentration of Hasidim even before its religious leaders took such high-profile steps as the creation in 1919 of a centralized yeshiva known generally as the *mesivta* of Warsaw.⁷⁸ At the

---

74 Cf. Gershon C. Bacon, *The Politics of Tradition: Agudat Yisrael in Poland, 1916–1939* (Jerusalem: The Magnes Press, 1996), 127–31.
75 Zemba, "'Shtiblakh'", 359.
76 Ibid. On the perceived danger presented by Orthodoxy's political successes no less than by its failures, namely, the seductions of Orthodox political involvement itself, see Bacon, *The Politics of Tradition*, 61, 96–99.
77 Zemba, "'Shtiblakh'", 360.
78 In this respect, the case of interwar Warsaw as presented by Zemba suggests at least a partial reversal of a mid-19th-century process recently reconstructed by Glenn Dynner in his "Hasidism and Habitat" (see n. 3). Examining the views of leading Polish Jewish *tzaddikim*

same time, Zemba suggests, growing numbers of religious leaders themselves converged on the capital in the interwar period, drawing after them growing circles of young scholars who specifically sought them out. Their homes came to serve in turn as additional social sites for ideologically committed Orthodox youth and thus, like the *shtiblekh*, nodes sustaining a Hasidic alternative to secular modernity.[79]

In short, even as Warsaw offered a unique space for Jewish nationalist activism and its public staging, so too did the city offer a virtually unparalleled concentration of Orthodox institutions, talent, and commitment that together allowed the flourishing of robust resistance or indifference to secular values, including Jewish nationalism. Having said all this that, however, the interwar period in Warsaw also saw some countervailing developments. Warsaw seems to have been a center for grass-roots Hasidic *moderation* on the question of Jewish territorialization and self-determination in Palestine particularly, as we shall see below.

Fourth, and finally, there is a more amorphous factor that ought to be considered: some sources suggest that, ironically, the self-contained and thickly Jewish settlement sustained by Warsaw seems to have worked to *blunt* the sort of inter-ethnic experience that scholars have identified as among the most important factors generating national consciousness in minority groups.[80] Lower-class Warsaw Jews in particular seem to have had far fewer opportunities to interact with non-Jewish Poles socially (leaving aside the criminal underclass, where there was perhaps much *more* interethnic contact). This factor intersected nicely with the city's socialist subculture: for some Jews,

---

across the 19th century regarding the prospects for proper religious life in village, city, and shtetl settings, Dynner underscores the inability of Hasidic communities to fully overcome the religious dangers of city life and a concomitant choice by "the vast majority of aspiring Polish *tzaddikim*" to locate their courts in small towns (this included such already-established major figures as the *Gerer* rebbe R. Yitshok Meir Alter who left Warsaw for the small town of Ger *after* becoming a rebbe in his own right); Dynner, "Hasidism and Habitat," 116, 111. Dynner convincingly attributes this choice to a threefold political-religious calculus that saw in the shtetl something that could not be achieved in the city: domination of the entire Jewish community, the possibility of avoiding interaction with acculturated Jews, and easier boundary-maintenance between Jews and non-Jews; ibid., 118, 110. The process traced by Zemba represents only a partial reversal of this process: not the return of Hasidic leaders to the city but rather the collapse of Hasidic assumptions about the normative security afforded by the shtetl, a point that accords as well with Stampfer, "Hasidic Yeshivas."

79   Zemba, "'Metivta,'" 366–67.
80   Cf. Landau-Czajka, *Syn będzie Lech*, 113, and sources cited there.

Warsaw was a space in which discontent with one's economic lot translated experientially into a vague anti-state sensibility coupled with sharp antagonism to middle-class Jewish neighbors. When the aforementioned memoir by Zonshayn turns to Zamenhof street, it depicts a Jewish bourgeois artery crosscut by poorer side-streets like Miła, Wolińska, and Niska, from which angry Jewish proletarians would periodically pour forth to demonstrate against "the *burzhoyen*."[81] A study of Jewish Communism in interwar Poland notes a related phenomenon: many new Jewish recruits to Communism were drawn from youth who arrived in Warsaw as labor migrants. Given that they most likely sought work in Jewish niches, they would have experienced the city in ways that resonated above all with ideologies of class conflict *within* Jewish society.[82]

That Jewish national consciousness was positively correlated to a heightened interaction between Jews and non-Jewish Varsovians, and conversely blunted for those Warsaw Jews who were *most* embedded in intra-Jewish settings ridden by class tensions, is further supported by the converse phenomenon. Evidence suggests that one of the reasons for *greater* Jewish-nationalist sensibility among what contemporaries called "bourgeois" Jewish circles was that those circles had *more* opportunity to interact with ethnic Poles, and thus to experience anti-Jewish animus directly. The memoirs of the journalist Yitshok Borenshteyn relate that the Warsaw Opera became a site of bitter confrontation between Jews and Poles when the famous tenor Ignacy Dygas played the Jewish father Eliezer in the Warsaw Opera's production of Jacques Halévy's "La Juive" (Żydówka). Dygas—by Borenshteyn's account a "fanatic" anti-semite—took the opportunity to play the role as a caricature stage-Jew. According to Borenshteyn, this angered the Jews in the gallery seats, drew great applause from "the goyim" in the parterre below and loge seats above, sparked a coordinated Jewish on-site demonstration three days later which included Jewish members of the orchestra, and elicited bitter shouting matches between Poles and Jews. One can only assume that the Jewish audience at the opera house was, crudely speaking, largely bourgeois. Borenshteyn's fascinating portrait of the opera house as a setting of routine ethnic self-segregation but potential interethnic conflict suggests the value of studying similar public spaces of sustained Jewish-Polish proximity and interaction.[83]

---

81 Zonshayn, *Yidish-varshe*, 44.
82 Schatz, *The Generation*, 62–63.
83 Borenshteyn, *Varshe*, 39–40. Of course, for circles who made conscious efforts to find sympathetic and anti-anti-semitic interlocutors or comrades—like active assimilationists or anarchists—the effects of interaction with (carefully selected) non-Jewish

These sources point to the need for more research on the differential effects of various spatial arrangements on ideology and self-identity in Warsaw or, in more agency-centered terms, on how individuals could organize their own spatial agendas in the city to accord with their ideological agendas. Thus, to return to the memoirs of the Warsaw Hasid-turned-anarchist Hirshauge, the reader is struck by the sheer number and succession of spaces in which Hirshauge was able to insulate himself from the problem of national identity that loomed so large for so many of his contemporaries. Hirshauge's initial crisis of faith took place in the sequestered Hasidic spatial subculture described above, the "*sharfe shtiblekh*" of Warsaw's " 'secondary courtyard[s].' "[84] Here, the problem of Jewishness was a problem of belief and unbelief, not a problem of Jews and Poles: Hirshauge's anarchism began as an anti-religious turn mediated by the classic work of anarchism as a simultaneously theological and political revolt against authority, Bakunin's *God and the State*; and he contends that this was true of a whole stratum of his fellow Hasidic youths.[85] Troubled by unorthodox doubts, Hirshauge began to seek out fellow doubters in an unexpected space: he began to take long walks in ethnically *Polish* neighborhoods where he could immediately identify any other "long-coated, ear-locked" young men as fellow agonized "seekers of truth."[86] A third space hosted a next stage in the evolution of such seekers' religio-political underground culture: the library of "the Great Synagogue," where visitors could read in shifts from 4:00 to 6:00 and 6:00 to 8:00, and where Hirshauge could always find "more than a *minyan* [a quorum of ten] of young, male 'God-seekers' studying anarchist works."[87] Eventually, Hirshauge and two fellow Hasidic "seekers" found a veteran Jewish anarchist, the aging Hebrew gymnasium teacher and long-time anarchist Arn Pinchas Gros, to lead them through the canon of 19th-century radical thought; this took place in a fourth insulated space, Wednesday instructional meetings at Gros' apartment. Through Gros, Hirshauge and his friends began to meet other anarchists and syndicalists of different background (though all, apparently, Jewish) for whom the movement was primarily a political-economic one rather than a revolt against religion.[88] Finally, as they made the transition to this primarily sociopolitical anarchism, they began to visit a fifth space: the syndicalist *berze*

---

        interlocutors could be just the opposite: a confirmation that one's aspiration to transcend either Jewishness or nationality as such were not delusory.

84   Hirshauge, *Troym*, 11.
85   Ibid., 7–9.
86   Ibid., 12.
87   Ibid., 13. Presumably he means the Główna Biblioteka Judaistyczna, which abutted the Great Synagogue.
88   Ibid., 17–21, 26–37.

or open-air meeting site at Leszno Street between Bankowa and Orla streets in the evening.[89] Although he and his friends were now tasked with distributing *Walka Klas*, the newspaper of the Anarchistyczna Federacja Polski (AFP), it is not clear when Hirshauge actually learned Polish or began to meet any actual non-Jewish Poles. And when he did, the Poles in question seem to have been either police and other members of the hated state or fellow anarchists, whose comradely relations with their Jewish counterparts remained an article of faith for Hirshauge well after the Holocaust.[90] Although Hirshauge eventually encountered Polish Jewry's "national question" (he notes that "in our circles it was an ideational duty to learn [Esperanto]"),[91] he seems to have done so only well after he had become a fully committed anarchist with ready answers to its challenges. What is important here is that the attainment of this unshakeable anarchist consciousness seems to have had much to do with the ways in which Warsaw's diverse spaces allowed for a paradoxically purely intra-Jewish process of self-education in which, at every stage, Hirshauge was able to essentially ignore the national question.[92]

Finally, thinking in terms of Warsaw as a specific sort of political space, we can return to the question of Jewish engagement with *Polish* national identity in the capital. In terms of its particular assimilationist subculture, Warsaw naturally also served as a particularly important center for organized assimiliationist political-cultural activism in the interwar period. Alongside Lwów, Warsaw was both the institutional and social center of organized "neo-assimilationist" sociopolitical endeavor in that period, as embodied in the Żagiew and ZAMZ assimilationist and anti-Jewish-nationalist scouting and academic-youth organizations. These and similar organizations hewed a complex and evolving relationship to the question of nationhood, but evidently continued to advocate a full-fledged Polish nationality for Jews predicated on an unalloyed devotion to Polish culture, the Polish state and national community.[93]

---

89 Ibid., 38–42.
90 Ibid., 38.
91 An invented language constructed by the Russo-Polish Jewish doctor and linguist L.L. Zamenhof. Although there is no sustained study of the place of Esperanto in interwar Polish Jewish culture, many sources suggest (as does this one) that its study was strongly associated with revolutionary-left leanings. Cf. one of the youth autobiographies in Jeffrey Shandler (ed.), *Awakening Lives: Autobiographies of Jewish Youth in Poland before the Holocaust* (New Haven, CN: Yale University Press, 2002), 93, 95, 108.
92 Cf. Dynner, "Hasidism and Habitat," 110–111.
93 Lichten, "Jewish assimilation in Poland," 108–9, 118, 122–24; see esp. 123 for discussion of some evolution in how these circles addressed the persistence of Jewish "community" within the framework of a supra-ethnic but wholly Polish-national-cultural nationality.

Furthermore, Jewish engagement with Polish nationhood in Warsaw may have gone well beyond the circles of committed assimilationists. Interwar Warsaw was a center of Endek anti-Semitic nationalist agitation, which could only drive Jews toward greater self-consciousness about their national difference. But it was also the center of the state's official national cult, and Jews of every background were drawn en masse into this cult at least at major ritual junctures. Thus, the city's Jewish communal institutions participated en masse in the Warsaw's 1928 Polish independence celebrations, with special emphasis laid on the participation of children.[94]

Of course, from the fact of such participation it does not follow that the participants were meaningfully and lastingly transformed into Polish nationalists, much less that their participation demonstrated a preexisting Polish-national consciousness. Jews had all sorts of practical reasons to participate demonstratively in patriotic events such as the 10th anniversary of independence or Josef Pilsudski's birthday.[95] But it is worth asking whether the presence and splendor of the Sanacja's (officially non-antisemitic) nationalism on streets of Warsaw made it possible for a substantial number of the city's Jews to imagine themselves as Poles in national terms, at least at particular junctures. Certainly, there is reason to think that at least in 1926–1927, Warsaw was a particularly strong site of the brief but powerful buoying of hopes for genuine Jewish incorporation into a multiethnic Polish political nation following Pilsudski's coup from the center.[96] But even after the deflation of the May 1926 hopes, there are good reasons to imagine that both the particular sociology of Warsaw's

---

94 B-i, "Eikh hagagah varsha ha-yehudit et hag polin," *Davar*, 4 December 1928.

95 And even more so his funeral: it is suggestive that proclamations addressed to the Jewish population of Tomaszów Lubelski by the community leadership regarding a day of mourning for the Marshal demanded that "the entire Jewish population" take part in a public procession and not only forbade laughter or bad behavior but also forbade Jews from watching passively from "the sidewalks, windows, and balconies." "Yuden birger!" and "Obywatele Żydzi!," YIVO Archives, Poland Collection, RG 28, f. 375. The rather practical, defensive concerns framing this manifestation of patriotism are only implicit. More explicit is a 1933 Yiddish-language communiqué from the Jewish community council of Tomaszów Mazowiecki warning local Jews to contribute to a national loan campaign because "in the circles of the local government organs there is powerful anger against those citizens who have promised nothing or little for the national loan" and "there is a tendency to direct consequences against those persons who have not properly fulfilled their civic duty." "Tsu der higer yudisher befelkerung!," YIVO Archives, Poland Collection, RG 28, f. 377.

96 Landau, "Hafikhat Mei 1926—tsipiot be-yahadut polin le-tmurah medinit be-tahalikh hit-badutan," *Gal-Ed* 2 (1975): 255–64, esp. 258.

Jewish community and the particular significance of Warsaw as the center of Polish nationhood's self-representation allowed for serious Jewish imaginative engagement with Polishness as a national identity. In 1928, a *Davar* correspondent complained that Jewish spokesmen of all stripes were going beyond requisite demonstrations of Jewish civic loyalty and instead casting Jews as members of the Polish nation.[97]

Even if we leave aside the pertinent question of whether such belief or investment can really be measured or indeed whether belief is a useful category for thinking about the performance of nationhood, we can point to concrete ways in which Jews in Warsaw could publicly *insist* on their place in the national cult. Once again, Hirshauge's anarchist memoir captures this reality with the amusing but revealing story of the 1936 funeral of an old revolutionary named Moyshe Koyfman ("Moyshl Mezritsher"). As a young man, Koyfman had joined the PPS' Jewish section. Later activities as an agitator on the borderline of anarchism and Communism, both illegal, earned him arrest by the new Polish state. But because the former Tsarist regime had punished him for his PPS membership years earlier, he had received from that same Polish state a decoration as a former Polish political arrestee. This he wore on his lapel, and he maintained membership in the organization of former Polish arrestees, "to which, incidentally, there belonged the former fighters for Poland's independence of all streams." When Koyfman died in 1936, Communists claimed his body and arranged a funeral procession into Warsaw with the corpse clothed in the hammer and sickle. But in Warsaw, his coffin was seized by what Hirshauge describes generally as an organization for former Polish-national political prisoners (presumably the PPS-affiliated Stowarzyszenie or Związek byłych Więźniów Politycznych) aided by the police, and Koyfman was conducted to a Jewish burial under the banner of the organization. Members of an anarchist organization, who also claimed Koyfman as theirs, joined the procession closely watched by police. The final act came when Koyfman, an uneducated man who had never learned to speak Polish properly, was eulogized as a "Polish patriot."[98] At the risk of generalizing from a story so richly weird, it seems that such ironclad claims on national inclusion in the Polish national political cult for Jewish individuals were more common, hence more visible and publicly meaningful, in Warsaw simply by dint of the higher proportion of Jews there who had, like Koyfman, played a role in pre-independence Polish socialist-nationalist endeavor.

---

97   B-i, "Eikh hagagah varsha."
98   Hirshauge, *Troym*, 23–26.

Jewish Nationalism and Zionism between Subculture and Shared Horizon

Thus, on the one hand, Jewish nationalism enjoyed a visibility in interwar Warsaw that was perhaps unequalled anywhere in Europe. But on the other hand, it did not command the streets and dominate public political culture in the way that it did in Tel Aviv, or in the way that religious Orthodoxy once commanded the streets of Polish Jewish towns and neighborhoods, or Jewish socialism the streets of early twentieth-century Jewish New York.[99] And this evidently became more rather than less the case as the interwar period wore on.

Both the general Zionist movement and the Folks-partey suffered dramatic declines in the latter half of 1920s. The collapse of the Folkists as a political movement was permanent, and since its support had been overwhelmingly Warsaw-centered to begin with, its decline was by definition a Warsaw-centered phenomenon.[100] In the case of the Polish Zionist organization, the downturn was not nearly as total or permanent. 1926–1927 was a moment of unprecedented crisis: the number of Polish Jews who bought the *shekel* to attain membership in the Zionist organization dropped from 110,000 to a mere 10,670; there was a wave of bitter recrimination by several thousand returnees from Palestine ("*yordim*"); there was a general collapse of Zionist activity; and there were widespread reports of a general backlash against Zionism's inflated promises among Polish Jews even in the movement's traditional centers.[101] This precipitous reversal played out quite visibly in Warsaw too, where, for instance, a mock trial of "*yordim*" turned into a forum for public expressions of bitter disappointment toward organized Zionism.[102] Even after the crisis of 1926–27 abated and the early 1930s brought a substantial turnabout in public attitudes toward the Zionist project and its relevance for Polish Jews, the local mainstream Zionist organization never fully recovered. But by 1928, the worst was over, and the early 1930s brought a substantial recovery in the fortunes of Polish Zionism; thus, in the 1930 Sejm elections, the Zionists managed to beat both the Agudah and the Bund in Warsaw,[103] and the early 1930s saw explosive

---

99   See Tony Michels' incisive portrait of the latter public dominance in idem, *A Fire in Their Hearts: Yiddish Socialists in New York* (Cambridge, MA: Harvard University Press, 2005).

100 Kalman Weiser, "Folkists," YIVO *Encyclopedia of Jews in Eastern Europe*, 1: 520–21.

101 Oppenheim, *Tenuat he-halutz be-polin (1917–1929)*, 379–409.

102 Ibid., 394–95.

103 Jolanta Żyndul, "Rzeczpospolita," in *Atlas Historii Żydów Polskich* (Warszawa: Demart, 2010), 264. My thanks to Dr. Michał Fedoryński, a dear family friend, who included this impressive atlas in his steady stream of gifts from the burgeoning world of Polish Judaica.

growth in the He-halutz pioneer movement and in Revisionist Zionism (see below).

Nevertheless, the mainstream organization (itself split between the two quarreling 'Al ha-mishmar and 'Et livnot movements) never regained its early 1920s strength.[104] Because Warsaw remained the national center of Polish Zionism, this anemia seems to have been widely felt among Zionists there. As the Warsaw activist Mojżesz Polakiewicz put it in a frank letter in May 1932 (at a relative high-point in post-1925 Polish Zionist fortunes), "it's now generally a difficult time for the Zionist Organization in Poland. From one side—the poverty and despondency of the Polish Jews, and from the other side—the organizational disorder and the internal dissonances in the organization."[105]

In this context of post-1925 weakness, punctuated by intermittent crisis, Zionism in Warsaw seems to have contracted into what might best be characterized as a subculture (or a set of distinct but interlinked subcultures). A baseline sense of Zionism's overall quantitative strength in Warsaw ca. 1930 is conveniently provided by the 1931 census data on mother tongues. To reiterate, Poland's Zionist movement asked Polish Jews to declare Hebrew their mother-tongue as a demonstration of national commitment. In Warsaw, 19,180 census respondents obliged. We can assume that virtually every one of these 19,180 persons was a committed Zionist of some sort and that, in turn, some portion of these 19,000 or so respondents was active in a broad array of institutions and practices that, taken together, seem to have comprised a specifically Zionist subculture (or subcultures)[106] in Warsaw.

---

104 Scott Ury, "Zionism and Zionist Parties," YIVO Encyclopedia of Jews in Eastern Europe, 2: 2128–29.
105 Mojżesz Polakiewicz to Yitzhak Grinboym, 4 May 1932, Central Zionist Archives (hereafter CZA), Grinboym Collection, A127, f. 1685 [Ben Gurion University Archives, http://bgarchives.bgu.ac.il/archives/grin/grin.html, accessed 6 January 2011].
106 Interwar Warsaw may have boasted at least six distinct Zionist subcultures, and arguably many more: the subculture of "bourgeois" Zionism (a world of movement institutions and practices apparently dominated by largely middle-class adults), itself divided into two competing movements; the socialist-Zionist young people active in such labor-Zionist-identified movements as Hitahdut and Poalei-tsion Right/Tseire tsion, which themselves stood in a complex relationship of cooperation but not unity; the He-halutz pioneer movement in and around Warsaw whose resolute focus on emigration and the transformation of young people into Jewish pioneers and agrarian socialists placed it in an agonistic if broadly cooperative relationship to general Zionism; the romantic-cum-Marxist Zionist youth movement Ha-shomer ha-tsair, which for both political and sociological reasons stood in a tense relationship to all of the preceding; the subculture of the religious Zionist Mizrahi movement; and the apparently altogether separate schismatic subculture

The various streams in Warsaw Zionism each boasted an array of party-affiliated clubs like the socialist-Zionist "Borochov Homes" at Gęsia 14 and Przejazd 1. They staffed and supported the Hebraist schools that comprised some of interwar Zionism's most sustained and intensive points of contact with a mass base, from the Tarbut schools of the secular center and left to the Takhkemoni and Yavneh institutions of the religious Zionist Mizrahi.[107] The various Zionist youth movements in the city maintained clubs like that of He-halutz ha-tsair where, in the romantic recollections of one participant, there gathered youngsters "dressed in their patch-covered holiday clothes" from "all the cellars and attic apartments in the capital: from Wolińska, Ostrowska, Niska."[108] No doubt, the Zionist subculture sustained in these institutions was also maintained, to various degrees, by less visible personal networks and familial settings.

Significantly, this was a subculture that *felt* itself to be one. Another member of one of the He-halutz branches in the city recalls his group's quarters in an impoverished part of Warsaw as a kind of Hebraist outpost in strange if not hostile territory. Within its walls, its 45 members lived a Hebrew-language life centered around ongoing contact with "the Land-of-Israel reality and with everything that was being created in the kibbutz [movement] [in Palestine]." Beyond its walls, the work of preaching its message was difficult: "It is not easy to go outside onto the Jewish street and call [people] courageously and with inner certainty to a life-course bound up with suffering and difficulties."[109]

For all the gloominess in these Zionist reflections, several facts militate against any overly grim assessment of Zionism's post-1926 status in Warsaw. First, of course, insofar as it was 'only' a subculture, it was in a position no different from that of its chief political-ideological competitors in the city, the Bund and the Hasidic-orthodox community (which for all its apparent prewar dominance seems to have dropped to an ever more subcultural status in the course of the interwar period).[110] Second, Zionism's return to a subcultural status by the late 1920s—or perhaps indeed its inability to move beyond

---

of the Left Poalei-tsion Marxist Zionist party. To these we might no doubt add the subcultures of other Zionist youth groups. This is further complicated by significant change over time in the internal structures and relative weight of each of these various groupings.

107 Avraham Levinson, *Toldot yehudei varshah* (Tel Aviv: 'Am 'Oved, 1953), 239–65 contains valuable if scattered information on the institutional loci of interwar Warsaw Zionism.

108 "Bilder fun halutsim-lebn in varshe: in varshever *snif*," in Leyb Shpizman (ed.) *Halutsim in poyln*, vol. 1, reprinted in *Dos amolike yidishe varshe* (Montreal: Farband fun Varshever Yidn in Montreal, 1966), 828.

109 M. B-i, "Di shoen hobn gekisheft," repr. in ibid., 829.

110 Hirshauge, *Troym*, 11; Kaniel, "Bein hilonim."

FIGURE 16.13   *Tearoom of a Po'ale Tsiyon ("Workers of Zion") home for workers in the Praga suburb, Warsaw, ca. 1920s. On the wall are portraits of Karl Marx and Ber Borokhov. Archives of the YIVO Institute for Jewish Research, New York. Courtesy of YIVO.*

a subcultural status despite the promise of the immediate post-World War I period—was not really a decline when measured against its pre-1918 situation: there is simply no comparison between the movement's public visibility, voice, and intermittent but real popular strength in the interwar period and its pre-war situation as a disorganized, under-institutionalized insurgent movement of isolated *polu-inteligent* newcomers to the city, a few students, and a self-contained community of largely Litvak *hovevei-tsion*. In that sense, the frustration voiced by Warsaw Zionists in the 1930s should probably be understood against the backdrop of the movement's heightened expectations in the 1918–1925 period. Third, Zionism even at low ebb dwarfed any other Jewish nationalist subcultures (if we exclude the Bund from that category) in the city. Among these we might include the circle of Yiddishist intellectuals, activists, and writers such as Noyekh Prilutsky, Hillel Tsaytlin, and H.D. Nomberg who stood at the center of Warsaw's Folks-partey and thereafter at the center of the *Moment* newspaper. There were also the more loosely-knit circles of socialist-nationalist Yiddishists, who in contradistinction to the Bund embraced the rhetoric of Jewish nationalism and who combined an unalloyed Yiddishist cultural nationalism with contradictory tendencies toward territorialism, left-wing Poalei-tsion Zionism, diasporism, and Communism. Linked to specific sites such as Warsaw's Union of Jewish Writers and Journalists ("Tłomackie 13") and the *Literarishe bleter* literary journal, these circles (which included such figures as the editor and literary critic Nahman Mayzl, the poet Meylekh Ravitsh, and the Yiddishist activist Zelig Melamed) might have constituted a subculture of their own too, though there is no research on their interwar personal lives and networks to speak of.[111] Other such nationalist subcultures no doubt remain to be discovered (there is some evidence of an incipient territorialist subculture, with its own youth group and journal, taking shape in Warsaw in the mid-1930s, for instance). But the fact remains that by the 1930s, Zionism was the only major Jewish nationalist movement in the city; it remained a serious contender for popular support, whereas the array of diaspora nationalist visions that had seemed poised to take support from it in the immediate wake of the First World War had simply evaporated.

There is much more research to be done on Warsaw's Zionist subculture, starting with the question of whether and to what degree it was one subculture or rather many, and proceeding to such neglected questions as its generational dynamics (were the boys and girls who filled Zionist-socialist movements the sons and daughters of the city's middle-class general Zionists?), its class dimensions, the specific spaces and practices that constituted it, and so on. But given the concerns of the present chapter, a different facet of the history of Zionism in Warsaw commands more attention: the ways in which Zionism (or the emergent *fact* of Jewish society-building in Palestine) remained a shared political horizon for many Varsovian Jews well *beyond* the boundaries of the 6%-strong subculture outlined above.

He-halutz, Revisionist Zionism, Palestinism: Negotiated Zionism in Warsaw

In this regard, we should start by recalling that the deep decline of Zionism after the perceived failures of the Fourth Aliyah was counterbalanced in the early 1930s by two unlooked-for, grass-roots alternative Zionisms that flourished across Poland: the explosive growth of the He-halutz pioneer movement and, at the other end of the political spectrum, the dramatic growth in popular Polish Jewish support for right-wing Revisionist Zionism. After undergoing a crisis of contraction in the later 1920s like the rest of the Zionist mainstream

---

111 Though there is much of value in Natan Cohen, *Sefer, sofer ve-'iton* (Jerusalem: Magnes, 2003), passim.

(though never to the point of complete collapse), He-halutz rebounded to tens of thousands of members in Poland by the early 1930s.[112] Its bitter opponents in the Revisionist camp could claim some 450,000 (!) supporters in Poland by 1935 and some 40,000 Polish members in its Betar youth organization by 1934.[113]

Warsaw was not excluded from these developments, which lent both new life and new tensions to the Zionist subculture in the city. Thus, Warsaw's Zionist subculture was substantially invigorated by the growth of the He-halutz movement there in general and the growth of the Grokhov [Grochów] *kibbutz hakhsharah* in particular. The *kibbutz hakhsharah*, or training kibbutz, was one of the core institutions of the He-halutz movement from the 1920s on. Multiplying across Poland, these *kibbutzei hakhsharah* were youth communities (usually farms) where *halutzim* were supposed to prepare themselves for a new life of hard physical labor, economic communism, radical Hebraism, and ethical communitarianism in the Yishuv's emerging kibbutz movement. One such farm was founded on a very small scale in the rural Grokhov suburb outside Warsaw in 1919.[114] Refounded in 1928 on a more substantial basis, Grokhov remained by far the smallest of He-halutz's training-kibbutz blocs. But in the early 1930s, it grew by a factor of three. By August 1933, it boasted some 345 members; by 1934, 602.[115] Of course, many of these young people were no doubt not from Warsaw. But the farm's rapid growth—and its extension into the heart of Jewish Warsaw in the form of supplementary urban branches and the movement's central office—rendered it a visible improvement in the Zionist subculture's fortunes. Grokhov became a point of pride and pilgrimage for the city's Zionists (and, as we shall see, others as well).

---

112   Shmuel Ettinger gives a total of roughly 40,000 in Poland for 1933 in his introduction to Yisrael Otiker, *Tenuat "he-halutz" be-polin: gidulah ve-hitpathutah be-shanim 1932–1935* (Tel Aviv: Hotsa'at ha-Kibuts ha-Meuhad, 1972), unpaginated introduction. Yisrael Oppenheim reports 29,000 Polish members in 1935; see idem, *The Struggle of Jewish Youth for Productivization: the Zionist Youth Movement in Poland* (Boulder, CO: East European Monographs, 1989), 64. Significantly for our focus on Warsaw, He-halutz grew just as quickly in Congress Poland as in the *kresy* in this period; see Otiker, *Tenuat "He-halutz,"* 39.
113   Ury, "Zionism," in YIVO *Encyclopedia of Jews in Eastern Europe*, 2: 2129; Emanuel Melzer, "Betar," ibid., 1: 173.
114   Emanuel, "An'idee [sic], vos boyt zikh (tsu der hayntiker fayerlekhkayt in grokhov)," *Moment*, 29 May 1928.
115   Otiker, *Tenuat "He-halutz,"* 131. The latter figure is from Oppenheim, *Struggle*, 66; the dating is unclear but seems to refer to 1934. The disparity might also stem from a difference between the numbers on the actual Grokhov farm and the numbers affiliated with the Grokhov *bloc*, which included 13 sections all told; Oppenheim's figure refers to the bloc as a whole.

The marked reinvigoration of Zionist sentiment in the early 1930s—albeit in new (and mutually opposed) forms—point us toward the final aspect of the career(s) of Jewish nationalism in interwar Warsaw that demands our attention: a variety of underexplored phenomena that suggest a substantial reservoir of growing and sometimes quite deep popular *interest* in Zionism and in the terms of Jewish nationalism among Varsovians who stood well beyond the institutional and ideological bounds of the organized movement. Such engagement was acute in the early 1930s, when large-scale emigration to Palestine once again began to seem a legal and practical possibility and the Yishuv began to seem much more politically and economically attractive than Poland. Thus, in June 1932, the same Warsaw Zionist activist Mojżesz Polakiewicz who had spoken candidly about the anemia of organized Zionism in Warsaw wrote in a private letter: "Here it's heaven and earth and ... certificates [for emigration to Palestine]. Everywhere, in Warsaw and in the provinces, in the larger as well as the smaller towns. The issue of certificates has become the talk of the day [...]."[116] He went on to warn that the Revisionists were successfully making hay out of real and perceived problems with the distribution of the coveted certificates, thus suggesting simultaneously the fragility of the popular warming toward organized Zionism and the breadth of the general Jewish reorientation toward Zionism in the larger sense: if the organized Zionist movement could not satisfy expectations, the beneficiaries would be an opposing group of Zionists. A year later, the Palestinian Labor Zionist leader Berl Katznelson sounded similar notes when, in his otherwise grim and urgent reports from Poland, he noted in a letter from Warsaw that "[o]ur movement is growing and expanding. He who has not seen it with his own eyes cannot imagine the size of the masses of people of every sort swarming to us."[117]

Here, a point about chronology—and about the largely synchronic structure of this chapter—is in order. It is clear that the 1929–1935 period marked a distinct moment in the history of nationalist sentiment among Warsaw Jewry in which a wide array of factors made the question of national identity ever more difficult to ignore for Warsaw Jews of *every* political and political-cultural orientation. This, in turn, was part and parcel of a general shift visible across Polish Jewry, as exemplified by the swelling of interest in emigration to Palestine, the He-halutz movement, Revisionism and many other contemporaneous

---

116 Polakiewicz to Yitzhak Grinboym, 29 June 1932, Grinboym Collection, A127/1685 [Ben Gurion University Archives, http://bgarchives.bgu.ac.il/archives/grin/grin.html, accessed 6 January 2011].

117 Katznelson to Histadrut Executive, 18 October 1933, in Anita Shapira and Eshter Raizen (eds.), *Igrot B. Katznelson*, vol. 6 (Tel Aviv: 'Am 'Oved, 1961–), 137.

developments. But more generally, I would argue that the whole of the interwar period saw a *steady* nationalization of the Polish Jewish political horizon and a concomitant *narrowing* in the possibilities of ignoring the national question. In both Warsaw and across Poland, this was neither universal nor unpunctuated (1926–1928 being an obvious moment of partial reversal), but there is nonetheless good warrant for treating the entire interwar period as one in which nationalism loomed ever larger as a decisive political determinant of Jewish destiny and hence an unavoidable horizon of Jewish political life: one could be nationalist or anti-nationalist, but it became impossible to *ignore* nationalism.[118]

Thus, though especially acute between 1931 and 1934 and strongly linked to enhanced prospects of *aliyah* after 1931, this revival of engagement with Zionism in the broad Polish Jewish public was neither an altogether new phenomenon nor one solely framed by the increasing desperation of Polish Jews in the 1930s. It seems clear that large numbers of Polish Jews well beyond Zionist circles took a special interest in the life, achievements, and travails of the new Jewish society emerging in Palestine (the Yishuv), that this interest began well before the 1930s and only deepened as time went on, and that it was not purely a matter of political concern but the mark of a more general nationalization of identity beyond Zionist circles.[119] Public interest in the Yishuv included both the dramas of Yishuv life and its everyday features. The June 1933 murder in Tel Aviv of labor Zionism's rising political star Haim Arlozorov apparently touched off fierce debate well beyond Zionist circles in Warsaw. The journalist Yitshok Borenshteyn recalls roiling exchanges at the Tłomackie 13 Jewish

---

118 Here I would go so far as to include the much-debated 1936–1939 period. The recent work of Jack Jacobs and others on Bundist political success in that period has led Jacobs to argue that the late 1930s shift marked a mass embrace of Bundist politics rooted in longstanding Bundist institution-building, recruitment, and indoctrination efforts. The argument for the importance of these longer-term developments (and concomitant arguments for the import of deeper sociological/class shifts by Gertrud Pickhan among others) seems convincing enough, but the issue remains one of degree: evidence suggesting that more of the 1936 and 1938 support for the Bund than we might have thought can be attributed to real ideological conviction does not disprove the older thesis that much of that support came as a matter of Polish Jewish political despair and frustration with other options; it simply suggests that we revise our sense of the proportions. For many reasons, the latter argument, articulated most compellingly by Mendelsohn and by the honoree of this volume, Antony Polonsky, remains compelling.

119 This is a central concern in my current research; see now the very interesting work of Irith Cherniavsky, "'Aliyat yehudei polin be-shnot ha-shloshim shel ha-meah ha-'esrim'" (PhD dissertation, Hebrew University Jerusalem, 2010), 79–104. I thank Dr. Cherniavsky for sharing her work with me.

literary club, hardly a redoubt of Zionism.[120] At the same time, there was strong Polish Jewish interest in the *everyday* life of Palestinian Jewry and in such central aspects of the Yishuv's Zionist project as Tel Aviv ("the first Jewish city") and in the kibbutz movement. Many Varsovians travelled to Palestine on tours in the early 1930s. Some used their tourist visas simply as cover for illegal immigration, but others went as actual tourists, and these benefitted from an increasingly regularized tourist agenda that combined traditional pilgrimage sites with Zionist/New Yishuv sites and attainments.[121] Contemporaries were well aware of this popular interest: it is telling that not only the Zionist *Haynt* but also the broadly non-Zionist *Moment* offered regular coverage of Jewish life in Palestine already in the 1920s.[122]

By the same token, the Grokhov *kibbutz hakhsharah* may have served as a site of special interest for the region's Zionists, but it also drew the attention and respect of other curious Varsovians. One memoirist who lived at Grokhov in the 1930s recalls: "Kibbutz Grokhov was famous among the Jews of Warsaw, who took pride in it. On the Sabbath and holidays, hundreds of Jews and also Christians would visit the kibbutz."[123] An early article in the non-Zionist *Moment* from 1922 noted that "the work and striving of [this] handful of our better youth" at Grokhov remained "totally unfamiliar to the broad Jewish

---

120   Borenshteyn, *Varshe*, 64.
121   See the cruise-ship lists in CZA, Jerusalem, Immigration Department (of the Jewish Agency), Record Group S6, f. 187 I, many of which list city of origin and in some cases birthplace; Warsaw is well-represented. My current project addresses Palestine tourism by Polish Jews in depth.
122   Readers could find similar sorts of interest in Jewish Palestine in the non-Jewish Polish press as well. In 1933, Stanisław Mackiewicz-Cat's maverick conservative Vilna journal *Słowo*, which enjoyed nation-wide readership, carried a detailed and highly sympathetic reportage on Jewish settlement in Palestine by the rising young publicist Ksawery Pruszyński; the reportage, which was then collected and published in Warsaw as the book *Palestyna po raz trzeci* (1933 and again in 1936), was addressed to general Polish readers but shared many tropes with the general Polish Jewish engagement with Palestine sketched here. On the reportage, see Jerzy Jaruzelski's introduction to the republication of the 1936 version of the book: Ksawery Pruszyński, *Palestyna po raz trzeci* (Warszawa: Czytelnik, 1996); on the circulation of *Słowo*, see George J. Lerski with Piotr Wróbel and Richard J. Kozicki, *Historical Dictionary of Poland, 966–1945* (Westport, CN: Greenwood Press, 1996), s.v. "Mackiewicz-Cat, Stanislaw"; for an analysis of the travelogue's themes in comparative context, see François Guesnet, "Sensitive Travelers: Jewish and non-Jewish Visitors from Eastern Europe to Palestine between the Two World Wars," *The Journal of Israeli History* [part of section on "East European Jewry, Nationalism and the Zionist Project," ed. Kenneth B. Moss], 27.2 (September 2008): 178–81.
123   Shabtai Ben-Nahum, "Sadot grokhov shemurim be-zikhroni," in *Be-shadmot Grokhov*, 273.

public."[124] By contrast, a second article in *Moment* from 1928, celebrating the laying of a cornerstone for a central building at Grokhov, maintained that the farm had "begun to win for itself ever newer (alts-nayere) circles. From time to time, the plowed field manifests plowed-up, opened-up Jewish souls, of the sort that was long closed off to us."[125] This latter article is not a straightforward source; it was in fact a celebratory piece by a founding member of the kibbutz. But the author himself acknowledged elsewhere in the article that this public interest had not come easily or quickly, noting that at the beginning "our Jewish Warsaw was as cold as the snows over Grokhov's fields." And the very choice of the non-Zionist *Moment* to carry this laudatory piece is itself striking. Even the Warsaw branch of the Jewish tourism society the Żydowskie Towarzystwo Krajoznawcze/di Yidishe Gezelshaft far Landkentenish, which generally maintained a distant relationship to Zionism, included a trip to Grokhov farm in its 1930 schedule of local tours.[126]

One way in which Warsaw clearly did distinguish itself with regard to non-Zionist engagement with Jewish life in Palestine was as a setting for the gradual evolution of a new relationship in the interwar period between polonized Jewish economic and professional elites and the Zionist project. Take, for instance, the Warsaw Bnei Brith Jewish fellowship organization. In the interwar period, the Warsaw Bnei Brith was a gathering place for what we might call a polonized but Jewishly engaged white collar elite—what seems to have been an important slice of Warsaw's most substantial Jewish merchants and professionals. In the interwar period, the organization self-identified as a meeting

---

124   Avrom Roz_feld [?], "Af der halutsim ferme in grokhov," *Moment*, 3 May 1922.
125   Emanuel, "An'idee [sic], vos boyt zikh (tsu der hayntiker fayerlekhkayt in grokhov)," *Moment*, 29 May 1928.
126   "Yidishe gezelsh far land kentenish, varshe. Der oysflug referat organizirt folgen[dik]n tsikl oysflugn in May 1930," mimeograph, Warsaw, YIVO Archives, Poland Collection, RG 28, f. 438. On the ZTK and its ideology in general, see Samuel Kassow, "Travel and Local History as a National Mission: Polish Jews and the Landkentenish Movement in the 1920s and 1930s," in Julia Brauch, Anna Lipphardt, Alexandra Nocke (eds.), *Jewish Topographies: Visions of Space, Traditions of Place* (Aldershot: Ashgate Publishing, 2008), 241–64. The ZTK's complex relationship to Zionism is exemplified by the following: its leadership included the Left Poalei-Tsion Emmanuel Ringelblum and the pro-Zionist Filip Friedman, but also the diasporist-localist Mikhl Burshtin and Leon Vulman; some of the aforementioned did give lectures on Palestine within the ZTK's lecture series framework; but the ZTK's journals of the early 1930s *Landkentenish* and *Landkentenish/Krajoznawstwo* make no mention of Zionism in any of the hundreds of pages I have read—this in the years of the peak strength of Poland's He-halutz and Zionist youth and scouting groups in Poland. My current project will take this up in greater detail.

place of Zionist and non-Zionist Polish Jews, where questions of "assimilation and Zionism" were not to be avoided but rather discussed openly. From the early 1920s, the organization developed a particular interest in the founding and early work of the Hebrew University of Jerusalem. After 1929, the Warsaw Bnei Brith consciously engaged with—and mirrored—the Jewish Agency, created as a framework in which Zionists and non-Zionists could work together on behalf of Jewish settlement in Palestine. Most significantly, by 1932, the organization had formally committed itself to the principle that the creation of a national home for Jews in Palestine was a matter of a concern not only for Zionists but for all Jews—a commitment that the writer of the 1932 organizational history called the fruit of a "deep evolution" of the last 10 years.[127]

There is also scattered evidence that signals an as-yet largely unstudied growth in pro-Zionist sentiment in a very different part of Warsaw's Jewish community, its internally variegated Hasidic subculture. Avraham Levinson's memoir-history of Jewish Warsaw is richly suggestive on this score. He identifies the Ahaves-Tsion *beys-medresh* on Pańska Street as having a largely Hasidic congregation but a generally "Zionist approach."[128] More sweepingly, he contends that it was among Warsaw Hasidim particularly that there first took shape a more positive relationship to the project of a Jewish national home in Palestine after the Balfour Declaration of 1917: he notes that it was a circle of wealthy Hasidic activists at the Skernevits shtibl at Nalewki 43 who in 1921–1922 created the "Bayis ve-nakhole" organization for orthodox agricultural settlement in Palestine, and asserts the evolution of positive attitudes toward Jewish society-building in Palestine among such leading Hasidic *admorim* in interwar Warsaw as the Radziminer Rebbe Menahem Mendl Guterman and the Aleksander Rebbe Shmuel Tsvi Dantsiger.[129] Contemporary and retrospective Hasidic sources lend weight to these claims. Thus, in a 1922 letter by Warsaw-based followers of the Gerer Rebbe justifying to other Hasidic leaders the creation of a fund for the support of orthodox Jewish settlement in Palestine, the authors admitted that this was in part a defensive move necessitated by broad pro-Zionist enthusiasm among Warsaw's religious Jews in the wake of the Balfour Declaration: "And who here does not know about the war that we fought even against Warsaw rabbis, who ruled that one may say Hallel [a selection of psalms of praise recited on Jewish holidays when joyful prayer is appropriate] on the yearly anniversary of the Balfour Declaration, and it was a hard war because it was as though the entire community [kol ha-kahal] had

---

127 *Stowarzyszenie Humanitarne "Braterstwo—B'nei-B'rith" w Warszawie 1922–1932* (Warszawa: [Bnei Brith], 1932), 48–53.
128 Levinson, *Toldot*, 250.
129 Levinson, *Yehudei varshah*, 269–70.

been seized by a convulsion [....] and from the camp of the *haredim* were lost thousands of souls every day and they joined [the Zionists], and thus we were compelled to save the religion and to lay still greater emphasis on the Fund for the Land of Israel."[130] The 1930s saw a much more open and sustained chorus of calls within Agudah ranks for more full-fledged commitment to Jewish mass settlement and society-building in Palestine, and here again, it seems clear that Warsaw played a disproportionately central role: at the 1935 meeting of the Agudah's international executive board, it was decided to relocate the movement's "international Center for Land of Israel Matters" to Warsaw "which is already today the center of that work."[131]

Of course, to continue with the diachronic dimension, this second six-year upswing in broad support for Zionism (or, to use a then-emergent term which demands much more analysis, "Palestinism") was also subject to change. Famously, the 1936–38 period brought a second crisis of support for Zionism in the context of the Arab Revolt in Palestine and the consequent sharp reduction in aliyah possibilities, which intersected with a sharp upswing in Jewish support for the Bund. How far this meant a *permanent* loss of interest in Palestine as a possibility and in Jewish nationhood as a political horizon is, however, an open question.[132] In any event, Warsaw remained a center for demonstrative Jewish nationalist politics, as when, in 1936–1937, the city hosted several bizarre processions of young people—one estimated at 5000 youths—pointedly setting out by foot from Warsaw to Palestine to protest British immigration limitations.[133]

In June 1935, the leading Polish Jewish bureaucrat-planner of the Joint Distribution Committee, Alexander Giterman, wrote a long private letter to the *Sokhnut* official Werner Senator. Writing in response to Senator's efforts to revive the Jewish Agency idea of cooperative work—and fund-raising—between Zionist and non-Zionist Jews in the diaspora on behalf of the Yishuv, Giterman suggested that the Zionist establishment was missing the forest for the trees. Focusing on long-time supporters of the Zionist project, they were missing what Giterman saw as a much more important shift in Polish Jewish

---

130 Mendl Piekarz, *Hasidut polin ben shte ha-milhamot u-ve-gezerot 1939–1945 ("ha-Shoah")* (Jerusalem: Mosad Bialik, 1997), 233–34. In accord with this account are the postwar memoirs of the aforementioned Avraham Zemba, who asserts that the Balfour Declaration generated enthusiasm among "the Jewish masses" broadly and allows that this enthusiasm could be "used" by "the secular-nationalist groups" ["ha-kvutsot ha-le'umiot ha-hiloniot"] to "influence the [Hasidic] youth and attract them"; Zemba, "Metivta," 364.

131 Cited in Fund, *Pirud o hishtatfut*, 102.

132 See note 85.

133 "'Daily Herald' 'al 'tsoadei ha-yeush'," *Davar*, 28 December 1936; "Od kevutsah shel 'tsoadei yeush'," *Davar*, 3 August 1937.

life. In the face of "the rise of open and concealed Nazism" in Europe and "the broadened absorptive possibilities of Palestine," Giterman asserted, many elements of the Polish Jewish community which yesterday were "distant or even hostile" to Zionism were now "psychologically ready" and even eager to take part in a "practical Palestinist [*palestinezishe*] movement."[134] From his vantage in Warsaw, where as the chief representative of American Jewish philanthropy in Poland he seems to have had substantial access to the highest circles of Jewish society, Giterman attributed such readiness to substantial parts of the Warsaw Jewish "financial aristocracy" and—strikingly—"the substantial majority of the Jewish intelligentsia in Poland." Given Giterman's access to both circles, and his own distance from Zionism, his suggestion that by 1935 there had been a sea-change in national (and personal) attitudes and hopes regarding Poland and Palestine among at least two important strata of Warsaw Jews deserves further investigation. One of the people whom he cited in 1935 as a good prospect for Senator's attention, Antoni Eiger, was by 1937 active in Jewish Agency circles. So too was a striking cross-section of Warsaw Jewish leaders from Rafal Szereszewski to Natalia Lichtenbaum, the chief doctor of the Bund's Medem Sanatorium, to the religious thinker and former Folkist Hillel Tsaytlin.[135]

Giterman's letter encapsulates the ways in which Warsaw may have served, throughout the entire interwar period, as a particular sort of site for a *renegotiation* of relations to the idea of Jewish nationhood on the part of "formerly distant and even hostile elements" who had once aspired to achieve Polishness in the capital of that cultural dispensation. More broadly, the sources examined in this last section of the present chapter suggest how historians of Polish Jewry and of Jewish nationalism alike might usefully begin to rethink the meaning and extension of Jewish nationalism not merely in terms of organized Jewish nationalism, nor even merely in the broader terms of how Jewish public debate and political thought was inflected by ideas of nationhood or oriented toward the discourse of the nation, but in the classical terms of intellectual history: as a set of ideas and claims about the world and one's own future in it about which growing numbers of Polish Jews had good reason to think seriously.

---

134 Giterman to Senator, 12 June 1935, CZA, Collection of the Section for the Organization of Non-Zionists (Sokhnut), S29, f. 51.

135 Protokół posiedzenia Komisji-Matki, wyłonionej przez zebranie wyborcze platników "K-H" [Keren ha-yesod] w. Kongresówce i na Kresach Wschodnich i Zachodnich, odbytej w lokalu "K-H" przy ul. Królewskiej Nr. 16, 15 July 1937, CZA, Collection of the Section for the Organization of Non-Zionists (Sokhnut), S29, f. 51.

PART 2

Destruction of the Metropolis and Its Aftermath

∴

FIGURE 17.14 *Tłomackie Street Synagogue (1875; Leandro Marconi), Warsaw. Archives of the YIVO Institute for Jewish Research, New York.*
COURTESY OF YIVO.

CHAPTER 17

The Polish Underground Press and the Jews: The Holocaust in the Pages of the Home Army's *Biuletyn Informacyjny*, 1940–1943

Joshua D. Zimmerman

The attitude and behavior of the Polish underground's principal military force, the Home Army, to the Jews during World War II, has received considerable scholarly attention in recent years.¹ The main reason for the increased interest seems to be that the gap in understanding between Jewish and Polish academics is wider on the topic of the Polish underground than on any other issue in Polish-Jewish relations during the Holocaust.² Among the topics that have been addressed in this scholarship is the reaction of the Polish underground press to the tragedy of Polish Jewry.³

While several works have brought forth a fuller picture of the overall views in the Polish clandestine press, the dizzying array of underground titles analyzed has obscured the distinction between the mainstream and radical periodicals,

---

1 Scholarly works showing the latest research, including Dariusz Libionka, "ZWZ-AK i Delegatura Rządu wobec eksterminacji Żydów Polskich," in Andrzej Żbikowski (ed.), *Polacy i Żydzi pod okupacją niemiecką 1939–1945: studia i materiały* (Warszawa: IPN, 2006), 15–136; Barbara Engelking and Dariusz Libionka, *Żydzi w Powstańczej Warszawskie* (Warszawa: Polish Center for Holocaust Research, 2009); Dariusz Libionka, "Polska konspiracja wobec eksterminacji Żydów w dystrykcie warszawskim," in Barbara Engelking et al. (eds.), *Prowincja Noc* (Warszawa: Wydawnictwo IFiS PAN, 2007), 443–504; Adam Puławski, *W obliczu zagłady* (Lublin: Instytut Pamięci Narodowej, 2009); and Joshua Zimmerman, "The Attitude of the Polish Home Army (AK) to the Jewish Question during the Holocaust: the Case of the Warsaw Ghetto Uprising," in M. Baumgarten and P. Kenez (eds.), *Varieties of Antisemitism* (Newark, DE: University of Delaware Press, 2009), 105–26.
2 See Robert Cherry, "Contentious History: A Survey on Perceptions of Polish-Jewish Relations during the Holocaust," *Polin* 19 (2007): 335.
3 Scholars who have addressed this topic include the late Lucjan Dobroszycki, Shmuel Krakowski, Paweł Szapiro, and Andrzej Friszke. Most recently, the German historian Klaus-Peter Friedrich has offered a detailed examination of the general topic. See, for example, Klaus-Peter Friedrich, "The Nazi Murder of the Jews in Polish Eyes: Views in the Underground Press, 1942–1945," *Polin* 22 (2010): 389–413, and idem, *Der nationalsozialistische Judenmord und das polnische-jüdische Verhältnis im Diskurs der polnische Untergrundpresse (1942–1944)* (Marburg: Verlag Herder-Institut, 2006).

as well as between short-lived titles and those in circulation throughout the war. The present essay examines a single, prominent newspaper printed by the Polish Home Army (AK), titled *Biuletyn Informacyjny* (hereafter, *Biuletyn*), and the way in which it reported on Jewish matters from the outbreak of war to the Warsaw Ghetto Uprising in April–May 1943. *Biuletyn* was distinguished from other periodicals by being the largest circulating clandestine paper in German-occupied Poland. It was printed between 1939 and 1945, and was regarded as the official voice of the Polish underground resistance movement linked to the Polish government-in-exile. *Biuletyn* was, according to Andrzej Kunert, "the most important and most widely read underground paper in occupied Poland."[4] It began circulation as the organ of the underground's Warsaw branch and, in April 1941, became the Polish underground's central organ under the auspices of its VI Department—the Bureau of Information and Propaganda (BIP).[5]

Biuletyn was part of a wide network of underground publications in German-occupied Poland—scholars have counted between 1097[6] to 1123[7] clandestine periodicals that circulated for various lengths of time, with varying degrees of influence. At its height, in 1944, 615 titles were in circulation, up from 55 in 1939, 241 in 1940, 336 in 1941, 388 in 1942, and 506 in 1943.[8] Despite the high numbers of individual titles, only 17 underground periodicals were published regularly.[9] What is more, *Biuletyn* was one of only three underground titles that circulated uninterruptedly throughout the war period, the others being the Home Army's *Dziennik Radiowy* and *Szaniec*, the organ of the extreme right-wing National Radical Camp (ONR).[10] Of the 615 titles appearing in 1944, about half were printed in Warsaw. Warsaw's primacy is further reflected in the fact that it housed 147 illegal printing presses by 1944, while the next largest printing

---

4 A. Kunert (ed.), *Słownik biograficzny konspiracji warszawskiej, 1939–1944*, 3 vols. (Warszawa: Instytut Wydawniczy Pax, 1987), vol. 2, 77.

5 Maria Straszewska, "'Biuletyn Informacyjny' 1939–1944," *Przegląd Historyczno-Wojskowy* 2 (2001), special issue 1 (190): 11, 18; Grzegorz Mazur, *Biuro Informacji i Propagandy SZP-ZWZ-AK, 1939–1945* (Warszawa: Instytut Wydawniczy Pax, 1987), 57; Kunert (ed.), *Słownik*, vol. 2, 77.

6 Stanisława Lewandowska, *Polska konspiracyjna prasa informacyjno-polityczna 1939–1945* (Warszawa: Czytelnik, 1982), 267–68.

7 1123 titles are listed in Lucjan Dobroszycki, *Centralny katalog polskiej prasy konspiracyjnej 1939–1945* (Warszawa: Wydawnictwo Ministerstwa Obrony Narodowej, 1962).

8 Lewandowska, *Polska konspiracyjna prasa*, 265.

9 Dobroszycki, *Centralny katalog*, 301.

10 Dobroszycki, "The Jews in the Polish Clandestine Press, 1939–1945," 290; and Dobroszycki, *Centralny katalog*, 35, 61, 212.

center, Kraków, housed only 27.[11] Given its distinction as the largest armed resistance group in German-controlled Europe by 1944, with an estimated 350,000 fighters,[12] it is not surprising that the Home Army put out more press titles than any other underground organization, with over 200 papers to its name.[13]

Biuletyn's first issue appeared in Warsaw on November 5, 1939, in a mimeograph form with a circulation of 90 copies, and came out continuously until it was forced to relocate to Kraków in October, 1944. *Biuletyn* became a weekly as early as 1939,[14] with a print run of 500 in the first half of 1940,[15] 19,000 by the end of 1941, 24,000 in 1942, and 25,000 by the beginning of 1943. From the middle of 1943 until the Warsaw Uprising in August 1944, *Biuletyn* had a print run of 43,000, making it the largest underground periodical in occupied Poland[16] or possibly in the whole of occupied Europe.[17] On the first day of the Warsaw Uprising, August 1st, 1944, *Biuletyn* printed its 241st issue; and throughout the Warsaw Uprising it appeared openly as a daily. By comparison, other main underground papers included the Home Army's *Wiadomości Polskie* (Warsaw, 1939–1944), with a print run of between 7,000 to 10,000, or *Trybuna Wolności* (Warsaw, 1942–44) the PPR's main organ, with a print run of 5,000.[18]

During the war years, *Biuletyn* devoted substantial coverage to the emerging Jewish tragedy. Of 241 issues between 1939 and August 1, 1944, the subject of the Jews appeared in 103 issues, or a full 43% of the paper.[19] A recent study

11 Lewandowska, *Polska konspiracyjna prasa*, 256–57, 261.
12 Tomasz Strzembosz, *Rzeczpospolita podziemna: Społeczeństwo polskie a państwo podziemne, 1939–1945* (Warszawa: Wydawnictwo Krupski i S-ka, 2000), 224.
13 According to Lewandowska, *Polska konspiracyjna prasa*, 267, 244 of 1097 underground papers were printed by the Home Army. My count of Dobroszycki's list of 1123 titles, however, puts the number at 197. See Dobroszycki, *Centralny katalog*. According to Lewandowska, the next largest underground organizations produced the following amount of titles: the Delegate's Bureau (72), the Peasant Party (183), the Polish communist underground (160), the PPS-WRN [the organ of the PPS titled WRN] (38), and the National Democratic Party or *Endecja* (51).
14 Straszewska, 'Biuletyn Informacyjny,' 6, Foreword.
15 Eadem, "'Biuletyn Informacyjny' 1939–1944," *Najnowsze dzieje Polski* 11 (1967): 132.
16 Marek Ney-Krwawic, *Komenda Główna Armii Krajowej 1939–1945* (Warszawa: Instytut Wydawniczy Pax, 1990), 184.
17 Barbara Wachowicz, *Kamyk na szańcu: gawęda o druhu Aleksandrze Kamińskim w stulecie urodzin* (Warszawa: Oficyna Wydawnicza Rytm, 2002), 211.
18 Lewandowska, *Polska konspiracyjna prasa*, 253.
19 The figure derives from a reading of the entire extant run of *Biuletyn* housed at the Archive of New Records (AAN), the National Library and the Jewish Historical Institute in Warsaw; the Jagiellonian University Library and State Archives in Kraków, the United

found that the *Biuletyn* reported more on the Jews than any other underground paper.²⁰ The coverage ranged from dry reporting to compassionate feature articles. The paper also used its pages to print notices from the civilian underground warning that blackmailing Jews constituted treason and would be punished with the full force of the law.

In stark contrast to the image of the Home Army in Jewish collective memory and Jewish historiography, *Biuletyn* put forth what is arguably the most sympathetic treatment of the Jews in the entire underground Polish press.²¹ *Biuletyn*'s exceptional treatment, I argue in this chapter, hints at the need to examine the scope and influence of a liberal wing within the Home Army, which has received little or no attention in English-language studies.²²

Significant for understanding the *Biuletyn*'s positions on Jewish matters was the fact that it was printed and distributed by the Polish underground's Bureau of Information and Propaganda (BIP), itself under the direct command of the underground's chief headquarters in Warsaw. Under the leadership of Col. Jan Rzepecki (1899–1983), BIP became a center for the Home Army's liberal wing, predominantly sympathizers with the left-wing Democratic Party (SD) and Polish Socialist Party (PPS). Rzepecki himself was, according to one scholar, a "brilliant officer and intellectual, liberal and left-leaning in his political outlook, who had assembled in BIP an outstanding group of collaborators."²³

Throughout the war, *Biuletyn* was run by an editor-in-chief and editorial staff of some twelve individuals. The editor and some twelve editorial assistants were, in general, university graduates with degrees in the humanities and social sciences, were left-leaning politically, and had been active in the Polish scout movement. Aleksander Kamiński (1903–1978), the founder and editor until 1944, was born and raised in Warsaw, where he graduated from Warsaw University's department of history. He became a leader in the Polish scout movement and, beginning in 1931, was assigned the position of director of the scouts' national minorities division. It was in this capacity that Kamiński became the chief supervisor of the Union of Jewish Scouts in the

---

States Holocaust Memorial Museum Archive in Washington, DC, and the Hoover Institution Archives in Stanford, CA. A nearly complete reprint was published in *Przegląd Historyczno-Wojskowy*, special issue vols. 1–4 (2001–2004). No issues from 1939, however, have been preserved. See ibid., vol. 2 (2001), no. 190 (special issue vol. 1) (2001): 7.

20   Friedrich, "The Nazi Murder of the Jews in Polish Eyes," 394.
21   Ibid., 392, concurs with this view.
22   As noted above, a re-evaluation has begun to take place in Polish scholarly circles in the last decade.
23   Jan Tomasz Gross, *Fear: anti-Semitism in Poland after Auschwitz* (New York: Random House, 2006), 19.

1930s.[24] When he started printing the *Biuletyn* in November 1939, Kamiński drew upon his prewar Jewish connections, as well. His first editorial assistant, Stanisław Berezowski (1910–1986), was a fellow scout and university graduate.[25] Born in Kraków to a middle-class, educated family, Berezowski graduated from the Jagiellonian University in 1934 with degrees in philosophy and political science.[26] Prior to the war, Berezowski landed a faculty position at Warsaw University.[27] Other editors included university graduates with degrees in economics, literature, graphic design, archeology, psychology & history.

Not only was Kamiński himself directly involved in aiding Jews, for which he was recognized after the war by the State of Israel, but two of his editors were active in this regard as well. In the early period, *Biuletyn* welcomed to its staff Ewa Rybicka (1909–1943), a graduate of Warsaw University and a distinguished psychologist.[28] With the onset of the Nazi Final Solution, Rybicka became "deeply involved with unusual dedication" in the rescue particularly of Jewish children and, in late 1942, joined Żegota, the Polish Council to Aid the Jews.[29] Another editor, Tadeusz Kwaśniewski (1915–1943), was a graduate of Warsaw University in history and similarly became involved with Jewish matters. Kwaśniewski had been a scout leader before the war who, like Kamiński, was an instructor for the Union of Jewish Scouts. Utilizing the Jewish connections he had developed, Kwaśniewski acted as liaison between the Jewish Fighting Organization in the Warsaw ghetto and the Home Army's high command.[30]

In addition to editors involved in Jewish rescue, the editorial staff included one Pole of Jewish background and one Jewish resident of the Warsaw ghetto who acted as chief correspondent of Jewish affairs. The former included Wiktoria Goryńka (1902–1944), a graphic artist by profession who joined the editorial board in the early period and, according to one source, was in hiding for much of the war due to her Jewish origin.[31] The only member of the Jewish community on the editorial staff was Jerzy Grasberg, a pre-war Jewish

---

24 Kunert (ed.), *Słownik*, vol. 2, 76–77.
25 Władysław Bartoszewski, "Z kart wojennej służby Aleksandra Kamińskiego," *Tygodnik Powszechny* (April 30, 1978), 1; Lewandowska, *Polska konspiracyjna prasa*, 67.
26 Kunert (ed.), *Słownik*, vol. 3, 38.
27 W. Bartoszewski, *Tygodnik Powszechny* (April 30, 1978), 1; Lewandowska, *Polska konspiracyjna prasa informacyjno-polityczna*, 67.
28 *Polski Słownik Biograficzny* 23 (1991), 299.
29 Ibid., also Teresa Perkerowa, *Konspiracyjna Rada Pomocy Żydom w Warszawie 1942–1945* (Warszawa: Państwowy Instytut Wydawniczy, 1983), 101.
30 Perkerowa, *Konspiracyjna Rada*, 50; *Polski Słownik Biograficzny* 16 (1971), 344.
31 For the reference to Goryńka's Jewish origin, see Straszewska, "*Biuletyn Informacyjny*, 1939–1944," 12.

scout under Kamiński's command who functioned as the paper's specialist on Jewish affairs.³²

Biuletyn Informacyjny on the ghettoization of Polish Jewry, 1940

In the early period of the war, prior to the formation of the Warsaw ghetto, *Biuletyn* gave sporadic coverage of Jews. As ghettoization proceeded more systematically in smaller urban centers in the spring and summer of 1940, however, *Biuletyn* reported on these developments with alarm. Coverage of Jewish matters in *Biuletyn* first appeared in January 1940, when the paper warned against any collaboration with the Germans, reminding its readers that "any direct or indirect cooperation with the Germans in the persecution of the Jews is exactly the same as any other form of collaboration with Poland's mortal enemy."³³ In April 1940, *Biuletyn* printed a report on "sadistic German soldiers" who tormented Jews in a small town in the Podlaskie region.³⁴ Another piece from June 1940 reported that on June 15th, 1940, the Jews of Kutno, a city in the Łódź province with a Jewish population of 6,700, had been crammed into a ghetto on the site of a former sugar refinery.³⁵ The item was a factual report without comment and with no subsequent notice. In the summer of 1940, reports emphasized the increasing brutality towards the Jewish population of Warsaw. "Despite the fact that the Jewish community provides a few thousand people daily for labor to the Germans," *Biuletyn* stated in June 1940, "... people in the Jewish district fall prey to regular hunts for [additional] Jews who are taken for labor.... often with sadistic tormenting."³⁶

Biuletyn also covered the ill-treatment of Jews by the Soviet authorities in eastern Poland. For example, the subject appeared in an August 1940 issue on Soviet deportations of Polish citizens, more and more of whom it claimed were Jews. It noted a dire situation in which the Soviet authorities tried to

---

32   Ibid.
33   *Biuletyn Informacyjny* (19 January 1940), cited in Tomasz Szarota, *U progu zagłady: zajścia antyżydowskie i pogromy w okupowanej Europie* (Warszawa: Wydawnictwo Sic!, 2000), 74.
34   "Żydzi w 'Gubernii'," *Biuletyn Informacyjny* (5 April 1940), 5, in Archiwum Akt Nowych, Warsaw (henceforth AAN), Zbiór Prasy Konspiracyjnej (Underground press collection, henceforth ZPK), 71/1.
35   *Biuletyn Informacyjny* (28 June 1940), 3, in AAN, ZBK, 71/1. The event is confirmed in Geoffrey P. Megargee (ed.), *The United States Holocaust Memorial Museum Encyclopedia of Camps and Ghettos, 1933–1945*, vol. 2, ed. Martin Dean, *Ghettos in German-Occupied Eastern Europe* (Bloomington, IN: Indiana University Press, 2012), 36.
36   "Żydzi," *Biuletyn Informacyjny* (26 July 1940), 6, in AAN, ZBK, 71/1.

send a group of Jewish refugees back to German-occupied Poland. When the Germans refused the Soviet request, "about 20 train cars, after long waits at different stations, were sent somewhere into the interior [of Russia]."[37]

More alarming to *Biuletyn* was the situation of Jews in Łódź. The Jewish community there had been herded into a walled ghetto between February and April 30th, 1940, when the ghetto was sealed. A few months later, *Biuletyn* printed a shocking report of conditions in the Łódź ghetto where the Jews were "absolutely isolated. The acute shortage of foodstuffs provided by the Germans is leading to the spread of epidemics. Despite the efforts of the ghetto authorities, the mortality rate is alarming."[38]

News of the Łódź ghetto as well as ghettoization in small towns was overshadowed by the increasingly precarious situation in Warsaw. In July 1940, *Biuletyn* announced that "after a long period of indecision, the Germans have decided to create a ghetto in the capital. The thicket of details about the exact boundaries is not yet known."[39] Shortly thereafter, *Biuletyn* reported on the cruelty of Nazi policies, alerting its readers that a "German anti-Jewish event" had taken place on July 5th in which the slogan "Down with the *Żydo-komuna* [Judeo-Communist] and Stalin" had been used to incite anti-Jewish violence.[40] The topic that began to most gravely concern *Biuletyn*, however, was the rumor about plans for a ghetto in the capital.[41] In September 1940, *Biuletyn* reported that the German authorities had closed down Polish public schools in the area of the proposed ghetto while some Jews were being removed from apartments in certain areas of Warsaw.[42]

"A Gigantic Crime": The Creation of the Warsaw Ghetto

In anticipation of a walled ghetto for Europe's largest Jewish community, *Biuletyn*'s editorial staff began to identify a larger aim in Nazi Jewish policies amid the haze of anti-Jewish regulations. When the German authorities

---

37 Ibid., (9 August 1940), 7, in AAN, ZBK, 71/1.
38 "Wiadomości z Łodzi," in ibid., (2 August 1940), 4, in Hoover Institution Archives (henceforth HIA), Stanford University, Jan Karski Collection, microfilm reel 1 ("Polish underground publications").
39 *Biuletyn Informacyjny* (6 July 1940), 6, in AAN, ZBK, 71/1.
40 Ibid. (12 July 1940), 4, in AAN, ZBK, 71/1. The latter incident is described in Szarota, *U progu zagłady*, 63.
41 "Ghetto," *Biuletyn Informacyjny* (23 August 1940), 5, in AAN, ZBK, 71/1.
42 Ibid. (6 September 1940), 6, in AAN, ZBK, 71/1.

announced the construction of the Warsaw ghetto in October 1940, *Biuletyn* responded with a scathing editorial entitled "Nationality quarters." Referring to the some 180,000 Jews living outside the decreed ghetto boundary, and the thousands of Poles who would have to similarly relocate,[43] *Biuletyn* described the decree as "the realization of Hitlerism's barbaric intentions, affecting almost 200,000 inhabitants." It continued,

> Both Poles and Jews have been sentenced to a misery and homelessness that is difficult to describe. Removing the roofs from above people's heads, from those often devoid of livelihood, brings with it a sizable... calamity. Warsaw, subject to an orgy of a two-way population removal, has before itself a tragic future to look forward to.[44]

After the ghetto was sealed on November 16th, 1940, *Biuletyn* printed the following editorial on November 28th, 1940:

> Beginning on Monday the 25th of this month, the Warsaw ghetto became completely sealed. Entering and exiting the ghetto requires authorized papers. In this manner, the Hitlerites' insane plan to enclose 410,000 people into a tiny isolated area, completely devoid of free space and greenery [has been achieved]. The methodical plundering of Jews has not ceased while repeated raids on Jews used for labor outside the ghetto continues.... The Warsaw ghetto has become... a gigantic crime: upwards of 400,000 people have been condemned to the inevitable consequences of epidemics and slow death from hunger.[45]

Between the creation of the Warsaw ghetto and Operation Barbarossa in June 1941, *Biuletyn* provided extensive coverage of harrowing conditions in the Warsaw ghetto. A piece in February 1941 voiced alarm at the dumping of Jewish refugees into an already overcrowded ghetto in Warsaw. We read in its pages that the ghetto population had increased by 50,000 in the previous month, the result of refugees arriving from small towns outside Warsaw.[46] In March, 1941,

---

43 In the end, 138,000 Jews and 113,000 Poles were uprooted due to the ghetto decree. See Israel Gutman, *The Jews of Warsaw, 1939–1943* (Bloomington, IN: Indiana University Press, 1982), 60.
44 "Dzielnice narodowościowe," *Biuletyn Informacyjny* (18 October 1940), 7, in AAN, ZBK, 71/1.
45 "Dookoła Ghetta," in ibid. (28 November 1940), 7, in AAN, ZBK, 71/1.
46 "Ghetto," ibid. (6 February 1941), 6, in AAN, ZBK, 71/2. According to Gutman, *The Jews of Warsaw*, 63, the population of the Warsaw ghetto increased by 65,000 between January and March of 1941.

we read that the German authorities in Warsaw were instigating "vociferous antisemitic actions" by distributing "leaflets with antisemitic content," including graphic images that "fortunately are not the works of Polish artists."[47] In the same month, the paper informed its readers about the alarming events in Lublin, in which 34,000 Jews were placed in a newly formed ghetto.[48]

Biuletyn also reiterated its warning to Poles against any collaboration with Germans against the Jews. In March, it printed a statement by the Polish government-in-exile banning Poles from joining a German-organized Polish force to guard Jews serving in forced labor units. "The Government of the Republic of Poland," the statement read, had instructed Poles to "withhold from any and all... participation in anti-Jewish actions organized by the Germans." The article then proclaimed that the Polish underground military and civilian organizations inside occupied Poland loyal to the Polish government-in-exile "call upon all Poles to categorically reject any thoughts of entering into the ranks of auxiliary service for the German police." It concluded with an appeal to all underground press publishers to reprint the appeal.[49]

As ghettoization proceeded at an alarming pace, *Biuletyn* published an extraordinary piece of investigative reporting. Appearing in May 1941, it provided a detailed, factual account of the dreadful living conditions to which Jews were subjected. The piece began by dividing the history of Polish Jewry under German occupation into two periods: "incapacitation" and "isolation." In general, Nazi Jewish law, *Biuletyn* maintained, sought to undermine Polish Jewry economically and socially. The "capstone" of this period, *Biuletyn* stated, was "external and ostentatious degradation: arm bands, separate streetcars, denial of entry into city squares, orders to step out of the way and bow before Germans."[50] In addition, daily searches of Jewish apartments and the plundering of Jewish property contributed to incapacitation. "All of this was simply preparation," *Biuletyn* maintained, for phase II: "the complete isolation of Jews by enclosing them in the ghetto."

Applying this periodization to the history of Warsaw Jewry, *Biuletyn* presented alarming statistics about living conditions. Whereas the population density in Warsaw was 70 persons per hectare, it was sixteen times greater in

---

47 *Biuletyn Informacyjny* (20 March 1941), 10, in HIA, Jan Karski Collection, microfilm reel no. 1 ("Polish underground publications").
48 Ibid. (27 March 1941), 10, in AAN, ZBK, 71/2.
49 Ibid. (6 March 1941), cited in Andrzej Kunert (ed.), *Polacy-Żydzi, 1939–1945: wybór źródeł* (Warszawa: Oficyna Wydawnicza Rytm, 2001), Doc. II/3, 189 (English trans., 190).
50 "Żydzi," *Biuletyn Informacyjny* (23 May 1941), 5, in AAN, ZBK, 71/2. The latter piece is reprinted in Władysław Bartoszewski and Zofia Lewinówna (eds.), *Ten jest z ojczyzny mojej: Polacy z pomocą Żydom 1939–1945*, 2nd ed. (Kraków: Znak, 1969), 907–09.

the ghetto (1,110). And this overcrowding was getting worse. *Biuletyn* reported that the transport of thousands of Jews from the outlying province into the ghetto had increased the population to almost 500,000. The result, *Biuletyn* stated, was "hunger and poverty beyond the pale." It continued:

> Along the crowded streets wander... pale-faced, emaciated people, paupers sit beneath the walls and lie; one frequently sees people collapsing from hunger. Each day the population of the foundling houses increases by several newborns, each day several people die in the street. Infectious diseases spread, particularly tuberculosis. Concurrently, the confiscation of property from the wealthy Jews by the Germans is unceasing. Their treatment of Jews continues to be extremely inhumane.[51]

Unable to conceal its outrage, *Biuletyn* concluded:

> It is useless to review the legal strictures and restrictions that have been issued by the invaders—they are in conflict with the basic laws of Poland, of international law, and also all remaining laws, both those of God and of man. The treatment of Jews by the Germans gives total proof of their incredible bestiality and barbarity.[52]

"The Murder of Jews by Poison Gas is Taking Place": Operation Reinhard and the Beginnings of Mass Murder, June 1941–July 1942

In the wake of the German invasion of Soviet Russia in June 1941, *Biuletyn* documented and reported on the dramatic deterioration of the situation of the Jews. In its reports after the invasion, *Biuletyn* noted increasing anti-Jewish repressions.[53] In a December 1941 piece on health conditions in Warsaw, the paper noted that since 1939 mortality rates had increased in Warsaw while birth rates had declined. *Biuletyn* nonetheless qualified the general portrait, stating, "Among the Jews the situation is incomparably worse." The paper went on to print health statistics showing that the number of live Jewish births had

---

51 "Żydzi," *Biuletyn Informacyjny* (23 May 1941), 6, in AAN, ZBK, 71/2.
52 Ibid.
53 "Kraj," *Biuletyn Informacyjny* (14 August 1941), 10, in HIA, Jan Karski Collection, microfilm reel 1 ("Polish underground publications").

dramatically decreased while the mortality rate had increased significantly in comparison to the general population.⁵⁴

It was not until the beginning of 1942, however, that *Biuletyn* began to print stories on the shift in Nazi Jewish policies from ghettoization to mass murder. In its first story on the topic printed on January 15, 1942, *Biuletyn* used eyewitness testimony as evidence. The eye witness, a Jew who had seen German atrocities in the East, told the following to *Biuletyn*:

> It amazes me that here, in Warsaw, you do not appear to know what the Germans are doing in Russia, and even in Eastern Poland: they are murdering, literally, whole [Jewish] towns—men, women, the elderly, children and infants. Nothing like this has ever happened since the Middle Ages.⁵⁵

Later in January 1942, *Biuletyn* reported on the shocking results of German Jewish policies in the East in a frantic tone. The dramatic population shifts that had taken place in the wake of the German invasion included the decline in the population of Minsk from 240,000 to 92,000, and of Smolensk from 160,000 to 41,000, while "the Jewish population 'has disappeared' completely from the majority of cities and towns. For example, in Borysov, Mołodeczno and Mogilev—not a single Jew is left."⁵⁶ What is more, Jewish small towns east of Warsaw along the Bug were being subjected to "slaughter" (*mord masowy*). The report continued: "People are taken away supposedly for labor—then, afterwards, they are shot or poisoned with gas."⁵⁷ In a story on the region of Vilna, *Biuletyn* maintained that "the occupier's use of unprecedented terror against the Jews" had crossed a threshold never before seen in history.⁵⁸ *Biuletyn* subsequently informed its readers that large numbers of Jews were being shot "for no reason whatsoever."⁵⁹ In a piece titled "Cases of Bestiality," a Jewish mother and her four year-old child were randomly killed on the street while a

---

54 "Warszawa," ibid. (4 December 1941), 8–9, in Archiwum Państwowe, Kraków (APK), Prasa Konspiracyjna (Underground press), 5.
55 Ibid. (15 January 1942), 5, in United States Holocaust Memorial Museum (USHMM) Archives, RG 15.080M *172, microfiche 43/142.
56 Ibid. (29 January 1942), 7, in HIA, Jan Karski Collection, microfilm reel 1 ("Polish underground publications").
57 Ibid. (19 February 1942), 9, in USHMM Archives, microfilm reel 1, RG 15.079M, microfilm reel 1, Ringelblum Archive I, folder 1355, I/719.
58 "Wileńszczyzna," ibid. (12 March 1942), 7.
59 "Niepokój w Lubelszczyźnie," in ibid. (19 March 1942), 8.

similar fate befell a ten year-old Polish boy for gathering bits of coal found on the street.[60]

When the Final Solution was launched in the spring of 1942, the Home Army's central organ gradually identified this new phase in the Nazi persecution. "In the territories of Poland," *Biuletyn* stated in early April 1942, "one is aware—in connection with Hitler's latest speeches—of an increase in German bestiality towards the Jews. According to reports from various regions, the Germans are shooting any Jews they come across on streets and in small towns for no apparent reason."[61] In the same issue, readers were informed of deteriorating conditions in the Warsaw ghetto, whereby "the poor Jewish masses are starving—in the ghetto upwards of 1000 people per week are dying."[62]

As the Final Solution took shape, *Biuletyn* reported on the shocking events in Lublin, where mass deportations from the ghetto had begun in March 1942. The descriptions of the liquidation actions in the Lublin ghetto include the first mention of the death camp in Bełżec, which had begun operating that month. It described how Jews were ordered to congregate in one place. "The sick, indolent and those lingering about were shot on the spot. All the children from the orphanage numbering 108... were taken outside the city and murdered." It continued:

> Around 2,500 people have been murdered. The remaining population numbering some 25,000 is being deported to camps in Bełżec and Trawniki. In these camps—according to the most reliable testimonies—the murder of Jews by poison gas is taking place.... Jews in the small towns outside Lublin are being murdered in the same manner (Opole, Wąwolnica, Nałęczów, Biłgoraj).[63]

In addition to Lublin, the paper cited evidence about the first experiments with the use of hermetically sealed gas vans for mass murder in Chełmno back in January and described mass graves in the forests outside of the camp.[64]

Meanwhile, in the same month, *Biuletyn* ran not only its largest story to date on the situation of the Jews but made it the cover story for the first time.

---

60   "Przykłady bestialstwa," ibid. (26 March 1942), 7.

61   "Kraj," ibid. (2 April 1942), 7.

62   "Warszawa," ibid. (2 April 1942), 7.

63   "Mordowanie Żydów w lubelszczyźnie," ibid. (16 April 1942), 6–7, in USHMM Archives, RG 15.080M *172, microfiche 50/142.

64   Ibid. (23 April 1942), 7, in USHMM Archives, microfilm reel 1, RG 15.079M, Ringelblum Archive I, folder 1355, I/719.

Divided into four parts, it began with an update on the conditions of the Jews in the Warsaw ghetto. Its dire tone set the stage for what was to come. "Extreme poverty," it began, "hunger, cold and horrific hygienic conditions have once again created an atrocious situation here."[65] The paper then pointed its readers to recent municipal population figures demonstrating an alarmingly high mortality rate in the ghetto. The number of deaths, it reported, was 44,272 in 1941, or 10% of the ghetto population. In contrast, the mortality rate among Warsaw Jewry in 1939 was 1.5%. "The Germans," *Biuletyn* concluded, "are consciously striving to exacerbate already horrendous conditions. And to this end, they are continuing to reduce the area of the ghetto combined with further resettlements of Jews from the surrounding small towns."[66] The article continued with sections on Jews in the eastern territories as well as the tragic situation of deportations from the Lublin ghetto. Here, devastating reports filled *Biuletyn*'s pages, portraying mass killings of unarmed Jews. One of the most frightening images of the Holocaust appeared for the first time: that of Jews being burned alive in a sealed synagogue: "In Białystok, a few hundred Jews were locked inside a synagogue while Germans set it ablaze."[67]

After a litany of shocking figures on the destruction of small Jewish communities in the east, *Biuletyn* concluded with an analysis of the unprecedented crimes against the Jews. In an unusually emotional editorial, *Biuletyn* evaluated the situation just as the Final Solution was beginning to be carried out. Hitler's public threats to "exterminate" European Jewry were now becoming state policy, the article began. Then, after quoting Hitler's blood-curdling speech of January 30th, 1942 threatening the complete annihilation of the Jews, *Biuletyn* had some words for the German leader and his people:

> The extermination of the Jews is, in the literal sense of the word, now taking place. While the initiator is Hitler, we cannot close our eyes to the fact that these crimes have taken such a monstrous form only because of those people ready and willing to carry out Hitler's intentions. This butchery rests not only on Hitler. Rather, the whole German nation bears responsibility for it. The sea of blood will be an eternal blot on this nation...[68]

---

65 "Żydzi," ibid. (30 April 1942), 1. The article has been reprinted in full in Bartoszewski, Kunert (eds.), *Polacy-Żydzi, 1939–1945*, Doc. II/7, 200, as well as in Bartoszewski and Lewinówna (eds.), *Ten jest z ojczyzny mojej*, 912–15.
66 Ibid., 2. [ref. to "Żydzi," ibid. (30 April 1942)?].
67 Ibid., 2.
68 Ibid., 3.

More reporting on massacres of Jews appeared in the pages of *Biuletyn* in early June and early July. "The slaughtering of the Jews on Polish lands," the journal stated, "now assumes the distinct character of a system: Jews able to work are preserved. The Germans either murder the remaining Jews or send them to camps, where they are, step by step, killed. Such was the case with the Jews of Lublin mentioned earlier in these pages."[69] In its following issue, *Biuletyn* ran a piece on the Warsaw ghetto. It expressed horror at the emerging trend of summary executions of Jews in the ghetto. "For some time," *Biuletyn* reported, "murdering Jews point-blank on the streets and leaving them dead on the pavement has become a prevalent 'fashion' for Germans." Ninety-four Jews had been executed on June 8th and 9th for being found outside the ghetto.[70]

Such compassionate reporting adds a much needed corrective to popular understandings of Polish-Jewish relations during the Holocaust. Yet it is also important to note that such shocking news was usually confined to the back pages, potentially lost among many news flashes. Take, for example, a piece of news from early July 1942, that appeared on p. 7: "In Kraków, Tarnów and other cities in western Małopolska, there are reports of mass murder committed against Jews. A new method is now being used: hanging [Jews] on trees and poles along the roads."[71] Prior to July 1942, when mass deportations began from the Warsaw ghetto, stories on the situation of the Jews in Poland and Europe were placed on the front page in only one out of 132 issues of the paper.

"With Absolute Prussian Brutality": From the Great Deportations to the Warsaw Ghetto Uprising, July 1942 to April–May 1943

Just when it was nearly inconceivable that conditions for Polish Jewry could deteriorate further, the throttle of the Final Solution machine was turned up to full speed. On July 22nd, 1942, German authorities in Warsaw ordered the "resettlement to the East" of 6,000 Jews per day. When the head of Europe's largest ghetto, Adam Czerniakow, realized "resettlement" meant death, he committed suicide. Total chaos ensued as mass deportations began. When the actions ceased in September, Warsaw's population had declined by a staggering 300,000.

---

69 "Likwidowanie Żydów," ibid. (18 June 1942), 7, in USHMM Archives, RG 15.079M, microfilm reel 1, Ringelblum Archive I, folder 1355, 1/719.
70 "W Getcie," ibid. (9 July 1942), 7.
71 "Kraj," ibid. (2 July 1942), 7.

In its first issue after the deportation began, dated July 30th, 1942, *Biuletyn* ran a story with first-hand descriptions. One of the distinctive features of *Biuletyn* was that it had a correspondent reporting from inside the Warsaw ghetto. That *Biuletyn* reporter was Jerzy Grasberg, a resident of the Warsaw ghetto who, beginning in 1941, served as the *Biuletyn*'s editor on Jewish affairs.[72] A Warsaw native who had been a student at Warsaw University, Grasberg had formed a group of Jewish scouts who had worked closely with Aleksander Kamiński, *Biuletyn*'s editor-in-chief, before the war.[73] Grasberg's wife, a resident in the Warsaw ghetto who survived the war, has confirmed that Kamiński and her late husband had been close friends prior to 1939.[74] Kamiński himself spoke warmly about his friend, Grasberg, in a postwar testimony.[75]

With a correspondent from inside the ghetto, the Home Army's central organ was able to provide a vivid and dramatic depiction of events. Relying on Grasberg's reporting, *Biuletyn* gave a hurried, almost frantic description of the events of the week of July 22–29 in Warsaw. "The main event which has shocked this city for a week now is the German-led commencement of the liquidation of the Warsaw ghetto," the paper reported, "carried out with absolute Prussian brutality."[76] A description of the deportations followed:

> The *aktion* began without any advance warning on the 22nd of this month and was initiated with the utmost ruthless terror. In the night, a special Ukrainian detachment along with SS units entered the ghetto. They began chaotically forcing people from their apartments and in the

---

[72] Sources confirming Grasberg's position within *Biuletyn Informacyjny* include the writings of Maria Straszewska, secretary to the paper's editor-in-chief throughout the war. In her essay on the history of *Biuletyn Informacyjny*, Straszewska maintains that Grasberg was the "editor on Jewish affairs" for the paper. See *Przegląd Historyczno-Wojskowy* Vol. 2 (2001), Nr. Specjalny 1 (190): 12. Two secondary sources that confirm Grasberg's position include Engelking and Libionka, *Żydzi w Powstańczej Warszawie*, 44; and Teresa Prekerowa, "Wojna i okupacja," in Jerzy Tomaszewski et al. (eds.), *Najnowsze dzieje Żydów w Polsce* (Warszawa: PWN, 1993), 308.

[73] Anka Grupińska, *Ciągle po kole: rozmowy z żołnierzami getta warszawskiego* (Warszawa: Twój Styl, 2000), 282.

[74] Interview with Luba Gawisar in ibid., 158.

[75] "Relacja Aleksandra Kamińskiego z 1946 r. w odpowiedzi na ankietę Komisji Historycznej," *Harcerstwo* 1 (January 1985): 29–30.

[76] "Początek likwidacji ghetta," *Biuletyn Informacyjny* (30 July 1942), 6, in USHMM Archives, RG 15.096M, microfilm reel 1, Muzeum Tatrzanskie, Zakopane, (Underground press collection), reel 1. Reprinted in Bartoszewski and Lewinówna (eds.), *Ten jest z ojczyzny mojej*, 917–18.

process people were murdered for the most trivial reasons or for no reason at all. Throughout the night, and all the next day, the sounds of rifles and machine guns could be heard as Jews were murdered in homes, in courtyards and on the streets. It was not until the second half of the day of pogroms that a notice was posted explaining the reason for the 'aktion': that inhabitants of the Warsaw ghetto were being removed from the city.[77]

The piece continued that "the mood in the ghetto is grim. The streets—empty. Windows—not a single person can be seen." For 6,000 Jews were being deported daily.

As to the fate of the deportees one week into the deportations, *Biuletyn* could only state that they were going somewhere to the east according to the Germans. Regarding the real fate of these deportees, *Biuletyn* reported, "the most pessimistic speculations are circulating."[78] *Biuletyn* referred to the way the Jewish Police and *Judenrat* were being used as a form of "satanic German ingeniousness." Regarding Adam Czerniakow, the Judenrat chief, *Biuletyn* stated: "The head of the Judenrat, Czerniakow, protested against the atrocities committed in the only manner available, and one which creates respect for him—by committing suicide."[79]

Throughout the summer of 1942, column after column appeared on deportations from the Warsaw ghetto. "On July 22nd," *Biuletyn* continued its coverage, "the diabolical liquidation *aktion* in the Warsaw ghetto began."[80] It noted that while the Jewish Police continued to take part, the Germans coerced them by threatening to kill their families unless a minimum daily quota of deportees was filled. The number of Jews deported, the paper stated, was now approaching 70,000. What was new in the August 8th edition was speculation on the fate of deportees. "While precise details and certainty are being determined, first-hand accounts give no doubt that the transports of Jews are being directed via various routes towards two main death camps in Bełżec and Sobibór." The paper was inaccurate about the details because the actual destination of the Warsaw ghetto deportees was a death camp that had only come into use that very month—Treblinka, some fifty miles north of Warsaw.

---

77   Ibid.
78   Ibid., 7.
79   Ibid.
80   "Postępy likwidacji ghetto," ibid. (6 August 1942), 7, in United States Holocaust Memorial Museum (USHMM) Archives, RG 15.080M *172, microfiche 43/142.

Biuletyn described the prevailing atmosphere in the ghetto: "In the face of this desperate situation, the mood in the ghetto is one of total gloom as acts of insanity are growing in numbers."[81] It continued that the "sadistic cruelty" towards the deportees "has not let up in the least bit. Shooting of a certain number of people on the ghetto streets continues which are now practically empty, creating a haunting impression."[82] It continued with a frightening portrayal of astronomical food prices due to the complete stoppage of imports into the ghetto, adding, "the number of suicides and displays of insanity are on the rise." *Biuletyn* estimated that somewhere between 120,000 and 150,000 Jews had now been deported. A frightening report about Bełżec also appeared, which the paper characterized as a death camp specifically for Jews.[83] Here, readers are informed that, according to one eye-witness, Jews were being killed in gas chambers, and a description follows based on that testimony.

Biuletyn continued its reporting on the deportations from the Warsaw ghetto under the paper's section on news from the capital. "Deportations from the Warsaw ghetto have continued unabated," the article read. "The most intense actions were taken Friday the 7th and Saturday the 8th [of August 1942] in which between 10,000 and 15,000 Jews were deported."[84] A dire report the following week informed its readers that "as we write, the number of people deported from the Warsaw ghetto now approaches 200,000."[85] Now, for the first time, *Biuletyn* reported that Warsaw Jewry was perishing in "gas chambers" in Treblinka outside of Warsaw. It recounted how throughout the night deep ditches were dug in the ground into which the murdered were dumped. The paper continued in its first September issue that after a brief pause "the Germans resumed liquidating the ghetto with absolute fierceness."[86] Only now, the paper reported, employees of the Judenrat and their families were being forced onto the train. In its subsequent issue, *Biuletyn* reported on the increasingly tragic situation in the ghetto, stating that the Germans had plastered new notices informing the ghetto inhabitants that exemptions from deportation enjoyed by employees of workshops had been lifted.[87] Furthermore, readers were informed, the ghetto had been totally sealed off from the outside. Not

---

81 Ibid., 7.
82 "Początek likwidacji ghetta," ibid. (13 August 1942), 7, in USHMM Archives, RG 15.070M, microfilm reel 1.
83 "Obóz w Bełżcu," ibid. (13 August 1942), 6.
84 Ibid., 7.
85 "Postępy likwidacji ghetta," ibid. (20 August 1942), 8.
86 "Dalsza likwidacja ghetta," ibid. (3 September 1942), 8.
87 "Dalsza likwidacja ghetta," ibid. (10 September 1942), 7.

only were rumors circulating of plans for the total liquidation of the ghetto, but new notices had appeared that the death penalty would be imposed on any Pole who gave assistance to Jews fleeing the ghetto.[88]

The so-called Great Deportations came to a halt on September 13th, 1942, having gutted Warsaw's population by some 300,000.[89] In its first issue following the cessation of deportations, *Biuletyn* ran several items ranging from the situation of the Jews in France to the deportations from Warsaw. It began by reprinting a declaration by the Polish underground's Directorate of Civil Resistance (KWC). "For a year now," the declaration stated,

> a monstrous plan by our enemy for the annihilation of the Jews has been taking place on Polish soil. All the atrocities ever committed pale in comparison to this mass murder which has no precedent in the history of the world. [The victims are] infants, children, youth, adults, the elderly, crippled, ill, healthy, men, women, Catholic converts, and practicing Jews who, for no reason other than the fact that they belong to the Jewish nation, are mercilessly slaughtered by poison gas, by being burned alive, thrown out of windows.... The number of those killed in these various ways now exceeds one million and increases with each day.... Unable to actively prevent this, the Directorate of Civil Resistance in the name of the whole of Polish society protests against the crimes committed against the Jews. This protest represents the voice of all Polish political and social groups. As in the case of Polish victims, the actual responsibility for these crimes rests on the perpetrators and their collaborators.[90]

In the same issue, *Biuletyn* ran a story on Auschwitz. What is extraordinary is the precision of the characterization of the range and purpose of this death camp. It stated that a separate section had been built for Jews from all over Europe. On p. 7 of the paper, it issued the following shocking report: "Gas chambers have been installed in which over 1,000 Jews perish daily. The corpses are incinerated in three crematoria."[91] The same issue of the paper reported on the deportation of French Jewry with the cooperation of the French authorities,[92]

---

88   Ibid., 8.
89   *Encyclopaedia Judaica*, 2nd ed. (2007), vol. 20, 672.
90   "Oświadczenie," *Biuletyn Informacyjny* (17 September 1942), 2, in USHMM Archives, RG 15.070M, microfilm reel 1. Reprinted in Bartoszewski and Lewinówna (eds.), *Ten jest z ojczyzny mojej*, 919–20.
91   "Oświęcim," ibid. (17 September 1942), 7.
92   Ibid., 6.

as well as the tragic fate of Polish Jewry, stating, "From all corners of Poland we are receiving reports of the continued extermination of the Jews."[93]

In a devastating report in the following issue, *Biuletyn* informed its readers on p. 7 of the increasing pace of German exterminationist actions: "Death camps in Bełżec, Treblinka and Sobibór are working day and night. In Radom," the paper continued, "only about 7% of the Jewish community remains. About 1,000 people were shot on the spot and the remaining 22,000 deported to Treblinka. In Kielce, the entire ghetto was liquidated in a single night (August 19th) with 1,200 shot on the spot and 16,000 deported.... While fragmentary and incomplete, these reports illustrate the scale of the crimes being carried out by the Germans."[94]

The theme of German exterminationist polices continued from issue to issue as the Polish underground authorities received reliable eye-witnesses testimony. For the first time, a column on Auschwitz referred to it as "Auschwitz—A Death Camp." Here, *Biuletyn* wrote of Auschwitz-Birkenau as a death camp for Jews, noting that only 2,000 Jews had been sent to Auschwitz by the end of 1941. Yet "in the course of 1942 about 30,000 Jewish men and 15,000 Jewish women and children" had arrived. The vast majority "... went directly to the gas chambers."[95] A table followed, maintaining that 35,000 "unregistered Jews" had arrived at Auschwitz as of July 1, 1942, for which there was no record of their whereabouts.[96] In a report on the Warsaw ghetto, *Biuletyn* stated accurately that some 90% of the ghetto had been wiped out, with between 30,000 and 40,000 Jews remaining, all between the ages of 15 and 45, who were employed in factories aiding the German war effort. Regarding the 300,000 Jews deported, *Biuletyn* stated that "the vast majority were murdered primarily in the gas chambers of the Treblinka concentration camp." A haunting description of the ghetto followed: "The streets and homes of the Warsaw ghetto are deserted, plundered, quiet, making a devastating impression."[97]

Despite its unwavering sympathy for the Jews, *Biuletyn* stopped short of calling on Polish society to physically intervene. Echoing the Home Army

---

93   Ibid., 7.
94   "Likwidacja Żydów," ibid. (1 October 1942), 7, in USHMM Archives, RG 15.096M, microfilm reel 1.
95   "Oświęcim—obóz śmierci," ibid. (8 October 1942), 3, in USHMM Archives, RG 15.070M, microfilm reel 1.
96   Ibid., 4.
97   "W ghetcie—'Spokój'," in ibid. (8 October 1942), 7–8. The figure of 90% accords exactly with the recently published Yad Vashem guide to the ghettos. See *Yad Vashem Encyclopedia of the Ghettos during the Holocaust* (Jerusalem: Yad Vashem, 2009), 914.

commander's order from November 1942, *Biuletyn* made the following revealing statement in a front-page editorial: "If the occupiers decide to direct the same methods they are using against the Jews against the Polish people, they will meet with ferocious resistance..."[98] In a piece on conditions in East Galicia, *Biuletyn* perpetuated uncritically the stereotype of Jewish support for the Soviets when it commented that "Jews are not liked [in East Galicia]" because during the Soviet occupation they exhibited "a harmful attitude (*postawa fatalna*)—yet despite this, the [local] population sympathizes with them and even gives aid."[99]

By November 1942, *Biuletyn* continued to report on atrocities in the Warsaw ghetto but surmised that the German plan was likely to retain the remaining population. The paper accurately estimated the ghetto population to have stabilized at about 40,000. The fact that these ghetto inhabitants, between the ages of 15 and 45, were working in war-essentials factories for the Germans made them indispensable, *Biuletyn* argued. Therefore, the Germans "this time, perhaps, do not intend to wholly destroy the ghetto."[100]

Meanwhile, on November 27th 1942, the Polish national council in London delivered a formal recommendation to the Polish government-in-exile that it demand Allied intervention to halt the German crimes against the Jews.[101] Rather than praise the action, *Biuletyn* harshly criticized the government-in-exile for what it argued was a too-little, too-late declaration. The Home Army paper boldly posed the following question:

> We, here in Poland, raise the question: what does this four months-long delayed response to what is going on with the Jews in Poland mean? Since June 22nd, news has been coming from Poland on this issue in numerous telegrams sent abroad... but the general subject was covered in silence. The answer to this riddle is simple: the reports from Poland **were not believed.** They were treated as unaccountable exaggeration. **The minds of normal people cannot accommodate the news coming out of Poland.** And only the arrival of extensive correspondence containing documents,

---

98 "Wytrwamy!," ibid. (29 October 1942), 1–2, in USHMM Archives, RG 15.080M *172, microfiche 64/142.

99 "Małopolska," ibid. (12 November 1942), 5–6, in USHMM Archives, RG 15.080M *172, microfiche 65/142. I am grateful to Julian Bussgang for assistance with rendering into English the term "postawa fatalna."

100 "Dalsza likwidacja ghetta," ibid. (19 November 1942), 7–8, in USHMM Archives, RG 15.080M *172, microfiche 66/142.

101 *Encyclopedia of the Holocaust*, vol. III, 1178.

photographs, descriptions, and testimonies have opened eyes to what the Germans are really capable of.[102]

Two weeks later, however, *Biuletyn* concluded that the Polish government's declaration to the Allies was, in itself, a positive development. The declaration was subsequently noted in a positive manner. *Biuletyn* continued to report on massive crimes being committed against Polish Jews. The paper stated that "world opinion is being stirred by German bestiality being conducted against the Jews," and that governments were officially taking note.[103] The Polish government's declaration was, at the very least, influencing world opinion, according to the paper.

Documenting Jewish Armed Resistance

The above story was followed by the first reports of active Jewish resistance to German liquidation actions in the provinces. The paper noted, in December 1942, that in the eastern Polish province of Polesia, "Jews are putting up active resistance in the face of German liquidation actions."[104] With horror, *Biuletyn* noted that German extermination plans in the General Government had been so thorough that most Jews had already been murdered. In southeastern Galicia, liquidation actions were not only in full force but were intensifying: there, authorities were shooting Jews on the spot and pursuing those in hiding. In Hrubieszów and Chełm, "one hears gun shots day after day in which the last Jews are being found."[105] But "active Jewish resistance" was taking place in the provinces of Białystok and Grodno.[106] And in January 1943, *Biuletyn* reported that during German anti-Jewish action in Częstochowa, "shots at the police by the Jews took place."[107]

The most prominent article in *Biuletyn* on Jewish resistance came in the wake of the first armed self-defense actions in the Warsaw ghetto when the

---

102 "Dopiero teraz uwierzono," *Biuletyn Informacyjny* (10 December 1942), 4 [emphasis in the original], in USHMM Archives, RG 15.080M *172, microfiche 67/142. Interestingly, it was on the day the latter issue appeared that the Polish government-in-exile in London made its memorandum public.

103 "Punkt szczytowy," ibid. (24 December 1942), 4, in USHMM Archives, RG 15.080M *172, microfiche 68/142.

104 Ibid. (17 December 1942), 3.

105 "Likwidacja Żydów na ziemiach wschodnich," ibid., 6.

106 Ibid.

107 Ibid. (28 January 1943), 8, in USHMM Archives, RG 15.080M *172, microfiche 71/142.

newly formed Jewish Fighting Organization (ŻOB) prevented a German liquidation action on January 18th 1943. A distinct shift in *Biuletyn's* characterization of the Jews, from passive to active, comes through. The report stated that German police entered the ghetto the night of Sunday, January 17th and began surrounding apartment houses in preparation for deportations. Jews were forced out of their houses and gathered outside.

> In a few locations, gun shots fired towards the German gendarmes while hand grenades were hurled in their direction, killing and injuring German and Jewish police. Faced with resistance, the German police returned fire, killing some, but feared stepping into homes [from which shots were being directed at them]. That is why only some 5,000 Jews were deported in the course of Monday and Tuesday whereas trains for twice that amount had been prepared. Organized strongholds defended themselves on Monday and Tuesday, right before two elite SS units in trucks entered the ghetto on Wednesday with machine guns and grenade launchers.... **They were met with active resistance using such primitive weapons as rods, crowbars, and stones.** The SS bloodily suppressed the latter. German losses include dozens of SS and police. The German actions were halted on Thursday and the ghetto expects more at any moment. The heroic stance of those who did not lose a sense of honor in the saddest times for the Jewish people builds respect and has inaugurated a glorious chapter in the history of Polish Jews.[108]

Biuletyn directed its readers to more and more cases of Jewish armed responses to the Final Solution in the first months of 1943. In a six-paragraph article in February 1943, the paper reported that Jews had taken up arms in many locations. The sounds of gun shots and explosions, similar to those heard in the Warsaw ghetto in mid-January, are echoed through all of Poland, *Biuletyn* stated. "Polish society now recognizes this decisive proof of a brave resolve to resist. The Germans do not hide their astonishment and still cannot believe [this is taking place]. At the same time, from the other side of Poland, alongside the deplorable liquidation actions against the Jews, reports are streaming in about manifestations of [Jewish] resistance."[109] The article followed with a discussion of armed revolts in Lwów in January. Active armed resistance was also reported in Sandomierz, Mińsk Mazowiecki and Krynki. Most recently,

---

108   Ibid. [emphasis in the original].
109   "Żydzi stawiają opór," ibid. (25 February 1943), 6, in USHMM Archives, RG 15.080M *172, microfiche 73/142.

Biuletyn stated, there were signs of resistance in Zagłębia Dąbrowa.¹¹⁰ Although the article admitted that it lacked sufficient evidence, it referred to "the first acts of sabotage" carried out in the Warsaw ghetto. The paper concluded that "all these cases reveal that there has been a transformation in Jewish society which has brought about a resolute will to resist, to fight with the criminal Germans."¹¹¹

Meanwhile, the coming of the year 1943 saw more extensive coverage of Nazi exterminationist policies. In its inaugural issue of 1943, *Biuletyn* reported on further massacres against the Jews. "The mass murder of Jews still continues unabated," *Biuletyn* stated, adding that "slaughter in Treblinka is happening around the clock."¹¹² It then reported that the last Jews of Lublin to be shot were the head of the Judenrat, and "the Jewish Gestapo agent, Grajer."¹¹³ In its last issue of January 1943, readers of *Biuletyn* were informed that at the end of December 1942 and the beginning of 1943, "the Germans have begun the final liquidation of the Jews in various locations in the General Government," citing the cities of Radom, Częstochowa, and Radomsko.

Confronting Polish Society—the *szmalcownicy* (*blackmailers*)

Until Fall 1942, *Biuletyn* made no mention of Polish involvement in anti-Jewish actions, either through participation in local pogroms or denunciations. With no mention of the outbreak of pogroms in Polish towns in July 1941 such as Jedwabne, readers came away with the impression that anti-Jewish policy was an exclusively German-Jewish problem. But *Biuletyn* broke its silence on October 15th 1942, when it reported on the liquidation of the ghettos of Wołomin and Stoczek, towns northeast of Warsaw: "The liquidation of ghettos in the majority of cities has now begun to encompass the destruction of Jewish communities in cities and towns in the whole of Poland." No liquidation actions had been as horrendous as in the towns of Wołomin and Stoczek,

---

110 Ibid.
111 Ibid., 7.
112 "Dalsze mordowanie Żydów," ibid. (7 January 1943), 7, in USHMM Archives, RG 15.070M, microfilm reel 1.
113 Shama Grajer (sometimes spelled "Grayer") was deputy head of the Jewish Police in the Lublin ghetto and was a notorious Gestapo agent. See Isaiah Trunk, *Judenrat: the Jewish Councils in Eastern Europe under Nazi Occupation* (New York: Bison Books, 1972), 487. On the Lublin ghetto (although Grajer is not mentioned), see Megargee (ed.), *The United States Holocaust Memorial Museum Encyclopedia of Camps and Ghettos, 1933–1945*, vol. 2, 675–78.

it stated. Although Poles are not mentioned by name, what follows was the description of a German *aktion* with substantial participation of local Poles:

> The fire brigade ... as well as the dregs of society in Stoczek actively took part in the destruction of the Jews, earning for themselves a disastrous page in [the town's] history, coming to the aid of the murderers, hunting down those in hiding, and taking part in looting.[114]

In a subsequent issue, *Biuletyn* printed a correction to the above story. An eyewitness to the liquidation of the Stoczek ghetto claimed that the Fire Brigade had tried to prevent anti-Jewish violence and looting by direct German orders. *Biuletyn* printed a retraction, but concluded: "*Biuletyn* corrects the above-mentioned error in full, excluding the Wołomin Fire Brigade from the circle of scum that was active in the liquidation of the Jews and plundered their property, bringing shame on the Polish Nation."[115]

The most pressing and delicate issue regarding Polish attitudes and behavior, however, was the problem of Polish blackmailers. In the wake of the Great Deportations from the Warsaw ghetto in July–September 1942, and the increasing number of Jews hiding on the Aryan side of Warsaw and other ghettos as liquidation actions spread across Poland, the problem of Polish blackmailers became increasingly acute. It was not until 1943 that the Polish underground authorities issued an official declaration condemning Polish blackmailing and warning that such actions constituted treason against the Polish state.

In March 1943, *Biuletyn* used its pages as a vehicle to condemn Polish blackmailers or *szmalcownicy* who preyed upon Jewish fugitives from the ghettos and camps. The declaration, issued by the Polish underground's Directorate of Civil Resistance (KWC), stated that blackmailing Jews would be punished to the full extent of the law.[116] The underground declared that despite the fact that some Poles were giving food and shelter to Jews,

> there nonetheless can be found those individuals bereft of respect and conscience ... who have created a new source of income for themselves by blackmailing those Poles who help Jews and Jews themselves. The

---

114 "Likwidacja getta w Wołominie i Stoczku," *Biuletyn Informacyjny* (22 October 1942), 6, in USHMM Archives, RG 15.070M, microfilm reel 1.

115 "Dopiero teraz uwierzono," ibid. (10 December 1942), 4, in USHMM Archives, RG 15.080M *172, microfiche 67/142.

116 "Ostrzeżenie," ibid. (18 March 1943), 2, in USHMM Archives, RG 15.080M *172, microfiche 74/142.

KWC warns that this type of extortion is recorded and will be punished to the full extent of the law... either at this time or in the future.[117]

Biuletyn accompanied the Declaration with an editorial reinforcing its support for the Declaration. "We are empowered to confirm that all types of this sort of extortion, coercion, bribery and swindling are consistently recorded [and] the offenders will at the proper moment be subjected to the severest consequences."[118] As blackmailing continued to plague Jews in hiding and their Polish helpers, Biuletyn printed announcements on several occasions from the Directorate of Civil Resistance informing readers that the death penalty had been either carried out or ordered on individual Poles for handing over Jews to the Gestapo. Prominent was the announcement printed on Biuletyn's front page on September 16th, 1943. The Polish underground's court in Warsaw, the paper informed its readers, had carried out the death penalty on August 25th, 1943 on Bogusław Pilnik. The announcement, intended to bring maximum public shame and thus to deter others, named the offender's parents and the street address in Warsaw. It stated the crime as "handing over Polish citizens of Jewish nationality into the hands of the German authorities."[119]

Meanwhile, the paper continued to disseminate news of the Final Solution in the weeks leading up to the Warsaw ghetto rising. In a devastating piece on the fate of Polish Jewry in the Volynia region, Biuletyn reported, in an emotionally charged article, that "the relentless extermination of the Jews in Volynia began in September 1942. Ruthless units, made up of a few German SS divisions, assisted by Ukrainian militants, initially murdered the whole Gypsy community in Volynia. Then, in turn, it murdered the Jewish people from the Volynian ghettos." The method of killing was by machine guns. "In this way entire Jewish communities of men, women and children were murdered."[120]

---

117   English translation from Bartoszewski, Kunert (eds.), *Polacy-Żydzi, 1939–1945*, Doc. II/13, 221.

118   "Hieny," *Biuletyn Informacyjny* (18 March 1943), 7, in USHMM Archives, RG 15.080M *172, microfiche 74/142. Partially reprinted in Bartoszewski and Lewinówna (eds.), *Ten jest z ojczyzny mojej*, 924.

119   "Obwieszczenie," *Biuletyn Informacyjny* (16 September 1943), 1, in USHMM Archives, RG 15.080M *172, microfiche 88/142. For an English translation of the announcement, see Władysław Bartoszewski and Zofia Lewin (eds.), *Righteous Among the Nations: How Poles helped the Jews 1939–1945* (London: Earlscourt Publications, 1969), 683. Biuletyn printed similar announcements in the following issues: 9 March 1944, 30 March 1944, 20 April 1944, and 6 July 1944.

120   "Tragedia Żydów wołyńskich," *Biuletyn Informacyjny* (25 March 1943), 7, in USHMM Archives, RG 15.080M *172, microfiche 75/142.

The report added that "at the present, all the ghettos in Volynia are already liquidated," and that "theoretically there are no more Jews in Volynia." However, *Biuletyn* did report that there was armed resistance in the ghetto of Łuck, while some Jews managed to flee and form partisan groups in the forests.[121] "It must be said," *Biuletyn* concluded, "that the Polish and Ukrainian peoples regard this German murder with widespread disgust and complete condemnation."[122]

While *Biuletyn* could state in the above-cited March 1943 issue that Poles overwhelmingly opposed Nazi Jewish policies in southeastern Poland, the paper was forced to qualify its position one month later when it revealed new evidence on Polish blackmailers. In a supplement inserted into the April 15th, 1943 issue, *Biuletyn* hammered away at those Poles who were blackmailing Jews for their silence or, worse, handing them over to the Gestapo. In a powerfully worded editorial, *Biuletyn* began, in an openly frustrated tone, "And once again, when conversation turns to blackmailing in our midst, blood floods our brain, the hand begins to itch and the mouth repeats some rather unpleasant expressions."[123] The statement continued:

> It is strange how luxuriously that poisoned flower of foul deeds and cowardliness has proliferated on our war-torn soil and in particular in the Warsaw region. Here... in the capital the worst, most vicious dregs of society are preying on the most unfortunate of our countrymen!
>
> In the last few days, reports have come into our possession of terrible facts about sophisticated blackmailers operating at the cost chiefly of Jews in hiding in various places. Such... scoundrels, without one iota of conscience, forge documents of a gendarme or a German Gestapo man and proceed to sniff out Jewish families hiding outside the ghetto. [Once he finds them], he begins a cruel game of dealings in human lives. Presenting himself to the Jew as an SS man, a Gestapo agent or a German gendarme, they take from them their entire supply of cash, all their possessions, especially of jewelry, and all for the price of—silence! They advise the Jewish family to move from their apartment allegedly to hide traces of themselves. And in their new apartment, the blackmailers begin again their disgraceful dealings a second time.[124]

---

121   Armed resistance in the Łuck ghetto is confirmed in Megargee (ed.), *The United States Holocaust Memorial Museum Encyclopedia of Camps and Ghettos, 1933–1945*, vol. 2, 1413.
122   "Tragedia Żydów wołyńskich," as above, fn. 120.
123   "Piętnujemy!" ibid. (15 April 1943), 1.
124   Ibid., 1–2.

Biuletyn's contempt for these individuals was revealed in the descriptions above. Yet the paper went further when it concluded,

> Here are the facts that lately abound in the area of Warsaw! Enough of this!.... What does it lead to, such failure of the most basic moral restraints! Thus, no wonder that every decent Pole, every Pole who has never blemished his hands in a deal even with such a beastly individual, should be obliged to report to our underground authorities the concrete and proven facts about such 'deeds' on the parts of these outcasts of society.
>
> With bullets and steel, we must burn out the scoundrels of this type from the body of society. Let no trace of them remain on the tortured body of our homeland! Neither now nor in the future will there ever be a place for these hyenas and scoundrels who profit from the misfortune of others.[125]

In contrast to Polish blackmailers, Jews who resisted the Nazis continued to be portrayed as heroes. Although the first issue of April 1943 ominously reported that "the Warsaw ghetto lives in fear of liquidation," Jews were continuing to strike back: three German guards were shot on March 13th and March 14th.[126] On March 29th, according to the paper, two more German guards were killed.[127] In mid-April 1943, the paper expressed alarm at the continuing problem of Polish blackmailers.

The Warsaw Ghetto Uprising: "A Severe Blow to the Prestige of Hitlerian Germany"

The reaction of the Polish underground press to the Warsaw Ghetto Uprising has been well documented.[128] The treatment here will consequently be only cursory. Consistent with its earlier reporting, *Biuletyn* wholeheartedly supported the ghetto fighters. Whereas until the Warsaw Ghetto Uprising, *Biuletyn*

---

125 Ibid., 2.
126 "Ghetto warszawskie," in ibid. (1 April 1943), 8, in USHMM Archives, RG 15.080M *172, microfiche 76/142.
127 "Ghetto warszawskie," ibid. (8 April 1943), 7, in USHMM Archives, RG 15.080M *172, microfiche 76/142.
128 See Paweł Szapiro, *Wojna żydowsko-niemiecka: Polska prasa konspiracyjna 1943–1944 o powstaniu w getcie Warszawy* (London: Aneks, 1992).

merely reported on the Holocaust, the uprising marked a new phase—that of direct calls for aid. In its first issue printed after the uprising began (its April 20th edition went to press prior to the rising), *Biuletyn*'s editor-in-chief, Aleksander Kamiński, penned a front-page article titled, "The Last Act of a Great Tragedy."[129] "For nearly a year," Kamiński began, "the Polish people ... have been a witness to crimes of a nature that have not been seen in modern times—the organized and planned massacre of the entire European Jewish nation."[130] The piece maintained that the response of the Jews to German attempts to deport the remaining inhabitants of the Warsaw ghetto constituted the second act of this Jewish tragedy. The first act was the ghettoization of European Jewry and the creation of death camps. "The defense of the Warsaw Ghetto," *Biuletyn* stated, "is a severe blow to the remaining prestige of Hitlerian Germany." Kamiński praised the Jewish fighters for their "glorious battle" and added a stern warning to the German people: "The entire German nation will need to answer for this before a world tribunal...." *Biuletyn* concluded with a call for Poles to aid the ghetto population. For it was their "duty to aid those Jews who are fleeing from the burning ghetto, until such time as the reborn Republic will restore full security, true freedom and the rule of our traditional European culture."[131] At the height of the uprising, in early May 1943, *Biuletyn* furthered the call for aid, writing: "Let's remember that our duty is to provide assistance in sheltering and protecting [the Jews] from the Germans!"[132] In his study on the reaction of the Polish underground press to the Warsaw ghetto uprising, Paweł Szapiro found that 63 underground papers published 194 articles on the ghetto rising.[133] Among Home Army papers, Szapiro notes, *Biuletyn* put forward the most unambiguous call for aiding Jews fleeing the ghetto.

---

129 Authorship is confirmed in Wachowicz, *Kamyk na szańcu*, 624.
130 "Ostatni akt wielkiej tragedii," *Biuletyn Informacyjny* (29 April 1943), 1, and also in Bartoszewski, Kunert (eds.), *Polacy-Żydzi, 1939–1945*, Doc. II/20, 237.
131 Ibid., 2.
132 *Biuletyn Informacyjny: Z Frontu Walki Cywilnej* (6 May 1943), reprinted in *Przegląd Historyczno-Wojskowy* 4, Nr. Specjalny 3 (2003): 1638.
133 See Paweł Szapiro, "The Question of Aid to the Fighting Ghetto in the Press of the Home Army and of the Bureau of the Delegate of the Government," in Daniel Grinberg (ed.), *The Holocaust fifty years after: 50th anniversary of the Warsaw ghetto uprising* (Warsaw: Jewish Historical Institute, 1993), 211.

Conclusions

What factors explain *Biuletyn*'s relatively consistent pro-Jewish orientation? First, the paper's editor-in-chief, Aleksander Kamiński, undoubtedly played a central role. Kamiński had had close prewar ties with the Jewish community and was politically oriented towards the democratic left, a milieu that had consistently supported Jewish civil rights before the war. Among his pre-war Jewish friends was Jerzy Grasberg, a student at Warsaw University who had joined a Jewish scout organization that acted under Kamiński's leadership. When the Warsaw ghetto was sealed in November 1940, Kamiński maintained ties with Grasberg, whom he recruited to provide reports on Jewish conditions for *Biuletyn*. Grasberg eventually functioned as the paper's Jewish correspondent. Luba Gawisar, Grasberg's wife during the war, knew Kamiński and referred to him as "a very close friend" of her late husband's before and during the war. Aleksander Kamiński belonged, Gawisar wrote, to what she referred to as "the liberal wing of the AK."[134] Kamiński was also a leader of BIP's Warsaw division, known for its high proportion of democratic-minded individuals, some of whom were Jewish or of Jewish background, such as Ludwik Widerszal and Jerzy Mazowiecki.

Another factor that may have played a role was *Biuletyn*'s status as the Polish underground's central organ. As David Engel has demonstrated, the official bodies of the Polish government-in-exile consciously aligned themselves on Jewish matters with its British and American allies, favoring equality under the law and full civil rights.[135] Like other clandestine periodicals, *Biuletyn* was scrutinized in bi-monthly reports sent to London and was expected to adhere to democratic principles. The Polish prime minister, W. Sikorski, acknowledged pressures from the allies in the formulation of his views in a September 1942 letter to the Home Army commander in Warsaw. "We must remember," Sikorski wrote, "that the position of the Anglo-Saxon world concerning anti-Semitism is unequivocal. The best means of assuring full support for our interest is by our

---

134 Luba Gawisar, "Im avrei ha-irgun lohem b-tzad ha-'ari'," *Mibi-fenim* 45.3–4 (August 1983): 297.

135 See David Engel, *Facing a Holocaust: The Polish Government-in-Exile and the Jews, 1943–1945* (Chapel Hill, NC: University of North Carolina Press, 1993), and David Engel, *In the Shadow of Auschwitz: The Polish Government-in-Exile and the Jews, 1939–1942* (Chapel Hill, NC: University of North Carolina Press, 1987).

showing and granting equal rights [for the Jews]."[136] The latter consideration, however, should not obscure the fact that the *Biuletyn*'s expressions of moral outrage at Nazi Jewish policy and Polish blackmailers were genuine. Nor has evidence surfaced connecting Kamiński's views with pressure from London.

Recently, Klaus-Peter Friedrich has argued for a third causal factor in understanding *Biuletyn*'s exceptionally sympathetic reporting on the Jews: it was "due to an appreciable extent to the personal involvement of a portion of its editorial staff who were Polonized Jews."[137] But Friedrich's otherwise well-documented article provides no sources or further comment. It is true, as I have demonstrated above, that *Biuletyn*'s editors included Wiktoria Goryńska, a Pole of Jewish background, and Jerzy Grasberg, correspondent in the Warsaw ghetto. I would argue, however, that the involvement of these two figures was a symptom of the editor-in-chief's dedication to reporting fairly on Jewish matters, rather than the actual cause of that reporting.[138]

Scholars nonetheless agree that *Biuletyn*'s treatment of the Holocaust was unique in the Polish underground press. As the late Lucjan Dobroszycki wrote, "*Biuletyn Informacyjny* gave up-to-date information on the situation of the Jews in Poland, condemned the crimes perpetrated by the Germans, appealed to its readers to help the victims, and warned that measures would be taken against those who collaborated in any way with the Germans in the extermination of the Jews."[139] *Biuletyn*'s extraordinary attention to the tragedy of Polish Jewry as well as its bold condemnation of Poles who collaborated in any way with the Nazis therefore call into question the notion of an undifferentiated, monolithic Home Army disposition with respect to Poland's Jews.

---

136 Prime Minister Sikorski, London, to General Rowecki, Warsaw, 25 September 1942, reprinted in Ber Mark, *Uprising in the Warsaw Ghetto* (New York: Schocken Books, 1975), 107.

137 Friedrich, "The Nazi Murder of the Jews in Polish Eyes," 394.

138 For more on the editorial board, see "Tadeusz Kwaśniewski (1915–1943)," *Polski Słownik Biograficzny* 16 (1971), 344–345; "Ewa Rybicki (1909–1943)," *Polski Słownik Biograficzny* 23 (1991), 299–300. For other editors, see entries in Kunder (ed.), *Słownik*.

139 Dobroszycki, "The Jews in the Polish Clandestine Press, 1939–1945," 294.

CHAPTER 18

"The Work of My Hands is Drowning in the Sea, and You Would Offer Me Song?!": Orthodox Behavior and Leadership in Warsaw during the Holocaust

Havi Dreifuss

Introduction

The world and religious life of observant Jews during the Holocaust have never stood at the center of Holocaust research, and in spite of decades of intensive study of the subject, there are still fundamental issues that have not been examined in depth.[1] Historians have rarely integrated the religious narrative into the general historical one,[2] whereas works written by ultra-Orthodox authors have principally emphasized personal and religious miracle stories while ignoring other aspects of the religious confrontation with the Holocaust, thus

---

* I would like to thank the anonymous readers of this article, whose notes helped me to improve it. My research assistant, Nir Itzik, assisted in the final stages of preparing this publication, and his devoted and precise work was most helpful. Responsibility for its contents naturally remains exclusively my own.

** Reuven Ben-Shem, *Yoman*, Yad Vashem Archive, O.33/959, 7 Aug. 1942. The original quotation comes from a *midrash* dealing with the Almighty's reaction to the angels' desire to offer praise at the splitting of the Red Sea: 'At that hour the ministering angels sought to sing before the Holy One, blessed be He. The Holy One, blessed be He, said to them: The work of My hands is drowning in the sea, and you would offer me song?', Babylonian Talmud, *Sanhedrin* 39*b* (cf. *Megilah* 10*a*).

1 Dan Michman, *Ha-sho'ah ve'hekerah: hamsagah, minuah, vesugiyot yesod* (Tel Aviv: Moreshet, 1998), 194; idem, 'Ha-mehkar al orah hayav shel ha-tsibur ha-dati tahat ha-shilton ha-natsi', in Israel Gutman and Gideon Greif (eds.), *The historiography of the Holocaust period: proceedings of the Fifth Yad Vashem International Historical Conference, Jerusalem, March 1983*, (Jerusalem: Yad Vashem, 1988), 742–43.

2 Ibid. It should be noted that this trend has changed in recent years; see for instance David Zilberklang, 'Ha-sho'ah be-mahoz lublin', PhD diss., Jerusalem, 2003; Sarah Bander, *Mul mavet orev: yehudei bialistok ba-milhemet olam ha-sheniyah* (Tel Aviv: Am Oved, 1997), 29–30, 47–8, 52–3, 96–9. An impressive integration of religious life into the general story appears in the detailed monograph written by Michal Unger on the Lodz ghetto, in which several chapters are devoted to religious life; Michal Unger, *Lodz: aharon ha-geta'ot be-polin* (Jerusalem: Yad Vashem, 2005), 440–69.

effectively filtering out many aspects of the lives of religiously observant Jews during the war.[3] As a result, the few works that have actually dealt with religious life during the Holocaust have not created an acceptably balanced, broad, and complex examination of the subject.[4]

An outstanding example of this is provided by the research—or, to be more precise, the very fragmentary research—on Orthodox behavior and leadership during the Holocaust.[5] A large number of the books about rabbis during the Holocaust have focused on the emotive issue of the rescue of several celebrated individuals, and have principally dealt with the escape of the Gerer Rebbe, the Belzer Rebbe, and the Satmar Rebbe from German-occupied territories.[6] Although it is impossible to ignore the importance of the actions

---

3   See for instance Yehiel Grantstein, *Ha-gevurah ha-aheret: ha-yehudi ha-dati ba-ma'avak gevurah uva-meri neged gezerot ha-natsim be-shnot ha-sho'ah* (Jerusalem: Mahon Zeher Naftali, 1988); id., *Mekadshei ha-shem: entsiklopediyah*, 3 vols (Benei Berak: Ganzah Kidush H'shem, 2006); Yehoshua Eibeshitz, *Be-kerovai akadesh: asufah al ma'asei kidush ha-shem umesirut nefesh bimei ha-hurban shel yameinu* (Jerusalem: Ha-mahon L'limod Korot Ha-sho'ah Al Shem Hedva Eibeshitz, 2005).

4   A remarkable example of this is provided by the Orthodox and academic authors who have written about the "role" played by the Zionist leadership in sabotaging attempts to rescue European Jews during the Holocaust. See Moshe Shenfeld, *Serufei ha-kivshanim ma'ashemim* (Benei Berak: Hog Bni Tora SH"I Zeiri Agodat Israel B' Eretz Israel, 1975); Shalom Shalmon, *Pishei ha-tsiyonut ba-hashmadat ha-golah*, 4th expanded edn. (Benei Berak: Shalom Shalmon, 1989). See also Hayim Nirel, *Haredim mul sho'ah: ha-ashamot ha-haredim kelapei ha-tsiyonut ba-aharayut la-sho'ah* (Jerusalem: Carmel, 1997); Dina Porat, 'Amalek's Accomplices—Blaming Zionism for the Holocaust: Anti-Zionist Ultra-Orthodoxy in Israel during the 1980s', *Journal of Contemporary History* 27.4 (1992): 695–735.

5   Several definitions of Orthodox society may be found in the scholarly literature. According to Jacob Katz, Orthodox society is a traditional Jewish society that adapts itself to modernity by means of internal variation. A similar definition appears in a work by Eliezer Schweid, who defines it as a movement that prefers the traditional past to the modern present in an intense and sharply-defined manner, in spite of its membership of the very present that it rejects; Schweid, *Bein hurban lishuah* (Tel Aviv: Ha-kibbutz Ha-meuchad, 1994), 9. In the context of this article, in spite of the internal variation within the ultra-Orthodox world, between *Hasidim* and *mitnagedim*, between *Hasidim* and Lithuanians, and so on, I am dealing with non-Zionist Orthodox Jews. See Israel Bartal, 'True Knowledge and Wisdom: On Orthodox Historiography', *Studies in Contemporary Jewry* 10 (1994): 178–92; Jacob Katz, 'Orthodoxy in Historical Perspective', *Studies in Contemporary Jewry* 2 (1986): 3–17; Ada Rappoport-Albert, 'Hagiography with Footnotes: Edifying Tales and the Writing of History in Hasidism', *History and Theory* 27 (1988): 119–59.

6   Although the dates of their escapes, as also the related circumstances, were completely different, the stories of these rabbis have often been linked together, both by the ultra-Orthodox community and by the wider community. While the ultra-Orthodox world-view has

of these prominent figures, who re-founded their Hasidic courts at the end of the war, any discussion that focuses exclusively on them and their deeds inevitably ignores the activity of tens of thousands of other souls during the war.

Other scholars who have studied religious behavior during the Holocaust have amassed an encyclopaedic amount of information about the fate of rabbis and yeshivas in occupied Europe,[7] or have discussed the behavior of the rabbinic leadership, examining the activities of particular rabbis,[8] specific occupied regions,[9] or the role played in rescue work by religious leaders who lived outside the occupied areas during the war.[10] Notwithstanding the

---

regarded their escapes as 'a miracle of saving the Torah', others have accused them not only of abandoning their followers in occupied Europe but also of ordering many Jews to remain in dangerous regions. On this subject, see Mendel Piekarz, *Hasidut polin bein shetei ha-milhamot uba-gezerot tav-shin-tav-shin-heh (ha-sho'ah)* (Jerusalem: Mosad Bialik, 1990), 412–34; Eliezer Schweid, 'Nes ha-hatsalah shel ha-rabi mibelz: ha-hitmodedut ha-te'ologit shel manhigei hasidut belz im ha-sho'ah be-hitarutah', *Mehkarei yerushalayim be-mahshevet yisra'el* 13 (1996): 587–611; Moshe [Prager] Yehezkeli, *Nes ha-hatsalah shel ha-rabi migur* (Jerusalem: Yeshoron, 1959); Esther Farbstein, 'Eyes of the Community: The Rescues of Hasidic Leaders', in eadem, *Hidden in Thunder: Perspectives on Faith, Halachah and Leadership during the Holocaust* (Jerusalem: Mosad H'rav Kuk, 2002). A veritable confrontation between the two views appears in *Kivunim* 11 (spring 1981) and 14 (winter 1982). For a similar phenomenon see also Bryan Mark Rigg, *Rescue from the Reich: How One of Hitler's Soldiers Saved the Lubavitcher Rebbe* (New Haven: Yale University Press, 2004).

7   Shmuel K. Marisky (ed.), *Mosdot torah be-eiropah be-binyanam ube-hurbanam* (New York: Ogen 'al yede ha-histadrut ha-'Ivrit be-'Ameriqah, 1955); Menashe Unger, *Admorim shenispu* (Jerusalem: Mosad Ha-rav Kuk, 1969); Avraham Fuchs, *Yeshivot hungariyah be-gedulatan ube-hurbanam* (Jerusalem: Fuchs, 1978); see also idem, *Ha-sho'ah be-mekorot rabaniyim* (Jerusalem: n.p., 1995).

8   See for example Judith Tydor Baumel, 'Esh kodesh: sifro shel ha-admor mipiasets'na umekomo be-havanat ha-hayim ha-datiyim be-geto varshah', *Yalkut moreshet* 29 (spring 1980): 173–87; Yeshayahu Jelinek, 'Ha-rav viesmandel ve"tokhnit ha-rabanim": mezimah anti-tsiyonit?', *Yalkut moreshet* 58 (1994): 83–92; Natan Cohen, 'Bein ke'ev ha-hisaredut le-simhat ha-hatsalah: koroteihem shel shenei rabanim mehungariyah be-tkufat ha-kibush ha-natsi', *Dapim le-heker ha-sho'ah* 20 (1996): 113–25; Esther Farbstein, 'Yomanim ufirkei zikhronot kemekor histori: yomano shel rav be-"beit avadim konin"', *Kovets mehkarim yad vashem* 26 (1998): 71–98.

9   Dan Michman, 'Ha-manhigut ha-rabanit be-holand be-tekufat ha-sho'ah', *Dapim le-heker ha-sho'ah* 7 (1989): 81–106; Sarah Kaplan, 'Diyunim hilkhatiyim saviv "gezerat ha-shehitah" be-germaniyah ha-natsit', *Mikhlol* 19 (Kislev 2000): 55–68; Ya'akov Geller, *Ha-amidah ha-ruhanit shel yehudei romaniyah be-tekufat ha-sho'ah 1940–1944* (Lod: Orot Yadot H'magrab, 2003).

10 See for example Efraim Zuroff, 'Ha-tsibur ha-ortodoksit be'arh"b vehurban yahadut eiropah: va'ad ha-hatsalah shel ha-rabanim ha-ortodoksim be'arh"b be'tekufat ha-sho'ah

genuine contribution made by these studies towards greater understanding of the behavior of particular rabbis, they offer no general evaluation of rabbinic behavior during the Holocaust. In addition, the few attempts to map this complex subject[11] have not provided an adequate response to this gap in the research; and some have treated it in a superficial if not simplistic manner.

This gap in research is all the more surprising in the light of the abundant historical sources available to those who are interested.[12] Alongside sources written by Orthodox individuals[13]—including diaries and contemporary memoirs[14]—there is also an impressive memoir literature,[15] which, although

---

(1939–1945)', PhD thesis (Jerusalem: H'oniversita H'evrit, 1997); Hayim Shalem, *Et la'asot le'hatsalat yisra'el: agudat yisra'el be'erets yisra'el le'nokhah ha-sho'ah 1942–1945* (Jerusalem: Kiriat Sede Boker: Machon Ben-Gurion L' Hekher Israel, H'Zionot Ve Moreset Ben-Gurion, Oniversitat Ben-Gurion Ba Negev, 2007).

11 Yeshayahu Wolfsberg-Aviad, 'Ha-yahadut ha-ne'emanah ba-milhamah', in Yisra'el Gutman and Livia Rothkirchen (eds.), *Sho'at yehudei eiropah: reka, korot, mashma'ut: mivhar ma'amarim* (Jerusalem: Yad Vashem, 1973), 504–14; Joseph Walk, 'Ha-hanhagah ha-datit be'tekufat ha-sho'ah', in Yisra'el Gutman (ed.), *Demut ha-hanhagah ha-yehudit be'aratsot ha-shelitah ha-natsit: hartsa'ot ve'diyunim be'kinus ha-bein-le'umi ha-shelishi shel hokrei ha-sho'ah* (Jerusalem: Yad Vashem, 1980), 325–35.

12 The abundance of Orthodox writing on the Holocaust must be emphasized, notwithstanding the general impression of Orthodox silence on the subject. It should also be remembered that a great deal of *haredi* discussion of the Holocaust occurs in the public sphere, including weekly Torah portion handbills, rabbinic sermons, *haredi* newspapers and internet sites. For a historiographical description, see Havi Ben Sasson, 'L'historiographie orthodoxe et la Shoah: ses repercussions dans le monde universitaire', *Revue de l'histoire de la Shoah* 188 (Janvier-Juin 2008): 453–77.

13 See for example the diary of Hinde Schwartz of Lesko, Yad Vashem Archive 033.755; the diary of Sarah Fishkin of Rovzhivitz, Yad Vashem Archive 033.222 (part of this diary has been published in *Yalkut moreshet* 2/4 [July 1965]: 21–35); the diary of Rabbi Guzhik of Dukla, Yad Vashem Archive 033.1609; and the writings of Rabbi Hayim Yitshak Volgelernter, Jewish Historical Institute, 302.46. See also published sources like Shimon Huberband, *Kiddush Hashem: Jewish Religious and Cultural Life in Poland during the Holocaust* (New York: Yeshiva University Press, 1987); Rabbi Yehoshua Moshe Aharonson, *Alei merurut* (Benei Berak: Yad Vashem, 1996); Moshe Flinker, *Young Moshe's diary: the spiritual torment of a Jewish boy in Nazi Europe. Introductions by Shaul Esh and Geoffrey Wigoder* (Jerusalem: Yad Vashem, 1965) (reprint Ra'na'na: Docostori, 2002).

14 On the differences between the two, see my book, *'Anu yehudei polin?': ha-yahasim bein yehudim upolanim be'tekufat ha-sho'ah min ha-hebet ha-yehudi* (Jerusalem: Yad Vashem, 2010), 24, 177–79.

15 A selected and partial list includes Yehezkel Harpnes, *Be'kaf ha-kela: yoman memahanot ha-hashmadah* (Benei Berak, 1981); Pearl Benisch, *To Vanquish the Dragon* (Jerusalem: Feldhim, 1991; Heb. edition 1994); Rivkah Vollve, *Ve'emunatkha ba-leilot* (Jerusalem:

written with clear educational goals, including *kevod elohim haster davar*,[16] when examined critically can provide valuable historical information about the rabbis and their lives, as well as about the lives of other religious individuals during the Holocaust. Even purely hagiographical works can assist the scholar in locating historical information, as long as he or she is aware of the methodological problems that arise from the obvious and tacit aims of such sources, as well as other problems. In addition, rabbinic sermons,[17] responsa literature,[18]

Rivkah Velber, 1997); Yehoshua Eibeschitz, *Ka'arar ba-aravah: korot hayim shel serid ha-kivshanim* (Jerusalem: H'mhon L'limod H'shoa al shem Hedva Eibeschitz, 1998). On the literary characteristics and the testimony of the ultra-Orthodox community, see Michal Zemer-Sha'ul, 'Pe'er tahat efer: nitsulei ha-sho'ah zikhronah vehitmodedut im hashlek-hoteiha—perek merkazi be'shikum ha-hevrah ha-haredit ha-ashkenazit be'"yishuv" u've'medinat yisra'el', unpublished PhD thesis (Ramat Gan: Bar Ilan University, 2009).

16   Literally: 'It is the glory of God to conceal a thing' (Proverbs 25:2). In the context of this article I cannot engage in a full discussion of this principle, which is fundamental to Orthodox historiography and results in downplaying controversies, concealing negative discoveries that might stain the reputation of Torah figures, and hiding things that might seem to contravene halakhah. For a discussion of this genre see David Asaf, '*Kvod elohim hester davar*: perek nosaf ba-historiografiyah ha-ortodoksit shel ha-hasidut be'erets yisra'el', *Cathedra* 68 (Tamuz 1993): 57–66; Kimi Kaplan, *Be'sod ha-siah ha-haredi* (Jerusalem: Merkaz Zalman Shazar L' toldot Israel, 2007): 140–66; Yisra'el Bartal, '*Zikhron ya'akov* le'rabi ya'akov lifshits: ha-historiografiyah ha-ortodoksit', *Milet: Open University Studies in Jewish History and Culture* 2 (1984): 409–14, in particular the scholarly literature listed in n. 6. See also Ben Sasson, 'L'historiographie orthodoxe' (above, n. 13).

17   Besides the famous work *Sacred Fire: Torah from the Years of Fury, 1939–1942* by Rabbi Kalman Kalonymus Shapira (Jerusalem and Northvale, NJ, 1960), and the sermons of Rabbi Kahlenberg, *Yedei mosheh: derashot be'mahaneh hesger be-tsarfat bimei ha-sho'ah*, ed. Esther Farbstein (Jerusalem: H'merkaz L' hiker H'shoa, 2005), see for example Rabbi Shelomoh Zalman Unsdorfer, *Siftei shelomoh* (Montreal, 1972); Rabbi Shelomoh Zalman Ehrenreich, *Derashot lehem shelomoh* (Brooklyn, NY, 1976); Rabbi Avraham Yosef Lichtenstein, *Sefer she'erit yekutiel* (Brooklyn, NY: Yatza L'or Al Yedi Bno Hill Lichtenstein, 1978).

18   It seems, however, that some of the responsa literature was written after the Holocaust and should be regarded more as memoirs than as primary sources; alongside these works, however, are queries that were sent to rabbis during the Holocaust, some of which received answers. For responsa literature composed after the Holocaust, see Rabbi Efrayim Asheri, *Sefer she'elot uteshuvot mi ma'amakim: she'elot uteshuvot ve'inyanim she'amdu al ha-perek be'yamei hereg ve'ovdan shel shenot tav-shin-alef-tav-shin-heh be-geto kovno*, 5 vols. (New York: Groys, 1949–79); Rabbi Shimon Efrati, *Mige ha-haregah: she'elot uteshuvot* (Jerusalem: Yad Vashem, 1960); Rabbi Tsevi Hirsh Meisels, *She'elot uteshuvot mekadshei ha-shem*, 2 vols. (Chicago: Dfus Ben Zion Lavkawits, 1955–67). For examples of responsa from the war years, see Rabbi Mordechai Brisk, *Sefer berit eitanim* (Netanya: Kolel Avrechim, 2002); Rabbi Yehoshua Grinwald, *She'elot uteshuvot hesed yehoshua* (New

and halakhic (ritual legal) works from after the war[19] contain a great deal of information about the lives and fates of rabbis and religious communities during the Holocaust; in recent years, unique sources have been discovered that focus on the lives of rabbis in the Holocaust, consisting of introductions to rabbinic works.[20]

In the following pages I will try to extract, from these and many other sources, unknown aspects of the lives of rabbis in Warsaw during the war, including the unusual concentration of rabbis in Warsaw during the war, their areas of activity, their successes and failures, and their different reactions to information about the mass murder of European Jews in general, and of the Jews of Warsaw in particular. Moreover, I will argue that, from the viewpoint of Torah scholars, the weakness of religious life in the ghetto and throughout the Jewish world was not the *result* of the tragedy but its *cause*. In other words, from their perspective, this was not a case of physical crisis leading to Jewish alienation from the world of Torah, but the opposite: the abandonment of religion caused all the disasters that had befallen the Jews.

The Concentration of Rabbis in Warsaw at the Beginning of the German Conquest

In the secret archive of the Warsaw ghetto, founded by Dr. Emanuel Ringelblum and known as the Oneg Shabat archive,[21] there is a list of about 130 rabbis who

---

York: Dfus H'ahim Slezinger, 1948); Rabbi Shemuel Shmelke Segal Litsh, *Sefer eleh divrei shemu'el* (New York, 1983).

19 Thus, for example, after the war a huge body of halakhic literature was composed on the issue of freeing *agunot* (women whose husbands had disappeared) so that they could remarry. Since the halakhic process involved in freeing an *agunah* requires an exact description of the information amassed, these halakhic sources include a large amount of data about life during the Holocaust and afterwards. In addition to the works listed here, see also Rabbi Yitshak Ya'akov Weiss, *She'elot uteshuvot minhat yitshak*, 10 vols. (London, 1958; Jerusalem: Minhat Yitshak, 1990); Rabbi Meshulam Rota, *She'elot uteshuvot kol mevaser* (Jerusalem: Mosad H' Rav Kuk, 1973).

20 A remarkable project directed by Ms. Esther Farbstein and the Centre for Holocaust Studies at the Jerusalem Mikhlalah (advisor: Dr Natan Cohen). Farbstein has discovered the widespread phenomenon of ultra-Orthodox writing about the Holocaust in the introductions to rabbinic works. These introductions have been collected and published on a CD, *Korot ha-sho'ah be'mevo'ot la-sifrut ha-rabanit korot ha-sho'ah be-mevo'ot la-sifrut ha-rabanit* (Jerusalem: Reuven Mas, 2008), part of which has been translated into English.

21 For information on the archive and those who maintained it, see Samuel Kassow, *'Who Will Write Our History?': Emanuel Ringelblum, the Warsaw Ghetto and the Oyneg Shabes Archive* (Bloomington: Indiana University Press, 2007).

gathered in the city during the occupation, including Hasidic *rebbe*s (leaders), community rabbis, and *morei tsedek* (auxiliary rabbis).[22] Study of the list reveals that over 90 of them were refugees in Warsaw who had been living elsewhere in Poland before the war. What is more, of the 26 Hasidic *rebbe*s resident in the city during the Holocaust, not one had lived there previously.[23] How can this remarkable concentration of Torah scholars in the city be explained, and what were the factors that caused so many *rebbe*s to flee to occupied Warsaw? The answer to these questions lies in the ordeals endured by the Jews of Poland—including the rabbinic leadership—at the beginning of the war, as well as in the nature of the roles that these individuals played within and outside their communities before the outbreak of war.

At the outbreak of the Second World War, about 300,000 young men fled to the east, including public figures, community leaders, and rabbis. There were several reasons for this chaotic flight: some people were fleeing from the German bombardment, others were obeying the call of Polish army leaders to make a stand on the River Bug, while some feared that their anti-Nazi activities before the war would place them in immediate danger. Whatever the reasons, the first days of the war were marked in Poland by mass flight that caused considerable change in the Jewish communities and led to panic among the established and accepted public leaders, and to swarms of refugees.

The leaders of the Orthodox communities were no different in their fears and expectations, but their degree of mobility was directly determined by the positions they occupied before the war. Community rabbis, most of whom had families, saw their destiny as bound up with that of their flock and had very little realistic chance of fleeing, since they were economically dependent on their communities; in addition, only the most famous could expect to find shelter easily in another community. Accordingly, it seems that most—though not all—remained in their homes or returned to them very soon. The position of the auxiliary *morei tsedek* was more difficult, since their activity was characteristically tied to a particular locality; their chances of leaving their homes and finding refuge in another town were even more remote. In contrast, the situation of the Hasidic *rebbe*s was completely different: first, as heads of groups that transcended local communities, they were less tied to the

---

22 *Morei tsedek* (lit. 'teachers of righteousness') made halakhic decisions on everyday questions of ritually permitted and prohibited matters, but did not act as judges in monetary cases.

23 The archive includes two copies: a handwritten list with 126 names and a typed list with 129 names; list of rabbis in Warsaw, Oneg Shabat archive M10.ARII/210. It should also be noted that dozens of other rabbis are known who do not appear on the list.

place in which they lived, since they regarded themselves as connected to their Hasidim everywhere rather than to the Jews in whose vicinity they happened to reside. In addition, many had Hasidim in neighbouring towns who regarded an opportunity to host them as a great honour; as a result, a large proportion of the Hasidic *rebbe*s moved, congregating in the larger cities. Yeshiva rabbis were in an especially advantageous position to flee: flight to the east was relatively easier for them. They served in an organized framework, most of their students did not have their own families, and the students' relatives lived far away. It is not surprising that among those who fled eastwards—especially to Vilna—there were many yeshiva students, alongside *halutzim* (Zionist pioneers) and other Jews.[24]

An analysis of the mobility patterns of Polish rabbis, as well as German attacks on religious Jews at the beginning of the German occupation of Poland,[25] helps explain the impressive concentration of Torah scholars in Warsaw, as is evident from the list of rabbis mentioned above. It seems that, as a result of these processes, a large number of religious leaders flocked together in the first weeks of the war, creating a sizeable Orthodox community in Warsaw. They included rabbis who had lived in Warsaw before the war, rabbis who had fled there upon the outbreak of hostilities, and numerous Hasidic *rebbe*s.

---

24   For a detailed description of these phenomena, see my article '"Ketson asher ein lo ro'eh?" rabanim uma'amadam ba-sho'ah', in Asaf Yedidya, Natan Cohen, and Esther Farbstein (eds.), *Zikhron ba-sefer*, 143–67.

25   Besides the official orders placing Orthodox Judaism in the 'eye of the storm', such as Heydrich's telegram that established that the Judenrat would be composed 'as far as possible of authoritative figures and the remaining rabbis', attention should also be paid to the appalling violence directed against religious Jews as a result of what was almost the first encounter of masses of German soldiers with Jews who appeared to them to resemble the propaganda figures on which they had been nurtured. I cannot here expand upon the story of the humiliations and tortures to which rabbis were subjected at the beginning of the war, including beard-cutting and other atrocities, but it should be noted here that several religious Jews were murdered by Germans in the first days and weeks of the occupation. On the German soldiers' encounter with the figure of the religious Jew, see for example Farbstein, *Be-seter ra'am*, 61–7; Yehudit Levin and Daniel Uziel, 'Anashim regilim ve'tatslumim regilim', *Yad Vashem Studies* 26 (1998): 201–22; Omer Bartov, *Hitler's Army: Soldiers, Nazis, and War in the Third Reich* (New York: Oxford University Press, 1991), 79–106; Saul Friedländer, *The Years of Extermination: Nazi Germany and the Jews, 1939–1945* (New York: Harper Collins Publishers, 2007), 27–9; Alexander B. Rossino, 'Destructive Impulses: German Soldiers and the Conquest of Poland', *Holocaust and Genocide Studies* 11.3 (1997): 351–65.

Even before the war, rabbis resident in Warsaw had played a central role in the Jewish life of the city and had been very active in various religious, educational, and social spheres. They included Rabbi Alexander Zysze Frydman (1897–1943), a Torah scholar, journalist, and haredi leader who was active in education; Rabbi Menahem Ziemba (Prager) (1884–1943), an Orthodox leader, public activist, and noted Torah scholar who was a member of the Rabbinical Council of Warsaw from 1935; and Rabbi Szimszon Sztokhammer (1899–1944), an Orthodox journalist, member of the orthodox political party Agudat Yisra'el and member of the Rabbinical Council of Warsaw from 1934.

These rabbis continued and even increased their religious and public activities during the war, adapting them to the special reality of Warsaw under occupation and, later, the Warsaw ghetto. Thus, for example, Rabbi Frydman expanded his educational activity and engaged in welfare and other assistance. He was an ultra-Orthodox representative of the Joint, and, together with his colleagues in the welfare organization and in his religious activities, set up a network of kitchens for Torah students and founded an extensive system of underground education, which spread to the ghettos of Lublin and Kraków. In September 1941, when the Germans permitted the establishment of an official educational system in the ghetto, the rabbi became the ultra-Orthodox representative on the Judenrat, and served as the head of its Religious Council, established in February 1942.[26] Rabbi Ziemba continued to serve on the Rabbinical Council of Warsaw during the war, and in spite of being beaten and humiliated at the beginning of the occupation, continued to play an active role in public life. Thus, for example, at the end of March 1943, Rabbi Ziemba, together with other rabbis, decreed a public fast and composed a special prayer for Rosh Hodesh (first day of the new month) Nisan.[27] Rabbi Sztokhammer also

---

26   See for instance his words in the minutes of a meeting on the rescue of Jewish detainees arrested for crossing the ghetto boundary, 15 Jan. 1942 at the offices of the Jewish Self-Help organization at Tłomacka Street, Yad Vashem Archive M10.ARI/210. According to Farbstein, Rabbi Frydman was also responsible for the underground publication *Kol bamidbar* (see below, n. 59). During the great deportation of summer 1942, his wife and only daughter were sent to Treblinka. He survived thanks to working in Schult's shop, where he continued his educational and religious activity. In March 1942, Rabbi Alexander Zysze Frydman was transferred to a camp in the Lublin region and was murdered there during the mass murder called Aktion Erntefest—'Harvest Festival'—by the Germans. During this blood-drenched operation, about 42,000 Jews were murdered on 3 November 1943 in the Lublin district camps, about 18,000 of them at Majdanek, including many survivors from the Warsaw ghetto.

27   Note that Rabbi Ziemba's name appears in a list of rabbis of the quarterly published in the newspaper *Gazeta Żydowska*, 4 February 1941. There is also evidence that he studied and

continued his religious work through his legal (halakhic) and educational activity. He served as the secretary of the Warsaw Rabbinate and was appointed to the Religious Department of the Judenrat, where he worked to expand the religious services available in the ghetto. He was also very active in working to free *agunot* (abandoned wives without the ability to remarry) and helped to set up the soup kitchen for Torah scholars in the ghetto.[28]

Their activities were reinforced during the war by Ultra Orthodox (*haredi*) educators and businessmen who had fled to Warsaw at the outbreak of hostilities, such as Rabbi Eliezer Gerszon Friednson (1899–1942), who had escaped to Łódź with his family at the beginning of the war. Rabbi Friednson was a prominent educator in the orthodox Beit Ya'akov school network for girls, one of the projects of Agudat Yisra'el in Poland between the world wars, and was also a member of the central committee of the youth movement Tse'irei Agudat Yisra'el. Before the war he displayed a lively interest in the literary world and in young people's lives,[29] and he continued his educational and public activity in occupied Warsaw. He was involved, for example, in running three public kitchens at which the underground educational activities of the Beit Ya'akov network took place.[30] Rabbi Aryeh Zvi Frumer of Koziegłowy (1884–1943), one of the greatest Torah scholars of the interwar period in Poland, also fled to Warsaw. He replaced Rabbi Meir Shapira, the founder of Yeshivat Hakhmei Lublin—the flagship institution of higher Orthodox education in Poland

---

taught the laws of martyrdom; see Hillel Seidman, *The Warsaw Ghetto diaries* (New York: Feldheim Publishers, 1997), 117–120. On 19 Nisan 1943, during the Warsaw Ghetto uprising, Rabbi Menahem Ziemba was killed. In 1958, following efforts by World Agudat Yisra'el, his bones were brought to Israel and he was laid to rest in Jerusalem.

28 See for instance the prayer that was composed at the 'rabbis' shop' on Nowolipki Street, where Rabbi Sztokhammer, Rabbi Frydman, and the Piaszener Rebbe spent time: 'A prayer in time of war', Yad Vashem Archive, M.10/AR.II/371; see also the letter of patronage (a public committee established to support a certain activity) of Torah scholars, headed by Rabbi Sztokhammer, 5 February 1942, Yad Vashem Archive, M.10/AR.II/104. During the Warsaw Ghetto uprising, Rabbi Sztokhammer was deported to camps near Lublin. Evidence about him has come from Poniatowa, Budzyn, and Majdanek, as well as contradictory testimony concerning his murder in 1944.

29 Before the war Rabbi Friedenson had founded a series of newspapers for ultra-Orthodox youth and organized the founding conference of *Banot Agudat Yisra'el* (1936). A few months before the war he had set up the Union of Ultra-Orthodox Authors of Poland (*Igud Ha-soferim Ha-haredim Be'Polin*).

30 For his activities during the war, see for example the testimony of Ya'akov Zilberberg, archive of the Jewish Institute of Warsaw, 301.2586. Rabbi Friedenson died in unclear circumstances during the Warsaw Ghetto uprising.

between the world wars—after the latter's death in 1935, and continued to be active in the fields of Torah study and education in the ghetto.[31]

Several Hasidic *rebbes* who had avoided settling in the metropolis before the war now found refuge there and joined the activities of their rabbinic colleagues. One of those who moved to the city was Rabbi Yitshak Menahem Mendel Danziger (1880–1942), the Alexander Rebbe, who was the grandson of the founder of the dynasty and who became *rebbe* upon his father's death in 1924. Before the war, he was known for his engagement in exoteric and esoteric study as well as his educational initiatives. In the first days of the war he and his family were attacked by the Germans, prompting his followers to smuggle him first to Łódź and then to Warsaw. Rabbi Ya'akov Yitzhak Dan Landau (1882–1943), the Strykówer Rebbe, considered one of the greatest Torah scholars of Poland, also escaped with his family to Warsaw from Zgierz after the Germans confiscated his property. Rabbi David Bornstein (1876–1942), the Sochaczewer Rebbe, arrived in the capital at the beginning of the war. He was the grandson of the founder of the dynasty Rabbi Avraham Bornstein, the author of *Avnei nezer*, a famous collection of responsa, the great-grandson of the Kotzker Rebbe, and one of the best-known Hasidic *rebbes* in Poland between the wars. He was a member of the Rabbinical Association of Poland (Agudat Ha-rabanim Ba-polin), a presidential member of the Council of Torah Sages (Mo'etset Gedolei Ha-torah), and a leader of Agudat Yisra'el. At the beginning of the war, Rabbi Bornstein suffered a violent attack at the hands of the Germans, and was consequently smuggled by his Hasidim to Warsaw, where he hid in the house of one of his followers. Other refugees in Warsaw included the family of the Gerer Rebbe, including his brother Rabbi Menahem Mendel Alter (1877–1942), who was the youngest son of the 'Sefat Emet' (Rabbi Yehudah Aryeh Leib Alter). He was a member of the Council of Torah Sages of Agudat Yisra'el, and in 1934 was elected chairman of the Rabbinical Association of Poland; he served simultaneously as the rabbi of Kalisz. Rabbi Alter is regarded as one of the founders of ultra-Orthodox journalism in Poland, and was known for his campaign to safeguard *shehitah* (ritual slaughter) between the wars. At the outbreak of war he learned that he was wanted by the Germans, left his hometown, and fled to Warsaw.

Like the rabbis who had lived in Warsaw before the war, and like others who fled there during the German occupation, these *rebbes* played an important part in public activity—both religious and social—in the Warsaw ghetto. Thus, for example, the Alexander Rebbe continued to emphasize the importance of

---

31   After the liquidation of the ghetto, Rabbi Frumer was deported to Majdanek, where he was murdered.

prayer in the ghetto and was active in the Halvayat Ha-met (burial) society.[32] The Strykówer Rebbe continued his activity among his Hasidim in the Warsaw ghetto and helped other religious refugees in the framework of the Ezrat Torah society, established to support Torah scholars.[33] Rabbi David Bornstein, the Sochaczewer Rebbe, continued Hasidic ritual practices such as the *tish* (Hasidic gathering; lit. "table") in the ghetto, and his Hasidim flocked to his door; like him, many of them were engaged in education.[34] Rabbi Menahem Mendel Alter, the brother of the Gerer Rebbe, was active in organizing and supporting Torah students, and ran several *minyanim* (prayer quorums) in his house.[35]

It should be emphasized that there is evidence that the followers of at least some of these rabbis attempted to get them out of the Nazi-occupied areas, as well as evidence of their refusal on principle to save themselves. Thus, for example, the son of the Alexander Rebbe, Rabbi Yerahmiel Yisra'el Yosef, sent several letters in which he recorded attempts to persuade 'His Holiness my Father the *Rebbe*, may he merit a long life, amen, to save himself and my righteous mother and myself, by means of three travel documents that they have succeeded in securing', and the *rebbe*'s stubborn refusal to leave occupied Poland:

> All the kind urgings and pleas were in vain, for His Holiness my Father the *Rebbe*, may he merit a long life, amen, told them with absolute finality that they should speak of this no more. '*Vos vilt its haben fun mir? Ikh zol mikh roteven, ven alle yidn zeinen in aza et tsorah? Nein!* [What do you want from me? Should I save myself, when all the Jews are in such

---

32 See for instance the letter from the members of the *Halvayat ha-met* organization to Czerniaków, Yad Vashem Archive, M10.ARII/119. The signatories to the letter include the Strykówer Rebbe, the Sochaczewer Rebbe, and the Aleksander Rebbe. The latter was captured by the Germans during the great deportation of summer 1942; he was sent to Treblinka and murdered there.

33 During the Warsaw Ghetto uprising, the Strykówer Rebbe was captured by the Germans and severely beaten. He was sent to several camps and eventually murdered during the so-called 'Harvest Festival' of November 1943.

34 The book by Rabbi Aharonson, a Hasid of the Sochaczewer Rebbe, contains valuable information about his *rebbe*'s activity in the ghetto; see notes 43, 44, and 72. Evidence of his involvement in the care of the dead appears in *Gazeta Żydowska*, 12 June 1942. The Sochaczewer Rebbe survived the horrors of the great deportation, but fell ill and died at the end of 1942. He is buried in the Jewish cemetery of Warsaw.

35 See for instance the short biography of him and three other rabbis, Yad Vashem Archive, M10.ARII/281. In early August 1942 Rabbi Alter was captured by the Germans and sent to Treblinka, where he was murdered.

trouble? No!] I dwell among my people. We have lived together with these Jews, and with these Jews we will die for the sanctification of God's Name.'[36]

It should be noted that, although his Hasidim present this letter as referring to the entire range of horrors of the Holocaust, it seems more likely that in mentioning his escape and the troubles of the Jews the *rebbe* was referring to the difficult situation in Poland at the beginning of the war as opposed to the German policy of systematic extermination, which had not yet been implemented. Likewise, it is difficult to know whether the attempts to rescue the *rebbe* were realistic, though it is important to emphasize that he himself refrained from taking advantage of this narrow opportunity of escape.

Thus, although there were rabbis—particularly heads of yeshivas and Hasidic *rebbe*s—who fled from occupied Poland during the first weeks, months, or even years of the war, it seems that most of the religious leaders remained under the yoke of the Nazi occupation. A minority—those who had a realistic chance of escape—stayed voluntarily, but most had no more choice than the wider Jewish population. At the same time, the war brought about a change in the distribution of rabbis throughout occupied Poland, with many rapidly gathering in the capital. Thus the particular characteristics of the posts that rabbis held before the war, with the associated variation in degree of mobility and their status among Polish Jews, led to an unprecedented concentration of Torah scholars in Warsaw during the Holocaust.

The Rabbinic Milieu and Its Spheres of Activity

An analysis of the character of the rabbinic life that developed in Warsaw during the war reveals that within a short time these figures created a distinct and unique social and spiritual milieu. Thus, for instance, in addition to co-operation in the public sphere and consultation on halakhic issues, it seems that as early as the bombardment of Warsaw in September 1939 many rabbis congregated in what came to be known as 'the rabbis' cellar' (*rabonim keller*). During the mass

---

36 Yitshak Menahem Mendel Danziger, *Akedat yitshak* (Jerusalem: n.p., 1953), 4. Evidence concerning other Hasidic *rebbe*s who could have escaped exists for Rabbi Hayim Yerahmiel Taub, Rabbi Shelomoh Hanokh of Radomsko, Rabbi Yisra'el Shapira of Grodzisk, and Rabbi Kalman Kalonymus Shapira, the author of *Esh kodesh*. It is difficult to know which of these possible chances for escape were realistic.

deportation, many of them found temporary refuge in Schultz's workshop with the help of Rabbi Avraham Hendel.[37]

In addition, analysis of the different levels of their activity shows that some of the rabbis continued creative intellectual work that was completely separate from their experiences during the war and to some extent served as a continuation of Torah life before the crisis. The significant difference in this religious creativity was not the actual engagement in the halakhic sphere, but the seizing of the opportunity offered by the concentration of the Torah world in Warsaw as an immediate consequence of the war. An excellent example of this is the project documented by Rabbi Yehiel Ya'akov Weinberg,[38] president of the Warsaw Union of Rabbis (Agudat Rabanei Varshah), to publish a book of novel interpretations (*hidushim*) of Maimonides' rulings on the subject of the removal of *hamets* (leaven) and its burning:

> All the outstanding scholars of Poland sent in *hidushim* on this subject ... we handed over this book to a secret press hidden in one of the cellars in Pawia Street. If the book had been published it would have astounded the world in the width of variation of its styles of *pilpul* and different

---

37 Rabbi Avraham Hendel (1894–1973), an ultra-Orthodox businessman, a Sokolower Hasid, and a close friend of the family of the Gerer Rebbe. Before the war he was a successful industrialist and owned a leather tanning and shoe-making factory. On the outbreak of war, the Germans confiscated his property and appointed the German Fritz Schultz to manage it on their behalf; in fact, however, Hendel continued to run the business. During the mass deportation from the Warsaw ghetto in the summer of 1942, Hendel sheltered many Jews in the factory, especially leading ultra-Orthodox figures and rabbis, and the place became known as 'the rabbis' workshop'. After the liquidation of the ghetto, Rabbi Hendel escaped to the Aryan side and hid there until August 1944. During the Polish uprising of the summer of 1944 he was captured and deported to Dachau. After the war he was known for his work with survivors, and in 1947 he immigrated to Palestine. His diary and writings from the war remain in the possession of his family and have not yet been published.

38 Rabbi Yehiel Ya'akov Weinberg (1884–1966) was a leading halakhic decisor (*posek*). From the mid-twentieth century he served as the head of the Berlin Rabbinical Seminary founded by Rabbi Esriel Hildesheimer. Since he was a foreign citizen, he was expelled from Germany and in 1939 made his way to Warsaw. There he was elected president of the Warsaw Union of Rabbis and the larger Rabbinical Association of Poland. Thanks to his (now Soviet) citizenship, he was sent to a labour camp, where he survived the Holocaust. See also Marc Shapiro's biography of Weinberg, *Between the Yeshiva World and Modern Orthodoxy: The Life and Works of Rabbi Jehiel Jacob Weinberg 1884–1966* (Oxford: 1999).

methodological approaches, and the world would have been amazed at the creative fertility and awareness of the talmudic thinking.[39]

The spiritual engagement of other rabbis was directly influenced by the reality of the war. Some of them, probably those who had engaged in practical kabbalah before the war, tried to work on the mystical plane with the aim of exerting direct influence on the terrible crisis.[40] Others tried to cope with the reality of the war by logical means and to explain it in the light of the Torah world, such as the Sochaczewer Rebbe, as recorded by his student, Rabbi Aharonson. According to the latter, the *rebbe* was already interpreting 'the secret meaning of the Holocaust and its horrors' as a call to *tikun olam* ('healing of the world') at the beginning of the war. When this student asked whether it was not possible to heal the world not only by means of the way of death and suffering but also by means of 'the way of life and the good way,' the *rebbe* answered that Heaven did not always grant this to individual Jews. In Rabbi Aharonson's words:

> I stood there, shaken and terrified at the *rebbe*'s words, may the memory of the righteous be a blessing. Absolute silence reigned in his room, except for the beating of my heart, and the *rebbe* added a few more words: "We learn this from the first section of the Torah, about the righteous Abel and the evil Cain. See, the blood of the righteous son is spilt like water, while the murderer Cain lives and walks around." The *rebbe*, may the memory of the righteous be a blessing, said more, but I cannot write

---

39   Weinberg (ed.), *Yad sha'ul* (Tel Aviv: published privately by the family of the author, 1953), 11. Cited in the database *Korot ha-sho'ah be'mevo'ot la-sifrut ha-rabanit* (above, n. 21). There is also indirect evidence of *hidushim* (lit. "innovations") composed by Rabbi Aryeh Zvi Frumer during the war, which have not survived. See also his unique collection at Yad Vashem archive P.51. Shapiro's bibliography of Weinberg (op cit.) has many advantages, but some problems too. Weinberg edited and wrote many parts of *Yad sha'ul*. See http://www.hebrewbooks.org/36723.

40   Weinberg, *Yad sha'ul* (above, n. 40), 9–10. Similar claims were made about the Koshnitzer Rebbe, Rabbi Aharon Yehiel Halevi, known as Rabbi Areleh. Similarly, in late September 1941 the city's rabbis came up with a plan to arrange a wedding in the Jewish cemetery 'of a poor young man and a virgin immediately after Yom Kippur, at the community's expense. This *segulah* [mystical remedy] is tried and tested, and certainly, with God's help, will be effective in stopping this plague.' Yad Vashem Archive, M10.ARII/142. See also the diary entry for 27 October 1941 by Adam Czerniaków, see idem, *The Warsaw Diary of Adam Czerniakow: Prelude to Doom*, (New York: Stein and Day, 1982), 293 (October 27, 1941).

it down. When I left his room, I knew that I had to prepare myself for the very worst.[41]

However, the main area of Torah study in which the rabbis of Warsaw were forced to be active was in adapting the halakhic world to the terrible reality of the war. Thus, for example, rabbis ruled that the fast of Tisha Be'av could be replaced by studying the talmudic tractate *Ta'anit* (which deals with public fasts), dealt with questions about marriages in the ghetto, and composed special prayers for the wartime situation.[42] Some of the halakhic decisions dealt with the tensions that arose not only between man and his Maker but between individuals, and were rendered in the rabbinic courts that continued to function in the city, sometimes in the rabbis' homes. It thus seems that a large number of the rabbis who congregated in Warsaw continued their religious activities and strove to establish a 'heavenly Warsaw' at a time when everyday existence there was too hard to bear.

Alongside this impressive spiritual activity, the rabbis' involvement in other, practical spheres should be noted, especially in the welfare organizations, the educational frameworks, and questions of the burial of the dead. It is important to note that the rabbis principally focused on helping Torah scholars and the religiously observant community and devoted much effort to religious education in the ghetto—both underground and, later on, permitted. Some of them helped to set up soup kitchens that distributed kosher food to religious refugees and Torah students;[43] others devoted themselves to the maintenance of educational institutions for boys and girls, Beit Ya'akov institutions, *hadarim* (religious elementary schools), and yeshivas;[44] and there were those

---

41 Aharonson, *Alei mererut*, 259. In these words Rabbi Aharonson hints at a recurrent feature in other Orthodox writings: the internal censorship adopted by religious writers when describing the horrors of the Holocaust. Orthodox writing about the war seems to have extended the halakhic principle *halakhah ve'ein morin ken* ('this is the halakhah but we do not teach it') to personal memories and interpretations. For another example, see the allusions made by Rabbi Ya'akov Avigdor in relation to the recommendations made by a rabbinical court to young girls that they escape to the Aryan side and pretend to be Christians; idem, *Abir ya'akov* (New York: n.p., 1949) (no page numbers).

42 Announcement about *Tisha Be'av*, Yad Vashem Archive, M.10/AR.I/599.86; Aharonson, *Alei mererut*, 230; prayer for wartime, Yad Vashem Archive, M.10/AR.II/371.

43 'Questions about *kashrut* from refugees in Warsaw', Yad Vashem Archive, M.10/AR.I/190.

44 For instance, Rabbi Orlian, one of the key figures in the Beit Ya'akov educational network, who served as the director of the flagship institution of the Beit Ya'akov Teachers' Seminary in Kraków before the war, fled to Warsaw after being severely beaten in his home town. Throughout the war he tried to keep in touch with the girls from the seminary

who concentrated on the preparation and burial of the dead.[45] These activities largely represented a continuation of pre-war involvement in these areas, both in terms of the people concerned and in terms of the methods that the rabbis employed.[46]

However, the vibrant religious life in the ghetto—in both the spiritual and practical realms—obscures neither the difficult challenges facing the rabbis as a result of the war nor the price paid by the religious world and its members. The rabbis seem to have found it more and more difficult over the years to continue to strengthen the faithful when they themselves were in crisis. In the words of the Piaczener Rebbe:

> ... and in particular, as the troubles continue, even someone who started by strengthening himself and the rest of Israel becomes exhausted from providing strength and weary of comforting; even if he wants to make an effort and say some words of comfort and strength, he has nothing to say, for during the long days of trouble he has already said and repeated everything that he was capable of saying, and his words have become old and have no effect any more, neither on him nor on those who hear him.[47]

Orthodox Judaism, like every other social and religious sector among the Jews of Warsaw, did not just accumulate a list of impressive successes in the spiritual and practical spheres but also had to deal with failures and crises, both internal and external. Thus, for example, there is no doubt that during the war there was a continuous decline in observance of the commandments, as well as a decline in the size of the religious population in the ghetto. In truth,

---

and advised them on both educational and religious matters. Rabbi Avraham Weinberg, a brilliant scholar, continued to give *shiurim* throughout the war, and his students seem to have continued with Torah study and preserved their traditional dress up to the uprising in April 1943. During the suppression of the uprising, a bunker was uncovered at 24 Miła Street where his students met after he had been murdered during the mass deportation. See the photograph album of Jürgen Stroop in Andrzej Wirth (ed.), *The Jewish Quarter of Warsaw Is No More! The Stroop Report* (New York: Pantheon Books, 1979), pictures 12, 34 (no picture numbers and no pagination).

45 Manifesto of *Hesed shel Emet*, Yad Vashem Archive, M10.ARII/210; report of the Society for the Care of the Bodies of the Jewish Poor, *Levaiyat Ha-met*, 20 April 1942, ibid., document 119.

46 Gershon C. Bacon, *The politics of tradition: Agudat Yisrael in Poland, 1916–1939* (Jerusalem: Magnes Press, 1996).

47 Shapira, *Sacred Fire: Torah from the Years of Fury, 1939–1942*, 293 (Parshat Zachor, 28 February 1942).

Orthodox Judaism had been facing increasing secularization for decades; but the war presented special difficulties:

> And another thing that everyone knows, that for many years sons of religious fathers to our regret have abandoned Torah and the way of their fathers and have become freethinkers, may the Lord have mercy; but to balance this God has inspired the hearts of sons of secular fathers so that of their own accord they draw near to Torah, and they have withstood trials, as long as they have cleaved to the Torah and been pious, and these young men have filled the gap left in the camp of God's servants and in the houses of the faithful, but this is not happening any longer. There are many young men who abandon Torah because of trouble and hardship, but not one single son of a secular father draws near, simply because there are no places for Torah students to gather, and there are no *batei midrash* and *shtiblach* ... and the reason for all this abandonment now is simply the bitter troubles of Israel that can scarcely be borne, may the Lord have mercy, so that even when God has mercy and saves us with whoever is left, then, God forbid, there will be nobody to fill the *hadarim*, and there will not be enough students to make it worth setting up yeshivas for them.[48]

Indeed, both religious sources[49] and those written by "freethinkers"[50] bear witness to the continual decline of religious society—as a society—in the ghetto during the war. It is not certain that carelessness about commandments at a time of extreme crisis necessarily indicates a weakening of religious faith.[51]

---

48 Ibid., 204–9 (Shabat Parshat Ekev, 16 August 1941).

49 In addition to the references in this article, see also other sermons of the author of *Sacred Fire: Torah from the Years of Fury, 1939–1942*, 26 (Parshat Va Yigash, 16 December 1939); 87 (Emor, 11 May 1940); 159 (Shabat Parshat Va Yeshev, 21 December 1940); Huberband, *Kiddush Hashem: Jewish Religious and Cultural Life in Poland during the Holocaust*, 175–87.

50 In addition to the references in this article, see also Marek Edelman in conversation with Anka Grupińska, *Ciągle po kole: rozmowy z żołnierzami getta warszawskiego* (Warszawa: Wydawnictwo Twój Styl, 2000), 16–17; the diary of Hayim Aharon Kaplan (unpublished), Moreshet Archive, D.2.470, 14 April 1941.

51 It should be remembered that the religious world—both at the practical level of observing the commandments and at the conceptual level of religious thought—is not dichotomous; and even under regular circumstances there are different levels of punctiliousness of religious observance and different levels of engagement with the spiritual world. During periods of extreme crisis, such as the Holocaust, a diminution in the observance of practical commandments does not necessarily indicate a contraction of the religious

But there is no doubt that alienation—even if only in practical terms and due to physical and institutional disintegration—from the Torah world had significantly diminished the circles that had previously been close to the rabbis.

However, it is difficult to find reliable evidence of cases of abandonment of faith among rabbis in Warsaw during the war. It may be conjectured that, as in other places,[52] such cases did exist, even if they did not occur among the rabbinic elite that had gathered in the city.[53] Some degree of participation in the general religious decline may be traced in the following joke, recorded in Hayim Kaplan's diary: 'A rabbi issued a halakhic judgment, but the parties to the dispute did not recompense him to his satisfaction. The rabbi expressed his dissatisfaction to them, remarking that the paltry sum was not even enough to purchase a kilo of pork fat.' Kaplan added, 'The God-fearing and devout Jews of Poland, masters of the Hebrew tradition, masters of a refined piety, masters of the faithful, have become corrupted in their spirit and religious devotion. Instead of suffering monetary loss [to comply with religion], they do not even observe Torah prohibitions.'[54]

---

sphere, just as a response to religious appeals does not necessarily prove a strengthening of faith. Thus, for example, eating non-kosher food might be done out of a deep religious recognition of the commandment that one should 'live by them' [the commandments], and participation by non-religious people in a public fast day does not necessarily prove that many people had strengthened their faith and moved closer to the religious world. In addition, in the reality of extreme crisis, halakhic decision-making itself tends to leniency in practical matters, so the relaxation of religious observance should not be treated as direct evidence of the weakening of faith. More nuanced research on the observance of practical commandments during the Holocaust, on changes that took place in the Jewish religious world during the war, and so on, lies outside the limits of this chapter and should be accompanied by consideration of the halakhic, conceptual, and practical complexity of the different sectors of the religious world.

52   See for instance Yehezkel Harpnes, *Be'kaf ha-kela* (above, n. 16), 26; the testimony of Abram Doktorczyk of Slonim about the rabbi of Ostrów Mazowiecka and his family, Yad Vashem Archive, M1E.567. A censored version of this event appears in Nachum Alpert, *The Destruction of Slonim Jewry: The Story of the Jews of Slonim during the Holocaust* (New York: Holocaust Library, 1989), 178.

53   See for instance the words of faith expressed in the poem 'Venatati nikmati be-edom', M10.ARII/356, in contrast to the expression of atheism in the poem 'Heikhan elokim', ibid., document 359.

54   The unpublished diary of Hayim Aharon Kaplan (above, n. 51), 29 June 1941. It seems reasonable to assume that there were some instances of betrayal and even co-operation with the authorities in the religious community, including its leaders. See for instance Huberband, *Kiddush Hashem: Jewish religious and cultural life in Poland during the*

Obviously, the failing strength of religious Judaism did not escape the notice of the city's rabbis, though it should be stressed that an analysis of their writings reveals that in the view of these Torah scholars the weakness of religious life in the ghetto and throughout the Jewish world was not the *result* of the tragedy but its *cause*. In other words, as mentioned earlier, this was not a case of physical crisis leading to Jewish alienation from the world of Torah, but the opposite: it was the process of the abandonment of religion that had caused all the current disasters that had befallen the Jews. Some rabbis explicitly claimed that the wartime reality was punishment for the community's sins,[55] while many others believed that the Jewish community's return to and strengthening of religion would lead directly to an improvement in the situation. This belief seems to have played a major role in increased activity by religious leaders in the public sphere and in their efforts to encourage the general community to observe the commandments.[56]

An example of this is the appeal made by the *rebbe*s and rabbis of the ghetto in September 1941, when there was a major typhus epidemic. The rabbis, who had met to take counsel, decided to issue an appeal to the Jews of the ghetto to maintain cleanliness and hygiene with reminders about the importance of keeping the Sabbath, giving charity, religious education, checking *mezuzot* (prayer scrolls affixed to doorways), prayer, study, and other observances, adding: 'in absolute confidence that by means of the above regulations we will be saved and inscribed and sealed for good.'[57] Thus a direct connection can be established between the rabbis' understanding of the situation in which they

---

    Holocaust, 136–46, as well as the list of 25 June 1942, Yad Vashem Archive, M10.ARII/446, which describes the questionable actions of the grandson of the famous rabbi of 'S.'

55 See for example the memoirs of Tadeusz Szymkiewicz, Yad Vashem Archive, O.33/258.

56 In this case too it is difficult to know how people reacted to these calls, but a critical echo can be heard in the diary of Ben-Shem, who records that during Yom Kippur 1942 he heard sayings of this type among labourers at the workshop in which he worked. In his words: 'I tried to explain to them and to point out their error in mistaking the result for the cause and the cause for the result. All these sins were the result of the cause, that God had organized the expulsion and not the reverse, but they stopped up their ears and would not hear that 'everything God has done is for the good', that it is forbidden to criticize His words, that only humans sin, and that evil and its cause is only to be sought among them.' It is thus clear that alongside the adoption of this faith-based attitude by simple people there were also those who criticized it; Reuven Ben-Shem, *Yoman* (above, n. 1), Yom Kippur 1942.

57 Yad Vashem Archive, M10.ARII/171. See also the underground Orthodox publication, *Kol ba-midbar*, Adar (February) 1942, in Yosef Kermish (ed.), *Itonut ha-mahteret ha-yehudit be'varshah*, v: *Detsember 1940–mars 1942* (Jerusalem: Yad Vashem, 1993), 221–3.

were living and their desire to act in the public sphere, even in matters with no obvious link to the world of Torah and religion.

It is difficult to know how this appeal was received either by religious or non-religious people in the ghetto, though it is clear that interventions by the rabbis in affairs outside the religious sphere were not always greeted with approval. Thus, for example, from the end of April 1941 the Germans declared the Sabbath, and not Sunday, to be the official day of rest in the ghetto. When it became clear that many people were not complying with this, the Orthodox leaders in the ghetto decided to fight against public desecration of the Sabbath, probably out of the belief that such desecration was one of the causes of Jewish misery. The religious department of the Judenrat suggested the establishment of a sort of 'Sabbath patrol', as well as the establishment of courts that would deal with those who did not respect the sanctity of the Sabbath.[58] As a result, an apparent overlap of interests was found between the Nazi oppressor and religious Jews, who needed an official permit from the authorities in order to set up patrols of this type. This proposal was greeted with anger and scorn by the Dror movement, which published a vitriolic response in its journal, entitled 'Keeping the Sabbath or Desecrating God's Name?', which attacked 'the cossacks of the Holy One, blessed be He' who were involving the Nazi murderers in religious legislation.[59] Of course, this conflict was not free of ideological and political dimensions, as can be seen from the treatment of this issue in another edition of the Dror journal, which reported that the Judenrat's religious department's proposal had been rejected by the legal department:

> Once again on the Sabbath observance issue. The stormy blood of the cossacks of the Holy One, blessed be He, finds no rest ... Rabbi Alexander Zysze[60] and the gang from the religious department! Don't pull the thread too hard, and don't go crawling to the Nazi oppressor over the heads of the Jewish people. Don't grace us with the commandment of Sabbath observance or with Hitler's tender mercies—you'd do better to engage in good and charitable deeds![61]

---

58   Proposal for *Mishmeret Ha-shabat* association and *Beit din la-inyanei shabat*, Yad Vashem Archive, M10.AR1/244.

59   *Yediot: biton tenuat dror* 10 (July 1942), in Yisra'el Shaham (ed.), *Itonut ha-mahteret ha-yehudit be'varshah*, vi: *Mars 1942–yuli 1944* (Jerusalem: Yad Vashem, 1997), 502.

60   Rabbi Alexander Zysze Frydman; see above, n. 27.

61   *Yediot: biton tenuat dror* 11 (July 1942), in Shaham (ed.), *Itonut ha-mahteret* (above, n. 60), 518.

Clearly, the anger felt by the members of the Dror movement was not only owing to the unusual proposal, but also—if not principally—to the religious leaders' attempt to intervene in the 'secular' public sphere. For the leaders of the secular population of the ghetto—or at least those who regarded themselves as worthy of holding such positions of power—the rabbis were meant to limit their activity solely to the religious sphere and to leave the public arena to others. The rabbis, on the other hand, saw it as not only their right but their duty to intervene on subjects that were outside the four cubits of halakhic decision-making. Considerable continuity of the political conflicts and opposing world-views that had existed among the different movements of interwar Poland is clearly visible here. However, it should be stressed that this confrontation, like the rabbis' involvement in public affairs,[62] underscores their position as public leaders and partners in the Jewish leadership of the ghetto.

The Rabbis of Warsaw as a Focus for the Transmission of Information about the Destruction of the Jews of Poland

Against the background of the terrible reality of the Warsaw ghetto, with which the rabbis and the wider community alike had to cope, the Germans began to implement their 'Final Solution' for the Jews of Europe, i.e., the total murder of the Jews. The massacre began with Operation Barbarossa in June 1941, with the slaughter of the Jews of the former eastern part of Poland and of the USSR in the death pits, and within a few months they expanded to other areas and implemented more sophisticated means of murder. In October 1941, the sites of the later extermination camps of Chełmno and Bełżec were established; and within a few months, the camps of Operation Reinhard had been built. On 8 December 1941, the Germans began to murder the Jews of the towns of the Warthegau region in Chełmno; in mid-March 1942 the deportation of the Lublin Jews to Bełżec began; and on 22 July 1942 the mass deportation of the Jews of the Warsaw ghetto commenced, during which about 300,000 Jews were sent to Treblinka.[63]

---

62 In addition to the instances already mentioned, another example is provided by Rabbi Frydman's participation in a meeting attended by other public representatives, concerning the rescue of Jewish detainees imprisoned for crossing the ghetto borders, held on 15 Jan. 1942; For another instance of rabbinic public activity, see n. 27 above.

63 For an overview of the development of the 'final solution', see Ian Kershaw, *Hitler 1936–1945: Nemesis* (London: Penguin Books, 2000); Christopher R. Browning, *The Origins of the*

Information about the mass murder of Jews in the East began to filter into the Warsaw ghetto towards the end of 1941. It began with rumours of mass killings of Jews in the East, often associated with pogroms by the local population (mainly Ukrainians and Lithuanians), with war crimes in the East, and with Nazi Germany's struggle against Bolshevism. In early 1942, several Jews who had escaped from the Chełmno extermination camp reached the Warsaw ghetto and recounted the murders that were taking place. At the same time, mainly in January and February 1942, dozens of postcards arrived in the ghetto from Jews who came from the towns of the Warthegau, who wrote to their relatives in the ghetto, both openly and by allusion, about deportations to Chełmno and the death that lay in wait for them. Information about the brutal deportation from Lublin also rapidly reached the ghetto and caused mass panic, since it had happened in a major city in the Generalgouvernement. Thus, starting in late 1941, abundant information about the mass murder of Jews both in and outside Poland was reaching the Warsaw ghetto.[64]

Recent research on this subject confirms the central role of rabbis in disseminating information about the slaughter and their role as recipients of information about the enemy from many informants in Poland in general and in Warsaw in particular.[65] Further evidence of the role of rabbis in disseminating information comes from the extensive testimony of Tadeusz Szymkiewicz, who after the establishment of the ghetto was a neighbour of Rabbi Halberstam of Sosnowice,[66] whom he describes as a 'wonder-working rabbi' and 'tzaddik'. According to Szymkiewicz, he was invited to the rabbi's lodgings in December 1941 because the latter wanted to share some information. That evening, the rabbi told him that a reliable man had arrived from Sosnowiec and reported on a massacre of Jewish children. Szymkiewicz refused to believe the report, but promised to investigate and report back to the rabbi. The rabbi, for his part, (as Szymkiewicz later testified) told him to prepare for the future, since days were coming for which the description 'difficult' would be understated. 'I parted from him in silence, bereft of words,' Szymkewicz recalls.[67]

Final Solution: The Evolution of Nazi Jewish Policy September 1939–March 1942 (London and Lincoln, NB: University of Nebraska Press, 2004).

64 On the transmission of information and its reception, see my (unpublished) article, '"Nikarim divrei emet?" Hitkablutan shel yediot al odot helmno be'geto varshah ve'tehum ha-hitnasut shel ha-hakarah ha-enoshit'.

65 Esther Farbstein, 'To the Rabbi's House: Community Rabbis and the Reports of Mass Murder', in eadem, *Hidden in thunder* (above, n. 7), 17–57, esp. 48–51.

66 It seems likely that this refers to Rabbi David ben Sinai Halberstam.

67 Memoirs of Tadeusz Szymkiewicz (above, n. 57).

Throughout the war, rabbis continued to be figures of authority and leadership to whom the Jews of the ghetto were accustomed to turn. Some Jews seem to have believed that rabbis would have the ability to do something and make others act on this most appalling information.[68] Rabbinic leadership thus endured throughout the war years, and rabbis continued to be the main address for this vital information, for their followers, and perhaps for others.

In addition, an analysis of the rabbis' reactions to the terrible information that trickled through to the ghetto reveals that many expressed different reactions in public and in private. In public sermons and statements, the rabbis seem to have acted in accordance with the principle 'Repentance, prayer, and charity avert the evil decree'[69] and called upon the community to observe the commandments and pray that the evil decree be overturned—as they had in the past, albeit with greater urgency now. Thus, for example, when Rabbi Aharonson found out about Chełmno, he wrote to his *rebbe*, the Sochaczewer Rebbe, in cryptic style that 'Aunt Esther, from 7 Megillah Street, flat 4, is coming', alluding to the verse in the book of Esther: 'For we are sold, I and my people, to be destroyed, to be slain, and to be annihilated' (Esther 7: 4).[70] The *rebbe* immediately replied, equally cryptically, that there was a need to summon up one's strength and play grandfather's work 23, part 4, an allusion to Psalm 23: 4: 'Even though I walk through the valley of the shadow of death, I will fear no evil; For Thou art with me; Thy rod and Thy staff comfort me.'[71]

---

68   See for instance the letter from Rabbi Silman of Grabów (21 Jan. 1942), Yad Vashem Archive, M10.AR1/549.2; the letter of M. Jachimiak of Grabów (22 Jan. 1942), ibid., document 549.3; the letter of I. Gutfreund of Zduńska Wola (21 Feb. 1942), ibid., document 571.

69   From the prayer *Unetaneh tokef*, recited on Rosh Hashanah and Yom Kippur.

70   A similarly cryptic hint seems to have been sent by Rabbi Ziemba in an attempt to tell world Jewry of the mass deportations from the Warsaw ghetto. In a telegram he wrote that Mr. Amos was keeping his promise from fifth-third, alluding to Amos 5: 3: 'The city that marched out a thousand strong shall have only a hundred left, and that which marched forth a hundred strong shall have only ten left for the house of Israel.' Melekh Neustadt, *Hurban umered yehudei varshah* (Tel Aviv: Ha-Va'ad ha-Po'el shel Ha-histadrut Ha-klalit shel Ha-ovdim b'Eretz Yisrael, 1946), 406.

71   Aharonson, *Alei mererut* (above, n. 14), 206. See also the sermon by the author of *Sacred Fire* for Shabat Parshat Matot (11 July 1942): 'But with what shall we strengthen ourselves over the martyrs who have already been killed, may God have mercy, our dear relatives and all Jews, some of whom were as close as our very souls, and with what shall we raise ourselves up a little from the terrible rumours, old and new, from the collapse of our bones and the melting of our hearts? With the knowledge that we are not alone in our troubles, that [God], may He be blessed, as it were suffers with us, "I am with him in sorrow."' *Sacred Fire: Torah from the years of fury, 1939–1942*, 191 (Mattoth, 11 July 1942).

At the same time, people who consulted with the rabbis on a personal basis, asking what they should do in the face of the approaching danger, seem to have received varied answers, the gist of which was that they should try to save themselves, even at the price of compromising their traditional Jewish observance. Thus, for example, Rabbi Laznowski records that the Sochaczewer Rebbe permitted him to cross over to the Aryan side, saying that 'in the ghetto it is definitely [a case of] *pikuah nefesh* (the need to save a life), and leaving it is a doubtful [case of] *pikuah nefesh*'.[72] In other words, even though the rabbis continued to call for a strengthening of faith in public, some do not seem to have hesitated to advise Jews to search for practical means of escape.

An analysis of the rabbis' reactions to information about the slaughter, and in particular about the mass deportation, as they themselves witnessed terrible brutality and the deaths of masses of Jews, also reveals their difficulties in coping—as individuals, as public leaders, and as religious people—with the murderous reality. Thus, for instance, once Szymkiewicz realized that the terrible reports were reliable, he went back to tell Rabbi Halberstam, who tried to cheer him up by saying that he would pray to God to save the Jews. Szymkiewicz observed that even this saintly man, who was used to talking to God in a natural way, harboured doubts as to the efficacy of his prayers.[73]

Not surprisingly, other rabbis also experienced a significant crisis when faced with mass murder. It is recorded of the Sochaczewer Rebbe that during the war he exchanged the prayerbook of the Ari (the sixteenth-century kabbalist R. Isaac Luria), from which he used to pray for an ordinary prayerbook, thus abjuring a prayerbook that contained kabalistic *kavanot* (mystical intentions). His reason: 'For one can see nothing at all, there is a great

---

72   laznowski, *Peri yitshak* (Benei Berak: n.p., 1976) 95. There is also indirect evidence concerning Rabbi Ziemba, who apparently said 'When the enemy wants the bodies, the commandment is to sacrifice the souls. If there are bodies, there will be souls.' For example, Aviva Kerwasser Sadan recorded: 'Papa returns from the house of the Piaczener Rebbe after evening prayers with a sad face... he gathers us, the daughters, around him and says, "Difficult days are approaching for the Jews of Warsaw. According to the *rebbe*'s advice you must escape from the ghetto as soon as possible. All your lives you girls have been faithful to the Torah and the commandments, but from this moment on you are exempt from this. In the name of heaven you are commanded in relation to one thing alone: to save your lives... after the storm has passed, come home."' Aviva Kerwasser Sadan, *Lihyot al kav hakets* (Kiriat Haim, n.p., 1955), 210. See also the memoirs of Tadeusz Szymkiewicz (above, n. 56), who reports that his saintly neighbour from Sosnowiec rejected the attempt at armed opposition, claiming that the Jews had no weapons, but said that those who had the chance to escape should take it, and that perhaps a few would be saved in this way.

73   Memoirs of Tadeusz Szymkiewicz (above, n. 56).

concealment... the Ari, may his memory be a blessing, asked in his Sabbath songs [*zemirot*] that [God] would "reveal to us the [secret] reasons",[74] but we do not understand the reason.'[75] The *rebbe* seems to have realized that the events happening around him were completely beyond comprehension.[76] It should be stressed that although these sources bear witness to a change in the rabbis' outlook, it was not outright apostasy but rather a change in the tenor of their conversation with the Master of the Universe. New patterns of confrontation with God in the face of the terrible reality can thus be detected in the religious community.[77] Particularly impressive evidence of the ultra-Orthodox confrontation with the crisis and the sense of abandonment is preserved in the diary of Reuven Ben-Shem, which records a meeting with the brother of the Gerer Rebbe during the deportation:

> And at the head of them all [Hasidic and non-Hasidic Orthodox Jews] he stands, the son of the Gerer Rebbe, the great rabbi in Israel, according to his wealth and his intellect and his presence in Warsaw, the capital. The *rebbe*'s daughters and sons-in-law are also here. And behold, they have already set up a *minyan*, and this evening they prayed 'Lechu nerananah' [the first psalm in the Sabbath evening service] at the *minyan* with song, and they sang '*Gut shabes!*', as they used to in the ordinary time of peace. The [sound] rang out after the prayer as though in a real *shtibl*... since I had made myself known to the *rebbe*... I asked him after we left the service, '"The work of my hands is drowning in the sea and you would offer me song?"' And he answered me, saying that God has the right not to listen to the song, but we are forbidden to stop the song, even for a moment.[78]

---

74 From the Ari's song for the third Sabbath meal (*se'udah shelishit*), 'Asader le'se'udata', written in Aramaic and replete with kabbalistic allusions.

75 Grantstein, *Mekadshei ha-shem* (above, n. 4), vol. 1, 127.

76 Additional evidence of this *rebbe*'s personal crisis is the description of his meeting with his relation by marriage, the Strykówer Rebbe, after their children had been sent to Treblinka. They embraced each other, and the Sochaczewer Rebbe wept, '*Mehutan! Vi halt men dos oys?*' [How do we keep going on?]; ibid., 128.

77 On a similar change, see Avihai Tsur, '"Hu yitbarakh mistater be'beit goali": torat ha-yisurim shel ha-admor mipiatsenah', *Dapim le-heker ha-sho'ah*, Me'asef 25 (2011): 151–90.

78 Ben-Shem, *Yoman* (above, n. 1), 7 Aug. 1942. In this context, it is interesting to note the continuation of the conversation, as well as Ben-Shem's own reservations: '"Annihilation, annihilation", I sighed. "God's salvations are like the twinkling of an eye," he answered. Not 'in the twinkling of an eye' but 'like the twinkling of an eye;' in other words, not after the twinkling of an eye, not 'in the twinkling' but 'like the twinkling,' i.e., together with

Ultimately, the fate of the rabbis who had gathered in Warsaw was no better than that of their flocks. On the eve of the great deportation, dozens of Jewish leaders were taken hostage, including a number of rabbis. These hostages, particularly the rabbis, were severely beaten by the Germans and were only released after several weeks back into the ravaged and ruined ghetto.[79] Most of the rabbis lived in terror of mass deportation. As in other circles, such as the youth movements and the political parties, who tried to protect their members during the deportation, the ultra-Orthodox tried to obtain work permits for their religious leaders in order to protect them from deportation to Treblinka. Unfortunately, dozens of rabbis were lost during the mass deportation;[80] others were murdered during the liquidation of the ghetto during the uprising,[81] while those who had survived in the Lublin camps were exterminated by the Germans in November 1943 during the 'Harvest Festival'.

Conclusion

The sources at our disposal bear witness to the fact that during the Holocaust Orthodox Judaism continued to sustain a vibrant religious life, which sometimes reached a unique florescence thanks to the concentration of Torah scholars in the Polish capital. This religious community was characterized both by continuity with pre-war life in terms of activity in the public sphere, and by crisis and change. The changes were produced by the difficult physical reality of wartime, which necessitated innovative halakhic decisions and the adaptation of the Torah world to everyday life, as well as to the religious possibilities created by the unusual concentration of rabbis in the city. Analysis of the rabbinic elite in wartime Warsaw reveals the continual dialogue in which the rabbis engaged, their separate, bounded milieu in the ghetto, their central

---

the twinkling. I was silent for a while, and when they went, I whispered to him that the twinkling of the eye of the Almighty lasts a long time, God willing they would not fail us now. God willing.'

79 On the brutal beating of these rabbis, see the contemporary writings of Dr. Polisiuk, Archive of Beit Lohamei Ha-geta'ot, collections 3182.

80 In addition to the rabbis whose stories are recorded above, Rabbi Huberband, Rabbi Yitshak Meir Kanel, Rabbi Ya'akov Gezundheit (the grandson of the last official Rabbi of Warsaw), and many others.

81 For example, Rabbi Maisel, of whom Yitshak Katzenelson and Tuvia Borzykowski speak with great admiration. See the diary entry for 12 August 1942, in Yitzhak Katznelson, *Vittel Diary* (Bet Lohami Hagettaot: Ha-kibbutz Ha-meuchad Publishing House, 1972), 114–20; Borzykowski, *Bein kirot noflim* (Tel Aviv: Ha-kibbutz Ha-meuchad, 1970), 42–3.

role in the processing of information about the mass destruction, and their difficulties—as human beings, as religious individuals, and as public leaders—when faced with the prospect of certain death that began to crystallize within the Warsaw ghetto.

An important question that arises is how far these rabbis succeeded in extending their influence during the war, and how similar this group's activities were to those activities in which they had engaged before the war. The available sources suggest that most of the rabbis did not increase their sphere of influence. Thus, for example, although many were involved in welfare and support activities, they seem to have continued to serve as spiritual leaders mainly for portions of their communities from before the war and did not extend their influence to the masses of refugees.[82] Although evidence can be found that shows that some freethinkers turned to them or responded to their appeals,[83] it would be difficult to argue that the rabbis became resources for many people who had not been close to them in the past. Yet, it should be remembered that the continual shrinkage of groups within the rabbis' orbit should be examined not only in the light of questions about atheism and ideological alienation from religion, but also against the background of the terrible material crisis that produced a general sense of impotence that included the religious sphere. In addition, the available sources do not allow us to discern whether the concentration of rabbis in the city led to the migration of Hasidim from one *rebbe* to another; nor to estimate the degree to which patterns of religious leadership were disrupted during the war. Nevertheless, in spite of the changes that took place in Jewish society during the war, the rabbis continued to lead discreet sectors of Jewish society.

Analysis of the activities of the rabbis gathered in Warsaw during the war thus underlines their part in Jewish leadership and their ways of coping with the impossible reality forced upon them. This not only enables us to fill a gap in research, but also to cast light upon the internal coping mechanisms of Jewish society both in crisis and in normal times. The foregoing analysis also

---

82 See, for example, Ben-Shem, *Yoman* (above, n. 1), October 1941, who claims, against the background of the third Rosh Hashanah of the war, that 'religious faith has not acquired any followers in this war.' For a discussion of rabbinic authority for refugees during the war, see Rabbi Avraham Barukh Rosenberger, *Sefer she'elot uteshuvot birkat avraham*, vol. 2 (Gamzu: n.p., 1979), section 49.

83 Memoirs of Tadeusz Szymkiewicz (above, n. 56); Shemuel Vinter gives a critical account of a public fast and prayer decreed by the surviving rabbis of the ghetto, in which non-religious people took part, see Shemuel Vinter, 'Mitokh yomano shel shemuel vinter', in Nahman Blumental and Yosef Kermish (eds.), *Ha-meri ve'ha-mered ba-geto varshah* (Jerusalem: Yad Vashem, 1965), 193 (diary entry of 5 February 1943).

reveals the strength of Jewish authority in this metropolis in the grip of crisis and want, as well as the complex relationships formed there. It suggests that the rabbis' activities during the war should be acknowledged as an additional type of Jewish leadership during the Holocaust, and that their patterns of activity should be understood within a continuum of Orthodox life in Poland in general, and in Warsaw in particular. The questions and the challenges that the rabbis were forced to confront during the war created a unique reality and must be incorporated into the study of the Holocaust, the modern Jewish world, and Jewish Warsaw.[84]

Translation by Lindsey Taylor-Guthartz

---

84   Thus, for instance, the rabbis' behavior during the Holocaust should be compared to the steps taken by halakhic decisors at other times of crisis. See for example the involvement of Rabbi Yisrael Friedman of Ruzhyn in the Ushyts affair, as well as the long debate on rabbis' positions—both principled and practical—on the issue of conscription to the Russian army; David Asaf, *The Regal Way: The Life and Times of Rabbi Israel of Ruzhin* (Stanford, CA: Stanford University Press, 2002); Mordechai Zalkin, 'Bein "benei elohim" le'"benei adam": rabanim, bahurei yeshivot veha-giyus la-tseva ha-rusi ba-me'ah ha-tesha-esreh', in Avriel Bar-Levav (ed.), *Shalom umilhamah ba-tarbut ha-yehudit* (Jerusalem and Tel Aviv: Merkaz Zalman Shazar L' toldot Israel 2006), 165–222.

CHAPTER 19

The Warsaw Ghetto in the Writings of Rachel Auerbach

Samuel Kassow

1

As one of only three survivors of the Oyneg Shabes archival project, Rachel Auerbach had the rare opportunity not only to retrieve her wartime reportages but to rewrite and publish them in such books as *B'hutsot varshe*, *Varshever tsvoes* and *Baym letstn veg*.[1] The differences, some subtle, some great, between her wartime writings and their postwar versions reflect a personal journey of survival and an evolving search for the meaning of Holocaust memory. As she handed over her first cache of writings to the Oyneg Shabes on July 26, 1942, in the chaos of the deportation to Treblinka, she attached a note that exposed her feelings: raw fear, violent anger, despair. "I am handing over this unfinished essay to the archive. The fifth day of the 'Aktion'. Perhaps such horrors have already occurred before in Jewish history. But such shame, never. Jews as tools [of the killers]. I want to stay alive I am ready to kiss the boots of the worst scoundrel (*dem gemaynstn kham*) just to be able to see the moment of revenge. REVENGE REVENGE remember."[2]

In that same note, she also wondered whether her writings would share the same fate as the scribblings of a coal miner trapped in a mining accident with no survivors, whose body would never be found. Would anyone read them, would anyone care? And besides, she complained, she had lost her ability to write coherently. Her style, she felt, was confused, disjointed. Had it not been for Ringelblum, she would have written nothing. And yet again, maybe it was best if she died. As a survivor, what good would she be to anybody?

By early 1944, living under false papers on the Aryan side, she was writing her memories of the Warsaw Ghetto at the request of the Jewish National Committee. This time there were no questions, no doubts about why she was

---

1 *B'hutsot varshe* (Tel Aviv, 1954); *Varshever tsvoes* (Tel Aviv, 1974); *Baym letstn veg* (Tel Aviv, 1977).
2 Ringelblum Archive, *Jewish Historical Institute*. Part One, Document 655.

writing. She owed it to the dead to tell what had happened. But her writing had to be exact:

> The mass murder, the murder of millions of Jews by the Germans, is a fact that speaks for itself. It is very dangerous to add to this subject interpretations or analyses. Anything that is said can quickly turn into hopeless hysteria or endless sobs. So one must approach this subject with the greatest caution, in a restrained and factual manner... this had been my intention: not to express but to transmit, to note only facts but not to interpret.[3]

She quickly added that she realized immediately that this mandate was impossible—even for herself. Her postwar books and articles were masterly reportages of what she saw in the ghetto, conveyed in evocative, powerful language that made her writings an indispensable source for any cultural or social history of the Warsaw ghetto. But she not only described. She also tried to explain. She wanted to ensure that the Jewish people remembered the Holocaust, not only to keep faith with the dead but also to use its lessons to strengthen the nation and tighten the bonds between Israel and the Diaspora.

For Auerbach, memory and mourning demanded a painful return to the intense, vibrant world of pre-war Jewish Warsaw. After the war, one of Auerbach's leading mentors, the Yiddish poet Melekh Ravitch, had called Warsaw a sprawling mosaic of different Jewish tribes and subcultures.[4] Auerbach took its shattered bits and shards and reconstructed a mosaic of memory based on a poignant evocation of dozens of individual vignettes. And thus she spoke for those who had no one to remember them: the ordinary Jews she came to know in the ghetto as she ran the soup kitchen on Leszno 40 and the Jewish writers, artists and actors whose milieu she shared in the 1930s and in the ghetto.

Jewish Warsaw was the largest Jewish community in Europe. It was a sprawling, intense, dynamic community whose Jewish population had skyrocketed from 40,000 in 1862 to 350,000 by the eve of World War II. Warsaw was a powerful magnet that attracted Jewish migrants from the Hasidic shtetls of central Poland, and Litvaks from Lithuania and White Russia. Caftaned Hasidim, Polish-speaking doctors and lawyers, tough porters and teamsters, underworld characters and writers, all were just a small part of the tableau that was Jewish Warsaw. As it grew, Warsaw became an important manufacturing center, as

---

3 B'hutsot varshe, 7.
4 Melekh Ravitch, *Mayn leksikon*, vol. 2 (Montreal, 1947), 101.

well as a railroad hub and a bustling beehive of wholesale and retail commerce. Its streets drew Jewish merchants from all over Poland to place orders for finished suits, coats, shoes and textiles from the big wholesale warehouses. In his memoirs the well-known Jewish journalist Bernard Singer recalled that "the Nalewki sold clothing and socks (*koronki*), Gęsia traded Łódź and Russian products, Franciszkanska dealt with leather, the Grzybów with iron...."[5]

But at the same time, its theaters, newspapers, cafes, publishing houses and libraries turned Warsaw into a cultural center for Jews and Poles. While the Poles showed no interest in Warsaw's thriving Yiddish culture, the city's Jews not only flocked to the Yiddish cultural institutions but were also often the most dependable patrons of Polish theater and literature.[6] Unlike cities such as Vilna or Białystok, a significant proportion of Warsaw Jewry—especially the middle and professional classes—was Polish-speaking.

And after Poland became an independent state, Jewish Warsaw took on a new role. It helped turn Jews from Galicia, Congress Poland and the Litvak Jews of the northeast borderlands into "Polish Jews." As the Yiddish literary critic Nakhman Mayzel noted, it was not easy to throw these fractious Jewish cousins into a common "melting pot."[7] But in time, the melting pot began to create a new identity, thanks in no small measure to the centripetal influence of the capital which contained the headquarters of the political parties, the editorial offices of the largest daily newspapers, the Jewish social welfare organizations that employed large numbers of the professional intelligentsia. "Tłomackie 13," the home of the Jewish Writers and Journalists Club, became a byword throughout Jewish Poland. From hundreds of remote Jewish shtetls, letters would arrive inviting writers and journalists to come and lecture. Actors from the leading Warsaw Yiddish theaters—Michael Weichert's Yung Teater, Zygmunt Turkow's VIKT—would tour the provinces.

As Auerbach struggled to describe the destruction of Warsaw Jewry, her story elided into a plaidoyer for Warsaw's particular place in the history of Polish Jewry. Warsaw Jewry had shown so much cultural vitality and had built such an active network of institutions that Auerbach characterized Jewish Warsaw as "a state within a state."[8] The more one knew about what the Germans had wiped out, the more one could grasp the enormity of the national *khurbn*. As

---

5   Bernard Singer, *Moje Nalewki* (Warsaw, 1959), 8.
6   For more on this see Michael Steinlauf, "Jews and Polish Theater in Nineteenth Century Warsaw," *Polish Review* 32.4 (1987): 439–458. Polish theaters were even more popular with Jewish theater goers in the interwar period.
7   Nakhman Mayzel, *Geven amol a lebn* (Buenos Aires, 1951), 17.
8   *Varshever tsvoes*, 23.

a writer Auerbach excelled in evocative descriptions of particular people and human relationships rather than at philosophizing or abstract speculation. What made her essays special was the fact that in her hands the descriptions of people and relationships came together in an evocation of Jewish Warsaw and the pain of its loss.

Other Jewish intellectuals besides Auerbach also tried to grasp the terrible implications of the destruction of the Jewish metropolis. Abraham Lewin, a teacher and an important collaborator of Emanuel Ringelblum's secret ghetto archive, made a poignant entry in his diary in December 1942. Most of Warsaw Jewry had already been murdered, and Lewin mourned the almost total destruction of the Jewish intelligentsia. The city had been the nerve center of the most vibrant Jewish community in the world. How could the Jewish people recover from such a disaster, Lewin asked?[9]

In his Song of the Murdered Jewish People, itself a chronicle of the murder of Warsaw Jewry, as well as in his *Vittel Diary*, the poet Yitzhak Katzenelson posed the same question as Levin. With Polish Jewry gone, what could take its place? The Jewish people would survive, but Polish Jewry was its spiritual core, its *Bet Hamidrash*.[10]

The religious journalist Hillel Seidman, in his Warsaw Ghetto diary recalled how a friend had once told him that when the Prophet Elijah would visit the earth to blow the ram's horn and announce the coming of the Messiah, the spot he would choose to stand on would be the corner of Gęsia and Nalewki streets, the heart of Jewish Warsaw. Why? Because it was the epicenter of Jewish spirit and Jewish energy.[11]

In a post war essay comparing the Vilna and the Warsaw ghettos the Yiddish literary critic Shloyme Belis wrote:

> Is it not symbolic? Warsaw struggled, Vilna furnished the song. Is that not a reflection of the entire history of these two great Jewish centers?... Warsaw earned its place [in East European Jewish history—SK] because

---

9   "Warsaw was in fact the backbone of Polish Jewry, its heart, one could say. The destruction of Warsaw would have meant the destruction of the whole of Polish Jewry, even if the provinces had been spared this evil.... One can say that with the setting of the sun of Polish Jewry the splendor and the glory of world Jewry has vanished. We, the Polish Jews were after all the most vibrant nerve of our people." Abraham Lewin, *A Cup of Tears: a Diary of the Warsaw Ghetto*, ed. Antony Polonsky (Oxford, 1989), 232. This is the diary entry of December 29, 1942.
10 Yitzhak Katzenelson, *Vittel Diary* (Tel Aviv, n.d.), 186.
11 Dr. Hillel Seidman, *Togbukh fun varshever geto* (Buenos Aires, 1947), 265. Diary entry of January 15, 1943.

of its quantity as well as its quality... Because of its enormous Jewish population she took the first place in the Jewish world...[12]

For Yiddish journalist Leo Finkelstein, writing in a memorial book dedicated to Warsaw Jewry, Warsaw's strength derived not from *zkhus oves* but from *zkhus otzma*, not from its historical tradition but from its sheer mass and power. Warsaw, he believed, was not burdened by a legacy of encrusted tradition and thus could serve as a path breaker in the modernization of Jewish life. For Finkelstein, a defining characteristic of Warsaw was streets full of Jewish crowds—the 100,000 Jews who came to the funeral of the Yiddish writer Yitzhak Leibush Peretz; the throngs of Hasidim who would jam the railway station to welcome the Gerer Rebbe; the masses of supporters of the Jewish Socialist Bund who would march down the Przejazd on May Day; the packed Yiddish theaters filled with Jews enthralled by Ansky and Asch.[13] In March 1942, in his important Vilna ghetto diary, Herman Kruk, who had run the Bund's Grosser library in Warsaw and fled to Vilna when the war began, nostalgically recalled what he most missed about Warsaw—the pulsing spirit of its "mass meetings" and demonstrations.[14]

However, before the outbreak of the war one could also note growing uncertainty and even pessimism about Jewish Warsaw. Economic anti-Semitism led to the ongoing impoverishment of Polish Jewry. It became harder to fund Jewish schools, theaters and publishing. There was growing worry about the ongoing linguistic acculturation of Warsaw Jewry, as more and more Jewish children were receiving their primary education in the Polish language, rather than Yiddish.[15] In the halls of Tłomackie 13, the renowned locale of the Jewish Writers and Journalists union, arguments flared about whether Warsaw was

---

12 Shloyme Belis, *Portretn un problemen* (Warsaw, 1964), 314.
13 Leo Finkelstein, "Iber un ariber varshever yidishe gasn," in Melekh Ravitch, *Dos amolike yidishe varshe* (Montreal: Farband fun Varshever Yidn in Montreal, 1966), 585.
14 Herman Kruk, *Togbukh fun vilner geto* (New York, 1961), 195.
15 In a March 1936 article in *Haynt*, the biggest Yiddish daily newspaper, the Yiddish poet Yisroel Stern wrote that when he found himself on the poor streets of Jewish Warsaw—Smocza and Miła—he would fall into a profound depression when he heard small Jewish working class children now speaking to each other in Polish. Jews, Stern warned, could no longer comfort themselves that the masses—the Jewish poor, the working class—still remained true to Yiddish. He likened the Polonization of poor Jewish children to an invidious plague or to a slowly gathering flood that posed a real and present danger to Polish Jewry.

still the cultural center of Yiddish literature and theater.[16] Many leading talents had left for other places: the Soviet Union, the United States, and Australia. Some writers vehemently insisted that the future of Yiddish lay in the Soviet Union, where the state supported Yiddish culture and schools. Other voices touted the United States, where Jews had more freedom and greater economic opportunities. What kind of future did Jews have in a Poland that was becoming increasingly nationalistic and anti-Semitic?

Auerbach freely admitted that before the war she herself had felt pessimistic about the future of Warsaw as a Jewish, and more specifically a Yiddish, cultural center. She herself had been far from secure before the war. She was a prolific writer, but had no steady job. She lived from translations, honoraria from articles, and proofreading. Her personal life had become equally unstable. She was married to the brilliant but volatile poet Itzik Manger. It was thanks to that relationship that Auerbach came to know broad circles of the Warsaw Jewish intellectual elite in the 1930s; however, Manger was a Romanian citizen who was forced to leave Poland in 1938. For a time Auerbach, too, weighed the possibility of leaving Poland. But by 1939 she wrote to Melekh Ravitch that, despite everything, she was determined to stay in Poland. If Yiddish had any future at all, it was in Poland and nowhere else, she declared.[17]

In her essays written in 1943 and 1944, as well as in her post-war writings, Auerbach revised her previous skepticism about Jewish Warsaw and about the future of Polish Jewry. It would be easy to dismiss Auerbach's change of heart as a post-Holocaust need to sanctify what had been destroyed. But a careful comparison of her wartime and postwar writings leads to a more nuanced assessment.

In 1943 and 1944, both Emanuel Ringelblum and Rachel Auerbach were living on the Aryan side of Warsaw, Ringelblum in a hideout and Auerbach successfully passing as a Pole. Both decided to memorialize the Warsaw Jewish intelligentsia by writing dozens of essays and sketches of Jewish painters, writers, poets, scholars, and actors who had been murdered. Like Ringelblum, Auerbach believed that she had a personal mission to ensure that these cultural figures would not be entirely forgotten. And like Ringelblum, this need became even more pressing when one remembered just how short-lived

---

16   There are many excellent memoirs of Tłomackie 13, where Auerbach was a frequent visitor. See for example the memoir of Zusman Segalowicz, *Tlomackie 13: fun farbrentn nekhtn* (Buenos Aires, 1946); an excellent scholarly study of literary Warsaw and Tłomackie 13 is Natan Cohen, *Sefer, Sofer v'iton: merkaz ha-tarbut ha-yehudit b'varsha* (Jerusalem, 2003).

17   Ravitch, who had been the secretary of Tłomackie 13, had emigrated to Australia in 1934. On Auerbach's letter to Ravitch see Cohen, *Sefer, Sofer v'iton*, 257.

modern secular Yiddish culture had been. Fewer than sixty years separated Sholom Aleikhem's first literary journal from the destruction of Yiddish-speaking East European Jewry. But as her essays and vignettes accumulated, they turned into an eloquent social history of Warsaw's Jewish cultural milieu, an incisive commentary on an entire Jewish city. Where else but in Warsaw could one see such a concentration of creative energy, such a network of theaters, newspapers, schools, institutions that employed the Jewish creative intelligentsia and such a synergy of talent? The dazzling creative intensity of the Warsaw Ghetto—beautifully described by Auerbach—proved beyond a doubt just how rich Jewish Warsaw really was.

A kaleidoscope of charismatic, talented, and often eccentric personalities emerge from Auerbach's essays. One fascinating figure was Miriam Orleska, the actress who played the role of Lea in the popular play *The Dybbuk*. In the ghetto, Orleska continued to act; and she also worked in the Aleynhilf, the most important social welfare organization in the ghetto. Auerbach described the starving religious poet Yisroel Shtern, the devoted librarian Leib Shur, who hanged himself surrounded by his beloved books. She wrote about Menakhem Kipnis, the singer and collector of Yiddish folk songs, who had the good luck to die a natural death before the beginning of the deportations to Treblinka. A choir of cantors accompanied his body to the cemetery.

Auerbach described the saintly Rosa Simchowicz, a teacher who had been devoted to the Yiddish schools and who before the war had published many works in Yiddish on child psychology and pedagogy. In the ghetto, Simchowicz continued her selfless devotion to her craft. Despite a raging typhus epidemic, Simchowicz refused to sit behind a wooden barrier when she spoke to lice-infested mothers and their children. She soon contracted typhus and died.[18] One of the finest singers in the ghetto was the fabulously gifted 17 year old Marysia Eisenstadt, whose father was the composer and choir director David Eisenstadt. Auerbach described in detail her many visits to their home, where the older Eisenstadt set the poems of many modern Yiddish poets to music. Marysia, his only child, gave recitals of arias and folk songs. When Marysia and her parents boarded the train to Treblinka, the Germans separated the girl from her parents. She fought back and was shot on the spot. Auerbach noted that, as was the case with so many other Jewish artists and writers, Eisenstadt's compositions were lost forever.[19]

Another young genius mentioned by Auerbach was the 17-year-old David Tseitlin (Zeitlin), the youngest of a well known Warsaw family of writers and

---

18 *Varshever tsvoes*, 254–260.
19 Auerbach, *Baym letztn veg*, 192–95.

FIGURE 19.15   *Ruins of the Tłomackie Street Synagogue, Warsaw, 1940s. Archives of the YIVO Institute for Jewish Research, New York.*
COURTESY OF YIVO.

poets. Had David survived, Auerbach believed, he would have become one of the greatest Yiddish poets.[20] He was the son of journalist Elkhanon Tseitlin and the grandson of Hillel Tseitlin, the writer and essayist. Of the entire Tseitlin clan, only the writer Aaron Tseitlin survived.

Auerbach also told the story of the Jewish sculptors and artists who formed a tight circle in the ghetto. Somehow they managed to earn money by painting posters for various Jewish institutions and backdrops for cafes and restaurants. When the liquidation of the ghetto began, one of the painters, Roman Rosenthal, took all of them into a German workshop that seemed to offer protection against deportation to Treblinka. For a few days they lived there with their families, overjoyed that they had some security. Then one day in late August, the SS pounced and took them all to the death trains.

Another essay described Shie Broyde, her boss in the Aleynhilf who had translated Plato's dialogues into Yiddish and who, had he only survived, would have enriched the Yiddish language. This was a basic motif of Auerbach's essay on the intelligentsia: "If only". What she heard and saw in the ghetto represented a flowering of Jewish genius, a bright flame just before the final destruction.

---

20   Ibid., 27.

Another set of Auerbach's essays discussed two leading ghetto intellectuals, Emanuel Ringelblum and Menakhem Linder. In addition to their important work in the Oyneg Shabes archive and in the Aleynhilf, Auerbach stressed their valiant struggle to raise the status of Yiddish in the ghetto.[21] Ringelblum, Linder and others founded the IKOR, a Yiddish Cultural Organization that encouraged the use of Yiddish in house committees and the Aleynhilf. It organized children's plays, memorials for Yiddish writers, and public lectures. Auerbach felt a particular affinity with Menachem Linder because of the many similarities in their biographies. Like Auerbach, Linder came from East Galicia, where the Jewish intelligentsia had shown very little interest in Yiddish culture. And like Auerbach, Linder became a dedicated Yiddishist. He was a gifted economist and statistician and played an important role in the Yiddish Scientific Institute. In the Warsaw Ghetto, Ringelblum entrusted Linder with overseeing the economic research of the Oyneg Shabes archive.

Linder, Auerbach recalled, was an idealist and a dreamer. He was thrilled that in the ghetto the Polish-speaking Jewish intelligentsia was returning— or so he thought—to Yiddish culture. He was happy that the IKOR's events attracted a large audience. Maybe, Linder thought, Yiddish had more staying power than had been widely thought.[22]

The verve and optimism shown by Ringelblum and Linder certainly had an impact on Auerbach as she began to develop a new respect for the vitality of the Jewish masses and their ability to resist the pressures of assimilation.

Even before the war, it should be said, Auerbach was determined to defend the Jewish masses against what she felt to be unfair attacks. An example was her reaction to a series of reportages written by Wanda Melcer that appeared in the mid 1930s in Poland's most prestigious literary journal, the liberal *Wiadomości Literackie*.[23] They were subsequently collected in a book entitled

---

21   *Varshever tsvoes*, 169–208, 241–52.
22   Auerbach wrote that Linder "believed that out of the curse of the ghetto would come a blessing in the form of a general shift of the Jewish intelligentsia to the living language of the masses. that a new energy would invigorate a Jewish creative spirit forged and tempered by the ordeals [of the war], ibid. 248. On the night of April 17, 1942, Gestapo agents knocked on Linder's door, politely asked him to come with them and told him to take a toothbrush and a change of clothing. They shot him in the street. Badly wounded, he lingered for some time before he died. It was after curfew and no one could come to help him.
23   Many intellectuals of Jewish origin worked for *Wiadomości Literackie* and much of its readership was Jewish. On the one hand *Wiadomości Literackie* combatted Polish anti-Semitism, but on the other hand, it often published articles that sneered at Jewish "hypersensitivity", provincialism and backwardness. It also totally ignored Yiddish literature, even as it printed frequent reviews of literature and poetry from Latin America

Czarny Ląd (The Dark Continent). These reportages were not about Africa but about the "Dark Continent" of the thickly populated Jewish streets of North Warsaw. Wanda Melcer, an assimilated Polish-Jewish writer, described the lives of the Yiddish-speaking Jewish masses as an anthropologist might describe exotic tribes in New Guinea. The Jews were portrayed as backward and mired in superstition. Several Jewish writers, including Auerbach hit back at Melcer, accusing her, and by extension the entire *Wiadomości Literackie* milieu, of arrogance, condescension and ignorance.

But it was really through her work in the Aleynhilf and in the soup kitchens that Auerbach developed close contacts with Jews she had seldom had contact with before—ordinary Warsaw Jews and religious Jews, whom she never would have met under normal circumstances and who left a deep impression on her.[24] An example was a Gerer Hasid, Leib Kozlowski, who had edited a religious youth journal before the war and who was the subject of one of her essays.[25] His religious devotion did not keep him from taking a deep interest in modern secular culture and in Yiddish literature.

It was then that she understood that Jewish life was so deeply rooted, and Jews were so numerous, that the Jewish people could have counted on the cultural capital of Polish Jewry for generations to come.

> ... despite everything we were surrounded by enormously powerful and dynamic Jewish folk masses.... the Jewish masses were face to face with the spontaneous processes of emancipation and assimilation. But despite everything the masses were too numerous and too rooted in their culture for these processes to threaten the basic character of the nation. The religious strata ... constituted an enormous reservoir of human resources and spiritual energy, and they were able to make up any losses we suffered [due to acculturation]—and then some.

---

or Asia. The relationship between this liberal and urbane tribune of high culture and the Jewish intelligentsia was very complex. See Magdalena Opalska, "*Wiadomości Literackie*: Polemics on the Jewish Question, 1924–1939," in Yisrael Gutman et al. (eds.), *The Jews of Poland Between the Two World Wars* (Hanover, NH, 1989), 434–53. For more specifically on the Melcer controversy see the excellent study by Katrin Steffen, *Jüdische Polonität* (Göttingen, 2004), 160–61. On Auerbach's rejection of Melcer, see *Baym letstn veg*, 48.

24 Auerbach noted that the Aleynhilf was one institution where religious and secular Jews worked side by side and many unlikely friendships developed here. Opposites, she noted, attracted. Ibid. 43.

25 Ibid., 42–48.

> We thought that we had arrived (in Jewish Warsaw) too late, after the best was already over. In fact the blooms faded only to prepare for the next harvest of fruit, had it not been for the terrible catastrophe that befell us.[26]

Before the war, she admitted, she concentrated on the fading blossoms and the falling leaves. She had failed to see that this was a necessary prelude to a new second growth. No, she had been wrong about Warsaw and, having survived, at the very least she could make others see what might have been. She would fight to preserve their memory.

To that end, as soon as the war ended, Auerbach took on the mission to carry on Ringelblum's legacy and to find the archive buried under the trackless rubble of what had been the Warsaw ghetto. The Yiddish writer Mendel Mann recalled Auerbach's talk at the third anniversary commemoration of the ghetto uprising. After many tiresome speeches full of political posturing, Auerbach, the only woman on the podium got up to speak:

> She did not make any speeches, she did not "explain the meaning" of the uprising. She implored! With a stubbornness that deeply affected me, she demanded, she called: Remember, she cried out, there is a national treasure under the ruins.... Even if there are five stories of ruins, we have to find the archive. I'm not making this up. I know what I'm talking about! This isn't just talk! This is coming from my heart. I will not rest and I will not let you rest. We must rescue the Ringelblum archive![27]

Mann remembered that Auerbach met with a cool reception. People had their own troubles, they didn't need an archive to tell them what they had gone through.

But Auerbach disagreed. The archive was more important than ever. Some postwar memoirs were appearing that were presenting a distorted picture of the ghetto. Some were written by converts like Ludwik Herszfeld, who disdained the Jewish masses. Others seemed driven mainly by a desire to settle narrow political scores. Auerbach held up the model of the Oyneg Shabes, where she felt that a shared sense of national mission had trumped such narrow agendas. In the aftermath of the catastrophe, a wounded nation had to look to its record, the good as well as the bad. To tell the whole truth, to add and subtract nothing, was a debt owed not just to the victims who had died but

---

26   *Varshever tsvoes*, 22.
27   Mendel Mann, "Rokhl Auerbach tsu ir bazukh in pariz," *Unzer vort*, August 6, 1966.

to the nation that had to recover and rebuild. Auerbach hallowed the exploits of the ghetto fighters and the partisans, but she could not allow their story to overshadow and diminish the memory of the 99 percent who had no weapons.

Like much of the Oyneg Shabes staff, Auerbach was close to the circles of the pre-war YIVO, with its traditions of *zamling* (ethnographic collecting) and of bringing together scholars and the masses.[28] Auerbach's work followed in the footsteps not only of Emanuel Ringelblum but also of YIVO director Max Weinreich, who had made special efforts to incorporate the insights of Sigmund Freud and social psychology into the study of Polish Jewry. In a world hitherto dominated by traditions and ideologies that stressed the primacy of the collective over the individual, Max Weinreich—in his youth studies (*yungforshung*) project, for instance—argued that one could not understand *klal yisroel* (the collective) without grasping the needs of *reb yisroel* (the individual): the aspirations, drives, obsessions and hopes of the many individuals who made up the Jewish mass in Poland.[29] Auerbach, who had received her degree in psychology and who had written extensively on the field in the pre-war Jewish press, needed little convincing. In her masterly 1935 review of Shie Perle's wonderful novel of adolescent awakening *Yidn fun a gants yor*, she lambasted a prudish Bundist critic who criticized the book because it raised the theme of adolescent sexuality.[30]

And so, too, in her Holocaust writings she highlighted the complex interplay of psychological factors in individuals, families, and entire social groups. She told a complicated story: resilience, vitality and self-sacrifice on the one hand, corruption and moral collapse on the other.

Auerbach stressed the Germans' brilliant use of psychological factors to effect the destruction of Warsaw Jewry and to use the Jews' strengths against them. The Germans played with the Jews and with their natural human instincts for self-preservation and hope. In her brilliant observations of the mass hysteria that gripped the Warsaw ghetto in the summer of 1942, Auerbach described how the very qualities that had served Jews so well in the past—practicality, pragmatism, hard-headedness, *seykhel* and natural optimism—now accelerated their journey into the abyss.

---

28 Indeed the very structure of Auerbach's wartime writings emphasized the close links of the Jewish intelligentsia and the masses. The first title of her essays on the murdered writers, musicians and artists was "Tsuzamen mitn folk" (Together with the People), Yad Vashem Archive, P/48.
29 See for example Max Weinreich, *Der veg tsu unzer yugnt* (Vilna, 1935).
30 See Rachel Auerbach, "Shie Perles yidn fun a gants yor," *Literarishe Bleter* 49 (December 6, 1935).

And still other Jews. Broad-shouldered, deep-voiced, with powerful hands and hearts. Artisans, workers. Wagon drivers, porters, Jews who, with a blow of their fists, could floor any hooligan who dared enter their neighborhoods.

Where were you when your wives and children, when your old fathers and mothers were taken away? What happened to make you run off like cattle stampeded by fire? Was there no one to give you some purpose in the confusion? You were swept away by the flood, together with those who were weak.

And you sly cunning merchants, philanthropists in your short fur coats and caps. How was it that you didn't catch on to the murderous swindle?[31]

Would other peoples, confronted with a similar massive assault have acted better? She did not think so. Did Warsaw Jewry eventually recover from the shock and fight back? Yes. Should one blame the Jewish masses for not having fought back earlier? Only those who had not been there, Auerbach implied, would do so. Was armed resistance the only way the Jews stood up to the Germans? Absolutely not.

2

Auerbach, like her fellow Oyneg Shabes collaborator Peretz Opoczynski, was a superb observer of the Jewish everyday. She had a fine sense of the nuances of the behavior and speech of different classes of Polish Jews, whether they lived in small towns or in urban centers like Warsaw. Like Ringelblum, she was a native of southeast Galicia. Before moving with her family to Lwów, she had spent her childhood in a remote village—not a shtetl—in Lanowitz (Łanowce), Podolia, where she acquired a love of Jewish folklore and the Yiddish language. The great Jewish folklorist and ethnographer, Shmuel Lehman, had interviewed her many times about the folksongs and customs of the rural Jews of Podolia.[32]

Like many other Galician Jews, Auerbach combined this deep Jewish identity with a first-class Polish education and cultural sensibility. At Lwów University in the early 1920s, Auerbach befriended the young poetess Dvora Fogel and the budding writer and painter Bruno Schulz, and then joined the editorial board of *Tsushtayer*, a literary journal that tried to bring the

---

[31] From "Yizkor" as translated by Leonard Wolf in David Roskies (ed.), *The Literature of Destruction* (Philadelphia and New York, 1988), 461.

[32] See her essay about Lehman in *Varshever tsvoes*, 133–61.

Polish-speaking Galician Jewish intelligentsia closer to Yiddish.[33] In the mid 1930s she moved to Warsaw from Lwów and became the companion of the brilliant and tempestuous Yiddish poet Itzik Manger.

Thus, much of the power of Auerbach's reportage stemmed from her ability to navigate cultural boundaries, which derived from a life that straddled different worlds: village, shtetl and city; Yiddish and Polish; Poles and Jews; Galicia and Warsaw; the milieu of the Jewish literary elite and the world of the Jewish masses; religious and secular; Diaspora nationalists and Zionists. This negotiation and mediation would continue after the war as Auerbach saw herself speaking up for the murdered victims in her controversies and arguments with Ben Zion Dinur about the agendas of Yad Vashem and Jacques Steiner over his book *Treblinka*.[34]

At the end of September 1939, after Poland's capitulation, Auerbach was about to flee to Lwów when she received an unexpected summons from Emanuel Ringelblum to stay in Warsaw and run a soup kitchen. Most of the Jewish elite had run away, but Ringelblum reminded Auerbach that not everyone had the right to flee.

Ringelblum thus brought Auerbach into the far flung network of the Aleynhilf, the "Self Help" of the Warsaw ghetto, with its hundreds of house committees, dozens of soup kitchens, and day care centers for children. The leaders of the Aleynhilf saw the organization as the conscience of Warsaw Jewry; as its legitimate tribune; as a rival to the Judenrat and as a revival of the traditions of World War One. Then, the Jewish intelligentsia in occupied Warsaw had used soup kitchens to begin new schools and libraries, to organize political parties, and to convince the masses to *zaml*, to collect historical sources. Yitzhak Leybush Peretz, whose soup kitchen occupied the same building where Auerbach would work in the Warsaw Ghetto, had stressed the interdependence of relief and *zamling*. In the Second World War, by the same token, the Aleynhilf made the functioning of the Oyneg Shabes archive possible. Ringelblum used the soup kitchens and refugee centers to gather information and find writers—as well as to save the cadres of the Jewish intelligentsia by giving them jobs. In 1941 he recruited Auerbach to the Oyneg Shabes by asking her to write an essay and reports about her soup kitchen. As Auerbach

---

33   Rachel Auerbach, "Nisht oysgeshpunene fedem," *Di goldene keyt* 50 (1964): 131–43.
34   On the controversy with Dinur see Boaz Cohen "Rachel Auerbach: Yad Vashem and Israeli Holocaust Memory," *Polin* 20 (2007): 197–222. On the Steiner controversy see Samuel Moyn, *A Holocaust Controversy: the Treblinka Affair in Postwar France* (Hanover, NH, 2005).

would stress after the war, had it not been for Ringelblum she would not have written anything.[35]

Auerbach's soup kitchen on Leszno 40, which fed 2000 Jews a day, offered her a unique vantage point to observe and get to know a large number of "customers." The story that Auerbach told provided a gripping, behind-the-scenes look at the desperate battle that the ghetto was fighting against hunger. Auerbach investigated the "social history" of hunger by telling a story of a soup kitchen as a microcosm of human relationships and human choices. The dead who ended up in the pits of the Gęsia cemetery were not an undifferentiated mass but individuals whose idiosyncrasies Auerbach recorded. She deftly caught the phrases or the habits that made them memorable: the young mother, expelled from her shtetl, who arrived at the soup kitchen with four children in tow, and a tot who was suckling at her breast; a family of solid, rugged Jewish boys from a country farm, who had also been expelled into the ghetto. Each day they would take a bowl of soup for their aged father. When they mentioned him, they never failed to add: *im tsu hundred un tsvantsig*; solid, members of the Jewish middle class, now reduced to desperate poverty.[36]

Auerbach, as the director of the soup kitchen, confronted serious psychological pressures and moral challenges. Like other figures in the Aleynhilf, she had seen herself as an honest public servant imbued with the moral code of the progressive Jewish intelligentsia. Very quickly, however, she discovered that for the masses of starving desperate people who came to the kitchen each day, she represented authority and power. In their eyes she had become an arbiter of life and death. Like Ringelblum, she had come from a milieu that was imbued with love for the "Jewish masses." Now these masses, these ordinary Jews, stormed her office, blocked her in the corridors, and begged for extra soup tickets. They looked at Auerbach as someone who could save them. Some confronted her in silent supplication, others yelled and loudly reminded Auerbach of their former status. Then there were the children, who would come in packs and cajole her in Yiddish-accented Polish (*plosze pani* [sic]—please ma'am) for some extra food.

And it seemed to her then that the kitchen only prolonged the agony but actually saved no one.[37] Should she favor a chosen few or dole out equal rations

---

35   For more on the Aleynhilf see Samuel Kassow, *Who will write our History?* (Bloomington, 2007), 90–145.

36   *Varshever tsvoes*, 63–133.

37   In a diary entry of February 2 1942, Auerbach wrote that "I have been slowly coming to the conclusion that the whole balance of this self-help activity is simply that people die more slowly. We must finally admit to ourselves that we can save nobody from death, we

and save no one? Ringelblum asked the same question. Increasingly frustrated, Auerbach singled out a chosen few for special care: the poet Israel Stern for instance; or a German-speaking refugee from the Sudetenland, Brocksmeier, who had survived Dachau and whom Ringelblum wanted to keep alive as a witness. This former athlete, the "Datch" as he was called in Warsaw Yiddish, won Auerbach over with his impeccable manners, good nature and spry sense of humor. For Auerbach he became a litmus test and a challenge. She bent her rules and gave him extra food. When he began to become apathetic, a common sign of starvation, she would yell at him that she could feed him but that he had to summon up the will to live. It was important, Auerbach felt, to win at least one victory. But here too she failed. In her diary entry of August 4, 1941 she noted, "What is the use of all of our work if we can't save even one person from death by hunger?" Ringelblum liked her reportages of the soup kitchen and gave her other assignments for the archive, such as a request to document the cultural and literary life of the ghetto. In September 1942, Ringelblum and Shmuel Winter asked Auerbach to interview Abraham Krzepicki, who had escaped from Treblinka.

In February 1943, Auerbach escaped to the Aryan side. Helped by Polish friends, she procured Aryan documents and became a courier for the Jewish underground.

On the Aryan side, after the ghetto uprising, Auerbach wrote a constant stream of essays for "Arkhiv Hemshekh", the underground Jewish archive on the Aryan side.[38] With the help of Polish friends, Auerbach buried her writings in two different locations in Warsaw, on the grounds of the Zoo and in a field in the southern district of Mokotów. Both caches survived the war. As Auerbach wrote, "I had better luck in saving paper than in saving people."[39]

One of the more striking features of Auerbach's writings from this period is her portrayal of Poland and the Poles. As a courier who distributed money and aid to hidden Jews, Auerbach was in constant contact with a category of Poles whom most Jews in the war never had a chance to meet: the liberal, intellectual elite. Her descriptions of such individuals as Jan Żabiński and his wife are particularly instructive and insightful. Żabiński had been the Director of the

---

don't have the means to. We can only put it off, regulate it, but we can't prevent it. In all my experience in the soup kitchen I have not been able to rescue anybody! And nobody could accuse me of caring less than the directors of other soup kitchens." See Ringelblum Archive, Part One, No. 654.

38 See Rachel Auerbach, "Arkhiv hemshekh oyf der arisher zayt," Yad Vashem Archive, Rachel Auerbach Collection, P-16-32.

39 *Baym letstn veg*, 301.

Warsaw Zoo as well as an officer in the Polish Underground. During the war he and his wife helped many Jews, including Auerbach herself.[40]

Her intense devotion to the memory of Jewish Warsaw in no way diminished her deep empathy for Polish Warsaw and for its sufferings. In *Varshever tsvoes*, she penned a sympathetic portrayal of Warsaw's mayor, Stefan Starzyński, who called on his fellow citizens to resist the Germans and who led the city during the days of the terrible siege in September 1939. Right after a terrible bombardment of Jewish neighborhoods, Starzyński paid a visit and stroked the heads of Jewish children. Perhaps, Auerbach speculated, as he walked through those Jewish streets, Starzyński was thinking about how before the war Poland had treated its Jews as second-class citizens. Perhaps the terror of the siege had one silver lining. For a brief moment, the fight against a common enemy brought Poles and Jews together and offered another glimpse into the heart of "what might have been." Before the war, Starzyński had not been known as a philosemite. But like so many others, Auerbach speculated, perhaps the war caused him to "grow beyond himself."

Many people would naturally wonder, Auerbach noted, why Starzyński and his fellow Poles defended Warsaw in September 1939. It was such a hopeless fight that led to so many needless civilian casualties. But Auerbach, steeped in admiration for Polish Romanticism and the pathos of carrying on a hopeless fight for the sake of honor, emphasized Starzyński's heroism.

> Romanticism? Idealism? May those who scoff at that get the contempt they deserve. Other European peoples [did not fight]. But we Polish Jews understood (what the Poles did), we were at their side and we understand today.[41]

But however much the Poles suffered, the stark difference between their fate and that of the Jews under German occupation could never be far from Auerbach's mind. This can be seen in one of her greatest wartime essays, "Yizkor," which was written in November 1943. This was a time of growing German terror against the Polish population, when the Nazis engaged in public shootings of hostages to retaliate for attacks by the Polish Underground. One day Auerbach was in a Warsaw trolley car and saw a Polish woman weeping over her son, whom the Germans had just shot. At least this woman, whose lips moved like Hannah's in the Bible, could mourn in public. Auerbach could not.

---

40   Ibid., 233–49. Żabiński and his wife's acts form the plot of the recent bestseller by Diane Ackerman, *The Zookeeper's Wife* (Norton, 2007).

41   *Varshever tsvoes*, 43.

That night she went to her room and began to write her great elegy for Warsaw Jewry, "Yizkor." Usually she wrote in Polish; this time she wrote in Yiddish.

> I may neither groan nor weep. I may not draw attention to myself in the street. And I need to groan; I need to weep. Not four times a year. I feel the need to say *Yizkor* four times a day.[42]

She poured out her soul as she tried to describe the murder of Warsaw Jewry: the toddlers, the children whom she remembered from the ghetto schools, the tough Jewish workers, the hardened women shopkeepers, young scouts, courting couples, intellectuals, all gone, gone. Even if a few individuals survived, the vibrant, raucous and diverse mosaic of Warsaw Jewry had been pulverized. "Yizkor" humanized the victims by recalling not only their individuality but also their city, the specific urban milieu that had shaped them and that had made them "Varshever".

In other essays she wrote in 1943–44, Auerbach indeed regretted the lack of armed resistance until January 1943. But "Yizkor" was different. Unlike the works of some other Oyneg Shabes writers who observed the Deportation (Shie Perle, Israel Lichtenstein, or Peretz Opoczynski), Auerbach's "Yizkor" was suffused with empathy rather than anger. By using the imagery of a flood, a natural disaster, she anticipated future questions that those who were not there would pose. What had happened to those millions of Polish Jews? Why had they let themselves be fooled? Those tough, bright resourceful Jews—why didn't they resist?

No, the mass murder was not a metahistorical event. But its enormity was too horrible and too unprecedented to allow for glib theories and facile questions that might compromise the memory of the Jewish masses that she cherished so deeply. How does one resist a flood or an earthquake? What befell the Jewish masses was so unthinkable and so calamitous that they were psychologically unprepared. Implicitly, Auerbach was anticipating the invidious distinctions that many would make after the war between the few who fought back with weapons and the masses who had allegedly died without a fight. It was the people she wrote about in "Yizkor," not the fighters who had risen up just months before.

And in the end this secular writer could only repeat the words of the traditional Yizkor prayer. For Auerbach, Yizkor was a return, not to religion but to the murdered world of her birth, to a folk community that did not have to

---

42   "Yizkor," *Against the Apocalypse*, 459–60.

invent new words to describe pain and loss. They were already there, in the prayers. Like her murdered friends, Auerbach was *tzuzamen mitn folk*.

•••

In the tension between Auerbach's wartime writings and postwar emendations, one can discern a marked shift not in subject matter but in emphasis and attitude. In her wartime writings and reportages for the archive, Auerbach judged herself harshly. The soup kitchen had been a failure, the Aleynhilf largely an exercise in futility.

After the war, when she retrieved these wartime writings, she took a more positive view of what she had done. She admitted that no one who depended *only* on the soup kitchen could have survived. But the kitchens had provided a critical margin for those who had some other source of food and had helped many people to survive. The Aleynhilf had done yeoman work in keeping up the struggle for human dignity.

By the same token, she changed her views on the state of Polish Jewry and its cultural future. In the 1930s, she shared the doubts of many of her friends about the future of Yiddish culture in Poland. But as she redacted her wartime writings, she realized that here too she had been too pessimistic. After the war, as she reread her essays on the Warsaw Jewish cultural elite, she asserted that this new generation of writers, poets, artists and singers would have taken the place of those who had gone before—if only the Germans had not killed them all. Furthermore, she wrote, her work in the Aleynhilf was an epiphany. The Jewish masses had more strength than she had ever believed, and they would have provided a deep reserve of people and spirit to counteract assimilation and cultural decay.

In post-war Poland and especially in Israel, she discovered a new sense of purpose: to ensure that the study of the Holocaust and the memorialization of the victims would not only render them their due but also strengthen Jewish unity and national cohesion. To that end, after her immigration to Israel in 1950, she helped organize the collection of survivor testimony and support for Yad Vashem, the Israeli Holocaust Archive and Museum.

To the very last, Auerbach tried to protect Ringelblum's legacy. And just as the bulk of the Oyneg Shabes archive remains untranslated and inaccessible to English language readers, so are the writings of this remarkable writer.

CHAPTER 20

Stories of Rescue Activities in the Letters of Jewish Survivors about Christian Polish Rescuers, 1944–1949

Joanna B. Michlic

Introduction

This chapter considers the early postwar memories of Jewish survivors and their rescuers in Warsaw and Warsaw province, and the relationships between rescuers and their Jewish charges in the immediate postwar period. With the exception of studies of anti-Jewish violence, an early postwar social history of Polish Jewry has largely eluded close treatment by historians, as has a similar treatment of early postwar Polish society.[1] In general, the period 1945–1949 is under-researched in comparison with the post-1950 and post-1956 periods. While the history of Polish rescuers has been raised in several publications in Poland in the past, they have mostly been of a popular nature, and with the subject heavily politicized and emotionally charged. In his essay *Polish-Jewish Relations since 1984: Reflections of a Participant*, Antony Polonsky predicts a bright future for the study of Polish-Jewish relations.[2] One can only hope, given the recent more sophisticated and analytical research on rescue activities and the concerted efforts of scholars in Israel, Poland and the West, that a nuanced, comprehensive and synthetic portrait of this important aspect of wartime and postwar Polish-Jewish relations will emerge, for the subject at this stage is in its infancy.

---

1 There is a vast literature in Polish, English and Hebrew on the Kielce pogrom and the historiography of this best-known single act of anti-Semitic violence of that period. For the most recent, albeit problematic, work in Polish pertaining to the subject, see Łukasz Kamiński and Jan Żaryn (eds.), *Wokół pogromu kieleckiego* (Warszawa: Instytut Pamięci Narodowej, 2006). On anti-Jewish pogroms in the early post-war period and the prevailing atmosphere, see Jan T. Gross, *Fear: Anti-Semitism in Poland after Auschwitz. An Essay in Historical Interpretation* (New York: Random House, 2006).

2 Antony Polonsky, *Polish-Jewish Relations since 1984: Reflections of a Participant* (Cracow, Budapest: Wydawnictwo Austeria, 2009), see especially the conclusions, 41–52.

In this chapter, I analyze the early postwar correspondence addressed to the Central Committee of Polish Jews (CKŻP)[3] located at Sienna St. no. 60 in Warsaw, to the American JOINT Distribution Committee (AJDC, the JOINT)[4] with its headquarters at Chocimska 18 in Warsaw, and to the little known Warsaw based *Komitet Pomocy Polakom* (*Committee to Aid the Poles*), also referred to as *Komisja Pomocy Polakom* or *Komisja Pomocy Aryjczykom*. This Committee was established on the initiative of William Bein, second Director of the Warsaw branch of the JOINT, with the assistance of CKŻP.[5] It began its work on November 15, 1946, and ended its activities, like the JOINT, in late 1949. The *Komitet Pomocy Polakom* had four main goals: to distribute financial aid, food and clothing among rescuers, to provide Christian holiday greetings and gifts to those rescuers who were known to have provided great service to the Jewish cause, to bring rescuers to the public eye, and to draw up a comprehensive chart of rescue activities by Poles. The latter two aims never came to fruition.

The large and unique collection of letters, petitions and accompanying notes, written between late 1944 and 1949, is scattered among different sections of the archives of the CKŻP, at the Jewish Historical Institute in Warsaw. Its authors were Christian Polish rescuers, rescued Jewish survivors, both adults and older children, and relatives of Jewish survivors living in and outside of Poland. A large number of the rescuers, both the authors of their own letters and those individuals referred to in the letters of Jewish survivors, constitute a group of "dedicated" individuals, committed to saving Jewish fugitives

---

3   On the activities of the Central Committee of Polish Jews in Poland (CKŻP), see Lucjan Dobroszycki, *Survivors of the Holocaust in Poland: A Portrait Based on Jewish Community Records 1944–1947* (Armonk, NY, and London: M.E. Sharpe, 1994); Natalia Aleksiun, *Dokąd dalej? Ruch syjonistyczny w Polsce (1944–1950)* (Warszawa: Wydawnictwo Trio, 2002); and August Grabski, *Działalność komunistów wśród Żydów w Polsce (1944–1949)* (Warszawa: Wydawnictwo Trio, 2004). This chapter draws upon CKŻP 301: Collection of Personal Testimonies of Jewish Survivors of the Holocaust; and 303/VIII/—Department of Social Welfare.

4   On the history of the JOINT in the postwar period, see Yehuda Bauer, *Out of the Ashes. The Impact of American Jews on Post-Holocaust European Jewry* (Oxford and Toronto: Pergamon Press, 1989); and on the JOINT in pre-1945 Poland, idem, *American Jewry and the Holocaust: The American Jewish JOINT Distribution Committee 1939–1945* (Jerusalem: The Institute of Contemporary Jewry, Hebrew University; Detroit: Wayne State University Press, 1981), 67–106.

5   On the subject of *Komitet Pomocy Polakom* see Joanna B. Michlic, "'I will never forget what you did for me during the war': Representations of Rescuers and Relationships Between Rescuers and Jewish Survivors in the Light of Correspondence to the Central Committee of Polish Jews and the JOINT, 1945–1949," *Yad Vashem Studies* 39.2 (Fall 2011): 169–208.

regardless of the dangers and without any prior assurance of reward, or any intention to profit from human misfortune. This group stands out in sharp contrast to the group of so-called "rescuers for profit,"[6] and those other individuals who ruthlessly took advantage of Jewish fugitives by abandoning, denouncing and even murdering their former charges.[7] Some rescuers' letters present a bill of wartime expenditures to the Jewish organizations, emphasizing their own impoverishment as a result of the war and their rescue activities. In some cases, it is difficult to establish the veracity of the rescuers' accounts, or possible levels of exaggeration, because there is no supportive letter from a former Jewish charge to confirm their assertions. Some letters of former rescuers are characterized by an embittered, angry and ironic tone directed at their former charges or at the Jewish committees, revealing disappointment, confusion, and discrepancies in their evaluations of expectations. Another, smaller category of letters reveals opportunistic attempts at gaining undeserved assistance and attitudes of greed tinted by anti-Jewish prejudice.

Historical Background: The Secret Cities of Warsaw

By the end of 1940, Poland's capital, Warsaw, underwent a major transformation and became a divided city of three quarters, Polish, German and Jewish. The establishment of the Warsaw ghetto was the chief marker of this transformation.[8] The Germans sealed the ghetto on November 15, 1940, closing all

---

6   For the first discussion of providing shelter for payment, see Nechama Tec, *When Light Pierced the Darkness* (New York and Oxford: Oxford University Press, 1986), 87–98. See also *Zagłada Żydów: Studia i materiały* 4 (2008); Jan Grabowski, "Rescue for Money: Paid Helpers in Poland, 1939–1945," *Search and Research. Lectures and Papers* 13 (Jerusalem: Yad Vashem, 2008).

7   For the discussion of such cases based on written testimonies and oral histories, see Joanna Tokarska-Bakir, "The Unrighteous Righteous and the Righteous Unrighteous," *Dapim: Studies on the Shoah*, 24 (2010): 11–63. The article appeared first in Polish as "Sprawiedliwi niesprawiedliwi, niesprawiedliwi sprawiedliwi," *Zagłada Żydów: Studia i materiały* 4 (2008): 170–217. On the problem of the murdering of Jewish fugitives in the countryside, see Jan Grabowski, *Judenjagd. Polowanie na Żydów 1942–1945: Studium dziejów pewnego powiatu* (Warszawa: Stowarzyszenie Centrum Badań nad Zagładą Żydów, 2011); and Barbara Engelking, *Jest Taki Piękny Słoneczny Dzień ... Losy Żydów szukających ratunku na wsi polskiej 1942–1945* (Warszawa: Stowarzyszenie Centrum Badań nad Zagładą Żydów, 2011).

8   On the history of the Warsaw Ghetto, see, for example, Barbara Engelking and Jacek Leociak, *Getto warszawskie: Przewodnik po nieistniejącym mieście* (Warszawa: Wydawnictwo Instytut Filozofii i Socjologii [IFiS] PAN, 2001); Israel Gutman, *The Jews of Warsaw, 1939–1943: Ghetto,*

twenty-two gates that evening. Thus 400,000 Jews, who constituted one-third of Warsaw's prewar population, were confined to a small area surrounded by an 18-kilometer long wall. The ghetto covered 307 hectares of built-up land on which 1,483 houses were located. Slave labor, hunger, and recurring epidemics of typhus were the main features of daily life behind the ghetto walls during its first two years of existence. Death by starvation and disease also plagued the imprisoned Jewish community, and the poor and those prone to sickness deteriorated fast, as did those forced Jewish refugees from smaller towns and villages in Warsaw province who, as newcomers to the capital, lacked life-saving social ties and connections. During 1941 alone, one hundred thousand ghetto inhabitants perished from infectious diseases and starvation. But the watershed occurred during the summer of 1942, when the Nazis launched Operation *Reinhard*, designed to exterminate the entire Jewish population.[9] On July 22, 1942 the Warsaw ghetto fell victim to "the Great Deportation" plan. In less than three months, the Germans shipped two hundred and fifty thousand Warsaw Jews from the infamous *Umschlagplatz* embarkation point to the death camp in Treblinka. On January 18, 1943, the Germans launched a short Second Deportation (January Action) during which another five thousand Warsaw Jews were sent to Treblinka, while on that same day the underground Zionist Jewish youth organization, *Hashomer-Hatzair*, staged the first short-lived armed resistance action against the Germans. The spring of 1943 witnessed the final end of the Warsaw ghetto. On April 19, the Warsaw Ghetto Uprising, headed by Mordecai Anielewicz (1919–1943), Commander of the Jewish Fighting Organization (*Żydowska Organizacja Bojowa, ŻOB*), broke out. The Uprising, which historians recognize as the first uprising against the Germans in Nazi-occupied Europe, lasted almost a month but was inevitably crushed by the German military might under the command of General Stroop. The Uprising ended on May 16, 1943, when the Nazis blew up the Great Synagogue

---

Underground, Revolt (Bloomington: Indiana University Press, 1989); and Samuel Kassow, *Who will write our History? Emanuel Ringelblum, the Warsaw Ghetto, and the Oyneg Shabes Archive* (Bloomington: Indiana University Press, 2007). On the history of Jews in Warsaw province, see Barbara Engelking, Jacek Leociak, and Dariusz Libionka (eds.), *Prowincja noc: Życie i zagłada w dystrykcie warszawskim* (Warszawa: Wydawnictwo IFiS PAN, 2007). Hereafter Engelking et al., *Prowincja noc*.

9 On the history of Operation Reinhard, see Yitzhak Arad, *Belzec, Sobibor, Treblinka: The Operation Reinhard Death Camps* (Bloomington: Indiana University Press, 1999); Dieter Pohl, *Von der "Judenpolitik" zum Judenmord: Der Distrikt Lublin des Generalgouvernements, 1934–1944* (Frankfurt am Main and New York: Peter Lang Verlag, 1993); and Dariusz Libionka (ed.), *Akcja Reinhardt: Zagłada Żydów w Generalnym Gubernatorstwie* (Warszawa: Instytut Pamięci Narodowej, 2004).

on Tłomackie Street and burnt the ghetto into rubble and cinders. But in its ruins, between ten and twenty thousand Jews were still hidden. These fugitives referred to themselves, and later became known, as the "Robinson Crusoes" of the ghetto. But most of Jewish fugitives who had managed to escape the ghetto before the outbreak of the Uprising lived on the Aryan side.

Prior to the "Great Deportation" and in its aftermath, many Warsaw Jews intensified their search for a safe shelter on the forbidden Aryan side of the capital and outside of it. The last fugitives escaped the ghetto on the eve of, and even during, the Warsaw Ghetto Uprising.[10] The next watershed in the history of the remaining Jewish fugitives, both those in hiding and those passing off as Christian Poles on the Aryan side, as well as of the non-Jewish Warsaw civilian population, began on August 1, 1944 with the outbreak of the 63-day Warsaw Uprising.[11] Like the Warsaw Ghetto Uprising of April 1943, the Germans ruthlessly crushed it. As a punitive measure, the Germans also turned 25 percent of the remaining capital into rubble. Among the massive military and civilian casualties, estimated at 200,000, were many Jewish fugitives. After the capitulation act of October 2, the Germans expelled the remaining 550,000 Varsovians from the capital. They were first sent to the transit camp *Durchgangslager 121* in Pruszków, and then were divided into three groups awaiting different fates. Among the expellees were Jewish survivors. Some of the latter who were fortunate enough to pass themselves off as Christian Poles with the help of Christian Polish rescuers or on their own initiatives were sent to forced labor in Germany with other Warsaw expellees. Others who successfully passed as Christian Poles and were not betrayed by their fellow Christian Polish expellees were dispersed and released into the Generalgouvernement with the rest of the civilian refugees. The Germans shipped the third group of Varsovian expellees to concentration camps. On January 17, 1945, the day that Warsaw was liberated from the German yoke, those Jews who had managed to survive in the rubble of the Warsaw ghetto and those who had remained in hiding on the Aryan side with or without the help of Christian rescuers began to emerge.

---

10   For a general discussion of survival strategies amongst Jewish adults and children in Warsaw, and the Warsaw district, see Małgorzata Melchior, "Uciekinierzy z gett po 'stronie aryjskiej' na prowincji dystryktu warszawskiego—sposoby przetrwania," in Engelking et al., *Prowincja noc*, 321–72; and Joanna Nalewajko-Kulikov, *Strategie przetrwania: Żydzi po aryjskiej stronie Warszawy* (Warszawa: Wydawnictwo IFiS PAN, 2004).

11   On the Warsaw Uprising, see, in English, the classic historical study by Jan M. Ciechanowski, *The Warsaw Rising of 1944*, new ed. (London and New York: Cambridge University Press, 2009; 1st ed. 1974) and Norman Davis, *Rising '44: The Battle for Warsaw* (New York: Viking, 2004).

In the course of the first four years of the war, Warsaw transformed itself into "a secret city,"[12] or more precisely into four "secret cities," each with its own particular set of aims and needs. Warsaw was first and foremost the heart of the Polish military, political and cultural underground, but, at the same time, it was a vibrant center of illegal black marketeering, offering major profit-making within the city limits and beyond the city. Warsaw was a major dynamic center of Jewish rescue activities because, as any other metropolis, it guaranteed relative anonymity for Jews to hide and pass themselves off as Aryans. Not only did Jewish fugitives from the capital seek refuge in their hometown, but also Jewish fugitives from other cities and towns like Częstochowa, Cracow and Lublin and from as far away as the *Kresy* (Eastern Polish Territories) viewed the capital as potentially the safest shelter. Simultaneously, Warsaw grew into a major center of highly developed networks of blackmailers and denunciators of Jewish fugitives.[13] This large world of professional and amateur blackmailers and denunciators represented a life-threatening danger for the "secret city" of Jewish fugitives and their "dedicated rescuers." Keeping constant vigilance and living in a state of isolation from one's neighbors and even relatives was the core strategy to neutralize the blackmailers, denunciators and dangerous neighborhood gossip that could lead to betrayal. Unfortunately, this strategy did not always prove effective. The "secret city" of blackmailers, denunciators, hostile former neighbors, employees and acquaintances forced the "secret city" of rescuees and rescuers to be ever prepared to flee, both within and out of Warsaw, to the countryside in Warsaw province and beyond. Blackmail and the threat of denunciation heavily depleted the financial and material resources of Jewish fugitives and their "dedicated rescuers," often leading to their deaths. Even among those Jewish fugitives and their rescuers who successfully defended themselves, the actions of blackmailers caused a great deal of moral, physical and mental suffering.

The 1948 testimony of Helena Kaletska, a 38 year-old educated Jewish woman who lived on the Aryan side in Warsaw after escaping her hometown ghetto in Opatów, near Kielce, poignantly captures the atmosphere surrounding the "secret city" of Jewish fugitives and their rescuers. Kaletska, familiar

---

12   Gunnar S. Paulsson, *Secret City: The Hidden Jews of Warsaw 1940–1945* (New Haven and London: Yale University Press 2002), uses the term "secret city" to describe the survival of Jewish fugitives on the Aryan side.

13   On the problem of denunciation and blackmail, see Barbara Engelking-Boni, *Szanowny panie Gistapo: Donosy do władz niemieckich w Warszawie i okolicach w latach 1940–1941* (Warszawa: Wydawnictwo IFiS PAN, 2003); and Jan Grabowski, *"Ja tego Żyda znam": Szantażowanie Żydów w Warszawie, 1939–1943* (Warszawa: Wydawnictwo IFiS PAN, 2004).

with Warsaw thanks to her studies in the capital prior to the outbreak of the war on 1 September 1939, gives a detailed and chilling account of the various attitudes towards Jewish fugitives during the Warsaw Ghetto Uprising of April 1943.

> "The stance taken by the Poles regarding the uprising was not monolithic. Some voiced their admiration for the Jewish heroics. By and large, however, the Poles laughed at how "Moyshek and Yisroelik," who were never required to serve in the army, had taken up arms. Many laid blame on the Poles who had helped the Jews. A certain Mrs. Piatowa from no. 17 [?]a[?]necka Street told me that during a religion lesson....., a pupil from the upper grade asked the priest, "Are the Germans doing a good thing by murdering the Jews?" The priest thought for a moment and then replied, "Yes, because if it wasn't good, God wouldn't allow it.....

We, the Jews who were on the Aryan side, were quite depressed and shocked."[14] To grasp the intricate inner working of the "secret city" of rescuing and its early postwar memories, we shall now turn to the early postwar correspondence of the rescuers and Jewish survivors. I begin this investigation with the following questions: Who were the "dedicated rescuers"? How did they cast their rescue activities in the early postwar period? How did the Jewish survivors relate to their rescuers in the immediate postwar period? And what image of rescuers emerges from letters of Jewish survivors written on their own initiative?

Rescue as a Humanitarian Act to the Jewish Nation, a Christian Duty (Agape), and a Commitment to Prewar Friends and Employers

News about the material and financial assistance extended by the newly re-established Jewish organizations spread among former rescuers through different channels, mainly by word of mouth. Some rescuers initially made enquiries to local Jewish committees as to whom they might write for help concerning their wartime deeds, and as to whether there were specific instructions on how to apply for assistance. Some wrote only in 1947 or 1948, when they felt hard-pressed by severe privation, illnesses, and devastating family situations caused by the abject conditions prevailing in the early postwar period. The common

---

14   Testimony of Helena Kaletska, July 14, 1948, Łódź, Interviewer M. Royak, (Yiddish), Archive of the Jewish Historical Institute Warsaw, file no. 301/4062, 31–32.

explanation for writing a request to Jewish organizations for material or financial aid is expressed in the statement: "the state of emergency I am in forces me to ask for help." Among those uttering this statement, many are Polish women, wartime widows left with children of various ages, and Polish women caring for their children, sick husbands, elderly parents and other relatives. In the early postwar period, though Polish women faced high unemployment, they were often the chief breadwinners of families and were forced to look for jobs and other means of financial support.[15] In petitions and letters, they present their wartime rescue activities in a modest manner; carefully delineating their rescue activities and providing a list of names of rescued Jews, their Aryan names, and prewar and wartime addresses. They emphasize that the promise of financial gain was not the driving force of their rescue activities. Such insistence indicates that in the early postwar period, Christian Polish petitioners to CKŻP felt it necessary to disassociate themselves from the group of "rescuers for profit," and that they were clearly aware that many members of their community had benefited materially from the predicaments of Polish Jews under the Nazi occupation, and that many had extended help to Jewish fugitives for profit rather than out of humanitarian concern. Some of the "dedicated rescuers" had already acquired first-hand knowledge of the "rescuers for profit," as they were extending help to Jewish fugitives who had been previously robbed of everything by profit seeking and opportunistic Poles.

A significant number of the "dedicated rescuers" who are the authors of these letters are individuals motivated mainly by the humanitarian desire to save innocent human life. In her letter of September 14, 1946, Janina Wójcikowa describes the humanitarian motives that drove her to rescue many Warsaw Jews. She provided a temporary shelter in her Warsaw apartment to Dr. Rudolf Kirszblum (Antony Głowacki was his Aryan name), acted as his messenger during the war, and assisted Kirszblum's wife who was hidden in another rescuer's home, at Mrs. Palestrowa's house at Łowicka St. no. 53 in the capital. Wójcikowa also provided shelters to the two sisters Mirka and Franciszka Ubfalowna and to their families, to Mrs. Dyzenhausowa and her son, and to

---

15   On the situation of women in postwar Polish society, see H. Jędruszczak, "Miasta i przemysł w okresie odbudowy," in Franciszek Ryszka (ed.), *Polska Ludowa 1944–50: Przemiany społeczne* (Wrocław: Zakład Narodowy Im. Ossolińskich, 1974), 339–40; Dariusz Jarosz, "Kobiety a praca zawodowa w Polsce w latach 1944–1956 (główne problemy w świetle nowych badań źródłowych)," in Anna Żarnowska and Andrzej Szwarc (eds.), *Kobieta i praca: Wiek XIX I XX.*, vol. VI (Warszawa, Wydawnictwo DiG, 2000), 217–44. On the standards of living, see also B. Brodziński, *Stopa życiowa w Polsce w latach 1945–1963* (London: n.p., 1965).

Mrs. Bronisława Kotlińska whose daughter Wójcikowa had managed to place in the well-known Boduen children's orphanage in Warsaw where approximately two hundred Jewish children were hidden. She safeguarded the belongings of Mrs. Koperowa, the shop owner at Poznańska 38 in Warsaw, and also hid the belongings of Bela Altmanowa. She sheltered Irena Rybicka, the wife of Szymon Reinberg in her own home for a year, and when the woman was arrested in a German round-up on the streets of Warsaw, she sent parcels to her to the notorious Pawiak prison in Warsaw.

Wójcikowa stresses that she returned all belongings that were given to her for safe-keeping to their rightful owners. To lend credibility to her statement, she promises that her prewar Jewish friends can confirm her loyalty towards the Jewish nation. Her request for financial aid is modest and unspecified. She plainly states the reasons why she is turning for help to the Jewish committee: the complete theft and loss of everything during the Warsaw Uprising of August 1944. Like other "dedicated rescuers," she speaks about her wartime Jewish charges in a deferential and respectful way, and about her own activities in a modest manner.

> Many other individuals whose names I have already forgotten, had also benefited from my 'services' that I had provided without any expectation of making profit, but only on humanitarian grounds. I never counted on receiving any awards and for that matter I did not expect that I would remain alive at the end of the war. In any case, two individuals who know me well from prewar social circles, and who are at present employees of the Central Committee [CKŻP], Pola Kirsztajnowa (Zofia Grabowska) and along with my friend Florentyna Kleniecowa, can confirm my loyalty to the Jewish nation. My present situation and difficult material conditions are forcing me to turn to the Central Committee for material help. The salary of my husband is very modest and is not sufficient to cover our basic costs of living, especially since we had been completely robbed and lost everything in the Warsaw Uprising.[16]

Wójcikowa's letter contains short handwritten notes and scribbles written by her former Jewish charges. As a rule, such notes served at the time as a proof of the truthfulness of the petitioner's statement. Barbara Grösglik, author of one of those notes, praises Wójcikowa: "I state the truthfulness of the above details and personally and wholeheartedly ask for a positive realization of

---

16   Letter of Janina Wójcikowa of September 14, 1946 to the CKŻP, Archive of the Jewish Historical Institute Warsaw, File no. 303/VIII/421, 71–72.

the above request. I stress that my little daughter is alive today only thanks to Mrs. Wójcikowa."[17]

Some "dedicated rescuers" were guided not only by humanitarian factors, but also by a Christian belief in charity for the needy. Cecylia Piotrowska and her family, including her husband and four children, belonged to this latter group. In her letter of August 8, 1947, the Christian idea of love as duty (*agape*) is elaborated in a striking, powerful way:

> We are Christians and we consider every human being our brother. When the brother is in danger, one must help him even at the price of risking one's life. This is not only a humanitarian duty but first and foremost a religious obligation..... They often warned me that I was exposing my own children to grave danger. I was aware of that but I also knew that if they [the children] were to be killed, they would have died for a good cause: saving a human being in the name of God who is Love.
>
> I never expected any rewards. Many of my acquaintances, particularly those observant Catholics did the same and because of the same reasons. During the Nazi terror, someone painted a Star of David on the doors leading to my sister's apartment. This was a warning directed at her so that she would cease hiding Jews. I could say many things about those who saved Jews because of their convictions. They put their lives in danger and paid for their actions with their lives, freedom, and wealth. They expected neither payment nor glory. But I have no right to write about them. Nevertheless, after a long hesitation I finally decided to write about my and my dearests' lives, so the truth will be known: Only great Love, love of God and people can save humanity from bestiality and hatred.[18]

The rescue activities of Piotrowska family seem to stretch even beyond the concept of Christian charity, and can be viewed as an example of pure *agape*. In their wartime apartment at Wspólna 61 in Warsaw, they provided long-term shelter to Sydonia Neumann, a prewar music student of Mr. Piotrowski who had been Professor at the Cracow Music Conservatory. The young woman lived with them for more than three years. During the "Great Deportation" in the summer of 1942, the Piotrowski family took in Neumann's friend Mieczysław Chlewicki and a twelve year-old girl, both escapees from the Warsaw ghetto. While Chlewicki remained in hiding with Piotrowski family, the girl was

17 Ibid., 72.
18 Letter of Cecylia Piotrowska to the CKŻP, August 8, 1947, Archive of the Jewish Historical Institute Warsaw, File no. 303/VIII/235, (5–6), 74–75.

immediately placed in the hands of another rescuer, Maria Bortnowska, of the Information Bureau of the Polish Red Cross, who, in turn, placed the girl in a monastery near Lublin under the assumed name Kasia Wiśniewska. At the same time during 1942, Piotrowska accepted another Jewish fugitive, Roman Welczer, a friend of her son Jerzy, who arrived in her Warsaw apartment from the Przemyśl ghetto in south-eastern Poland. Welczer, whom Piotrowska treated as if he was her own son, had to leave the apartment after only two months because of a denunciation. Welczer and Piotrowska's other son, Zbigniew, were both killed during the Warsaw Uprising in late September 1944. Piotrowska also provided temporary shelter to Dr. Władysław Molkner and Nobert Grunbaum-Drzewocki; both men had been blackmailed in their previous apartment and had had to leave it instantly. In October 1942, Piotrowska managed to smuggle a Jewish woman who spoke poor Polish out of the Tarnów ghetto to Warsaw. Piotrowska also safeguarded various precious belongings of Jews, including those of Dr. Lilienfeld-Krzewski, but many of these items—though hidden from the Nazis and Polish blackmailers—were lost during the Warsaw Uprising when Piotrowska's apartment was burnt down. Piotrowska also engaged her teenage children Stanislaw and Marysia in rescue activities. They were responsible for obtaining false birth certificates for Jewish fugitives.

In May 1947, Iwo Trunk, another of Piotrowska's charges, corroborated her statement and spoke about her as an ideal and rare rescuer.

> During the time of the greatest adversity during the war, I myself experienced a lot of good in her home; I received not only moral but also material support. This was not an unusual action on her part. Through her home many Jews passed, and they owed their lives to her. If there were more Poles like her, certainly more Jews would have been saved. I emphasize that she did all that out of purely selfless reasons.[19]

Many "dedicated rescuers" from different social backgrounds were motivated by prewar friendships with Jews and by positive prewar professional and social relations with Jewish employers. Because of his prewar friendships, Leonard Wołomski extended help to both those Jews whom he knew and to strangers.[20] As a tram controller he could easily enter the Warsaw ghetto, where he delivered food, correspondence, and packages. He smuggled Jews in and out of the

---

19   Statement of Iwo Trunk, May 8, 1947, Łódź, Archive of the Jewish Historical Institute Warsaw, File 303/VIII/235, 77.
20   Letter of Leonard Wołomski to the CKŻP, Gdańsk-Wrzeszcz, Archive of the Jewish Historical Institute Warsaw, File no. 303/VIII/421, 52–55.

ghetto. During the Warsaw Ghetto Uprising, Wołomski, who also worked as a house administrator, helped Jews obtain false birth certificates and *kennkartes* (IDs), two absolutely necessary documents for Jewish fugitives wishing to live as Christian Poles on the Aryan-side. His behavior towards Jews passing as Poles on the Aryan side was also an important part of his rescue efforts. He supported them by treating them in public as ordinary Polish friends and acquaintances, signaling to other Poles that they should not suspect them and leave them alone. Wołomski smuggled food and letters to the Radom ghetto and took part in a rescue effort to smuggle fourteen Jews out of that ghetto. However, the latter effort failed. In his statement of July 21, 1947, Dr. Henryk Szipper, a survivor who knew Wołomski between 1942 and 1944, adds that Wołomski built a secret room in his wartime apartment in the House of Tram Drivers at Cegielna 10 in Warsaw, where he sheltered many Jews.[21]

Leokadia Wesołowska was nanny to Elżbieta Steinberg, the daughter of Szymon and Irena Steinberg.[22] Szymon Steinberg, a Warsaw lawyer, was killed in 1939 soon after the war broke out. Wesołowska remained a devoted and loyal employee of Irena Steinberg and her actions extended far beyond the call of duty.[23] Though she was not obliged to, Wesołowska moved into the Warsaw Ghetto with the widow and daughter. Fortuitously, the three women escaped the ghetto and managed to live together on the Aryan side for a certain amount of time. However, when they began to be suspected by their neighbors, Wesołowska and the four-year-old Elżbieta separated from Elżbieta's mother, living as aunt and nice. In the aftermath of the Warsaw Uprising, Wesołowska and Elżbieta were reunited with the girl's mother and lived together as a three-woman family unit. They were first based in Izabelin, sixteen kilometers north-west of Warsaw and then moved to Wieliczka near Cracow. Wesołowska protected the Jewish mother and daughter from the dangerous curiosity of strangers, providing the Steinbergs with a strong "Polish alibi," her presence itself serving as a proof of the Catholic Polish identity of the two Jewish women. While she lived in the Warsaw ghetto, Wesołowska also extended help to other Jews, delivering them food and letters. In a brief statement, one of her

---

21   Statement of Dr. Henryk Szipper, July 21, 1947, Szklarska Poręba; Archive of the Jewish Historical Institute Warsaw, File no. 303/VIII/421, 56–57.

22   Letter of Leokadia Wesołowska, January 8, 1947, Warsaw; Archive of the Jewish Historical Institute Warsaw, File no. 303/VIII/241, 8.

23   The historian Philip Friedman was the first scholar to discuss the issue of loyalty and total dedication and altruism of some former housekeepers towards their Jewish employers. See Philip Friedman, *Their Brothers' Keepers* (New York: Crown Publisher, 1957), 82–94, 150–54.

beneficiaries, Dr. Kalinowski from Warsaw, fully corroborates everything that the 60-year-old Wesołowska wrote in her statement of January 1947. He insists that she is a modest person and her presentation of her rescue activities in her letter is only a small fraction of all the good deeds she has performed.[24]

"They Treated Us as if We were Their Family, Completely Selflessly, since We Possessed nothing except for Our Misfortune:" Portraits of "Dedicated Rescuers" by Their Jewish Charges

Jewish survivors wrote letters about their rescuers either on their own initiative or because the rescuers asked them to do so. Some former Jewish charges, including children, also encouraged their former rescuers to apply for recompense to the CKŻP for what they had selflessly done for them during the war. As with other correspondence, the letters of Jewish charges requesting support for their rescuers vary in length: some are brief statements of a single page accompanied by a signature, while others are more lengthy and elaborate. Many of these letters give the impression of being composed in a hurry, en route to beginning a new life; or of their authors' already having gone to live in a faraway place. Nonetheless, the authors of these letters feel obliged to make official statements in support of their former rescuers. Their preoccupation with the relocation and search for their own families in Poland and abroad do not stop them from maintaining some form of contact with their former rescuers. This indicates that among many survivors there was a consensus that those who had risked their lives on their behalf and who had not used or abused them in any way should be acknowledged and their kindness repaid with kindness. The survivors felt compelled to act according to the traditional Jewish concept of *mitzvah goreret mitzvah* (one good deed produces another good deed).[25]

Dire poverty and a lack of basic goods and supplies were a problem for both Poles and remnants of Polish Jews in the immediate postwar period. Those who came from destroyed cities such as Warsaw, and those who were resettled in western and central parts of Poland as repatriates from the *Kresy*, seemed the most destitute. In the ruins of Warsaw, young and old had to begin their lives from zero. The language in which the rescuers describe their life conditions reveals the extent of the poverty and destruction, "I am naked and

---

24 Statement of Dr. Kalinowski, January 8, 1947, Warsaw; Archive of the Jewish Historical Institute Warsaw, File no. 303/VIII/241, 8.

25 *Mishnah Pirkei Avot* 4:2.

barefoot" (*Jestem naga i bosa*), and "I am totally burnt" (*Jestem całkowicie spalona*).

The Jewish survivors generally recognize that their rescuers, many of whom were widows of varying ages and women who were sole breadwinners of families, were in urgent need of material assistance. Therefore, in their petitions they pay special attention to descriptions of the wartime predicaments and the significance of their rescuers' actions, and highlight the selfless dedication and commitment of the rescuers. Moreover, they always take care to convey the former rescuer's drastic current material, medical and social situation. Not infrequently, they suggest specific forms of remuneration for the rescuer, such as food, clothing, underwear and financial payments, similar to the assistance that they themselves had received from the Department of Social Welfare of the Central Committee of Polish Jews and the JOINT.

The characteristic portrait of the "dedicated rescuer" that emerges from the former Jewish charges' letters is that of an exceptional individual who had extended help not only to one but to many Jewish fugitives, and who had provided more than just one form of assistance. The list of activities which can be classified as part of the rescue effort is long, and includes: smuggling food into the ghetto, smuggling Jews out of the ghetto, preparing, delivering and paying for false documents, sheltering, feeding, washing and cleaning, safeguarding precious belongings, curtailing blackmail, sending postcards, letters and packages as proof of the Christian Polish identity of the Jewish charges who had been forced to relocate or who had been taken to prisons or concentration camps as Christian Poles, and being a messenger among Jews in hiding on the Aryan side and handling their personal and business affairs. As a rule, such rescuers had acted with the cooperation of only very few members of their own immediate family, such as a spouse or a child, or may even have acted entirely on their own.

In their letter of March 11, 1947, three survivors, Hela and Natan Rokacz and Małka Mróz-Podemska, stress the compassionate attitude of their rescuers as the main reason they had been able to survive the war. The Wiśniewski couple had sheltered Hela and Natan Rokacz along with their two children and Małka Mróz-Podemska, in their Warsaw apartment on Emilii Plater Street no. 8, Apt. 38, from April 20, 1943 through January 17, 1945. The survivors highlight the fact that the Wiśniewskis had also sheltered two of their other relatives, Marian Rokacz and Lola Liberman-Rokacz, who like them were fugitives from the Warsaw ghetto. The other two had already left Poland and could not, therefore, be included as eyewitnesses to the Wiśniewskis' good deeds or included with the co-authors of the letter, which states:

> These people [the Wiśniewscy couple] shared all the meager food that they had with us, and throughout the entire time exhibited a compassionate attitude towards us, and thanks to that we managed to survive the occupation. After we left the ghetto, these people made false documents (*kennkarte*) for us, for which they paid with their own money. At present, the Wiśniewskis are in a dire situation, because Mr. Wiśniewski returned from German captivity only a month ago, and because everything they had was destroyed in the Uprising [Warsaw Uprising of August 1944]. Because of that, we would like to request that the Wiśniewskis receive temporary assistance in the form of money, food and clothes.[26]

Another former Jewish charge assisted by the same Wiśniewskis wrote a brief note in which he emphasizes in a rather grand style that:

> The citizen Antoni Wiśniewski is a symbol of friendship extended to the Jews during the most challenging years of conspiracy. His apartment on Emilii Plater Street was always like a "small ghetto" through which many Jews passed. The Wiśniewskis took good care of me and my mortally sick child when we reached [their home] after we had escaped the ghetto through the sewers. The citizen Wiśniewski also acted as a driver bringing various Jews and their goods from the provinces, and often smuggled Jews with "bad looks" [i.e., Jewish appearance] in his car from one apartment to another. The citizen Wiśniewski always fulfilled all his responsibilities, risking his own life and the lives of his dearest.[27]

Hinda Żaboklicka, a survivor who was still living with her rescuers, the Tekla Saliccy family, in March 1947 in the village of Złotokłos, 15 kilometers south of Warsaw, writes a deeply moving letter about the Saliccys' acts of selfless devotion both towards her and another unidentified member of her family. According to the letter, the rescuers were her prewar teachers. In late 1942 they smuggled Hinda from the Kałuszyn ghetto, twenty-eight kilometers north of Warsaw, and brought her to their home. Given the description of the weather

---

26 Letter of Hela and Natan Rokacz and Małka Mróz-Podemska, to the CKŻP in Warsaw, March 9, 1947, written in Łódź where the three survivors had moved to after the war; Archive of the Jewish Historical Institute Warsaw, File no. 303/VIII/241, 24.

27 A brief, typed-in note signed by an individual [an unclear signature], and also signed by H. Skolnicka and Zofia Wodzinowska of the CKŻP; Archive of the Jewish Historical Institute Warsaw, File no. 303/VIII/241, (755), 28.

conditions and other details in Hilda's letter, this most likely occurred after November 25, 1942, during the first deportation of the three thousand Jews of Kałuszyn to Treblinka, including Hilda's parents. The Saliccy were not afraid to keep her throughout the rest of the occupation, despite pressure from their neighbors to get rid of the Jewess. To ensure greater safety, they succeeded in getting her a false identity card in the name of Sabina Jabłońska. In her letter to the CKŻP, she uses both her original name and her acquired Aryan name.[28] This is how Hinda/Sabina remembers the Saliccys' behavior towards her and evaluates their rescue efforts:

> I must stress that they walked on foot about thirty kilometers to Kałuszyn in rain and in snow and they searched for us all over our village. They made such a sacrifice, as if we were their closest family. They took us home, ignoring the danger to their own lives, and they shared everything they had with us. They treated us as if we were their family, completely selflessly, since we did not possess anything except for our misfortune. They kept us and tried to provide us with everything in spite of the testing conditions. Mr. [Salicki] refused to work for the Germans because he did not want to have anything to do with them. He hated them like we did. . . . . People from the area were saying that he was hiding Jews. I walked freely within their property, but [the Saliccy] stated that God's will is stronger than that of the murderers and did not give us up. . . . . . I wish I were able to repay even just a tiny part for saving my life in such difficult times when they could have been killed at any moment. Only a biological mother is capable of such acts, but here as complete strangers they had acted just as selflessly.[29]

Similarly, Róża Stettner and A. Finkelsztejn wrote a passionate letter detailing the various rescue activities of the lawyer Grażyna Szmurtowa, who conducted most of her rescue actions in the small town of Legionowo, located twenty-three kilometers north-east of Warsaw, where she lived until 1944. These two survivors took upon themselves the recording of Szmurtowa's good deeds, which were extended not only to them and their families but also to other Jews. Thus, they write both as individuals and as representatives of that

---

28 On the problem of retaining and using 'Aryan names' among the survivors, see Irena Hurwin–Nowakowska, *Żydzi Polscy (1947–1950): Analiza więzi społecznej ludności żydowskiej* (Warszawa, Wydawn. Instytutu Filozofii i Socjologii PAN, 1996). This book is based on the author's impressive PhD dissertation, written in 1950.

29 Letter of Hinda Żaboklicka, March 24, 1947; Archive of the Jewish Historical Institute Warsaw, File no. 303/VIII/238, (690).

entire group of survivors whom Szmurtowa rescued. According to their letter of September 28, 1946, Szmurtowa emerges as a selfless, altruistic and compassionate person who assisted many Jews in many ways. She sheltered Jews for shorter and longer periods in her own home, as well as finding them safe hiding-places in other people's homes. She never took a penny for her services. In addition, she safeguarded belongings of various other Jews during the war, and made their belongings accessible to them when they were in urgent need to pay for shelter or when they were being blackmailed for their lives. Szmurtowa even declined to accept any financial help from the Jewish organization after the war, accepting only two supplies of clothes, two towels, two blankets and three tubes of toothpaste. The survivors' letter reads:

> Mrs. Szmurtowa belongs to that group of individuals of Aryan origin who helped the Jews by ignoring all the rules and orders of the Nazi occupier, risking her own life and the lives of her family. Her home was open to the people from the ghetto.... She safe-guarded the remnants of the belongings of the miserable ones, which allowed many to save themselves from the claws of their tormentors. She gave shelter for two weeks to Jean Lagnean, a Jew from Avignon, and a soldier of the French army. He subsequently went off and returned back to her home on many occasions. She kept him and fed him generously. Szmurtowa also helped Regina Wiśniewicz, (who now lives at Zachodnia Street in Łódź), and her four-member family. They are alive today only thanks to her.
>
> She hosted my old mother and sister in her home for a long time, without asking them for any payment. She fed them and carefully hid them from the eyes of her neighbors in one of the buildings belonging to her property. However, after a few visits from the gendarmerie, when it became too dangerous for them to remain there, she found them a shelter in Warsaw where the family subsequently remained. She did a lot of good things for Róża Stettner and her daughter, by placing both of them in the homes of friends of hers who lived in the countryside. Today, Mrs. Szmurtowa is completely destroyed by the war and has to support her old aunt and her own two daughters who are still at school. We would like the directors of the Committee [CKŻP], who always relate to such matters positively, to help Mrs. Szmurtowa and her family by supplying them with clothes that are so hard to obtain these days. In this way the Jews whom she has sheltered will be able to repay her at least in part for what she did for them.[30]

---

30   Letter of Róża Stettner of Jabłonna, near Warsaw and A. Finkelsztejn of Legionowo, September 28, 1946, to the CKŻP. The handwritten note of December 17, 1946, written by

On March 31, 1947, ten Jewish survivors from Sosnowiec and Katowice wrote a collective letter to the CKŻP in Warsaw asking for support, reward and protection of their wartime savior Leon Bukowiński from Warsaw.[31] They call him a "sincere patriot who provided indispensable help to people of a different religious background."[32] Bukowiński, an educated middle-class man with a wife and two sons, belonged to the Polish underground in occupied Warsaw. His position in the Polish police (*granatowa policja*)[33] gave him that rare opportunity to perform rescue activities in which ordinary civilians had no chance to succeed. As the letter informs us, Bukowiński issued false documents, relocated many Jews from dangerous hiding places (*spalone*) to new safe shelters, warned Jews on the Aryan side about blackmailers, and frequently shut down blackmail circles.

> We cite names of individuals who we know personally whom Bukowiński helped: 1. Marian Borkowski wel Borensztein, his wife and two year-old child lived in the Bukowiński family home between August 1942 and the entry of the Soviet Army into the city; 2. Ruchla Gluglich [Glaglich?]—he curtailed blackmail; 3. Wolf Berliński—risking his life [Bukowiński] carefully prepared and executed [Berliński's] escape from Pawiak prison; 4. Leokadia Berlińska—he curtailed many blackmails and prevented her arrest 5. Liberowa and her son—he defended them from blackmailers while smuggling them to Praga, a neighborhood of Warsaw. He had to use a weapon against the blackmailers at Washington Avenue. 6. The Iger family from Sosnowiec numbering eight persons—he found a safe shelter for all of them at Korawa Street [?] in Warsaw. 7 and 8. Jasiński and Mirosława Poznańska and her husband, he transported these three persons from Częstochowa to Warsaw. 9. Feliks Rockman, lawyer, and his

---

an official of the CKŻP in Warsaw [signature illegible] states that altogether she received 25 items in two deliveries; Archive of the Jewish Historical Institute Warsaw, File no. 303/VIII/239, 107–8.

31 For an account of rescue activities events presented by Bukowiński himself, see Leon Bukowiński, *Pamiętnik z okresu okupacji*; Archive of the Jewish Historical Institute, CKŻP, File No. 301/4424, 5.

32 A collective letter of six Jewish survivors living in Sosnowiec March 31, 1947 to the CKŻP, signed also by four Jews in Katowice, 3 April, 1947; Archive of the Jewish Historical Institute Warsaw, File no. 303/VIII/222, 76–77.

33 On the *granatowa policja*, see Adam Hempel, *Pogrobowcy klęski: Rzecz o policji 'granatowej' w Generalnym gubernatorstwie, 1939–1945* (Warszawa: Państwowe Wydawnictwo Naukowe, 1990).

brother Stanislaw with wife—he protected them against blackmail. 10. The Bober family from Ostrołęka—he assisted them and took special care of an eight-year old child whose parents had perished."[34]

Some survivors who had already moved abroad, and were either waiting in DP camps in Germany to travel to their final destination[35] or were already engaged in building a new life overseas, also wrote letters to the CKŻP, delineating how they had been rescued, requesting material assistance for their former rescuers. Like some survivors still living in Poland, these survivors had remained in direct communication with their Polish rescuers and were concerned about their well-being and wished to alleviate their current hardship. Some who had the means to personally assist their rescuers and who promised such assistance for the future nonetheless wrote to the CKŻP in Warsaw asking for help for their rescuers on their behalf. They argued that it was too difficult to send personal parcels from the West to Poland because of long postal delays and the high likelihood of such gifts being misplaced or lost.

In his letter of February 2, 1947, composed in Hanover, Germany, Israel Dorembus speaks movingly about the rescuer of his family, Stanisław Bandurski of Warsaw. It was thanks to this man's efforts that Dorembus and his wife, father and sister were able to separately escape the Warsaw Ghetto in September and October of 1942. Stanisław Bandurski, as Dorembus states, was a total stranger whom the Dorembus fugitives did not get to know until after he had smuggled them out of the ghetto to the Aryan side. Over the next two years, up till the Warsaw Uprising of August 1, 1944, Bandurski made sure that the Dorembus family was safe, constantly assisting them in various life-saving ways. He organized false identity cards for all four fugitives, and was in charge of the relocation of Mr. Dorembus and his wife from the first shelter after smugglers had discovered it. He was not afraid of claiming that Dorembus's wife was his niece from that part of Poland incorporated in 1939 into the Reich, nor of finding her a job as a housekeeper with some of his relatives, nor of finding a job for Israel. Israel Dorembus acknowledges that it was only thanks to

---

34   Ibid., 76.
35   On the *She'erit Hapletah* in early postwar Germany, see Zeev W. Mankowitz, *Life Between Memory and Hope: The Survivors of the Holocaust in Occupied Germany* (Cambridge: Cambridge University Press, 2002); Hagit Lavsky, *New Beginnings: Holocaust Survivors in Bergen-Belsen and the British zone in Germany, 1945–1950* (Detroit: Wayne State University Press, 2002); and Atina Grossmann, *Jews, Germans and Allies: Close Encounters in Occupied Germany* (Princeton and Oxford: Princeton University Press, 2007).

Bandurski that they survived the most challenging two years of their lives until they were taken to Germany in the aftermath of the Warsaw Uprising.[36]

Another case is that of Dr. Sarah Spiegel, who in May 1947, at her comfortable new home on New York's Upper West-Side, composed a letter praising her rescuer Marian Wróbel. Wróbel, a Varsovian like herself, was both her former prewar patient and a prewar friend of her husband. Spiegel briefly relates the circumstances in which she met Wróbel in Warsaw after she had escaped the Warsaw Ghetto in early 1943. On May 3 1943, she was forced to leave her previous shelter at the apartment of other Christian friends. She found herself on the street, fearful and without the slightest idea of whom to turn to for help. Fortunately, she suddenly remembered Wróbel and made a quick decision to approach him for help. Spiegel stresses that Wróbel took her in without hesitation, and in spite of his difficult marital and family circumstances and the dire wartime conditions, sheltered her in his apartment for fourteen months until July, 1944. Spiegel emphasizes that:

> for all his efforts and worries [Wróbel] did not ask for, nor did he receive, any recompense in money or other material form from me, except for my gratitude for his noble actions in saving my life. At present, I am in communication via letters with Mr. Wróbel, and I am aware that his material situation is bad. If the CKŻP in Warsaw compensates this kind of individual, who contributed to saving the Jews from the Nazi destruction, then Mr. Marian Wróbel of Bolecha St. no. 57, Apt. 42 in Warsaw should be enlisted as one of the most deserving people. He should be offered material help.[37]

"She Looked after Her with Dedication and with All of Her Heart:" Depictions of Rescuers by Relatives of Survivors

The same image of an exceptional, selfless individual, risking his or her life to save Jews emerges in the various letters written by relatives of rescued Jews. Albert Meszorer, a Warsaw lawyer, describes his son's rescuer, Stanisława

---

36   Letter of Israel Dorembus, February 2, 1947, Hannover (Germany) to CKŻP; Archive of the Jewish Historical Institute Warsaw, File no. 303/VIII/221, 19–20. In Hannover, Germany, Dorembus worked for UNRRA and enjoyed a steady income. In the letter he declares that he will repay the CKŻP the sum of money that they will offer to his rescuer.

37   Letter of Sarah Spiegel, May 17, 1947, of 315 West 98 Street, New York, NY, to the CKŻP; Archive of the Jewish Historical Institute Warsaw, File no. 303/VIII/241, 80.

Szaniawska, as a woman who looked after his son impeccably and who bestowed upon his son kindness from the depths of her heart. Mrs. Szaniawska, an educated woman, was a widow whose husband, a writer, had been killed by the Germans. In December 1942, she took in the then ten and a half year-old Józef Lucjan Meszorer. In spite of the fact that Józef's parents had lost contact with her and therefore could not pay the boy's living costs, she continued to shelter him. Not only did she provide him with food and clothes, but she also tutored him. At the same time, she sheltered a little Jewish girl who was considered to have a "bad" Semitic appearance. According to Albert Meszorer, she also extended help to other Jews on a selfless basis. When Meszorer reclaimed his son from the rescuer in 1945, he paid her a certain sum of money to cover expenses incurred towards his son's upbringing during the occupation. Nonetheless, in his letter of March 20, 1949, to the *Komisja Pomocy Polakom*, he insists that Szaniawska should be offered additional material help, food and clothes, for three reasons: her rescue actions during the war, her very modest living standards, and her status as a widow of a citizen killed by the Germans.[38]

Anna Baćkowa, the mother of a child survivor, praises the elderly couple, Stanisława and Władysław Zbysz, who had saved her daughter Diana, born in 1934. The girl had arrived at their Warsaw apartment in October 1943, where she remained until the end of the Warsaw Uprising of August 1, 1944.

> She [Stanisława Zbysz] looked after the child very well and acted out of selfless motives, since I was in a terrible material situation and could not pay her. At present, Stanisława Zbysz and her husband, both in their seventies, live in poverty because the husband suffers badly from severe asthma. Therefore I am asking for assistance for them with clothes, food and financial help.[39]

In her letter of April 14, 1947, Helena Arkin Okońska, sister of Artur and Wiktor Arkin, praises Agnieszka Wróbel, a young woman thanks to whom both brothers found shelters and survived on the Aryan side in Warsaw.[40] Wróbel was a messenger between the Warsaw Ghetto and the Aryan side, and

---

38 Letter of Albert Meszorer, March 20, 1949, to the *Komisja Pomocy Polakom* at the CKŻP; Archive of the Jewish Historical Institute Warsaw, File no. 303/VIII/239, 78.

39 Letter of Anna Baćkowa, December 28, 1946, Warsaw, to the CKŻP; Archive of the Jewish Historical Institute Warsaw, File no. 303/VIII/242, (519), 17. Stanisława Zbysz requested help from JOINT on March 25, 1947. Her letter is enclosed with Baćkowa's.

40 Statement of Helena Arkin-Okońska, April 14, 1947, Warsaw; Archive of the Jewish Historical Institute Warsaw, File no. 303/VIII/421, 78–79.

smuggled food into the ghetto. Helena Arkin Okońska elaborates events and conditions under which Wróbel conducted rescue activities, which the rescuer briefly touches upon in her own letter to the CKŻP of the same date.[41] From Helena Arkin's letter we learn that Wróbel was blackmailed many times over while delivering food to Artur Arkin in his shelter on the Aryan side. The blackmailer Stefania Dammowa of 18 Nowogrodzka Street also blackmailed Wiktor Arkin, who was hiding at Agnieszka Wróbel's apartment. After the Warsaw Uprising, Wróbel took her Jewish charges to her sister's home in Limanowa in the Beskidy Mountains, where she also offered shelter to two other Jews, Helena Arkin Okońska and Bronislaw Luidor. Jewish survivors and rescuers often recall blackmail as the ominous daily challenge. In addition, young Jewish women fugitives and their "dedicated rescuers" recall struggling not only with financial blackmail but with attempts at sexual assault.[42]

Conclusions

Noe Grüss, one of the leading historians of the Jewish Historical Commission[43] set up in Poland in November, 1944, viewed accounts concerning rescue activities as "the files of innate human kindness in the archives primarily registering the murder and destruction of individuals, families and entire generations."[44] While these letters of both rescuers and rescued Jews undoubtedly corroborate acts of kindness and dedication, they also constitute rare and salient data

---

41   Letter of Agnieszka Wróbel, Warsaw, to the CKŻP, April, 14, 1947; Archive of the Jewish Historical Institute Warsaw, File no. 303/VIII/421, 76.

42   Curriculum Vitae of an unnamed mature Christian Polish woman, a member of the lower middle class, living in Warsaw. She rescued two young Jewish women, Regina and Ewa Greiss of Strachobiczyn in Lviv Voivodeship, who had taken the "Aryan" names Maria and Krystyna Kawecka. They had arrived at her place in April 1943 from a previous shelter where they were robbed of their belongings and even of the clothes they wore. The rescuer recalls attempts of taking sexual advantages of the two Jewish women by Polish men who knew where they were hidden; Archive of the Jewish Historical Institute Warsaw, File 303/VIII/243, 6–14.

43   For discussion of the origin and make-up of the Jewish Historical Commissions, see Laura Jockusch, "Khurbn Forshung—Jewish Historical Commissions in Europe, 1943–1949," *Simon Dubnow Institute Yearbook* 6 (2007): 441–73, and Natalia Aleksiun, "The Central Jewish Historical Commission in Poland 1944–1947," *Polin: Studies in Polish Jewry* 20 (2007): 74–97.

44   Noe Grüss, *Dokumenty wrodzonej szlachetności*, [undated, early postwar, one and a half page essay]; Archive of the Jewish Historical Institute Warsaw, File no. 303/XX/292, 44, 45.

for the study of the intricate map of wartime relations between Christian rescuers and rescued Jews, and into their surrounding local neighborhoods and communities. They throw light onto interactions between individual Christian Poles and Polish Jews immediately after the war, and onto fresh, raw postwar memories of the wartime experiences. They constitute precious material for the study of both social mentalities and economic conditions of early postwar Polish society, both in large cities such as Warsaw and in small towns and rural areas. A thorough analysis of this correspondence will contribute to the creation of a more systematic typology of the rescuers from Warsaw and Warsaw province, and other urban and rural regions of Nazi-occupied Poland. It will enable us to probe major issues such as the profile and motivation of "dedicated rescuers," the role of gender in rescue activities, and the impact of ethnicity, religion, social status and other forms of self-identification on rescue activities. Moreover, it will enable us to produce a chart of commonalities and differences among rescue activities in Warsaw and Warsaw province and those in other regions of Nazi-occupied Poland.

The portrait of the selfless "dedicated" rescuer that emerges from the letters of Jewish survivors, their relatives and members of Jewish organizations, is on the one hand fairly uniform. The selfless rescuer, both in and outside of Warsaw, is usually an individual who extended rescue activities to several rather than just a single Jewish fugitive; and who provided several forms of assistance, such as sheltering and feeding Jewish fugitives, finding them shelter in other people's homes when necessary, safeguarding their belongings, arranging false papers, assisting in proving their Christian Polish identities, and transporting them from one hiding-place to another. Neighbors and professional blackmailers frequently harassed the selfless rescuer. Nevertheless, such a rescuer typically managed to stand up to social pressures, fear, and threats of denunciation, and continued to engage in rescue activities. This also corroborates the thesis, first raised in *Dzieci żydowskie oskarżają*, published in 1946 by Maria Hochberg Marianska, of a low societal approval of rescue activities directed towards Jews.[45]

On the other hand, the portrait of the selfless rescuer is varied with respect to social and professional background, gender, age and marital status. Many

---

45 Maria Hochberg-Mariańska was herself a Jewish survivor and a member of the Council to Aid Jews, Cracow branch, during the war. In her introduction to Maria Hochberg-Mariańska and Noe Grüss (eds.), *Dzieci żydowskie oskarżają* (Kraków: Żydowska Komisja Historyczna w Krakowie, 1946), she raises the problem of low societal approval of rescue activities. See also English edition: Maria Hochberg-Mariańska and Noe Grüss (eds.), *The Children Accuse* (London and Portland, OR: Vallentine & Mitchell, 1996), 24.

selfless rescuers were prewar friends of Jewish charges and their families, and were individuals with a prewar history of professional and social relations with Jews. Many were women who were either widows or sole family breadwinners. What emerges on the whole is that the "dedicated rescuer" is a special individual who in his or her relations with the Jewish fugitives transcends ethnic and religious boundaries. They clearly stand out from the community to which they belong and appear to be a minority driven by a set of qualities and values atypical to that community. This picture is confirmed in survivors' and rescuers' testimonies from the same and later periods.

CHAPTER 21

The Politics of Retribution in Postwar Warsaw: In the Honor Court of the Central Committee of Polish Jews

Gabriel N. Finder

> *The question of the guilt and accountability of Jews who in one way or another collaborated with the Germans has created heartache enough in all circles of the Jewish community.*—Shaye Shechatov, former judge in the Honor Court of the Central Committee of Polish Jews[1]

Fresh from their conquest of Poland, the German occupation authorities ordered Adam Czerniaków to present a list of twenty-four candidates for the Warsaw Jewish Council (Judenrat), which was to replace the prewar denominational Commune Council. Czerniaków had been a member of the Commune Council's board since 1937 and had been appointed its president by the mayor of Warsaw, Stefan Starzyński, on 22 September 1939, after the board's head, Maurycy Mayzel, had left Poland in the first days of the war. The occupation authorities accepted Czerniaków's list on 13 October, 1939. It included prominent and well-respected members of the Jewish community, complemented by representatives of various political viewpoints. Officially established in the General Government (Generalgouvernement) by decree of the governor-general, Hans Frank, on 28 November 1939, the function of Jewish councils (Judenräte), which represented local Jewish communities in their relations with the occupation authorities, was to execute German orders and directives. Despite their veneer of independence, the Jewish councils worked under extreme pressure, distress, and threats of violence both to their members and their communities.[2]

The prevailing opinion in the Warsaw Ghetto of the Judenrat and its chairman, Czerniaków, was negative. The Judenrat's onerous and unfair tax policy,

---

1 Shaye Shechatov, *Yorn fun kamf un gerangl* (Ramat Gan: Lior, 1973), 72. The chapter in which this citation appears is called "Kolaboratsye bay yidn" (Collaboration of Jews) and was first published separately in the Mexican Jewish periodical *Faroys* (1 September 1955): 8–12.
2 Isaiah Trunk, *Judenrat: The Jewish Councils in Eastern Europe under Nazi Occupation* (Lincoln, NB: University of Nebraska Press, 1996 [orig. 1972]).

of which the poor bore the brunt, its conscription of overwhelmingly poor residents into forced labor contingents, and its tolerance of corruption within the ranks of the Jewish Order Service (Służba Porządkowa), the Jewish police force in the ghetto, which operated under its auspices, all elicited antipathy in the ghetto. The disdain of the ghetto's inhabitants was magnified by inflated and unrealistic expectations of the Judenrat's ability to improve the lot of Warsaw's Jews when, in fact, its freedom of action was severely restricted by the Germans. The Ghetto residents' unfavorable encounters with the Judenrat's officials and personnel only served to further tarnish its reputation. For his part, Czerniaków evoked contempt for his emotional distance from the Jewish masses, his appointment of the assimilated and rich to posts in the Judenrat, and his perceived conciliatory approach to the Germans. His suicide on the second day of the great deportation from the Warsaw Ghetto, on 23 July 1942, which signified his refusal to comply with German orders to cooperate in the deportation of his fellow Jews to their certain deaths, softened the opinions of some, but certainly not all, of his detractors.[3]

The Germans ordered the Judenrat to establish the Order Service when they decided to create a ghetto in Warsaw. The superintendent of the Jewish police force was Józef Szeryński (Szynkman), who before the war had been a colonel in the Polish police. He was a Jew who had converted to Catholicism and had no ties to the Jewish community. According to historian Barbara Engelking, "Szeryński was an effective and experienced civil servant; however, he could not resist the temptation of what on the surface seemed like power."[4] The primary duties of the Order Service were to maintain order in the ghetto and provide auxiliary units of the German police. Initial reactions in the ghetto to the Jewish police formation, which comprised roughly 2,500 men in July 1942, were favorable. But, with the passage of time, its reputation deteriorated as a result of its Mafia-like methods (for example, providing protection to businesses for bribes and expelling residents from their apartments during so-called disinfection procedures unless they purchased disinfection certificates), its heavy-handed use of force, and its perceived hostility to the community. Perceptions

---

3   Ibid., 261; Barbara Engelking and Jacek Leociak, *The Warsaw Ghetto: Guide to the Perished City*, trans. Emma Harris (New Haven and London: Yale University Press, 2009), 153–59, 160–61, 164–65; Samuel D. Kassow, *Who Will Write Our History? Emanuel Ringelblum, the Warsaw Ghetto, and the Oyneg Shabes Archive* (Bloomington and Indianapolis: Indiana University Press, 2007), 94–95, 111; Yitzhak Zuckerman ("Antek"), *A Surplus of Memory: Chronicle of the Warsaw Ghetto Uprising*, trans. and ed. Barbara Harshav (Berkeley and Los Angeles: University of California Press, 1993), 194–96.

4   Engelking and Leociak, *The Warsaw Ghetto*, 190.

of Szeryński and his commanders, who were assimilated Jews, became overwhelmingly negative owing to their imperiousness.

Dislike of the Jewish police and its command turned to hatred during the Great Deportation in the summer of 1942. Prodded by Jakub Lejkin, deputy head of the Order Service, some Jewish policemen, in an effort to save themselves and their families, zealously and brutally apprehended inhabitants of the ghetto and escorted them to the Umschlagplatz, while Szeryński oversaw the operation with apparent indifference to their fate.[5] In 2005, Polish sociologist Ewa Koźmińska-Frejlak interviewed Jerzy Lewiński, a former Jewish policeman. According to Lewiński, out of a couple of thousand Jewish policemen in the ghetto, most removed their uniforms or merely went through the motions once the deportation started, and some even went out of their way to shelter and save fellow Jews. By contrast, only two hundred or so desperate Jewish policemen, under intense German pressure, acted badly. Nevertheless, the disreputable actions of a few became the dominant image of the Jewish police in the ghetto.[6]

The Warsaw Ghetto was plagued, moreover, by the existence of a large number of informers in the service of the Germans. As Engelking explains, "Some did it in the belief that the Nazis would win the war and that therefore for the sake of the future of the Jews (both individually and collectively) it was necessary to ensure good relations with the authorities. Others collaborated in exchange for money and an improvement in their living conditions, from opportunism, from fear, or to protect themselves and their families."[7] Abraham Gancwajch headed the Office to Combat Profiteering and Speculation, known by its unofficial name the "Thirteen" (Trzynastka), which was subordinate not to the Judenrat, the Polish police, or the German civil administration but directly to the German Security Police (Sipo). The Germans initiated the creation of the "Thirteen" ostensibly to combat profiteering and speculation in the ghetto. In reality, it wrote weekly reports on the mood in the ghetto for the Sipo, while its agents blackmailed and denounced ghetto inhabitants, including extorting payments from "fat cats" (this was the term used by one contemporary observer) involved in smuggling and illegal trading. Gancwajch, who believed that a German victory was inevitable and that Jews had better adapt to this prospect, had close contacts with the Germans and oversaw the operation of

---

5 Ibid., 190–218; Kassow, *Who Will Write Our History?*, 93, 111, 129–31, 313, 327, 343–44.
6 Ewa Koźmińska-Frejlak, "Świadectwo milczenia: Rozmowa z Jerzym Lewińskim, byłym funcjonariuszem Służby Porządkowej getta warszawskiego," *Zagłada Żydów* 2 (2006): 245–79, 273–75.
7 Engelking and Leociak, *The Warsaw Ghetto*, 218.

various shady institutions in the ghetto.⁸ The Germans cultivated other spies in the ghetto, the so-called Jewish Gestapo. Agents like Alfred Nossig advised the Germans and kept tabs on the mood in the ghetto for them.⁹ Needless to say, the inhabitants of the ghetto held the "Thirteen," its leader Gancwajch, and Jewish Gestapo agents in contempt.

The disreputable behavior of the Judenrat, the Order Service, the "Thirteen," and suspected Gestapo spies not merely earned the enmity of the ghetto population but also provoked underground circles to charge them with collaboration. Exemplary of the underground's contempt for Judenrat officials is an article published in *Jutrznia* (Dawn), the underground paper of the Zionist organization Gordonia:

> Leaving aside the personal history and uprightness of a Judenrat man, the mere fact of belonging to this institution makes him objectively a Nazi agent, and so the most miserable traitor, who must in the future face his deserved punishment. The Jewish masses must be aware of this dispassionately viewed role of the Judenrat. They must approach it with profound, well-founded hatred and contempt, they must sabotage its decrees, they must at every turn unmask its role and remember well who collaborated with it, so that none escapes punishment.¹⁰

The Jewish Fighting Organization (Żydowska Organizacja Bojowa, ŻOB) particularly despised the Order Service and targeted specific Jewish policemen for assassination.¹¹ The ŻOB was motivated not only by vengeance but also by the tactical necessity of removing the mortal threat posed by a Jewish fifth column to the budding insurgency in the ghetto. In its founding statute, the ŻOB proclaimed its objective, in anticipation of the Germans' intention to destroy the Jewish community, to protect it from internal "criminals and agents, collaborators with the occupier."¹² Three or four members of the ŻOB's command staff passed death sentences on several putative collaborators from the

---

8   Ibid., 218–28. See also Christopher Browning and Israel Gutman, "The Reports of a Jewish 'Informer' in the Warsaw Ghetto—Selected Documents," *Yad Vashem Studies* 17 (1986): 247–93.

9   Engelking and Leociak, *The Warsaw Ghetto*, 228–32.

10 Cited in ibid., 157.

11 Zuckerman, *A Surplus of Memory*, 192.

12 Cited in Bernard Mark, "Statut Żydowskiej Organizacji Bojowej," *Biuletyn Żydowskiego Instytutu Historycznego* 3 (39) (1961): 39–62, quote on 59.

Judenrat, the Order Service, the "Thirteen," and the so-called Jewish Gestapo.[13] Estimates range from a dozen to some thirty suspected collaborators who were executed by the ŻOB. The Jewish Military Union (Związek Żydowski Wojskowy, ZŻW), founded by Revisionists and Betar, passed its own death sentences on collaborators. Between August 1942 and the Warsaw Ghetto Uprising in April 1943, the ŻOB's targets included Szeryński, who narrowly escaped death (Szeryński later committed suicide), Jakub Lejkin, deputy head of the Order Service, Izrael First, director of the Economics Department of the Judenrat, who was a feared intermediary between the Germans and the Judenrat, and Alfred Nossig. Announcements of death sentences, which were signed in the name of the ŻOB, contained stern warnings to other collaborators.[14] The death sentences passed on collaborators helped establish the authority of the ŻOB in the Warsaw Ghetto. As Yitzhak Zuckerman, a legendary commander of the ŻOB, recollected in his memoir, the "Jewish Fighting Organization . . . [was] tangible for the public, because they knew it issued death sentences, and they thought that anyone who issued death sentences was really an organization of fighters."[15]

Jewish vigilantism could be justified while the fighting raged. But as the end of the war approached, it became untenable, as the ŻOB's surviving leaders came to realize. In either late January or early February 1945, Zuckerman rescued a former Jewish policeman in the Warsaw Ghetto from an angry mob of fellow Jews and had him arrested by the Polish Security Office militiamen, but somehow the arrested man was freed. Zuckerman then dispatched his own people to find him. They located him and alerted the Russian army to arrest him, but he was set free once again. Then, one day in April the same former ghetto policeman entered Zuckerman's room while he was lying ill in his bed. The man could have killed Zuckerman then and there, but instead he said to him, "I came to you to judge me!" Zuckerman pulled his pistol out from under his pillow and listened to the man's story. He had agreed to become a Jewish policeman to save his mother, but it had been in vain. After the war, he had come to hate himself, and now he was coming to Zuckerman's apartment to plead with him to end his life. When he finished telling his story, Zuckerman

---

13 Zuckerman, *A Surplus of Memory*, 210–12, 246–47.
14 See Engelking and Leociak, *The Warsaw Ghetto*, 215, 230, 755–56; Mark, "Statut Żydowskiej Organizacji Bojowej," 61–62.
15 Zuckerman, *A Surplus of Memory*, 273. This opinion was shared by Jerzy Lewiński; see Koźmińska-Frejlak, "Świadectwo milczenia," 276. See also Israel Gutman, *Resistance: The Warsaw Ghetto Uprising* (Boston and New York: Mariner Books, Houghton Mifflin, published in association with the United States Holocaust Memorial Museum, 1994), 169–71.

ordered him to leave. He had decided not to shoot him, but not because he had forgiven him. Zuckerman is emphatic on this score: "No, I didn't forgive him, absolutely not." It seems that Zuckerman was reexamining his view of vigilante retribution:

> Beginning at that time, early January 1945, I decided I wouldn't issue any more death sentences. Objectively, it was right to execute that person, definitely—yes! But there's no end to that, once you start. So I wanted to try him, but he escaped that. Now he came because his conscience oppressed him and he wanted to commit suicide. Should I have killed him? In those days, I was becoming increasingly aware that we had to put an end to issuing sentences and their partisan execution.[16]

It is plausible that Zuckerman's attitude began to shift after a dramatic encounter in the offices of the Central Committee of Polish Jews (Centralny Komitet Żydów w Polsce, CKŻP) in January 1945, after the Soviet liberation of Warsaw. The CKŻP became the principal postwar representative body of Polish Jewry until 1950. During a meeting of the CKŻP's executive committee, Zuckerman, who was popularly known by his nom de guerre, "Antek," requested the floor to denounce Michał Weichert, who was then leading efforts to provide relief to Jews returning to Kraków from the camps. The ŻOB had passed a death sentence on Weichert, accusing him of collaboration with the Germans on account of his leadership of the Jewish Social Assistance Society (Jüdische Soziale Selbsthilfe, JSS) in Kraków, which in the view of underground leaders had played into German hands under Weichert. According to Leon (Arieh) Bauminger, whom the committee was dispatching to Kraków to oversee the reorganization of the Jewish community there, Zuckerman, after his denunciation of Weichert, turned to him and urged him to assassinate Weichert after his arrival in Kraków.

> 'Lonek, take my pistol, and if you reach Kraków, put a bullet in his head.' And Antek slid his pistol over the table to me. I answered: 'Antek, I don't know Dr. Weichert and I don't know about his activities during the occupation because I was away for three-and-a-half years in the Kovno Ghetto. In addition, now with the end of the war, I don't shoot Jews. There are courts now, and if he is a traitor, he will be punished.' And I slid the pistol back to Antek.[17]

---

16   Zuckerman, *A Surplus of Memory*, 636–37.
17   Arieh Bauminger, "Reshit darko shel 'Ha-Ichud' be'polin: pirkei zichronot," part 1, *Masu'ah* 19 (1991): 226; cited in part in David Engel, "Who is a Collaborator? The Trials of Michał

Thus it seems that there was a growing sentiment among the emerging leadership of the surviving remnant of Polish Jewry that vengeance wreaked on putative Jewish collaborators needed to be pursued in court rather than on the street. At first, the Jewish leadership was content to see suspected Jewish collaborators stand trial in Polish criminal courts. Indeed, thirty of at least forty-four accused Jewish collaborators were ultimately convicted in Polish courts.[18] But, as David Engel shows, the postwar Jewish leadership decided by 1946 "to develop its own mechanism for holding Jews to account for their wartime behavior" because "there was a sense that the existing general Polish mechanisms had not proven sufficient for Jewish communal purposes."[19] The reason is that Polish courts acquitted some high-profile Jewish defendants, including Weichert—to the chagrin of Jewish leaders. As Engel argues, it was Weichert's acquittal in January 1946 that prompted the CKŻP to revise its policy of leaving the punishment of putative Jewish collaborators to the Polish legal system and, in turn, to establish, with the approval of the Polish government, a Jewish tribunal or honor court for this purpose.[20]

Jewish honor courts were established in the immediate aftermath of the Holocaust in the Netherlands, in Jewish displaced persons' (DP) camps in the American zones of occupation in Germany and Italy, and in Poland. Although they varied somewhat from locale to locale, they were essentially administrative tribunals mandated by local Jewish communities to investigate Jews whose behavior under Nazi occupation was called into question, and to condemn and sanction those whose actions were deemed reproachable. They were all dismantled by 1950. Germane to this context were the trials of some thirty postwar immigrants, mostly from Eastern Europe, by Israeli courts from the 1950s until 1972 under Israel's 1950 Nazi and Nazi Collaborators Law.[21]

In October 1946, the CKŻP announced the establishment of an honor (or civic) court (*sąd społeczny* or *sąd obywatelski* in Polish, *birger-gerikht* or *eren-gerikht* in Yiddish), with its seat in Warsaw.[22] The court's mandate was

---

Weichert," in Sławomir Kapralski (ed.), *The Jews in Poland*, vol. 2 (Cracow: Judaica Foundation Center for Jewish Culture, 1999), 339–70, cite on 340.

18 See Gabriel N. Finder and Alexander V. Prusin, "Jewish Collaborators on Trial in Poland, 1944–1956," in Gabriel N. Finder et al. (eds.), *Making Holocaust Memory* (*Polin: Studies in Polish Jewry* 20 [2008]), 122–48.

19 Engel, "Who is a Collaborator?," 341.

20 Ibid., 361.

21 Trunk, *Judenrat*, 548–69; Gabriel N. Finder, "Honor Courts," in *YIVO Encyclopedia of Jews in Eastern Europe*, 1: 751–53.

22 More than a dozen judges served on the Honor Court during its three-year existence. A panel of five judges heard each case. Some judges came originally from Warsaw; the others hailed from various parts of Poland. That said, all judges on the Honor Court

to determine whether the conduct of Jews whose behavior during the Nazi occupation of Poland was called into question had indeed, in the language of Article 2 of the Honor Court's charter, failed to rise to the level of "comportment befitting a Jewish citizen, through membership or harmful activities in Jewish Councils, the Order Service, the administration of concentration camps or all other forms of collaboration with the occupier to the detriment of the [Jewish] community."[23] In the words of Marek Bitter, a representative of the communist Polish People's Party (Polska Partia Robotnicza, PPR) in the CKŻP, who introduced the motion to create the Honor Court, "the thought of cleansing the atmosphere [is] now ripe."[24] The immediate objective of the CKŻP in establishing the Honor Court was to prevent Jews tainted by collaboration from occupying influential posts in the reconstituted postwar Jewish community. According to the CKŻP's second annual report, the tasks of the Honor Court were "cleansing the Jewish community of people who for one reason or another collaborated with Nazi authorities during the occupation" and "unmasking traitors to the Jewish nation, who have tens and hundreds of victims on their conscience and still pass or want to pass for respectable people or want to play a certain role in the life of our community."[25] Although the charter did not require former members of Jewish Councils or the Order Service to submit petitions for rehabilitation in order to clear their names, the Honor Court encouraged such petitions.[26]

---

resided in Warsaw after the war, and like many Jews who were not originally from Warsaw, judges who came from other cities made it their home and became part of the city's reconstructed postwar Jewish population.

23 Centralny Komitet Żydów w Polsce, *Regulamin Sądu przy Centralnym Komitecie Żydów w Polsce*, Archiwum Żydowskiego Instytutu Historycznego (Archives of the Jewish Historical Institute, Warsaw, hereafter AŻIH), collection of the Central Committee of Polish Jews, hereafter CKŻP] 313/150, 4–10.

24 Protokól posiedznenia Prezydium (CKŻP), 8 October 1946, AŻIH/CKŻP, 313/3, 172; cited in Gabriel N. Finder, "The Trial of Shepsl Rotholc and the Politics of Retribution in the Aftermath of the Holocaust," *Gal-Ed* 20 (2006): 63–89 (English section), esp. 69.

25 Sprawozdanie z 2-letniej działalności C.K.Ż.P," prepared by J[oel] Lazebnik, n.d. [1947], Archiwum Akt Nowych (AAN), Polska Partia Robotnicza (PPR) 295/IX/408, 61 (Polish version); Barikht-referat vegn tsvey yor tetikeyt fun tsentral-komitet fun di yidn in poyln," prepared by Y[oel] Lazebnik, n.d. [1947], AŻIH/CKŻP, 303/27, 12–13; cited in Finder, "The Trial of Shepsl Rotholc," 69.

26 Article 13 of the charter empowered prosecutors, personnel in the Legal Bureau of the CKŻP who were attached to the Honor Court, to move the court to consider petitions for rehabilitation. An internal memorandum reflected the court's approach to this issue: "Every member of the [Jewish] community has the right to appeal to the court for

Between November 1946 and December 1949, the Legal Bureau (Wydział Prawny) of the CKŻP opened files on thirty-one suspected Jewish collaborators from Warsaw. As it turns out, there were more than twice as many files opened on Jews from the Warsaw Ghetto as on Jews from other ghettos or camps. By comparison, the lawyers assigned to the Honor Court opened files on only fifteen Jews from the Łódź Ghetto, the second largest ghetto after the Warsaw Ghetto. The overwhelming majority—twenty-three—of those investigated for their actions in the Warsaw Ghetto were ordinary men suspected of persecuting fellow Jews during their service in the ghetto police force. Three putative Gestapo informants, two agents in the "Thirteen," two supervisors of German shops located in the ghetto, and the owner of a factory who allegedly exploited Jewish workers were also investigated. Two of the suspects were women, both accused of being German informants. There were no investigations of members of the Warsaw Judenrat because none survived.[27]

Only three of these investigations led to a trial. For the rest, the Legal Bureau filed petitions to close roughly half the files owing to the lack of incriminating evidence to proceed to trial, and the Honor Court returned the files of four suspected collaborators to the Legal Bureau and the Jewish Historical Commission, the successor to the Central Jewish Historical Commission, for further investigation, while the remaining files were closed for technical reasons, usually because the suspect had died since the war, lived abroad and therefore beyond the reach of the Honor Court, or could not be located.

The Honor Court seems to have enjoyed the support of a broad cross-section of the postwar Jewish community in Poland, including the Jews of Warsaw. For example, for four days in November 1946 six hundred people crammed into the makeshift courtroom in the offices of the CKŻP to observe the first trial conducted in the Honor Court, the trial of Stanisław (Shepsl) Rotholc of Warsaw, a successful prewar boxer accused of excessively brutal behavior while serving in the ghetto police.[28] According to Shaye Shechatov, an alternate judge on the Honor Court who observed the trial from the gallery, many of its observers

---

rehabilitation." Tezy wpisane do księgi zasad Sądu Obywatelskiego przy C.K.Ż.P., AŻIH/ CKŻP, 313/150, 13.

27   Barbara Engelking compiled a list of thirty-one members of the Judenrat in Warsaw. Of these, she established that twenty-seven perished, with the fate of only four of its members unknown. Engelking and Leociak, *The Warsaw Ghetto*, 168–70.

28   Finder, "The Trial of Shepsl Rotholc," 75.

reacted emotionally to the proceedings. At one point, according to Shechatov, "those in attendance wanted to pounce on the defendant."[29]

Of the three trials of alleged collaborators from the Warsaw Ghetto held in the Honor Court, two, in particular, electrified the postwar Polish Jewish community in Warsaw: the trials of Shepsl Rotholc and of Wiera Gran, a popular prewar cabaret performer suspected of close ties with the Gestapo. Indeed, when the CKŻP announced its intention in October 1946 to bring putative collaborators to justice before an honor court, it identified only three by name, thereby signaling their singular importance to future prosecution efforts. Two of the three came from the Warsaw Ghetto: Rotholc and Gran. (The third was Michał Weichert from Kraków.) Moreover, both Rotholc and Gran were the objects of intense grassroots whispering campaigns among survivors.[30] Rotholc was convicted, although his sentence was eventually commuted; Gran was acquitted. The defendant in the third trial of an alleged collaborator from the Warsaw Ghetto was Abram Wolfowicz (Wolański), who, like Rotholc, was a former member of the Order Service. Like Rotholc, he was convicted, but his conviction was overturned on appeal.

Shepsl Rotholc (1912–1996) was a celebrated featherweight boxer in the 1930s who fought for the Jewish workers' club Gwiazda and the Polish national team. He became a Jewish folk hero and a symbol of Jewish pride. He joined the Order Service in 1941 and became a *grayek*—a policeman who profited from the smuggling of goods into the Warsaw Ghetto.[31] Anxious after the war to clear his name, he sent a written request for rehabilitation to the CKŻP's internal disciplinary interparty court, but since this court examined the conduct only of members of the committee's constituent parties, his request was redirected, apparently in October 1946, to the Central Committee's embryonic Honor Court.[32] Rotholc's indictment, prepared by the CKŻP's Legal Bureau, charged him with membership in the Warsaw Ghetto police from its formation in 1941 to the liquidation of the ghetto in April 1943. The indictment further accused Rotholc, while a policeman, of beating and terrorizing Jews in the

---

29   Shechatov, *Yorn fun kamf un gerangl*, 81. However, not all Jews supported the establishment of the Honor Court. Natan Gross, a survivor from Kraków who moved to Łódź after the war and directed important Yiddish-language films in immediate postwar Poland, called those who founded and participated in the Honor Court "zealous Jews." Letter to the author, 26 April 2000.

30   Finder, "The Trial of Shepsl Rotholc," 66–67; Agata Tuszyńska, *Oskarżona: Wiera Gran* (Kraków: Wydawnictwo Literackie, 2010), 147–71.

31   Finder, "The Trial of Shepsl Rotholc," 63–66; see also Diethelm Blecking, "Stanisław Rotholc," in *YIVO Encyclopedia of Jews in Eastern Europe*, 2: 1599.

32   Finder, "The Trial of Shepsl Rotholc," 67.

Warsaw Ghetto. In addition, the indictment declared that the Order Service was a collaborationist organization that had been detrimental to Jewish society.[33]

During his trial in November 1946, Rotholc insisted on his innocence. He claimed that he had joined the ghetto police so that he could provide for his family. He denied that he had ever beaten anyone or that he had been an active participant in deportations from the ghetto. But he did not rest his defense on a claim that he had merely gone through the motions with no intent to harm anyone. In fact, by his own account he had capitalized on the authority vested in policemen to rescue relatives and acquaintances from the Umschlagplatz. His judges viewed him in a vastly different light, however. Despite his protestations, his replies to their questions created an impression of a man who was morally evasive, self-serving, and vainglorious. In their eyes, the Nazi occupation had debased Rotholc, and his debasement had irrevocably impaired his capacity to grasp even now, after the war, the gravity of his choice to join and then to remain in the ghetto police after the trains started rolling to Treblinka.

The Honor Court's judges found Rotholc guilty under the terms of its charter. The judges accepted the testimony of witnesses for the prosecution who testified that Rotholc had beaten them, but, in the end, their testimony played virtually no role in the verdict. Moreover, while giving credence to prosecution witnesses who placed Rotholc in the midst of clearance operations during the Great Deportation, the court found that the evidence adduced at trial was insufficient to establish his exact role in it. It is not surprising that the judges denounced the Jewish police in scathing terms. But the formal and most formidable basis of Rotholc's conviction was not his membership in the Order Service per se but his continued service in it during the Great Deportation and after September 1942, "when the true objective of resettlement and the fate of his brothers were already clear to everyone and also to him." In effect, the Honor Court imputed to Rotholc knowledge of when he ought to have grasped

---

33   File of Shepsl Rotholc, Sąd Społeczny przy CKŻP, AŻIH/CKŻP, 313/109, 116; cited in Finder, "The Trial of Shepsl Rotholc," 75. The declaration that the Jewish police force in the ghetto was a collaborationist organization ran parallel to the practice of the Polish Supreme National Tribunal (Najwyższy Trybunał Narodowy, NTN), which was established specifically for the purpose of prosecuting major Nazi perpetrators. Rulings by the NTN declared entire groups criminal on the grounds that they had "acted in the interests of Nazi Germany." These groups included Ukrainian SS formations, the Ukrainian Insurgent Army, which was responsible for the brutal ethnic cleansing of Polish settlements in Volhynia and East Galicia, and the Selbstschutz, paramilitary police consisting of ethnic Germans. Alexander V. Prusin, "Poland's Nuremberg: The Seven Court Cases of the Supreme National Tribunal, 1946–1948," *Holocaust and Genocide Studies* 24.1 (2010): 1–25, esp. 5–6.

the Germans' genocidal intentions. The court justified the imputation of such knowledge to him on the grounds that his lengthy membership in a working-class Jewish sports club should have sensitized him to the plight of his fellow Jews and, by implication, motivated him to take up arms in the Jewish armed resistance. In the final analysis, the court ruled that it was clear that "policemen who remained at their posts after 5 September 1942 had delivered a contingent [of Jews for deportation] and thus directly cooperated as accomplices in the operation leading to the killing of Jews."

The Honor Court did pay lip service to extenuating circumstances in the defendant's favor—his limited intellectual capacity and the fact that he had applied to the CKŻP at his own initiative with a petition for consideration of his request for rehabilitation—but these played no role in the verdict or in sentencing. Indeed, the court failed to take into account evidence that Rotholc had smuggled his immediate family to the Aryan side or that he had risked his life to save his niece and the former manager of his sports club from the Umschlagplatz. Deciding that Rotholc no longer deserved an unrestricted place in postwar Jewish society, the Honor Court meted out the harshest sentence authorized by its charter, formally expelling Rotholc from the Jewish community for two years, revoking his right to participate in communal activities for three years, and ordering publication of his conviction in the Jewish press.[34] Sometime after his trial, Rotholc was taken into custody by the security services but was released shortly thereafter.[35]

Two years later, however, the Honor Court commuted Rotholc's sentence after the communist authorities offered athletes who had been disqualified from participation in sports for political reasons the possibility of reinstatement. The government agency responsible for sport reminded the CKŻP of Rotholc's importance to Polish sport and commended his remorseful behavior since his conviction in the Honor Court. Formally speaking, the Honor Court responded to Rotholc's lawyer's petition for commutation, which seems to have been coordinated with the authorities' indirect appeal to the court to reconsider its verdict. In his defense of Rotholc, the lawyer, Bolesław Kobryner, pointedly accused the court of making Rotholc a scapegoat in a patently unfair trial.[36]

Kobryner's assertion was not entirely without merit. Rotholc's conviction was, indeed, almost certainly a foregone conclusion. After all, the Honor Court

---

34   File of Shepsl Rotholc, Sąd Społeczny przy CKŻP, AŻIH/CKŻP, 313/109, 282–88; cited in Finder, "The Trial of Shepsl Rotholc," 84–85.
35   Blecking, "Stanisław Rotholc," 1599.
36   Finder, "The Trial of Shepsl Rotholc," 88–89.

was under pressure to censure Rotholc since he was the first defendant to stand trial before it; and it was important to the CKŻP, the court's patron, to make an example of him. Shaye Shechatov, an alternate judge on the Honor Court, who, it will be recalled, was not a member of the particular judicial panel that passed judgment on Rotholc, later ascribed the verdict and sentence partly to the pressure exerted by the large number of spectators who attended the trial and demanded revenge. Shechatov added that the judges who heard his case were torn by the facts of the case, in particular by evidence of general moral decline in the ghetto, thanks to which many Jews joined the Order Service— that is to say, Rotholc was no different from hundreds of others who shared his predicament. Moreover, the harshness of his punishment, which represented the maximum level of punishment permitted by the Honor Court's charter, left them feeling uneasy. As it turns out, then, irrespective of government pressure, the judges were inclined to commute Rotholc's sentence on their own.[37]

In any event, Rotholc's trial raised important questions of first impression: Who should be censured? What were the standards of culpability? Would the principle of personal responsibility prevail or would guilt by association be sufficient to convict? The judges who heard Rotholc's case provided preliminary answers to these questions. Members of the Order Service were clearly subject to censure. As far as former Jewish policemen were concerned, the standard of culpability to be applied seemed to be deontological, that is to say, based on the nature of a ghetto policeman's duty and obligation; thus the applicable standard was what a Jewish policeman, acting under the color of authority, should have done, knowing what one knew or ought to have known. But guilt by mere association—in this case, mere membership in the Order Service—was not sufficient to convict. It is further noteworthy that in its ruling the Honor Court intimated that in future cases of Jewish policemen it would be inclined to make distinctions between those who abandoned their posts between the end of July and the beginning of August 1942, before the completion of the Great Deportation of Jews from Warsaw to Treblinka, and those who remained at their posts even after it was concluded.

Wiera Gran (1916–2007) was a popular prewar singer in Warsaw's cabarets. From the spring of 1941 to the spring of 1942 she appeared in the Sztuka café in the Warsaw Ghetto. During the Great Deportation she fled from the ghetto to the outskirts of Warsaw, where she survived in hiding. Already during the war she was suspected of revealing to the Gestapo the identities and locations of Jews in hiding, due to her evidently close ties to Jewish Gestapo agents in the ghetto, among the members of the "Thirteen." The procurator's office attached

---

37   Shechatov, *Yorn fun kamf un gerangl*, 79–81.

to the special state courts established to try suspected collaborators dismissed her case in late 1945 due to the absence of any indication of the commission of a crime. The Union of Professional Musicians cleared her name in early 1946 and restored her professional rights to appear on stage again. But rumors in the Jewish community about her suspected links to the Gestapo persisted, and the CKŻP's Legal Bureau launched an investigation of her in the fall of 1946, shortly after the establishment of the Honor Court. She gave a statement to the Legal Bureau's prosecutor in which she protested her innocence, but to no avail. After she was indicted in August 1947, she steadfastly refused to cooperate further with the Honor Court. The indictment accused Gran rather vaguely of having "collegial relations with individuals who were evident Gestapo agents, thereby committing a foreseeable criminal act" in violation of the Honor Court's charter. The indictment referred to the testimony of several witnesses in support of its allegation. It further alleged that Gran, after finding refuge on the Aryan side, continued to associate with known Gestapo agents, insinuating that they offered her protection, enabling her to walk freely on the streets in spite of the fact that she was a well-known artist and had typically Jewish facial features.[38]

Gran's trial opened in October 1947. Partly because of the large number of witnesses for both the prosecution and the defense, and partly because prosecutors made repeated efforts to pressure Gran to testify, the trial lasted until January 1949. She testified briefly on the last day of the trial, admitting that suspected Gestapo agents attended her performances but denying any contacts otherwise with them.[39]

The Honor Court decided "that the acts of which she was accused had not been proven and to acquit her of the charges leveled against her" (*że zarzucone Wierze Gran czyny nie zostały udowodnione i z postawionych jej zarzutów uniewinnić*). The court found that the testimony of key prosecution witnesses that she had been a Gestapo informant was based mostly on hearsay and therefore unreliable. It also deemed important the absence of Gran's name from any state-sponsored lists of collaborators or underground publications denouncing collaborators. A large part of the verdict was devoted, however, to an assessment of Jewish life in the Warsaw Ghetto. The court took note of the step-by-step nature of the extermination of Polish Jewry, annihilation in the gas chambers preceded in all ghettos in general and in the Warsaw Ghetto in particular by the "material and moral destruction of the Jewish people." According to the court, this process entailed the establishment of not only the Judenrat and the Jewish Order Service but also the recruitment of "the worst

---

38   File of Wiera Gran, Sąd Społeczny przy CKŻP, AŻIH/CKŻP, 313/36, 83.
39   Ibid., 301.

elements" in Jewish society in the service of the Gestapo. Many of these elements, the court averred, came from artistic circles that performed in cafés that were frequented by known Jewish spies for the Gestapo. Gran, a member of these circles, "by entering the café 'Sztuka,' had social contacts with individuals in the service of the Gestapo." By her own account, Gran even attended a party hosted by the Jewish Gestapo agent Szymanowicz, and in the company of another suspected Gestapo agent, a female dancer, visited nightclubs. Although there was no solid evidence of her own cooperation with the Gestapo, such incidents were sufficient "to cast an unfavorable shadow on Gran and became the source of unsubstantiated accusations." The Honor Court was constrained from seeing in such contacts criminal liability per se, but it did consider them a "serious matter." In this vein, it openly lamented in its verdict the existence of the Judenrat, the Order Service, and Gestapo agents in the ghetto, which comprised "a separate tragic chapter in the martyrdom of Jewish ghettos."[40]

The third trial in the Honor Court of a resident of the Warsaw Ghetto was the trial of Abram Wolfowicz (b. 1917). In his reminiscences more than three decades after the end of the war, Yitzhak Zuckerman recalled Wolfowicz as follows: "There was one Jewish policeman named Abraham Wolfowicz (there were two brothers with that name who were known for their cruelty) who was brought to me right after the war. His defense was that he wanted to save his mother. But he didn't."[41] Immediately after the war, Wolfowicz produced attestations from the Union of Participants in the Armed Struggle for Independence and Democracy (Związek Uczestników Walki Zbrojnej o Niepodległość i Demokrację), the communist association of Polish veterans, and the main board of "Maawak" (Zarząd Główny "Maawak"), the association of Jewish veterans associated with the Zionist party Ichud in Poland, that he had participated in the Warsaw Uprising. He was nonetheless indicted in the Honor Court in the spring of 1948. The indictment did not specify any questionable deeds on Wolfowicz's part; rather, the core accusation of the indictment was his membership in the Order Service until the beginning of June 1942, although the indictment noted the lack of any evidence that he took part in the Great Deportation from 22 July to 6 September 1942. The indictment noted,

---

40   Ibid., 308–15. Although Gran was cleared by the Polish authorities and acquitted by the Honor Court, her reputation in the Jewish world both in and outside Poland never recovered from the accusations that she was a collaborator. Tuszyńska, *Oskarżona: Wiera Gran*, 321–85.

41   Zuckerman, *A Surplus of Memory*, 208–9.

moreover, his failure to request rehabilitation after the war.⁴² This charge was reminiscent of the deontological standard applied to Rotholc in justification of his conviction in the Honor Court. However, when Rotholc was indicted (and subsequently convicted), this deontological standard applied from the Great Deportation onward, whereas in Wolfowicz's case the prosecution sought to apply it even prior to the commencement of the 1942 deportation.

In comparison with the trials of Rotholc and Gran, Wolfowicz's trial in May 1948 was unremarkable. By his own account, Wolfowicz donned the cap of the Order Service on the instructions of the communist underground because it afforded him the opportunity to move freely within the ghetto and to enter the Aryan side, which he used to establish contact with the communist underground and save several people from deportation, including his mother, whom he moved to the Aryan side before he himself fled there. But he otherwise merely went through the motions and never participated in the roundup of Jews. Witnesses testified that they saw him wear the cap of a Jewish policeman in the ghetto, but no one saw him take part in roundups or act brutally. In its verdict, the Honor Court made note of the fact that Wolfowicz, acting under the color of the authority vested in him as a ghetto policeman, had rescued two girls from deportation and then his mother and hadn't exploited his position in the Order Service, that there was no evidence that he had taken part in the Great Deportation, and that he had acted bravely in the Warsaw Uprising. The Honor Court nonetheless convicted him of membership in the Order Service, ruling that "at a critical time, he was a member of the Order Service and wore the dishonorable and unbefitting cap of the [Jewish] militia." His punishment was a formal rebuke (*upomnienie*), the least severe sanction authorized by the Honor Court's charter, but a sanction nonetheless.⁴³ Wolfowicz's attorney appealed the verdict, emphasizing the court's favorable assessment of his client's actual behavior in the ghetto. It should be noted that, unlike Rotholc's case, there is no evidence in Wolfowicz's file of any outside intervention in his case. Upon the recommendation of the prosecution, in January 1949 the Honor Court accepted Wolfowicz's appeal and overturned his conviction without comment.⁴⁴ The ruling on appeal indicates that two years after its judgment in Rotholc's case and eight months after its initial verdict in Wolfowicz's case, the Honor Court and the lawyers from the CKŻP's Legal Bureau now had second thoughts, at least in the cases of ghetto policemen, about applying a strict

---

42 File of Abram Wolfowicz (Zdenek Wolański), Sąd Społeczny przy CKŻP, AŻIH/CKŻP, 313/137, 99.
43 Ibid., 116–17.
44 Ibid., 137.

deontological standard without serious consideration of what those under suspicion for collaboration actually did and did not do.

The fifteen files closed on grounds of insufficient evidence to proceed to trial are in and of themselves instructive indicators of the court's evolving standards of wartime accountability. Take, for example, the cases of Józef Teszner and Jerzy Lewiński, respectively. To clear his name, which was under attack, Józef Teszner, the director of the secretariat of the Central Committee of Polish Jews, submitted a petition of rehabilitation to the Honor Court shortly after its creation. Teszner had been employed in the administration first of the Warsaw Judenrat and then the Order Service, but by his own account his employment in both institutions had been strictly administrative and he had never participated in any field operations. He gave a statement on his own behalf and more than half a dozen former inhabitants of the Warsaw Ghetto gave statements that supported his claim. On the recommendation of the prosecutors, the Honor Court decided in February 1948 to close his file owing to the lack of any evidence that he had acted to the detriment of the Jewish people.[45]

Lewiński, who, it will be recalled, was interviewed by Ewa Koźmińska-Frejlak in 2004, was a lawyer and activist in the Polish Socialist Party (Polska Partia Socjalisticzna, PPS) who increasingly favored Zionism before the war. He joined the Order Service in the Warsaw Ghetto and remained in it through September 1942, after which he escaped from the ghetto. He claimed that he was in contact with the Socialist underground during the war. After the war he served as a prosecutor in Łódź. He was appointed prosecutor by the Minister of Justice in the war crimes trials of Hans Biebow, administrator of the Łódź Ghetto, and Walter Pelzhausen, commandant of the Radogoszcz prison. From 1947 to 1948, Lewiński was president of the Main Board of the Trade Union of Court Employees. From 1948 he was a member of the Polish United Workers' Party (Polska Zjednoczona Partia Rabotnicza, PZPR)—the ruling Communist Party. Upon his own application for rehabilitation, he was investigated by the Central Party Court of the Polish Socialist Party in 1948. The party court found that Lewiński did not participate in the deportation of Jews in the summer of 1942 and that, although he benefited materially from his membership in the Order Service, he had also distributed underground publications in the ghetto, helped organize shelter for homeless children in the ghetto, and, particularly after 22 July 1942, the beginning of the Great Deportation, protected those threatened by deportation. Although, in the party court's opinion, Lewiński had made a political mistake by joining the Order Service and staying in it without an order from the underground until September 1942,

---

45   File of Jozef Tezner, Sąd Społeczny przy CKŻP, AŻIH/CKŻP, 313/130, 21, 24.

his positive deeds deserved consideration, as did his faultless attitude as a citizen. The party court ordered that Lewiński should resign from posts held in and on behalf of the party while submitting to party disciplinary measures, including self-critique. In spite of the favorable adjudication of his case in the Central Party Court, to Lewiński's chagrin the CKŻP's lawyers decided to investigate him.[46]

After questioning several witnesses who testified in Lewiński's favor, in December 1949 the CKŻP's prosecuting attorney moved the Honor Court to close his file, repeating more or less the reasoning of the PPS Central Party Court. In this case, however, the prosecution went so far as to cast doubt on a statement by Marek Edelman, famed commander in the Warsaw Ghetto Uprising, who stated that he had seen Lewiński in the ghetto during the deportation operation of the summer of 1942. The prosecuting attorney observed that Edelman did not have precise information about Lewiński's actions during this time and that, under questioning in November 1949 in the trial of Weichert, Edelman had testified that he could not remember Lewiński's conduct during the Great Deportation. In the conclusion to his motion to the Honor Court, the prosecutor maintained that since it ensued from the witness statements that Lewiński did not take part in the Great Deportation, there was no basis for an indictment against him.[47] In other words, parallel with the ruling of the Central Party Court, in this case the CKŻP's lawyers, with the blessing of the Honor Court, genuinely took into account mitigating circumstances even when the suspect continued to serve in the Order Service over the course of the Great Deportation until September 1942. In Rotholc's trial, by contrast, which had taken place three years earlier, the Honor Court had paid mere lip service to the significance of mitigating circumstances in favor of the defendant.

In sum, in the cases of Rotholc and Gran, there was intense pressure coming from the Jewish leadership and the Jewish public on the CKŻP's lawyers to indict and on the Honor Court's judges to convict. A conviction in Rotholc's case was predictable, but the judges harbored reservations. Subsequent pressure by the regime led to the commutation of Rotholc's sentence, but the opportunity to revise the sentence was in line with the judges' own second thoughts. A conviction in Gran's case was to be expected, yet she was acquitted. The indictment of Wolfowicz was probably unwarranted; the overturning of Wolfowicz's conviction and light sentence on appeal was consonant with the court's evolving approach to cases of policemen who seemed to be guilty,

---

46 File of Jerzy Lewiński, Sąd Społeczny przy CKŻP, AŻIH/CKŻP, 313/65, 34–38, 43. See also Koźmińska-Frejlak, "Świadectwo milczenia," 246–49.

47 File of Jerzy Lewiński, 50–51.

at most, of going through the motions. The lawyers' decisions to forego indictments of Teszner and Lewiński point to their growing demand for tangible evidence of collaboration, even under the open-ended standards of the Honor Court's charter, even if this did not coincide with popular communal notions of accountability.

In the final analysis, of the thirty-one individuals suspected of collaboration in the Warsaw Ghetto, only two were convicted, and the conviction of one was eventually nullified, while the sentence of the other was subsequently modified. If their assessment of Jewish behavior in the Warsaw Ghetto, which represented a kind of moral bellwether, since the Warsaw Jewish community had been the standard bearer of Polish Jewry until its destruction, is any indication, the CKŻP's Legal Bureau and Honor Court acted with a fair degree of moderation after Rotholc's trial in 1946 to the end of 1949, when the court was dismantled. (The exception to this trend was the high-profile case of Weichert in December 1949 for his activities in Kraków).[48] For the most part, with the partial exception of Rotholc's trial—partial because they succumbed to intense pressure to convict him but not without enunciating reasonable rules for making distinctions between defendants in future cases—the judges approached their mandate in earnest and took pains to distinguish between questionable and unsavory behavior in the Warsaw Ghetto on the one hand and reproachable and intolerable behavior on the other.

It seems fair to say, therefore, that the cases from the Warsaw Ghetto show that sometime not too long after the establishment of the Honor Court, the lawyers from the CKŻP who were assigned to it and the judges who served on it became increasingly convinced of the existence of a middle ground, to borrow from Jan Gross's finely grained study of collaboration, "situated between collaboration and resistance," that they needed to take into account "in order to make better sense of the experience of war and occupation in twentieth-century Europe."[49] Gross suggests that terms suitable to describe this middle ground are cooperation, collusion, compliance, and complicity.[50] The open-ended quality of its charter notwithstanding, the Honor Court generally, though not always, construed collaboration as meaning complicity and only complicity.

---

48 On Weichert's trial, see Engel, "Who is a Collaborator?," 361–68.
49 Jan T. Gross, "Themes for a Social History of War Experience and Collaboration," in István Deák, Jan T. Gross, and Tony Judt (eds.), *The Politics of Retribution in Europe: World War II and Its Aftermath* (Princeton, NJ: Princeton University Press, 2000), 31.
50 Ibid., 35 n. 49.

This approach did not square with the policy of the court's architects, the Jewish leadership in postwar Poland, which by the end of 1948 was in the hands of Jewish communists. During a meeting in 1948 with the secretariat of the Honor Court, CKŻP officials upbraided the judges for their conciliatory approach. Hersh Smolar, a doctrinaire communist who would eventually take over the chairmanship of the CKŻP, complained that ever since Rotholc's trial the court had been following "the wrong path," that the "civic character of the court was being lost," and that the court was assuming the character of a state court, "guided by legal norms instead of civic ones." At the same meeting, Marek Bitter, who had played an important role in founding the Honor Court, expressed his own frustration with its direction, insisting that it "must be a civic institution."[51] In other words, the court's application, in Bitter's view, of more or less formal legal standards was out of tune with the intentions of its patrons in the Jewish leadership.

On the one hand, a consensus had formed within Poland's postwar Jewish leadership, which by this time, late 1948, was dominated by communists, that an administrative purge of collaborators from within the ranks of the surviving Jewish community was imperative. On the other hand, the judges on the Honor Court and even the lawyers assigned to it took seriously—indeed, too seriously for the likes of Smolar and Bitter—the agonizing task of identifying internal enemies with a degree of due process and resisted the pressure of the court's patrons in the CKŻP to force the evidence into a Procrustean bed of political and moral assumptions. To be sure, the Honor Court conducted what were fundamentally political trials, but it did not, apart from rare exceptions, operate under the assumption that the end justified the means—this to the consternation of the communist-led CKŻP.[52]

The chagrin of Jewish communists in the leadership of the CKŻP is not surprising. Unlike the tendency by 1948 in many countries in Western and Eastern Europe to bring the trials of Nazi perpetrators and collaborators to an end and to offer them amnesty in an effort to gain their implicit support for postwar regimes, the prosecution of Nazi persecutors and collaborators in Poland did not abate until much later. "In fact," writes historian Alexander Prusin, "among the former Soviet satellites, Poland was the most consistent in investigating and prosecuting war crimes: between 1944 and 1985, Polish courts tried more than 20,000 defendants, including 5,450 German nationals."[53] To put it another

---

51 Protokół posiedzenia Prezydium CKŻP y Prezydium Sądu Społecznego, 3 March 1948, AŻIH/CKŻP, 303/9, 129–30; cited in Finder, "The Trial of Shepsl Rotholc," 87–88.
52 Ibid., 88.
53 Prusin, "Poland's Nuremberg," 1.

way, some 14,000 Polish citizens faced charges for convictions during this time period. In this context, Smolar and Bitter's expressions of dissatisfaction with the modus operandi of the Jewish Honor Court and their promotion of the wholesale administrative purge of collaborators from within the Jewish community help bring home an important point: given the spirit of the times, the second half of the 1940s in communist Eastern Europe in general and in Poland in particular, one might be excused for expecting to find the uncompromising application among Jews, embittered as they were by the questionable behavior of their wartime leaders and functionaries, of a draconian standard that reflected communist bias towards putative Jewish collaborators.

However, the cases tried in the Jewish Honor Court of putative collaborators in general and of Warsaw Jews in particular defied these expectations. The Honor Court did not operate like Polish courts sitting in judgment over defendants accused of collaboration whose real offense was their opposition or perceived threat to the regime.[54] The Honor Court did not conduct "show trials" in this sense. By contrast, within broad limits it considered each case more or less on its merits and acted with a fair degree of integrity, managing to resist internal pressure coming from ordinary survivors as well as from the postwar Jewish leadership.

At first glance, it seems paradoxical that while Jewish communist leaders were demanding that the Honor Court convict putative Jewish collaborators, Polish Communist Party officials were loath, except in rare cases, to exercise pressure on the Honor Court. After all, Jewish communists took their cues from the party, and one might expect that the party, which consolidated its hold on power after the parliamentary elections in 1947, just as the Honor Court was shifting into high gear, would desire to see suspected Jewish collaborators punished and neutralized no differently from ethnic Poles accused, justly or wrongly, of collaboration. But, in fact, the regime took only minimal interest in the pursuit of alleged Jewish collaborators. In its own hunt for collaborators, the regime was mainly concerned with the neutralization of real and potential political enemies who might challenge its dubious authority to rule the country.

The CKŻP operated under a different sort of political pressure. In the evolving collective memory of postwar Polish Jewry, all Polish Jews had acted with dignity in their struggle for their very existence, a substantial proportion of them had taken various measures short of combat to thwart the Nazis' genocidal campaign, and a significant number of them had taken up arms against

---

54   On Polish postwar political trials, see Jerzy Poksiński, *"My sędziowie, nie od Boga…" Z dziejów Sądownictwa Wojskowego PRL 1944–1956* (Warszawa: Gryf, 1996).

the German enemy. Not only Jewish leaders but also the Jewish man in the street put great stock in the promotion of this stereotype, which, they reckoned, would legitimize the claim of Jews who chose to remain in the country to a stake in the promised new postwar Polish society. However, the effort to refashion Jewish reality in Poland after the Holocaust on the basis of this stereotype could not be completely insulated from the vexing challenge of Jewish accommodation and even collaboration during the war. Although so-called "traitors to the nation" comprised only a tiny fraction of the Jewish population, their continued presence constituted a source of vexation and embarrassment to all Polish Jews, but especially to the Jewish leadership, which felt obliged to prove its antifascist credentials to Communist Party officials and, as a result, pressured the Honor Court to stigmatize putative collaborators and declare them persona non grata.

Ironically, the party did not really care very much what the Honor Court did or, for that matter, about Jewish collaborators, as they posed no threat to the regime. They may have been major criminals in the eyes of Jewish leaders, but from the vantage point of the communist authorities they were insignificant and barely worthy of their attention.[55] The regime's indifference to the pursuit and punishment of Jewish collaborators testifies to the marginalization of Jewish communist leaders in the evolving political system. They were increasingly restricted to their specific fields of action, where they exercised a certain degree of autonomy, but when push came to shove, their actual power, even in the Jewish sector, was limited owing to the party's indifference to their concerns.[56]

As a result, the Honor Court, including both its judges and the lawyers assigned to it, assumed the appearance of a somewhat subversive institution—subversive because its members undermined, probably unconsciously, the Jewish leadership in its efforts to promote precisely the "Jewish stereotype ... that all Jews exhibited high moral standards in the darkest hour," as Antony Polonksy and Monika Adamczyk-Garbowska put it, a stereotype these two eminent scholars deem "in part the product of dismay at the absence of large-scale resistance."[57] Without a doubt, this stereotype was largely inspired

---

55   Finder and Prusin, "Jewish Collaborators on Trial in Poland," 146–48.
56   See Natalia Aleksiun, "The Vicious Circle: Jews in Communist Poland, 1944–1956," in Ezra Mendelsohn, (ed.), *Jews and the State: Dangerous Alliances and the Perils of Privilege* (*Studies in Contemporary Jewry* 19 [2003]), 157–80.
57   "Introduction," in Antony Polonsky and Monika Adamczyk-Garbowska (eds.), *Contemporary Jewish Writing in Poland: An Anthology* (Lincoln, NB: University of Nebraska Press, 2000), xxvi.

by events in the Warsaw Ghetto. However, the Honor Court's lawyers and judges, for their part, acknowledged at least implicitly that many Jews in the Warsaw Ghetto and elsewhere were degraded by the Nazi occupation; that, as Yitzhak Zuckerman put it, "there are hints of a moral decline in the [Warsaw] ghetto," which ensued from "hunger, epidemics, and oppression," as well as "instances of moral dignity."[58] As a result, it became incumbent on the CKŻP's lawyers and the judges on the Honor Court to distinguish misguided—even deeply misguided—men and women from profoundly bad ones, to distinguish accomplices from instigators.

Unfortunately, there are no statements in the archival record that clarify the reasons that these lawyers and judges increasingly adopted a conciliatory approach. I would hazard one possible explanation. The process embodied by the Honor Court was not just about avenging the past but also about creating a space for Jews in a future Poland. Postwar Polish Jewry was a community that was well aware of its own attenuation, if not potential disappearance. During this liminal and critical period, the second half of the 1940s, in which any sustainable future for Polish Jewry hung in the balance, an honest exhumation of the behavior of the Jewish community's members under Nazi occupation was imperative to its emotional viability in the future. But a reckoning with the past did not necessarily entail committing communal suicide. The personnel of the Honor Court seem to have intuited the potential implications of a draconian approach to its task—pitting Jews against Jews—and thus to have rejected it in favor of a conciliatory approach that, alongside cleansing the Jewish community of its worst elements, aspired to preserve more or less of what remained of the community after the devastation wrought by the Holocaust in Warsaw and elsewhere in Poland.

---

58   Zuckerman, *A Surplus of Memory*, 277.

CHAPTER 22

The End of a Jewish Metropolis? The Ambivalence of Reconstruction in the Aftermath of the Holocaust

David Engel

To think of Warsaw as a Jewish metropolis in the wake of the city's thorough destruction and the annihilation of its Jewish community by German hands between 1942 and 1944 is to defy both intuition and common wisdom. In 1945, the Jewish Warsaw that has been the subject of this conference—the Warsaw that was, as the conference organizers put it in their initial prospectus, the 'locus of a Jewish knowledge explosion' in the nineteenth and early twentieth centuries; a 'center of editing and publishing' for Jews in Poland and beyond; a primary focus of Jewish economic activity; the home of a 'dynamic [Jewish] religious life' alongside modern Jewish mass political movements and a plethora of 'voluntary associations in the spheres of philanthropy, education, social life, entertainment, and culture'; and a 'target and starting point of migrations'—lay buried deep beneath the rubble of the former ghetto, with what virtually all observers regarded as a scant prospect for even a partial revival. Such appears to have been the unanimous view of the handful of foreign Jewish journalists and emissaries from abroad who traveled to the city during 1945 and 1946 and recorded their observations in print. S. L. Schneidermann, Henryk Szoszkies, Jacob Pat, Moshe Yishai, Shimon Samet, Ya'akov Zerubavel—all described their visit to Poland's capital as an encounter with the dead.[1] Their descriptions of those encounters, moreover, educed hardly any sense of Warsaw Jewry's former vitality. As these reporters walked through what remained of the streets of the former ghetto, they imagined the battles that a handful of Jewish fighters had waged against their would-be

1 S.L. Shneiderman, *Tsvishn shrek un hofenung* (Buenos Aires: Tsentral-Farband fun poylishe yidn in Argentine, 1947), 47–89; Henryk Szoszkies, *Poyln 1946* (Buenos Aires: Tsentral-Farband fun poylishe yidn in Argentine, 1946), 72–81; Jacob Pat, *Ash un fayer (Iber di khurves fun poyln)* (New York: Tsikho 1946), 7–19; Moshe Yishai, *B'tsel ha-sho'ah: rishmei shelihut be'polin* (Israel: Lohamei ha-geta'ot, 1973), 30–37; Shimon Samet, *B'vo'i lemohorat: masa be'polin* (Tel Aviv: T. Leynman, 1946), 243–44; Ya'akov Zerubavel, *Barg hurbn: kapitlen poyln* (Buenos Aires: Tsentral-Farband fun poylishe yidn in Argentine, 1946), 35–53.

murderers: it was the deeds of the few who had died with weapons in hand that the name 'Warsaw' evoked in their accounts, not the shops of the Nalewki, the Great Synagogue on Tłomackie Street, the Orgelbrand Press, the Instytut Nauk Judaistycznych, the *Yidisher kunst-teatr*, or the offices of *Haynt* and *Der moment*. That representation contrasted sharply with their depictions of other features of the postwar Polish Jewish scene. Whereas efforts to revive Jewish communities in Łódz and Kraków, to establish a new Jewish center in Lower Silesia, and to reconstruct the foundations of Jewish society under the so-called people's regime figured in their reportage as proof of Polish Jewry's indomitable spirit and unshakable determination to rise from the ashes, Warsaw took on the exclusive image of a memorial site for the recent catastrophe—hardly one befitting a metropole, Jewish or other.

And yet, it seems that, for a brief moment following the end of the Second World War, the possibility that Warsaw might actually emerge from the catastrophe as the demographic, institutional, and cultural heart of a reborn Polish Jewry could not be dismissed out of hand. Numbers tell part of the story. To be sure, the available population estimates for the period in question vary widely, and their reliability is by no means assured. Nevertheless, rough estimates are possible, and certain broad trends can be discerned.

To begin with, it appears fairly certain that more Jews emerged from hiding in Warsaw than in any other Polish city or town. Perhaps a quarter, maybe even a third of all Jews who survived the war on Polish soil did so in the Polish capital.[2] It is not difficult to imagine why such should have been the case. Most obviously, there was a far greater pool of potential survivors there than anywhere else. On the eve of Operation Reinhard, fully 25 percent of the Jewish population in the entire Generalgouvernement was confined in the Warsaw ghetto. More than twice as many Jews lived there as in the second-largest ghetto on Polish soil, Łódz, which was located in territory annexed to the Reich.[3] Moreover, although initial opportunities for hiding on the Aryan side were not necessarily greater there than in certain other urban ghettos, longterm survival prospects for Warsaw Jews benefited from the proximity of a ramified

---

2 On the number of Jews who survived on Polish soil, see David Engel, *Bein shihrur li-verihah: nitsolei ha-sho'ah be'polin veha-ma'avak al hanhagatam* (Tel Aviv: Am Oved, 1996), 39–40, 154–55. On the number who survived in Warsaw, see Gunnar S. Paulsson, *Secret City: The Hidden Jews of Warsaw 1940–1945* (New Haven: Yale University Press, 2002), 210–30.

3 Yisrael Gutman, *Yehudei varshah 1939–1943: geto, mahteret, mered* (Tel Aviv: Sifri'at po'alim, 1977), 79–80; Ruta Sakowska, *Ludzie z dzielnicy zamkniętej* (Warsaw: PWN, 1993), 28–33; Lea Preiss, "Pelitim be'mirkam ha-hayim ha-yehudi'im ba'ir varshah u'va-geto" (unpublished PhD dissertation, Hebrew University of Jerusalem, 2006), 31–115.

underground support network. For example, *Żegota*, the clandestine Council for Aid to Jews affiliated with the Polish government-in-exile's representation in the occupied homeland and two Jewish underground political formations, served by its own estimates at least five times more Jews in hiding in Warsaw than in Kraków, its secondary locus of operations.[4] It stands to reason, therefore, that Warsaw should have been the initial demographic center of the remnants of Polish Jewry following liberation.

And indeed, there are signs that during the winter and spring of 1945 a significant number of Jews—significant, at least, in relation to the total number of identifiable Jews living on Polish soil at the time—made the effort to rebuild both their individual lives and their central collective institutions in the Polish capital. In February, the Central Committee of Polish Jews transferred its base of operations from Lublin to Warsaw, ensconcing itself in a building on Szeroka Street in Praga that had served before the war as a Jewish community center and *mikveh*. At the same time, Committee personnel observed that 'every day new groups of Jews liberated from the concentration camps arrive in Warsaw,' even though 'there is simply no place for them to rest their heads.'[5] In early June, the Committee noted that the number of such returnees to Warsaw was 3,000, nearly 18 percent of the 16,900 returnees who had registered with various provincial and local Jewish committees during the previous three months.[6] That percentage comported roughly with the general distribution of Jews throughout Poland at the time. According to Central Committee figures, 7,111 out of the 55,519 Jews who had registered with local or provincial Jewish committees by August 1945 had done so in Warsaw.[7] These figures suggest that, at the time, nearly 13 percent of Polish Jews had sought residence in the capital—a higher proportion than the approximately 11 percent who had lived there before the war. In fact, in a strictly demographic sense, Warsaw's position among Jews in postwar Poland was comparable to or greater than the current status of many indisputable world metropoles in relation to the

---

4 Paulsson, *Secret City*, 3; Teresa Prekerowa, *Konspiracyjna Rada Pomocy Żydom w Warszawie 1942–1945* (Warsaw: Państwowy Instytut Wydawniczy, 1981), 305–22; Yisrael Gutman and Shmuel Krakowski, *Unequal Victims: Poles and Jews during World War II* (New York: Holocaust Library, 1986), 265–66.

5 Jonas Turkow, *Nokh der bafrayung* (Buenos Aires: Tsentral-Farband fun poylishe yidn in Argentine, 1958), 185–86.

6 "Protokół z posiedzenia w sprawie pomocy dla powracających z Niemiec z dnia 2.VI.1945r." Microfilm copy in Information Center of the Interuniversity Project for the Study of Illegal Jewish Immigration to Palestine, Tel Aviv (henceforth IC), record group 35, reel 22.

7 Lucjan Dobroszycki, *Survivors of the Holocaust in Poland: A Portrait Based on Jewish Community Records 1944–1947* (New York: M. E. Sharpe, 1994), 74–75.

populations of their countries. Prague, for example, is home today to about 12 percent of residents of the Czech Republic, Greater London to a similar percentage in the United Kingdom, Tokyo to 10 percent of Japanese, Lima to 9 percent of Peruvians, Johannesburg to 8 percent of South Africans, and Paris to only slightly more than 3 percent of Frenchmen.

Still, these early figures notwithstanding, Warsaw did not maintain its position as even a local metropolis for postwar Polish Jews, even though Jews were clearly among those former capital residents whom the new regime, intent on reconstructing the *Polish* metropolis, celebrated for their determination to 'return to the desolate ruins of the city' because 'life without Warsaw was unthinkable' for them.[8] What eventually undermined Warsaw's position as a *Jewish* metropolis was the rapid rise of other urban concentrations—first in Łódź, then in Dzierżoniów, Wałbrzych, and Wrocław, all of whose Jewish communities exceeded that of Warsaw in size. Łódź, for which, in contrast to Warsaw, fairly reliable month-to-month statistics are available virtually from the moment of liberation, appears to have overtaken Warsaw as the site of the largest settlement of Holocaust survivors in Poland by February or, at latest, March, 1945. By June, its Jewish population was perhaps triple that of the capital, surpassing 20,000.[9] By the middle of the following year the number grew to more than 50,000, while over the same interval Warsaw's Jewish population appears to have remained fairly steady, with movement into the city from the surrounding province more or less offset by emigration or relocation within Poland.[10] That interval also witnessed the rapid growth of the Lower Silesian Jewish centers, thanks mainly to the arrival of repatriants from the Soviet Union. In July 1946, Wrocław reported a Jewish population of nearly 18,000, with another 13,000 in Dzierżoniów and 9,000 in Wałbrzych (all within 60 kilometers of one another).[11] These communities also supplanted Warsaw as the chief sites of Jewish cultural production. Łódź was home to the country's most widely-circulated Jewish newspaper, *Dos naje lebn*, as well as to the Central Jewish Historical Commission, a Yiddish-language film production company,

---

8   Bolesław Bierut, *Sześcioletni plan odbudowy Warszawy: Szatę graficzną, wykresy plany i perspektywy opracowano na podstawie materiałów i projektów Biura Urbanistycznego Warszawy* (Warsaw: Książka i Wiedza, 1949), plate 14.

9   Wojewódzki Komitet Żydowski w Łodzi, Wydział Ewidencji i Ruchu Ludności, "Sprawozdanie za okres od dnia 1 stycznia do 30 czerwca 1945 r.," IC 35/17.

10   Wojewódzki Komitet Żydowski w Łodzi, Wydział Statystyczny, "Ruch ludności żydowskiej, miesiąc lipiec 1946 r.," IC 35/17; Centralny Komitet Żydów Polskich, Komitet w W-ie, "Ruch ludności żydowskiej, lipiec 1946," IC 35/19.

11   Wojewódzki Komitet Żydowski na Dolny Śląsk, "Liczba ludności żydowski, miesiąc lipiec 1946 r.," IC 35/21.

and the country's largest Jewish publishing house and professional Jewish theatre company. It was the place to which Poland's postwar Jewish intelligentsia and artistic elite gravitated.[12] In Lower Silesia, so-called Jewish culture houses quickly obtained a reputation as venues where Jewish artists could find a regular sympathetic audience, turning Wrocław and the surrounding communities into magnets for Jewish actors, dancers, and musicians. The availability and artistic level of Jewish cultural activity in Dzierżoniów, reported Jacob Pat in early 1946, had no parallel in any other Polish city, including Warsaw.[13]

What accounts for Warsaw's eclipse? Should the geographical redistribution of Poland's postwar Jewish population that turned Warsaw into, at most, the fifth-largest Jewish community in the country by the second half of 1946 be understood primarily as a more-or-less instinctive, unprompted response by Holocaust survivors and repatriants to variations in objective material conditions in different towns and regions—what the east European political jargon of the time would have termed a 'stychic' process? Or was it more the outcome of direction from above, something that Poland's new rulers effectively imposed upon a Jewish population that, if left to its own devices, would likely have distributed itself differently, in a way that restored Warsaw to its former metropolitan status?

Both possibilities are plausible. There were, after all, sound, tangible, reasons for preferring settlement in Łódź or Lower Silesia over Warsaw. Whereas Warsaw was liberated from German occupation in a state of nearly total devastation, its leading competitors emerged from the war relatively unscathed. Both housing and employment were thus more readily available outside of the capital than in it. Additionally, although more Jews who survived the war *on Polish soil* did so in Warsaw, an incommensurably greater proportion of Jews living in Poland in 1946—greater perhaps twenty-five times over—were prewar residents of areas captured by the Red Army in September 1939 and annexed to the Soviet Union later that year who had passed the war years as refugees or deportees in Central Asia or Siberia.[14] For these Jews, returning to Poland did not mean returning to their former homes, which were now by and large under Soviet rule. Warsaw would thus likely have held a sentimental attraction for relatively few of them, making them less willing to tolerate the city's material discomforts than were, presumably, those who regarded it as home. It may well be, then, that Jews would have spread themselves over postwar Poland more

---

12   See, for example, the description in Shneiderman, *Tsvishn shrek un hofenung*, 182–87.
13   Pat, *Ash un fayer*, 212–13.
14   Engel, *Bein shihrur li-verihah*, 40.

or less as they did in any case, whether state or Jewish community officials encouraged them to do so or not.

But on the other hand, Poland's postwar regime was hardly one to entrust so crucial an economic determinant as distribution of the country's labor force to the marketplace alone. In particular, it was concerned to settle the newly-acquired western territories, including Lower Silesia, with enough Polish citizens to solidify its claim upon the region and to turn it into a significant economic resource.[15] This consideration led the Polish government to deny, as a matter of policy, repatriants from the Soviet free choice of destination within Poland or the ability to evenly disperse throughout the country, directing them instead to territories that were not part of Poland before 1945. Approximately 157,000 Jews in areas of the USSR other than the Ukrainian and Belorussian Soviet Republics were included in the Polish-Soviet repatriation agreement of July 1945, substantially more than the number of ethnic Poles eligible to return to Polish rule. Accordingly, the majority of postwar Polish Jewry found itself subject to official pressure regarding where it ought to live, pressure that led away from Warsaw.[16]

The available documentary evidence strongly suggests that such pressure was applied not only for the purpose of directing Jewish repatriants to the western territories but also in order to move as many Jews as possible, repatriants and former residents alike, away from the Polish capital. Indeed, that evidence contains indications that the government wished from the outset to hold the Jewish population of Warsaw to a minimum and that the Central Committee of Polish Jews eventually helped it pursue that goal. The actor and Central Committee member Jonas Turkow, for example, who arrived in Warsaw with the Committee in early February, 1945, encountered institutionalized discrimination against Jews seeking housing. He reported that the local housing office systematically refused to find lodging for former Jewish residents; in his words, 'all... free space was distributed exclusively to Christian Poles, even if they had not lived in Warsaw previously,' while 'Jews would be allocated a room only when a Jewish officer in the Soviet army intervened on their behalf, and even then only after arguments and harsh words.'[17] More significantly,

---

15   Jan Czerniakiewicz, *Repatriacja ludności polskiej z ZSRR 1944–1948* (Warsaw: Państwowe Wydawnictwo Naukowe, 1987), 194.
16   Engel, *Bein shihrur li-verihah*, 120–25; Yosef Litvak, "Polish-Jewish Refugees Repatriated from the Soviet Union at the End of the Second World War and Afterwards," in Norman Davies and Antony Polonsky (eds.), *Jews in Eastern Poland and the USSR, 1939–46* (London: Macmillan, 1991), 235.
17   Turkow, *Nokh der bafrayung*, 186.

government funds for assistance to Jews living in the capital and for the reestablishment of a Jewish community there were scarce compared with monies made available in other locations. On 14 April 1945, the Central Committee informed the Provincial Jewish Committee of Warsaw that it was cutting its previously-approved aid budget, maintaining promised levels of support only for children.[18] In May 1945, two articles in *Dos naje lebn* indicated that Łódź was to be the principal site where 'the sacred obligation of rebuilding [our] magnificent cultural institution[s]' would be fulfilled, whereas Warsaw was slated to become 'a cultural center for the entire [Warsaw] Province.'[19]

The following month the Central Committee gave the Łódź Provincial Committee a special allocation of 400,000 złotys for assistance to returnees from labor and concentration camps; that amount was nearly the sum contributed by the Central Committee to the Warsaw Provincial Committee's *entire* budget for that month, even though at the time Warsaw was absorbing almost the same number of camp returnees as Łódź.[20] Indeed, throughout 1945 and 1946, per capita subventions from the Central Committee to the Warsaw Provincial Committee were consistently lower than to other Provincial Jewish Committees, sometimes by 40 percent or more.[21] Additionally, the approximately 150,000 Jewish repatriants from the Soviet Union who arrived in Poland during the first half of 1946 appear to have been deliberately directed away from the capital. Central Committee plans for housing repatriants, drawn up in March 1946 in consultation with the State Repatriation Office, envisioned Warsaw absorbing 3,000 Jews arriving from the USSR; and in April the figure was reduced to 1,000. In the end, the actual number resettled in Warsaw came to about 2,000, even though Provincial Committee records show that 26,000 Jewish repatriants had applied to it for aid by the end of July 1946.[22] Even if

---

18 "Protokół posiedzenia Prezydium Komitetu Żydowskiego w Warszawie z dnia 18 kwietnia 1945r." IC 35/3.

19 *Dos naje lebn*, 20 May 1945 (Melech Karpinowicz, "A binyan far a yiddish teater"); 31 May 1945 ("Kultur-arbet fun yidishn komitet in varshe").

20 "Protokół z posiedzenia w sprawie pomocy dla powracających z Niemiec z dnia 2.VI.1945r.," IC 35/22; "Protokół Nr. 21 posiedzenia Komitetu Żydowskiego w Warszawie z dnia 13.6.1945 r.," IC 35/3. Cf. "Protokół z posiedzenia Prezydium CKŻP," 30 May 1945, IC 35/12, which foresaw a more proportional distribution of Central Committee funds for assisting camp returnees.

21 The relevant financial reports are dispersed throughout IC 35/3.

22 "Protokól Nr. 76 posiedzenia Prezydium Komitetu Żydowskiego w Warszawie z dnia 30.III.1946 4.," IC 35/6; E. Sommerstein and P, Zelicki to W. Wolski, 12 April 1946, IC 35/22; I. Falk and Zelicki to Wolski, 13 May 1946, ibid.; "Protokół Nr. 7 Narady przewodniczących Powiatowych Komitetów w Woj. Kom. Żyd. w Warszawie z dnia 20 lipca 1946 r.," IC 35/6.

that figure is exaggerated (and the Warsaw Provincial Committee was notorious for poor management, including sloppy record keeping),[23] it seems fairly certain that significant numbers of repatriants who, all things being equal, might well have chosen to settle in Warsaw, were induced through manufactured inequalities to settle elsewhere.[24]

Why should Poland's state and Jewish leaders have sought to minimize Warsaw's postwar Jewish population? The documentary record offers no unequivocal answer to that question.[25] Nevertheless, such a policy makes sense in view of the regime's demonstrated determination to represent itself as authentically Polish. Although at the beginning of its rule it found itself heavily dependent upon Jews for staffing key positions in the state service, it was keen to replace them as soon as dependable cadres of ethnic Poles could be cultivated. In the same fashion, it would hardly have suited the regime's purposes were the Polish capital once again to have displayed a significant Jewish presence.

It thus seems no accident that President Bolesław Bierut's five-year plan for rebuilding Warsaw designated the Muranów district, the heart of the interwar Jewish city, for a complete makeover in which "the newly reconstructed quarter will in no way recall the former tight, cramped blocks of narrow tenement houses."[26] And indeed, the promise was fulfilled. Nalewki Street disappeared as a thoroughfare, mostly buried under buildings built along the new Nowotki Street, with a vestigial 250-meter alley renamed 'ulica Bohaterów Getta,' as if to underscore that the old Jewish neighborhood was now to serve as a site for commemorating the recent destruction, nothing more. Warsaw, the great Jewish metropolis, was to remain obliterated not merely physically but in memory as well.

---

23 See, for example, "Sprawozdanie z ogólnej kontroli działalności Wojewódzkiego Komitetu Żydowskiego w Warszawie, przeprowadzonej w okresie 21/V-18/VI 1946 roku." IC 35/5.

24 For example, only about 2.5 percent of the total budget for assistance to repatriants from the Soviet Union was allocated to Warsaw. "Preliminarz budżetowy na cele repatriacji za m. maj 1946 r.," IC 35/22.

25 The most thorough search to date of that record, Neli Oren-Monivitz, "Mediniyut ha-mimshal ha-komunisti be'polin kelapei ha-yehudim ba-shanim 1944–1951" (unpublished Ph.D. dissertation, Tel Aviv University, 2009), turned up no clear policy statement.

26 Bierut, Sześcioletni plan, 11.

CHAPTER 23

The Reconstruction of Jewish Life in Warsaw after the Holocaust: A Case Study of a Building and Its Residents

Karen Auerbach

In 1948, with the Polish capital still in ruins after its wartime destruction, a handful of Jewish families began moving into a once-elegant apartment building at 16 Ujazdowskie Avenue in the heart of Warsaw. Three years earlier, the parents were among the remnants of Polish Jewry who emerged from forests and hiding places, were freed from Nazi camps, or returned from wartime exile in the Soviet Union. Now, as ten families of Jewish background moved into the building's apartments in 1948 and the following two years, the parents brought with them nine infants born in the war's early aftermath and two Jewish children who were adopted after surviving in hiding in L'viv. Eight other children were born just before or during the war in Poland, the Soviet Union and France. By the time the last family moved there in 1950, Jewish residents lived in ten of the building's twenty-three apartments.

The families' common address resulted from the social, political, and professional ties that connected one neighbor to another. Parents in all ten families worked for publishing institutions of the postwar Polish government, and in five of those families, they were founding editors and directors of the postwar Polish communist party's ideological publishing house, *Książka i Wiedza* [Book and Knowledge].[1] The neighbors shared bonds of political passion and publishing work, friendship and casual acquaintance, and a common Jewish background that led to an understanding of where they had come from and what they had lost during wartime.

---

1 The postwar communist party's ideological publishing house was known as Książka [Book] until the fall of 1948, when it absorbed the Polish Socialist Party publishing house, Wiedza [Knowledge], to become Książka i Wiedza [Book and Knowledge]. That change followed the dissolution and absorption of the Polish Socialist Party into Poland's communist party, called the Polish Workers' Party, to form the Polish United Workers' Party. To avoid confusion, I will refer to the communist party's publishing house as Książka i Wiedza regardless of time period.

The Jewish parents at 16 Ujazdowskie Avenue were entirely secular, nearly all of them radically so. Although they did not hide their Jewish roots from their children, they distanced themselves from that identity in postwar Poland. Yet the spaces they shared within the walls of their apartment building reflected the ties that continued to connect them with other Jewish families. The common setting of their homes, schools, social circles, and workplaces preserved the presence of the Jewish past in everyday life.

The building's Jewish families were not typical of Poland's Jewish population before or after the Holocaust, since nearly half of the parents were Communists. Nor were their networks exclusively Jewish. The connections that brought together the Jewish families at 16 Ujazdowskie Avenue included some of their non-Jewish neighbors, among them one who was involved in Communist underground circles that provided help to Jews during the Holocaust. But their ideology amplified the secularizing influences that shaped postwar Polish Jewry more broadly. The families' histories underscore the paths by which Polonizing Jews sought entrance into nineteenth- and twentieth-century Polish society as well as the ambiguous fate of those aspirations. Despite the drastically reduced size of the Polish Jewish population after the Holocaust, the early postwar pogroms, and the antisemitic politics that prompted periodic Jewish emigration waves, remnants of Polish Jewry continued to live, work and raise their children in Poland. Their gradual integration into Polish society over the course of the postwar generations coexisted with the antisemitism and emigration that underscored the limits of integration and the informal nature of communities that was central to the reconstruction of Jewish life in Poland after the Holocaust.

If, as Jacob Katz argued, the greater role that the distant past played in traditional Jewish life deepened the dislocations of modernity, then the rupture with the past in Warsaw after the Holocaust was even deeper, and the changes more rapid, than during the more gradual transformations over the course of prewar modern European Jewish history. When we look at postwar Polish Jewry not as a negligible population entirely cut off from prewar Jewish life, but rather as one that underwent accelerated transformations as a result of the Holocaust—in size, communal and cultural identifications, language and other factors—then we can begin to place the postwar period into a broader Jewish historical context.

In postwar Poland, as in Western and Central Europe in previous periods, the transformation for many Jews from shared spaces associated with observance and institutions, to informal spaces as a boundary of community—whether literal (e.g., workplaces or an apartment house) or figurative (e.g., social circles)—reflected not only rupture but also elements of continuity in identification and community. The history of the Jewish families at 16 Ujazdowskie Avenue and the shared spaces of their lives provide access to this paradoxical development, creating a different picture of Jewish life in postwar Poland than that provided by institutional histories.[2] As in previous periods and in other countries, Jews in Poland after the Holocaust often created informal communities even as they suppressed outward manifestations of their Jewish background in their everyday lives and were no longer connected to one another through Jewish institutions. The transformation from shared spaces associated with religious observance and Jewish institutions to more informal spaces as a boundary of community underscored both rupture and continuity.

Scholarship about shared spaces as a boundary of community in Jewish life in both the pre-modern and modern period sheds light on these kinds of changes in postwar Poland. These studies often emphasize neighborhoods as well as the symbolic space of literature and text as composing boundaries of communities, drawing on studies of "the connection between spatial practices and identity formations" in the humanities more generally, as Charlotte Fonrobert and Vered Shemtov have explained.[3] In pre-modern Jewish societies, common living spaces among Jews developed not only when external authorities restricted where Jews could live, but also because of the communal character of many Jewish rituals and customs. These shared spaces, in turn, reinforced the cohesiveness of the Jewish population, reflecting the process by which "society produces spaces, and these very spaces produce the society," as Barbara Mann has argued.[4] Charlotte Fonrobert's studies of the *eruv* as a delineation of Jewish space that served a symbolic role in conceptualizing Jewish

---

[2] For histories of Jewish communal institutions in postwar Poland, see Grzegorz Berendt, *Życie żydowskie w Polsce w latach 1950–1956* (Gdańsk: Wydawnictwo Uniwerystetu Gdańskiego, 2006); Grzegorz Berendt, August Grabski, and Albert Stankowski, *Studia z historii Żydów w Polsce po 1945 r.* (Warsaw: Żydowski Instytut Historyczny, 2000); Alina Cała, "An Attempt to Recover Its Voice: The Towarzystwo Społeczno-Kulturalne Żydów w Polsce, the Jewish community, and the Polish State, 1956–1960," *Polin* 19 (2007): 557–68; August Grabski, *Działalność komunistów wśród Żydów w Polsce (1944–1949)* (Warsaw: Trio, 2004); Audrey Kichelewski, "A Community under Pressure: Jews in Poland, 1957–1967," *Polin* 21 (2009): 159–86; and Joanna Nalewajko-Kulikov, *Obywatel Jidyszlandu: Rzecz o żydowskich komunistach w Polsce* (Warsaw: Neriton, 2009).

[3] Charlotte Fonrobert and Vered Shemtov, "Introduction: Jewish Conceptions and Practices of Space," *Jewish Social Studies* 11.3 (2005): 1–8.

[4] Barbara E. Mann, *A Place in History: Modernism, Tel Aviv, and the Creation of Jewish Urban Space* (Stanford, CA: Stanford University Press, 2006), 1. See also Barbara E. Mann, *Space and Place in Jewish Studies* (New Brunswick, NJ: Rutgers, 2012), esp. 116–27.

community point to the mutually reinforcing connections among Jewish observance, space and community in traditional Jewish societies. The physical boundary of the *eruv* community, in Fonrobert's analysis, was intended to unify the community rather than separate the Jewish population from outsiders. The underlying significance of the *eruv* in understanding traditional Jewish society, then, is to "underscore the importance of neighborhood for conceiving of community," writes Fonrobert. She and other contemporary scholars have viewed shared living quarters as a kind of substitute or symbolic nation in the diaspora. Thus interpreted, the *eruv*, like the ghetto, was an institution that both underscored Jewish exclusion and integrated Jews into the streetscape as a community.[5]

In the modern period, from London to Vienna to St. Petersburg, the neighborhood remained a boundary of community even after neither religious observance, nor restrictions on where Jews could live, determined those boundaries any longer.[6] In medieval Europe the cathedral or church and its adjacent square were the "focal point of religious and public life" in urban centers—a way of life that found its echo in the synagogue and its adjacent courtyard as the focus of Jewish communal life[7]—and in the modern city, common spaces that shaped and reflected community continue to play a role, however altered, in everyday life. In St. Petersburg in the last decades of Imperial Russia, for example, Benjamin Nathans finds that residential clustering of Jews increased between 1869 and 1910 and that Jews were more segregated residentially from non-Jews

---

5 See Fonrobert and Shemtov, "Introduction: Jewish Conceptions and Practices of Space"; Charlotte E. Fonrobert, "The Political Symbolism of the Eruv," *Jewish Social Studies* 11.3 (2005): 11; and Charlotte E. Fonrobert, "From Separatism to Urbanism: The Dead Sea Scrolls and the Origins of the Rabbinic Eruv," *Dead Sea Discoveries* 11.1 (2004): 43–71.

6 See Marsha Rozenblit, *The Jews of Vienna, 1867–1914: Assimilation and Identity* (Albany, NY: SUNY, 1983), 71–98; Benjamin Nathans, *Beyond the Pale: The Jewish Encounter with Late Imperial Russia* (Berkeley and Los Angeles: University of California, 2002), 113–122; Gary B. Cohen, *The Politics of Ethnic Survival: Germans in Prague, 1861–1914*, 2nd revd. ed. (West Lafayette, IN: Purdue University, 2006), 101–2; and Stanley Waterman and Barry A. Kosmin, "Residential Patterns and Processes: A Study of Jews in Three London Boroughs," *Transactions of the Institute of British Geographers*, New Series, 13.1 (1988): 79–95. Waterman and Kosmin warned against confusing residential concentration with segregation; living together, which they termed congregation, did not necessarily imply social isolation. Rather, they interpreted the behavior as a desire to live among other Jews rather than a desire to separate oneself from non-Jews.

7 Alfred Haverkamp, "Jews and Urban Life: Bonds and Relationships," in Karin Birk, Werner Transier, and Markus Wener (eds.), *The Jews of Europe in the Middle Ages (Tenth to Fifteenth Centuries)* (Ostfildern: Hatje Cantz, 2004), 55–69.

than other ethnic minorities were. Clustering developed to some degree in this city "beyond the Pale" because early Jewish residents settled in neighborhoods where trades in which they tended to work were already established. Yet these concentrations developed among all segments of the city's St. Petersburg Jewish population despite the absence of residential restrictions, and despite increasing linguistic assimilation and the integrationist goals of St. Petersburg Jewish elites. This development is all the more striking because there was no earlier period of Jewish settlement in St. Petersburg during which residential restrictions or settlement patterns rooted in pre-modern Jewish communal life could have set a precedent for later clustering, as it did in Vienna.[8]

In fact, Nathans found that residential clustering in St. Petersburg was even higher in roughly the same period than in Vienna, where Jewish residential concentrations remained apparent particularly in the former medieval Jewish district of Leopoldstadt. This Viennese neighborhood, along with two nearby districts, continued to be home to large Jewish concentrations from 1867 through the First World War regardless of the residents' economic status, and not only among new immigrants.[9] In Prague, Jews in districts studied over a similar period as in Vienna generally lived in the same apartment houses as other Jews regardless of whether they identified with surrounding Czech or German culture.[10] In contemporary London, too, despite the high degree of integration, Jewish residential clustering as late as the 1980s was greater than for other minority groups, including groups of recently arrived non-Jewish immigrants. Jews in Greater London concentrated in Barnet and adjacent

---

8   Nathans, *Beyond the Pale*, 113–22.
9   Rozenblit, ibid.
10   "Religion clearly affected residence patterns and family life among the Prague Germans at the end of the century more strongly than did the simple Czech-German national divide. At least in the Old Town and New Town, the census returns suggest that households that were largely or wholly German in their loyalties were generally found in the same apartment buildings with Czech households, but German Catholics tended to reside with Czech Catholic neighbors and seldom lived in the same buildings with Jews, whether German or Czech in their national loyalties. For their part, the Jews in the sampled parishes resided primarily along with other Jewish families, whether German- or Czech-speaking. While German Jews found great acceptance in German public life in Prague, they and the German Catholics seem to have kept some distance from each other in the most intimate areas of private life. Besides the residential patterns, few Jews converted or married non-Jews in Prague before World War I. The separation of the German Jews' family life from German Christians helped them to preserve a distinct Jewish group identity even while they participated extensively in non-Jewish public affairs." Cohen, *Politics of Ethnic Survival*, 101–2.

boroughs in the Northwest, reaching as high as 17 percent of the population in Barnet. The clustering was even more noticeable at the street level; in the Edgware district of Barnet, for example, most Jews lived on streets where 70 percent of their neighbors were also Jewish.[11]

The specific reasons for Jewish residential clustering and its significance differ according to location and period. In Central and Western Europe, for example, particularly in Vienna, Berlin, Paris, and London, immigration waves from Eastern Europe between 1881 and the First World War, as well as during the interwar period, complicated earlier shifts in Jewish settlement patterns among more established Jewish residents. St. Petersburg provides perhaps the best analogue to post-war Warsaw. The Jewish population in the imperial Russian capital was a largely "new" population which developed beginning in the 1860s because of a new government policy of "selective integration."[12] This policy lifted restrictions on residence outside the Pale of Settlement for Jews who had served in the military, worked as merchants or in other specified occupations, or had acquired a university education. Yet residential segregation developed in St. Petersburg even though no earlier Jewish residential district had established a precedent for later settlement patterns for Jews who were more integrated into surrounding society.[13]

Like St. Petersburg, Warsaw only began to develop as a center of Jewish life in the second half of the nineteenth century. Warsaw's earliest known Jewish community, in the late fourteenth or early fifteenth century, probably consisted of no more than fifteen families, but in the early sixteenth century the city prohibited Jewish settlement, although some Jews lived in private enclaves of noblemen and others (see chapter 1 in this volume). For payment they were also allowed to live and trade elsewhere in the city when the Polish Parliament, the *Sejm* (diet), convened. In addition they settled in right-bank Praga as early as the mid-seventeenth century, and a legal community was established there in 1775. Only after the late-eighteenth-century partitions of Poland, when Warsaw initially came under Prussian rule, was the prohibition against permanent Jewish settlement lifted, and a *kehillah* and institutions of Jewish life established. The Jewish population and its institutions grew, and a cemetery was founded in 1806 (a Jewish burial ground already existed in right-bank Praga). Under Russian rule, following the Napoleonic wars, the Jewish

---

11   Waterman and Kosmin, "Residential Patterns and Processes: A Study of Jews in Three London Boroughs."
12   Nathans, *Beyond the Pale*, 17, 45–79.
13   Nathans, *Beyond the Pale*, 113–22.

population increased from 12,000 (17 percent of Warsaw's population) in 1805, to 72,000 (32 percent) in 1864.

In the second half of the nineteenth century Warsaw developed into Europe's largest Jewish center following the 1862 liberalizing decrees for Jews in the Russian-controlled, semi-autonomous Polish kingdom. A mix of Hasidim, *mitnaggdim*, and *maskilim* in the first decades of the nineteenth century gave way to a predominately Hasidic population among an increasing large minority of polonized Jews. Beginning in 1868, an influx of Jews from the Russian interior, so-called Litvaks, deepened internal Jewish divisions. The Jewish population reached 301,268 (38 percent) by 1911. Warsaw' role as a center of Jewish culture and politics continued into the interwar period. Despite the absence of restrictions on where Jews could live, the population was concentrated in the neighborhoods of Muranów and Grzybów.

In postwar Warsaw, Jewish residential concentrations are difficult to quantify. Interviews and documents in the Ministry of Interior Affairs archive confirm the presence of clusters of Jewish residents in at least five other buildings aside from the one at 16 Ujazdowskie Avenue, while informal conversations indicate a higher number. A building on Jagiellońska Street in right-bank Praga was assigned to Jewish communal authorities after the war for the allocation of apartments, while residents of another apartment house, on Konopnicka Street, included numerous employees and members of Jewish institutions. The latter was home to Ignacy Ekerling, a former driver for Jewish institutions who was accused of the 1957 murder of the son of an antisemitic, prewar nationalist, and in 1972, the security police counted thirty-five Jewish families who lived in the building before emigrating in the 1950s and late 1960s.

During the repatriation wave of 1956 to 1960, when Polish citizens remaining in the Soviet Union were allowed to return to Poland, among them about 18,000 Jews, the Social-Cultural Association of Jews in Poland [Towarzystwo Społeczno-Kulturalne Żydów w Polsce, TSKŻ], the umbrella organization for postwar Polish Jewish life, was assigned a handful of apartments clustered together in buildings in Bielany and other neighborhoods for Jewish repatriates who were newly employed for the Folks-shtime and the Social-Cultural Association's other workplaces. Other apartment houses were not associated with Jewish communal life and point to informal networks that connected Jewish families. A building on Puławska Street was home to party officials, among them at least four Jewish families, while at least three Jewish families lived in a prewar apartment house on Litewska Street. Informal conversations point to the presence of clusters of Jewish residents in a handful of other buildings as well, including in the Mokotów neighborhood and on Ordynacka Street in the city center.[14] The building at 16 Ujazdowskie Avenue was but an extreme example of this clustering.

The Postwar Transformation of Warsaw and Its Jewish Population

Few cities in Nazi-occupied Europe were destroyed on the same scale as Warsaw during the Second World War, and nowhere else was the size of a city's murdered Jewish population so large. Accelerated changes in Warsaw's physical appearance and social structures after its wartime destruction were even more acute among the capital's Jewish population, and with the city's reconstruction, the absence of Jewish neighborhoods was one of the most significant transformations.

Even those who lived in the capital before the war were surrounded after the Holocaust by a new streetscape. A woman whose mother lived in the predominantly Jewish neighborhood of Muranów before the Holocaust and continued to live in her old-new neighborhood after the war with her family recalls: "As soon as we walked down Zamenhof Street, she immediately cried! And at the ghetto monument she said: 'This is not the Warsaw that I remember from childhood. My school stood over there, I played with my friends over there—it does not exist! All of this is so foreign now!' And it was an ironic fate that we would live after the war on the terrain of the former ghetto, in the same area where mother lived before the war."[15]

The accelerated transformation of Warsaw Jewry into a largely polonized population distanced from Jewish institutions, which began among an increasing minority of Jews even before the Second World War, was intensified by the emigration of most survivors in the early postwar years.[16] That transformation was not only rooted in the vastly diminished size of the postwar Jewish population, however. Although most surviving Jews left Poland by 1950, small

---

14 See the archives of the Instytut Pamięci Narodowej [Institute for National Remembrance, IPN], collection of the Ministerstwo Spraw Wewnętrznych [Ministry of Internal Affairs, MSW], archival no. MSW SGO 0747/30, folder 21; and interviews by the author with Helena Datner, Warsaw, May 16, 2004; and May 20, 2004; Stanisław Krajewski, Warsaw, July 11, 2004; and Aleksander Bilewicz, Warsaw, May 27, 2004, and June 3, 2004.

15 Interview by Joanna Wiszniewicz with "Henia," in Joanna Wiszniewicz, *Życie Przecięte: Opowieści pokolenia marca* (Wołowiec: Wydawnictwo Czarne, 2008), 84.

16 See Albert Stankowski, "Nowe spojrzenie na statystyki dotyczące emigracji Żydów z Polski po 1944 roku," in Grzegorz Berendt, August Grabski and Albert Stankowski (eds.), *Studia z historii Żydów w Polsce po 1945 r.* (Warsaw: Jewish Historical Institute, 2000), 103–151.

populations of observant Jews and others with strong ties to Jewish institutions did reestablish communities in Poland. Yet in Warsaw, the devastated infrastructure and severe housing shortage discouraged survivors from resettling there in the early postwar years, at a time when they were first making decisions about where to rebuild. In later years, for Jews who sought to maintain Jewish religious life, the stronger presence of central political authorities in the capital provided an incentive to live elsewhere.

These individual choices, as well as the planned resettlement of the Jewish population by government authorities and the Jewish communal leadership immediately after the war, led to the development of more traditional Jewish communities in Poland's newly acquired western territories in and around Wrocław and Szczecin, including the largely Jewish small town of Dzierżoniów, as well as in Łódź. The Polish authorities' expulsion of ethnic Germans from the new western regions meant that there were empty homes for new settlers, not only Jews but also, in even greater numbers, ethnic Poles from Poland's former eastern territories, which it had lost to the Soviet Union. Łódź, meanwhile, had survived the war mostly intact, and cultural institutions were based there in the initial postwar years as the government began rebuilding on the ruins of Warsaw. Directing Jews to Łódź and cities in the new western territories therefore made resettlement less of a burden on the state and on state-funded Jewish communal institutions. Postwar religious and secular Jewish communal institutions were more central to Jewish life in these cities than they were in the capital. In Warsaw, the absence of a Jewish quarter of any significant size reflected not only its wartime destruction, the vastly diminished size of the surviving Jewish population, and the uprooting that led to new residential patterns for those who returned or moved to the city, but also the distance from Judaism and Jewish traditions among most surviving Jews who lived in the capital after the Holocaust.

The histories of the Jewish families at 16 Ujazdowskie Avenue underscore the challenge of including in postwar Polish Jewish history the experiences of those Jews who rebuilt outside of Jewish institutions and who remained in Poland after the early postwar years. Only five of the ten families, as well as one parent in a sixth family, appear in registries of the surviving Jewish population in the early postwar years. The experiences of those who maintained distance from their Jewish background often do not emerge in records or in the narrative of postwar Polish life until they left Poland during the emigration waves of 1956–1960 or 1968–1970.

Postwar Poland's Jewish institutional leadership recognized the difficulty of ascertaining how many Jews lived in postwar Warsaw compared with elsewhere in Poland. A population count by the Social-Cultural Association for

Jews in Poland shortly after the emigration wave of 1956–1960 included detailed demographic counts for Poland's Jewish communities but only a general estimate of 10,000 for Warsaw.[17] Here was an acknowledgment of the ambiguities of who could be considered Jewish in postwar Poland and of the assimilating tendencies of the Jewish population in postwar Warsaw. Bernard Mark, director of the Jewish Historical Institute, wrote in his diary in 1966 that the absence of formal affiliation with Jewish institutions among many of Jewish background, who rebuilt their lives at a distance from Jewish identity both culturally and psychologically, made it difficult to estimate the Jewish population, and he highlighted Warsaw. "They say that the number of Jews in Poland... consists of 25,000. I think that the number is higher, since we do not know about all Jews. There are those who do not have any contact and do not come to the Jewish theater, they do not receive *matzah* and they do not even come to the ghetto [uprising] commemoration."[18]

To be sure, shared Jewish spaces in postwar Warsaw were not entirely disconnected from communal institutions. In the early postwar period, returning Jews settled on or near Jagiellońska Street in Praga, on the right bank of the Vistula River, where Warsaw's early Jewish communal institutions were based. Later, observant Jews and those involved in secular Jewish institutions carved out formal Jewish spaces that became a drastically scaled-down version of the "Jewish street." Communal life often took place in or near prewar spaces, providing a degree of continuity between the thriving Jewish life of prewar Warsaw and its postwar shadow. The Jewish Historical Institute was housed in the former library of the destroyed Great Synagogue, while the Nożyk Synagogue, the only active synagogue in postwar Warsaw, had been established in 1902 on Twarda Street in a largely middle-class Jewish neighborhood around Grzybowska Square. The Okopowa Street cemetery, where generations of Warsaw Jews were buried, continued to serve as the graveyard for the postwar capital's Jewish community.

Certain spaces affiliated with Jewish institutions became sites of interaction between Jews active in communal life and those who were distanced from

---

17   Archive of the Jewish Historical Institute, TSKŻ Wydział Organizacyjny, 114, "Ankiety TSKŻ 1961 r., wszystkie oddziały TSKŻ w Polsce." According to Albert Stankowski, in 1967 the Social-Cultural Association of Jews in Poland asserted that 6,200 Jews had contact with Jewish institutions.

18   Diary of Bernard Mark in the Goldstein-Goren Diaspora Research Center at Tel Aviv University, Bernard and Ester Mark Bequest, P-69, 1997, entry of January 14, 1966. I am grateful to Joanna Nalewajko-Kulikov and Audrey Kichelewski for calling my attention to this diary and its archival location.

them. The Amica restaurant which was established in the late 1950s by the Social-Cultural Association of Jews in Poland; the monument to the Warsaw ghetto uprising in Muranów, the largest prewar Jewish neighborhood; and the Jewish theater played a role in the lives of some Jews even when they otherwise had little or no affiliation with the post-war Jewish community.

The murder of nearly a third of Warsaw's prewar Jewish population was one element of a much broader transformation of the postwar capital. In Communist Eastern Europe after the Second World War, the socialist ideology of the new governments sought to dissolve the bonds of community, and those changes manifested themselves in cityscapes, even more so in cities such as Warsaw where that ideology shaped their rebuilding after wartime destruction. In postwar Warsaw, social ties borne of prewar communities were partially broken by wartime displacement and resettlement. Although many residents lived there before the war, the postwar capital was in some sense a new city superimposed on the ruins of the old, not only in its landscape but also in its social structures. In Poland more generally, notes Krystyna Kersten, "traditional structures and patterns of life were destroyed or badly eroded.... The uprooting of millions of people from their environments and the necessity of adjusting to a new situation had an immeasurable effect on attitudes and behavior." Kersten argues that regardless of whether the "historic turning-point of 1944–45" could be seen as a political revolution, "we can state without doubt that it caused fundamental changes in the structure of society."[19] In Warsaw, the physical devastation of the capital and its population, particularly during the city's uprising against Nazi rule in 1944, led to a "defeat of hope, of a certain order, of a system of values," Kersten argued.[20] Some historians later viewed the quixotic patriotism of the uprising as unnecessarily exacerbating the city's wartime fate, the 1944 uprising's disastrous consequences producing widespread political realism.[21]

The virtual emptying of the capital after the Nazis quashed the uprising and Warsaw's post-war repopulation in largely new physical surroundings deepened the societal rupture. Moving into new buildings in the postwar capital were not only the city's surviving prewar residents but also tens of thousands

---

19 Krystyna Kersten, *The Establishment of Communist Rule in Poland, 1943–1948*, translated and annotated by John Micgiel and Michael H. Bernard (Berkeley, Los Angeles and Oxford: University of California Press, 1991), 165.

20 Kersten, 169.

21 See, for example, Włodzimierz Borodziej, *The Warsaw Uprising of 1944*, translated by Barbara Harshav (Madison, WI: University of Wisconsin Press, 2005); and Jan M. Ciechanowski, *The Warsaw Rising of 1944* (Cambridge: Cambridge University Press, 2002).

of peasants from the Polish countryside, who helped to repopulate the capital. The new postwar government pursued rapid industrialization and provided economic incentives for peasants to move to the capital, both to rebuild the capital's infrastructure and to work in its newly constructed factories.

The combination of peasants-turned-workers, rapid industrialization, the Nazis' murder of much of the prewar Polish intelligentsia and most of Warsaw Jewry, the postwar presence of intellectuals associated with the new government, and the city's physical reconstruction under a Communist regime, all altered the character of Warsaw's physical appearance and society despite threads of continuity with the prewar capital. The transformation of public and private spaces reflected the government's conscious attempt to break society's ties with past traditions. In Warsaw, as in the Soviet Union and throughout postwar Eastern Europe, the Communist government's planning of living quarters was part of an attempt to reshape society, identity and the bonds of community.[22]

Typical housing conditions in Warsaw in the first postwar decade recalled the communal apartments of the Soviet Union, even if the arrangement in Poland resulted as much from pragmatic needs as from government planning. Few families had their own apartment in the first postwar years, and several families often crowded into one apartment while waiting years, often more than a decade, to be assigned an apartment. The confinement of individual family space to "a room or a nook behind a partition"[23] within an apartment and the sharing of common kitchens and bathrooms eroded the boundaries of private and public space. Only with the Five-Year Plan for Housing, announced in 1960, did the state's construction of new housing projects on the city's outskirts begin to accommodate more residents, soon bringing the number of

---

22   See Victor Buchli, *An Archaeology of Socialism* (Oxford, New York: Berg, 1999), esp. chapter 4, "The Narkomfin Communal House and the Material Culture of Socialism"; Stephen Kotkin, *Magnetic Mountain: Stalinism as a Civilization* (Berkeley, Los Angeles and London: University of California Press, 1995), especially Part II, "Living Socialism: The Little Tactics of the Habitat," which focuses on the industrial city of Magnitogorsk; Katerina Gerasimova, "Public Privacy in the Soviet Communal Apartment," in David Crowley and Susan E. Reid (eds.), *Socialist Spaces: Sites of Everyday Life in the Eastern Bloc* (Oxford and New York: Berg, 2002), 207–30; David Crowley, "Warsaw Interiors: The Public Life of Private Spaces, 1949–65," in Crowley and Reid Socialist Spaces, 181–206; Gerasimova, "The Soviet Communal Apartment," in Jeremy Smith (ed.), *Beyond the Limits: The Concept of Space in Russian History and Culture* (Helsinki: SHS, 1999), 107–31.

23   Błażej Brzostek, *Za progiem. Codzienność w przestrzeni publicznej Warszawy lat 1955–1970* (Warsaw: Trio, 2007) 48. My thanks to Zosia Wójcicka for calling my attention to this study.

residents per room back to prewar levels.[24] Newcomers to Warsaw and others who did not have connections with influential individuals often lived even longer in apartments shared with other families

Yet individual efforts to maintain communal connections outside the reach of politics included carving out private space within homes despite the government's ideological blurring of distinctions between public and private. Postwar transformations in the urban character and social structures of Warsaw underscore the tensions between the state's attempt to control space in order to reshape society, on the one hand, and individual efforts to create autonomy over this space to limit the intrusion of politics into everyday life, on the other.

The Jewish Families of 16 Ujazdowskie Avenue

The neighborhood around Ujazdowskie Avenue was one of the few that avoided complete destruction in Warsaw's city center, and in the summer of 1947 the Polish communist party's publishing house, Książka i Wiedza, began reconstructing the partially destroyed building at 16 Ujazdowskie Avenue, which the government had allocated to the publishing house for its employees.[25] The first residents began moving into the building's apartments in early 1948, at first Książka i Wiedza editors and directors, and later those from other publishing institutions.

The Jewish families at 16 Ujazdowskie Avenue had taken diverse prewar, wartime and postwar paths. At least thirteen of the eighteen parents—those who survived the Second World War as adults—grew up speaking Yiddish, usually in addition to Polish, as they became increasingly integrated into Polish culture before the war. Four others grew up in more polonized families, including one parent whose mother was not Jewish and another who married a non-Jewish man after her wartime survival on the "Aryan" side of L'viv. Twelve of the parents lived in the Soviet Union during the Second World War, but even among them, most had few surviving family members while the spouses of three residents were killed in Nazi-occupied Poland. Yet grandmothers survived in two of the families and lived with them on Ujazdowskie Avenue after the war, while three generations and two branches of another family lived in the building.

---

24 See Crowley, "Warsaw Interiors", as above, footnote 22.
25 Archiwum Akt Nowych, Komitet Centralny, Polska Partia Robotnicza, 295/XVII-24, 51. The building was later formally assigned to the publishing cooperative RSW-Prasa.

Informal connections were essential to finding adequate housing in the devastated capital, and social or political networks linked several of the building's residents to one another, including at least two other non-Jewish families. But the cluster of Jewish families at 16 Ujazdowskie Avenue resulted even more so from a concentration of Jewish employees in postwar publishing institutions, particularly Książka i Wiedza. Their work developed in part from prewar political and publishing work. Eight of the nineteen parents of Jewish background at 16 Ujazdowskie Avenue were prewar Communist party members who were involved in illegal prewar publishing and propaganda activities, which led to their assignment in party publishing posts after the war. Two other residents among the ten Jewish families joined the reconstructed Polish communist party late in the war.

The families' association with the Communist government and the deeper degrees of secularization as a result of political ideology reflect, in exaggerated form, typical patterns of family life, social circles and education among the rest of Warsaw's postwar Jewish population. Jewish tradition, culture and other markers of Jewish identity were almost entirely absent in the homes of all but one of the families from Ujazdowskie Avenue, even as the parents were part of Jewish social circles that signaled their isolation from non-Jews. Their children, too, remained connected with other Jewish youth as a result of their attendance at secular schools where Jews were overrepresented among students, despite their lack of connection to or understanding of their Jewish background.[26] None of their children knew that so many of the other families had Jewish roots, but they were aware that some neighbors shared their own Jewish background.

Life-cycle events were characterized by distinctiveness from most other Polish families not because of the presence of Jewish ritual but rather the very absence of ritual. None of the children in the families recalled any weddings,

---

26 Joanna Wiszniewicz examined the Jewish children's attendance at these schools, which were operated by the Society for the Friends of Children [Towarzystwo Przyjaciół Dzieci]. See "Jewish Children and Youth in Downtown Warsaw Schools of the 1960s," *Polin: Studies in Polish Jewry* 21 (2008): 204–29. The society maintained a secular curriculum even at times in the early postwar years and the late 1950s when the government permitted Catholic religious instruction in schools. My archival research on these schools drew on Wiszniewicz's work; see Karen Auerbach, "A Window on Postwar Warsaw: The Jewish Families of 16 Ujazdowskie Avenue," Ph.D. thesis (Brandeis University, 2009), chapter 3. Wiszniewicz's interviews provide extensive evidence of Jewish attendance at these schools. Nearly all of my own interviewees who grew up in Poland after the Holocaust also attended the Society for the Friends of Children schools and indicated that many of their childhood friends were of Jewish background like themselves.

funerals, or births characterized by Jewish customs in their childhood or teenage years. Nor did they report any Jewish holidays being overtly celebrated in the home, even secular variants. Even among the Bergman-Rudnicka family, where Jewishness was more openly expressed than among their neighbors, family life was marked mainly by the absence of rituals rooted in the past. In the Bergman and the Tyszelman families, no second-generation member recalls their parents sitting *shivah*, reciting *kaddish* or lighting *yahrzeit* candles on the anniversary of the deaths of their grandmothers, who were the only surviving grandparents among the Jewish families at 16 Ujazdowskie Avenue. None of the second-generation members in any of the families report having visited cemeteries on All Saints' Day as children. Aside from the Bergman and Tyszelman families, such rituals would have been difficult to observe, since there were few graves of parents and siblings to visit, and since the dates to commemorate the anniversary of those murdered during the Holocaust were most likely unknown. The nearly complete absence of graves as a result of the anonymity of Jewish wartime deaths itself signified difference from most of their non-Jewish neighbors.

Among most other Poles, in contrast, the secularization of everyday life and culture that the Communist system sought to impose on Polish society had not erased the influence of Catholic identity, and religious elements continued to shape family life even among secular families. Name days, connected with Catholic saints, were celebrated more often than birthdays, and individuals continued to visit graves on All Saints' Day and Easter Sunday. Extended families, regardless of religious observance, still gathered on Christmas and Easter. Thus, Jewishness was, paradoxically enough, expressed through the absence of ritual.

Among individuals of Jewish background, despite the virtual absence of ritual associated with births, deaths and other life-cycle events, families sometimes adopted secularized Catholic rituals not related to the life cycle, including Christmas trees in their homes for their children, though sometimes with a red star at the top. Most of the families gathered during *wigilia*, Christmas Eve dinner, with their few surviving relatives or with close friends, also of Jewish background. Children in three of these families celebrated name days in addition to birthdays, and photographs show a young Halina Adler holding hands with other children of Książka i Wiedza employees during a Christmas party. Yet the absence of extended family still made these celebrations among the Jewish families of 16 Ujazdowskie Avenue different from their non-Jewish neighbors, who were likely to gather with extended families at home.

The more ideological families at 16 Ujazdowskie Avenue also created new family rituals through the celebration of political holidays. Among the seven families at 16 Ujazdowskie Avenue in which at least one parent was an ideological Communist, the parents were connected by a shared political faith that replaced religious rituals of family life. May 1, when the Communist countries marked International Workers' Day as a national holiday, became an annual event celebrated communally, and sometimes earnestly at least in the first postwar decade. Photographs from the 1950s, for example, show the Adler and Bergman families attending the May 1 parades together with other employees from Książka i Wiedza.

Indications of the families' Jewish background were not entirely absent from the home, and the Jewish past continued to be present on the margins and under the surface of their parents' post-war lives. Alexandra Bergman's husband Stefan, his mother Paulina, and his sister Luba Rudnicka occasionally spoke Yiddish with one another and with Stefan's wife Aleksandra, and for one boy who lived upstairs at 16 Ujazdowskie Avenue, the Yiddish sometimes spoken in the Bergman family stood out in his memory; it was his own mother's native tongue but one that he almost never heard in his own home. In another family of Jewish background that lived at 16 Ujazdowskie Avenue in the early postwar years, an Auschwitz survivor, Genia Adler, wrote to her husband just after Christmas in 1959 that she and Aleksandra Bergman had attended the Jewish theater in Warsaw two nights in a row for a performance of the Yiddish classic *Green Fields*,[27] perhaps responding to their longing for their murdered families at a time when most Polish families were celebrating Christmas together. On another floor at 16 Ujazdowskie Avenue, Samuel Neftalin sometimes sang in Yiddish while shaving, to his wife Nina's dismay,[28] but Nina and her sons nevertheless gave Samuel a Hebrew book for a birthday present when the two boys, Jurek and Piotr, were still young.[29] In the Adler home, meanwhile, a handful of books on Hebrew grammar and Yiddish literature were scattered among classics of Polish literature and Marxist philosophy.[30] Easter was a family occasion for none of the ten Jewish families, but two children of Jewish background who grew up in the building, Bernard Kruc and Liliana Tyszelman, recalled that their parents sometimes had *matzah*

---

27 Letter from Genia Adler to Emil Adler, December 27, 1959. Personal papers of Emil and Genia Adler.
28 Interview with Jurek Neftalin, Warsaw, Nov. 14–15, 2006.
29 Interview with Piotr Sztuczyński, Warsaw, Nov. 10, Nov. 20 and Nov. 24, 2006.
30 A list of every book which the Adlers took with them upon their departure from Poland was included in their emigration papers. Personal papers of Emil and Genia Adler.

in their homes around that time.[31] Yet the parents seemed to create a barrier between their own occasional connections to their Jewish background, on one hand, and the absence of such connections for their children. Only as adults did Liliana Tyszelman, Bernard Kruc, and others of their generation understand the connection between their parents' peculiar Easter-time ritual of obtaining *matzah* for the home and the Jewish holiday of Passover.

The transformation of home life among the Jewish families 16 Ujazdowskie Avenue resulted largely from the ideology of at least one parent in seven of the ten families as well as the secularizing policies of People's Poland. These changes in family life were one aspect of the intrusion of political ideology into private life in post-war Poland, an impact that was strongest among pre-war Communists, whose politicization of their private lives before the Second World War was now officially sanctioned and reinforced by educational and government policy. Whereas other families in post-war Poland, both Jewish and non-Jewish, often sought to limit the imposition of politics on their private lives, ideological Communists embraced the erosion of barriers between the political and private spheres, at least initially. This transformation of family life was even more significant among Jewish Communist parents compared with their non-Jewish Communist comrades, because of the destruction of extended prewar families and communities during the Holocaust as well as the stigma associated with Jewish expression in the post-war political conditions.

Throughout the children's early years in the first post-war decade, the blurring of the political and the personal was particularly evident in the strong connections between work and private life, beginning with the very setting of their families' everyday lives. Apartments were sometimes allocated to work institutions or government agencies for their employees, so work colleagues became neighbors as well, and the very nature of their relatively privileged material surroundings was often dependent on a parent's political connections.

In highly ideological work institutions such as Książka i Wiedza, where parents in five of the ten families at 16 Ujazdowskie Avenue worked when they moved into the building, the personal and the political were even further intertwined. Parents who believed in communist ideology shaped their families' lives according to the tenets of their secular faith. Among Jewish survivors starting life anew, political comrades became both social circle and family in the early postwar period, connections that were often maintained for decades and disrupted only by the emigration waves of 1956–1960 and 1968–1970.

---

31   Telephone interview with Bernard Krutz, July 8, 2007, and interview with Liliana Tyszelman, Warsaw, Dec. 1, 2006.

The strong connections between personal and political life among the majority of the Jewish families at 16 Ujazdowskie Avenue meant that shifts in political winds affected their home lives to an even greater degree than among other Jewish families in post-war Poland. As individuals of Jewish background, meanwhile, antisemitism during periods of political upheaval underscored the gap between political ideology and reality, and affected them more personally. The political and the personal were therefore inextricably linked among Communist Jewish families when it came to shifts in how parents and children alike related to their Jewish background.

In 1956, the parents' generation at 16 Ujazdowskie Avenue was reacting to the political upheavals on both personal and political levels just as their children, most of them born during or just after the Second World War, were reaching an age when they were beginning to understand and question their surroundings. Their parents' political questioning and greater openness in expression in 1956, including about Jewish issues, took place as the children were beginning to develop their own world views. Daniel Passent, for example, was a hidden child in wartime whose uncle Jakub Prawin, a top government official in People's Poland, was raising him in postwar Poland after Daniel's parents were killed during the Holocaust. Passent, who recalls regular visits with his uncle to Emil Adler's apartment at 16 Ujazdowskie Avenue and later on Plac Narutowicza, recalls overhearing his uncle discuss with friends the impact of the political changes in the mid-1950s and saying, "We'll see if they allow a Jew" to hold the important position for which he was being considered. Only then, Passent recalled, did he realize that his uncle, too, was Jewish.[32]

Of the ten Jewish families that lived at 16 Ujazdowskie Avenue in post-war Warsaw, the Sławnys were the only ones to leave Poland between 1956 and 1960, but all of the families were affected by the waves of Jewish emigration and repatriation in those years. Salomea Falk's brother and his family left for Australia in 1957, leaving Salomea, her husband Ernest and their young son Feliks with no extended family in Poland. Zina Tyszelman's eldest sister emigrated to Israel, leaving behind her two sisters and their families as well as the grave of their mother, who died in 1952.

Furthermore, at least one parent in at least seven of the ten families visited Israel in 1957 and 1958, not to emigrate but to visit relatives whom they had not seen for a decade or more. At least one parent in six of the ten families had a sibling who had left for Palestine before the Second World War or in

---

32   Interview with Daniel Passent, Warsaw, Aug. 29 and Oct. 23, 2004. Passent is now a prominent writer and columnist for the weekly magazine *Polityka*, where he also worked during the Communist period.

the immediate aftermath of the Holocaust. Parents in two other families had cousins there. Salomea Falk and Zina Tyszelman both traveled to Israel in 1957 to visit their siblings who had recently left Poland as well as cousins whom they had not seen since before the war.[33] When two other mothers who lived at 16 Ujazdowskie Avenue in the first postwar decade, Stanisława Kruc and Stefania Fedecka, visited Israel in the same period, they brought with them their young children,[34] who had their first contact with an openly Jewish society. Fedecka's only child recalled the embarrassment he felt during his visit to Israel at being the only one among his male cousins who was uncircumcised.[35]

When the Polish government's antisemitic campaign in March, 1968, scapegoated Jews as the main element in student anti-censorship protests, the Jewish identity that was present in the shadows of the children's everyday life rose to the surface. They were confronted with a Jewish past about which most of them knew little. More than twelve thousand Jews, and as many as twenty thousand, emigrated in the following two years.[36] At 16 Ujazdowskie Avenue, three families left Poland after the events of March 1968, and another two families were split between emigration and Poland. Four families remained entirely in Poland.

Yet the departures did not put an end to Jewish integration in Poland. As the children who remained entered adulthood, they overcame much of the isolation from Polish society that had shaped their parents' lives. Both the

---

33   IPN BU 1368/633, "Stanisława Kruc, Akta Osobowe Cudzoziemca," document dated January 23, 1957 seeking permission to visit her brother in Israel. "I have not seen my brother since 1939 and recently I found him," Kruc wrote in seeking a travel visa to Israel. "He is one of the only ones from my family who remained."

34   IPN BU 1368/633, "Stanisława Kruc, Akta Osobowe Cudzoziemca," document dated March 18, 1957; and interview with Stefan Sztetner, Paris, March 15, 2007.

35   Interview with Stefan Sztetner, Paris, March 15, 2007.

36   There are no decisive data on the number of émigrés after the start of the antisemitic propaganda in 1967 and in the wake of the March protests in 1968. The Dutch embassy in Poland, acting on Israel's behalf, issued about 20,000 visas, although it is difficult to confirm how many recipients used the documents, since most émigrés traveled to other countries instead of to Israel. Albert Stankowski, using varied archival sources, gives the figure of 12,927 for the number of émigrés between 1968 and 1972, and 11,185 for the years 1967 to 1970, without determining a figure for the entire period between 1967 and 1972. Stankowski's numbers are conservative, and Eisler, in particular, is critical of the lower estimates. He places the number of émigrés at fifteen thousand to twenty thousand. See Stankowski, "Nowe spojrzenie na statystyki dotyczące emigracji Żydów z Polski po 1944 roku," in Grzegorz Berendt, August Grabski and Albert Stankowski (eds.), *Studia z historii Żydów w Polsce po 1945 r.* (Warsaw: Żydowski Instytut Historyczny, 2000); and Jerzy Eisler, "1968: Jews, Antisemitism, Emigration," *Polin. Studies in Polish Jewry* 21 (2009): 55.

absence of Jewish identity on the surface of their childhoods and its presence beneath the surface led to their assimilation as adults. They grew up in homes where Polish culture filled the gaps formed by their parents' suppression of their Jewish past. At the same time, the very spaces that connected them to other Jews in childhood limited the presence of antisemitism, which often preserves Jewish identity in the absence of any positive connection. Certainly some among them recalled encountering discrimination during the first postwar decades, but clusters of Jews among classmates, friends, and neighbors surrounded them in childhood with a concept of Polishness that did not exclude them.

Despite the antisemitic campaign of 1968, the spaces of everyday life that set them apart from other Poles at home, at school, and among friends in previous decades eventually helped those who remained in Poland after 1970 to fulfill their parents' hopes that their families would no longer experience life as the "other" in their native country. Of the nine children who grew up at 16 Ujazdowskie Avenue and remained in Poland after 1970, six married non-Jewish spouses, while those who had children raised them as Christians or with no religion at all. Of the two who married spouses of Jewish background, one left Poland in the 1980s.

But postwar Polish Jewish history is full of paradoxes. Even as Jewish families at 16 Ujazdowskie Avenue and elsewhere assimilated into surrounding society as children who grew up in Poland after the Second World War reached adulthood, some among them began to explore their Jewish background, if often only marginally. Their explorations eventually strengthened the Jewish presence in Poland, creating identities that blurred boundaries between Christian and Jewish, insider and outsider.

CHAPTER 24

In Search of Meaning after Marxism: The *Komandosi*, March 1968, and the Ideas that Followed

Marci Shore

"It is surely our lot—we, the plague-stricken sons—to live to the end and die with that 'Christian' blemish. We have been thus marked."[1] Adam Michnik, writing after the death of his close friend who was, like himself, the child of Polish-Jewish communists

The history of communism is a generational history. In Warsaw, embedded in this generational history is one story among many of Polish Jewry. For Aleksander Wat and Bruno Jasieński's generation of Polish intellectuals "of Jewish origin," born at the turn of the twentieth century, communism was something they came *to*. By the time any hope in some incarnation of Marxism had passed, it was too late: after Marxism there was nothing. The pressing question was how to live—or rather, how to die—with the guilt.

For Włodzmierz Brus, Zygmunt Bauman and Bronisław Geremek's generation, born between the two world wars, the story was a different one: engagé in the Stalinist years of their youth, the pressing question of later years was how to reconcile historical determinism with personal responsibility.

And for the generation of Adam Michnik, born after the Second World War, Marxism was the starting point, the context of their youth. Too young to have been implicated in the crimes of Stalinism, theirs was a guilt only by contiguity. (Perhaps they found themselves in a Freudian family romance that could only end in parricide?) For these children of *"żydokomuna"* who came to form the core of the *"komandosi"* of March 1968, the pressing question was rather: if Marxism, in all its contested versions, had failed, then what?

---

* My thanks to Jan T. Gross, Irena Grudzińska-Gross, Aleksander Smolar, and Timothy Snyder for reading earlier drafts of this essay, and Stanisław Krajewski and Krzysztof Michalski for serving as interlocutors. I would also like to thank the ever-stimulating and ever-congenial Institut für die Wissenschaften vom Menschen in Vienna, where I wrote this paper.

1 Adam Michnik, "Odlot malowanego ptaka," *Gazeta Wyborcza* (15 March 2009).

The members of this latter generation—or rather this milieu within a generation—were by and large born to the communist intelligentsia; they were raised in the capital; they had enjoyed privileged childhoods under Stalinism. Yet what was intellectually formative was less the Stalinism of their childhood than the revisionist Marxism of their youth, inaugurated by the Polish October of 1956. Inspired—that is, made possible—by Khrushchev's admissions that under Stalin there were "excesses," the Polish October promised a new era, and a new kind of Marxism. Revisionism was an attempt to reform communism as practiced, to reclaim a Marxism cleansed of bureaucracy, of "errors and distortions," of Stalinist terror: an attempt to reconcile determinism and responsibility. "The glue of our political education was *faith in the possibility of liberalizing socialism*," Barbara Toruńczyk wrote.[2] For Toruńczyk and her friends, the children of ideologically committed communists, communism was something they knew both from school and from home. (Jewishness—and certainly Judaism—by and large was not.) And as they neared adulthood, the questions they asked came from the confrontation between ideology and reality. For Toruńczyk, generational cohesion came from having grown up reading the same books: the ones published after 1956. There were not, after all, so many of these books; it was possible to read them all, to share a set of references.[3]

A Revisionist Adolescence

Most important of all were books by Leszek Kołakowski. In the decade following the Polish October, Warsaw University's star philosopher was a Marxist still. His 1957 essay, "The Concept of the Left," was an attempt to define the Left after Stalinism: what it was and what it ought to be. The overtone was Hegelian: the Left meant negation. This did not meant "destruction," but rather a negation of the existing social reality; negation was the opposite not of "construction," but of "*affirming existing conditions.*"[4]

Negation for Kołakowski was bound up with utopia, conceived as radical transformation, "a total negation of the existing system." For the Left, utopia was a necessity, something it could not do without: "The Left gives forth

---

[2] Barbara Toruńczyk, "Opowieść o pokoleniu marca: przesłanie dla nowej lewicy (część pierwsza)," *Krytyka Polityczna* 15 (summer 2008): 208–30, quotation on 228.
[3] Ibid., 225.
[4] Leszek Kołakowski: "Sens ideowy pojęcia lewica," *Aneks* 2 (summer 1973): 136–56. Quotations taken from Leszek Kołakowski, "The Concept of the Left," in *Marxism and Beyond*, trans. Jane Zielonko Peel (London: Pall Mall Press, 1969), 87–103, quotation on 87–88.

utopias just as the pancreas discharges insulin—by virtue of an innate law. Utopia is the striving for changes which 'realistically' cannot be brought about by immediate action, which lie beyond the foreseeable future and defy planning."[5] Yet was the impossible really impossible? Kołakowski insisted on the need to articulate goals *before* they were attainable—in order that they might some day become attainable: "It may well be that the impossible at a given moment can become possible only by being stated at a time when it is impossible ... *The existence of a utopia as a utopia is the necessary prerequisite for its eventually ceasing to be a utopia.*"[6] In other words, the demands of the Left *must be premature.*

Kołakowski positioned the authentic Left in opposition both to Stalinism and to the Right. The latter for Kołakowski included "bourgeois rule;" the "obscurantism of the clergy;" and those with "no scruples" who were not averse to exploiting antisemitism. The Left, in contrast, was "free of sacred feelings;" it had no emotional investment in the continuation of the current reality. It was fearless, unafraid of history and confident that both social relations and human nature could and would be changed. The Left stood for free speech and secularization, for the abolition of social privilege, for the largest possible role of the working class in government, for the elimination of antisemitism and all racisms, for "the victory of rational thought."[7] This was the Left that, while representing pure negation, stood for the antithesis of nihilism.[8]

Two years later, in 1959, Kołakowski approached the imperative of negation differently. "The Priest and the Jester" began with a discussion about eschatology: Could the best human values ever be fully realized? Was human history moving towards justice and equality? Would ultimately everything make sense and have a purpose? Would we achieve a world where good would be rewarded and evil would be punished, where everyone and everything would find its place in the correct order of things?

No longer did Kołakowski have an answer to this question. He wanted, rather, to describe the perpetual conflict in philosophy: "the conflict between a quest for the absolute and flight from it."[9] Here, too, there were Hegelian overtones: only by negation of the existing order did human history move forward. "All realms of culture," Kołakowski wrote,

---

5   Kołakowski, "The Concept of the Left," 90.
6   Ibid., 90–91.
7   Ibid., 96.
8   Ibid., 100.
9   Leszek Kołakowski, "The Priest and the Jester," in *Marxism and Beyond*, 29–57, quotation on 52.

... exemplify the paradox whereby everything that is new grows out of the endless need to question all existing absolutes. And though every new current of thought that tries to break away from acknowledged finalities establishes its own ultimates and though every rebellion is therefore metamorphosed into a conservative state, still, it makes room for the next phase, where its own absolutes will in turn be the target of criticism.[10]

These two forces—those of the absolute and the attempt to subvert it—were embodied in two historical characters: the priest and the jester. The priest guarded the absolute and its sanctity, while the jester held nothing sacred, instead "expos[ing] as doubtful what seems most unshakable, reveal[ing] the contradictions in that which appears obvious and incontrovertible."[11] Unlike the priest, the jester could provide no grounding structure of his own, he could only undermine. The Left needed both priest and jester, and Kołakowski believed that Marxism could provide both.

For Kołakowski's then future students, the priest and the jester was to be a lasting intellectual paradigm. Yet in politics the spirit of a self-questioning revisionist Marxism was much more ephemeral. The Polish October brought freedom that lasted for but a moment. Afterwards repression returned en force. These were the years when Toruńczyk and her friends could feel themselves "almost palpably ... beginning to suffocate."[12]

At this time, in 1962, the fifteen year-old Michnik, together with his friends Jan Gross, Jan Kofman, and Aleksander Perski, precociously embarked on their own exploration of revisionism and its discontents. "We knew," Michnik recalled, "that in Poland there was a dictatorship based on lies, only I was a rebellious communist, I was interested in Trotsky and the differences between the young Marx and the older Marx."[13] "In Marxist literature *The Revolution Betrayed* interested us much more than *The Communist Manifesto*," Gross explained, "and party discipline we regarded as a societal misunderstanding."[14] Michnik and his friends went to Polish United Workers' Party ideologist and Marxist philosopher Adam Schaff. According to Jacek Kuroń, Schaff welcomed

---

10   Ibid.
11   Ibid., 54.
12   Toruńczyk, "Opowieść o pokoleniu marca," 215.
13   Anna Bikont, "Moi chłopi wymordowali moich Żydów," *Gazeta Wyborcza* (5 February 2008).
14   Jan T. Gross, "Opozycja polityczna w wspołczesnej Polsce," *Aneks* 15 (1977): 11–29, here 25.

their proposal, being of the mind that "Marxist thought, even revisionist Marxist thought, was currently worth its weight in gold."[15]

In this way the Klub Poszukiwaczy Sprzeczności (Club of the Seekers of Contradictions) came into being. In time Michnik, Gross, Kofman and Perski were joined by Seweryn Blumsztajn, Irena Grudzińska, Jan Lityński, Barbara Toruńczyk and others who met on Thursdays in Warsaw University's philosophy department. They invited speakers like the sociologist Zygmunt Bauman, the historian Andrzej Walicki, the economist Włodzimierz Brus, and the poet Witold Dąbrowski.[16] They read Czesław Miłosz's *The Captive Mind*. They represented a young elite: most of the club's young members were the children of prewar communists—and most (although certainly not all) were "of Jewish origin." They were educating themselves: they would read the sources, discuss the literature, and then decide whether or not they were—or would be—communists.[17]

A young man named Henryk Wujec, who had organized his own Catholic discussion club, received an invitation from the Club of the Seekers of Contradictions: the young rebellious Marxists wanted to meet with their Catholic counterparts. Wujec accepted. "We looked at them," Wujec remembered, "and wondered how it was possible to become a Marxist, and they looked at us and wondered how it was possible to believe in God."[18]

It was in 1965, during Toruńczyk's and Michnik's first year at Warsaw University, that Jacek Kuroń and Karol Modzelewski risked their freedom for a Marxist gesture of opposition: they wrote an open letter calling for a new revolution, a true workers' revolution against the Party bureaucracy, which they claimed had merely become a new class exploiting workers and peasants. The teenaged Adam Michnik decided to join their protest; the result was his first arrest.[19]

Michnik was undeterred; his critical grappling with Marxism continued. "At his place we talked about ideas," Bronisław Świderski said of discussions with Michnik, "as if they were unattainable girls." This was in contrast to Świderski's

---

15 Jacek Kuroń, *Autobiografia* (Warsaw: Wydawnictwo Krytyki Politycznej, 2008); fragment "Michnika poprawka z fizyki" (odc. 9): http://www.krytykapolityczna.pl/Autobiografia/Michnika-poprawka-z-fizyki/menu-id-232.html [accessed 8 March 2010].

16 Adam Michnik, "Wolność, sprawiedliwość, miłosierdzie. Rzecz o Jacku," *Gazeta Wyborcza* (28 September 2006).

17 On the Klub Poszukiwaczy Sprzeczności, see Andrzej Friszke, *Anatomia buntu: Kuroń, Modzelewski i komandosi* (Kraków: Wydawnictwo Znak, 2010), 359–74.

18 Henryk Wujec, interview with Paweł Smoleński, *Gazeta Wyborcza* (15 July 2005).

19 Michnik, "Wolność, sprawiedliwość, miłosierdzie."

own home, where his relationship with his parents existed almost wordlessly. His battles with his father were of an odd sort, "since he never talked, they were my monologues."[20]

The tenth anniversary of the Polish October fell on the year following Kuroń and Modzelewski's open letter. On that occasion, Michnik organized a meeting at Warsaw University with speeches by Krzysztof Pomian and Leszek Kołakowski. In these years it was not only Kołakowski's essays, but also his person, who played a special role. "The thought and person of Leszek Kołakowski," Marcin Król wrote, "made up the greatest spiritual adventure of my youth. And after all, my fascination was not something exceptional. In Warsaw, in the mid-1960s, Kołakowski unquestionably ruled souls."[21] "We called Kołakowski 'master,'" Krzysztof Michalski recounted, "and it was without irony. One had to be an idiot not to notice his greatness. For that department he was something in the way of a sun, around which the others revolved, like planets."[22]

And so the meeting Michnik organized was extremely well attended. Kołakowski expressed nostalgia for the feeling of national unity brought by the Polish October a decade earlier. The aftermath had been a bitter disappointment. Poland suffered from material poverty, miserable automobiles, low rates of housing construction, and high rates of infant mortality. Thirteen years after Stalin's death, Poland remained a country in which there were no free elections, no freedom of association, no freedom of criticism, and no freedom of information. The theory that socialism by its nature required the absence of political freedoms had come to dominate. Moreover, if the era of Stalinist horrors had passed, so had the era of ideological sincerity. In the present day, Kołakowski told his listeners, Party representatives tended to be chosen by the principle of "negative selection," according to which "fawning, cowardice, absence of initiative, [and] willingness to eavesdrop" were qualifying factors. Poland suffered from "spiritual pauperization."[23]

---

20   Wojciech P. Duda, interview with Bronisław Świderski, "Po Śladach," *Przegląd Polityczny* 70 (1 May 2005).

21   Marcin Król, "Leszek Kołakowski i zmierzch filozofii racjonalistycznej," *Zeszyty lierackie* 3 (summer 1983): 25–51, quotation on 25.

22   Krzysztof Michalski, interviewed by Andrzej Franaszek i Grzegorz Jankowicz, *Tygodnik Powszechny* (8 September 2009): http://tygodnik.onet.pl/33,0,32785,1,artykul.html [accessed 8 March 2010].

23   "Odpis tajne wystąpienie profesora U.W. Leszka Kołakowskiego na zebraniu dyskusyjnym zorganizowanym w dniu 21. 10. 1966 w Instytucie Historycznym UW przez Zarząd ZMS Wydziału Historycznego UW na temat 'Kultura polska w ostatnim 10-leciu,'" 22 October 1966, Warsaw, Archiwum Dokumentacji Historycznej PRL-u, Warsaw. K. 103, S V/16.

Marzec 1968

As a philosophical argument, what Kołakowski said that day was in essence banal, as Bronisław Świderski later recalled. They had found themselves in a terrible situation "in which the most intelligent people can say nothing other than banality, yet suddenly it's revealed that banality is such a great threat to the system."[24] Six days later, Leszek Kołakowski was expelled from the Polish United Workers' Party.[25] For many of his students, their professor's expulsion marked their "official divorce" from Marxism.[26]

"The PRL," Andrzej Friszke described the *komandosi*, "was their state, their parents co-created and ruled it."[27] They had "an absolute sense of security (naive, as it turned out)," Aleksander Smolar later wrote.[28] They were unafraid of the regime. Theirs was an optimism engendered by "youth, lack of memory, a sense of security," Irena Grudzinska explained.[29] (Perhaps their parents, survivors of the Second World War and in many cases of interwar Polish prison, were the source of this security. Yet it was, paradoxically, a sense of security that those parents themselves rarely shared. His mother, Świderski described, "believed only her own fear... For her every moment was a game of life and death.")[30] Her generation, Toruńczyk wrote forty years later, had often been portrayed as the postwar-born children of prewar communists, often of Jewish origin, raised in the privilege and security that came from having influential parents, the *"bananowa młodzież"* ("banana youth") who grew up in Warsaw's nicest neighborhoods. Perhaps, Toruńczyk acknowledged, such a description

---

24 Duda, "Po Śladach,"
25 "Leszek Kołakowski do Biura Politycznego KC PZPR, 23 November 1966," in Józef Stępień (ed.), *Listy do Pierwszych Sekretarzy KC PZPR (1944–1970)* (Warszawa: Wydawnictwo FAKT, 1994), 251–54, esp. 253.
26 Toruńczyk, "Opowieść o pokoleniu marca," 229.
27 Friszke, *Anatomia buntu,* 404.
28 Aleksander Smolar, "Years of '68," *Eurozine,* http://www.eurozine.com/articles/2008-05-26-smolar-en.html [accessed 3 June 2010]. Published in German as "1968: Zwischen März und Mai," *Transit* 35 (summer 2008): 142–54. Irena Grudzińska makes this point as well in an interview with Shana Penn, "Należeliśmy do komunistycznej elity, dzięki czemu czuliśmy się chronieni i bezpieczni," in Shana Penn, *Podziemie kobiet,* trans. Hanna Jankowska (Warsaw: Rosner & Wspólnicy, 2003), 190.
29 Irena Grudzinska Gross, "1968 in Poland: Spoiled Children, Marxists, and Jews," in Vladimir Tismaneanu (ed.), *Promises of 1968: Crisis, Illusion, and Utopia* (Budapest and New York: Central European University Press, 2011), 43–53, quotation on 48.
30 Duda, "Po Śladach."

was true enough. It failed, though, "to solve the puzzle, why the spark of rebellion came from us."³¹

The catalyst was a play, a performance of Adam Mickiewicz's Romantic national drama *Dziady* (*Forefathers' Eve*), prematurely shut down by communist censors. The Polish Writers' Union protested. In a speech given at the Writers' Union, Kołakowski noted that presently, any expressed criticism was regarded as an anti-socialist attempt to restore capitalism in Poland. "But we must not submit to that blackmail," he said.

> In fact, if we were to believe that socialism could exist only in conditions of cultural repression, then we would have to believe that socialism is either impossible or only a parody of its own principles. Yet we have no reason to reach such a gloomy verdict. We want to attempt some form of socialist life in which the intolerable and destructive state of affairs under which cultural creativity and reflections on such are felt by the government as a permanent threat, requiring counter-action by means of violence and intimidation, will be abolished. We want this situation abolished, and we want that in the name of socialism, and not against socialism."³²

At Warsaw University, students joined the Writers' Union in protesting the closing of *Dziady*. "We regarded ourselves as socialists," Jan Gross explained, "but we couldn't understand why, for the nationalization of the means of production, society should pay with freedom and free speech."³³

Kuroń, Modzelewski, and Michnik were among those who organized a protest. It resulted in their imprisonment, as they had known it would.³⁴ Students demonstrated against the arrests of their classmates. Communist police forces beat the students. In the report of one western journalist, some of the students fled the university campus to a church across the street. Sympathetic priests found hiding places for them. Policemen impersonating students pursued the students into the church, and the journalist wanted to know: how could the priest distinguish the students from the policemen? And the priest replied that

---

31 Toruńczyk, "Opowieść o pokoleniu marca," 228.
32 Leszek Kołakowski, "Przemówienie na walnym nadzwyczajnym zebraniu Oddziału Warszawskiego Związku Literatów Polskich wygłoszone dnia 29 lutego 1968 r.," in *Obecność: Leszkowi Kołakowskiemu w 60 rocznicę urodzin* (London: Aneks, 1987), 7–9, quotation on 9.
33 Jan T. Gross, "Opozycja polityczna w wspołczesnej Polsce," *Aneks* 15 (1977): 11–29, esp. 25.
34 Adam Michnik, "Wolność, sprawiedliwość, miłosierdzie."

it was easy: "every policeman who comes into this church crosses himself."³⁵ The demonstrating students were an urban elite, children of the communist intelligentsia. The communist policemen were not.

Seweryn Blumsztajn, Jan Gross, Irena Grudzińska, Irena Lasota, Jan Lityński, Aleksander Smolar, Henryk Szlajfer, and Barbara Toruńczyk were also among those arrested. Grudzińska had been translating Trotsky's *The Revolution Betrayed*.³⁶ Now she found herself in communist prison. The experience was traumatic. Antisemitism was an interrogation technique: the arrested students were told they were foreign, other; that they were not Poles; that they did not belong. Michnik's interrogators told him that he was a Jew and should leave Poland. Why did he not go to Tel Aviv? He would happily leave for Tel Aviv the next day, Michnik retorted, if they would leave for Moscow.³⁷ Worse, though, were interrogators' attempts to manipulate them into testifying against one another—and against themselves. Interrogators fabricated *grypsy*, making a prisoner believe the notes were from a friend in another cell. Sometimes the deception was successful: sometimes the young people in prison told their interrogators too much.³⁸ "There are things," Barbara Toruńczyk wrote of her time in prison forty years later, "which each of us has dragged with us nearly our entire lives, we will never forgive ourselves."³⁹

Outside of the prison, as well, antisemitism was a favored tactic. The communist regime blamed the student demonstrations on Zionist conspirators. Opposition to censorship was cast as a Zionist plot against Poland. Among the Polish United Workers' Party's slogans that spring were "Cleanse the party of Zionists!" and "Provocateurs, away from the academy!" "We demand the unmasking and punishment of Zionist instigators!" and "Down with Kołakowski, Brus and company!"⁴⁰

---

35   Quoted in Thomas W. Simons, *Eastern Europe in the Postwar World* (New York: St. Martin's Press, 1993), 136.
36   Friszke, *Anatomia buntu*, 700.
37   Quoted in ibid., p, 733; original in Adam Michnik, "Pewien polski etos. Rozmowa Dany Cohn-Bendita z Adamem Michnikiem," in Andrzej Romanowski (ed.), *Diabeł naszego czasu: publicystyka z lat 1985–1994* (Warszawa: Niezależna Oficyna Wydawnicza, 1995), 406.
38   Friszke, *Anatomia buntu*, 599–883.
39   Quoted in ibid., 683.
40   Teresa Torańska, *Jesteśmy: Rozstania '68* (Warsaw: Świat Książki, 2008), 227. In the Polish original: "Oczyścić partię z syjonistów!", "Prowokatorzy, precz z uczelni!" "Żądamy zdemaskowania i ukarania syjonistycznych rozrabiaczy!" and "Precz z Kołakowskim, Brusem i spółką!"

"Nevertheless," Aleksander Smolar wrote forty years later, "the anti-Semitic campaign of the authorities of the time does not provide a let-out from an answer to the question: why were so many Jews, Jewish Poles, Poles of Jewish descent, Poles with Jewish roots (what difficulties the Polish language has with Jewishness!) among the initiators of the '68 movement? Not just in Poland, but also in the Paris May, or the American '68 movement, or maybe elsewhere too."[41] Irena Grudzinska poses this question as well: "what led all these young people—Jews or of Jewish origin, born after the Holocaust, to be so prominently involved in student protests?"[42]

In a March 1968 speech, Władysław Gomułka spoke about opening the borders in order that those who "regard Israel as their homeland" could leave Poland.[43] Many of the arrested students emigrated following their release, as did many who were not arrested but were expelled from university. Some 13,000 people—mostly Polish Jews from the intelligentsia, many lifelong communists—left Poland. Leszek Kołakowski left, as well, settling eventually in Oxford.[44] Krzysztof Michalski, then a student in the philosophy faculty, was among those who stayed. Yet nothing was ever the same again. "March 1968 ended everything," he remembered, "It was a catastrophe for Polish sciences and humanities, for all of Polish intellectual life. Our department went from being one of the best in Europe to being a real hole."[45]

In Torunczyk's opinion, by March 1968 Marxism had already ended for her generation. In contrast to their contemporaries in the West, the Polish students who demonstrated that year no longer truly believed Marxism could be reformed. This was in contrast, too, to their counterparts in Czechoslovakia, for whom hope in a better version of Marxism lasted until the Warsaw Pact—that is, Soviet—invasion that August. It was a difference that resembled, as Torunczyk described it, "a different tempo among performers of the same

---

41 Smolar, "Years of '68."
42 Grudzinska Gross, "1968 in Poland: Spoiled Children, Marxists, and Jews," 49.
43 Władysław Gomułka, "Przemówienie na spotkaniu z warszawskim aktywem partyjnym," 19 March 1968, in Władysław Gomułka, *Przemówienia 1968* (Warszawa: Książka i Wiedza, 1969), 74–75.
44 On the events of March 1968, see Andrzej Friszke, *Anatomia buntu*. passim; Dariusz Stola, *Kampania antysyjonistyczna w Polsce 1967–1968* (Warsaw: ISP PAN, 2000); Franciszek Dąbrowski, Piotr Gontarczyk, and Paweł Tomasik, *Marzec 1968 w dokumentach MSW* (Warsaw: Instytut Pamięci Narodowej), vol. 1: *Niepokorni* (2008). vol. 2: *Kronika wydarzeń* (2009).
45 Krzysztof Michalski, interviewed by Andrzej Franaszek and Grzegorz Jankowicz, *Tygodnik Powszechny* (8 September 2009); http://tygodnik.onet.pl/33,0,32785,1,artykul .html [accessed 8 March 2010].

musical composition."⁴⁶ Even so, in Poland as well that year brought a "caesura in consciousness."⁴⁷ For Gross, March 1968 was the "definitive end of revisionism"—but not only that. For while the end of Marxist revisionism might well have come in any case, the specific circumstances—the "flood of lies, xenophobia and antisemitism"—was a shock. March 1968, Gross explained, was "a generational experience."⁴⁸ "And for many of us," Grudzinska wrote, "it was the moment in which personal fate met with historical fate."⁴⁹

The Shaking of Utopia

Jan Gross, together with Irena Grudzińska, Aleksander Smolar, his brother Eugeniusz Smolar and his sister-in-law Nina Smolar, were among those who left prison—and left Poland. A few years later, now in emigration, together with Krzysztof Dorosz and Irena Grosfeld-Smolar, they began the London-based journal *Aneks*. It was a small group, with family ties.⁵⁰ Marxism—accounting with Marxism—was a point of departure. The first issue of *Aneks*, published in 1973, began with a self-introduction: "Doubtlessly most of us are closest to the socialist tradition."⁵¹ Now the editors felt a need to familiarize themselves with different perspectives. It could not be otherwise: they were living in West European exile.

"The West," Aleksander Smolar wrote,

> churned up by 1968, fascinated me; but I also felt lonely and alien. The people I met in Bologna and Paris were often near to me in age, sensitivity, and literary taste, but at the same time terribly distant. This began at the level of language. For them, the basic category was revolution. Milan Kundera contrasted the Paris uprising and its 'explosion of revolutionary lyricism' to the Prague Spring and its 'explosion of post-revolutionary skepticism.' What he said about the Czechs and Slovaks was also relevant

---

46   Toruńczyk, "Opowieść o pokoleniu marca," 221.
47   Ibid., 224, 221.
48   Jan T. Gross, "Opozycja polityczna w współczesnej Polsce," *Aneks* 15 (1977): 11–29, esp. 26. See also Marcin Król, *Czego nas uczy Leszek Kołakowski* (Warszawa: Czerwone i czarne, 2010), 105–6.
49   Grudzinska Gross, "1968 in Poland: Spoiled Children, Marxists, and Jews," 45.
50   Andrzej Paczkowski, "O 'Aneksie' po latach," *Zeszyty Literackie* 84 (2003): 136–42, quotation 137. See also Andrzej Paczkowski, "'Aneks' 1973–1989," *Res Publica* 9 (1990): 28–37.
51   Zespół Redakcyjny, "Od Redakcji," *Aneks* 1 (1973).

to Warsaw and Poland. Except that the Polish intellectuals already had hopes for 'socialism with a human face' behind them. The Western prisoners of semantics—Marxists, Leninists, Trotskyites, Maoists, situationists, anarchists, and even socialists—were describing the world in the same language as Brezhnev and Gomulka. That was enough to block conversation, not to mention agreement.[52]

Aneks's early issues reflected both an intellectual passage from revisionism to "post-revisionism," and this separation from the editors' West European contemporaries.[53] In summer 1973 the second issue of *Aneks* included a special section titled "Lewica i utopia" ("the Left and utopia"). In his introduction, Aleksander Smolar (writing under the pseudonym "Adam Kalm") wrote of how, in Eastern Europe, something had broken in leftist thought in the middle of the 1960s. Now it was the relationship between the Left and utopia that created an additional difference between Europe's east and west. Utopia meant harmony; it meant the co-existence of all values—freedom and equality, security and dynamism, fraternity and individual development, perfect organization and the destruction of the state as a repressive organization. In Western Europe, Smolar believed, the "New Left" continued to believe in utopia as such.

Among the slogans of the May 1968 Sorbonne demonstrations was "*Soyons réalistes, demandons l'impossible!*" Eleven years earlier Kołakowski had insisted that the demands of the Left must be premature, that "the impossible at a given moment can become possible only by being stated at a time when it is impossible." Now in Eastern Europe this confidence had already passed. For in communist countries, the "New Left" now parted with utopia. "When one believes in the possibility of absolute attainment," Smolar now wrote critically, "one has decided to bear all costs—including human ones."[54]

Following the introduction was Kołakowski's 1957 essay "The Concept of the Left," arguing for the necessity of utopia. While the essay belonged to an era now passed, *Aneks*'s editors "regard[ed] the text as worthy of revisiting."[55] They

---

52 Aleksander Smolar, "Years of '68."
53 I have borrowed the term "post-revisionism" in this context from Andrzej Paczkowski, see his "'Aneks' 1973–1989," 30.
54 Adam Kalm [Aleksander Smolar], "Lewica i utopia: zamiast wstępu," *Aneks* 2 (1973): 74–79, quotation on 76.
55 Ibid., 79.

were thinking through utopia—under the guidance of someone who understood just how powerful a temptation utopia could be.[56]

By the 1970s, Kołakowski's belief in the necessity of utopia was increasingly overshadowed by his growing conviction that the costs would always be too high. In a 1974 essay on the "revolutionary spirit," published in *Aneks*, Kołakowski compared the categories of absolute salvation espoused alike by revolutionary Marxism and early Christianity:

> In the most general terms, revolutionary mentality is a way of thinking distinguished by the particularly intense belief, that man's total salvation is possible and that this state of salvation stands in absolute opposition to the present state of servitude, such that there is no continuity between them and no intermediary states; moreover, that this total salvation is the single self-sufficient goal of humanity, that all other values must be made to comply as means. There is only one goal and one value, and that is total negation of the existing world. Whatever cannot be made to serve as a means of attaining that value no longer counts at all, it must be regarded as part of today's rotten world. Suffering and hardship are an inherent part of the path to salvation, but for that reason are also meaningful and are rewarded hundreds of times over. In short, revolutionaries do not believe in purgatory: they believe in the way of the cross, they believe in heaven and hell, in a kingdom of total salvation and a kingdom of total evil. They reason according to the principle 'all or nothing.'[57]

Kołakowski was by now resigned: there would never be any single leap "from the depths of hell... to the peaks of heaven."[58]

The response to this impossibility, though, should not be a fatalistic appeasement of all evils. While there were no laws of history that guaranteed progress, this did not mean that a world better than the current one was not possible.[59] Human beings, fated to make compromises, *could* learn better the

---

56   "...mało komu," Kołakowski well understood, "udaje się całkowicie skutecznie opierać się pokusie utopii...." ("There are few who succeed entirely in resisting the temptation of utopia....") Kołakowski, *Czy diabeł może być zbawiony i 27 innych kazań* (London: Aneks, 1984), 7.
57   Leszek Kołakowski, "O duchu rewolucyjnym," *Aneks* 4 (1974): 3–15, quotation on 4.
58   Ibid., 15.
59   Leszek Kołakowski, "Dlaczego potrzeba nam pieniędzy?" *Aneks* 5 (1974): 10–30, quotation on 30.

art of balancing opposing dangers.⁶⁰ Kołakowski's 1979 essay for *Aneks,* "Jak być konserwatyno-liberalnym socjalistą?" ("How to be a conservative-liberal socialist?"), was a codification of these ideas into a political manifesto— a political manifesto that opposed political ideologies. He began on a sober note: while countless evils were capable of coexistence, many goods limited or excluded one another. There was no such thing, for instance, as a society that enjoyed full freedom and full equality. The task of the state was to provide for society's security, which meant that people should not starve for lack of work or die of curable illnesses for lack of money. Security meant more state regulation, whereas freedom meant less: the truth was that security could only be increased at the cost of freedom. More security, Kołakowski believed, was often worth this cost, yet "[t]his limiting of freedom...should be called the limiting of freedom, not a special form of freedom."⁶¹ All improvements in human life needed to be paid for at the expense of other aspects of human life. Yet it was morally unsustainable to draw from this the conclusion that every form of inequality was unavoidable and every form of exploitation justified. The moral imperative was not to abandon efforts at improvement, but rather to maintain an awareness of the price we were paying. Alas, Kołakowski acknowledged, "there exist[ed] no *happy ending* to human history."⁶²

Understanding Totalitarianism, or towards a Philosophy of the Opposition

Barbara Toruńczyk spent the first half of the 1970s reading Theodor Adorno and Hannah Arendt, for whom the destruction of subjectivity was among totalitarianism's defining features. At the time these authors were not available in Polish translation.⁶³ *Aneks* in part compensated, publishing in the 1970s and 1980s Arendt and other authors such as Zygmunt Bauman, Nadezhda Mandelshtam, Samuel Huntington, Arthur Koestler, Raymond Aron, Aleksandr Solzhenitsyn, Vasily Grossman, Zbigniew Brzeziński, George Orwell, and Isaiah Berlin. "Our *maîtres à penser*," Toruńczyk explained, "became, alongside Kołakowski (whose every word was always important to us), Miłosz, Wat, Orwell, Hanna

---

60   Kołakowski, *Czy diabeł może być zbawiony*, 157.
61   Leszek Kołakowski, "Jak być konserwatyno-liberalnym socjalistą?" *Aneks* 20 (1979): 3–6, quotation on 5.
62   Kołakowski, "Jak być konserwatyno-liberalnym socjalistą?" 3.
63   Toruńczyk, "Opowieść o 1968," 272–305.

Arendt, Raymond Aron—intellectuals, who tried to define the traits of ideological dictatorship."[64]

The pages of *Aneks*, like the pages of many underground publications in Poland in the 1970s and 1980s, revealed a shift from critiques of Marxism to critiques of totalitarianism as such. Grudzińska published essays in *Aneks* analyzing the language of communist censors—themselves subject to the regime, never entirely sure when the Party line would change. As a result, the censor's world was a world without a real language.[65] For Grudzińska, the erstwhile translator of Trotsky's *The Revolution Betrayed*, the focus was no longer an examination of Marxism in any of its forms, but rather an examination of the power mechanisms of a totalitarian regime.

This was true as well of Jan Gross's work about the Soviet occupation of eastern Poland, which began to appear in *Aneks* in 1979.[66] Amidst graphic descriptions of Soviet violence, Gross posed questions about the "essence of 20th-century totalitarianism." He was struck in particular by the countless cases in which victim and perpetrator knew each other personally. Mechanisms of terror, put at the disposal of the new regime's adherents, were used to settle personal scores; the ever-present possibility of informing meant that every person was threatened at every moment. While at a given time certain groups might be targeted more than others, one's fate tended to lie in the hands of one's fellow citizens: for terror was arbitrary and the criteria for imprisonment were fluid. "The public sphere and the private sphere cease to be divided in the sense," he wrote, in a modification of an Arendtian motif, "that the adjudication of even the most intimate matters is the prerogative of the state. The individual is an instrument by means of which the fate of the collectivity is constructed. What follows is a nationalization of the private sphere."[67] This made for a certain egalitarianism: at any given moment every person was at once infinitely helpless as to his own fate and infinitely powerful as to the fates of others. Each person was always both vulnerable to arrest and capable of

---

64 Ibid., 288. See also Barbara Toruńczyk, *Żywe cienie* (Warszawa: Fundacja Zeszytów Literackich, 2012).

65 Irena Grudzińska-Gross, "Świat zaaresztowanych słów," *Aneks* 21 (1979): 92–106, quotation on 105. See also Grudzińska-Gross's linguistic analysis of the communist regime's anti-Solidarity propaganda: "Manipulacje pod płaszczykiem," *Aneks* 29–30 (1983): 217–23.

66 See Jan T. Gross "W zaborze sowieckim," pt. 1, *Aneks* 22 (1979): 16–44 and pt. 2, *Aneks* 28 (1982): 61–96.

67 Ibid., 94 and Jan T. Gross, *Revolution from Abroad: The Soviet Conquest of Poland's Western Ukraine and Western Belorussia* (Princeton: Princeton University Press, 1988).

using the state apparatus against a fellow citizen. The result of such "egalitarianism" was social atomization.

Both those like Gross, Grudzińska, and Smolar who left Poland, and those like Blumsztajn, Lityński, and Michnik who stayed, devoted themselves to the opposition. And the shift from critiques of Marxism to critiques of totalitarianism stood, too, at the center of Komitet Obrony Robotników (The Workers' Defense Committee, KOR). In June 1976, Edward Gierek, who in 1970 had replaced Gomułka as General Secretary of the Party, raised food prices. In Radom and elsewhere workers protested; in the wake of the brutal repressions that followed, many workers found themselves unemployed—or imprisoned. In response, intellectuals formed the Workers' Defense Committee, articulating the demands of the workers on the workers' behalf, protesting the increase in food prices; the meat shortages; the poor health services; the housing shortages; the increase in the working day; the extensive privileges enjoyed by authorities; the violence and abusiveness of the police; and the throttling of culture and scholarship by censorship. It was the moment when intellectuals and workers joined forces; and it was the precedent for the creation of Solidarity four years later, in the wake of Pope John Paul II's first papal visit to Poland. Solidarity grew into a mass social movement. It was a name with real content: people of the right and left, Marxists and Catholics, intellectuals and workers—together some ten million people—united against an oppressive regime. "History has taught us," Solidarity's program declared, "that there is no bread without freedom."

Erstwhile firm oppositions between Left and Right, Catholicism and Marxism now "melted into air." Once all-meaningful, these categories came to be seen as relics of a by-gone era, by now anachronistic.[68] The old division between "progressive" and "Catholic" intellectuals, Gross wrote shortly after the founding of KOR, had been broken. He quoted Kołakowski, who had recently written that the whole "secular humanism in battle with Catholic obscurantism" no longer applied; it referenced a no-longer existing world.[69] "The enemy of the Left," Michnik wrote, "is not the Church but totalitarianism."[70] And the opposition defined itself above all as being anti-totalitarian.

Anti-totalitarianism meant not only overcoming the ossified division between Left and Right, but also restoring subjectivity to the individual. KOR's

---

68 Adam Michnik, *Takie czasy... rzecz o kompromisie* (London: Aneks, 1985), quotation on 12.
69 Jan T. Gross, "Opozycja polityczna w wspołczesnej Polsce," *Aneks* 15 (1977): 11–29, here 28–29.
70 Adam Michnik, *The Church and the Left*, trans. David Ost (Chicago: University of Chicago Press, 1993), 182.

focus was the "concrete person" who needed help: be it by means of money, advice, employment, legal aid or medical assistance.[71] The opposition distinguished itself from the regime in turning from "the people" to individual "persons." This was Kuroń's great contribution as well. "For Jacek did not love mankind," Michnik later wrote, "Jacek loved people, real people, people of blood and bones, in their searching and wandering, in their struggle with suffering, with the hardship of existence, with disease, with death."[72]

KOR's only doctrine, Michnik insisted, was the call to build "society's subjectivity."[73] The imperative was to end people's passivity, to build social ties, to make society *active*, Jan Lityński argued. The point was to instill in people a "feeling of freedom, [of] the possibility of thinking, speaking, and writing in accordance with their conscience."[74]

Konstanty Gebert, who was a few years younger, agreed. Despite the authorities' efforts, Gebert maintained in an essay published by the underground press, martial law had only increased Polish society's awareness of its "own political subjectivity."[75] Moreover, the restoration of subjectivity was not only a means to an end, but more importantly, an end unto itself: "our aim should not be an attempt to conclude a compromise with the government… but to increase the scope of our own subjectivity… society's subjectivity cannot be the object of bargaining or an instrument of realizing some other goal. On the contrary: it's a goal unto itself."[76]

The restoration of subjectivity went hand-in-hand with an embrace of pluralism and an accompanying refusal to subscribe to any over-arching vision of a new harmonious order. For Michnik, this was the lesson of Kołakowski's anti-utopian critique. Another lesson Michnik took was that totalitarian regimes required hatred not only against external enemies, but also against their own people in order to "desolate them internally, overpower them spiritually." This was totalitarianism's "secret weapon": the spiritual poisoning of the individual

---

71 Jan Józef Lipski, "Etos Komitetu Obrony Robotników," *Aneks* 29–30 (1983): 30–46, quotation on 30.

72 Adam Michnik, "Wolność, sprawiedliwość, miłosierdzie. Rzecz o Jacku," *Gazeta Wyborcza* (28 September 2006).

73 Michnik, *Takie czasy… rzecz o kompromisie*, 12.

74 Jan Lityński, *Solidarność—problemy, znaki zapytania, próby odpowiedzi* (Warsaw: Wydawnictwo Przedświt, 1984), quotation on 15–16. "poczucie wolności, o możliwość myślenia, mówienia, i pisania w zgodzie z sumieniem."

75 Dawid Warszawski [Konstanty Gebert], *Przerwa na myślenie* (Kraków: Miesięcznik Małopolski, 1986), 50.

76 Warszawski, *Przerwa na myślenie*, 51.

that deprived him of dignity.[77] It could only be combated by respect for the individual. The Polish opposition's new formula—"żyj jak wolny człowiek" ("live like a free person"), Jan Gross wrote in the pages of *Aneks*, was restoring to people a sense that they were not objects, but rather subjects. Members of KOR were "living like free people in a free country."[78] To live in freedom meant to live in responsibility. "Today, when no one is able to appreciate the vital significance of eternal conditions," Henryk Szlajfer wrote, quoting the nineteenth-century Polish historian Michał Bobrzyński in an essay for an underground journal, "we can use external conditions as an excuse to avoid responsibility; however. . .it is exactly this responsibility on which we should lay the greatest emphasis."[79]

Epilogue

In 1990 *Aneks's* editor Aleksander Smolar brought his journal to a gracious end. The function *Aneks* had fulfilled, he wrote in a note to his readers, would now be fulfilled by new publications that would emerge in the new Poland. "The discontinuation of this journal," he added, "does not end the active public engagement in Polish issues of those people associated with it. But those will be other adventures."[80] They have been.[81]

---

77   Quoted in Michnik, *Takie czasy . . . rzecz o kompromisie*, 133.
78   Jan T. Gross, "Opozycja polityczna w wspołczesnej Polsce," *Aneks* 15 (1977): 11–29, esp. 28–29.
79   Jan Kowalski and Andrzej Malinowski (Henryk Szlajfer), "Under the Military Dictatorship: Between 'Freeze Frame' and 'Restoration,'" in M. Bernard and H. Szlajfer (eds.) *From the Polish Underground: Selections from* Krytyka *1978–1993* (University Park, PA: Pennsylvania State University Press, 1996), 1–67, quotation on 4; originally published in *Krytyka* 12 (1982).
80   Aleksander Smolar w imieniu Zespołu Redakcyjnego, "Do Czytelników Kwartalnika 'Aneks'," reprinted in Andrzej Paczkowski, "'Aneks' 1973–1989," 37.
81   On the *pokolenie marca* after 1989, and its dialogue with a younger generation, see especially Barbara Toruńczyk's exchange with Krytyka Polityczna leader Sławomir Sierakowski: Barbara Toruńczyk, "Opowieść o pokoleniu marca: przesłanie dla nowej lewicy (część pierwsza)," *Krytyka Polityczna* 15 (2008): 208–30; Toruńczyk, "Opowieść o 1968," 272–305; Sławomir Sierakowski, "Zakładnicy własnego zwycięstwa," *Krytyka Polityczna* 16/17 (2009): 306–13.

Some Reflections

When in Warsaw in 1991, the American journalist Shana Penn interviewed Irena Grudzińska. Penn was surprised to learn that in 1969 Grudzińska had emigrated from Poland: the other Solidarity activists had spoken of Grudzińska as if she had been in Poland the whole time. "I live abroad as if I were Madame Bovary," Grudzińska explained to her, "I'm not in the place where I physically am."[82]

What was striking about the *komandosi* was their commitment to Poland. This was true of those who stayed and those who emigrated alike: the extraordinary devotion of the "March emigration"—precisely those whom Władysław Gomułka accused of not regarding Poland as their homeland—was one among many painful ironies of Polish-Jewish history. "I continue to think," Świderski explained in an interview thirty-five years after his emigration from Poland, "that Michnik and his group, these are one hundred percent self-conscious Poles—in distinction to the majority of inhabitants of our homeland... Precisely that surplus of conscious 'Polishness' in Michnik's group was defined by Gomułka and Moczar in March as 'Zionism' and 'a fifth column.'"[83] In 1968, these young people were not acting as Jews, but as young members of a Polish intelligentsia they conceived of as morally obliged to represent universal values.[84] Even while *Aneks* found its place as a European journal, publishing Czech, German, Russian, and French authors in translation, its gaze never strayed from Poland. The editors followed every twist and turn of the Polish opposition, lived every incremental victory and defeat, reflected repeatedly on the meaning for Poland of 1939, of 1945, of 1956, 1968, 1970, 1976, 1980. By all possible means they strove to support Solidarity. Wherever they found themselves, they *lived Poland*.

It was true as well, that the explorations of Jewishness on the part of both this generation's émigrés and those who remained in Poland were always already very much about Polishness. For this generation, Jewishness—like Catholicism, like the very notion of moral values—was always very much about Polishness. This is true as well of the angst-laden and deeply probing discussions about Polish-Jewish relations, which became animated in the 1980s. At a 1984 Oxford University conference organized by Antony Polonsky, Jan Gross delivered a lecture on Polish-Jewish relations during the Second World War in which he posed the painful question of why more Poles did not help

---

82   Shana Penn, *Podziemie kobiet*, 203–4.
83   Duda, "Po Śladach."
84   Grudzinska Gross, "1968 in Poland: Spoiled Children, Marxists, and Jews," 48.

save Jews. The explanation could not be simply that it was so dangerous, for after all, Gross pointed out, "the Poles lived dangerously in those days and were proud of it."⁸⁵ The deeper reason, Gross argued, was more likely a lack of social approval.

Gross's explorations of antisemitism, then and later, were always bound up with his explorations of totalitarianism—it was totalitarianism that was his milieu's true preoccupation. Their reaction to the antisemitism they faced in 1968 was not the reaction of Jews whose feelings were personally hurt as much as it was the reaction of principled and idealistic young leftists who believed that antisemitism was a symptom of fascism, a manipulation tactic of totalitarianism. When in 1986 Gross published a version of this lecture in *Aneks*, he introduced the text by expressing his concerns about the reception of his original Oxford lecture—which was translated into unauthorized Polish and reached people he knew in Poland, who declared that the text was an "intellectual aberration, that under the influence of the film *Shoah* the blood of the Maccabees in me has raised its voice." "And because I believe that everything one writes is addressed first and foremost to friends," Gross responded, "I understood that my text did not defend itself on its own and that it was necessary to support it with a declaration of good will. Which I do. Above all I would like to assure readers that my article is a reaction to the call of the blood of the Piasts rather than the blood of the Maccabees."⁸⁶ Gross was not alone among his friends in never having lost the striking sense of belonging to the intelligentsia from the capital, of being morally obligated by the historic role of Polish intellectuals to be the "conscience of the nation."

Striking, too, about this generation is the unusual role played by Leszek Kołakowski. "In my generation," Michnik wrote, "each of us is to some extent Kołakowski's pupil."⁸⁷ In the 1970s and 1980s, now a professor at Oxford, Kołakowski published seventeen texts in *Aneks*; he was the journal's most frequent contributor, both a patron and a "guru," as Andrzej Paczkowski described him.⁸⁸ He was a philosopher who was read by philosophers and

---

85 Jan T. Gross, "Polish-Jewish Relations during the War: An Interpretation," *European Journal of Sociology* XXVII (1986): 199–214.
86 Jan Tomasz Gross, "Ten jest z ojczyzny mojej…, ale go nie lubię," *Aneks* 41–42 (1986): 13–35, quotation on 15.
87 Michnik, *The Church and the Left*, 191.
88 Andrzej Paczkowski, "O 'Aneksie' po latach," 140; Andrzej Paczkowski, "'Aneks' 1973–1989," 35. Wydawnictwo Aneks, the journal's affiliated publishing house, also published Kołakowski's books. "Mamy do czynienia niewątpliwie z daleko posuniętą 'kołakowszczyzną,'" Paczkowski writes (36). ("We're dealing undoubtedly here with a "Kołakowski-fête taken quite far.")

non-philosophers alike.[89] Toruńczyk believed it was the great good fortune of her own milieu to have had Kołakowski as their leader. (The French students did not—instead they had Sartre, who "led them astray.")[90] It was Kołakowski who gave them the jester and the priest, teaching them both to be skeptical of seeming certainties—and to be aware that skepticism had its limits. While dismantling dogmas, he never placed doubt in ethical values. "That shaking of trust in a system of values, but not the values themselves," Toruńczyk wrote, "is surely a characteristic of our generation."[91]

Kołakowski insisted that there was a distinction between good and evil transcendent of any momentary partialities. Whether one attributed this distinction to religious tradition or to Kantian reason mattered little. The critical point for Michnik was that there be a moral boundary, a boundary that stood above any ideologies that might seem momentarily compelling, be they ideologies of the Right or the Left.[92] This was the imperative of the post-Marxist years: that in rejecting the validity of grand narratives, one not reject the validity of moral values. The impulse to "take apart" must have its limits; it was imperative to maintain faith in the categories of "good" and "evil" as having tangible meaning that could be grasped and held.

In this connection, a third striking characteristic of the *komandosi* reveals itself: an intellectual split with their West European counterparts, the veterans of 1968 in Paris and elsewhere. Like Kołakowski's own post-Marxist philosophy, post-modernism was a reaction to 1968, to the death of Marxism as the last grand narrative. In France, following Sartre's reign came that of Michel Foucault and Jacques Derrida, each of whom in his own way did away with the stable subject—and with the possibility of stable meaning. French post-modernism was the decisive break with Hegel, and Derrida opposed linear narrative as totalitarian, as connected with the illusion of a unifying first principle that did not exist. For Derrida not only was God in particular dead, but the very notion that there could exist a transcendental signified of any kind was a chimera. In reality there was nothing to anchor us: no center, no "privileged

---

89   See the comments, for instance, by Agnieszka Holland and Aleksander Smolar in "Pogrzeb prof. Leszka Kołakowskiego," *Gazeta Prawna* (29 July 2009): http://www.gazetaprawna.pl/wiadomosci/artykuly/341008,pogrzeb_prof_leszka_kolakowskiego.html [accessed 8 March 2010].

90   Toruńczyk, "Opowieść o pokoleniu marca," 226.

91   Ibid.

92   Adam Michnik, "Kłopot," in *Obecność: Leszkowi Kołakowskiemu w 60 rocznicę urodzin* (London: Aneks, 1987), 198–219, see 214–15.

reference," no "absolute *archia*."⁹³ There were no origins to ground meaning and no telos to direct it; rather meaning was always already present in excess, always already in conflict with itself, subverting itself, leading us to an impasse. For Derrida this stance was not only philosophical, but also ethical: he understood it as a means of deconstructing ideologies, as an antidote to the way of thinking that had led to Stalinism and Nazism.⁹⁴

Kołakowski's jester was post-modernist *avant la lettre*. Yet Kołakowski's loyalty to the jester was a qualified one. Kołakowski taught him—the "człowiek z rozpadliny" ("person from the chasm"), Michnik once wrote, "—that the priest and the jester must *meet*, one defends against fanaticism, the other against nihilism."⁹⁵ What Derrida called "the transcendental signified" was for Kołakowski "the absolute," and throughout his life Kołakowski remained reluctant to abandon such a possibility in its entirety. "A philosophy that tries to dispense with absolutes and with the prospect of finality," he wrote in "The Priest and the Jester," "cannot, by the nature of things, be a consistent structure, for it has no foundations and does not want a roof; it undermines existing structures and rips off existing roots."⁹⁶ And this came at a cost.

In the 1970s, Adam Michnik became the secretary of the then aged but ever irreverent Antoni Słonimski. At the end of his life Słonimski, the Skamander poet, returned to the role he had played in his youth: that of Poland's consummate jester. The anti-utopianism that Michnik had learned from Kołakowski insulated him, Michnik believed, against all "pleasant falsehoods about oneself and one's human condition."⁹⁷ It was an anti-utopianism that was not nihilism, but was on the contrary the only way to rescue moral values. Solidarity's idea of "self-limiting revolution," of living "as if" one were a free individual reflected this stance.

Against post-modernism's mournful loss of the subject, Kołakowski's students insisted on the possibility of a substantive subjectivity. And against post-modernism's loss of faith in stable meaning, Kołakowski continued to instill in his erstwhile students "faith in the meaning of big questions."⁹⁸ Unlike Hobbes

---

93   Jacques Derrida, "Structure, Sign, and Play in the Discourse of the Human Sciences," in idem, *Writing and Difference*, trans. Alan Bass (Chicago: University of Chicago Press, 1978), 279–93, quotation on 286.
94   On Derrida's explicit engagement with ethics, see also Jacques Derrida, "Like the Sound of the Sea Deep Within a Shell: Paul de Man's War," *Critical Inquiry* 14.3 (1988): 590–652 and Jacques Derrida, *On Cosmopolitanism and Forgiveness* (New York: Routledge, 2001).
95   Adam Michnik, "Książę i żebrak," *Aletheia* 1 (1987): 153–73, quotation on 157.
96   Kołakowski, "The Priest and the Jester," 55.
97   Michnik, *Takie czasy... rzecz o kompromisie*, 7.
98   Marcin Król, *Czego nas uczy Leszek Kołakowski*, 207. See also 107–8, and 252.

or Kant or Hegel, Kołakowski, Król wrote, never created any overarching system. Yet he always insisted that the search for meaning was essential. Even if the answers were impossible, the search had to continue. Giving up on meaning—on the possibility of absolute truth—would be giving up on humanity. In an essay confronting the angst-laden history of Polish Jews' engagement in communism, Aleksander Smolar called for an end to taboos, for an open discussion, for "faith in the liberating power of truth."[99] "As in a Freudian dream, the secrets of our parents' past... weighed heavily on the lives of an entire generation," Grudzińska wrote.[100] Faith in truth—understood in part as committed to impassioned discussion against the silences of their parents—was central to developing a critique of totalitarianism. Perhaps, Kołakowski taught, one would never find answers, but it was an ethical imperative to keep asking the questions.[101]

And so the *komandosi* belonged not to a generation of faith and disillusionment—nor to a generation—unlike Kołakowski's own—whose most pressing question was about guilt, or about how to sift through the layers of Stalin, Lenin, Marx, Engels, and eventually Hegel to return to something pure. Rather theirs was a generation of critique and a search for alternative values. They differed, perhaps, from their Western counterparts in coming much less under the influence of Foucault and Derrida than of Arendt and Kołakowski—perhaps because the contiguity with totalitarianism was too close for totalitarianism to have ever been an abstraction. They treated matters of knowledge, truth, and subjectivity as moral issues. They were not all "of Jewish origin." Yet this makes it no less true that in posing epistemological questions as explicitly ethical ones, as a group they embodied a postscript—or perhaps simply a continuation—of a rich tradition of Jewish learning in the Polish lands.

---

99   See also Aleksander Smolar, "Tabu i niewinność," *Aneks* 41–42 (1986): 89–133, quotation on 130. An English version appeared the following year, see Aleksander Smolar, "Jews as a Polish Problem," *Daedalus* 116.2 (1987): 31–73.
100 Grudzinska Gross, "1968 in Poland: Spoiled Children, Marxists, and Jews," 44.
101 On this point see also Leszek Kolakowski, *Husserl and the Search for Certitude* (South Bend, IN: St. Augustine's Press, 2001).

CHAPTER 25

"Context is Everything." Reflections on Studying with Antony Polonsky

Yohanan Petrovsky-Shtern

Antony dropped this thought on one of his seminars in passing—among many other lucid asides that we, his students in NEJS graduate school, heard from him over the years. But this one deeply struck me then and still fascinates me today. Antony rarely speaks about context per se but he always builds contexts for us. He dissolves methodology in story-telling. Antony uses contexts to explain how historical events occurred or did not occur and what path they followed or should have followed. Why such powerful Jewish nationalism in Galicia?—Look at the rising Polish and Ukrainian nationalism around. Why the pogroms in the 1880s?—Think about the influx of déclassé individuals into Russian cities after the emancipation of the peasants. For Antony, context is a key methodological tool—a magical key to the murkiest dungeons of East European Jewish history.

One needs to know the context in order to build on it. Antony is a master of contexts—especially those neglected, dismissed, or forgotten. Antony reminds the new "revisionist" historians of East Europe—among them, Gershon Hundert and Moshe Rosman—that such phenomena as productive interaction and symbiotic relationships between Jews and Poles are, of course, a step forward in our understanding of two-thirds of early modern Jewry; and yet, the suspicion, animosity, and violence in the relations between neighboring peoples is difficult to ignore. We need to deal with the Haidamaks and Jedwabne, if we seek to create a balanced portrayal of the East European Jewish community. In doing so, Antony brings back the historiographic achievements of the entire generation of Polish and Russian scholars who never made it through the Holocaust—Emanuel Ringelblum, Majer Bałaban, and Simon Dubnow. Alienated from academia, these scholars produced a grand historical narrative centered in Jewish communal developments. Their communal context, Antony claims, enabled the much more nuanced approach to East European history that has been optimized by the "revisionists," myself including.

Antony brings in contexts to express the nuances. Jews in Austrian Poland, Russian Poland, Prussian Poland and the Polish-Lithuanian Commonwealth, *Rzecz Pospolita*, created a Jewish communal and cultural life each different from the other. Why so? Consider the Austrian, Russian, and Prussian context, answers Antony in his magnum opus *The Jews in Poland and Russia*. This consideration becomes for him a major modus operandi—hence we get volumes of POLIN focusing on Belorussia, Prussia, Galicia, and Ukraine. Furthermore, Antony brings in scholars from these and other countries—more often than not preoccupied with their own communities—puts them together between the bindings of the volumes of POLIN, and facilitates a conversation. Antony helps them realize that they are the context for one another.

Thus, contextualization becomes an ethical imperative. By bringing in a variety of contexts, Antony demonstrates to what extent East Europeans used or lost their historical opportunities—and why. He tells a wide range of Polish public figures, scholars, and intelligentsia: modern Jewish history is one of your primary contexts. You will know yourself much better if you study it. Antony turns to his Jewish history students: Austrian, Russian, Polish, Czech, and German contexts will help you to make sense of what you have found in Jewish communal history. Context takes you out of the ghetto—and helps transcend inter-ethnic bias. Context has a redemptive quality.

Antony applied it indiscriminately for the benefit of his very different audiences. In the spring of 1997, at his regular undergraduate lecture on *gzerot takh ve-tat*—the catastrophe of 1648–1649—with about a hundred students before him, Antony laid out contexts like a virtuoso. First, he spoke about the Polish *Korona*, its vast territory, its new quasi-colonial possessions in the east, its pompous magnates and szlachta oppressing the peasantry, and its new system of private ownership of towns. Then he turned to the Ukrainian/Ruthenian/Orthodox Christians: their situation under the Catholic magnates, their harsh corvée (labor service), their dependence on and aversion to the towns, and their run-away serfs-turned-Cossacks. Then, Antony spent quite some time talking about the Polish borderland with the Crimean Khanate, the freebooters, the Cossacks, and their complex relations with the Polish Kingdom they were called on to defend and with the Tatars from whom they had to defend the Polish borders—including the painful problem of registered and non-registered Cossacks. Finally, the Jews in the service of the Polish magnates entered the scene: as intermediaries between rural and urban, as tax collectors; and as lease-holders of towns, villages, mills or whatever could be economically significant. At this point the incendiary, bitterly offended and humiliated Bohdan Khmel'nyts'kyi entered the picture—and that was enough to make the tinderbox explode. The Cossacks rebelled, the Tatars joined the war on their side, the peasants rose in their support, the Poles refused to take the situation seriously and did not mobilize in a timely manner, Muscovy watched from afar, and the Jews...

Well, there is no need to continue. Antony's reconstruction conjured up the unique logic of the unfolding events. No viewpoint was privileged. No narrative received exclusive treatment. And new contexts, one of Muscovy and the other Austrian, contributed key variables to the reconstruction, eliminating any threat of determinism. Of course, Antony followed this multi-optical portrayal with excerpts from Jewish chronicles, voices from the depth of the abyss. I still remember leaving the room, standing in front of the Lown Building at the top of the Brandeis campus with a deep sense of the intellectual wizardry I had just experienced.

Such contextualization helped Antony—on more than one occasion, I think—get through many an uneasy situation. "How can you talk this way about thousands of victims," one of the graduate students interrupted indignantly when we were quantifying the death toll of the pogroms of 1919. We were very uneasy. Antony was lost, but only for a second. "Look, when we talk about one death, it is a tragedy. When we discuss thousands of deaths, it is statistics." Perhaps not the most satisfying answer, but it was timely and calmed the rising tension. Of course there were moments when Antony could not be so objective. In the middle of the class on the Vilna ghetto, he began reciting Sutzkever's poem in Yiddish—and in the middle of it started to stumble, as if he could not get to the end of the line. Professor Polonsky could not read a line in Yiddish? My fellow student Glenn Dynner, sitting next to me, leaned over and whispered: "He's crying." Of course he was, yet I, myopically, had not realized it.

Antony's keen interest in context followed him everywhere. "By the way, is it true that 'khappers' were only significant during the Crimean War?" he asked me in a letter from September 15, 2000, trying to put into perspective dozens of hair-raising tales of those burly catchers sent to kidnap Jewish children and bring them to conscription posts. When one rather influential professor did not seem to like my dissertation chapter that was, I felt strongly, built on a meticulous reconstruction of the internal documents of the Russian main staff before and during World War I, Antony magnanimously provided reassurance "The chapter is excellent and if [he] does not really like it...."

I only later understood that Antony's ability to put things in context was part and parcel of the Anglo-Saxon tradition of "ironization," i.e., allowing oneself an ironic distance from subject matter that would otherwise be too stressful. Antony helped me many times by teaching me—without any didactic pressure—this kind of ironic approach. I needed that lesson, particularly from 1998 to 2003, when I was a mere greenhorn who recklessly threw himself into fierce academic competition and was sometimes stymied. "In other words," commented Antony in a letter on November 15, 2000, "it could be worse, as the man said when a chair fell on his head, it could have been a piano." He added with a statement particularly dear to my Slavic heart: "The vodka will have to remain in the freezer, but we will drink it in the end." I did my best to be stoic, it did not always work, and in a very personal letter to Antony I quoted Kipling's "If" with its unforgettable lines on triumph and disaster. Antony reacted in a letter on November 17, 2000, this time with quite an unusual South African reference: "You will perhaps not be surprised that 'If' was the favorite poem of Hendrik Verwoerd, who was PM of South Africa when I lived there!"

It is a blessing that Antony came to Judaic Studies from his studies of the Polish armed resistance to the Nazis and Polish peaceful resistance to the communists. It is his formidable knowledge of European history that has made a long-lasting impact on the new generation of historians. If we want to understand how Antony integrates Europe into his research of East European Jewry, we need to turn to his early works, for example, on the inter-war "little dictators" of East Central Europe, and see how Antony integrates Jews into his study of Europe. Look at Antony's formidable output—dozens and dozens of volumes on history, society, literature, politics, and culture. To understand what the early twenty-first century historians of Eastern Europe strove to achieve, a future historian would need to exhaustively analyze Antony's contribution in its entirety.

After all, as Antony tirelessly teaches us, "context is everything."

Name Index

Abramovitsh, Sholem-Yankev (1835–1917) 78 n. 33, 88 n. 80, 181, 195–96, 265, 298, 315, 325, 342
Adamczyk-Garbowska, Monika (1956–present) 560, 560 n. 57
Adler, Genia (1918–2003) 585, 585 n. 27
Adorno, Theodor (1903–1969) 209 n. 7, 603
Alapin, Yisrael Borukh Hacohen (1840–1907) 188
Albek, Shalom (1858–1920) 186
Alter, Abraham Issachar Benjamin (1896–1943) 92
Alter, Abraham Mordecai (1866–1948) 125, 359
Alter, Isaac Meir (1799–1866) 8, 91–93, 112 n. 72, 113, 115, 115 n. 82, 122–24, 127, 158, 164–67, 177
Alter, Menahem Mendel (1877–1942) 361
Alter, Yehudah Aryeh Leib (1847–1905) 160, 165, 177, 477
Anielewicz, Mordecai (1919–1943) 518
Anski, Sh. (1863–1920) 227, 240, 240 n. 30, 240 n. 33
Arendt, Hannah (1906–1975) 603–04, 612, 218 n. 28
Arkin, Wiktor (1894–1982) 441, 535–36
Arnold, Stanisław (1895–1973) 375, 375 n. 13, 377, 377 n. 24 & 25
Arnshteyn, Mark (1879–1943) 232–33
Aron, Raymond (1905–1983) 603–04
Asch, Sholem (1880–1957) 205, 232, 254, 264–65, 267, 315, 338, 356 n. 26, 500
Askenazy, Szymon (1866–1935) 59 n. 52, 373, 373 n. 7
Atlas, Eliezer (1851–1904) 190
Auerbach, Rachel (1903–1976) 496–99, 501–14
Avraham ben Avigdor (d. 1542) 186 n. 22, 195, 195 n. 62
Azulay, Khayim Yossef David (Khida) (1724–1806) 185

Baal Makhshoves (Isidor Yisroel Eliashev, 1873–1924) 232

Bałaban, Majer (1877–1942) 371–73, 376–79, 381–88, 613
Baron, Salo (1895–1989) 155 n. 2, 386, 386 n. 60, 388, 388 n. 65, 388 n. 61
Batory, Stefan (1533–1586) 22–24
Bauman, Zygmunt (1925–present) 590, 594, 603
Bauminger, Leon (Arieh) (1913–2011) 385 n. 54, 544
Beer, Herz Jacob (1759–1825) 56, 56 n. 42 & 43, 58
Ben Yehuda, Eliezer (1858–1922) 185
Berenstein, Aharon (1812–1884) 189, 189 n. 35
Berezowski, Stanisław (1910–1986) 441
Bergelson, David (1884–1952) 302–03, 303 n. 14, 327 n. 15, 328 n. 20, 344
Berlin, Isaiah (1909–1997) 603
Berliński, Wolf (1823–?) 532
Bernstein, Yitzkhok (Ignac) (1836–1909) 86, 186, 186 n. 25 & 26, 204
Bersohn, Mathias (1823–1908) 85 n. 69, 186
Berson, Meir (1801–1873) 139
Bialik, Hayyim Nakhman (1873–1934) 205, 233, 265
Biebow, Hans (1902–1947) 555
Bierut, Bolesław (1892–1956) 565 n. 8, 569
Blumsztajn, Seweryn (1946–present) 594, 598, 605
Bobrzyński, Michał (1849–1935) 607
Boraisha, Menachem (1888–1949) 259, 269, 269 n. 49
Borenshteyn, Yitzkhok (1921–2006) 401, 401 n. 28, 417, 417 n. 83, 429, 430 n. 120
Bornstein, David (1876–1942) 162–63, 477–78
Bortnowska, Maria (1894–1972) 525
Bresler, Alter (1866–1930) 199, 199 n. 79, 200–01
Brodowski, Feliks (1864–1934) 233
Brus, Włodzimierz (1921–2007) 580 n. 21, 594
Brzeziński, Zbigniew (1928–present) 603
Buchner, Abraham (1789–1869) 87

Cahan, Abraham (1860–1951)   339
Chagall, Marc (1887–1985)   335, 335 n. 48, 342
Charney (Tsharni), Daniel (1888–1959)   344
Chlewicki, Mieczysław (1911–1939)   524
Cleinow, Georg (1873–1936)   279
Cylków, Izaak (1841–1908)   86, 147, 147 n. 71, 161
Czerniakow, Adam (1880–1942)   351, 450, 452, 478 n. 32, 481 n. 40, 539–40

Dąbrowski, Witold (1933–1978)   594
Dantsiger, Shmuel Tsvi (1860–1923)   432
Danziger, Yitshak Menahem Mendel (1880–1942)   477, 479 n. 36
Dawidsohn, Hayyim (1760–1854)   109, 116–19, 122, 158, 158 n. 9, 164, 172 n. 53, 357 n. 27
Dembiński, Bronisław (1858–1939)   373
Der Nister (Pinchus Kahanovich, 1884–1950)   302
Derrida, Jacques (1930–2004)   610, 611 n. 93 & 94
Dick, Isaac Meir (1814–1893)   265
Dinezon, Yankev (1856?–1919)   192 n. 52, 196–97, 227
Dinur, Ben Zion (1884–1973)   509, 509 n. 34
Dmowski, Roman (1864–1939)   248, 250
Dobkin, Eliahu (1898–1976)   402, 402, n. 31
Dobroszycki, Lucjan (1925–1995)   437 n. 3, 438 n. 7–10, 439 n. 13, 466, 466 n. 139, 516 n. 3, 564 n. 7
Drimer, Solomon of Sokołów (d. 1873)   113, 114 n. 77
Druyanov, Alter (1870–1938)   404, 404 n. 36
Du Plat, Col. (1829–1904)   103, 104 n. 41
Dua, Yankev-Kopl (1898–1942)   264
Dubnow, Simon (1860–1941)   65 n. 75, 121 n. 103, 229, 229 n. 7, 230, 240, 240 n. 30, 302, 317 n. 73, 325, 329, 536 n. 43, 613
Dunin-Wąsowicz, Krzysztof (1923–2013)   274 n. 13, 278 n. 31, 294
Dygas, Ignacy (1881–1947)   417

Edelman, Marek (1919–2009)   484 n. 50, 556
Ehrenburg, Ilya (1891–1967)   339
Ehrlich, Henryk (1882–1942)   334
Eisenbach, Artur (1906–1992)   8 n. 16, 9 n. 16, 44 n. 5, 45 n. 13, 58 n. 46 & 48, 65 n. 74 & 75, 66 n. 76 & 78, 131 n. 9, 132 n. 13, 145 n. 65, 372, 376, 377 n. 22, 386 n. 59, 5 n. 7 & 9
Eisenstadt, Marysia (1921–1942)   502
Eplberg, Heshl (1861–1927)   196
Epstein, Jozef (1937–present)   140

Fajans, Maksymilian (1827–1890)   147
Farbstein, Heshel (1870–1948)   469, 471 n. 17, 472 n. 20, 474 n. 24 & 25, 474 n. 26, 489 n. 25
Fedecka, Stefania (1919–present)   588
Fefer, Itsik (1900–1952)   344
Feinkind, Moses (1805–1869)   117, 119, 140
Feldman, Eliezer (1903–?)   376, 376 n. 19, 377 n. 24, 381 n. 39
Fiałkowski, Melchior (1778–1861)   146
Finkel, Eliezer David (1861–1918)   191, 267
Finkel, Ludwik (1858–1930)   373
Flatau, Itzig (Izaak) Jacob (turn of 19th century)   6, 46, 51, 54, 54 n. 35 & 36
Fogel, Dvora (1900–1942)   508
Foucault, Michel (1926–1984)   217 n. 24, 610, 612
Frankel, Samuel Antoni (d. 1833)   58, 62, 62 n. 62, 63, 63 n. 66
Frenk, Azriel Natan (1863–1924)   155 n. 1, 331, 331 n. 35
Friedman, A.A. (1888–1925)   207
Friedman, Filip (1901–1960)   268, 274 n. 10, 277 n. 25, 382, 385 n. 55, 431 526 n. 23
Friedman, Israel of Ruzhyn (1796–1850)   495
Friednson, Eliezer Gerszon (1899–1942)   476
Frishman, David (1859–1922)   189, 196, 213, 232
Friszke, Andrzej (1956–present)   437 n. 3, 594 n. 17, 596, 596 n. 26, 598 n. 36 & 38, 599 n. 44
Frumer, Aryeh Zvi of Koziegłowy (1884–1943)   476, 477 n. 31, 481 n. 39
Frydman, Alexander Zysze (1897–1943)   475, 475 n. 26, 487, 487 n. 60
Fuen, Shmuel Yosef (1818–1891)   185
Fürstenberg, Moses Aron (turn of 19th century)   54, 64

Gancwajch, Abraham (1902–1943)   541–42
Gandhi, Mahatma (1869–1948)   96–97
Gawisar, Luba (1924–2011)   451 n. 74, 465, 465 n. 165

NAME INDEX

Gebert, Konstanty (1953–present)   606, 606 n. 75
Geremek, Bronisław (1932–2008)   590
Gesundheit, Jacob (1815–1878)   8, 123, 140, 149, 154–60, 163, 163 n. 25, 164–79, 347, 349, 356, 362
Glatshtern, Hilel (Hilary) (1827–1874)   194
Goldman, Yitzkhok (1812–1888)   183, 185–90, 195–96, 199 n. 79
Gomułka, Władysław (1905–1982)   599, 599 n. 43, 605, 608
Gordin, Jacob (1853–1909)   233
Gordon, Judah Leib (1830–1892)   1, 7 n. 12, 83, 83 n. 55, 89 n. 87, 114 n. 78, 181
Gorky, Maxim (1868–1936)   233, 260
Goryńka, Wiktoria (1902–1944)   441, 442 n. 31
Gotlib, Meir (1866–?)   201, 201 n. 86, 202 n. 91
Gotlober, Avrom Ber (1811–1899)   181, 194
Gottlieb, Dov Beirish (1740–1796)   120, 120 n. 99 & 100
Goydo, Yitzkhok (1868–1925)   195, 199 n. 79
Gran, Wiera (1916–2007)   548, 548 n. 30, 551–54, 556
Grazovski, Yehuda (1862–1950)   185
Grinboym, Yitzkhok (1879–1970)   400, 409, 409 n. 55, 423 n. 105, 428 n. 116
Grodzenski, Chaim Ozer (1863–1940)   264
Gross, Jan (1947–present)   593
Grosser, Bronisław (1883–1912)   500
Grossman, Vasily (1905–1964)   603
Gros-Zimmerman, Moshe (1891–1974)   264
Grudzinska, Irena (1946–present)   590 n. 1, 594, 596, 596 n. 28 & 29, 598–600, 604, 604 n. 65, 605, 608, 608 n. 84, 612, 612 n. 100
Grünbaum, Yitzhak (1879–1970)   155, 254–56, 258, 258 n. 20, 260, 260 n. 26, 27 & 28, 262, 282, 382 n. 43
Gruszecki, Artur (1852–1929)   257, 257 n. 19
Guenzburg, Mordecai Aharon (1795–1846)   192, 192 n. 41
Guterman, Menahem Mendel of Radzymin (1860–1934)   432

Haffner, Falik (1908–1942?)   376, 377 n. 24, 385 n. 54
Halecki, Oskar (1891–1973)   375
Halévy, Jacques (1799–1862)   417

Handelsman, Marceli (1882–1945)   374–75, 374 n. 9, 375 n. 12, 377, 377 n. 24 & 25, 384
Hartglas, Apolinary (1883–1953)   260 n. 27, 267–68, 282
Heijermans, Herman (1864–1924)   233
Heller, Celia (1922–present)   406 n. 40, 407, 407 n. 45
Herszfeld, Ludwik (1884–1954)   506
Hirschbein, Peretz (1880–1948)   336, 341, 342 n. 63
Hirszhorn, Samuel (1876–1942)   281
Hoffmann, Nekhemya Dov (1857–1928)   190, 190 n. 40
Hofshteyn, Dovid (1889–1952)   302
Horowitz, David (1858–1914)   190
Huntington, Samuel (1927–2008)   603
Hurvitz-Zalkes, Shloyme (1878–1960)   203

Imber, Naftali Herz (1856–1909)   264
Imber, Shmuel Yankev (1889–1942?)   264, 266
Isserles, Moses (1520–1572)   99 n. 26 & 29, 100 n. 31, 119, 120 n. 99

Jabotinsky, Vladimir (1880–1940)   400–01
Jakubowicz, Szmul (1727–1801)   46, 52, 55, 55 n. 42, 56–58, 58 n. 46 & 48, 59–60, 63, 63 n. 68, 64, 66
Jakubowiczowa (Zbytkower), Judyta (1749–1800)   46, 55–59, 63, 63 n. 68, 64, 66
Janusz of Mazovia (1379–1429)   22
Jarzemski, Adam (Jarzębski)   24 no 23, 25, 27 n. 27
Jasieński, Bruno (1901–1938)   590
Jaskiewicz, Mikołaj (1717–1779)   107
Joselewicz, Berek (1764–1809)   5, 5 n. 8

Kacyzne, Alter (1885–1941)   342
Kagan, Yisrael Meir, the "Chofetz Chaim" (1838–1933)   359
Kahana, Shlomo David of Warsaw (1868–1943)   361
Kahanovski, Shmuel Nakhum (1856–1926)   195
Kaidanover, Tzvi Hirsch (d. 1712)   97, 97 n. 22
Kalish, Bunem (1851–1907)   261

Kalish, Isaac of Warka (1779–1848)   96 n. 16, 116
Kamiński, Aleksander (1903–1978)   439 n. 17, 440, 441 n. 25, 442, 451, 451 n. 75, 464–66
Kanal, Yitzhak Meir (1799–?)   361
Kantorovich, Pinkhes (1866–1927)   200, 200 n. 81
Karlinski, Ber (1886–1935)   191 n. 44, 204, 204 n. 88
Karo, Joseph (1488–1575)   99, 99 n. 28 & 29, 100 n. 30, 119, 120 n. 99, 373
Katzenelson, Yitzhak (1886–1944)   493 n. 81, 499, 499 n. 10
Katznelson, Berl (1887–1944)   428, 428 n. 117, 493 n. 81
Kazimierz, Jan (1609–1672)   22, 25, 373–74
Kempner, Stanisław (1857–1924)   290
Kermisz, József (1906–2005)   376, 377 n. 24 & 25
Kharik, Izi (1898–1937)   344
Kipnis, Menachem (1878–1942)   258, 258 n. 22, 259, 502
Klauzner, Yosef (1874–1958)   185
Kleinbaum-Sneh, Moshe (1909–1972)   262, 268, 270
Kletzkin, Boris (1875–1937)   195 n. 64, 198 n. 72, 199 n. 78, 213 n. 15, 306, 336, 338, 341
Kluger, Solomon (1783–1869)   113, 113 n. 75 & 76, 114, 121, 121 n. 102
Kochanowski, Jan Karol (1869–1949)   373, 375, 377, 377 n. 24
Koestler, Arthur (1905–1983)   603
Kofman, Jan (1941–present)   593–94
Kołakowski, Leszek (1927–2009)   591
Königsberger, David (1885–1942)   65
Körner, Moshe (1878–1937)   282
Kotik, Avraham (Avrom, 1898–1967)   v, 133, 133 n. 21, 196, 199, 199 n. 78, 200, 207, 209–24, 213 n. 15, 216 n. 19
Kotik, Ezekiel (1847–1921)   95 n. 13, 98, 98 n. 25, 216 n. 19, 224–26, 331 n. 31
Kotler, Aharon (1891–1962)   361
Kozlowski, Leib (?–1941)   505
Krämer, Mojżesz (1913–?)   376, 377 n. 24 & 25, 381 n. 39
Kraushar, Alexander (1843–1931)   279 n. 37, 280–81, 281 n. 43

Krinsky, Magnus (1863–1916)   202
Krochmal, Nachman (1785–1840)   73
Król, Marcin (1944–present)   595, 595 n. 21, 600 n. 48, 611 n. 98, 612
Kronenberg, Leopold (1849–1937)   59 n. 52, 75, 85 n. 75
Kruk, Herman (Hersh) (1897–1944)   339, 500, 500 n. 14
Kucharzewski, Jan (1876–1952)   248, 250
Kulbak, Moyshe (1896–1940)   302, 305
Kundera, Milan (1929–present)   600
Kuroń, Jacek (1934–2004)   593–94, 594 n. 15, 595, 597, 606
Kvitko, Leyb (1890–1952)   302
Kwaśniewski, Tadeusz (1915–1943)   441, 466 n. 138

Laeytan, Naftali Maskil (1829–1897)   185
Lagnean, Jean (1873–1945)   531
Lakhover, Fishl (1883–1947)   196
Landau, Abraham of Ciechanów (1789–1875)   115
Landau, Shaul (1936–2013)   349
Landau, Ya'akov Yitshak Dan (1882–1943)   477
Lasota, Irena (1945–present)   598
Leivik, H. (1888–1962)   336
Lejkin, Jakub (1906–1942)   541, 543
Lelewel, Joachim (1786–1861)   146
Lestschinsky, Jacob (1876–1966)   324–26, 325 n. 6, 326 n. 6, 330, 341, 342 n. 63, 345, 346 n. 78
Levin, Gershon (1868–1939)   204, 264
Levin, Yehuda Leyb (1844–1925)   134
Levinshteyn, Yossef (1834–1927)   185
Lewin, Aaron of Rzeszów (early 20th century)   358, 368, 499 n. 9
Lichten Joseph (1906–1987)   406, 406 n. 41, 408, 408 n. 48, 419 n. 93
Lichtenstein, Israel (1932–present)   513
Lidski, Yankev (1868–1921)   195, 198, 201 n. 88, 202
Lilienfeld-Krzewski, Karol (1893–1944)   525
Litvak, A. (Khaim-Yankev Helfand)   329, 330
Litvakov, Moyshe (1875–1939)   344
Lityński, Jan (1946–present)   594, 598, 605, 606, 606 n. 74
Lubomirski, Zdzisław (1865–1943)   292
Lunacharsky, Anatoly (1875–1933)   328

NAME INDEX 621

Mahler, Raphael (1899–1977)   28 n. 40, 46 n. 13, 70 n. 2, 74 n. 14, 109 n. 62, 126 n. 118, 342, 371, 375, 375 n. 12 & 13, 376, 376 n. 19, 20, 376 n. 22, 376 n. 25, 379, 379 n. 31, 381 n. 39, 385 n. 54, 387
Mandelkorn, Solomon (1846–1902)   191, 191 n. 43
Mandelshtam, Nadezhda (1899–1980)   603
Manger, Itzik (1901–1969)   501, 509
Mann, Mendel (1916–1975)   506, 506 n. 27
Mark, Bernard (1908–1966)   542 n. 12, 579, 579 n. 18
Mark, Yudel (1897–1975)   345
Markish, Peretz (1895–1952)   302, 336
Mayzel (Maisel), Nakhman Nachman (1887–1966)   330, 330 n. 28, 333, 333 n. 40, 334 n. 42, 336 n. 51, 338, 340, 341 n. 60, 342, 342, 343, 343 n. 25, 344 n. 68, 345, 498, 498 n. 7
Mayzel, Maurycy (1872–1941)   539
Medini, Khayim Khizkiya (1833–1905)   186
Meisel, Dov Berush (1798–1870)   8, 123 n. 109, 140, 146–49, 158, 158 n. 12, 159–62m 165–66, 168, 172 n. 53, 347–48, 348 n. 3, 349, 249 n. 7, 353–54, 356–57, 357 n. 27, 258, 366
Meisel, Eliyahu Hayyim (1821–1912)   354
Melamed, Zelig (1830–?)   327, 327 n. 15, 330, 338, 426
Melcer, Wanda (1896–1972)   504–05, 505 n. 23
Menahem Mendel of Kotzk (1787–1859)   90–91, 115, 115, n. 82, 126, 215, 215 n. 18, 225 n. 44
Mendele Moykher Sfoyrim see S.Y. Abramowicz
Mendelssohn, Moses (1729–1786)   72, 265
Meszorer, Józef Lucjan (1931–present)   72, 265
Michaelsohn (Mikhlzohn), Tzvi Yehezkel (1853–1942)   350, 351, 362
Michalewicz, Beinish (1876–1928)   334
Michnik, Adam (1946–present)   590, 590 n. 1, 593–95, 594 n. 15 & 16 & 19, 597 n. 34, 598, 598 n. 37, 605, 605 n. 68 & 70, 606, 606 n. 72 & 73, 608–09, 609 n. 87, 610, 610 n. 92, 611, 611 n. 95
Mickiewicz, Adam (1798–1855)   597

Miczyński, Sebastian (16th–17th c.)   25, 25 n. 24
Mikhoels, Solomon (1890–1948)   344
Miłosz, Czesław (1911–2004)   317, 594, 603
Minor, Zalkind (1826–1900)   134
Modzelewski, Karol (1937–present)   594, 594 n. 17, 595, 597
Molodowsky, Kadia (1894–1975)   317
Montefiore, Moses (1784–1885)   103, 103 n. 39 & 40, 104, 104 n. 41 & 42
Morgnshtern, Yude Leyb (1869–?)   187, 188
Morgulis, Mikhail (1941–present)   81
Muszkat, Jeszaja (d. 1866)   96, 109, 118, 122–23

Nahman of Bratzlav (1772–1810)   186, 186 n. 23
Nałęcz, Daria (1951–present)   254 n. 6, 255 n. 10, 263, 263 n. 39, 448
Narutowicz, Gabriel (1865–1922)   260 n. 26, 397
Natanson, Dov Ber (Bernard) (1832–1916)   184, 244 n. 50
Natanson, Ludwik (1822–1896)   139, 141, 244
Neufeld, Ignacy (d. 1880)   147
Neufeld, Reuven of Nowy Dwór (20th c.)   361
Neumann, Salomon (1819–1908)   52
Nicholas II, Tsar (1868–1918)   230
Niemojewski, Andrzej (1864–1921)   277
Niger, Shmuel (1883–1955)   197 n. 71, 298, 298 n. 1, 299, 300, 300 n. 3, 301, 310 n. 45 & 46, 312, 313 n. 59, 326, 326 n. 14, 327, 327 n. 15, 332, 332 n. 38, 344
Nikolaevich, Grand Duke Nikolai (1856–1929)   274
Nomberg, Hersh Dovid (1876–1927)   200 n. 82, 214, 232, 254–55, 425
Nossig, Alfred (1864–1943)   542–43
Nussbaum, Hilary (1820–1895)   21 n. 8, 74 n. 18, 85 n. 69, 86 n. 74, 87, 87 n. 78, 155, 168 n. 40

Oesterreicher, Leib (?–1944)   55
Opatoshu, Joseph (1886–1954)   304–36, 336 n. 51, 344
Opoczynski, Peretz (1892–1943?)   508, 513
Orgelbrand, Szmul (1810–1868)   182–83, 563
Orleska, Miriam (1900–1943)   502

Orwell, George (1903–1950)   603
Ostersetzer, Israel (1904–1942)   376, 377 n. 25, 382, 383 n. 44 & 45

Paczkowski, Andrzej (1938–present)   254 n. 7, 600 n. 50, 601 n. 53, 608 n. 80, 609 n. 88
Paprocki, Abraham (1813–1852)   77 n. 18, 87
Park, Robert (1864–1944)   129, 129 n. 3
Paskevich, Ivan (1782–1856)   96, 115, 374
Passent, Daniel (1938–present)   587, 587 n. 32
Pelzhausen, Walter (1891–1948)   555
Peretz, Yitzkhok Leybush (1852–1915)   181 n. 4, 187, 188, 196–97, 197 n. 71, 203, 205, 213, 227–28, 228 n. 2
Perle, Shie (Yehushe) (1888–1943)   216 n. 71, 316 n. 71, 342, 507, 507 n. 30, 513
Perlmutter, Avraham Tsevi (1843/46–1930)   349–50, 350 n. 9 & 10 & 11, 357–58, 358 n. 31, 366
Perski, Aleksander (1947–present)   593–94
Pinski, David (1872–1959)   197, 199, 200 n. 82, 232–33
Pomian, Krzysztof (1934–present)   595
Poniatowski, Stanisław August (1732–1798)   27, 29, 29 n. 43, 30, 46
Posner, Salomon Markus (1770–1848)   61, 61 n. 59, 62 n. 65, 67, 68 n. 83, 96, 104, 116, 216 n. 20
Poznański, Samuel Abraham (1864–1921)   366, 366 n. 77, 367, 367 n. 59, 411 n. 63
Prawin, Jakub (1901–1957)   587
Prilutski, Tzevi Hirsh (1862–1942)   231
Prylucki, Noah (1882–1944)   xiii, 300–01, 301 n. 11, 308, 317–19, 319 n. 83

Rabinovitz, Shalom ("Sholem Aleichem," 1859–1916)   200 n. 82, 203, 214–15, 215 n. 18, 225, 225 n. 44, 227–28, 232–33, 254, 298, 306, 325
Rabinovitz, Shaul Pinkhas (Shefer) (1845–1910)   184
Radziwiłł, Janusz (1612–1655)   24
Rakovsky, Puah (1865–1955)   263, 263 n. 37, 264, 400 n. 26
Rapport, Solomon Judah Loeb (1790–1867)   73

Ravitsh, Meylekh (1893–1976)   256 n. 13, 257 n. 18, 258 n. 22, 259 n. 24, 426
Reyzen (Reisen, Reyzn), Avrom (1876–1953)   196–97, 213–15, 213 n. 15, 256 n. 13, 258 n. 22, 259 n. 24, 251 n. 30, 265, 265 n. 41
Reyzen, Zalmen (1887–1941)   313, 313 n. 56, 315 n. 67, 316 n. 71
Ringelblum, Emanuel (1900–1944)   xi, 14 n. 26, 15, 20 n. 3, 21 n. 8, 28 n. 41, 56 n. 42, 42, 29 n. 46, 94 n. 8, 102 n. 33, 259, 306 n. 24, 342, 372, 374–76, 317 n. 17 & 19, 377, 377 n. 21 & 22 & 24, 378–79, 379 n. 29, 380, 385, 386 n. 59, 387–88, 431 n. 126, 447 n. 57, 448 n. 63, 450 n. 69, 472, 472 n. 21, 496, 496 n. 2, 499, 501, 504, 506–14, 518 n. 8, 540 n. 3, 613
Rokacz, Marian (1910–1987)   528
Rosen, Itshak Shimon (1923–present)   139
Rosen, Mathias (1804–1865)   75, 87, 139, 139 n. 41
Rosenstrauch, Markus (1802–?)   107
Rotholc, Stanisław (Shepsl) (1912–1996)   547–48, 548 n. 30, 31, & 32, 549, 549 n. 33, 550, 550 n. 34, 35 & 35, 551, 554, 556–58, 558 n. 51
Rotwand, Jakub (1818–1913)   87
Rubinstein, Yitzhak (1880–1945)   360, 360 n. 39
Ruderman, Pessakh (1854–1887)   189
Rybicka, Ewa (1909–1943)   441
Rzepecki, Col. Jan (1899–1983)   440

Salcstein, Hasid Getzl (1773–1841)   183
Samet, Shimon (1904–1998)   562, 562 n. 1
Schaff, Adam (1913–2006)   593
Schiffer, Fayvl (1809–1871)   191
Schiper, Ignacy (1884–1943)   48 n. 19, 64 n. 71, 94 n. 8, 137 n. 37, 148 no, 74, 318, 371–73, 376, 378–79, 382, 383, 383 n. 45, 387–88
Schlesinger, Akiva Joseph (1837–1922)   125, 125 n. 114
Schneersohn, Menachem Mendel of Lubavitch (The Tzemah Tzedek) (1789–1866)   98 n. 24, 114, 114 n. 29
Schorr, Moshe (1874–1941)   362, 362 n. 44, 367, 367 n. 30, 371–73, 378–79, 381, 381 n. 41, 382, 382 n. 43 & 44, 383 n. 49, 385, 387, 387 n. 62 & 63

NAME INDEX

Schulz, Fryderyk (b. 1762)   29, 29 n. 44, 34–35, 35 n. 55
Segalovich, Zusman (1884–1949)   254, 264
Seligfeld, Zimra (1900–1942)   258
Serdatski, Yente (1877–1962)   232
Shalit, Moyshe (1885–1941)   205 n. 104, 343, 343 n. 67
Shalkovich, Avrom Leyb (1866–1921)   195
Shapira, Meir (1887–1933)   476
Shapiro, Eliezer Yitzkhok (1835–1915)   187
Shatzky, Jacob (1893–1956)   1, 1 n. 2 & 3, 2, 9 n. 3, 20 n. 3, 74 n. 16, 75, 75 n. 19, 87, 87 n. 76 & 79, 94, 94 n. 11, 108 n. 59, 118 n. 52, 118 n. 95 & 97, 121 n. 104, 123 n. 109, 126 n. 116 & 117, 127 n. 121, 128 n. 2, 131 n. 10, 132 n. 13, 132 n. 17, 134 n. 24, 137, 137 n. 31 & 32, 139 n. 40 & 42, 140 n. 45 & 48, 148 n. 72 & 74, 154–55, 155 n. 1, 169, 169 n. 43, 175, 180 n. 2, 182, 182 n. 6 & 9, 183, 183 n. 12, 184, 184 n. 16, 187 n. 27, 188 n. 33 & 34, 189 n. 36, 191 n. 47, 193, 193 n. 56, 194 n. 56 & 60, 197 n. 69, 204 n. 99, 216 n. 20, 217 n. 22, 347, 347 n. 1, 348, 348 n. 4, 349, 349 n. 8, 362 n. 43, 374, 374 n. 10, 400 n. 26
Sheynhak, Yossef (1812–1870)   189, 189 n. 36
Shimin, Binyomin (1880–1942)   203–04, 204 n. 97
Shmeruk, Chone (1921–1997)   103 n. 38, 127 n. 121, 155 n. 2, 181 n. 4, 194 n. 60, 206 n. 106, 242 n. 37, 252 n. 3, 257 n. 16, 263, 263 n. 36, 301 n. 9, 320, 320 n. 89, 332 n. 36
Shrebrek, Shlomo (1876–1944)   195–96
Shtern, Yisroel (1894–1942)   502
Shtif, Nokhem (1879–1933)   302, 379 n. 33
Sikorski, Władysław (1881–1943)   465, 466 n. 136
Singer, Bernard (1893–1966)   268, 498, 498 n. 5
Singer, I.J. (1893–1944)   201, 201 n. 85, 300, 311, 314, 314 n. 64, 331, 331 n. 34, 336, 337, 345, 345 n. 73, 366, 366 n. 53 & 54
Słonimski, Antoni (1895–1976)   611
Slonimski, Hayim Zelig (1810–1904)   v, 7, 70–90, 72 n. 11, 73 n. 12 & 14, 74 n. 14, 75, 75 n. 21 & 22, 78 n. 33, 34, & 36, 79 n. 39 & 42, 81 n. 46 & 48, 82 n. 49 & 51, 83 n. 55 & 58, 84 n. 61, 85 n. 66, 86 n. 74, 87 n. 79, 88 n. 80, 81 & 84, 89 n. 85, 88 & 89, 193, 193 n. 57
Sloves, Chaim (b. 1905)   344, 344 n. 68, 345
Slutzki, David (d. 1889)   183, 183 n. 14
Smolar, Aleksander (1940–present)   590, 596, 596 n. 28, 598–99, 591 n. 41, 600–01, 601 n. 52 & 54, 605, 607, 607 n. 80, 610 n. 89, 612, 612 n. 99
Smolar, Eugeniusz (1945–present)   600
Sneh, Kleinbaum (1909–1972)   262, 262 n. 33, 268, 270
Sobieski Jan III (1629–1696)   22
Sofer, Moses (Hatam Sofer) (1762–1839)   123, 125, 125 n. 114
Sofer, Shimon (1820–1883)   353
Sokolov, Nakhum (1860–1936)   82 n. 51, 190, 190 n. 39, 191 n. 45, 193–94, 197
Solzhenitsyn, Aleksandr (1918–2008)   603
Sonnenberg-Bergson, Berek Szmul (1764–1822)   94
Spektor, Mordkhe (1858–1925)   186 n. 26, 196–97
Spektor, Yitzhak Elhanan of Kovno (1817–1896)   360, 360 n. 35
Starzyński, Stefan (1893–1939)   512, 539
Stein, Menachem (Edmund) (1893–1942)   382, 383 n. 44
Steinberg, Isaac Nakhman (1888–1957)   343, 343 n. 67
Steinkeller, Piotr (1799–1854)   58, 62, 62 n. 63 & 65
Stern, Abraham (1769–1842)   73, 73 n. 14, 74, 74 n. 14, 75 n. 22, 87, 126 n. 118
Sue, Eugène (1804–1857)   187, 198 n. 74
Świderski, Bronisław (1946–present)   594, 595 n. 20, 596, 608
Swiętochowski, Aleksander (1841–1938)   77
Symons, Simon (1863–1930)   46–48, 48 n. 17 & 18, 49, 50, 65
Szabad, Tsemach (1864–1935)   307
Szaniawska, Stanisława (1903–1980)   535
Szereszewski, Rafal (1896–1948)   434
Szeryński (Szynkman), Józef (1893–1943)   540–41, 543
Szlajfer (Szipper), Henryk (1947–present)   598, 607, 607 n. 79
Sztokhammer, Szimszon (1899–1944)   475, 467 n. 28

Tcherikover, Elias (1881–1943)   302
Tsaytlin, Hillel *see* Zeitlin, Hillel
Tseaylin, Aron, *see* Zeitlin, Aaron
Tugendhold, Jacob (Jakub, 1794–1871)   6, 74 n. 18, 87, 126, 126 n. 117 & 118
Tugendhold, Wolf (1796–1864)   83, 98
Turkow, Zygmunt (1896–1970)   498
Tyszelman, Zina (1917–?)   587–88
Tzukerman, Avrom (1843–1892)   187, 198 n. 73, 201

Veber, Mikhl (1859–1907)   189, 189 n. 38, 201, 201 n. 87 & 88
Vendroff, Zalmen (1877–1971)   264
Verne, Jules (1828–1905)   280, 280 n. 39280 n. 39
Von Beseler, Hans Hartwig (1850–1921)   280

Walden, Aharon (1834–1912)   115, 185
Wasserman, Elhanan (1874–1941)   361
Wat, Aleksander (1900–1967)   590, 603
Weichert, Michal (1890–1967)   340, 498, 544, 544 n. 17, 548, 556–57, 557 n. 48
Weinberg, Yehiel Ya'akov (1884–1966)   480, 480 n. 38
Weinreich, Max (1894–1869)   302, 308, 308 n. 33, 317 n. 73, 318, 321, 331 n. 33, 507, 507 n. 29
Weissenberg, I.M. (1881–1938)   232, 318
Wengeroff, Pauline (1833–1916)   98, 98 n. 25, 121, 121 n. 103
Wessely, Naftali Hertz (1725–1805)   72
Widerszal, Ludwik (1909–1944)   465
Winawer, Abraham (d. 1857)   115–17, 119, 126
Wiśniewski, Antoni (1718–1774)   528–29
Wisse, Ruth (1938–present)   229, 229 n. 6, 232 n. 12, 242, 242 n. 38
Władysław IV (1595–1648)   22, 25

Wojciechowski, Tadeusz (1838–1919)   373
Wolfowicz, Abram (b. 1917)   548, 553–54, 556, 556 n. 42
Wraxall, Nathaniel William (1751–1831)   29, 29 n. 45, 97 n. 21
Wujec, Henryk (1940–present)   594, 594 n. 18
Wurm, Dawid (1909–1941)   372, 385 n. 54

Yaavetz, Zeev (Volf) (1847–1924)   191
Yatzkan, Shmuel Yankev (1874–1936)   202, 255–56, 256 n. 13, 264, 266
Yogev, Gedalia (1929–1982)   42, 42 n. 1

Żabiński, Jan (1897–1874)   511, 512 n. 40
Zasławski, Aleksander (1577–1629)   35
Zbysz, Stanisława (1879–1967)   535, 535 n. 39
Zbysz, Władysław (1891–1968)   535
Zbytkower, Shmuel (1727–1801)   19, 40, 46, 52, 55, 55 n. 42, 129
Zeitlin, Aaron (1898–1973)   503
Zeitlin, Hillel (1878–1942)   425, 434
Zerubavel, Ya'akov (1886–1967)   338, 562, 562 n. 1
Zhitnitski, Hersh-Leyb (1891–1942)   264
Ziemba, Menachem (1883–1943)   363, 475, 475 n. 27, 490 n. 70, 491 n. 72
Zilberfarb, Moyshe (1876–1934)   330, 335, 336 n. 49
Zineman, Jacob (1893–1966)   259 n. 24, 260, 260 n. 25
Zuckerman, Yitzhak (1915–1981)   540 n. 3, 542 n. 11, 543, 543 n. 13 & 15, 544, 544 n. 16, 553, 553 n. 41, 561, 561 n. 58
Zweifel, Eliezer (1815–1888)   81, 81 n. 45
Zygmunt August II (1520–1572)   4, 22–24
Zygmunt III Vasa (1566–1632)   22, 25

www.ingramcontent.com/pod-product-compliance
Lightning Source LLC
Chambersburg PA
CBHW061339300426
44116CB00011B/1919